THE ROUTLEDGE COMPANION
TO LEAN MANAGEMENT

Interest in the phenomenon known as "lean" has grown significantly in recent years. This is the first volume to provide an academically rigorous overview of the field of lean management, introducing the reader to the application of lean in diverse areas, from the production floor to sales and marketing, from the automobile industry to academic institutions.

This volume collects contributions from well-known lean experts and up-and-coming scholars from around the world. The chapters provide a detailed description of lean management across the manufacturing enterprise (supply chain, accounting, production, sales, IT etc.), and offer important perspectives for applying lean across different industries. The contributors address challenges and opportunities for future development in each of the lean application areas, concluding most chapters with a short case study to illustrate current best practice. The book is divided into three parts:

- The Lean Enterprise
- Lean across Industries
- A Lean World

This handbook is an excellent resource for business and management students as well as any academics, scholars, practitioners, and consultants interested in the "lean world."

Torbjørn H. Netland is Chair of Production and Operations Management at the Department of Management, Technology, and Economics at ETH Zürich, Switzerland.

Daryl J. Powell is Lean Program Manager at the Subsea division of Kongsberg Maritime AS, Norway, and a visiting professor at the Faculty of Economics and Business at the University of Groningen, Netherlands.

THE ROUTLEDGE COMPANION TO LEAN MANAGEMENT

Edited by Torbjørn H. Netland and Daryl J. Powell

Routledge
Taylor & Francis Group

NEW YORK AND LONDON

First published 2017
by Routledge
711 Third Avenue, New York, NY 10017

and by Routledge
2 Park Square, Milton Park, Abingdon, Oxon OX14 4RN

Routledge is an imprint of the Taylor & Francis Group, an informa business

© 2017 Taylor & Francis

The right of Torbjørn H. Netland and Daryl J. Powell to be identified as editors of this work has been asserted by them in accordance with sections 77 and 78 of the Copyright, Designs and Patents Act 1988.

Library of Congress Cataloging in Publication Data
Names: Netland, Torbjørn H., editor. | Powell, Daryl J., editor.
Title: The Routledge companion to lean management/edited by Torbjørn H. Netland and Daryl J. Powell.
Description: New York, NY: Routledge, 2016.
Identifiers: LCCN 2016025506| ISBN 9781138920590 (hbk) | ISBN 9781315686899 (ebk) | ISBN 9781317416500 (epub) | ISBN 9781317416494 (mobi/kindle)
Subjects: LCSH: Management. | Industrial management. | Cost effectiveness. | Cost control. | Quality control. | Organizational effectiveness.
Classification: LCC HD31.R756 2016 | DDC 658.4/013–dc23
LC record available at https://lccn.loc.gov/2016025506

ISBN: 978-1-138-92059-0 (hbk)
ISBN: 978-1-315-68689-9 (ebk)

Typeset in Bembo
by Sunrise Setting Ltd., Brixham, UK
Printed and bound by CPI Group (UK) Ltd, Croydon, CR0 4YY

CONTENTS

Contents

CONTRIBUTORS

The Editors

Torbjørn H. Netland, Ph.D., is Chair of Production and Operations Management at the Department of Management, Technology and Economics at ETH Zürich, Switzerland. He was until recently an Associate Professor at the Norwegian University of Science and Technology (NTNU) and a Senior Researcher at SINTEF, both Trondheim, Norway. He has been a visiting researcher at the University of Cambridge, UK, and a Fulbright Research Fellow at Georgetown University, Washington, DC, USA. His research on corporate lean programs appears in several peer-reviewed journals. Netland serves on the Board of the European Operations Management Association (EurOMA) and the *Lean Management Journal*.

Daryl J. Powell, Ph.D., is Lean Program Manager at the Subsea Division of Kongsberg Maritime AS, which has its main office in Horten, Norway. He holds both an M.Sc. and a Ph.D. in lean, and has more than 10 years of experience working with lean implementations as both a practitioner and an academic. Currently he leads the global implementation of Kongsberg Maritime Subsea's corporate lean program. Powell is also a Visiting Professor at the Department of Operations at the University of Groningen in the Netherlands. His research appears in several peer-reviewed international journals. He is a member of the Editorial Advisory Board for the *International Journal of Lean Six Sigma*.

Introduction

Chapter 1   The Evolution of Lean Thinking and Practice

Daniel T. Jones is the Founder and Chairman of the Lean Enterprise Academy in the UK. He is also senior advisor to the Lean Enterprise Institute, a management thought leader, and a mentor on applying lean process thinking to every type of business. He is the co-author of *The Machine that Changed the World*, *Lean Thinking*, *Seeing the Whole Value Stream*, and *Lean Solutions*. He is the publisher of *Breaking through to Flow*, *Creating Lean Dealers*, and *Making Hospitals Work*. Jones also has organized Lean Summit conferences in Europe, including the Frontiers of Lean Summit, the First Global Lean Healthcare Summit, and the Lean Transformation Summit. Jones was the European Director of MIT's Future of the Automobile and International Motor Vehicle

Programs. He is advisor to the European Efficient Consumer Response movement and editor of the *International Commerce Review*. Jones holds a bachelor's degree in economics from the University of Sussex.

James P. Womack, Ph.D., is the founder and senior advisor to the Lean Enterprise Institute, Inc., Cambridge, MA, USA. He is a co-author of *The Machine that Changed the World*, *Lean Thinking*, *Lean Solutions*, and *Seeing the Whole Value Stream*. He has published several articles in the *Harvard Business Review*. Womack received a BA in political science from the University of Chicago in 1970, a master's degree in transportation systems from Harvard in 1975, and a Ph.D. in political science from MIT in 1982 (for a dissertation on comparative industrial policy in the US, Germany, and Japan). During the period 1975–1991, he was a full-time research scientist at MIT directing a series of comparative studies of world manufacturing practices. As research director of MIT's International Motor Vehicle Program, Womack led the research team that coined the term "lean production" to describe Toyota's business system.

Chapter 2   The Toyota Way: Striving for Excellence

Jeffrey K. Liker, Ph.D., is Professor of Industrial and Operations Engineering at the University of Michigan and President of Liker Lean Advisors, Ann Arbor, MI, USA. He is the author and co-author of numerous international bestsellers such as *The Toyota Way*, *The Toyota Way Fieldbook*, *The Toyota Product Development System*, *Toyota Culture*, and *The Toyota Way to Lean Leadership*, among others. He has a B.S. in industrial engineering from Northeastern University and a Ph.D. in sociology from the University of Massachusetts.

Part I: The Lean Enterprise

Chapter 3   Lean Production

Pauline Found, Ph.D., is Professor of Lean Operations Management at the University of Buckingham, Buckingham, UK. She is co-author of *Staying Lean: Thriving Not Just Surviving*, for which she holds a Shingo Research and Professional Publication Prize (2009). She was President of the POMS (Production and Operations Management Society) College of Behavior from 2009 to 2011.

John Bicheno is Professor of Lean Enterprise at the University of Buckingham, Buckingham, UK. Previously he was with the Lean Enterprise Research Centre, Cardiff, where for 12 years he was course director of the M.Sc. program in Lean Operations. He is has written 11 books on lean, one of which, *The Lean Toolbox*, has sold over 110,000 copies.

Chapter 4   Lean Leadership

Michael Ballé, Ph.D., is a business writer and executive coach with 20 years' experience in lean research and practice. He is also associate researcher at Telecom Paristech and co-founder of the Institut Lean France, Paris, France. He has co-authored three books (*The Gold Mine*, *The Lean Manager*, and *Lead with Respect*), and is the author of the Gemba Coach column at lean.org.

Chapter 5   Lean Innovation

Günther Schuh, Ph.D., holds the Chair of Production Engineering at the Laboratory for Machine Tools and Production Engineering (WZL) of RWTH Aachen University, Aachen,

Germany. He studied mechanical engineering and economics at RWTH Aachen University from 1978 until 1985 and received his doctorate in 1988. He became Professor for Economic Production Management at University of St. Gallen in 1993.

Stefan Rudolf, Ph.D., is Head of the Department of Innovation Management at the Laboratory for Machine Tools and Production Engineering (WZL) of RWTH Aachen University, where he started in 2009 as a researcher, and Managing Director of the Complexity Management Academy, Aachen, Germany. He studied mechanical engineering and economics at RWTH Aachen University and Tsinghua University, Beijing.

Christian Mattern is Research Assistant and Ph.D. candidate at the Department of Innovation Management at the Laboratory for Machine Tools and Production Engineering (WZL) of RWTH Aachen University, Aachen, Germany. Mattern holds a M.Sc. in mechanical engineering and business administration from RWTH Aachen University.

Chapter 6   Lean Product and Process Development

Monica Rossi, Ph.D., is a Postdoctoral Researcher at Politecnico di Milano, Milan, Italy. Since 2010, she has been engaged in research on lean product and process development. She has held visiting researcher positions at both Massachusetts Institute of Technology (MIT), USA, and Tokyo Metropolitan University, Japan.

James Morgan, Ph.D., has served in numerous lean product and process development leadership roles throughout his career, most notably when he was part of the team that led Ford Motor Company's product-driven turnaround during the recent global financial crisis. Jim is currently leading the Lean Product & Process Development initiative at the Lean Enterprise Institute, Cambridge, MA, USA.

John Shook is a business executive, industrial anthropologist, and author who currently serves as Chairman and CEO of the Lean Enterprise Institute, Cambridge, MA, USA, and Chairman of the Lean Global Network. Shook is a graduate of the Japan-America Institute of Management Science. He is the former director of the University of Michigan, Japan Technological Management Program, and faculty of the university's Department of Industrial and Operations Engineering. Shook learned about lean management while working for Toyota for nearly 11 years in Japan and the US, helping it transfer production, engineering, and management systems from Japan to New United Motor Manufacturing Inc. (NUMMI) and subsequently to other operations around the world. As co-author of *Learning to See*, he helped introduce the world to value stream mapping.

Chapter 7   Lean Systems Engineering

Cecilia Haskins, Ph.D., is an Associate Professor in Systems Engineering at the Norwegian University of Science and Technology (NTNU, Trondheim, Norway). Cecilia entered academia after more than 30 years in industry. Her educational background includes a B.Sc. in chemistry from Chestnut Hill College, an MBA from Wharton, University of Pennsylvania, and a Ph.D. from NTNU. She is a member of The International Council on Systems Engineering (INCOSE).

Bohdan W. Oppenheim, Ph.D., is a Professor of Mechanical and Systems Engineering at Loyola Marymount University, Los Angeles, CA, USA. He is the founder and co-chair of the

Lean Systems Engineering Working Group of INCOSE and serves as the local coordinator of the Lean Aerospace Initiative Educational Network. His 30-year industrial experience spans space, offshore, software, and mechanical engineering, including several major aerospace programs. Oppenheim has worked for Northrop, the Aerospace Corporation, and Global Marine, and has served as a lean consultant for Boeing and 50 other firms. His credits include six books, 30 journal publications and book chapters, and externally funded grants. He has a doctorate in dynamics from the University of Southampton (UK). He is a member of INCOSE.

Chapter 8   Lean Logistics

Michel Baudin is a trained engineer who got his feet wet in production in 1980, and later apprenticed under Japanese consultant Kei Abe. He has consulted on lean in many industries worldwide since 1987. Baudin has taught with UC Berkeley extension, the University of Dayton, and HKPC. He is the author of four books: *Manufacturing Systems Analysis with Application to Production Scheduling* (1990), *Lean Assembly* (2002), *Lean Logistics* (2004), and *Working with Machines* (2007). He is the owner of the Takt Time Group based in Palo Alto, CA, USA

Chapter 9   Lean Safety

Robert B. Hafey has worked in manufacturing operations and maintenance for 40 years. He is the owner of RBH Consulting LLC based in Chicago, IL, USA. The first part of his career was with US Steel Corporation followed by 20-plus years at Flexco. He has been an AME (Association for Manufacturing Excellence) volunteer for the past 14 years and acquired much of his lean knowledge through this involvement. He holds a B.S. in professional arts from the University of St. Francis.

Chapter 10   Lean Teams

Desirée H. Van Dun, Ph.D., obtained her doctorate in operations management and organizational behavior at the University of Twente, Enschede, in the Netherlands. She has been a management consultant since 2008 at House of Performance in the Netherlands, primarily in the service industry. Her professional interests include lean management, leadership, industrial and organizational psychology, organizational behavior, and change management.

Celeste P. M. Wilderom, Ph.D., holds the Chair in Change Management and Organizational Behavior at the University of Twente, Enschede, in the Netherlands. In 1987, she obtained her Ph. D. in psychology from the State University of New York, Buffalo (USA). She has been associate editor of the *British Journal of Management*, *Academy of Management Executive/Perspectives*, and the *Journal of Service Management*. Her current research pivots on effective leader- and followership.

Chapter 11   Lean IT

Pär Åhlström, Ph.D., is the Torsten and Ragnar Söderberg Professor and Vice President of Degree Programs at the Stockholm School of Economics, Stockholm, Sweden. He has published frequently on lean in manufacturing, product development, and services. He is the co-author of the bestselling book *This is Lean: Resolving the Efficiency Paradox*.

Ryusuke Kosuge, Ph.D., is an Associate Professor at Ritsumeikan University in Japan. He received his doctorate from the University of Tokyo, and was a visiting researcher at the

Stockholm School of Economics. His research interests focus on lean capability development in service settings.

Magnus Mähring, Ph.D., is a Professor at Stockholm School of Economics, Stockholm, Sweden. His current research interests include public sector digitalization, governance of IT projects and programs, and organizational practices involving IT use. He has published in various peer-reviewed journals.

Chapter 12   Lean Sales and Marketing

Brent Wahba, MBA, has been leading and coaching lean sales and marketing, product development, and strategy for over 20 years. He serves on the Lean Enterprise Institute Faculty, is the President of the Strategy Science Inc. consulting network (Dallas, TX, USA), and regularly writes/speaks about many business improvement topics. His book, *The Fluff Cycle*, specifically addresses lean sales and marketing concepts and organizational change. Wahba holds an M.S. in materials science and engineering from the Rochester Institute of Technology, and an MBA from the University of Rochester.

Chapter 13   Lean Branding

Laura Busche is the author of *Lean Branding*, part of Eric Ries' Lean Series. She is a consultant, researcher and entrepreneur with a fundamental interest in consumer psychology. Busche's multifaceted approach to branding emerged from the combination of a summa cum laude degree in business administration (American University), a master's degree in design management (SCAD), and doctoral studies in consumer psychology as part of a fellowship awarded by the Colombian government.

Chapter 14   Lean Accounting

Brian H. Maskell is the President of BMA Inc., Cherry Hill, NJ, USA, and has more than 30 years' experience in the manufacturing and distribution industry. Over the past 20 years, Maskell's consulting practice has worked with manufacturing and distribution companies, large and small, throughout the world, assisting these companies in lean transformation, lean accounting, lean manufacturing and distribution, lean healthcare, and lean business management. He is the author of many books within the field of lean accounting.

Chapter 15   Lean Auditing

James C. Paterson works as a consultant specializing in risk assurance, lean auditing, and other aspects of internal audit effectiveness. Paterson has worked as the Chief Audit Executive for the Internal Audit function of AstraZeneca Plc. In 2005, he led work to apply lean techniques to the internal audit function. His book *Lean Auditing* was published in 2015.

Chapter 16   Lean Remanufacturing

Elzbieta Pawlik works in the research and development department within the Lean Enterprise Institute Poland. She is also currently engaged in Ph.D. research at the University of Strathclyde in the UK. Pawlik's research interests focus on the application of lean management principles to support sustainable development.

Winifred Ijomah, Ph.D., is Director of the Scottish Institute for Remanufacture and has elements of her work incorporated in British Standards (e.g. BS 8887-2:2009—Terms and definitions). She is initiator and Editor-in-Chief of Springer's *International Journal of Remanufacturing* and heads the University of Strathclyde remanufacturing research group.

Jonathan Corney, Ph.D., is a Professor of Design and Manufacture at the University of Strathclyde in the UK. His research interests range from mechanical remanufacturing and intelligent CAD/CAM to design innovation and advanced manufacturing. He is currently deputy director of the Scottish Institute of Remanufacture.

Chapter 17   Lean and Green

Keivan Zokaei, Ph.D., is an Honorary Visiting Professor at University Polytechnic Madrid, Spain and Managing Director of Enterprize Excellence. He is a winner of the 2014 Shingo Research and Professional Publication Award. He has been a director at the Lean Enterprise Research Centre (LERC) in Cardiff. He has specialized in operations excellence, supply chain optimization, and "lean and green."

Ioannis Manikas, Ph.D., holds a bachelor's degree in agriculture and a master of science in the field of logistics from Cranfield University. He holds a Ph.D. from the Department of Agricultural Economics in Aristotle University of Thessaloniki and his primary interests include supply chain management, logistics, and agribusiness management. Manikas has conducted research for projects regarding supply chain modelling and development of IT solutions for agri-food supply chain management and traceability both in Greece and the UK. He also works as a self-employed project manager and consultant in the agri-food sector.

Hunter Lovins is the President and Founder of Natural Capitalism Solutions, Longmont, CO, USA, a non-profit formed in 2002. A renowned author and champion of sustainable development for over 35 years, Lovins has consulted on sustainable agriculture, energy, water, security, and climate policies for scores of governments, communities, and companies worldwide. Lovins has co-authored 15 books and hundreds of articles, and was featured in the award-winning film *Lovins on the Soft Path*. Her book, *Natural Capitalism*, has been translated into more than three dozen languages and summarized in *Harvard Business Review*.

Chapter 18   Lean Purchasing

Tim Torvatn, Ph.D., is an Associate Professor at the Norwegian University of Science and Technology (NTNU) in Trondheim, Norway. He took his Ph.D. in purchasing management at the same university. He also holds an MBA from Queen's University, Kingston, Canada. His research interests are in purchasing and logistics management, organizational and inter-organizational theory, and industrial networks.

Ann-Charlott Pedersen, Ph.D., is a Professor at the Norwegian University of Science and Technology (NTNU), Trondheim, Norway. Pedersen's research in the areas of purchasing and supply management, supplier relationships and development, supply networks and strategizing in networks has been published in several peer-reviewed journals.

Elsebeth Holmen, Ph.D., is a Professor at the Norwegian University of Science and Technology (NTNU) , Trondheim, Norway. Holmen has published papers on supplier relationships and supply networks, supplier development, supplier involvement in product development, capability development in networks, and, more generally, managing and strategizing in business relationships and networks.

Chapter 19   Lean Supply Chains

Jonathan Gosling, Ph.D., is a Senior Lecturer in Supply Chain Management at Cardiff University, Cardiff, Wales, and undertakes research in engineer-to-order environments. He is Deputy Head of the Logistics and Operations Management Section for Research, Innovation and Engagement. Prior to becoming an academic, he worked in the automotive industry as a supply chain analyst.

Maneesh Kumar, Ph.D., is a Senior Lecturer at Cardiff Business School, Cardiff University, Cardiff, Wales. He conducts cross-disciplinary research in the area of operational excellence including topics such as Lean Six Sigma, process/service innovation and knowledge management within SMEs, the automotive industry, service industries, and public sector organizations.

Mohamed Naim, Ph.D., is a Professor in Logistics and Operations Management. He is Deputy Dean of Cardiff Business School, Cardiff University, Cardiff, Wales. He undertakes theoretical and empirical research on supply chain resilience, applying whole systems approaches to creating sustainable value.

Chapter 20   Lean Distribution

Matthias Holweg, Ph.D., is Professor of Operations Management at Saïd Business School at the University of Oxford, Oxford, UK. Prior to joining Oxford, he was on the faculty of the University of Cambridge and a Sloan Industry Center Fellow at MIT's Engineering System Division. Holweg is widely recognized as a thought leader in the field of lean management.

Andreas Reichhart, Ph.D., holds a doctorate in management studies from the University of Cambridge, where he researched how automotive supply chains built up flexibility. After his Ph.D. studies he joined a global management consulting firm for five years, and he has been working for a leading online retailer in the areas of supply chain management, pricing, and product management since 2012.

Chapter 21   Lean After-Sales Services

Barbara Resta, Ph.D., has been Research Assistant at the University of Bergamo, Bergamo, Italy since 2012. Her main research activities are focused on the corporate social responsibility topic, with a particular attention to the textile industry, and on the investigation of the role of the human factor in lean management applications.

Paolo Gaiardelli, Ph.D., is an Associate Professor at the University of Bergamo, Bergamo, Italy. His research activities mainly focus on organization and management of after-sales service, with a specific interest in service chain configuration, organization, and performance measurement. Recently Gaiardelli has extended his research to lean management applications in product-service systems.

Stefano Dotti, Ph.D., is an Assistant Professor at the University of Bergamo, Bergamo, Italy. His academic research interest is mainly focused on the development of eco-friendly equipment and processes, with a specific interest in the textile industry. Lately Dotti has extended his research activities to lean management applications in production and product-service systems.

Dario Luise is a Dealer Development Manager at the Italian subsidiary of DAF Trucks N.V. Dario is responsible for ensuring the territory coverage and qualitative growth of sales and after-sales networks. This work is enabled by a significant competence in dealership organization and management, which he has acquired in over 30 years' experience in the automotive industry.

Chapter 22   Lean Global Corporations

Torbjørn H. Netland. See "Editors."

Part II: Lean across Industries

Chapter 23   Lean Healthcare

Daniel T. Jones. See Chapter 1 "The Evolution of Lean Thinking and Practice."

Chapter 24   Lean Construction

Glenn Ballard, Ph.D., is the Research Director of the Project Production Systems Laboratory at the University of California, Berkeley, USA. He is the co-founder and has been the Research Director of the Lean Construction Institute (LCI), a non-profit organization dedicated to applying lean theory, principles, and techniques to create a new form of project management to design and build capital facilities. Ballard is the leading expert on lean construction.

Chapter 25   Lean Engineer-to-Order Manufacturing

Daryl J. Powell. See "Editors."

Aldert van der Stoel, M.Sc., is a researcher at HAN University of Applied Sciences, Arnhem, the Netherlands, with expertise in lean and quick response manufacturing (QRM). Van der Stoel has been working closely with more than 50 small and medium-sized enterprises to evaluate the implementation and use of lean and QRM practices.

Chapter 26   Lean Mining

Behzad Ghodrati, Ph.D., is an Associate Professor of Maintenance and Reliability Engineering at Lulea University of Technology, Luleå, Sweden. He obtained his Ph.D. on spare parts planning from the same university. He was awarded a Postdoctoral Research Fellowship from the University of Toronto in 2008. Ghodrati has published widely within his field.

Seyed Hadi Hoseinie, Ph.D., is an Assistant Professor in the Department of Mining Engineering at Hamedan University of Technology, Hamedan, Iran. His research interests are: mining machinery, reliability centered maintenance, mechanical excavation, and mine automation. Hoseinie has published widely and he holds one patent.

Uday Kumar, Ph.D., is Professor and Head of Operation and Maintenance Engineering at Lulea University of Technology, Luleå, Sweden. He has published widely in peer-reviewed international journals, mainly in the field of reliability and maintenance. His research interests are product support, equipment maintenance, reliability and maintainability analysis, life cycle costing, and risk analysis.

Chapter 27   Lean Maintenance, Repair, and Overhaul

Mandyam M. Srinivasan, Ph.D., is the Pilot Corporation Chair of Excellence in Business at the University of Tennessee, Knoxville, TN, USA. He has many years of experience in the automobile industry. He has written five books on lean and global supply chains. Srini received his Ph. D. from Northwestern University.

Chapter 28   Lean Public Services

Zoe Radnor, Ph.D., is Dean of the School of Management at the University of Leicester, Leicester, UK, and a Professor of Service Operations Management. Her interest lies in performance, process improvement, and service management in public services. Radnor held a research fellowship that considered the sustainability of lean in public services. She has published over 100 articles, book chapters, and reports.

Chapter 29   Lean Armed Forces

Nicola Bateman, Ph.D., is a Senior Lecturer in Operations Management at Loughborough, Loughborough, UK. She has published in both lean operations and public service, presented to organizations such as the Confederation of British Industry, and participated in a Department of Trade and Industry (UK government) economic evaluation unit. Her current research includes the fire service and the use of visual tools to support lean environments.

Peter Hines, Ph.D., is the co-founder of the Lean Enterprise Research Centre at Cardiff University, Cardiff, Wales. He has undertaken extensive research into lean thinking and written or co-written several books including *Staying Lean* and *Creating a Lean & Green Business System*, both of which won a Shingo Research Award. Peter is Chairman of S A Partners, a specialist consultancy organization, as well as a visiting professor at Waterford Institute of Technology, Ireland.

Chapter 30   Lean Policing

Harry Barton, Ph.D., is Professor of Human Resource Management and Head of Research at Nottingham Business School (NBS), Nottingham Trent University, UK. His wider research interests are in the areas of international HRM, lean in public services, and police performance management. His research has resulted in both national and international publications.

Rupert L. Matthews, Ph.D., is a Lecturer in Operations Management at Nottingham Trent University. He researches in the areas of process improvement, organizational learning, small and medium-sized enterprises, supply chain disruption risk, and public sector operations, and teaches in the areas of operations, supply chain, and innovation management.

Peter E. Marzec, Ph.D., is a manager in KPMG's Lean Practice, and a visiting fellow at the Nottingham Business School. He attained his Ph.D. from the University of Nottingham and researches in the area of process improvement, knowledge management, entrepreneurship, and innovation.

Chapter 31 Lean Justice

Ana Lúcia Martins, Ph.D., is an Assistant Professor and Head of the Operations and Logistics area at University Institute of Lisbon, Portugal. She has published in several peer-reviewed journals, co-authored a logistics handbook, and participated in consultancy and research projects concerning lean in justice and healthcare.

Isabell Storsjö is a doctoral student in supply chain management and social responsibility at Hanken School of Economics, Helsinki, Finland. She is writing her doctoral thesis on collaboration in public service supply chains, particularly focusing on the justice system and judicial proceedings.

Simone Zanoni, Ph.D., is Associate Professor in Industrial Systems Università di Brescia, Brescia, Italy. He has published more than 50 papers in various journals, and serves as subject editor for several journals. Zanoni has experience of applying lean principles across a variety of sectors from several consultancy projects.

Chapter 32 Lean Public Water Supply

Kirstin Scholten, Ph.D., is Assistant Professor in Operations Management in the University of Groningen, the Netherlands. She has a background in supply chain management, specializing in supply chain resilience and disaster management. She is a member of EurOMA and a winner of the first Nigel Slack Teaching Innovation Award.

Benjamin Ward is a graduate of the Master of Supply Chain Management program at the University of Groningen, Groningen, the Netherlands. He conducted his thesis research with the Waterbedrijf Groningen, the focal company of this chapter. Ward is now pursuing a supply chain career at one of the world's leading sports fashion and apparel companies.

Dirk Pieter van Donk, Ph.D., is Professor in Operations Management in the Department of Operations, University of Groningen, the Netherlands. His major field of research is supply chain management and integration in different contexts, incorporating aspects such as ICT and supply chain resilience. He has co-organized several EurOMA workshops and two annual EurOMA conferences.

Chapter 33 Lean Dealerships

David Brunt, MBA, works at the Lean Enterprise Academy, Herefordshire, UK, helping firms making lean transformations. He was the Porsche Improvement Process Manager at Porsche Cars Great Britain and carried out work to develop lean in after-sales, used car processing, and parts operations. Brunt has an MBA from Cardiff Business School, where he specialized in lean and supply chain management. He is co-author of the book *Manufacturing Operations and Supply Chain Management: The Lean Approach*.

Chapter 34 Lean Software Development

Mary Poppendieck has been in the information technology industry for over 40 years. She has managed software development, supply chain management, manufacturing operations, and new product development. A popular writer and speaker, Poppendieck is the co-author of four books:

Lean Software Development (2003), *Implementing Lean Software Development* (2006), *Leading Lean Software Development* (2009), and *Lean Mindset* (2013).

Chapter 35   Lean Printing

Ken Macro, Ph.D., is a Professor and Chair of the Graphic Communication department at the California Polytechnic State University in San Luis Obispo, California, USA, where he teaches lean printing and continuous improvement concepts. He is also the co-developer of the Customized Lean Implementation Plan (CLIP) model.

Chapter 36   Lean Retail

Paul Myerson, MBA, is Professor of Practice in Supply Chain Management at Lehigh University, Bethlehem, PA, USA and holds a B.S. in business logistics and an MBA in physical distribution. Prior to joining the faculty at Lehigh, Myerson had been a successful change catalyst for a variety of clients and organizations. He is the author of the books *Lean Supply Chain & Logistics, Lean Wholesale and Retail*, and *Supply Chain and Logistics Management Made Easy*, as well as a lean supply chain and logistics management simulation training game and training package.

Chapter 37   Lean Education

Vincent Wiegel, Ph.D., is one of the leading experts in the field of lean in the Netherlands and founder of and professor at the Research Group for Lean & World Class Performance, HAN University of Applied Sciences, Arnhem, the Netherlands. Wiegel is involved in lean education and initiates research into the effectiveness of lean implementations. Besides his wide range of general knowledge and experience, his specific expertise is in lean product development and lean in non-manufacturing environments such as healthcare and education.

Lejla Brouwer-Hadzialic, MBA, combines her economic background and years of management experience with her knowledge and understanding of applying Lean Six Sigma. She works at HAN University of Applied Sciences, Arnhem, the Netherlands. As certified Lean Six Sigma Black Belt, Brouwer-Hadzialic also trains and guides colleagues in continuous improvement projects. Her expertise in the service sector in particular relates to application, research, and development of lean (Six Sigma) in education. Furthermore, she is a co-creator of and a lecturer in the undergraduate course World Class Performance/Lean Management.

Chapter 38   Lean Schools

Jan Riezebos, Ph.D., is Associate Professor of Operations and Academic Director of Career Services and Corporate Relations, University of Groningen, Groningen, the Netherlands. He is an active researcher in the fields of lean production, planning and shop floor control, quick response manufacturing, and lean education. His research has resulted in several practical tools and methods that help organizations to apply lean.

Chapter 39   Lean Universities

Steve Yorkstone is an acknowledged authority on applying lean in universities, leading successful initiatives in a number of institutions. He currently works applying lean in Edinburgh Napier University, Scotland, UK. He is an editorial board member of the *Lean Management Journal*, and chairs an international community of practice for lean in higher education.

Part III: A Lean World

Chapter 40   A Lean World

Torbjørn H. Netland. See "Editors."

Daryl J. Powell. See "Editors."

PREFACE

Since the dawn of lean production in the 1990s, lean has continued to develop as the foremost philosophical management approach of the 21st century. The term itself was first introduced in the 1988 *MIT Sloan Management Review* article "The triumph of the lean production system" by John Krafcik, and two years later was popularized in the famous book *The Machine that Changed the World* by James Womack, Daniel Jones, and Daniel Roos. In fact, when the MIT's International Motor Vehicle Program suggested the term "lean" in the late 1980s, it was a result of five years of intensive international research collaboration within the global automotive industry. Since then, researchers and practitioners have continued to show how lean can improve the performance of companies across a wide array of industries outside of the automotive arena.

Even though lean and its early proof-of-concept clearly stems from "the industry of industries"—the auto industry—lean has now spread to all kinds of industries and application areas. Womack and Jones were the first to convey that such simple management ideas can significantly improve any company or economic activity, in their book *Lean Thinking* (1996). Having evolved from *lean production* through *lean thinking* to what we today call "lean management" or simply "lean," we have truly seen an evolution in the way that businesses are organized and run. Today, we have lean innovation, lean construction, lean logistics, lean healthcare, lean education, and the list continues to grow.

Interestingly, the augmentation of the lean concept has also provided the world with a great deal of confusion. Much of this confusion arises from the various abstraction levels that can be adopted in defining the lean approach. Many fall into the trap of defining lean in terms of a set of tools and techniques developed by Toyota Motor Manufacturing. Though the ad hoc adoption of these tools and techniques can generate limited gains and benefits for those who apply them, much greater rewards can be expected by adopting a principle-based lean approach that structures the application of tools in order to support the deployment of lean principles.

Lean is far from just another management fad. Its significance has been proven by both an abundance of successful practical applications and scientific research over a sustained period of time. Considering the spread of lean, it is timely to ask if the deployment of lean concepts implies the same across different application areas. This companion aims to do exactly that. By closely examining how lean has been developed and applied across numerous application areas, the chapters in this book provide the reader with a clearer understanding of what lean can be for his or her application area. Most chapters also include a short and helpful case study. The companion draws together contributions from a cross-section of established researchers regarded as experts in their respective fields.

The companion starts with two introductory chapters. In Chapter 1, Dan Jones and Jim Womack present their view of the evolution of lean thinking and practices. In Chapter 2, Jeff Liker expands on Toyota's role in the development of lean. The rest of the companion consists of three parts:

- Part I: The Lean Enterprise
- Part II: Lean across Industries
- Part III: A Lean World.

Part I of the book, "The Lean Enterprise," presents how lean has spread from *lean production* to the entire enterprise, including lean thinking in both primary and supportive business processes. Leading researchers provide short and informative chapters in their specific areas of expertise—ranging all the way from *lean production* to *lean corporations*.

Part II of the book, "Lean Across Industries," gives insights as to how lean has been developed and applied in diverse types of industries and sectors. Again, leading researchers provide short and informative chapters in their specific areas of expertise—ranging from *lean healthcare* to *lean universities*.

Part III summarizes the contributions from the individual chapters. We call this concluding chapter "A Lean World."

We hope this companion will be a helpful resource for practitioners, researchers, and consultants in the field of lean management.

Prof. Dr. Torbjørn H. Netland
Chair of Production and Operations Management, ETH Zürich, Zürich, Switzerland

Dr. Daryl J. Powell
Lean Program Manager, Kongsberg Maritime Subsea, Horten, Norway
Visiting Professor, University of Groningen, Groningen, the Netherlands

INTRODUCTION

1

THE EVOLUTION OF LEAN THINKING AND PRACTICE

Daniel T. Jones and James P. Womack

Introduction

Lean thinking and practice has arguably become the most successful approach to business improvement of our generation. It has outlasted many other improvement approaches and been taken up by organizations in all kinds of industries across the world. Almost every large organization now has some form of lean program or internal lean improvement group and lean has spawned an army of lean consultants. Interest in lean has also resulted in a huge and growing literature on all aspects of lean, and lean is beginning to be taught on university courses in engineering and management. But as lean spreads it has been reinterpreted many times, and has been bolted onto other improvement approaches like "Lean Six Sigma" and "LeanAgile." This has led to considerable confusion. For a precise definition of lean terms see Lean Enterprise Institute (2003).

What distinguishes lean thinking and practice is that it did not derive from theory, but through observing business practices at Toyota that deliver superior performance in terms of time to market for new products and better product quality using less capital and human effort and hence lower costs in production. This enabled Toyota to grow into the largest and most innovative car maker in the world. Although lean involves several different practices that lead to different ways of thinking about working together, it is the way these practices are combined and used that distinguishes lean as a different business system.

The full significance of lean as a business system is learned step by step through experience in using these practices, rather than through classroom learning. Lean is in fact both a personal journey and a path of organizational development. Although Toyota has had its setbacks, it has proven to be highly resilient by going back and deepening knowledge of the basic lean practices in the face of each of these challenges. Toyota also continues to act as a powerful reference model for lean practitioners in taking the next steps on their lean journeys and as a way to clarify the confusion that surrounds lean today.

The Birth of Lean at Toyota

Toyota was a successful textile loom maker in the 1930s and developed a device for stopping the loom immediately on detecting a broken thread, enabling one person to supervise several looms instead of just one. In 1935, Toyota decided to begin making automobiles. Toyota was determined to develop its own cars rather than license foreign designs and to fund this development itself rather than rely on banks. After a big strike in 1950 it also agreed with the unions not to make employees redundant in the future. Its response to this challenge was to create product development and production systems that could learn to improve product design and process efficiency faster using less resources in order to be able to compete with global car makers when the Japanese car market was opened and as they entered foreign markets. This story is told in Womack et al. (1990) and Shimokawa and Fujimoto (2009).

The Toyota Development System (TDS) was developed by Kenya Nakamura and Tatsuo Hasegawa. Powerful chief engineers, who are responsible for the success of their products and who negotiate for the necessary resources with department heads, lead the system. The chief engineers lead cross-functional teams, including production and suppliers, who initially spend more time exploring alternative design solutions using set-based concurrent engineering. This helps to avoid the rework and delays in realizing the chosen design solution. The progress of the work is reviewed on a daily and weekly basis in a visual management room, called *obeya,* where the team can respond quickly to delays and problems. Reusable knowledge is captured in many ways, including design check sheets, A3 reports, trade-off curves, and standard work sheets, so engineers can focus on developing new knowledge and deepening their own skills through solving new problems. These measures all contribute to being able to launch a new model every four years or less, rather than the eight to ten years that was common in the industry in 1990. More recently this system has also enabled Toyota to pioneer new technical innovations like hybrid engines and hydrogen powered cars. TDS is described in Morgan and Liker (2006) and the underlying concepts in Ward and Sobek (2014).

The challenge facing Taiichi Ohno, the architect of what became the Toyota Production System, was how to build several different products on the limited equipment that Toyota could afford at that time. Instead of resorting to producing in batches he carried out many pioneering experiments to build an integrated production system that was able to make a variety of products in single-piece flow in line with demand. This challenged the assumptions that there is a trade-off between quality and productivity and that bigger batches result in lower costs. His experiments led to the development of an interconnected set of practices called the Toyota Production System (TPS), described in Ohno (1978) and Shingo (1989).

After spreading the TPS thinking across Toyota's manufacturing operations, Ohno's group collected these practices and wrote them down for the first time in the early 1970s in order to teach them to their Japanese suppliers, and in the 1980s translated them into English as they opened their first joint-venture plant in the USA. The original TPS training material is contained in Narusawa and Shook (2009).

However, the distinguishing feature of Ohno's approach was to engage the whole workforce in seeking improvements, rather than relying solely on expert engineers. He challenged and taught front-line and support staff how to define and improve their own work, using the Training Within Industry system pioneered during World War II in the USA (see Dinero, 2005). This enabled the front line to establish a standard way of doing each task as a local base line for improvement, which in turn enabled them to see and respond quickly to any deviations from this standard. In analyzing the root causes of the many issues that interrupted their work he also taught them how to use the scientific approach to solving problems, using Deming's plan, do, check, act (PDCA) method (see Deming, 1982).

Indeed, it is the repeated daily practice of PDCA, using the perspectives of TPS, that develops the capabilities of individuals and teams to continually improve their work and improve the performance of the system as a whole. Toyota is often quoted as saying it "makes people in order to make cars." These enhanced problem-solving capabilities enabled Ohno to link activities together, remove all kinds of buffers and delays, and with much shorter lead times to use simpler planning systems driven by demand rather than by forecasts. This accelerating continuous improvement system is called *kaizen* (see Imai, 1991). The net result of deploying TPS was to achieve double the productivity and one-third of the defects of American assembly plants by the mid-1980s (see Womack et al., 1990).

Similar logic was used to develop very different approaches in other areas of the business, including production engineering of right-sized tooling, supplier coordination, and sales and marketing. Eiji Toyoda, the long-time president and then chairman of Toyota, also used these principles to build a management system to support kaizen and to focus and align activities towards key corporate objectives, which was finally written down in the Toyota Way (Toyota Motor Corp, 2001). Again, the key to doing so is building common capabilities at every level of management to plan and solve business problems using another version of PDCA, called A3 thinking, and a planning framework, called *hoshin kanri* (see Dennis, 2009 and Shook, 2010). It also involves a very different way of supporting, mentoring, and challenging front-line teams. The evolution and details of Toyota's management system are described in Hino (2002), Liker (2004), and Liker and Convis (2011).

The Evolving Understanding of Lean

Our understanding of lean has deepened over time. The MIT International Motor Vehicle Program (IMVP) benchmarked Toyota's superior performance and coined the term lean to describe this system in Womack et al. (1990). The results reported in this book caused quite a stir across the global auto industry and beyond. But it quickly became apparent that simply collecting and training with all the lean tools was not enough for others to follow Toyota's example. So we set out to observe Toyota's practices in more detail, along with some of the pioneering organizations who had learned directly from Toyota. From this, we were able to distil a set of five principles—value, value stream, flow, pull, and perfection—behind a lean system and a common action path to realize them in Womack and Jones (1996).

This triggered a wave of interest from practitioners across the world and led us to establish the Lean Enterprise Institute in the USA (www.lean.org), the Lean Enterprise Academy in the UK (www.leanuk.org), and 15 other non-profit institutes across the globe, now members of the Lean Global Network (www.leanglobal.org). Their mission is to research, teach, and publish do-it-yourself guides to the building blocks of lean, including Rother and Shook (1999), Rother and Harris (2001), Brunt and Kiff (2007), Baker and Taylor (2009), Dennis (2009), Glenday (2009), Smalley (2009), Shook (2010), Harris et al. (2011), and Jones and Womack (2011).

In observing the pioneer firms outside of Toyota building their own functional equivalent of Toyota's management system we discovered three challenges all firms face. The first is to build a daily management system to enable front-line team leaders and managers to make the work visible, to be able to respond to problems immediately, and review obstacles on a regular cadence. The basis for this is helping the team to define their standard work, improve on it, and gradually link these steps with upstream and downstream into a continuous flow. The next step is to link separate activities with customer demand using Kanban pull systems and to level the workload to establish stability and responsiveness. This all depends on team leaders and line managers developing the problem-solving skills of their subordinates, described in Sobek and Smalley (2008), Shook (2010), and Rother (2010).

The second challenge is that no one can see or is responsible for the horizontal sequence of activities that creates the value customers pay for, from concept to launch, from raw material to finished product, and from purchase to disposal. Vertically organized departments instead focus solely on optimizing their activities and assets to make their numbers.

To help teams see the end-to-end processes or value streams they are involved in, Toyota uses another tool which we call value stream mapping (see Rother and Shook, 1999; Jones and Womack, 2011). As teams map their value streams they realize the problem is not the people but a broken process and, having stabilized their own work, they then see new opportunities for collaboration to improve the flow of work and align it with the pull from real customer demand.

In industry after industry, we have seen value streams that used to take many months from beginning to end now take a matter of days, with far fewer defects and more reliable delivery. This is only possible because front-line staff know how to react quickly and tackle the root causes of problems that will arise in any tightly synchronized and interdependent system. It is also much easier to adapt to changing circumstances. Over time, these emergent capabilities achieve performance superior to systems designed and supported solely by experts. This is a key difference between value stream analysis and business process reengineering.

The third challenge is that the traditional approach to managing by the numbers and through functional politics at headquarters wastes a lot of management time, fails to align activities with corporate objectives, hides problems, and takes management away from front-line value-creating activities. Relying on expensive enterprise systems to force compliance with the command and control instructions from the top has in many cases made things worse and much harder to adapt to changing circumstances.

Toyota's planning process, *hoshin kanri*, is used to define the overall direction of the organization and to conduct a dialogue up and down the organization on proposed actions to achieve it, again based on PDCA (see Dennis, 2009; Shook, 2010). As a result resources and energies are prioritized and aligned through a visual process that reaches right down to the front line. This also lays the basis for collaboration across functional silos. Management in turn spends a lot more time at the front line, understanding its issues, eliminating obstacles and coaching problem solving. In this way management learns by helping colleagues to learn and does this by asking questions rather than telling them what to do. This builds very different behaviors and an environment where employees are challenged to fulfill their potential.

There have been several different descriptions of the lean business system, including three novels by Ballé and Ballé (2005, 2009, 2014), a collection of articles by Womack (2013), a CEO's perspective (Byrne, 2013) and a review of the spread of lean by Stoller (2015).

The Spread of Lean and Lean Consumption

Lean thinking and practice has spread across almost every sector of activity, from retailing and distribution to discrete and process manufacturing, service and repair, financial services and administration, construction, software development and IT, healthcare, and service delivery in government. It has even created a framework for improving the viability of digital start-ups. While the focus on value creation, value streams, and learning has been common, the sequence of improvement steps has varied for different types of activity. Fortunately, we have found that lean practices work equally well in different cultures.

The full potential of lean is realized when it is embraced by the whole supply chain. Toyota's aftermarket parts distribution system is still the global benchmark supply chain, delivering near perfect availability of the basket of parts at the point of use with only a tenth of the lead time and inventory in the pipeline from the point of production. Not surprisingly this inspired retailers like Tesco and Amazon to develop their own rapid response distribution systems that are essential for convenience retailing and home shopping. Manufacturers like GKN have also moved away from concentrating activities in focused factories in distant low-cost locations to creating rapid response supply chains to serve customers in each region. GE Appliances (now owned by Haier) is also using lean to design a new product range and production system for household appliances in North America, bringing this activity back from China.

While most of the attention has been focused on the upstream supply chain, lean actually begins with the customer's use of the product or service. We developed a framework for using lean to define value from the user's perspective (see Womack and Jones, 2005). Consumption is in fact a series of processes that interact with the provider's processes. Mapping both processes shows where they are broken and cause mutual frustration and unnecessary cost. This reveals opportunities for improving user experience at lower cost and even generating new business models. In the digital age it is now possible to track the customer's use of the product or service and enter into a two-way dialogue with them. In a very real sense customers and users are becoming an important part of the supply chain delivering today's products and services and co-developing tomorrow's solutions.

Conclusions

From this chapter it should be clear that lean is not just another improvement methodology, but a very different set of behaviors and a management system. It is not just a set of tools for production operations in the auto industry, but a much broader framework for creating more productive value creation systems in all kinds of sectors and activities. Readers should beware of the confusion that is caused by partial descriptions of lean, which often miss the key elements that make it work as a system.

Lean shares the same scientific approach to the analysis of work with many improvement methodologies, like BPR, Six Sigma, and TQM. But it differs from them in how it is used. Rather than relying on experts to design better systems, lean builds superior performance by developing the problem-solving capabilities of the front line, supported by a hands-on management system.

Lean is therefore a path or journey of individual and organizational learning and leads to more challenging and fulfilling work for those involved. It is learned by doing it and through repeated practice rather than by studying it in books or in the classroom. While it is driven by practice and not theory, lean raises many interesting new hypotheses about learning and collaborative working for different academic disciplines to think about and research.

References

Baker, M. and Taylor, I. (2009). *Making Hospitals Work,* Goodrich, Herefordshire, UK, Lean Enterprise Academy.

Ballé, M. and Ballé, F. (2005). *The Gold Mine*, Cambridge, MA, Lean Enterprise Institute.

Ballé, M. and Ballé, F. (2009). *The Lean Manager: A Novel of Lean Transformation*, Cambridge, MA, Lean Enterprise Institute.

Ballé, M. and Ballé, F. (2014). *Lead with Respect: A Novel of Lean Practice*, Cambridge, MA, Lean Enterprise Institute.

Brunt, D. and Kiff, J. (2007). *Creating Lean Dealers*, Goodrich, Herefordshire, UK, Lean Enterprise Academy.

Byrne, A. (2013). *Lean Turnaround*, New York, McGraw-Hill.

Deming, W. (1982). *Out of the Crisis*, Cambridge, MA, MIT Press.

Dennis, P. (2009). *Getting the Right Things Done*, Cambridge, MA, Lean Enterprise Institute.

Dinero, D. A. (2005). *Training Within Industry*, New York, Productivity Press.

Glenday, I. (2009). *Breaking through to Flow*, Goodrich, Herefordshire, UK, Lean Enterprise Academy.

Harris, R., Harris, C. and Wilson, E. (2011). *Making Materials Flow*, Cambridge, MA, Lean Enterprise Institute.

Hino, S. (2002). *Inside the Mind of Toyota*, New York, Productivity Press.

Imai, M. (1991). *Kaizen*, New York, McGraw-Hill.

Jones, D. T. and Womack, J. P. (2011). *Seeing the Whole Value Stream*, Cambridge, MA, Lean Enterprise Institute.

Lean Enterprise Institute (2003). *Lean Lexicon*, Cambridge, MA, Lean Enterprise Institute.

Liker, J. (2004). *The Toyota Way*, New York, McGraw-Hill.

Liker, J. and Convis, G. L. (2011). *The Toyota Way to Lean Leadership: Achieving and Sustaining Excellence through Leadership Development*, New York, McGraw-Hill.

Morgan, J. and Liker, J. (2006). *The Toyota Product Development System*, New York, Productivity Press.

Narusawa, T. and Shook, J. (2009). *Kaizen Express*, Cambridge MA, Lean Enterprise Institute.

Ohno, T. (1978). *The Toyota Production System*, New York, Productivity Press.

Rother, M. (2010). *Toyota Kata: Managing People for Continuous Improvement and Superior Results*, New York, McGraw-Hill.

Rother, M. and Shook, J. (1999). *Learning to See*, Cambridge, MA, Lean Enterprise Institute.

Rother, M. and Harris, R. (2001). *Creating Continuous Flow*, Cambridge, MA, Lean Enterprise Institute.

Shimokawa, K. and Fujimoto T. (2009). *The Birth of Lean*, Cambridge, MA, Lean Enterprise Institute.

Shingo, S. (1989). *The Toyota Production System*, New York, Productivity Press.

Shook, J. (2010). *Managing to Learn*, Cambridge, MA, Lean Enterprise Institute.

Smalley, A. (2009). *Creating Level Pull*, Cambridge, MA, Lean Enterprise Institute.

Sobek, D. and Smalley A. (2008). *Understanding A3 Thinking*, New York, Productivity Press.

Stoller, J. (2015). *The Lean CEO*, New York, McGraw-Hill.

Toyota Motor Corp (2001). *The Toyota Way*, Tokyo, Toyota Motor Corporation.

Ward, A. C. and Sobek II, D. K. (2014). *Lean Product and Process Development*, Cambridge, MA, Lean Enterprise Institute.

Womack, J. P. (2013). *Gemba Walks*. Cambridge, MA, Lean Enterprise Institute.

Womack, J. P. and Jones, D. T. (1996). *Lean Thinking: Banish Waste and Create Wealth in Your Corporation*, New York, Simon & Schuster.

Womack, J. P. and Jones, D. T. (2005). *Lean Solutions: How Companies and Customers Can Create Value and Wealth Together*, New York, Simon & Schuster.

Womack, J. P., Jones, D. and Roos, D. (1990). *The Machine that Changed the World*, New York, Rawson Associates.

2

THE TOYOTA WAY

Striving for Excellence

Jeffrey K. Liker

The Problem? The Misunderstanding of Lean and "How it Applies Here"

Lean (along with its variations, such as Six Sigma, theory of constraints, Lean Six Sigma, and specialties in different industries like agile IT development, lean construction, lean healthcare, lean finance, and lean government) has become a global movement. As with any management movement, there are true believers, resisters, and those who get on the bandwagon but do not care a lot one way or the other. There are a plethora of service providers through universities, consulting firms of various sizes, and not-for profit organizations, and there is a book industry.

For zealots like me, this is, in a sense, a good thing—there are consumers of my message. But there is also a downside. As the message spreads and goes through many people, companies, and cultures, it changes from the original, like the game of telephone in which the message whispered to the first person bears little resemblance to the message the tenth person hears.

In the meantime, well-meaning organizations that want to solve their problems are searching for answers. What is lean? How do we get started? How do these tools developed within Toyota for making cars apply to my organization? How do these methods apply in our culture, which is very different from Japanese culture? Do the tools have to be used exactly as they are in Toyota, or can they be adapted to our circumstances? And how does Toyota reward people for using these tools to improve?

These are all reasonable questions and, unfortunately, there are many consultants and self-appointed "lean experts" ready to answer them, often in very different ways. But the starting point should be the questions themselves. Are these the right questions? As reasonable as they may seem, I believe they are the wrong questions. The underlying assumption in each case is that lean is a mechanistic, tool-based process to be implemented as you would install a new piece of computer software. Specifically, the assumptions can be summarized as follows:

1   There is one clear and simple approach to lean that is very different from alternative methodologies.
2   There is one clear and best way to get started.
3   Toyota is a simple organization that does one thing—makes cars—and it uses a core set of the same tools in the same way, every place.

4 The tools are the essence and therefore must be adapted to specific types of processes.

5 Because lean was developed in Japan, there may be something peculiar about it that needs to be modified to fit cultures outside Japan.

6 Toyota itself has a precise method of applying the tools in the same way in every place that others need to copy.

7 The formal reward system is the reason people in Toyota engage in continuous improvement and allocate effort to support the company.

In fact, none of these assumptions are true, and that is the problem. The gap between common views of lean, and the reality of how this powerful thing Toyota has been pursuing for almost one century *actually* works, is preventing organizations from accomplishing their goals. The Toyota Way, by contrast, is a generic philosophy that can apply to any organization, and if applied diligently, will virtually guarantee improvement (Liker, 2004). It is a way of looking at organizations, a philosophy, and a system of interconnected processes and people who are striving to continuously improve how they work and deliver value to customers.

Having dismissed the common and simplistic notion that it is a program of tools for taking waste out of processes, in this chapter I wish to convey the deeper meaning of the Toyota Way. I will briefly describe the origin of the Toyota Way within Toyota, the principles I have distilled, and what it looks like to pursue it in practice.

The Toyoda Family: Generations of Consistent Leadership

To understand a company's culture, we should always begin with its roots—the core values of its founders—and Toyota is no exception. Many companies have drifted so far from their roots that the initial values are barely visible, but Toyota has maintained a remarkable degree of continuity of culture over most of a century, starting with its founder, Sakichi Toyoda.

Sakichi Toyoda: Creating Looms and Values

Sakichi Toyoda was born in 1867, the son of a poor carpenter in a rice village. He learned carpentry from the ground up, and he also learned the necessity of discipline and hard work. A natural inventor, he saw a problem in the community. Women were "working their fingers to the bone" using manual looms to make cloth for the family and for sale, after a full day of work. To ease the burden, he began to invent a new kind of loom. His first modification used gravity to allow weavers to send the shuttle of cotton thread back and forth through the weft by manipulating the foot pedals instead of by using their hands. Immediately, women worked half as hard and were more productive. Sakichi Toyoda continued to make improvement after improvement, some small, some big, and in 1926 formed Toyota Loom Works.

He was a devout Buddhist and always lived strong values. One of his favorite books was called *Self-Help*, by British philanthropist Samuel Smiles ([1859] 1982). Smiles dedicated much of his life to mentoring juvenile delinquents so they could become successful contributors to society. He wrote about the inspiration of great inventors who, contrary to popular opinion, were not always privileged and gifted students, but achieved great things through self-reliance, hard work, and a passion for learning. This fit well the story of Sakichi Toyoda, who raised himself from a poor background as a carpenter's son, and did not appear particularly outstanding, but who through the passion of contributing to others, the hard work of learning the fundamental skills of carpentry, and a clear picture of the problems he wanted to solve, relentlessly made improvement after improvement, each to solve the next problem.

As Sakichi Toyoda grew, his ambitions and contributions also grew. He began to envision a fully automatic loom and each individual innovation moved him nearer to that idea, continually improving toward his vision. He started by helping the women in his family, then the community, then helping to industrialize Japanese society, and ultimately contributing to all society. He is considered by many to be the father of the Japanese industrial revolution and is given the title "King of Inventors" in Japan. Along the way, he cultivated himself and his own values. These values eventually became the guiding principles of Toyota Motor Company, and included: contribute to society, put the customer first and the company second, show respect for all people, know your business from the ground up, get your hands dirty, work hard with discipline, work as a team, build in quality, and continually improve toward a vision.

Built-in quality was most evident in one of his most influential inventions—the loom that could stop itself when there was a problem. Every innovation by Sakichi Toyoda was problem-driven based on what he learned from earlier innovations. After the loom was reasonably automatic and could run at a relatively high speed, he noticed that when a single thread broke on the weft to make cloth, the cloth would be defective. A human had to stand and watch the loom and stop it when that happened, which he considered a tremendous waste of human capability. Yet another invention used gravity. This time, he added a piece of metal onto each thread in the weft. When a thread broke, the metal would interfere with the threads and stop the loom. He called this *jidoka*, a word which was formed by adding to the Chinese kanji for automation a symbol for a human. Thus, he had put human intelligence into automation so the loom could stop itself when there was a problem. He later added to this a small metal flag that would pop up, signaling "I need help." Jidoka would become a pillar of the Toyota Production System, conveying the notion of stopping when there is a quality problem and immediately solving the problem.

Based on the teachings of Sakichi Toyoda, the Toyota Precepts were created, which still guide the company today (Toyota, 2012):

1   be contributive to the development and welfare of the country by working together, regardless of position, in faithfully fulfilling your duties;
2   be ahead of the times through endless creativity, inquisitiveness, and pursuit of improvement;
3   be practical and avoid frivolity;
4   be kind and generous; strive to create a warm, homelike atmosphere;
5   be reverent, and show gratitude for things great and small in thought and deed.

In 1937 Toyota Motors was formed by Kiichiro Toyoda as a division of Toyota Loom Works. Kiichiro's father, Sakichi, had asked him to do something to contribute to society and Kiichiro chose automobiles, a highly risky major challenge. Automobile companies are very capital-intensive and it seemed Toyota was a lifetime behind Ford Motor Company, which at the time was pumping out over one million vehicles per year and getting all the attendant economies of scale. Why would a tiny start-up in an obscure part of Japan have any chance of competing, outside perhaps of the protected market in Japan? Like his dad, Kiichiro Toyoda saw a need, an opportunity, and believed in his team. One of the decisions in the start-up of the company was that Kiichiro, a mechanical engineer, and his team would learn about all the technologies from the ground up and get their hands dirty. This reflected the Toyota principle of self-reliance. Another core principle was announced in a speech Kiichiro gave in which he said: "I plan to cut down on the slack time in our work processes . . . As the basic principle in realizing this, I will uphold the 'just in time' approach."

What was this "just in time" approach? Operations management courses in MBA programs would not teach JIT for decades and there were no books or articles about it. It seems he made it up! And he was not exactly sure what it was. Taiichi Ohno, a brilliant young manager in Toyota Automatic Loom Works, was given the assignment to develop the manufacturing system that would become the next great innovation in Toyota beyond automatic looms—the Toyota Production System (TPS).

The methodology for Ohno's innovation was the same as Sakichi Toyoda's for the loom—relentless *kaizen*. Kaizen literally means "change for the better," but in Toyota's case it means systematically working toward a challenge overcoming obstacle after obstacle one at a time. When Ohno started, he was running the machine shop for engine and transmission components and just started trying things—small experiments—to solve problem after problem. Nothing was worth talking about for Ohno until he actually tried it on the shop floor. Like Sakiichi Toyoda, the more problems he solved, the more problems were revealed.

For example, the factory was organized in the traditional way by type of process—lathes over here, drilling machines over there—and there were specialist workers for each machining department. Ohno's idea was to create a cell for a product family and have all the machines set up in sequence to make complete parts. He wanted the cells to build to *takt*—the rate of customer demand—with no inventory in the cell except one part here or there as a buffer between machines. He also wanted the flexibility to adjust the number of people in the cells based on the rise and fall of customer demand without losing productivity. This meant that as demand went down, there would be fewer people and some would have to operate more than one type of equipment, such as a lathe and a drill.

The concept of a cell building to takt was a magnificent idea, but proved to be much harder to implement than Ohno expected. Lathe operators did not want to operate drilling machines and vice versa. His solution? Go to the *gemba* (where the work is done) every day and spend time with the workers showing them, and getting them to try the new system. Over time, they found it was a better way to work as it produced higher quality with less wasted effort, and was even safer. Ohno learned a critical lesson—simply thinking of an idea is only the start and the real work is the time-consuming process of training and developing people through repeated practice so the new system becomes "the way we work."

Much later, after the bugs had been mostly worked out, the system was put into writing, and represented as a house (see Figure 2.1). The term "system" is not incidental, but very intentional. The two key pillars were Kiichiro Toyoda's just-in-time and Sakichi Toyoda's jidoka (built-in quality). If Toyota was going to work with very little inventory and build in quality at every step, the foundation had to be extremely stable. There had to be reliable parts delivery, equipment that worked as it was supposed to, well-trained team members, and essentially no deviations from the standard. Ideally, the foundation would provide the ability to build consistently to a leveled production schedule, without huge ups and downs, supporting the customer takt. Leveled production would provide a steady rhythm for the factory.

To maintain this high level of stability, quality, and just-in-time production would require intelligent team members who were vigilant in noticing all the many problems that occurred every day and who took the time to think about and test countermeasures to address deviations from the standard as they occurred. At the center of the house are highly developed and motivated people who are continually observing, analyzing, and improving the processes. These individuals are focused on the purpose, and on correcting any deviations from the standard that adversely affect the purpose. The process gets closer to perfection through continuous improvement by thinking people; therefore, some in Toyota have described TPS as the *Thinking* Production System.

The purpose of the system is represented by the roof—best quality, lowest cost, on-time delivery, in a safe work environment with high morale. The house was a type of system—weak pillars, unstable foundations, a leaky roof, and the house will come tumbling down. Perfect

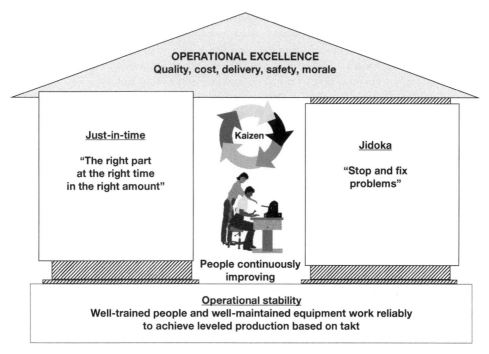

Figure 2.1 The Toyota Production System house

Source: Liker (2015).

adherence to the TPS vision was never possible, but it provided a picture of perfection that could always be striven for—the purpose of kaizen.

What is Lean?

It is very difficult to define "lean," but let's start with the term's origin as a descriptor of organizational excellence. It is not a term you will hear a lot around Toyota. It was first introduced in 1990 in the book *The Machine that Changed the World* (Womack et al., 1990), which was the result of a five-year study at the Massachusetts Institute of Technology (MIT) comparing the American, European, and Japanese auto industries. The researchers consistently found, regardless of the process or metric, that the Japanese automotive companies were far superior to the European and American companies in a wide range of areas, including manufacturing efficiency, product quality, logistics, supplier relationships, product development lead time and efficiency, distribution systems, and more.

The message was that the Japanese had developed an integrated enterprise based on a fundamentally different way of looking at the company, work processes, and people that can be best viewed as a new *paradigm* of management. The word "lean" was suggested by then graduate student John Krafcik (1988), who argued that lean means doing more with less, like a superior athlete, and that the Japanese, especially Toyota, were doing more of everything they needed to do for the customer with less of almost everything. It was a holistic concept for the enterprise, not a toolkit for a specific type of process. It applied both to routine work, such as is done on the assembly line, and to very non-routine work requiring specialized knowledge, like engineering design and sales.

The concept of "waste" in lean is central but often misunderstood. Waste is more than specific actions or objects that need to be eliminated. Waste is anything that causes a deviation from the perfect process. The perfect process gives the customer exactly what they want, in the amount they want, when they want it, and all steps that deliver value do so without interruption.

The concept of "one-piece flow" is the ideal. Each step in the value-adding process does what it is supposed to do perfectly without the various forms of waste that cause processes to be disconnected by time, space, or inventory. Toyota often uses the metaphor of a free-flowing stream of water without stagnant pools. Of course, one-piece flow requires perfection in everything that is done by people or technology and is therefore an impossible dream. Toyota says this is their "true north" vision which is not achievable, yet always the goal—striving for perfection while recognizing there is no perfect process.

I submit that any organization should desire this state of perfection, regardless of the specific product, service, or culture of the organization. The organization that can deliver pure value to its customers without waste, while continuously innovating to improve the product, service, and processes, will be successful. This ideal, or some would say *idealistic*, vision arose in Toyota from some very special people, starting with the great inventor Sakichi Toyoda.

Womack and Jones (1996) then built on *The Machine that Changed the World* with the book *Lean Thinking*. Lean was even more than a highly effective system for delivering value to customers—it was a different way of thinking about the total enterprise. They made clear in that book that the lean model was not based on Japanese automotive companies in general, but on Toyota specifically. Toyota had the best performance at the time of any of the Japanese auto companies and was the best model for "lean thinking."

The Toyota Way: A Philosophy and Way of Thinking

The Toyota Way begins with a passion for solving problems for customers and society. To do this requires deep respect for people and their ability to adapt and innovate. Building an enterprise that can withstand being beaten and battered by the harsh environment, decade after decade, requires a degree of adaptation that can only come from relentless kaizen from everyone possible. Since people are not born with the spirit or skills for kaizen, they must be taught them. As with any other advanced skill, teaching requires some direction and persistent practice.

If you believe findings by cognitive psychologists, such as Dr. K. Anders Ericsson, mastering any complex skill requires "deliberate practice" for 10 years or 10,000 repetitions (see Ericsson et al., 2007). Deliberate practice requires a self-awareness of weaknesses and drills to correct them, one by one, and is helped by a teacher who can see the weaknesses and suggest the drills. Ohno had been doing this throughout his career. As he learned, he then taught, not through lecturing, but at the gemba by challenging students, giving them (often harsh) feedback, and letting them struggle.

After the TPS was well established in Japan, Toyota had a dilemma. Could this finely tuned system work in a foreign country, without the Japanese workers and culture that seemed to fit so well with its principles? Toyota did what Toyota does—experimented. They decided not to go it alone and partnered with General Motors in a 50–50 joint venture called New United Motor Manufacturing Inc. (NUMMI). NUMMI started up in 1984 hiring back over 80 percent of the workers from the GM plant in Freemont, California that had been closed down in 1982. A reason for closing down the plant was horrible labor relations that led to low productivity and quality. With these workers and the Toyota Way, NUMMI quickly became the best automotive assembly plant in North America in quality, productivity, low inventory, safety—in short, more like a high-performing Toyota plant in Japan than a low-performing GM plant. Toyota learned a lot and then decided to start up its own plant in Georgetown, Kentucky (TMMK) which started production in 1988.

Fujio Cho was selected as the first President of TMMK. If anything it had surpassed the performance of NUMMI and all seemed well. But Fujio Cho saw a weakness. As the Japanese trainers left and Americans were increasingly taking over responsibility for the plant they needed explicit training in the Toyota Way. He realized there was more to Toyota's company philosophy than is captured in the TPS, which is mainly a prescription for manufacturing. The broader philosophy was learned tacitly in Japan, by living in the company and repeatedly hearing the stories and being mentored. What he experienced in America was a lot of variation in the understanding of the core philosophy which Toyota expected all of its leaders to embrace.

Fujio Cho's work over a period of about 10 years led to many versions of a document that never got approved. Toyota works toward consensus, and it could not get consensus. When Fujio Cho became President of Toyota Motor Company globally in 1999, he revived the effort, this time for the company as a whole. He still struggled to get consensus because others said the philosophy was a living and breathing entity and could not be frozen in time as a document. He finally got agreement to call the document "The Toyota Way 2001," with the understanding that it was the best they had in 2001 and could be modified in the future (it has not been so far).

It is represented as a house (see Figure 2.2). The two pillars are continuous improvement and respect for people. Continuous improvement means just what it says: everybody, everywhere, constantly challenging the way they are currently working and asking, "Is there a better way?"

Respect for people goes far beyond treating people nicely. In Toyota, respect means challenging people to be their best, and that means they are also continually improving themselves as they improve the way they work to better satisfy the customer. Respect for people is intentionally generic. It is not only respect for people who are employed by Toyota. It starts with the purpose of the company, which is to add value to customers and society by providing the best means of transportation possible. Respect for society includes respect for the environment, respect for the communities in which Toyota does business, and respect for the local laws and customs of each community.

It is difficult to respect people who are treated as temporary, disposable labor. So Toyota makes a long-term commitment to its employees and to the communities where it sets up shop. Though it does happen, people rarely lose their jobs. Even in the Great Recession, Toyota carried tens of

Figure 2.2 The Toyota Way 2001 house

Source: Liker (2015).

thousands of people globally who they did not need to make vehicles at the low level of demand (see Liker and Ogden, 2011). They worked on continuous improvement and on developing people through education and training, waiting out the bad economy and preparing for the inevitable pent-up demand when things got better. Toyota did not close factories, and this saved local communities from the devastating effects of massive job loss.

There is a particular right way to achieve continuous improvement and respect for people represented by the core values in the foundation of the house. It begins with developing people who will gladly take on a challenge, even when they have no idea how they will achieve it. Examples of challenges that Toyota has achieved from 2000 to 2016 include:

- 20 percent reduction in resources for new model development;
- 25 percent improvement in fuel economy with 15 percent more power;
- 40 percent reduction in cost of a new plant;
- 50 percent reduction in launching a new model, with almost zero downtime;
- eventual target of 75 percent reduction in part numbers.

Each of these remarkable achievements was the result of relentless kaizen. Someone got the assignment to achieve a breakthrough objective, they got a team together, and they followed a well-defined process to systematically improve, step by step, toward the challenge. The challenge provided the direction. Toyota Business Practices (TBP) provides the process (see Figure 2.3). Those familiar with improvement processes will recognize the plan-do-check-act (PDCA) cycle, which is often attributed to Dr. W. Edwards Deming. It is through many cycles of PDCA, essentially constant experimentation and study reflecting on what was learned at each step, that Toyota achieves its breakthrough objectives. And as the leaders work through obstacle after obstacle to meet the challenge, they develop as better leaders and people.

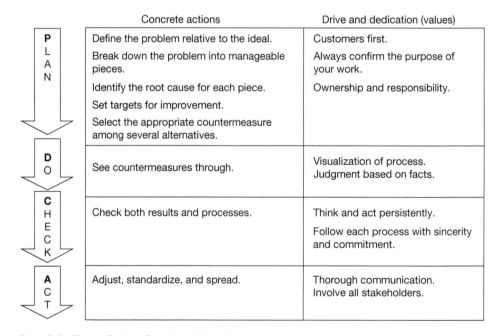

	Concrete actions	Drive and dedication (values)
P L A N	Define the problem relative to the ideal.	Customers first.
	Break down the problem into manageable pieces.	Always confirm the purpose of your work.
	Identify the root cause for each piece.	Ownership and responsibility.
	Set targets for improvement.	
	Select the appropriate countermeasure among several alternatives.	
D O	See countermeasures through.	Visualization of process. Judgment based on facts.
C H E C K	Check both results and processes.	Think and act persistently. Follow each process with sincerity and commitment.
A C T	Adjust, standardize, and spread.	Thorough communication. Involve all stakeholders.

Figure 2.3 Toyota Business Practices—Toyota's systematic improvement process

One hard-and-fast rule of TBP is to practice it at the gemba, or what Toyota calls *genchi genbutsu*, meaning, "go and see the actual place to observe directly and learn." Toyota leaders are obsessive about direct observation. In fact, they distinguish between data (abstractions of reality) and facts (direct observation of reality). Both are invaluable in understanding the current reality and determining what happens when you attempt some sort of intervention.

The final two values focus on people. People work to be the best contributors possible to the team. As stated in "The Toyota Way 2001," "We stimulate personal and professional growth, share the opportunities of development, and maximize individual and team performance" (Liker, 2004). The team is always given credit for accomplishments, while there is always an individual leader accountable for the results of the project.

Then we come right back to respect as the way in which improvement is carried out. This includes respect for stakeholders, mutual trust and responsibility, and sincere accountability. Accountability is described in the following way: "We accept responsibility for working independently, putting forth honest effort to the best of our abilities and always honoring our performance promises" (Liker, 2004).

What happened to the TPS, you ask? What about just-in-time (JIT) and built-in-quality and stable processes? In "The Toyota Way 2001," these are part of "lean systems and structure" which contributes to kaizen (see Figure 2.4). These are the tools and concepts which we should consider when working to meet the challenging objectives. At the start of this chapter, I argued that lean management has lost perspective. It almost seems to be an end unto itself. Companies think, "Let's implement JIT to reduce inventory" or "Let's install quality systems to build in quality" or "Let's put in standard work so that processes are stable." In the Toyota Way, however, these are but tools and concepts to consider when doing kaizen to strive toward excellence. The focus is on the objective and the right way to achieve the objective. Lean systems are side by side with innovative thinking and promoting organizational learning, and collectively, these contribute to kaizen. This is an entirely different mindset than the mechanistic view of implementing tools to get specific results.

Figure 2.4   Lean systems are a contributor to kaizen in the foundation of the Toyota Way

Applying the Thinking of the Toyota Way to your Organization

As we reflect on the beginning of the chapter, when we discussed the problem of companies and their many advisors viewing lean as a toolkit for waste reduction, perhaps it is clearer just how far afield these mechanistic "lean programs" have come from the rich tradition developed within Toyota. I hope the chapters in this book help put our readers back on track to the original purpose of the Toyota Way: to create a culture of people continuously improving to adapt and grow through the many challenges of the environment.

This is not to say that anywhere you go and anyone you meet in Toyota follows all of these principles to the letter. Think of "The Toyota Way 2001" as a holy document like the Bible or a governmental constitution. The fact that people deviate from the doctrine, or misapply it, is not an indictment of the doctrine. It is simply that we as humans are far from perfect, sometimes misinformed, sometimes using bad judgment, rarely being perfectly disciplined, and often giving in to immediate needs and desires. In fact, if we were perfect, we would not need any written or spoken doctrine. We would just be.

The Toyota Way is often spoken about as "true north," a beacon that guides daily behavior and helps us to detect whether we are on track or off track. The very basis of continuous improvement is to identify gaps between the actual and ideal and work relentlessly to reduce those gaps, including gaps in our own skills and behaviors.

If we think about trying to improve our bodies physically through exercise and healthy eating, we would all admit that we err from time to time—eating too much or skipping exercise. The vision is a great one, but the execution is often flawed. For those who have lost control of their bodies and are obese, it is extremely difficult to even get started. We have so far to go and need tremendous discipline and a great deal of social support. Those in relatively good shape may already have some of the skills and may have developed a degree of willpower. And the more we exercise that willpower to create positive habits, the easier it becomes to follow our daily regime.

Being mediocre as an organization with few well-defined habits and poorly defined processes is like being obese. It is painful to even think of getting started on the path to true north. But as we try, sometimes fail, but also have small wins, we get more and more skilled in overcoming our weaknesses. Success breeds success and diligent practice is the only true path to excellence.

Toyota is far from perfect, but is comparatively healthy in many parts of the organization and in many different cultures. It has passionately developed leaders who strive to live the values—striving for true north. They have the social support of senior leaders consistent in their vision of true north—consistent over decades of growth. Even for an organization very far from Toyota's maturity level, it is never too early to start the process of looking with brutal honesty at where you are and where you would like to get to—your true north. Then we need to take a first step, then a second step, and continuously improve our way to the vision.

As you think of how to get started in your organization, review the principles of the Toyota Way. Review Toyota Business Practices, which gives you an idea for getting started. Where will you start? Identify a challenge that will bring your organization to a new level of customer service. Define the ideal state. Understand the current state. Then break down the problem into manageable pieces—step by step. For each step, identify a short-term target and begin to experiment toward each target through PDCA cycles. Every step is worthwhile, successful or not, as long as you learn something. Additional guidance is provided by Mike Rother (2010) in his book *Toyota Kata*. He has gone deeper into the essence of Toyota thinking, providing practice routines to work your way toward the habit of daily improvement.

If you already have a lean program started, I encourage you to think about that program as part of the current state and compare it with the ideal state. What are the critical gaps in how the program is being executed? How are you doing at developing people in a respectful way? Where is a culture of continuous improvement starting to take root and where is there stagnation? Investigate personally at the gemba. You will begin to understand the true condition of your organization and yourself as a leader. Striving for perfection always begins with working on yourself as a role model for continuous improvement and respect for people.

References

Ericsson, K. A., Prietula, M. J., and Cokely, E. T. (2007). The making of an expert. *Harvard Business Review*, *85*(7/8), 114.

Krafcik, J. F. (1988). Triumph of the lean production system. *MIT Sloan Management Review*, *30*(1), 41–51.

Liker, J. K. (2004). *The Toyota Way*, New York, McGraw-Hill Professional.

Liker, J. K. (2015). *The Toyota Way 2001 House: Lean for the 21st Century.* Available at: www.gray.com/news/blog/2015/05/13/the-toyota-way-2001-house-lean-for-the-21st-century (accessed July 2016).

Liker, J. K. and Ogden, T.N. (2011). *Toyota, under Fire*, New York, McGraw-Hill Professional.

Rother, M. (2010). *Toyota Kata: Managing People for Continuous Improvement and Superior Results*, New York, McGraw-Hill.

Smiles, S. ([1859] 1982). *Self-Help*, London, John Murray Publishing.

Toyota (2012). *Toyoda Precepts: The Base of the Global Vision.* Available at: www.toyota-global.com/company/toyota_traditions/company/apr_2012.html (accessed July 2016).

Womack, J. P. and Jones, D. T. (1996). *Lean Thinking: Banish Waste and Create Wealth in Your Corporation*, New York, Simon & Schuster.

Womack, J. P., Jones, D. T., and Roos, D. (1990). *The Machine that Changed the World*, New York, Simon & Schuster.

PART I

The Lean Enterprise

3

LEAN PRODUCTION

Pauline Found and John Bicheno

Introduction

At the time of writing, it is more than one quarter-century since the term *"lean production"* was first introduced to the management lexicon by John Krafcik, a researcher from the Massachusetts Institute of Technology (MIT), who was working on the International Motor Vehicle Program (IMVP) (Krafcik, 1988). Womack, Jones, and Roos later popularized lean in the bestselling book *The Machine that Changed the World*. However, it was Richard Schonberger and Robert Hall who wrote the two books, in 1982 and 1983 respectively, that effectively launched (or relaunched) the concept that became known as lean production in the West. Schonberger (2007) noted that while *The Machine that Changed the World* is commonly perceived to mark the beginning of the lean movement, in reality lean manufacturing was actually already well established in the US in the early 1980s, albeit under different names.

In *The Machine*, the authors contend that the findings of the IMVP large-scale study revealed that there was a dramatic performance gap between Japanese and Western car producers and asserted that lean production should be universally adopted: "Our conclusion is simple: Lean production is a superior way for humans to make things . . . It follows that the whole world should adopt lean production, and as quickly as possible" (Womack et al., 1990, p. 225). The impact of *The Machine* has been far-reaching and the book led to the commissioning of two follow-up studies that provided further support for the existence of a substantial performance gap (Anderson, 1992; Oliver et al., 1994). These studies were publicized extensively to the manufacturing community at the time.

In the period since the introduction of lean, huge changes have taken place, yet it is also true that, for the majority of operations organizations, the lean potential has hardly been tapped. This chapter looks at the evolution and spread of lean and opens the discussion on lean as the dominant operations paradigm of the 21st century.

Evolution of Lean Production

Lean emerged in the West as a result of great interest in Japanese production and management methods stimulated by the second oil crisis when automotive production in the US fell by almost 22 percent as consumers turned to the more fuel-efficient small Japanese cars. The golden days of mass manufacturing in the US were over in 1976 as Chrysler declared bankruptcy and both GM and Ford were losing money. The interest in Japanese manufacturing techniques and, in particular, Toyota's production system, led to the publication of two English language articles in 1977, one by Sugimori et al. in the *Journal of Production Research* and the other by Ashburn in the *American Machinist* (cited in Schonberger, 2007) which raised concerns in US and European automotive companies, but it was an NBC-TV broadcast by producer Claire Crawford-Mason in 1980 entitled "If Japan Can, Why Can't We?" that prompted a quality revolution, which led to the five-year, five million dollar IMVP research program.

The ideas behind what is now termed "lean" originate from several sources, including great industrialists like Henry Ford in the US, Frank Woollard in the UK who developed the concepts behind flow manufacturing and moving assembly lines and management thinkers such as W. Edwards Deming and Peter Drucker who criticized mass manufacturing and won support in Japan to think differently. In Japan, one of the main sources is considered to be Sakichi Toyoda in the Toyoda loom factory, who originally developed the philosophy and methods associated with lean production at the turn of the 20th century; these influenced his son Kiichiro Toyoda to develop what is known as the just-in-time (JIT) method at the Toyota Motor Company in the late 1930s which became one of the pillars of the company.

The Second World War reconstruction of Japanese manufacturing and the lack of available capital resources and severe economic slump saw these ideas extended and combined with a discipline of daily improvements (*kaizen*) at Toyota that was supported by Eiji Toyoda, the new chairman, and enforced by chief engineer Taiichi Ohno, who had transferred from Toyoda Loom Works to Toyota Motor Company in 1943. The new approach, created by Taiichi Ohno, became known as the Toyota Production System (TPS). The philosophy and methods of TPS evolved over time, extending to Toyota's supply base in the 1970s, its distribution and sales operations in the 1980s, and became a competitive weapon as Toyota competed openly with US and European automakers. Toyota's business success and world-leading product quality is an established fact. Rother (2010) recently summarized Toyota's success into four key statistics: Toyota has shown sales growth for over 40 years (at the same time other car makers' sales have reached a plateau or declined); Toyota's profit exceeds that of other car makers; Toyota's market capitalization has for many years exceeded that of other car makers; and in sales rank Toyota has become the world leading car maker. This success is often attributed to the production system Toyota developed during 1950s and 1960s as a result of intense post-war competition.

TPS is characterized by a systematic approach to the organization of production that emphasizes the elimination of all forms of waste (Ohno, 1988). However, over time TPS has been discovered to be a complex, multifaceted element of Toyota's broader management system and culture, something that has been reflected in the prolific lean literature. In his book *The Evolution of a Manufacturing System at Toyota*, Takahiro Fujimoto (1999) describes how Toyota developed three layers of manufacturing capabilities: a routinized manufacturing layer, a routinized learning layer, and a non-routine and dynamic evolutionary learning capability which gives Toyota the capacity and strength to adapt and change over time. Spear and Bowen (1999, p. 99) attempted to codify TPS and describe four key rules that describe the tacit knowledge and guide the design, operation, and improvement of every activity, connection, and pathway of products and services and it is these rules that are the essence, or DNA, of TPS. These rules are as follows:

1   All work shall be specified as to content, sequence, timing and outcome.
2   Every customer–supplier connection must be direct.
3   The pathway for every product or service must be simple and direct.
4   Any improvement must be made in accordance with the scientific method, under the guidance of a teacher, at the lowest level in the organization.

In spite of a plethora of academic and practitioner books and articles on lean, however, there is still not a precise and agreed-upon definition (Shah and Ward, 2007). Referring to the old fable of the blind men touching an elephant and imagining very different animals, Shah and Ward suggest that over time commentators on lean have focused on single, visible aspects of the process while missing the invisible highly inter-dependent links of lean systems as a whole. As well as being a poorly defined construct, interpretations of lean have continued to evolve over time. Originally presented by Womack et al. (1990) as a counter intuitive alternative to traditional manufacturing, it is now presented, by some at least, as a new paradigm for operations management (Bartezzaghi, 1999; Holweg, 2007). In addition, lean has expanded beyond its original applications on the shop floor of vehicle manufacturers to other functional areas within organizations, to other manufacturers and to non-manufacturing organizations. Consequently, lean means different things to different people (see Table 3.1).

Lean is described as a philosophy (Bhasin and Burcher, 2006), a management system (Hines et al., 2004), and an operating system of production planning and control (Standard and Davis, 1999).

Lean Production as a Philosophy, Management and Operating system

Lean as an Operating System for Production Planning and Control

A shop floor-based view of lean still emerges as the prominent means of implementation. The essence of this view is smoothing and improving operational processes through the application of lean tools. Often, these are not even a set of tools but completely independently introduced by companies trying to emulate the TPS. For example, managers employ a variety of mapping tools

Table 3.1 Lean viewed as a philosophy, a management system, and an operating system for lean production planning and control

Lean philosophy
Systems thinking
Value for the customer
Waste elimination
Lead time reduction
Humility and respect for humans
Continuous improvement
Lean management
Hoshin kanri (policy deployment)
Value stream (cross functional and "gemba" management)
Visual management and visual controls
Kata
Leader standard work
TWI (Training Within Industry)
Lean operations
Value stream management
5S
Standard work
TPM (total productive management)/SMED (single-minute exchange of dies)
Pull systems/Kanban
Demand and capacity management

Source: Adapted from Slack et al. (2004).

to identify the value-added and non-value-added activities of each process. From this they can reduce the operating costs by eliminating non-value-added activities, waste, and reorganizing value-added activities. In these cases, the primary goal of the shop floor tool-based method is to efficiently improve the organization's performance at an operational level, by enhancing quality and reducing waste, inventories, and lead times (Manos and Vincent, 2012).

Womack and Jones began their book *Lean Thinking* with the words "Muda. It's the one Japanese word you really must know" (Womack and Jones, 2003, p. 15). Today there is widespread awareness of waste. Fujio Cho, former President of Toyota, defined waste as "anything other than the minimum amount of equipment, materials, parts, space and worker's time, which are absolutely essential to add value to the product" (Suzaki, 1987, p. 8). The concept of *muda* primarily originated from Taiichi Ohno's production philosophy in the early 1950s (Dahlgaard-Park, 2000) although Toyota also talks about three Ms—*muda* (waste), *muri* (overburden), and *mura* (unevenness). Knowing about all three gives a more complete understanding of lean; the three are interlinked and lean is about mobilizing people to reduce all three. While total quality management (TQM) was not mentioned in *The Machine that Changed the World*, possibly because TQM was not a well-known management philosophy in the West at that time (Dahlgaard and Dahlgaard-Park, 2006), the mention of muda in lean thinking is very significant as it links the two management philosophies and confirms that the aim of lean production is to eliminate waste.

Lean is often described as a pull system, compared with a materials requirements planning (MRP), or push, system. Toyota implemented a JIT pull system in post-World War II Japan as the capital resources to support the high levels of inventory that were often the consequence of push and MRP systems were not available. The concept behind JIT is described by Monden (1983, p. 2). JIT means "to produce the necessary units at the necessary quantities at the necessary time" and core to implementing a JIT and pull system is managing demand and capacity to reduce the lead time between customer order and cash received. Therefore, pull systems are based on responding to actual customer demand, not in response to orders *pushed* on to the shop floor from schedules based on forecasts. Pull is based on a sell-one (or use-one), make-one concept of small batches. To run a successful pull system, demand needs to be leveled as much as possible to eliminate spikes and to allow the products to flow without disruption and diversion, thus reducing the need for excess inventory. This is managed by understanding the "load" and the "capacity" of the system. Load is the amount of work imposed on the system and capacity is the resources available to do the work. Ohno used a simple formula to show that present effective capacity is the sum of work and waste:

Present capacity = work + waste.

While this is a simple way to demonstrate that you can get more work out of the current system by reducing the waste, this can be misunderstood and may suggest that you can increase capacity if you increase waste. There are actually three factors that influence queues or lead time. These are arrival variation, process variation, and utilization, as in the equations: *Utilization* = *load*/*capacity* and *load* = *real demand* + *mistake demand* (mistake demand could be rework, work done due to errors, failure demand). Therefore, *present capacity* = *base capacity* − *waste*. Hence, there are four things that should be tackled: arrival variation, process variation, mistake demand, and waste.

The key to realizing JIT is not relying on a central planning approach to production control which "pushes" a product through production by simultaneously scheduling the individual processes but, rather, that work (or value) should flow through the system at the pace of the demand without deviation, detour, or delay. Where flow is not possible, pull systems might use a *kanban* system as the way to manage JIT production. Kanban is a signal from a process to the preceding process to indicate that product has been consumed and that it is necessary to produce more to replenish the quantity withdrawn. The signal can be in the form of a card system, a square or, indeed, any suitable signaling system that is visual and recognizable by the operators (Harmon and Peterson, 1990). Kanban is not the only control system used in a lean environment. *Drum buffer rope* (DBR) and *constant work-in-process* (CONWIP) are often the most effective pull-oriented hybrid production control systems in other situations, such as process plants (Hopp and Spearman, 2000).

To be implemented successfully, JIT/pull systems need to be aligned to strategy, supported by senior management and operated by skilled people. Pull may not be the best strategy for all products; some products that are made infrequently may be better "made to stock" and replenished when needed. There are several lean tools that support small batches and pull systems, such as *single-minute exchange of dies* (SMED) to reduce changeover times, *total productive management* (TPM) to increase availability and 5S to organize the workplace. JIT is supported by *jidoka*, or autonomation, which may be interpreted as "automation with a human touch" that prevents defects from disrupting the flow from process to process. JIT and jidoka are the two pillars of the Toyota Production System (TPS) and, consequentially, in lean production systems (Bicheno and Holweg, 2008).

While, for many, lean production starts with "tools," Toyota did not start with this way. It started with the unremitting focus on how to use its resources to produce a product that is defined to be as close as possible to what the customer wants to buy and how to align the flow of production as close as possible to the flow of cash. The five lean principles (Figure 3.1) presented in the book *Lean Thinking*, by Womack and Jones (1996), represent a "roadmap" for those organizations attempting to implement lean or emulate TPS.

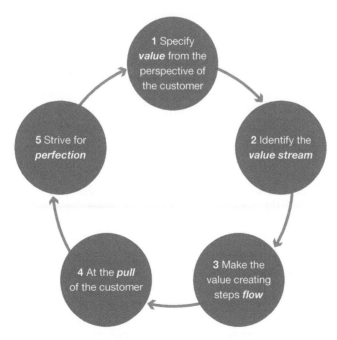

Figure 3.1 The five lean principles

Source: Based on Womack and Jones (1996).

The empirical data in *Lean Thinking* is based on case studies of companies that have successfully adopted the lean imperative to become lean organizations. The five lean principles defined introduced a structure, or framework, to better describe the approach at Toyota and the focus moved from the "tools" approach towards the principles of self-help, and respect and responsibility towards staff, customers, and society. At this point some lean commentators began to realize that "real" lean (Emiliani, 2007) is behavior-driven and linked to a mindset of creating thinking people who can solve real production problems and the focus shifted in the literature from tools to problem solving (Spear and Bowen, 1999; Hines et al., 2004, 2011; Liker, 2004; Spear, 2009) and becoming a learning organization (Senge, 1990).

Lean as a Management System for Process Improvement

The Japanese word *kaizen* quite literally means change, or changing (kai), for the better, or good (zen), and the term entered popular Western management terminology in the 1980s (Imai, 1986) to refer to problem solving and continuous improvement. Continuous improvement is the essence of the fifth lean principle: Strive for Perfection. This principle recognizes that lean is not a single project that has an endpoint, but rather a journey of daily improvements as identified by Eiji Toyoda and Taiichi Ohno in TPS. Problem solving, experimentation, and continuous improvement are part of the culture of the whole organization and built in to the day-to-day management system. Deming's improvement cycle, *plan, do, check* (or *study*), *act* (PDCA or PDSA) is often used by organizations as a vehicle by which to maintain and sustain improvement activities.

Not all of the quality influences on Toyota came from the West; one of the most influential Japanese authors on quality and problem solving is undoubtedly Kaoru Ishikawa who gave his name to the "*Ishikawa diagram*," more popularly known as the "fishbone" cause-and-effect diagram. The diagram is so-called because it resembles the skeleton of a fish when it is drawn. The method is used to determine problems within a workplace and then to identify the root cause of the problem before assigning it to a theme, or category. The head of the fish is the visual problem (symptom) and the skeleton forms the possible underlying causes, sorted into themes that resemble the spines of the fish skeleton. Along each spine the issues (causes) are highlighted. The original main themes used in such kaizen and problem solving were the methods used, the machinery used, the materials used, the measurements used, the management of the process (often known as manpower), and the working environment or mother nature (six themes that can all begin with the letter M), but these can be adapted to be specific to a particular setting and are used in many organizations as part of their kaizen and problem-solving events (Bicheno, 2006).

Kaizen is well established as an improvement methodology in manufacturing and is increasingly being used in the service sector. Three types of kaizen improvements are often employed within organizations to tackle different levels of problems (Figure 3.2):

1   Daily problem solving, which focuses continuously on small problems that can be tackled immediately, or over a few days.
2   Kaizen events (blitz) actions which usually last for one week and focus on medium-sized problems such as reducing changeover times. Kaizen events are not typically used in Japan. They are actually a US innovation, suited to using outside experts and consultants (cited in Stoller, 2015).
3   System kaizen for the few strategic, large problems that are longer in duration, possibly up to three to four months. The scope of the problem would be a process redesign at a departmental level.

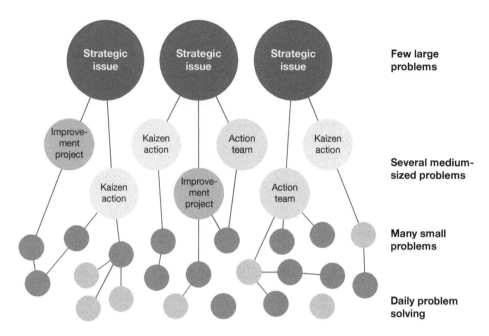

Figure 3.2   Cascade of problems and solutions

Source: Adapted from Dennis (2006).

Kaizen teams utilize a full range of problem-solving tools, such as fishbone diagrams, to determine the root cause of the problem. A very effective tool used in kaizen is the "5 Whys" technique to ask "why does this happen?" repeatedly until the root cause appears. Typically, a kaizen event includes a *value stream mapping activity* to describe the current state and identify problems or improvement opportunities. Central to kaizen is *genchi genbutsu* (go and see for yourself), and the concept of personal involvement. George Koenigsaecker, former CEO of the Danaher Corporation, who has led several successful lean transformations, expected executives from all the companies he managed to participate personally in at least ten kaizen events. His philosophy was that only by participating personally could an executive really know and understand the business and its internal and external issues (Koenigsaecker, 2009).

In recent years, *kata* has often replaced kaizen. Kata is described by Rother (2010) as a structured routine of continual improvements that are practiced every day under the guidance of skilled coaches to build new habits and ways of thinking. By practicing improvement kata daily obstacles are removed to enable an organization to move from its current condition toward a new target condition that is aligned to a long-term vision.

As a management system, lean focuses on supporting the lean principles and aligning the goals of the organization to the operational business improvement plans through a structured deployment of the strategic policies, known in the West as *policy* (or *strategy*) *deployment*. In Japan the term is *hoshin kanri*, meaning "shining needle," and refers to directional management. The methodology of hoshin kanri is to align visibly the key performance indicators (KPIs) of the business goals through a cascading system, where the top-level strategy is a function of all of the sub-strategies of the business hierarchy. Hoshin kanri is a strategic management system that shares the commercial vision and goals for the business with everyone providing clarity of purpose and communicating business priorities to all employees so that they can contribute to, and understand their role in, organizational improvement.

Lean management is also built on *visual management*, where performance is transparent so managers and team leaders can see easily how the business is performing and the improvement targets. Critical to this are standard work operations, visual controls, and mistake-proof devices (known as *poka yoke*). Performance boards are located in the workplace, or *gemba*, and managers are encouraged to spend time at the workplace practicing *genchi genbutsu,* going to the source to get the facts and then making informed decisions based on consensus of the solutions.

Leaders are encouraged to practice *leader standard work* (LSW) by creating standard routines for most leadership tasks, such as morning meetings, audit checks, and problem escalation procedures to reduce problems and ensure permanent fixes are introduced by those closest to the process.

Initially, lean production was seen to be incompatible with enterprise resource planning (ERP) and there were major debates in the literature about whether lean and MRP conflicted or complemented each other. However, new insights have shown that they can co-exist and most ERP vendors have now developed lean programs within their ERP systems that complement the shop floor and visual management systems (Powell, 2013).

Lean as a Philosophy

TPS was founded on two pillars, just-in-time, making only what is needed, when it is needed, and in the amount needed, and *jidoka*, automation with a human touch. Jidoka is putting people in charge of the process to identify problems and to stop the line if defective parts are detected. Combining the concept that quality must be built into products and operations systems with respecting people's judgment in recognizing poor quality/variation is key to improving productivity. To support this, a collaborative approach to team-based problem solving is required within a leadership culture that promotes transparency and open reporting of problems. A blame culture prohibits kaizen, and the use of specialists only to solve problems distances operator teams from suggesting and owning improvement solutions. The lean philosophy involves everyone: it is neither a top-down nor bottom-up approach but all-inclusive. Leaders at all levels are encouraged to coach and mentor less experienced people daily to transfer knowledge throughout the organization. The daily opportunity to learn, experiment, and improve engrains these activities in the organizational culture—one that accepts change rather than resists it.

A good example of a lean enterprise that views lean as a philosophy is GKN, a major British multinational corporation with operations in more than 30 countries and over 140 manufacturing businesses, which employs more than 50,000 people around the world. Founded in 1759, in South Wales, UK, GKN was one of the first companies of the modern industrial age. After more than 250 years, this global British engineering company operates in four divisions: GKN Aerospace, GKN Driveline, GKN Powder Metallurgy, and GKN Land Systems—and is a major first tier supplier to the automotive and aerospace industries with established solid foundations and policies in both lean and environmental fields.

Lean was introduced in 2004 in the GKN automotive sector to improve competiveness in that market and one of the early significant milestones was the support by senior leadership for the Site Continuous Improvement Leader (SCIL) training program. This series of training workshops takes promising manufacturing leaders and trains them to expert level over a period of a year. These leaders return to their home site and become the local lean change agents for their factory, focusing on the deployment of lean to manufacturing processes. This structure has become the backbone of lean deployment at GKN where all sites are required to develop an annual continuous improvement plan, aligned to their business objectives, which engages every employee in driving value through the business. In addition to the SCIL program, GKN also introduced a Mastering Continuous Improvement Leadership (MCIL) program that saw 350 leaders graduating in 2011.

Employee involvement is at the heart of GKN's lean enterprise model. Employees are able to submit improvement ideas and implement many of these ideas in the workplace. Leaders are encouraged to coach their teams at every opportunity, allowing team members to grow and thrive. Together these form a culture in which improvement is encouraged.

Although there are different views of lean production, these could also reflect the position of the organization on the lean implementation journey. Most organizations will start with an operations focus by implementing tools; this would progress to a management system and, ultimately, to an organizational culture where the philosophy of lean is embedded, if the organization completes the journey. Netland and Ferdows (2014) describe the pattern of performance improvement in Volvo and other major organizations and explain how the journey goes through four stages that represent an "S" curve in performance improvement, where the rapid gains appear to occur in Stage II. In this "S" curve stages I and II might reflect an operations approach to performance improvement, whereas Stage III is more reflective of a management system. For an organization to transition to the final stage and become a "cutting edge" plant, managers have to manage their own, and the organization's, expectations to ensure that the organization does not become complacent and slip back due to tool and change fatigue. Therefore, in "cutting edge" plants managers need to think strategically to leverage the gains and embed the changes into the culture and philosophy of the organization.

The Future of Lean Production

While lean production started as a description of TPS, the evidence in the literature demonstrates that it has evolved over time well beyond the traditional Japanese automotive manufacturing roots to an enterprise system focused on best practice and process improvement methodologies that has been adopted, and adapted, by public and private sector organizations around the world. In a study on the diffusion of lean, Samuel (2011) found that the period 1987–1995 was dominated by automobile and automotive supply chain publications. From 1995, publications on aerospace and electronic industries emerged, followed by retail, construction, financial services, and health. Since 2000, the body of lean literature in all sectors has increased substantially and spread from private sector manufacturing and service organizations to the public sector and public services in almost all departments. In addition, more recent publications on innovation, new product/service development, leadership, culture, and IT have taken lean beyond the traditional fields of operations and process improvement into more enterprise-wide areas as well as into start-ups and small to medium-sized (SME) businesses. Lean has extended into areas such as "lean and green" and combined with concepts such as *systems thinking* to push the boundaries of lean to solve 21st-century environmental concerns and compete on innovation.

So, 25 years on, lean has touched many aspects of our everyday lives beyond how companies structure, operate, and organize themselves. It is clear that lean has come a long way from its shop floor origins in the very best car-making companies. It continues to evolve today and to infiltrate our strategic and operational management thinking into the 21st century, yet so much potential remains untapped.

References

Anderson (1992). *The Lean Enterprise Report*, London, Anderson Consulting.
Bartezzaghi, E. (1999). The evolution of production models: Is a new paradigm emerging? *International Journal of Operations and Production Management, 19*(2), 229–250.

Bhasin, S. and Burcher, P. (2006). Lean viewed as a philosophy. *Journal of Manufacturing Technology Management*, 17(1), 56–72.

Bicheno, J. (2006). *Fishbone Flow: Integrating Lean, Six Sigma, TPM and TRIZ*, Johannesburg, South Africa, PICSIE Books.

Bicheno, J. and Holweg, M. (2008). *The Lean Toolbox: The Essential Guide to Lean Transformation*, Johannesburg, South Africa, PICSIE Books.

Dahlgaard, J. J. and Dahlgaard-Park, S-M. (2006). Lean production, six sigma quality, TQM and company culture. *The TQM Magazine*, 18(3), 263–281.

Dahlgaard-Park, S-M. (2000). From Ancient Asian Philosophies to TQM and Modern Management Theories. Licentiate Thesis, Linköping University, Linköping.

Dennis, P. (2006). *Getting the Right Things Done: A Leader's Guide to Planning and Execution*, Cambridge, MA, Lean Enterprise Institute.

Emiliani, B. (2007). *Real Lean*, Kensington, CT, Center for Lean Business Management.

Fujimoto, T. (1999). *The Evolution of a Manufacturing System at Toyota*, Oxford, Oxford University Press.

Hall, R. W. (1983). *Zero Inventories*, Homewood, IL, Dow Jones-Irwin/APICS.

Harmon, R. L. and Peterson, L. D. (1990). *Reinventing the Factory: Productivity Breakthroughs in Manufacturing Today*, New York, Free Press.

Hines, P., Holweg, M., Piercy, N. and Rich, N. (2004). From production toolkit to strategic value creation—a review of the evolution of contemporary lean thinking. *International Journal of Operations and Production Management*, 24(10), 994–1011.

Hines, P., Found, P., Griffiths, G. and Harrison, R. (2011). *Staying Lean: Thriving, Not Just Surviving*, Boca Raton, FL, CRC Press.

Holweg, M. (2007). The genealogy of lean production. *Journal of Operations Management*, 25(2), 420–437.

Hopp, W. J. and Spearman, M. L. (2000). *Factory Physics*, 2nd edition, New York, McGraw-Hill/Irwin.

Imai, M. (1986). *The Key to Japan's Competitive Success*, New York, McGraw-Hill/Irwin.

Koenigsaecker, G. (2009). *Leading the Lean Enterprise Transformation*, Boca Raton, FL, CRC Press.

Krafcik, J. F. (1988). Triumph of the lean production system. *MIT Sloan Management Review*, 30(1), 41–51.

Liker, J. K. (2004). *The Toyota Way: 14 Management Principles from the World's Greatest Automaker*, New York, McGraw-Hill.

Manos, A. and Vincent, C. (eds) (2012). *The Lean Certification Handbook: A Guide to the Bronze Certification Body of Knowledge*, Milwaukee, WI, ASQ Quality Press.

Monden, Y. (1983). *Toyota Production System: Practical Approach to Production Management*, Norcross, Engineering & Management Press.

Netland, T. and Ferdows, K. (2014). What to expect from corporate lean programs. *MIT Sloan Management Review*, 55(4), 83–89.

Ohno, T. (1988). *Toyota Production System: Beyond Large-scale Production*, New York, Productivity Press.

Oliver, N., Jones, D. T., Lowe, J., Roberts, P. and Thayer, B. (1994). *Worldwide Manufacturing Competitiveness Study: The Second Lean Enterprise Report*, London, Anderson Consulting.

Powell, D. (2013). ERP systems in lean production: new insights from a review of lean and ERP literature. *International Journal of Operations and Production Management*, 33(11/12), 1490–1510.

Rother, M. (2010). *Toyota Kata: Managing People for Continuous Improvement and Superior Results*, New York, McGraw-Hill.

Samuel, D. E. (2011). *Exploring UK Lean Diffusion in the Period 1988 to 2010*, Cardiff University.

Senge, P. M. (1990). *The Fifth Discipline: The Art & Practice of the Learning Organization*, New York, Doubleday/Currency.

Shah, R. and Ward, P. T. (2007). Defining and developing measures of lean production. *Journal of Operations Management*, 25(4), 785–805.

Schonberger, R. (1982). *Japanese Manufacturing Techniques: Nine Hidden Lessons in Simplicity*, New York, Simon & Schuster.

Schonberger, R. J. (2007). Japanese production management: An evolution—with mixed success. *Journal of Operations Management*, 25(2), 403–419.

Slack, N., Chambers, S. and Johnston, R. (2004). *Operations Management*, 4th edition, Harlow, UK, Financial Times/Prentice Hall.

Spear, S. (2009). *Chasing the Rabbit*, New York, McGraw-Hill.

Spear, S. and Bowen, H. K. (1999). Decoding the DNA of the Toyota Production System. *Harvard Business Review*, 77, 96–108.

Standard, C. and Davis, D. (1999). *Running Today's Factory: A Proven Strategy for Lean Manufacturing*, Dearborn, MI, Society for Manufacturing Engineers.

Stoller, J. (2015). *The Lean CEO: Leading the Way to World-Class Excellence*, New York, McGraw-Hill Professional.

Sugimori, Y., Kusunoki, K., Cho, F. and Uchikawa, S. (1977). Toyota Production System and Kanban system: Materialization of just-in-time and respect-for-human system. *International Journal of Production Research*, *15*(6), 553–564.

Suzaki, K. (1987). *New Manufacturing Challenge: Techniques for Continuous Improvement*, New York, Simon & Schuster.

Womack, J. P. and Jones, D. T. (1996). *Lean Thinking: Banish Waste and Create Wealth in your Corporation*, New York, Simon & Schuster.

Womack, J. P. and Jones, D. T. (2003). *Lean Thinking: Banish Waste and Create Wealth in your Corporation*, new edition, London, Simon & Schuster.

Womack, J. P., Jones, D. T. and Roos, D. (1990). *The Machine that Changed the World*, New York, Simon & Schuster.

4

LEAN LEADERSHIP

Michael Ballé

Introduction

Lean leadership is the skill of achieving goals by developing people. "Lean," to a large extent, remains an attempt to generalize Toyota's unique management method to other companies and other fields—from healthcare to start-ups. From the start, leadership has been central to Toyota's management worldview. When Eiji Toyoda, the architect of the Toyota we now know, described the evolution of Toyota's management perspective he did so by highlighting the contribution of individual leaders who shaped the company by the systems they developed: Kiichiro Toyoda's just-in-time system, Shotaro Kamiya's sales system, Masao Nemoto and Hanji Uemata's total quality control system, Taiichi Ohno's *kanban* system and so on. For his own contribution, Eiji Toyoda repeatedly highlighted the suggestion system: the efforts made to get improvement ideas out of every employee, and thus offering everyone the opportunity to lead in their role (Shimokawa and Fujimoto, 2009).

Leadership appears everywhere in Toyota's thinking. Each new car model is developed by an engineering leader, the chief engineer. Employees work in teams led by a team leader. The first managerial job is that of group leader. Indeed, as Toyota's current president, Akio Toyoda, explains in Jeff Liker and Gary Convis' seminal book on *The Toyota Way to Lean Leadership* (2012, p. x): "We say at Toyota that every leader is a teacher developing the next generation of leaders. This is their most important job." He also explains his particular vision of leadership:

> The job of a leader is not to put [people] in positions to fail, but to put them in challenging positions where they must work hard to succeed and still see how they could have been even better. Our goal is for every Toyota team member from the worker on the production shop floor to our most senior executives to be working continuously to improve themselves
>
> *(Liker and Convis, 2012, p. xii)*

In studying both Toyota and experiments to learn from Toyota in other fields, it becomes quickly apparent that leadership is a key to success. It also becomes clear that the form of leadership required for a lean approach to seeking superior performance differs clearly from other leadership styles. Undeniably, it makes sense to talk about a specific lean leadership, in both content and style.

Lean leaders are expected to contribute to the business by the initiatives they develop that the company will adopt as a whole. They're expected to develop these initiatives by leading *kaizen* efforts on the *gemba*, at group leader, team leader, and team member level, learn from these small, local improvement efforts, and integrate them to the way the organization works in order to keep it evolving.

What is Lean Leadership?

Lean, taken as a full approach, can be seen as a learning system to develop such leadership in everyone. Over the years, Toyota has developed a system, a method, to learn (and teach) how to lead in this specific lean way. This system is based on six lean leadership practices:

1 *Gemba:* Go and see the real things at the real place with the real people.
2 *Challenge:* Recognize business challenges and express them clearly at the gemba.
3 *Business:* Understand the outcomes sought from attacking these challenges.
4 *Kaizen:* Support individual kaizen initiative and build it into collective change.
5 *Deep thinking:* Nurture deep thinking at all levels to sustain smart improvement ideas.
6 *Organize for learning:* Organize for learning by encouraging a lean leadership style within the management line.

Gemba

The most radical departure of lean leadership from any other form is the commitment to lead from the ground up: leadership starts at the gemba. Gemba is the lean term for "real place," where customers use the products or service, where engineers design them, at the workplace where employees do the work, at suppliers where components are designed and made, and so on.

Going to the worksite and confirming things in person is already a leadership act. As Kiichiro Toyoda explained: "When a problem arises, the shortest route to final resolution is to return to the source and pinpoint what is truly wrong" (Toyota Motor Corporation, 2009, p. 2). After viewing the worksite, it is important for employees to carefully think through what they have seen, and then take action. By spending time on the gemba, one can confirm facts first-hand. One can also get others to agree on the problem before arguing about solutions, as well as evaluate strengths and weaknesses of products, services, processes, and people in order to scope the required speed of progress.

The key ability a leader learns at the gemba is to shift constantly from business-level challenges to the detailed processes and problems of day-to-day real life. This "helicopter vision" (helicopter as in going up high in the sky to down at ground level) is what develops a multifaceted, gritty, complex understanding of reality. Based on this, leaders can learn to make sensible decisions and develop their business judgment according to operational realities. "Go and see" is also a strong show of respect for the people doing the work, who then have the opportunity to contribute to the company's vision by offering their perspective and insight. Simply being on the gemba allows the leader to check his or her thinking about the big picture, while sending a strong message of commonality of purpose and destiny to all staff.

Challenge

Until someone builds a crystal ball, the future remains unknowable, and increasingly so in turbulent times where hyper-competition, globalization, and technological change combine in unexpected and surprising ways. A strength of lean is that it does not seek to optimize a static situation (likely to be drastically changed by events tomorrow) but to seek dynamic gains. This results in being more adaptive and better able to cope with whatever comes.

Rather than visualize a strategy as a destination (which markets do we want to conquer, which is the best organization to do so, who should we hire to execute the strategy, and so forth), lean leaders are taught to identify the key challenges they face as improvement directions: things we want to do better. In the fog of war, these improvement directions are rarely self-evident, if only because humans naturally shy away from problems they don't feel confident they can solve. Acknowledging this, Toyota has established a few general principles that tell you exactly where to seek profitable challenges:

1   *Complete customer satisfaction:* Address every customer complaint today, facing every dis-gruntled client. This tough discipline keeps managers and their teams focused on under-standing what customers really want and how to evolve our offer in the future—what improvement direction should we take to improve our customers' engagement?
2   *Increase the level of just-in-time:* Whatever the current level of just-in-time (the response time between asking for something and receiving it), whether a year or a minute, how can we halve it? Reducing batch sizes and increasing the frequency of pick-ups increase the need for precision in all logistics operations, which reveals deeper capability problems—mostly hard technical issues.
3   *Increase the level of jidoka:* Whenever a defect occurs, is it possible to spot it closer to where it was created? To stop sooner and to react faster both to get the process back working the way it should and to investigate the causes of the problem? Improving measuring methods and devices within the process highlights possibilities of deepening people's fundamental knowl-edge and technical inventiveness.
4   *Intensify workplace improvement activities:* By asking people to improve their standardized work through regular training and problem solving and looking for further potential by studying their own work methods and coming up with new ideas, particularly in the fields of safety and ease of work, it is possible to discover new directions to engage and involve people further as well as reduce overburden.

In any situation, in any location, one can challenge oneself in these terms: how can I further increase customer satisfaction (internal and external)? How can I increase the precision of my logistics to reduce lead times? How can I spot defects earlier, react faster, investigate deeper? How can I better encourage teams to study their own methods and tackle safety, quality, and pro-ductivity issues by themselves? By asking these core questions the lean leader will progressively discover true improvement directions, which he or she can then share with the shop floor and challenge their subordinates to do the same. In taking a page from great explorers, we don't know where the sources of the Nile are, but we know which direction to look for them.

Business

A problem common to lean leaders is that they don't know how to translate lean challenges in business terms. Therefore, they have a hard time garnering the necessary support to pull changes through. For instance, Eiji Toyoda explicitly adopted Ford's suggestion systems to encourage idea generation, and not for the ideas' monetary value—at the same time as Ford abandoned the system because payback was poor. Lean leadership is about people development. Thus, it supports the flow of ideas and their exchange irrespective of potential gain, that is very clear; however, convincing more traditional managers of the benefits is a tall order.

To explain the outcomes sought by lean leadership we can look at the ROCE, *the return on capital employed*. ROCE can be expressed as results/sales × sales/capital employed; in other words, margin multiplied by turns. Toyota's lean method is quite specific on how to grow each of these terms:

- *Sales* grow from the stock of satisfied customers who both repurchase and recommend products or services. Systematically putting customers first is the lean method to steadily grow sales, *even in very competitive, saturated markets.*
- *Profitability* comes from productivity, which is achieved by higher levels of jidoka. Learning what is needed to improve *right first time* (RFT) and *first pass yield* (FPY) has a dramatic effect on productivity as it reduces non-productive time created by dealing with defects, reworks, and all the resulting confusion.
- *Capital employed* use improves with just-in-time: by delivering on time, reducing inventory, and increasing frequency of supplier pick-ups (with the related impact of leveling supplier invoicing). This has dramatic effects on wasted capital use such as unnecessary warehousing, unneeded logistics personnel and equipment, over-capacity, inflexible machines, over-complex computer software, and so on.
- *Morale*, and the employee engagement which is the key to sales, margins, and more frugal use of capital, is achieved by spending time on the gemba. This results in increased sharing of overall challenges with teams and supporting them as they find local improvement solutions that better fit with their day-to-day working environment and conditions.

At a more general business level, lean leadership looks at developing *goodwill* capital (brand value and enterprise value) from *intellectual* capital (ideas and technologies), which, in turn, derives from *human* capital (skills and expertise) and *social* capital (cooperation and trust).

The outcomes sought through lean challenges are enhancing goodwill through better satisfied customers, each according to their chosen lifestyle, from increased intellectual capital (quality and innovation) by, in turn, systematically developing human capital (through jidoka and kaizen) and social capital (through just-in-time and kaizen). In other words, a lean leader is constantly seeking to more completely satisfy customers through more precise mastery of techniques and innovation from technical insights. This is made possible by learning to reduce lead times and stop at defect, realized in practice by ongoing kaizen by local teams, everywhere, all the time, in order to develop initiative and mutual trust.

Kaizen

The question remains: how can lean leaders achieve large-scale progress from small-step local improvements? The deeper question here is how to secure the link between individual intelligence, limited to one role, one job, one workstation, and collective intelligence represented by the procedures and habits of the organization as a whole. Unless you believe in the wisdom of crowds, this is unlikely to happen on its own. In effect, lean leaders are taught to systematically chaperone kaizen ideas into process changes. This leadership skill can be illustrated by the suggestion system.

Toyota's *suggestion system* has been consistently underrepresented in the lean literature but is clearly an important piece of the lean system puzzle. As Jeff Liker and Michael Hoseus describe in *Toyota Culture* (2008), suggestions are very carefully handled by the group leader (the first level of shop floor management). When a member has an idea (often triggered by a problem in working safely, delivering just-in-time, or quality issue), she sketches it on a suggestion form. This is often done with the help of either a team leader or supervisor who helps the person clarify their idea and demonstrate the improvement potential. The person then agrees a plan with the group leader to trial the idea where and when is most practical. If the trial process is successful (and it's the group leader's job to make sure it is), the new method is now presented to all other team members concerned and all collateral kinks are ironed out. At this point, the suggestion is accepted and standards are modified accordingly.

A determining aspect of lean leadership is therefore accompanying employee ideas through the steps of 1) clarifying, 2) testing, 3) convincing others until it is finally 4) adopted. Such skill requires an attitudinal shift for many leaders in realizing that, first, all ideas matter and performance is largely driven by engagement of employees with one another. Additionally, reinforcing both social and human capital should be done through discussing and testing kaizen ideas. Second, a department or a company can be described as the sequence of its change points, change by change. Kaizen improvements therefore need babysitting all the way from a local improvement to a change in the way the organization does things. Failing to understand this, leaders often bemoan that the results achieved in kaizen activities don't stick. The results stick if the leader has developed the knack to turn kaizen improvements into procedural changes (which often involves a degree of dickering with other departments and stakeholders).

Deep Thinking

Thinking is a recurring theme at Toyota, right from the early development of the lean system. "Good thinking, good products" was adopted as a company slogan as early as 1953. Taiichi Ohno is widely quoted in saying: "The Toyota style is not to create results by working hard. It is a system that says there is no limit to people's creativity. People don't go to Toyota to 'work', they go there to 'think'" (Yorke and Bodek, 2005, p. 238).

In "Learning to lead at Toyota," Steven Spear (2004) shares the blow-by-blow training of an American executive in Toyota's lean approach. He was first asked by his *sensei* (a Toyota Production System master) to observe an assembly line, come up with ideas on a weekly basis, convince the people to apply his ideas, and improve productivity. After successfully doing so, the executive was asked by the sensei to spend weeks observing how the equipment works to increase machine availability. After improving the use of the machine, the executive was taken to Japan and introduced to a production cell where he had to come up with improvement ideas every day. After proudly coming up with seven ideas for his first day on the line, the executive learned that two Japanese team leaders who were going through the same training had respectively come up with 28 and 31 change ideas. The lesson was clear: do not try to think of everything on your own, but rather work with operators to generate ideas.

The lean tradition has several techniques to help people generate new ideas within the routine of their day-to-day job:

1   *Visualize processes to reveal problems:* The main aim of visual management is to visualize the planned situation so that the gap from the actual is obvious to everyone and ideas can be generated on the spot to explain the difference. The principle here is not to solve every problem, but rather to observe and discuss what is going wrong and what can be done about it.

2   *Problem solve daily performance issues to teach standards:* Daily performance problems are the opportunity to learn to 1) formulate the problem, 2) explore the root cause, 3) try a countermeasure, and 4) study the impact of this countermeasure. Most daily problems are in fact gaps from standards: the standard doesn't exist, is not known, or is plain wrong. The aim of daily problem solving is not to solve all problems, but to take the time to analyze how

one problem is being solved. If the countermeasure is successful, standards should be updated, thus creating a continuous learning cycle.

3   *Quality circles to improve team functioning:* Teams are asked to 1) find improvement potential in their day-to-day work, 2) analyze their work method, 3) come up with original ideas, 4) propose a plan to implement these ideas, 5) test and measure the new way of doing things, and 6) evaluate the new method (Kato and Smalley, 2010). The aim here, again, is to increase the flow of ideas and engage teams in taking ownership of their own work environments.

4   *Cross-functional kaizen activities:* Most just-in-time problems can only be solved by increased cooperation across functions: sales, engineering, production, supply chain. Cross-functional kaizen activities are the opportunity to deepen collaboration in order to improve cooperation. Teamwork in lean is an individual skill: the ability to work well with others across boundaries. Cross-functional kaizen activities are the occasion to hone political skills and improve connectivity.

A common mistake is to see in the lean system a way of designing production systems for greater efficiency. Lean is a radically different approach in as much as Toyota showed us to be open minded about the final design, and also forcefully pursue improvement by getting all employees to think about what they do from the customer's perspective, both in terms of their own work and cooperation with their colleagues. As a Toyota executive once explained: "An environment where people have to think brings with it wisdom, and this wisdom brings with it kaizen (continuous improvement)"; producing units one at a time according to a steady flow is a puzzle that develops people. The T in TPS, he suggested, "actually stands for 'thinking'" (Ballé et al., 2006, p. 4).

Organize for Learning

Leaders are supposed to make the hard decisions and then get them done, decide and execute. Lean leadership is about setting dynamic challenges, creating consensus, and discovering how to solve hard problems through kaizen. Due to the mainstream focus on the discipline of execution, most leaders organize work—they choose people who take charge and get things done. With lean leadership the problem is completely different: the question is to find leaders who learn, support kaizen, and integrate the learning from kaizen efforts in the working of their organizations.

Psychologist Carol Dweck (2008) has shown that people divide into either "fixed mindset," the belief that basic abilities, such as intelligence or talent, are fixed, thus must be made the best of, or the "growth mindset," the belief that talents and abilities can be developed through effort. Fixed mindset people tend to aim to look smart at all times and never be caught looking dumb. Growth mindset people accept trying and failing until they get it right—they see the world as a work in progress. Lean leadership is specifically directed at growth mindset people, and doesn't work so well with fixed mindsets, which is tricky because many managers got the job for their ability to both optimize a given situation, and make the situation look good to their own superiors. Growth mindset people are not so easy to handle as they keep challenging what doesn't work and engage in messy experiments to find better ways of doing things. This often challenges the political status quo and improvement gets hit in the crossfire of the resulting political battles.

Organizing for learning rather than for work means first making sure all employees are part of stable teams of five to seven people and that their team leader is identified, and then picking growth mindset managers to encourage the flow of ideas and manage the shift from individual intelligence to collective intelligence. Contrarily, as happens with many lean programs, a fixed mindset manager will tolerate kaizen efforts if they're imposed by the top, but is very unlikely to draw the lessons and integrate them into his or her own way of running a department. Not surprisingly, many kaizen efforts in mainstream companies show promising results that disappear within the following weeks.

Experience shows that lean leaders have a very different style from the take-charge, get-things-done, firefighting leader we're accustomed to. Lean leaders are *adaptive leaders*—they're usually less charismatic, easier going with their teams, sometimes to the point of vagueness or reticence—they're certainly reluctant to take spot decisions. Their key talents, however, are the persistence to stick with issues over the long term, even when those appear to be intractable, the resilience to accept that not all people agree and that obstacles keep showing up, and the ability to somehow get teams to learn and progress. This last skill shows immediately on the gemba—some managers keep driving their teams forcefully. As a result, employees end up disengaged and create pushback while other managers in a more low-key style run teams that self-improve without seemingly taking any direct action. This is a lean leadership style.

Conclusion: Achieving Goals by Developing People

The lean leader is not the heroic character that takes the hard decisions and surrounds him- or herself by enforcers to make them happen. The lean leader develops his or her subordinates and expects them to train their own staff in their turn. The lean leader sets a direction for improvement and then supports people as they propose new systems, ideas, technical insights, to build progress together. The lean leader uses lean activities to develop people while obtaining results, not to obtain results regardless of what happens to people.

Leadership is an ambiguous topic because it usually blends leading a group to achieve goals for the community and seeking personal power out of ambition and for personal gain. Both history and present times show that humans will follow narcissistic leaders (Maccoby, 2007) sometimes with disastrous consequences. Power is necessary to get things done, but power corrupts and the temptation to enforce *compliance* over *competence* is ever present. As Eric Schmidt, former CEO of Google, phrases it, following the HiPPO, the *highest-paid person's opinion*, is a dangerous form of decision making (Schmidt and Rosenberg, 2014) and yet is common in many companies. Lean leadership is unique in its relentless focus on going and seeing facts at their source making the effort to listen to employees and taking into account their experience. Further, lean leaders refrain from wading in and doing other people's job for them and taking *their* decisions but, instead, develop the person in charge to make better decisions. Lean leadership is a structured approach to leadership that emphasizes competence over compliance and uses the hierarchy as a tool for training at all levels, rather than enforcement.

The beauty of lean leadership is that it can be learned and taught. Lean is a learning system in which tradition sets the questions to surface the deep business challenges. Here, the kaizen methods are known. Problem solving and kaizen activities are used in a deliberate, systematic way to develop people by encouraging them to think and to share their own ideas with their colleagues, both within their own teams and across boundaries.

Case Study: Lean Leadership in AIO

In late 2009, Cyril Dané knew he had a serious problem. Two years before, he and a partner had bought AIO, a company founded in 1978 to provide lineside equipment to local plants in the French South-West region. In the late 1990s, the shift to assembled mechanical factory structures such as shelves and other storing equipment from the traditional welded ones had given the small company some impetus, and in 2008, at the time of the change of leadership, it had reached a turnover of 2.7 million euros. The consequences of the Lehman Brothers meltdown were felt immediately: industrial investment in the region simply stopped. The few projects already in the works stumbled but would eventually be finished, but not new plants. Zero. By the end of 2009, the CEO was looking at a 30 percent drop in sales, and although these would rebound slightly with projects already in the pipeline, there was no hope the situation would right itself on its own.

Dané had been interested in lean from the start because he had realized that low inventory turns (five in 2009) would create a drain in cash he could little afford in the leveraged buyout (LBO) situation, with a rigorous cash reimbursement calendar and reduced turnover, and had been practicing "go and see" from the day he took over the company (Practice 1), getting involved with a local lean association and trying to learn to lead kaizen on his own. Eventually, he invited a sensei to look at his early lean efforts. The conversation didn't go quite as expected as the sensei kept returning to his challenge and to AIO's real value to society and customers. Nonplussed, the CEO explained that smarter lineside equipment made operations easier on the line and could lighten the ergonomic load on operators, but afterwards kept mulling the thought in his head. The advantage of his light assembly technology was that he could create flexible, dynamic equipment but the question bugging him was: how good at it was he? Quite stunned, Dané realized that his product challenge reflected a much greater business challenge (Practice 2)—how to respond to free falling sales—and beyond that a societal challenge—how to eradicate the ergonomic burden in any production facility.

In true lean spirit, he decided that the best thing to do was to "go and see" and look for some easy kaizen opportunity. Looking at the competition and the plant environment with a different pair of glasses, he found himself on a plane to Japan to participate at a "karakurikaizen" exhibition. *Karakuri* are simple mechanical devices to move parts around and support the operator's movements without hydraulics or electronics, by ingenious mechanical tricks. The CEO came back from the fair with an epiphany: these devices could radically reduce the ergonomic burden for operators in every industrial facility, if he could only learn how to make them and convince his clients.

Throughout 2010 he worked hard with his engineers to come up with the first karakuri solutions. By the end of 2011, he better grasped the outcomes he was seeking (Practice 3) and realized he had an entire new business line on his hands with a turnover of more than a million euros. He also came to terms with the fact that lean had to be embedded in his operations because of the very nature of this new product. Karakuri's work on the astuteness of their design and realization means mindfulness both from the engineer and from the operators who assemble the device, as well as a different relationship with customers as the final product is never fully finished: the customer is supposed to continue to kaizen it him- or herself to adapt it to changing conditions in the line. Interestingly, the very nature of bespoke products meant he had to support individual kaizen and initiatives (Practice 4) to explore the full range of what karakuri could do on a production line (and in a few cases, what it could not do). This is a rare case where the link between assembly kaizen and design (and vice versa) is highly visible.

In 2012, turnover from the new business was higher than the old—the most dire predictions of no new investment in industrial sites in the region were actually happening, and the future of the old business looked bleak. Thankfully, karakuri did quickly convince new clients and major players, in both the automotive and aerospace industries. AIO was contacted by Toyota which was keen to support its European production engineers in understanding how to make the best possible karakuri to kaizen their lines.

As a supplier to Toyota, Dané became more convinced than ever that lean was the way forward and, looking back on his growing business (in 2012 he had reached 3.5 million euros turnover), he saw that the flow of work through engineering to delivery was poor. He'd been focused on lead time to customers for a couple of years now and couldn't seem to crack the problem. Projects accumulated in engineering, then another queue would get them in production, and the overall flow was terrible. Overall, focusing on the new business, the CEO challenged himself and his teams in improving the flow. They established a kanban system for projects in engineering to limit projects-in-waiting on engineers' desks, and one in production. After the early improvements, one year or so down the line, they hit upon the real hidden rock in the flow: the supply chain.

Because the quality of the product depends on the "astuteness" of the mechanical engineering design, engineers were often tempted to use bespoke parts, which were then difficult to get from suppliers. Many engineering projects also had missing parts until late in the process, which kept them out of the production queue. This was not a matter of simply organizing things better, it touched the very nature of the products themselves. Step by step, through better visualization and kaizen, AIO's engineers, supply officers and assembly operators learned to work better together to use more standard components in products through practical assembly tricks without losing the astuteness that made the benefit to customers. The supply chain turned out to be a difficult nut to crack where much deep thinking was needed (Practice 5). Kaizen efforts would momentarily improve lead time, which would then slide back. Eventually, the management team came to grips with the fact that it could break the walls between engineering, supply, and production by creating autonomous cells, "*daisies*" as they called them to reflect the fact that engineers, production guys, and a supply chain person would sit around one large table in the open plan as petals on a daisy.

Leading a fast-growing small business is no walk in the park, particularly when one expands internationally and starts working with the big names of automotive and aeronautics, from Germany to the UK, and Dané confesses his focus was largely on the new business and not the old, where sales continued somewhat, although at a lesser level. Although unfortunate, this gives us a good opportunity to compare where lean thinking is being pursued to where it's not. Table 4.1 shows the inventory turns in the old and new business.

In other words, the inventory turns after leaning the new business are double what they were at the start of lean. In the same period AIO's sales doubled, and so did the earnings before interest, taxes, depreciation, and amortization. Beyond financial measures, the company itself is transformed. As a response to the hard supply chain/engineering/production it faced, the CEO encouraged one of his engineers to explore the possibilities of 3D printing. This has opened up a complete new field of creating in-house bespoke components adapted to karakuri. As it stands, 100 percent of new products have at least one 3D printed component in them—tested until failure in the lab. In other words, adopting new technologies to better relieve the ergonomic burden of operators. "Where I had to evolve most," confesses Dané (Practice 6), "is in how I chose people to give them responsibilities in the company":

> I used to hire people who would get things done, and this has not worked out too well. Now that the company has doubled in its number of people, I have to start thinking about management for the scale-up. I now know that I need to find people who are interested in what we do, able to learn and get on reasonably well with other members of the team. This has been a deep lesson, and I'm not through working it out yet. Practicing lean leadership has turned out very differently than I expected, far messier day to day than the structured kaizen approach I had originally envisaged, but also much more fun. We have huge challenges, but we also work much better together, we face our issues, and, oddly, my stress level has reduced as I'm more confident we'll make it together.

Table 4.1 Inventory turns in AIO in the non-lean and lean business divisions

	2009	2010	2011	2012	2013	2014
Old business (not lean)	4.8	6.1	5.7	4.0	2.4	1.3
New business (lean)	–	–	7.4	6.1	8.5	9.0

More than ever, AIO's mission is to eradicate ergonomic burdens and their health consequences for workers everywhere, all the time. Sure, it's still a very small company and anything can happen, but on the other hand anything can happen as any company scales up with lean thinking as its main strategy.

References

Ballé, M., Beauvallet, G., Smalley, A. and Sobek, D. (2006). The thinking production system. *Reflections*, 7(2), 1–12.

Dweck, C. (2008). *Mindset*, New York, Ballantine Books.

Kato, I. and Smalley, A. (2010). *Toyota Kaizen Methods: Six Steps to Improvement*, Boca Raton, FL, CRC Press.

Liker, J. K. and Hoseus, M. (2008). *Toyota Culture*, New York, McGraw-Hill.

Liker, J. K. and Convis, G. L. (2012). *The Toyota Way to Lean Leadership*, New York, McGraw-Hill.

Maccoby, M. (2007) *Narcissistic Leaders*, New York, Crown Business.

Schmidt, E. and Rosenberg, J. (2014). *How Google Works*, London, John Murray.

Shimokawa, K. and Fujimoto, T. (2009). *The Birth of Lean*, Cambridge, MA, Lean Enterprise Institute.

Spear, S. J. (2004). Learning to lead at Toyota. *Harvard Business Review*, 82(5), 78–91.

Toyota Motor Corporation (2009). *Sustainability Report 2009*, Toyota Motor Corporation.

Yorke, C. and Bodek, N. (2005). *All You Gotta Do is Ask*, Vancouver, PCS Inc.

5

LEAN INNOVATION

Günther Schuh, Stefan Rudolf, and Christian Mattern

Introduction

Mastering innovation processes is a crucial factor for companies in today's market environment. Across many industries, the effects of overcapacities, globalization, and increasing pricing pressure have led to an intensified competitive environment. Life cycles of products are continuously shortening and, at the same time, markets are becoming increasingly fragmented. Many companies have decided to respond to customer demand for higher individualization by extending their product program and introducing more product variants. As the number of sold units per variant decreases, the costs of development and production of those variants increase substantially. Consequently, the absolute return on engineering per project declines despite the company selling more units in total across all variants (Schuh et al., 2007).

In order to secure their market position and develop their business, companies need to differentiate themselves from their competitors through successful innovation. Research and development (R&D) processes must be accelerated to keep up with shorter life cycles, and higher dynamics as well as structures must be adapted to the challenges of product variety with a larger number of parallel projects, variants, parts, and components. The effectiveness and efficiency of R&D is thus a cornerstone of the strategy of successful companies and concepts of how to increase effectiveness and efficiency of R&D have simultaneously become a focal point of management science.

The introduction of *lean thinking* in production was a major step forward in effectiveness and efficiency. Thus, transferring the basic principles of lean thinking to the management of R&D represents the opportunity to repeat this success for innovation processes. Due to their universal nature, the principles of lean thinking are applicable to all corporate functions (Pfeiffer and Weiss, 1994). However, applying lean principles in R&D requires adjustment to the characteristics of the innovation process. Introducing lean and striving for elimination of waste in innovation processes does not necessarily crowd out creativity and inventiveness, which are the foundation for successfully realized innovations.

The principles of lean thinking have been described extensively for production processes and implemented in a multitude of applications. However, the concept of *lean innovation* is not yet elaborated to the same degree. The establishment of lean thinking principles in R&D is in progress and covered by numerous authors (e.g. Ward, 2007; Hoppmann, 2009; Sehested and Sonnenberg, 2010; Oppenheim et al., 2011), but it has not yet been carried out systematically.

In a recent benchmarking study, the Laboratory of Machine Tools and Production Engineering (WZL) of RWTH Aachen University interviewed 100 companies in automotive and engineered-product industries in cooperation with The Boston Consulting Group. The results show that only less than 20 percent of manufacturing companies use methods of lean thinking in engineering on a regular basis (Lorenz et al., 2015).

In this chapter, a holistic approach to lean innovation is described. The approach has been systematically derived from *Lean Thinking* by Womack and Jones (1996) and is structured along four domains with 12 dedicated guiding principles to shape innovation processes in a value-centered company—the "lean enterprise."

What is Lean Innovation?

The central idea of lean innovation is to identify and eliminate any kind of waste in innovation processes. Innovation processes are characterized by a high degree of planning uncertainty due to a low transparency of activities and a long-term planning horizon. In addition, innovations are usually driven by the creativity and experience of the involved individuals. The potential for automation is therefore lower compared with production processes because the sequence of activities is much less clearly defined. Furthermore, value-adding activities are not as easy to identify as they are in production (Oehmen and Rebentisch, 2010). For this reason, the concepts of lean cannot be taken over from production to product development without further adjustment. However, the five basic lean principles—customer value, value stream, process flow, pull, and perfection—can be transferred to R&D (McManus et al., 2005). Hence the general understanding of waste from lean management can be used to develop a definition of lean innovation. Lean innovation can be understood as the ambition to introduce lean thinking into the R&D of manufacturing companies from idea generation to the market-ready product. Originating from waste in production processes (Liker, 2004) the following seven types of waste can be identified in an innovation process:

1   *Overproduction* is reflected in R&D by *insufficient customer orientation*. Customer orientation is one of the fundamentals of lean thinking. Typical waste in R&D is the development of features that the customer does not appreciate or recognize. An innovation process based on lean principles should be composed of activities that all contribute to customer value. A prerequisite for that is a profound knowledge of the customer's needs.

2   *Transportation* is represented in R&D by *handovers* of responsibilities or information. Every handover interrupts the value stream and carries a risk of losing tacit knowledge. An innovation process following the principles of lean thinking should have an intelligent standardization of interfaces and a structured process organization.

3   *Inventory* has its counterpart in *partially completed tasks*. This includes any work packages or projects that are currently in process, but not completed yet. An excessive backlog of tasks can be a result of unutilized resources or a lack of proper resource allocation. The assignment of tasks needs to take the current workload and individual skills of the personnel into consideration.

4   *Waiting* as one of the basic types of waste can also be found in R&D. Time and resources are wasted whenever outstanding decisions for project approval or decisions on product specifications delay the project progress. Iterations and additional queries should be minimized in order to reduce time to market.

5   *Over-processing* can be seen in R&D as *rework* due to changes of requirements or additional efforts as a result of media discontinuity. A clear and stable definition of requirements as well

as data consistency and compatibility of IT tools are a prerequisite for efficient innovation processes.

6   *Motion* is represented in R&D by *switching between tasks*. Unplanned task switching can be a result of unclear prioritization of tasks and objectives. A systematically developed hierarchy of objectives helps to maximize transparency on priorities and to reduce unnecessary task switching.

7   The equivalent of *defects* is in R&D *malfunction* of products. Malfunctions of a product are oftentimes discovered late in the product development process. The correction of these errors usually involves tremendous effort and results in rework.

Analyzing waste in R&D is a difficult task as waste is less obvious when activities are characterized by creativity and iterations. However, keeping the analogy of production in mind can help to identify waste in R&D that corresponds to the types of waste in production. Based on the analysis of waste, the lean innovation approach has been developed according to the five basic lean principles (Womack and Jones, 1996). This approach provides a framework to establish lean principles in R&D. Schuh (2013) includes domains that are targeted on product configuration as well as those that focus on process improvements. These domains are derived from the basic principles of lean thinking and can be arranged as quadrants of a circle as shown in Figure 5.1, covering all fields of the innovation process. The four quadrants will be introduced briefly in the following paragraphs and discussed in more detail later in this chapter when we consider challenges and opportunities of lean innovation.

The first domain, *"prioritize clearly,"* addresses the strategic level of innovation management. The key topic here is to identify and prioritize the customer needs and to define a product

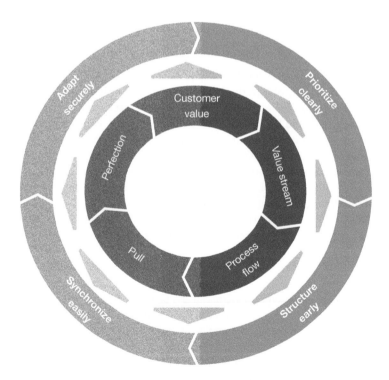

Figure 5.1   Lean innovation is based on a holistic transfer of the lean thinking principles

portfolio covering those needs. Similar to the lean concept in production, it is fundamental in innovation management to understand customer value and to direct all activities to increasing it.

The second domain, "*structure early*," is dealing with the product itself. The essential part of this domain is to find the right configuration of the product architecture. Once a product portfolio has been defined, the specific customer requirements have to be transformed to product features. In this domain, the main lever to control and adjust external and internal variety is product architecture design.

The third domain, "*synchronize easily*," covers the aspects of cooperation between the stakeholders in a company. Their activities need to be coordinated by a powerful project management and have to be concentrated on customer value creation. Although innovation processes are much more iterative and sometimes turbulent compared with production processes, concepts like the "*takt*" can be applied in order to define work cycles in the innovation process.

The fourth domain, "*adapt securely*," is about enabling the innovation management to adapt to internal and external dynamics as well as continuous improvement of products and processes. Striving for perfection requires constant effort toward improvement in the innovation process.

Dedicated principles have been formulated for each of these four domains. These principles have been substantiated with specific methods on how to implement them (see Schuh, 2013, for details). Companies that follow these principles and anchor them in their organization have proven to be more successful and innovative than others. This was shown in the consortium benchmarking study "Lean Innovation 2011," conducted by the Laboratory of Machine Tools and Production Engineering, which interviewed 70 European engineering companies. "Top performers" among the interviewed companies that are leading in terms of objective criteria like time to market, number of filed patents, or share of achieved project objectives are a few decisive steps ahead of the field in implementing lean innovation. Key findings of the study are that successful companies succeed in aligning their activities with customer demand and steering their project portfolio by the use of key performance indicators. For example, they stop product development projects with little prospect of success earlier than others, resulting in lower deviation from plans (Schuh et al., 2012).

Challenges and Opportunities

Each of the four domains of lean innovation addresses areas of action in an innovation system with specific challenges. In this chapter, the Lean Innovation Circle with four quadrants, as shown in Figure 5.2, serves as a structure to discuss the specific challenges in each domain.

The major challenge in the first domain "*prioritize clearly*" is to allocate resources of R&D toward the customer and according to the strategic targets and the core competencies of the company. A thorough understanding of what signifies value from the customer's perspective is fundamental for a systematic transformation of customer needs in project goals. In order to ensure the company's long-term success, a roadmap regarding future products and technologies is essential.

Clearly defined and communicated *critical success factors* (CSFs) allow the company to develop core competencies as an enabler for a sustainable competitive advantage. The relevant critical success factors can be determined by analyzing best-in-class players in a market. On this basis, a company can decide which of the CSFs to concentrate on as part of an innovation strategy. Concentrating on too many positions leads to an imprecise focus on core competencies, which further hampers the development of competitive advantage. The more precisely the CSFs are defined and the more balanced their number is, the more successful the company will be (Schuh, 2013).

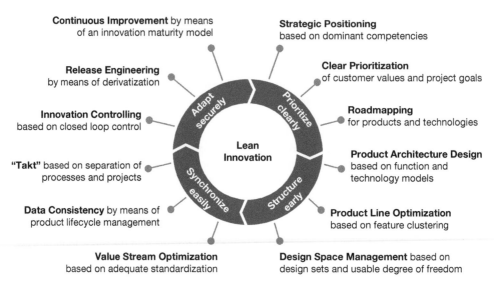

Figure 5.2 The 12 lean innovation principles

A well-defined innovation strategy must be operationalized and translated into project targets. Project portfolios can be utilized to evaluate projects based on objective criteria and to decide which projects should be realized. Detailed targets of single projects are deduced from an overall target system. The prioritization of targets based on customer demands can be supported by the methodology of *quality function deployment* according to Akao and King (1990). Unclear targets and target conflicts still offer large potentials in R&D for the increase of efficiency (Bullinger et al., 2009). Value driver trees enable analysis of complex dependencies between technical development targets and allow for early detection of conflicts. Proactive decisions are needed to resolve these contradictions and define acceptable trade-offs.

For a clear prioritization of resources, the decision makers require transparency on future developments regarding new products and technologies. A long-term roadmap containing all relevant information regarding upcoming technology trends is a beneficial tool to gain transparency on new and promising fields of action. The roadmapping process should be anchored in the organization with the involvement of top management due to its strategic relevance. Among the many types of roadmaps (e.g. Phaal et al., 2001), their relevant elements have been identified as the timeline, planning levels, integration of planning objects, and linkage between planning objects (Schuh, 2013). Based on a detailed roadmap, potential and sales opportunities can be identified early.

"*Structure early*" addresses the early phase of product development where guidelines for a value-oriented product design are specified. In this phase, the previously defined innovation strategy is implemented in the product program, alongside setting preconditions for avoidance of waste in later phases.

The product architecture defines the basic structure of all the products a company offers. Beyond single products, the product architecture also describes interrelations between products of different product lines. Therefore, the product architecture can be seen as the lever to realize economies of scale in a product program with high variety. Modular product platforms offer the potential of a high degree of commonality as well as reduced costs in engineering, procurement, and production. To achieve these advantages, it is important to differentiate between conventional product development and a product architecture development that is organized independently from specific projects.

As the product portfolio variety increases, it becomes increasingly difficult to keep an overview of the costs and benefits of each variant. The majority of companies do not have detailed information on their situation regarding the costs of complexity. An approach that can be used is the analysis of variants based on feature clusters to identify features that both differentiate the products from a customer's perspective and cause minimal costs of complexity. If these costs are taken into consideration, many variants usually turn out to be unprofitable (Schuh, 2012). Optimizing the product portfolio thus means to eliminate these variants.

Once the decision to develop a new product has been made and the project has started, the major challenge is to achieve maturity of the product as fast as possible, reducing time to market. In most new product development projects, decisions regarding solution alternatives are made based on intuition and individuals' experiences. *Design-space management* ensures that solution alternatives are selected based on a systematic and objective evaluation. Through evaluating the existing degrees of freedom, the number of remaining solution alternatives is reduced gradually and a too-early limitation of the design space is avoided.

The third domain, *"synchronize easily,"* entails process-related aspects of innovation projects. The interaction of all involved disciplines can be compared to the performance of a symphony orchestra. The synchronization of simultaneous activities is a key capability of innovative companies.

Creative and repetitive activities compose the value stream of an R&D project. Repetitive activities like administration processes should be standardized whereas creative activities should be steered by transparent targets and short control loops. The value stream can be visualized by using process modeling techniques. Based on modeling in swim lanes, for example, the weak points and waste in the value stream can be identified through value stream analysis. The value stream analysis, originally designated for applications in production, has to be adapted to the specifics of innovation processes. These specifics have been discussed in the previous section looking at typical types of waste compared with production.

When different people and functions work together in a product development project, a large amount of data, information, and knowledge needs to be shared. Data redundancies and inconsistencies cause waste in the value stream. In order to synchronize the activities, a consistent data backbone in common IT systems is required. Efforts for searching and adjustments add no value and can be reduced significantly by the use of a holistic product life cycle management (PLM) system. As the capability of IT increases, the implementation of up-to-date systems is essential for companies to be competitive.

The structure of conventional innovation processes usually follows the stage-gate process. Nevertheless, in many cases projects deviate from the defined goals. A promising approach to reduce deviation in time and budget is the synchronization of activities following a "takt." The time intervals between two milestones or stage-gates are harmonized in the concept of "takt." "Takt" sets the rhythm for independent work on defined tasks. Synchronization points at the end of each "takt" ensure coordination between different functions. Daily work and alignment meetings at synchronization points can be facilitated by using task boards clearly showing the current status of work packages.

"Adapt securely," as the fourth domain of lean innovation, includes principles that ensure adaptability of innovation management. Products have to be changed regularly due to new requirements, customer needs, and overall market trends. Continuous improvement of products and processes toward full implementation of lean innovation is needed to increase innovation productivity.

For a target-oriented improvement of existing processes, it is necessary to have a clear view on the results and the impact of previous and ongoing initiatives. Target values, available degrees of freedom and roles with clear assignments, competencies, and responsibilities need to be defined. This implies the necessity of innovation controlling with short control loops for quick reaction on changes and deviations from target values. When project teams are permitted to make their own decisions within specified limits, the whole system becomes self-regulating with external reference input.

Whenever product changes need to be made due to cost reduction measures or adaption to new market requirements, these changes should be released in a synchronized way. The components of a product should be clustered depending on their interrelations and the dynamics of customer needs. Release frequencies in general should be a multiple of each other and integrated in an overall planning of the product life cycle. Release engineering has to take account of the availability of internal resources as well as market trends.

Finally, continuous improvement as a core concept of lean thinking can be transferred to the lean innovation approach based on a maturity model as shown in Figure 5.3. The current maturity of lean innovation is classified in five levels from the lowest with no structured implementation of lean to the highest where lean innovation is fully anchored and adhered to within the organization (Schuh, 2013).

The major obstacle in implementing lean thinking in R&D is often insufficient involvement and, as a result, mistrust of the employees. Without early and open communication of the objectives and the background, successful lean innovation initiatives are threatened. In order to prevent failure of lean innovation projects, managers need to initiate discussions on the lean innovation concept and create an understanding, as well as confidence, among the employees.

The first step toward *lean initiated* is to mobilize influential people within the organization who support lean innovation as an idea personally and to formulate a clear mission statement with realistic objectives. The benefit of lean innovation is illustrated in first flagship projects that address identified deficits and realize "quick wins." After the first step has been taken, *lean organized* means that lean thinking is cascaded through the entire company and anchored in the organizational structure. Opinion leaders at lower levels of the hierarchy may serve as multipliers

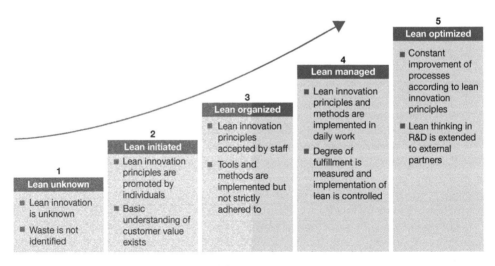

Figure 5.3   The lean innovation maturity model

Source: Schuh (2013).

and trainers who instruct their colleagues on the principles and methods of lean innovation. The next level, *lean managed*, includes a re-evaluation of the defined objectives as well as the implementation of a performance measurement system that quantifies the effects of the lean innovation initiative. The final level, *lean optimized*, is composed as a continuous improvement system, as well as the expansion of lean innovation principles to partner companies.

It is tremendously important to keep in mind that a fundamental change process like the introduction of lean innovation cannot be done in one single step. The lean innovation maturity model offers a framework for an incremental rollout of lean innovation with dedicated levels. Lean innovation affects many areas of a company and soft factors regarding employees that have to be particularly considered. Lean innovation is not just a concept that runs automatically once it has been implemented. Lean thinking in R&D is more dependent on the attitude of those who are carrying it into execution than in other fields.

The Future of Lean Innovation

The approach of lean innovation will be affected by major trends that shape the future of all producing companies on a global basis. IT-related trends will improve the ability of companies to collect and process, as well as analyze, data. The increasing integration of electronics and software in products affects product architecture design. A highly dynamic market necessitates new concepts for flexible innovation processes.

Increasing processing power and accelerated data transmission will enhance the ability to analyze market information and improve data handling in IT systems. Companies that have detailed knowledge of customer needs and regional differences and that are able to develop a sense of trends in global markets will have a competitive advantage in the future market environment. Innovative IT solutions for market intelligence will help to analyze large amounts of complex data. Market intelligence requires a well-defined organizational anchoring. Uncovered market segments can be identified with the help of collected data further interpreted in a portfolio analysis.

Further efforts need to be taken to improve the integration of IT structure which also offers large potential for improved efficiency in R&D. Data consistency across all corporate functions is not yet achieved in vast parts of the industry. Product-related data has to be organized in such a way that each involved function is able to filter out the relevant information. Media discontinuity along the value creation chain and incompatible software is a major reason for waste. Thus, the complete integration of product-oriented PLM systems and process-oriented *enterprise resource planning* systems is an inevitable step. Interfaces to *customer relationship management* systems that carry information on sold product configurations need to be defined.

Future improvements in terms of steering innovation processes can be expected as a consequence of better ability in data analysis. Value stream mapping as retrospective analysis is able to identify typical and recurring weaknesses. Modern methods of data analysis are a key element on the way toward the vision of a prospective method for project steering based on live tracking of the value stream. A forward-oriented method that supports proactive steering of the value stream will allow for anticipation of weaknesses and avoidance of waste in the early phase of project planning.

Intelligent product and process platforms will provide a sufficient degree of flexibility in certain areas of the product architecture whereas the rest of the architecture is structured with a clear focus on efficiency. Sections of the product architecture that do not contribute to customer differentiation should be structured efficiently. In this regard, new potential is opened up by the integration of electronics and information technology into formal, predominantly mechanical, systems. Instead of varying mechanical structure, product variety can be realized through modification of software. Methods for product architecture development must be refined with regard to interdisciplinary modular platforms.

Beyond conventional innovation processes structured in stage-gates, it is increasingly important for companies to manage radical innovations that are able to revolutionize traditional markets. Radical innovations are characterized by a high degree of uncertainty regarding market success, as well as the technologies applied. A key success factor in efficient development of radical innovation is the realization of agile processes that offer sufficient flexibility to respond to shifts in markets and available technologies. Agile processes focus clearly on customer value and integration of customer demand. The continuing need for adaptation is reflected in intense iterations with short sprints and daily scrums, which increases reactivity in R&D projects characterized by high uncertainty.

A large number of companies have already brought their innovation processes to the next level by successful implementation of the lean innovation principles. About one-third of automotive and machinery manufacturing companies make use of lean methods in product development on a regular basis. These practitioners of lean in R&D are able to develop their projects faster, and uphold milestones and cost targets more frequently (Lorenz et al., 2015).

Nevertheless, the concepts and ideas of lean innovation are subject to constant change. As discussed in this chapter, major trends will affect the field of innovation management in the near future. The principles and methods of lean innovation need therefore to be adjusted continuously. The presented approach offers a general framework for a systematic introduction of lean thinking in R&D as part of a transformation toward the "lean enterprise."

Case Study: Lean Innovation at StreetScooter

The project StreetScooter is an example of successful implementation of lean innovation principles. The objective of this project was to realize affordable electric vehicles. This spin-off from RWTH Aachen University was founded in 2010 and worked toward the production of a *short distance vehicle* in small series. In 2013, StreetScooter started production of a commercial vehicle that would be operated by the German mail service.

One of the reasons for the resounding success of the StreetScooter was its focus on a clearly delimited target group. Also, customer requirements were analyzed early by integration of potential customers in a benchmarking study. Comments and wishes of mail carriers were incorporated in the development of the vehicle concept. This is an essential element of the lean innovation principle *"clear prioritization of customer values and project goals"* in the first quadrant of the lean innovation circle (Figure 5.2). In the case example, a clear prioritization of customer values was conducted regarding requirements in terms of handling, durability, and other features, as shown in Figure 5.4. Economic efficiency in general is a crucial factor for commercial vehicles. The design was adjusted to the customer's willingness to pay and the features offered in the product were reduced to the essentials (Krumm, 2014).

The product architecture of StreetScooter was designed to facilitate a synchronized development in a network of university researchers and industry partners. Following the approach of an integrated product and process development in networks, the complexity of the product architecture is reflected in the network structure. As development networks need to be synchronized precisely, it is crucial to have a consistent data structure that allows local and distributed stakeholders to get the information they need and to bring in their results through a standardized interface. Here, the principle *"data*

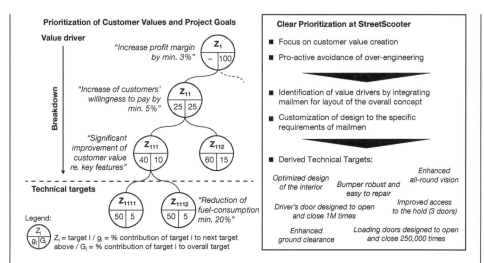

Figure 5.4   Clear prioritization at StreetScooter

Source: Kampker et al. (2014); Krumm (2014).

consistency" as part of the third quadrant, "*synchronize easily*," of the lean innovation circle has been addressed. To achieve a common data management system with StreetScooter, all development partners were obliged to use a mandatory collaboration platform and have a common perspective on variants using the classification system of feature and variant trees (Krumm, 2014).

The StreetScooter project is a good example of the successful implementation of lean innovation principles. Clear customer orientation, distinguishing between the essential and the inessential, and an integrated approach of product and process development in networks made it possible to start the production only 3.5 years after the formation of the company (Krumm, 2014). The challenges companies are facing today show great similarities to those StreetScooter overcame. Lean innovation, if adequately implemented, has the potential to give companies a substantial competitive advantage.

References

Akao, Y. and King, B. (1990). *Quality Function Deployment: Integrating Customer Requirements into Product Design*, Cambridge, MA, Productivity Press.

Bullinger, H. J., Spath, D., Warnecke, H. J. and Westkämper, E. (eds) (2009). *Handbuch Unternehmensorganisation: Strategien, Planung, Umsetzung*, Berlin, Springer-Verlag.

Hoppmann, J. (2009). The Lean Innovation Roadmap—A Systematic Approach to Introducing Lean in Product Development Processes and Establishing a Learning Organization, Doctoral dissertation, Institute of Automotive Management and Industrial Production, Technical University of Braunschweig.

Kampker, A., Burggräf, C., Nee, C. and Sarovic, N. (2014). *Wirtschaftliche Industrialisierung automobiler Kleinserien am Beispiel StreetScooter*. In: Brecher, C., Klocke, F., Schmitt, R. and Schuh, G. (eds), *Industrie 4.0: Aachener Perspektiven: Aachener Werkzeugmaschinenkolloquium*, Aachen, Shaker, pp. 171–189.

Krumm, S. (2014). Beherrschte Komplexität durch Lean Innovation am Beispiel des StreetScooter. *Complexity Management Journal*, Aachen, Schuh Group, 4–12.

Liker, J. K. (2004). *The Toyota Way: 14 Management Principles from the World's Greatest Manufacturer*, New York, McGraw-Hill.

Lorenz, M., Jentzsch, A., Andersen, M., Noack, B., Waffenschmidt, L., Schuh, G. and Rudolf, S. (2015). *The Lean Advantage in Engineering. Developing Better Products Faster and More Efficiently*, The Boston Consulting Group & WZL of RWTH Aachen.

McManus, H., Haggerty, A. and Murman, E. (2005). *Lean Engineering: Doing the Right Thing Right*. Proceedings of the 1st International Conference on Innovation and Integration in Aerospace Sciences, Queen's University Belfast.

Oehmen, J. and Rebentisch, E. (2010). *Lean Product Development for Practitioners: Waste in Lean Product Development*, Cambridge, MA, Center for Technology, Policy and Industrial Development, Massachusetts Institute of Technology.

Oppenheim, B. W., Murman, E. M. and Secor, D. A. (2011). Lean enablers for systems engineering. *Systems Engineering, 14*(1), 29–55.

Pfeiffer, W. and Weiss, E. (1994). *Lean Management: Grundlagen der Führung und Organisation lernender Unternehmen*, Berlin, Erich Schmidt.

Phaal, R., Farrukh, C. and Probert, D. (2001). Technology roadmapping: linking technology resources to business objectives. White Paper. Centre for Technology Management, University of Cambridge, 1–18. Available at: https://sopheon-wpengine.netdna-ssl.com/wp-content/uploads/Article-Technology-Roadmapping.pdf (accessed July 2016).

Schuh, G. (ed.) (2012). *Innovationsmanagement* (Vol. 3), Berlin, Springer.

Schuh, G. (2013). Einleitung. In: *Lean Innovation*, Berlin and Heidelberg, Springer, pp. 1–18.

Schuh, G., Bartoschek, M. and Nußbaum, C. (2007). *Assessing the Degree of Efficiency of Product Complexity. Proceedings of the 4th World Conference on Mass Customization & Personalization (MPC)*, Cambridge, MA.

Schuh, G., Arnoscht, J. and Aryobsei, A. (2012). Die Top Performer—Studie "Lean Innovation 2011." *Management und Qualität, 42*(2), 16–17.

Sehested, C. and Sonnenberg, H. (2010). *Lean Innovation: A Fast Path from Knowledge to Value*, Berlin, Springer Science & Business Media.

Ward, A. (2007). *Lean Product and Process Development*, Cambridge, MA, Lean Enterprise Institute.

Womack, J. P. and Jones, D. T (1996). *Lean Thinking: Banish Waste and Create Wealth in Your Corporation*, New York, Simon & Schuster.

6

LEAN PRODUCT AND PROCESS DEVELOPMENT

Monica Rossi, James Morgan, and John Shook

Introduction

A company is nothing without its products or services. So, it is no exaggeration to say that product development may be the most important process of any enterprise. Product development is a set of activities that begin with a perceived opportunity and end with the delivery of a finished product (Ulrich and Eppinger, 1995). A product, whether tangible (a physical product) or intangible (a service), can be new to the market, new to the company, new to technology, or a combination of these. It may derive from a radically new project or be an improvement of previous versions. Moreover, together with shorter product life cycles, rapidly changing market environments, increasing levels of competition, and a higher rate of technical obsolescence, a steadily widening variety of products makes product development crucial for competitive advantage of companies in all industries (Clark and Fujimoto, 1991; Ward et al., 1995; Womack and Jones, 1996; Morgan and Liker, 2006). Moreover, data consistently show that the majority of companies' investment costs and up to 70 percent of operating costs are determined during the product development process. This is also true for product quality potential.

Consequently, product development capability is arguably the most significant source of sustainable competitive advantage for any enterprise. The most successful companies execute product development systems that are both effective and efficient. However, organizations that succeed in developing new products with consistency, year after year, are rare. There is no shortage of studies on how to improve product development but, despite nearly 40 years of research, recent results reveal that these improvements have failed to materialize as expected in most companies and that product development is often ineffective or inefficient (e.g. Ballard, 2000; Rossi et al., 2011). Successful stories do exist, and they demonstrate that top companies are able to innovate in terms of providing the right product at the right time and place without requiring an overabundance of resources (e.g. Womack et al., 1990; Womack and Jones, 1996; Morgan, 2002; Morgan and Liker, 2006). Toyota Motor Company serves as a notable example of consistent success. Toyota is able to bring valuable products to the market much faster, with a higher success rate and higher quality, and with significantly less effort than its global competitors. Why? Toyota embraces the well-known *lean thinking* ideal for its entire enterprise, including innovation and product development. The adoption of lean thinking at the earliest phases of the product development process and its continued use throughout the process is known as *lean product development* (Womack et al., 1990).

Data have shown that lean product development is faster to market and has lower investment costs, higher quality, more efficient launches, and higher transaction prices and sales. However, only a few successful lean product development journeys have been publicly documented. This is probably because most companies are very secretive about their development performance and because product development complexity, uncertainty, and unpredictability make lean product development extremely difficult to measure and understand. Further, lean product development contains components that can seem counterintuitive and paradoxical. This chapter aims to help readers understand what lean product development is as well as the dramatic power it holds for companies.

What is lean product development? Why do companies that properly adopt lean product development achieve such competitive positions? Why do some lean product development implementations fail? What are the main challenges of starting a lean product development journey, and how can it be sustained? This chapter addresses these and other questions by describing the main traits of lean product development and suggesting how developers can take advantage of this innovative way of thinking.

What is Lean Product Development?

The Origin of Lean Product Development

In the early 1980s, research interest arose regarding the role of product development as leverage for companies' competitiveness. Focusing on the global auto industry, researchers from Harvard University found evidence that Japanese and Western (US and European) automakers had different engineering paradigms in terms of how projects were organized and managed. In contrast to their Western competitors, the Japanese enterprises exhibited faster development cycles and more efficient use of engineers as well as lower levels of specialization, and placed a premium on supplier capability (Clark et al., 1987). This pioneering work paved the way for extensive research that followed. In the landmark 1990 book *The Machine that Changed the World*, Womack, Jones and Roos identified lean production for the first time as a general concept of *doing more with less* (Womack et al., 1990). This book quickly became the reference for any lean thinking research or initiative, whether in academia or industry. Mainly, *The Machine that Changed the World* has for years been considered a breakthrough contribution to manufacturing. *The Machine that Changed the World* goes well beyond lean manufacturing; it is really about the *lean enterprise*, including marketing, management, supply chain, and product development.

By the mid-1990s, various pieces of related research had already arisen in the engineering community—such as design for manufacturing and assembly, variety reduction programs, standardization of parts and components, and modularity, among others. These can be viewed as collectively comprising an extensive toolkit of *lean engineering*. However, a limitation of these developments was that they remained isolated, with attention focused on engineering alone, largely disconnected from concerns of the broader enterprise. For example, researchers at Massachusetts Institute of Technology (MIT) investigating integrated product development in the aerospace industry promoted concepts of *concurrent engineering* as contrasting with conventional *sequential engineering* (e.g. Browning, 1996; Bernstein, 1998). This switch from sequential to concurrent engineering signaled a trend toward radically different ways of doing product development. Clark and Fujimoto (1989) published research that was extremely influential (also see Clark et al., 1987); however, their findings were only indirectly related to Toyota. Their work was followed by groundbreaking research on lean product development at the University of Michigan that focused on Toyota. Finally, researchers gave appropriate attention to lean product development in order to fully understand the role of effective product development in the entire enterprise system. Subsequently, researchers began to conduct more focused studies, which targeted Toyota to fully clarify its production process. It was around this time that lean product development as a real movement began, with the first academic–practitioner conference (the first Lean Product Development Conference: Principles and Practices from Toyota and its Suppliers), taking place in 2002 in Ann Arbor, Michigan, featuring presenters from Toyota and the University of Michigan.

At the time *The Machine that Changed the World* was written, there was much interest in the Toyota Production System (TPS) but little curiosity about the Toyota Product Development System (TPDS). At the beginning, the extent of the Toyota philosophy's impact on product development was unclear, as was the effect of TPDS on the entirety of Toyota's performance. Consequently, efforts to implement lean thinking were focused mainly on production. One of the first documented examples of TPDS is the incredible success story of the Prius (Liker, 2004). The aim was to introduce breakthrough fuel economy appropriate for the environmental concerns of the 21st century. Initially, the means of achieving the ambitious objectives set by company senior management were unknown. A team was formed, led by a talented *chief engineer* (see Box 6.1), and an aggressive timeline was established. Through intensive R&D, it was decided that adopting hybrid technology was the only feasible way forward. At that time, however, hybrid powertrain was an unproven system, so the project faced tremendous technical challenges. A team of engineers named Global 21 (G21) led the vehicle development project, working with a hybrid technology team named Business Revolution–Vehicle Fuel Economy (BR–VF). Working within the constraints of the challenging timeline, the G21 team, working with the broader engineering organization, made rapid decisions regarding which specific hybrid technology to adopt and then quickly started designing. Concurrently, the BR–VF engineers evaluated around 80 different hybrid types and progressively eliminated engines that failed to meet requirements, until they were left with 10 options. The team then narrowed this number to four higher-value alternatives, which were evaluated through computer simulation. This narrowing of alternatives through a process of elimination was a classic example of a *set-based* (to be explained later in this chapter) approach, and it enabled the team to confidently propose one alternative to the G21 team in May 1995. The development of the first mass-produced hybrid car was thus fully underway and Prius became an official development project in June 1995. Ultimately, the Prius became a historic runaway technical and market success with the radical product innovation made possible by the dramatic success of the development process.

Toyota is thus the pre-eminent exemplar of both lean production, the TPS, and lean product development, the TPDS. However, TPS and TPDS evolved quite separately and in distinct organizational units in the company. Most Toyota product development managers explain that they had very limited knowledge about TPS, and Toyota engineers did not see TPS as the launching point for their product development system (Morgan and Liker, 2006). Therefore, it would be wrong to consider lean product development a consequence of lean production and a mere translation of all the principles, theories, and models already consolidated in manufacturing into product development. It would also be incorrect to understand lean product development as limited to describing TPDS. Independent studies on lean product development arose in the United States from the avant-garde mind of Allen Ward, who was the first to describe the traits of lean product development. Ward had developed several key concepts of lean product development through his research at MIT (Ward, 1989) and the University of Michigan, but only found evidence of their application in reality when he and research associates at the University of

Box 6.1   The Chief Engineer

The common term *chief engineer* has a special meaning within lean product and process development (Shook, 2009). Chief engineers possess full ownership of a development project from concept through launch, yet may not have direct authority over the engineering and other resources necessary to execute the actual work of the project. To achieve this tricky responsibility without authority, chief engineers must thoroughly grasp the changing needs and wants of customers, possess the deep technical skills required to make product decisions (understanding trade-offs), and master the soft project management skills to effectively integrate the various functions involved in the project. Figure 6.1 depicts the concept of a chief engineering system. Across the bottom are the operating functional silos, the vital storehouses of profound technical knowledge and skills which companies may also refer to as *centers of excellence*. Cutting across are the chief engineer-owned product lines or value streams, which generate value for the customer while ensuring profitability for the enterprise. Clark and Fujimoto (1991) first described a version of this as the "heavyweight project manager" system.

Toyota's first chief engineer was Kenya Nakamura, who led the development of the company's first true passenger car, the Crown, introduced in 1955. Nakamura was recognized as Toyota's most brilliant production engineer. But when executive Eiji Toyoda assigned him the bet-the-company task of developing the Crown, Nakamura had no experience in product development. By selecting a production engineer as the first product chief engineer, Toyota recognized the critical interdependence between product and process development, embodying Al Ward's observation decades later that the aim of product development is the creation of successful value streams. Nakamura's actions were documented by his lieutenant, Tatsuo Hasegawa. Based upon his observations of Nakamura as well as his knowledge of product development from his previous experience in the aerospace industry, Hasegawa documented 10 rules of conduct required to successfully lead development

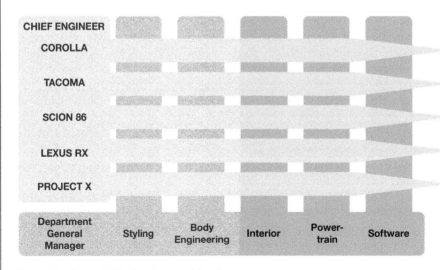

Figure 6.1   Toyota's chief engineer or "*shusa*" system

projects in a management system in which leaders have broad responsibility with very little direct authority:

1   Gain broad knowledge and point of view
2   Develop a clear vision
3   Conduct research that is broad and deep
4   Apply knowledge and skill toward achieving concrete results
5   Persistently repeat each task as necessary—never give up
6   Have confidence, believe in yourself
7   Never delegate responsibility
8   Create alignment with lieutenants and other key people
9   Never take the easy route to make it easy for yourself
10 Possess good character (further defined by another list of 10 characteristics).

Hasegawa became the model for future chief engineers at Toyota, partly due to his contribution in codifying the role of the chief engineer (known at that time as "*shusa*"), but also as developer of the first Corolla (eventually the bestselling vehicle of all time) with his inspirational design theme of *Utilize the Corolla for the happiness and well-being of everyone on Earth*.

Any large product development organization has the dilemma of requiring deep expertise in the various technologies that comprise its products while aligning that expertise in the service of the customer (as well as the organization). The chief engineer system is the lean product and process development answer to that vexing problem.

Michigan undertook a series of research visits to Toyota beginning in 1992. At Toyota, Ward found an exemplary model of successful application of the principles and practices of lean product and process development. Ultimately, Ward and numerous subsequent researchers concluded that its product development system was the main reason why Toyota could boast such outstanding results in business performance. It is now commonly accepted that excellence in product development has become more of a strategic differentiator than manufacturing capability alone (Morgan, 2002; Morgan and Liker, 2006).

How Product Development Differs from Manufacturing

Production deals with the flow and physical transformation of material into products and components. Material transformation can be seen and touched. This makes the application of lean principles easily visible and is one reason most lean transformation initiatives have started on the shop floor. Product development processes differ from factory processes in essential ways, driven primarily by the fundamental uncertainty inherent in developing products—at the beginning of the process, the exact content of the output is not known. Since product development processes deal with information, the ultimate output is the specification of a product (or service or process) rather than the product itself.

Whereas manufacturing is a repetitive, sequential, bounded activity that produces physical objects, product development is to varying degrees a non-repetitive, non-sequential, unbounded activity that produces information. In manufacturing, cycle time is typically measured in days or weeks, whereas in product development cycle time may be measured in months or years. Often, product development involves thousands of problem-solving and decision-making activities that combine creative thinking, experience, intuition, and quantitative analysis, the characteristics of which are iterative, cooperative, evolutionary, and uncertain. A large number of participants are involved, such as architects, project managers, discipline engineers, service engineers, and market consultants. Each category of professional has a different background, culture, and learning style.

Clearly, product development introduces forms of complexity and uncertainty that are challenging to manage and therefore require a kind of attention that differs from that needed in manufacturing. Fortunately, lean thinking has been demonstrated to be applicable and beneficial to both production and product development, despite the peculiarities and distinctions involved. So, how does lean thinking support such a complex process as product development? What *is* lean product development?

Defining Lean Product and Process Development

The original definition of lean thinking speaks directly to these questions. Creating more value from the perspective of the customer while at the same time using fewer resources (Womack and Jones, 1996) assumes direct application in the realm of product development. However, there are still questions regarding how to thoroughly and accurately define lean product development. This chapter borrows from observations common among thought leaders. There is no single, monolithic definition—instead, different researchers emphasize different aspects, with broad consensus on key, fundamental matters.

One of the main research streams, originating with Allen Ward, provides a succinct, profound view of the meaning of lean product development: product development should essentially create profitable value streams (Ward, 2007). Further, since product development is so strongly based on learning and the creation and use of knowledge, the *value* of product development is the generation of *reusable knowledge* (Ward, 2007). Ward's research included process development, introducing what practitioners and researchers refer to as *lean product and process development*.

Another influential view of lean product development is presented by Morgan and Liker (2006) who looked at product development as an interconnected structure consisting of a large number of resources, both human and technical, each involved in the complex and uncertain development process, and each contributing to value creation. Morgan and Liker (2006) draw upon sociotechnical system theory, from which they derived the three main perspectives to be integrated into product development: *people, processes,* and *technology* (see Box 6.2).

Since it is a complex discipline comprising many elements, critically it is the way all the system elements interact to create value that represents the unique character as well as the main challenge of lean product and process development. The way lean product development enables value creation with reduced consumption of resources may appear counterintuitive at first because it represents a dramatic shift from the traditional product development paradigm.

Traditional product development is an iterative approach in which designers and engineers move from point to point looking for feasible solutions. This is called *point-based concurrent engineering* (PBCE) (Ward et al., 1995; Sobek et al., 1999). In PBCE designers tend to make decisions very early in the development process. Conversely, in lean product development, designers delay decisions until sufficient knowledge and data are acquired. While delaying decisions, designers explore and test several alternative sets in parallel in order to obtain insight into the performance of these sets (Ward et al., 1995; Sobek et al., 1999). This approach is called *set-based concurrent engineering* (SBCE) (Ward et al., 1995; Sobek et al., 1999), and it represents a radical change in the traditional industrial paradigm: from a design-build-test to a *test-design-build* paradigm (see Box 6.3).

Box 6.2   Morgan and Liker's 13 Principles for Lean Product Development

Three primary subsystems are acknowledged to converge together to efficiently and effectively support value creation: *process, people,* and *tools and technology*; and 13 principles serve as a support of this whole system (Liker, 2004; Morgan and Liker, 2006).

Process:

1   Establish customer-defined value to separate value added from waste.
2   Front load the product development process to explore thoroughly alternative solutions while there is maximum design space.
3   Create a level product development process flow.
4   Utilize rigorous standardization to reduce variation, and create flexibility and predictable outcomes.

People:

5   Develop a chief engineer system to integrate development from start to finish.
6   Organize to balance functional expertise and cross-functional integration.
7   Develop towering competence in all engineers.
8   Fully integrate suppliers into the product development system.
9   Build in learning and continuous improvement.
10   Build a culture to support excellence and relentless improvement.

Tools and technologies:

11   Adapt technologies to fit people and process.
12   Align the organization through simple visual communication.
13   Use powerful tools for standardization and organizational learning.

This approach may seem cumbersome at first glance. Ward and his fellow researchers first found evidence of such an approach at Toyota, and the initial, misleading impression was that it was extremely inefficient because it involved a large amount of time and knowledge created during earlier phases of development. Contrary to this impression, the approach resulted in extremely high product development performance, which made Toyota the most efficient automaker in the world (Clark et al., 1987; Clark and Fujimoto, 1989; Womack et al., 1990). This led to SBCE being referred to as the *Second Toyota Paradox* (Ward et al., 1995). Whereas the first paradox is how lean production can seem highly inefficient compared with the mass-production paradigm, the second paradox is how set-based thinking appears on the surface to be inefficient compared with the point-based paradigm. In short, lean product development delivers value to the involved stakeholders through a profitable value stream; it avoids design costs late in the design process by postponing decisions as long as possible; it generates knowledge that is reusable; it consists of different kinds of resources; and it involves problem solving, continuous improvement, and continuous learning.

In summary, lean product and process development can be described in terms of three main components: lean product development is about (i) *creating value through* (ii) *a process that builds on knowledge and learning enabled by* (iii) *an integrated product development system (consisting of people, processes, and technology).*

Box 6.3   Set-based Concurrent Engineering

Sobek (1997) defined SBCE as a process in which *engineers and product designers reason, develop and communicate about sets of solutions in parallel and relatively independently*. This definition reflects the main traits of SBCE, which relies mainly on the use of design sets as alternative options in a design space; independent development of such sets from sub-functional teams; intensive communication of these sets between design teams; and progressive elimination of weak alternatives until a final robust solution is achieved (see Figure 6.2 for an overview of the SBCE principles and process). All these processes are supported by a strong use of formalized knowledge in the form of trade-off curves, limit curves, checklists, and standards, to mention some (Ward et al., 1995; Sobek et al., 1999). These forms make it easy to effectively capture, share, and reuse knowledge across design teams. Moreover, they facilitate the making of correct decisions based on data (Ward, 2007; Oosterwal, 2010). This approach fully embraces the test-build-design paradigm and overcomes the drawbacks of the design-build-test paradigm (trial and error).

Three basic principles can provide a deeper understanding of SBCE (Sobek et al., 1999; Ward, 2007; Kerga, 2013).

First, map the design space, or the *principle of exploration*. The first aim of SBCE is to develop an in-depth understanding of sets of designs. This principle is realized through its three subprinciples: (i) *defining feasible regions*, (ii) *exploring trade-offs by developing sets*, and (iii) *communicating sets of possibilities* (Sobek et al., 1999).

Second, integrate by intersection, or the *principle of set-based communication*. This guarantees, through inter-team communication, that the outlined design sets are feasible and compatible with all functional groups involved. This second principle relies on three subprinciples: (i) *looking for the intersection of feasible sets*, (ii) *imposing minimum constraints*, and (iii) *seeking conceptual robustness* (Sobek et al., 1999).

Third, establish feasibility before commitment, or the *principle of convergence*. This allows for the progressive elimination of inferior design solutions from sets and ensures the identification of high-value system solutions. This last principle can be explained through its three subprinciples: (i) *narrowing sets gradually while increasing details*, (ii) *staying within sets once committed*, and (iii) *establishing control by managing uncertainty at process gates* (Sobek et al., 1999).

SBCE has several advantages compared with PBCE. It improves efficiency and effectiveness in product development (Ward et al., 1995; Sobek, 1997; Sobek et al., 1999; Morgan and Liker, 2006; Ward, 2007; Kennedy and Harmon, 2008; Oosterwal, 2010; Raudberget, 2010; Kerga, 2013). More specifically, SBCE leads to considerable advantages, such as:

- the reduction of product and process costs by searching for cheaper alternatives, implementing the right features, and reducing late and costly rework;
- the reduction of development time by reusing previous knowledge and/or avoiding delays caused by changes in the late design phases;
- the enhancement of innovation potential by exploring different solutions and formulating successful ideas the first time;
- the establishment of better communication by effectively sharing data and proven knowledge among design teams (i.e. trade-off and limit curves);
- the avoidance of design risks by increasing the probability of success as a result of considering larger sets, front-loading previous knowledge, and establishing feasibility before commitment; and

- the facilitation of learning through extensive testing and visually representing lessons learned in trade-off and limit curves to enable future reuse (Kerga, 2013; Kerga et al., 2014).

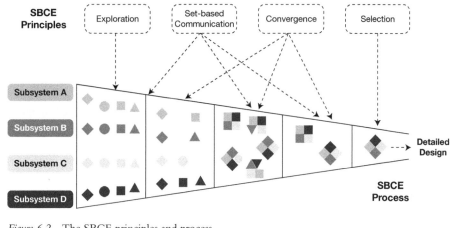

Figure 6.2   The SBCE principles and process

Creating Value

When an organization embraces lean thinking, delivering customer value becomes its core purpose (Womack and Jones, 1996), with value defined as everything the customer is willing to pay for. However, what does *customer value* mean in the context of lean product development?

In product development, *value* assumes a specific meaning. Creating value starts with identifying what customers really want and understanding and articulating customer-defined quality. So, who is it that determines what customers need? And how do they do it? Lean product development provides an answer to those questions, beginning with the prominent figure of the chief engineer (see Box 6.1) who plays the decisive role in defining value from the customer's perspective. Chief engineers spend extensive time with customers to gain a deep understanding of their experiences and to get a truthful and accurate idea of their expectations and true needs. This knowledge enables the company to delineate the functions and features of the final product to be delivered to the customer at the right time, at the right cost, and with the right quality.

Value is then actually created through an operational *value stream*, which consists of all the interconnected activities that contribute to value creation. Product and process development is crucial for the creation of customer value, because any decision made in product development affects the way value will be created and delivered along the value chain of the whole enterprise. It is in product development that value streams are generated for all the downstream operations, which thereby become product development's customers. Therefore, the challenge for product development is to create operational value streams that can guarantee the production and delivery of a product (or service) for which the customer is willing to pay. According to Ward (2007), *the aim of development value streams is to create profitable operational value streams*. In order to do so predictably, efficiently, and effectively, product development should rely on *usable knowledge* (Ward, 2007). Creating usable knowledge becomes paramount in lean product development, and the usable knowledge itself becomes value, not only for product development, but also for the entire organization.

Conversely, failure to generate customer-defined quality is *waste*. Waste (or *muda* in Japanese) is any activity that uses resources without adding any value for the customer. Within the product development process, activities do not create value directly. They create *processes that create value*. That's the meaning of Al Ward's insight (above) that the product of product development is an operational value stream, which directly creates value. Still, the classic categories of waste as famously introduced by Ohno (1988) can be useful, as a focus of lean product and process development to create operational value streams that are as waste-free as possible. With some adjustments, the concept of waste can be applied to lean product and process development:

- *Overproduction:* producing more, faster, or at an earlier stage than is required by the next process (or customer).
- *Waiting:* waiting on work to be completed by a previous process or person.
- *Conveyance:* the movement of documents/information/project tasks from person to person.
- *Processing:* performing unnecessary processing on a task.
- *Inventory:* buildup of more material or information than is needed.
- *Motion:* excess movement or activity during task execution.
- *Rework:* any kind of correction, such as late engineering changes.
- An eighth category of waste is *unused employee capabilities:* failing to develop and/or utilize human capabilities has been proposed by many.

As discussed above, product development consists of flows of knowledge and transformations of information and data; this makes it difficult to distinguish between *value-adding* and *non-value-adding* activities. Moreover, there is a third class of activities called *non-value-adding-but-necessary*, such as organizing files (Ward, 2007). Many empirical studies have indicated that organizations spend more than 50 percent of their time on pure *muda*; the rest of the time is split between non-value-adding-but-necessary activities and value-adding activities. Engineers should be focused on achieving the right customer value and avoiding wasting their time on non-value-adding activities, such as rework, additional costs, missed opportunities, and so on, which have considerable negative impacts on product development performance. The problem is that engineers and designers are very often not even willing to recognize that their jobs can produce waste (Browning, 2003; Rossi et al., 2011). Moreover, many organizations often limit their improvement efforts to *muda* reduction; however, this is not sufficient to guarantee sustainable success.

It can be quite easy for product development to eliminate *muda* from its own processes, but doing so may cause substantial waste elsewhere. It requires significant effort to generate a uniformly balanced flow of work, which actually leads to improved product and process development performance in the long run (Morgan and Liker, 2006). Therefore, it is vital to consider the *causes* of waste together with the waste itself; Toyota in particular focuses on so-called *muri* and *mura*. In product development, *muri*, or overburden, is overloading resources. This results in long queues that increase product development lead time, or introduces chaos into the development process which causes mistakes and errors. *Mura*, or unevenness, is an imbalanced work pace that among other problems forces people to hurry and then wait. Addressing these sticky sources of waste contributes to longer-term, sustainable success.

In summary, creating value in lean product and process development consists of enabling the whole enterprise to generate everything the customer is willing to pay for and of understanding the customer-driven quality and subsequently enabling the operations that produce and deliver such quality. The outcome of product development is the creation of successful operational value streams enabled by a relentless focus on creating usable knowledge. The usable knowledge in lean product development is effectively created through a process built on learning and knowledge, that is, through SBCE (see Box 6.3). The principles of SBCE will orient designers and managers toward the creation of high-value products and usable knowledge in product development.

Value as Knowledge and Learning

When Allen Ward first described the traits of lean product development he also referred to it as knowledge-based product development (Ward, 2007). The ability to accurately capture customer value and to deliver it through profitable operational value streams is related to the *doing more* part of the definition of lean thinking. A process strongly based on the relentless creation of reusable knowledge and continuous learning enables this to happen not only more effectively but also *with fewer resources*. Indeed, the ability to learn and to rely on proven knowledge fosters development of improved, more innovative, and highly valuable products (or services) for which the customer is willing to pay. Moreover, the fact that the process is firmly anchored in knowledge reuse and learning makes the value creation process highly efficient *and* effective.

The capability of companies to effectively acquire and reuse knowledge to create value is a paramount focus in lean product and process development. New knowledge is continuously created with each product developed; learning occurs continuously in the development process as it generates new knowledge that should be recognized and captured in order to be reused. Learning can be facilitated through several tools and methods, such as rapid learning cycles, scientific method/experimentation, observations at the source, design reviews, and lessons learned. Captured knowledge can be represented and reused in the form of trade-off curves, limit curves, standards, A3s, and checklists, among others. To effectively create reusable knowledge through validated learning, some basic learning models can be adopted, including: the Deming cycle, also known as *plan, do, check, act* (PDCA); *define, measure, analyze, improve, control* (DMAIC); and *look, ask, model, discuss, act* (LAMDA). These learning cycles, used continuously, serve as the basis for any kind of product development activity, improvement initiative, and problem-solving effort. They encourage shop-floor observations of problems, which usually arise because of gaps encountered between expectations and reality. They promote profound investigations of design-related problems and foster the reasoning related to appropriate engineering methods and tools to be adopted. The learning also occurs between people and teams, where much knowledge arises that should be confirmed, consolidated, represented, and reused on a continuous and endless basis (Ward, 2007).

Relying on learning and the creation of reusable knowledge enables the lean product development process to be both effective and efficient in delivering customer value. It is thanks to this strong commitment to learning and reusable knowledge creation that mistakes in the late phases of design are avoided—specifications are not frozen too early with the result that continuous and costly changes must be made to them, and decisions are made at the appropriate time and on the basis of proven knowledge and data. This focus on reusable knowledge and learning is represented in the subsystem of SBCE (see Box 6.3).

SBCE calls for no decision to be made before it is required and before sufficient knowledge is available—whether new knowledge generated through learning or previously generated knowledge. The heart of SBCE is the development of sets of designs, that is, multiple design options for a given design problem. Rather than a single solution, engineers explore and test several design alternatives in parallel, progressively eliminating options as they obtain enough knowledge about the performance of the sets, until only one solution remains.

SBCE is not just about developing alternative designs in parallel. It is also about learning; developing technical knowledge and knowledge about customers; making decisions at the right time and based on the best knowledge and data available; and properly using methods and tools to facilitate the exploration, communication, and convergence processes.

System Integration: Process—People—Technology

A powerful development system should enable effective and efficient value creation over the long term. Sociotechnical system theory posits that organizations should be able to find an appropriate fit between their social and technical systems that aligns with the organizational purpose and the external context (Morgan and Liker, 2006). What makes lean product development truly powerful is the combination of mutually supportive tools, processes, and human systems working in synergy to fulfill the purpose of the organization. Moreover, a proper integration of the three subsystems of people, processes, and tools and technology into a coherent enabling system makes this value creation successful and maintainable.

How are people, processes, and tools and technology relevant to a lean product development system?

Process refers to the sequence of tasks required to take a product from concept to launch. This entails the day-to-day activities by which information flows, designs evolve, tests are completed, prototypes are built, and finished products are developed. The process should aim at creating value for the customer while avoiding actions that cause waste. This occurs through a set-based thinking approach, particularly at the front-end phase of product development. The design and engineering process should then flow with a level workload and with a short task time that creates a cadence by which processes are synchronized across functions with rework minimized. Moreover, product design, processes, and engineering skills should be standardized to guarantee flexibility and predictable outcomes (Morgan, 2002; Morgan and Liker, 2006; Ward, 2007).

The *people* subsystem covers recruiting, selecting, and training engineers, along with the organizational structure, and learning patterns. It reflects the strength of the lean-thinking culture inside the organization. A crucial role in lean product development is assumed by the chief engineer, who is directly responsible for an entire project, from the beginning—starting with deep investigation at the customer side—to the end. With deep technical skills, chief engineers not only lead projects, but also act as technical-system integrators. The chief engineer facilitates the cross-functional integration and communication of different expertise within the organization, which often occurs within an *obeya* (literally "big room" in Japanese), a space that fosters collaboration and the exchange of knowledge. Training and the enhancement and development of technical competencies are fundamental to lean product development, together with the integration of all the people involved in the value chain, including suppliers. The entire enterprise benefits from a culture that supports and drives the development of people, who in turn drive the actual continuous improvement in a sustainable way.

The *technologies* subsystem not only includes tools such as computer-aided design systems, machine technology, and digital manufacturing, but also incorporates soft tools that support the efforts of people, either for problem solving, learning, or the use of standardized best practices. Lean thinking dictates that people should not adapt themselves to the acquired technology in the organization; rather, the proper technology should be adapted to enable people to do their jobs efficiently and effectively through a flowing, waste-free process. Simple visual communication tools, such as A3 sheets for problem solving and knowledge management, are recognized as effective (Sobek and Smalley, 2008). Moreover, tools and methods should support standardization and organizational learning in order to promote continuous improvement.

Morgan and Liker (2006) proposed a list of 13 principles that foster system integration as listed in Box 6.2.

Create Flow in the Development Process

A successful lean product and process development system will integrate the three central components outlined above—people, process, and technology—through a management system that makes value flow. Creating development process flow enables an enterprise to deliver a product to its customer with speed and precision.

The first step in creating development process flow is to align the organization around the product vision and how it will deliver unique new value to the customer. Next, each participant in the development process must understand and agree on their particular role and responsibility in delivering this value. This alignment up front in the process saves a great deal of rework later. The Chief Engineer Concept Paper (Morgan, 2002; Morgan and Liker 2006) is a tool that, used effectively, can help align the organization around product creation. This paper is typically relatively short and contains both quantitative and qualitative information about the product. It serves as an alignment tool for project onset and as a contract between the chief engineer's program and the functional departments throughout the duration of the project.

One process to reduce late engineering changes and related program disruption is called *compatibility before completion* or CbC (Morgan and Liker, 2006). By employing CbC individual developers ensure that their design is fully compatible with the larger system, including manufacturing, quality, and other requirements through a series of checkpoints built into the process (see also Box 6.3).

Another key to creating flow leading to faster development times is doing more work simultaneously by synchronizing work across functional activities (Morgan and Liker, 2006). Concurrent engineering is not new, but successful application can be elusive. Value stream mapping is a tool that can drive understanding on how the work actually gets done within each functional department as well as show cross-functional interdependencies. This encourages synchronization of activities across functions, thus leading to an increase in the amount of simultaneous engineering without increasing rework. As the organization matures and teams learn to do more with smaller quantities of stable data, shorter development cycles and faster times to market become possible.

An effective means of improving development capability is to identify those elements of the process that are "fixed and flexible" (Morgan, 2016). Fixed elements can be defined in terms of standards which represent the latest knowledge available to the organization (Morgan and Liker, 2006). These standards safeguard the quality of the product and the development process, but should be designed so that they minimize restrictions to innovation.

Finally, lean product development process flow is maintained by a management system that identifies and responds to abnormalities via prompt leadership support. Thus, the role of developing capability of people at all levels is critical and characteristic of a successful lean product and process development system.

Challenges and Opportunities

Lean product development can help organizations achieve outstanding results, as Toyota and many other companies across different industries demonstrate (Ward and Sobek, 2014). Notable examples include Ford's dramatic product-driven turnaround, Menlo Innovation's application of lean thinking to software development, and the transformation at Carel to demonstrate the power of lean thinking in product development. However, despite these successful examples, organizations still struggle to bring lean thinking into their product development and innovation processes. This occurs for a variety of reasons, further elaborated below.

First, as its definition and characteristics show, lean product development consists of beliefs and practices that can revolutionize the conventional industrial paradigm, but that can be seen as paradoxical. If this makes the hallmarks of lean product development extremely powerful on one side, at the same time it can make it challenging for some to understand and apply. For instance, not everybody agrees that spending more time at the start of the development process will improve a project's quality and performance outcomes. It is simply not intuitive to devote time to designing something that will almost certainly be discarded—but it is indeed this process that generates precious knowledge that will improve future projects. It is also uncommon to base the entire development process on continuous learning. This requires the creation of a deep culture throughout the organization. However, the approaches of lean product development need not be viewed as so controversial, although they may seem unusual in the beginning. They are so logical that they could be described as *common-sense* engineering instead of lean development (Morgan and Liker, 2006). This is a double challenge. On one hand, teach practitioners what can be achieved and how to apply lean product development. However, the challenge for companies is also *how to unlearn* ingrained thinking and development processes; that is, to abandon the current mindset and embrace the paradigm change. Altering mindsets and behaviors is not an easy task. Structured learning and educational initiatives have become paramount, and various effective methods have been proposed with this intent, such as serious games (Kerga et al., 2014).

Second, failures occur when companies implement subsystems or tools incorrectly or incompletely. This occurs frequently with SBCE practice, for instance, which cannot guarantee success in isolation, but is powerful when enabled by certain conditions: customer-value research; employee competencies; process practice; knowledge transfer; tools; methods; and technology adoption (Kerga, 2013). The challenge is, as with any major change, how to create and nurture the proper environment for a new approach or behavior to arise and succeed.

Lean product and process development is best understood as a comprehensive mindset: the coordinated implementation of a set of principles, tools, and logic is an everyday working framework. It should rely on an integrated structure of people, processes, and technology. Companies sometimes focus on only one or a few of the aspects and fail to benefit from the entirety of the system. Too often, lean product development devolves to chasing after some of the key methods or tools to be applied without a supportive structure, a long-term strategy, or any alignment with enterprise purpose. Each company is different, and each needs to seek its own lean product development system, consisting of the appropriate fit of people, processes, and tools, suitable for the reference context, and aiming at the achievement of the company's purpose. Systems evolve over time, and this dynamism leads organizations to constantly seek proper integration of the elements through continuous adaptations and improvements. This is truly challenging given the highly demanding and changing context industries are now facing. Regardless, the dynamics that led to the creation of lean product and process development remain and there are principles of lean product development that will not change: value, usable knowledge, set-based thinking, generating knowledge, and learning quickly.

The Future of Lean Product and Process Development

Creating value for customers is no longer a matter of providing physical products only. Today's world calls for new business models and innovations in the very meaning of product. In such a context, lean product development comes to the fore as it is not circumscribed by the conventional processes, such as engineering, of traditional product development. Embedded characteristics of lean product development resonate, such as cross-functional engagement, deep recognition of the external environment, and the concern with entire product life cycle. Product development and innovation are becoming extremely dynamic. The ability of organizations to learn and adapt quickly is paramount to keeping their lean product development system aligned with a company's purpose in its specific context. Building on learning and knowledge via SBCE and rapid learning cycles will be increasingly critical to guarantee the flexibility and adaptability that companies now require.

It can be expected that since customers will no longer be satisfied with provision of simple products (or services) only, innovation cannot be limited to physical product innovation. Customer value is changing, moving from a pure product (or service) to a solution. (This progression is sometimes referred to as product-oriented, use-oriented, and result-oriented product–service systems.) Consequently, the aim of product development has become delivering solutions to customers, often as a result of a problem-solving process. Lean product development will increasingly support the investigation and exploration of solution alternatives over simple product design alternatives; in this regard, SBCE will support the definition of solution design space, not only product design space.

More debate on the definition and implications of lean product and process development is necessary, along with research on subsystems and tools such as quick learning cycles, SBCE, people and social system development including the role and development of chief engineers, methods to validate the knowledge that is generated during the development process, and other areas. Moreover, we have referred to lean product *and process* development, but the majority of researchers and practitioners have underestimated the process view. Ward (2007) provided critical insights into how the creation of profitable operational value streams is crucial to product development, and enterprise, success. This view should be elevated and considered in all discussions of the future of lean product development.

As lean product and process development continuously evolves, integration with innovations in related methodologies should be explored. Design thinking, lean start-up, and TRIZ (theory of inventive problem solving), among others, represent significant efforts to tackle some of the same challenges as lean product and process development. We suggest that these disciplines would benefit from the structure and tools of lean product and process development.

Just as product development for practitioners in companies must be cross-functional, it must be interdisciplinary in academia. Lean thinking and practice overall has been led from the beginning by practitioners with academicians following. There may be little problem with that on the factory floor where the challenges are, however difficult, relatively straightforward. For product development, however, we suggest that academia needs to be more involved in not only documenting the innovations of industry but participating and even leading in the development of new methods and applications. Innovating new products and services that are truly valuable in the face of increasingly rapid change requires lean product and process development.

There is an increasing need for application among industry practitioners and clarity in academia. Researchers have lots of work to do, with experiments and practical experience accompanied by intense debate taking place to paint a clearer and more complete picture. Without question, lean product and process development will increasingly be the center of dialogue among practitioners and academicians, leading steadily to more widespread understanding and adoption of this most critical component of the lean enterprise.

Case Study: Lean Product Development in Carel Industries S.p.A.

Carel Industries is an Italian company operating in the heating, ventilation, air-conditioning, and refrigeration (HVAC/R) market. The company sells mainly in international markets (70 percent of sales are outside Italy) and operates through 18 subsidiaries in Europe, China, the United States, Brazil, South Africa, and Australia. Carel's purpose is to offer innovative humidification and control systems while continually striving to anticipate the needs of customers, enabling them to achieve superior results thanks to tailor-made solutions.

The company has defined a set of corporate values:

> We operate worldwide, offering everywhere the same superior class quality. We want to be closer to our customers for a better understanding of their needs. We pursue financial solidity. We invest in innovation with the objective to ensure higher energy saving. We offer integrated solutions.

In order to achieve these values, Carel has chosen to embrace the lean philosophy across the entire enterprise, beginning with product and process development (the opposite of the silo-thinking illustrated in Figure 6.3).

Carel's lean product development journey started at the end of 2007, and only after some months did the transformation extend to the manufacturing line. This makes the case of Carel unusual and instructive. The company understood that the lean revolution should be profound and that it should start from the very beginning of the value chain, product development, because this is where innovation takes place and where the competitive advantage is generated. The company invests 7 percent of its turnover in the innovation process annually (from €10 million to €13 million/year).

Carel has emphasized the creation of a lean culture, so that all employees are aware and motivated. In Carel's view, this is the only way that true lean culture change can be sustainable in the long term. Before launching any lean initiative, the company runs a thorough training program for the people involved, which sometimes lasts months. For this purpose, Carel uses its *continuous learning competence center*, physically located in a dedicated building close to the Italian headquarters.

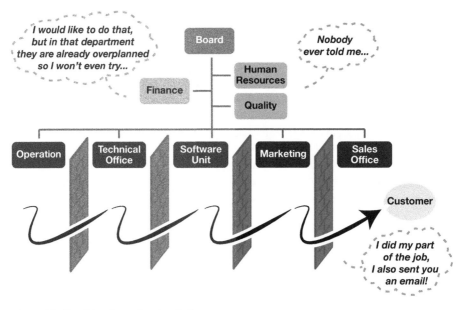

Figure 6.3   Breaking down functional silos

Carel delivers solutions to its customers as a combination of products, which are organized into platforms. Engineers know the customer application field intimately, so they can apply and implement what the customer wants. Product development begins with the development of the required technology, and the process then moves on to market-pull logic. In order to minimize product development lead time, the company adopts an on-the-shelf approach to enhance its technological knowledge. There is a manager for each platform, each with the goal of introducing highly standardized products into the market, which can in turn be used in as many market applications as possible. Each platform has its own value stream, where flow is synchronized with customer pull (a supermarket approach). The entire process is supported by a series of enabling practices. For example, the company makes an intensive use of visual communication in order to support project management and project meetings, for which it dedicates appropriate locations (*obeya* rooms; see Figure 6.4).

As one of the first steps of its lean journey, Carel introduced its competence centers, which collect cross-functional expertise from the project teams (see Figure 6.5).

The company is one of the first in the world to stress the concept of compact teams characterized by dedicated, autonomous, and collocated team members (see Figure 6.6). The main advantages of compact teams are the achievement of single-piece flow in product development and the effective increase of value-added delivery for stakeholders.

After adopting its lean product development strategy, Carel was able to significantly reduce project delays and project cost overruns, as well as to continuously meet product cost targets. As one piece of the strategy the company studied and adopted the SBCE approach. This revolution started in 2012 with a pilot project, and it is now spreading into existing and new mechanical product development projects. As a lesson learned, Carel established that it is mandatory to capture knowledge throughout

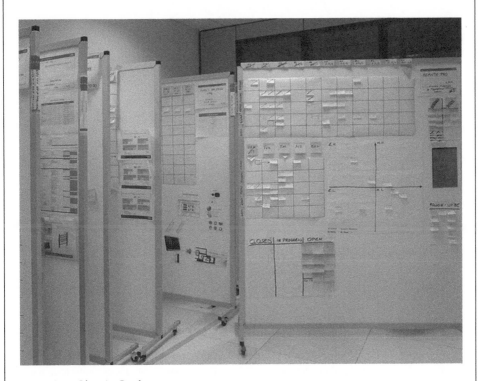

Figure 6.4   Obeya in Carel

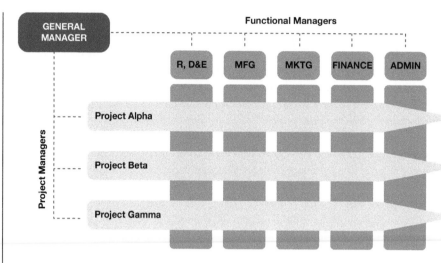

Figure 6.5   Lean project leader and the competence center

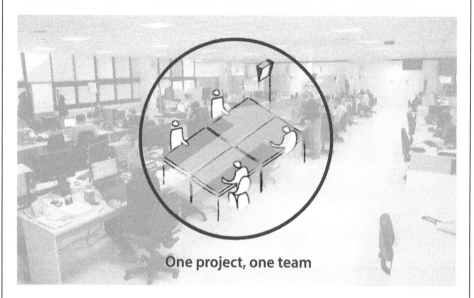

Figure 6.6   A compact team

the design and development process. This supports the effort to implement SBCE and moves Carel closer to becoming a true learning organization, day after day.

The strategy has brought surprising results across the whole enterprise. Carel estimates that for every hour spent on continuous improvement in production, three are saved in cycle times. In addition, production rejects have dropped by 59 percent, turnover per square meter has increased by 47 percent, service levels have risen by 9 percent, and the number of defects has been reduced by half. R&D project development time has been reduced by 20 percent, and output quality level has increased, as has the level of involvement and motivation of personnel. These results have been achieved by applying a new organizational matrix (cross-functional value stream concept) and

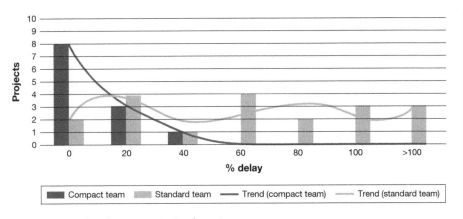

Figure 6.7   Results of new organizational matrix

compact multifunctional teams that work on one project at a time (one piece flow concept) (see Figure 6.7).

Carel's managers are pleased with the success their lean product development strategy has brought so far and determined to take it further in the future. According to Alberto Rosso, Lean Change Agent in Carel: "Even though we have achieved many good results, we are still investing a lot of resources on a daily basis in continuous improvement tasks, and this will help us grow with less waste."

References

Ballard, G. (2000). Positive vs negative iteration in design. In: *Proceedings of Eighth Annual Conference of the International Group for Lean Construction, IGLC-6*, Brighton, July 17–19.

Bernstein, J. I. (1998). Design Methods in the Aerospace Industry—Looking for Evidence of Set-Based Practices. Master's thesis, Massachusetts Institute of Technology.

Browning, T. R. (1996). Systematic IPT Integration in Lean Development Programs. Master's thesis, Massachusetts Institute of Technology.

Browning, T. R. (2003). On customer value and improvement in product development processes. *Systems Engineering*, 6(1), 49–61.

Clark, K. B. and Fujimoto, T. (1989). Reducing the time to market—the case of the world auto industry. *Design Management Journal*, 1, 49–57.

Clark, K. B. and Fujimoto T., (1991). *Product Development Performance*, Boston, MA, Harvard Business School Press.

Clark, K. B. Chew, W. B., Fujimoto, T. Meyer, J. and Scherer, F. M. (1987). Product development in the world auto industry. *Brookings Papers on Economic Activity*, 729–781.

Kennedy, M. N. and Harmon K. (2008). *Ready, Set, Dominate—Implement Toyota's Set-based Learning for Developing Products and Nobody Can Catch You*, Richmond, VA, Oaklea Press.

Kerga, E. T. (2013). *Set-based Concurrent Engineering (SBCE). A Learning Method to Increase Awareness Level in Industry & a Methodology to Identify and Prioritize Areas at a Product Level*. Ph.D. thesis, Politecnico di Milano.

Kerga, E. T. Rossi, M., Taisch, M. and Terzi, S. (2014). A serious game for introducing set-based concurrent engineering in industrial practices. *Concurrent Engineering: Research and Applications*, 22(4), 333–346.

Liker, J. K. (2004). *The Toyota Way: 14 Management Principles from the World's Greatest Manufacturer*, New York, McGraw-Hill.

Morgan, J. M. (2002). *High Performance Product Development: A Systems Approach to Lean Product Development*, Ann Arbor, MI, The University of Michigan.

Morgan, J. M. (2016, April) Embracing development conflict. *The Lean Enterprise Institute E-Letter.*

Morgan, J. M. and Liker J. K. (2006). *The Toyota Product Development System: Integrating People, Process, and Technology*, Cambridge, MA, Productivity Press.

Ohno, T. (1988). *Toyota Production System: Beyond Large-Scale Production*, Cambridge MA, Productivity Press.

Oosterwal, D. P. (2010). *The Lean Machine: How Harley-Davidson Drove Top-Line Growth and Profitability with Revolutionary Lean Product Development*, New York, American Management Association.

Raudberget, D. (2010). Practical applications of set-based concurrent engineering in industry. *Journal of Mechanical Engineering*, 56(11), 685–695.

Rossi, M., Kerga, E. T., Taisch, M. and Terzi, S. (2011). Proposal of a method to systematically identify wastes in New Product Development Process. In: *Concurrent Enterprising (ICE), 2011 17th International Conference on, Munich*, Germany, June 20–22, 2011, 1–9.

Shook, J. (2009). The remarkable chief engineer. Available at: www.lean.org/shook/DisplayObject.cfm?o=906 (accessed July 2016).

Sobek, D. K. II (1997). *Principles that Shape Product Development Systems: A Toyota and Chrysler Comparison*. Ph.D. thesis, Industrial and Operations Engineering, University of Michigan.

Sobek, D. K. II, Ward, A. and Liker, J. K. (1999). Toyota's principles of set-based concurrent engineering. *Sloan Management Review*, 40(2), 67–83.

Sobek, D. K. II and Smalley, A. (2008). *Understanding A3 Thinking: A Critical Component of Toyota's PDCA Management System*, Cambridge MA, Productivity Press.

Ulrich, K. T. and Eppinger, S. (1995). *Product Design and Development*, New York, McGraw-Hill.

Ward, A. C. (1989). A Theory of Quantitative Inference for Artifact Sets, Applied to a Mechanical Design Compiler. Ph.D. thesis, Massachusetts Institute of Technology.

Ward, A. C. (2007). *Lean Product and Process Development*, Cambridge, MA, Lean Enterprise Institute.

Ward, A. C. and Sobek, D. K. II (2014). *Lean Product and Process Development*, 2nd edition, Cambridge, MA, Lean Enterprise Institute.

Ward, A. C., Liker, J. K., Christiano, J. J. and Sobek, D. K. II (1995). The second Toyota paradox: How delaying decisions can make better cars faster. *Sloan Management Review*, 36(3), 43.

Womack, J. P. and Jones, D. T. (1996). *Lean Thinking: Banish Waste and Create Wealth in Your Corporation*, New York, Simon & Schuster.

Womack, J. P., Jones, D. T. and Roos, D. (1990). *The Machine that Changed the World*, New York, Rawson Associates.

7

LEAN SYSTEMS ENGINEERING

Cecilia Haskins and Bohdan W. Oppenheim

Introduction

Systems engineering (SE) has proven to be an established sound practice; but it is not always delivered effectively. A record of accomplishment of over 100 successful space launches between the years 2000 and 2015 demonstrates the result of systems engineering practiced well. However, recent US Government Accountability Office (GAO, 2008) and NASA (2007) studies of space systems criticized significant budget and schedule overruns, some exceeding 100 percent. These programs struggle with waste, poor coordination, unstable requirements, quality problems, and management frustrations. Ironically, the early years of American aerospace programs were quite lean and typified by small, collocated groups of enthusiastic engineers, little bureaucracy, and projects that were completed in record time.

Recent studies by the researchers at the MIT Lean Advancement Initiative (LAI) have identified a staggering amount of waste in government programs, concluding that value is created during only 12 percent of the program time—and the rest is waste (Oppenheim, 2004; McManus, 2005). This waste represents a vast productivity reserve in programs and an opportunity to improve program efficiency as illustrated in Figure 7.1.

Practices in classical systems engineering and program management (PM) have grown heavier and more wasteful over the past 60 years. At the same time, the number of top-level requirements in projects has grown, routinely reaching many hundreds and thousands. This drives the perceived

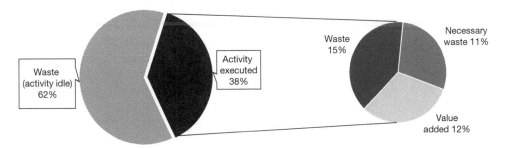

Figure 7.1   88 percent productivity reserve

Source: Oppenheim (2004); McManus (2005).

75

need for program bureaucracy and makes programs costlier, longer, and usually more frustrating to all stakeholders. This can be attributed to two influential factors: the uncompromising need for reliable system-level performance, and inefficient acquisition practices and incentives. Oppenheim (2015) outlines the history of this evolution that has created the paradox that plagues modern aerospace systems. On one hand, these projects are building some of the most technologically advanced and inspirational systems ever engineered by humans. On the other hand, current design and management processes manifest some of the least efficient organizational efforts ever practiced.

For comparison, it is fascinating to recall that the early Apollo program, without a doubt the most dramatically successful space program in the entire history of human civilization, started with only four requirements pronounced by President J. F. Kennedy (paraphrasing): "(1) take man to the Moon, (2) and back, (3) safely, (4) by the end of the decade!" Similarly, the highly successful U2 aircraft program started only with a few requirements defining the flight altitude, speed, endurance, and payload.

What is Lean Systems Engineering?

Systems engineering, which evolved from practices in the space industry to help deliver flawless complex systems, focuses on technical performance and risk management. Lean focuses on creating value through waste minimization, short schedules, low cost, flexibility, and attention to quality. The International Council on Systems Engineering (INCOSE) has developed the subsequent definition of *lean systems engineering* (LSE): lean systems engineering is the application of lean principles, practices, and tools to systems engineering in order to enhance the delivery of value to the system's stakeholders.

Lean thinking is the holistic management paradigm credited for the extraordinary rise of Toyota to the most profitable and near-largest auto company in the world (Womack and Jones, 1996). Toyota refers to its practice of combining excellent product development and SE as simultaneous engineering. For example, the Prius car design was completed nine months after the end of styling, a performance level previously unmatched by any competitor (Morgan and Liker, 2006).

LSE is the area of synergy of lean and SE with the goal to deliver the best life cycle value for technically complex systems with minimal waste. Emphatically, *LSE does not mean less SE*, or cutting corners. It means more and better SE, "with better preparations of the enterprise processes, people and tools; better program planning and frontloading; better workflow management; and leadership with higher levels of responsibility, authority, and accountability (RAA)" (Oppenheim, 2011: xv).

Challenges and Opportunities for LSE

In large projects, value formulation is a difficult process not only because of complex technology, but also because of unstable program funding, dissolved management, fragmented execution, and policy and politics. In many technologically complex programs customers lack expertise to describe their needs clearly and more often than not must be assisted in the task by value creators, or a proxy SE organization through extensive efforts of interaction, cooperation, and clarification.

> In lean systems engineering, both customers and contractors have a responsibility to formulate requirements as well as the state of the art permits, without blaming one another for inadequate effort while working together as a seamless team of honest, open, trustworthy partners who share the same goal.
>
> *(Oppenheim, 2011: 52)*

Requirements

In traditional SE, value to the customer is formulated using requirements, first the top level or customer requirements, then detailed derived requirements allocated for all subsystems at all levels of decomposition. The value proposition to be captured must involve not only explicit requirements and related documents, but also unspoken requirements defining needs, context, operations, interpretations, interoperability, and compatibility characteristics, as well as a good understanding of customer culture.

Experience indicates that many programs eager to get underway tend to rush through the process of capturing top-level requirements, resulting in incomplete, incorrect, or conflicted requirements that burden subsequent program phases with waste (Oppenheim et al., 2011). Poorly formulated requirements significantly increase program cost and lead time, and in extreme cases even cause cancellation of entire programs. Programs that require long durations often suffer requirement instability introduced by the need for changes which were unforeseen at the beginning of the program.

Requirement stakeholders often ignore the fact that a requirement is an imperfect and inherently ambiguous means to describe need. Typically, a requirement is a sentence containing several words. Written in a natural language, especially one as rich as English, where each word in a dictionary has several meanings, it is inherently ambiguous in the linguistic sense. Additional ambiguity arises because of handoffs: the person writing the requirement has in his/her mind the rich context of the need, while the person reading the requirement sees only the requirement text. Because of these structural communicative disjunctions, it is critically important not only to make every effort to make all requirements crystal clear and complete, but also to create means to clarify requirements without causing requirement creep, properly planning effective and efficient channels for clarifications.

Applying LSE we continue defining value using requirements, but in view of the above difficulties we place a significantly higher emphasis on the quality of the effort of formulating and clarifying the requirements, and make certain that all of the above potential pitfalls are minimized. We also promote development of a robust process for capturing and formulating requirements.

Interfaces

With "n" elements in the system, there are $n(n-1)/2$ possible simple connections or interfaces. A typical space vehicle or craft has tens of thousands of elements. This alone makes the interface definition effort formidable, as each interface is needed to write good specifications. Systems engineering practitioners anticipating interfaces understand the trepidation question: "Have we included all of them?," knowing that even one omitted interface may cause fatal failure. Particularly difficult to anticipate are the "wicked" human or higher-order interfaces. The Space Shuttle *Challenger* disaster serves as a dramatic example: engineers understood that the rubber O-rings in the Solid Rocket Boosters must not be used in cold weather, but they ignored the human interface between the O-ring and the shuttle flight management. The managers did not appreciate the risk of cold weather and ordered the flight, which led to the catastrophe (Challenger Commission, 1986).

Model-based systems engineering (MBSE), with its advanced functional and physical views of the system, greatly facilitates the management of interfaces, but cannot assure that all interfaces have been included. Model-based systems engineering can help in identifying possible interfaces by making the n-squared matrix easier to manage, but cannot fill in the details in each matrix cell. That task is still left to the experience and intuition of engineers. The problem is that the experience and intuition work well only for well-understood systems. This brings us to the following important conclusion: it is not realistic that all interfaces in a complex system can be anticipated and defined early in the program. Since all interfaces need to be defined in order to write a complete set of requirements, it follows that it is not realistic to develop good, detailed requirements at the beginning of a program.

The topic of interfaces is further complicated by two widespread industrial practices:

1   Distribution of production among as many contractor sites and supplier locations as possible, driven by political and financial pressures to "spread the wealth" and secure broad political support for the project.
2   Overwhelmingly popular corporate policy to "stick to core competencies and subcontract the rest," with the vast majority of system parts built by a complex network of suppliers. This complex multitier supplier network is largely driven by the fact that higher-tier costs are higher than those at a lower tier, and the time between building parts at higher tiers is so long that many organizations decide to outsource lower-level design activities to specialty con-tractors who survive because they focus on just one type of activity for multiple buyers.

These practices make the program coordination and system integration challenging and increase the need for excellent classical systems engineering and program management. More specifically, prime contractors perform system design, major structural design, and systems integration, and subcontract subsystems and components to the established vendor base for major subsystems (e.g. engines, avionics). These second-tier subcontractors then subcontract for components (such as valves, pumps, etc.). These third-tier contractors subcontract for smaller parts such as sensors, actuators, seals, and so forth. It is normal for a supplier network that builds a complex system to include four tiers of suppliers. Therefore, lean SE strongly recommends that system design is fully completed and stable before allocating lower-level requirements to subcontractors. Allocating only fully mature and stable requirements prevents costly, lengthy, and frustrating requirements instabilities (Oppenheim, 2015).

INCOSE LSE Working Group

Waste in classical SE emanates from a variety of causes: the conviction of the engineers that everything is unique, requires a unique solution, and a unique set of processes. The result of this mindset is projects that are poorly planned, executed in an ad hoc manner, exhibit poor communications culture, poor coordination, and poor organizational preparation (Oppenheim, 2004). INCOSE is the world authority on systems engineering, with the stated goal to advance the state of the practice. The LSE Working Group was formulated in 2006. In 2010 the group issued the *Lean Enablers for Systems Engineering* (LEfSE), which subsequently was recognized as the INCOSE product of the year, and later received the Shingo Research and Professional Publication Award. LEfSE is a checklist of nearly 200 actionable practices for SE and closely related aspects of product development and enterprise management, including supply chain management (INCOSE, 2011). A series of validating surveys confirmed that the LEfSE recommendations aligned closely with NASA and GAO benchmarking results (see Table 7.1).

Lean Enablers for Systems Engineering

The LEfSE practices are organized according to the six lean principles. The checklists cover a large spectrum of SE practices, with a general focus on improving program value and stakeholder

Table 7.1 NASA best practices compared with LEfSE recommendations (NASA, 2007)

NASA "Best practices"	LEfSE sample
Leading with vision: sharing the vision; providing goals, direction and visible commitment	3.2.6 Identify a small number of goals and objectives that articulate what the program is set up to do, how it will do it, and what success criteria will align the stakeholders
Focusing on requirements: mission success driven requirements and validation process	3.2 Clarify, derive, prioritize requirements early and often during execution
Achieving robust systems: use rigorous analysis; robust design; HALT/HASS testing	3.2.5 *Fail early—fail often* through rapid learning techniques (e.g. prototyping)
Models and simulation: model-based systems engineering with "seamless" models, validated by experts	3.2.4 Use architectural methods and modeling for system representations that allow interactions with customers as the best means of drawing out requirements
Visible metrics: effective measures, visible supporting data for better decisions at each organizational level	2.6 Plan leading indicators and metrics to manage the program 3.7 Make program progress visible to all
Systems management: managing for value and excellence throughout the life cycle	4.2 *Pull* tasks and outputs based on need and reject others as waste—prevents execution of unnecessary tasks
Building culture: based on foundation "systems" principles; continuous improvement	6.2 Build an organization based on *respect for people*

satisfaction, and reducing waste, delays, cost overruns, and frustration. The full text of the LEfSE (Oppenheim et al., 2011) is too long for the present chapter, but a brief summary is given here. The full text is available online.

Under the *value principle*, the enablers promote a robust process of establishing the value of the end product or system to the customer with crystal clarity. The process should be customer-focused, involving the customer frequently and aligning the enterprise employees accordingly.

The enablers under the *value stream principle* emphasize waste-preventing measures; solid preparation of the personnel and processes for subsequent efficient workflow and healthy relationships between stakeholders (customer, contractor, suppliers, and employees); detailed program planning; frontloading; and use of leading indicators and quality metrics.

The *flow principle* lists the enablers that promote the uninterrupted flow of robust quality work and first-time right; steady competence instead of hero behavior in crises; excellent communication and coordination; concurrency; frequent clarification of the requirements; and making program progress visible to all.

The enablers listed under the *pull principle* are a powerful guard against the waste of rework and overproduction. They promote pulling tasks and outputs based on need (and rejecting others as waste) and better coordination between the pairs of employees handling any transaction before their work begins (so that the result can be first-time right).

The *perfection principle* promotes excellence in the SE and enterprise processes; the use of the wealth of lessons learned from previous programs in the current program; the development of perfect collaboration policy across people and processes; and driving out waste through standardization and continuous improvement. A category of these enablers calls for a more important role of systems engineers, with RAA for the overall technical success of the program.

Finally, the *respect-for-people principle* contains enablers that promote the enterprise culture of trust, openness, respect, empowerment, cooperation, teamwork, synergy, good communication, and coordination—enabling people for excellence.

The LEfSE were developed to be used as a checklist of good holistic practices. Some are intended for top enterprise managers, some for programs, and others for line employees. Some are more actionable than others, and some are easier to implement than others. Some enablers may require changes in company policies and culture. However, employee awareness of enablers that are the least actionable and most difficult to implement is useful.

A major follow-up project jointly managed by INCOSE, Project Management Institute (PMI), and the MIT Lean Advancement Initiative (LAI), with the participation of nearly 180 industrial companies, developed additional *lean enablers*, this time for *integrated systems engineering and program management* (Oehmen, 2012; Conforto et al., 2013). The guide has been tailored for programs that operate under complex political and financial constraints and applies to a broad range—commercial and governmental, including hardware, aerospace, energy, and infrastructure. The LEfSE were incorporated into the set of 326 enablers that aid programs to improve cost, schedule, and quality performance.

The Future for LSE

When speaking of lean practices, one must not fail to mention the exemplary lean company SpaceX, an almost entirely co-located and vertically integrated small firm building rockets and spacecraft which is well ahead of large governmental space programs, breaking from traditional SE methods with its independently developed lean principles and practices. Companies such as SpaceX provide the inspiration for the development of future lean enablers. At the time of writing a major study of SpaceX operations is in preparation. The illustrative case study summarizes the SpaceX way.

Case Study: Lean Systems Engineering in SpaceX

According to its website, "SpaceX designs, manufactures and launches advanced rockets and spacecraft. The company was founded in 2002 to revolutionize space technology, with the ultimate goal of enabling people to live on other planets" (spacex.com). Its historical milestones include December 2010 when it became the only private company ever to return a spacecraft from low-Earth orbit; in May 2012, its Dragon spacecraft attached to the International Space Station, exchanged cargo payloads, and returned safely to Earth—a technically challenging feat previously accomplished only by governments. Since then Dragon has delivered cargo to and from the space station multiple times, providing regular cargo resupply missions for NASA. The company's comparatively small, talented staff includes former NASA engineer John Muratore, author of "X38 Program System Engineering Lessons" (Bilardo et al., 2008). Muratore (2014) recently told a class at Loyola Marymount University that "classical methods only work well when you are building something that is completely understood – otherwise you need a crystal ball. . . ."

SpaceX only formally manages the payload interface requirements and verification with the customer. It replaces lower-level requirements management, allocations, verifications, and artifact bureaucracy with intense engineering optimization, super-efficient prototype development, design iterations focused on best overall system performance, and extensive multi-dimensional mission assurance based on an extraordinary amount of testing of prototypes, subsystems, and entire integrated systems.

SpaceX uses a next generation testing infrastructure that permits rapid design-build-test prototyping cycles, rapid development and testing of software and software-hardware systems, and the use of 3D printers. It tests a fully integrated wet rocket in the "test what you fly" condition (in contrast to the traditional "test as you fly" which demands identical but not the same hardware and software to that used in flight). "Test what you fly" performs tests on the actual flight hardware and software, including testing on the launch pad. In order to enable such testing, SpaceX developed restartable engines and other multi-use hardware.

Rather than employ dedicated SE or PM organizations, SpaceX performs mission assurance with integrated SE and PM activities distributed throughout the company, using a unique system of integration and mission assurance responsibilities. For example, for each system element, SpaceX uses a life cycle integrator called "*responsible engineer*" who has full RAA for the element from early concept through prototype development and testing, design, production, integration, launch, and performance in flight, including disposal. This person knows the status of the element at any moment in time, and has the right to inquire, coordinate, and help stakeholders along the life cycle, and react immediately to any problems or delays. This practice enables excellent and efficient mission assurance for the element, traceability, configuration and risk management, and rapid decision making to optimize system design and qualify system parts. Intensive mission assurance and integration are also performed along several vertical dimensions: integration within a discipline (e.g. propulsion system), product integration, and integration for a flight. SpaceX engineers spend almost all their time on "great engineering," avoiding the frequent "bureaucracy of artifacts" of traditional SE and PM.

We estimate that SpaceX practices over 100 of the lean SE enablers. It is fascinating that these practices were developed at SpaceX totally independent of the INCOSE or PMI projects, as independent intellectual development. This is an independent validation of both the lean enablers and SpaceX practices. However, SpaceX has gone farther than the scope discussed in this chapter, and a future release of the lean enablers by INCOSE and PMI should address and incorporate these new revolutionary practices.

References

Bilardo Jr, V. J., Korte, J. J., Branscome, D. R., Langan, K., Dankhoff, W., Fragola, J. R., . . . and Sweet, R. E. (2008). Seven key principles of program and project success—A best practices survey. Available at: http://ntrs.nasa.gov/archive/nasa/casi.ntrs.nasa.gov/20080021182.pdf (accessed July 2016).

Challenger Commission (1986). *Report to the President by the Presidential Commission on the Space Shuttle Challenger Accident*, June 6, 1986, Washington, DC.

Conforto, E., Rossi, M., Rebentisch, E., Oehmen, J. and Pacenza, M. (2013). Survey report: Improving the integration of program management and systems engineering—Results of a joint survey by PMI and INCOSE. Presented at the *23rd INCOSE Annual International Symposium*, Philadelphia, June 2013.

GAO (2008). *Space Acquisitions—Major Space Programs Still at Risk for Cost and Schedule Increases*, GAO-08-552T. Washington DC. March 4, 2008. Available at: www.gao.gov/new.items/d08552t.pdf (accessed October 17, 2015).

INCOSE LSE WG (2011). Lean Systems Engineering Working Group website. Available at: www.lean-systems-engineering.org (accessed July 2016).

McManus, H. L. (2005). *Product Development Value Stream Mapping (PDVSM) Manual*. Release 1.0. Available at: https://dspace.mit.edu/bitstream/handle/1721.1/81908/PDVSM_V.1_2005.pdf?sequence=1 (accessed July 2016).

Morgan, J. M. and Liker, J. K. (2006). *The Toyota Product Development System: Integrating People, Process and Technology*, New York, Productivity Press.

Muratore, J. (2014, January 23). A traditional discipline of systems engineering in a non-traditional organization system. Lecture, Loyola Marymount University.

NASA (2007). *NASA Pilot Benchmarking Initiative: Exploring Design Excellence Leading to Improved Safety and Reliability*. Final Report, October 2007. Washington, DC, NASA.

Oehmen, J. (ed.) (2012). *The Guide to Lean Enablers for Managing Engineering Programs*. Version 1.0. Cambridge, MA, Joint PMI-MIT-INCOSE Community of Practice on Lean in Program Management. Available at: http://dspace.mit.edu/handle/1721.1/70495 (accessed July 2016).

Oppenheim, B. W. (2004). Lean product development flow. *Systems Engineering*, 7(4), 352–376.

Oppenheim, B. W. (2011). *Lean for Systems Engineering with Lean Enablers for Systems Engineering*, Hoboken, NJ, J. Wiley & Sons.

Oppenheim, B. W. (2015). *Program Requirements: Complexity, Myths, Radical Change, and Lean Enablers*. PMI White Paper. Available at: www.incose.org/docs/default-source/los-angeles/oppenheim_program-requirements.pdf?sfvrsn=2 (accessed October 17, 2015).

Oppenheim, B. W., Murman, E. M. and Secor, D. A. (2011). Lean enablers for systems engineering. *Systems Engineering*, 14(1), 29–55.

Womack, J. P., and Jones, D. T. (1996). *Lean Thinking: Banish Waste and Create Wealth in Your Corporation*, New York, Simon & Schuster.

8

LEAN LOGISTICS

Michel Baudin

Introduction

In lieu of an introduction, the following paragraphs are a précis of the chapter, which is itself a précis of the book by the same title (Baudin, 2005), giving you three options in depth of coverage.

Logistics comprises all the operations needed to deliver goods or services, *except* making of the actual goods or performing the services. In manufacturing, it covers material flows between plants and between production lines within a plant. It also includes information flows generated by processing of transactions associated with material flows, analysis of past activity, forecasting, and planning and scheduling of future activity, as well as fund flows triggered by the movements of goods and information.

Lean logistics is the logistics dimension of lean manufacturing. The logistics organization is the pit crew to production's race car driver. Its first objective is to deliver the right materials to the right locations, in the right quantities, and in the right presentation; its second, to do all of it efficiently. *Outbound logistics* is organized to serve as a source of market intelligence. Shortages are prevented by vigilance rather than inventory.

Lean logistics tailors approaches to demand structures of different items, as opposed to one-size-fits-all. It is a pull system: materials move when the destination signals that it is ready for them (Sugimori et al., 1977). Moving small quantities of many items between and within plants with short, predictable lead times requires pickups and deliveries at fixed times along fixed routes called "*milk runs.*" In turn, this supports the use of returnable containers.

Information systems for lean logistics combine visible management with computer systems. Toyota uses a worldwide network for logistics and markets in Japan through an internet portal (Fujimoto, 1999; Iyer et al., 2009). Production planning/scheduling involves leveled sequencing and pull systems, and uses the capabilities engineered into the shop floor. Materials requirements planning (MRP) provides suppliers with forecasts, *electronic data interchange* (EDI) and kanbans are used to issue orders, and auto-ID helps maintain inventory accuracy (Louis, 1997).

Option-specific components are ordered through the body-on-sequence system, and responsibility for commodities is delegated to suppliers through vendor-managed inventory or consignment. Suppliers are organized in tiers, and used as single sources. Customer/supplier collaboration extends from product design to emergency response, and suppliers organize mutual support in improvement efforts.

Objectives of Lean Logistics

The objectives of any business organization can be summarized in different ways from different perspectives. For manufacturing logistics, the most relevant are what we call "the two Fs": effectiveness and efficiency. Being effective, as Peter Drucker (2007) put it, means getting the right things done; being efficient means doing them without wasting resources. Effectiveness is about the "what"; efficiency, about the "how." Obviously, effectiveness takes priority, and efficiency at doing the wrong things is not an objective worth pursuing. Yet this is what most material managers in manufacturing companies are doing, when they worry more about keeping trucks full and forklift operators busy than about delivering the right parts in the right quantities at the right time and in the right presentation to production.

On the outbound side, a customer who orders a case is not usually forced to accept a truckload. However, in production, an operation that needs a small bin of parts—even if this bin must be fully stocked—sees full pallets arrive still shrink-wrapped, simply because it is convenient for the forklift driver to deliver them at that time and in that form.

By definition, logistics does not transform materials. Many lean manufacturing authors conclude from this that there is no value added in logistics. Logistics authors counter that, arguing that logistics provides the value of time and place. In addition, we also see value in presentation. These three types of logistics value added are dramatized with extreme examples in Figure 8.1:

- A beautiful maternity ward ready six months from now is no use if you are in labor today.
- Your bicycle is worth more in your hands at the start of the race than 50 miles away.
- Bullets in a sealed box offer no protection against a pouncing lion.

Figure 8.1 The value of time, place, and presentation

Source: Baudin (2005).

For the manufacturing organization as a whole, there is much more at stake in the quality of the service provided by the logistics organization than in the productivity of its members or the utilization of its equipment and facilities. Logistics operations occupy more space than production and are therefore highly visible. However, production operators outnumber logistics personnel about 10 to 1, and production machinery and its supporting facilities also represent an investment that is an order of magnitude larger than that used for transportation, storage, and retrieval.

If there is one forklift driver too many, the cost to the organization is in the tens of thousands of dollars per year, but shortages can cost millions. Yet, in his analysis of logistics performance, Frazelle (2002) proposes measures of logistics performance covering costs, productivity, quality, and responsiveness, but without ever suggesting that quality and responsiveness, measuring effectiveness, should be addressed before considering addressing costs and productivity related to efficiency.

In lean logistics, the functions of *materials supply and production* are not treated at the same level. As discussed in my book *Lean Assembly* (Baudin, 2002), materials supply is the pit crew to production's race car driver. Adopting this perspective does not mean neglecting efficiency, only putting it where it belongs: to be addressed after effectiveness.

The objectives of lean logistics can therefore be stated as follows:

1   Delivering the materials needed, when needed, in the exact quantity needed, and conveniently presented, to production for inbound logistics and to customers for outbound logistics.
2   Without degrading delivery, pursue the elimination of waste in the logistics process.

Inbound logistics is production's pit crew, and its emphasis is on the level of materials service as opposed to the efficiency with which it is provided. This is a key driver of lean logistics and the rationale behind many of its features.

Material Flow Concepts of Lean Logistics

First, outbound logistics is a source of market intelligence. Since outbound logistics is the tail end of the order fulfillment process and deliveries trigger the collection of revenue, there is generally no confusion within the company regarding the importance of this activity. There is, however, one aspect of it that makes it different from a mirror image of inbound logistics, and that is its role as a source of market intelligence.

Many companies, and not just lean manufacturers, mine their sales data. What is, however, specific to lean manufacturing is the realization that the physical organization of distribution can act as a screen, blocking access to market information and the design of creative ways to remove or work around these screens.

Second, lean logistics prevents shortages through vigilance, not inventory. Whether raw materials, work in process, or finished goods, the rationale for keeping inventory is shortage prevention. While keeping large stocks of coal, iron ore, or petroleum may work for this purpose, this approach breaks down as the product mix and the variety of materials and components used increase. Instead of a secure supply, the result, known as *"the paradox of stock,"* is warehouses that are full and contain ample supplies of all but one of the items needed for a product. As a result, not a single unit can be assembled and shipped.

The lean approach is instead to hold the minimum needed to support production but monitor it closely, plan production to smooth the consumption rate of each item over time, organize inbound logistics to make replenishment lead times more predictable, and respond with countermeasures at the first sign of problems. Spectacular examples of this approach include how

Toyota was able to maintain supply of parts from the Midwest to NUMMI throughout the Mississippi flood of 1993 and to restore full production in six weeks after the Aisin Seiki fire of 1997 cut off 99 percent of the supply of proportioning valves in Japan.

Logistics must be Tailored to Specific Needs, not One-size-fits-all

Most manufacturing organizations have only one way to do the work of logistics. One common pattern for inbound operations inside the plant is as follows:

1 Parts come in full truckloads from one supplier in each truck.
2 Operators use forklifts to unload the truck one pallet at a time.
3 After receiving, forklift operators put away pallets into single-deep pallet racks into any available slot, and log the location with a radio terminal.
4 The computer system issues work orders or routing slips.
5 The forklift operators retrieve full pallets from the warehouse and log this operation with a radio terminal.
6 They deliver full pallets wherever they can find space to set them down near the destination production area.

The same pattern is applied to all items, regardless of required quantities or frequency of use. The logistics organization is attached to this one-size-fits-all approach. Its management is particularly concerned that its members may not be able to deal with the complexity associated with a different approach for each category of items.

The lean logistics perspective is the opposite. Regardless of which single approach is chosen, it will be effective and efficient for some items and neither for others. If an assembly line consumes a pallet of an item every 20 minutes, then it makes sense to deliver this item by the pallet load. If, for a different item, a pallet holds 12 boxes and one box lasts a week, then deliveries should be for no more than one box. Since it makes no sense to use a forklift to deliver one box, other means of transportation should be used, such as a cart that can hold a mixed load of boxes of different items. Understandably, tailoring the approach to the needs results in a more complicated system, and the logistics organization may need more training to cope with it.

Milk Runs Smooth the Flows

The need to move small quantities of a large number of items both between and within plants with short, predictable lead times and without multiplying transportation costs has driven lean manufacturers to organize pickups and deliveries at fixed times along fixed routes called "milk runs." The term is a reference to the system used for home delivery of milk in the US until the 1960s. It is in fact not the standard meaning of "milk run," which is aviation slang for an easy trip, similar to a "cake walk." As shown in Figure 8.2, the milk run concept applies in different forms to inbound, outbound, and in-plant logistics, at least for some of the items consumed or produced.

Other metaphors could have been used to describe this approach. Inside a plant, dispatching forklifts on request to pickup locations can be viewed as a taxi system. On the contrary, milk runs can be viewed as buses, picking up and dropping off passengers at a series of stops at fixed intervals on regular routes. In Japan, this system is known as *junkai* (巡回), which means "tour."

The milk run concept is largely ignored in the logistics literature, and barely mentioned even in the literature on lean manufacturing in English. In Japan, it is described in articles in the magazine *Kojo Kanri* (Factory Management, published by Nikkan Kogyo Shimbunshu).

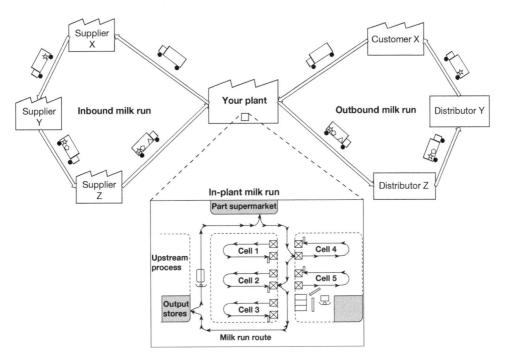

Figure 8.2   Inbound, outbound, and in-plant milk runs

Source: Baudin (2005).

Returnable Containers Improve Part Protection and Cut Costs

Until the 1960s, such foods as milk, yoghurt or beer were sold to consumers primarily in returnable bottles or jars, but the trend since then has been towards disposable containers. Some local breweries in Germany still use returnable bottles, and the reusable industry still has a foothold in many European countries. Today, however, the closest most companies get to reusing packages is recycling the materials they are made of.

In this context, it comes as a surprise that lean manufacturers are going in the opposite direction and favoring returnable over disposable containers for packaging parts in transit. In automobile plants, returnable plastic bins now dominate, even for shipments from overseas, and cartons are a vanishing minority. In other industries, one also sees plants where suppliers' disposable containers do not make it past receiving or past a consolidation center, and where parts are transferred to returnable bins at the point of entry.

There are many reasons for this:

1   Provided returnable containers are handled with sufficient care to make 20 round trips or more, they are cheaper to use than single-use containers that must be disposed of in an environmentally acceptable way.
2   Returnable containers can be fitted with item-specific dunnage that effectively protects the parts from one another, prevents operators from inserting wrong items, and makes the parts easier to count. However, item-specific dunnage is too expensive to be used only once.
3   Collecting returnable containers from industrial customers is easier than from consumers, because there are fewer of them, and milk runs provide an infrastructure for the return flow of empties.

4   The number of returnable containers in circulation for an item is controlled and caps the number of parts in the pipeline.

Like milk runs, however, returnable containers have yet to receive any attention in the literature on lean manufacturing and logistics. This may be due to the numerous practical challenges implementers face in managing the return flow of containers in usable condition at the right locations.

Information Flow Concepts of Lean Logistics

The material flow systems provide the muscles; the information flow system, the nerves. This section outlines the key concepts of the information systems that are part of lean logistics.

Lean Logistics is a Pull System

Lean manufacturing is often described as a "pull system," as opposed to the "push system" it replaces. This distinction is only relevant in the logistics domain. It is no more applicable to conveyance within a production line than to water flow within a pipe. However, it is applicable to the transportation of parts between plants or between lines within a plant.

The distinction between a pull and a push system is then simple (see Figure 8.3):

- In a pull system, parts do not move until the destination plant or production line signals that it is ready for them.
- In a push system, parts move as soon as they are ready, regardless of the conditions in the destination plant or line.

Many managers fail to work out the logical consequences of the pull concept. They want parts to move on as soon as they are ready, because they assume it will get them out the door in finished goods faster. However, in a pull system this is not supposed to happen. Instead, the parts stay in the output buffer of the line until a pull signal arrives. This output buffer is located right at the end of the line where it is visible, not in a separate room. If the line's production runs are for pallets and the pull signals for individual boxes, then boxes are what moves, as shown in Figure 8.4. The output buffer works like a retail store, from which the next line "buys" parts by issuing pull signals, and in which the parts that have not yet been bought remain on the shelves.

The pull system is an adaptation of commercial market mechanisms, where money is the pull signal. The move to a pull system on the shop floor is a partial reversal of the trend observed from the 1840s to the 1970s, away from market mechanisms and toward what Alfred Chandler called *the visible hand* of management to allocate resources and work within companies and industries.

The attempt to use MRP to plan and schedule the shop floor can be seen as the extreme of the visible hand reaching into operational details and prescribing from a central location which parts should be run when through each machine.

Pull systems allow local decisions to be made locally, using a logic that makes these decisions naturally consistent with global business needs. The concept is simple; making it work on the ground, with actual products, processes, people, and equipment is not.

Pull signals can take on a variety of forms, from empty containers or fixtures to cards called kanbans and electronic signals. We will discuss the selection of appropriate types for each application.

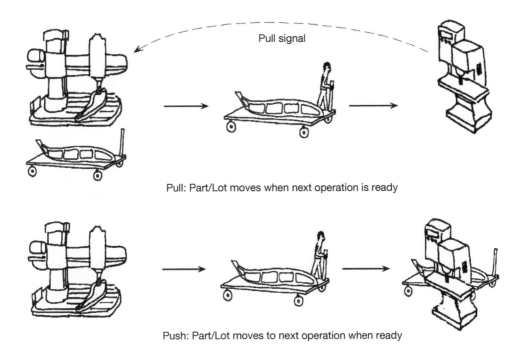

Figure 8.3   Push and pull concepts

Source: Baudin (2005).

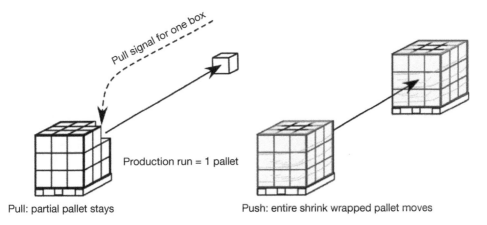

Figure 8.4   Quantities moved in pull versus push system

Source: Baudin (2005).

Information system = visible management + computer systems

In most businesses today, "information system" is synonymous with "computer system." However, in lean manufacturing, the information system combines visible management with computer systems. Successful 5S projects make plants not only clean but easy to navigate. A first-time visitor to a well-lit, clearly marked neighborhood supermarket can find butter without

Unmarked aisle   **Marked aisle**

Figure 8.5   Visible management in a supermarket

Source: Baudin (2005).

asking for help. However, the challenge of locating an item in an uncharted warehouse makes the maintenance of an accurate inventory database all but impossible. The difference is highlighted in Figure 8.5.

The computers available when lean manufacturing pioneer Taiichi Ohno was professionally active could not do much that was useful in a factory. If you tried to use them, the care and feeding of the computer systems became your full-time occupation, and applications that could justify their costs never materialized. It is little wonder that Ohno had little use for these machines. Many current practitioners of lean manufacturing retain an anti-computer bias to this day. While it is possible even for today's tools to become time sinks and money pits, they can be productivity boosters.

In 2000, Toyota launched its own internet portal named "Gazoo," with the goal of getting its fingers on the pulse of the market again. In its early days, Toyota sold cars in Japan door to door. This method was later abandoned as too expensive, but it had the advantage of providing better market intelligence than dealers. Gazoo restores this market visibility by allowing car users to communicate with Toyota through their clicks.

Production Planning and Scheduling

The order fulfillment process is industry-specific, and there is therefore no single approach that can be called "lean planning and scheduling." Instead, there are common principles that are applied in different ways depending on circumstances. Toyota's production planning and scheduling methods blend a flow of consumer orders aggregated through dealers into a final assembly leveled sequence. The assembly leveled sequence execution pulls parts in and triggers the production of thousands of items up the supply chain. This works for cars. To make injection-moulded plastic parts from a single resin, there is also a lean way to plan and schedule production. However, most of the specific features used for car assembly are irrelevant. Table 8.1 describes underlying principles that can be used across industries.

The Role of Manufacturing Execution Systems in Lean Logistics

Many enterprise resource planning (ERP) systems have modules to track shop floor activity. These modules have historically been ineffective, leading to the creation of another class of software, called *manufacturing execution systems* (MES), to fill the gap.

Lean manufacturing makes materials easier to track through the plant and the supplier network. Further, it makes tracking vital as a tool to exercise vigilance in preventing shortages.

In flow lines and cells, there is a visible mapping from physical location to process status. Since there is no backtracking or eddy flow, simply seeing where a part is enables you to tell exactly which operations already have been undergone and which still remain. Also, since parts through the line move one at a time, first-in-first-out, the time at which a part completed an operation can be inferred from data about the complete production run. If moves between lines are triggered by kanbans, then the "traveler" documents that accompany parts in job shops can be eliminated for all standard products. They will only survive in the form of "build manifests" for products with options or customization.

The MES is then used to print the kanbans and build manifests based on the *bills of materials* (BOM) in the ERP or the technical data management system.

While visibility on the shop floor eliminates work in process (WIP) tracking transactions through every operation in the computer system, the need remains for materials to check in and out of warehouse locations. Without this, it is impossible to maintain accurate inventory data.

Since, in principle, it tracks physical flows, the MES also should, but in most plants does not, have a key role in preventing shortages. Knowing how much of an item is on hand, the rate at which it is consumed, and the delivery schedule, it should be able to anticipate shortages and issue warnings to managers in a position to launch countermeasures. Yet even in factories with multimillion-dollar information systems budgets, shortages are not discovered until an operator reaches for a part and can't find one.

Monitoring Supplier Performance

The history of transactions with each supplier is summarized into supplier performance metrics that are used to certify suppliers. Suppliers are certified as trustworthy, needing assistance or guidance to achieve the certification, or as candidates for replacement.

The prices suppliers charge is what purchasing traditionally pays the most attention to, among other reasons because price data is the most readily available. Collecting performance data on delivery and quality is necessary to keep the company from hurting itself by always choosing the lowest bidder.

In most plants, the data to perform the required analysis exists, and what is lacking is the will to mine this data for multiple dimensions of supplier performance, categorize suppliers based on the results, and develop appropriate policies for each category.

Table 8.1 Principles for production planning and control in lean logistics

#1 Separate rate work and response work.	In telling the plant what to make, when to make it, and with what resources, the lean approach is also tailored to the different types of demand the plant faces.
	One key distinction is between items made on a routine basis, which we call "rate work," and items made irregularly, on request, which we call "response work." It is based on the product-quantity (P-Q) and seasonality analysis. It leads to the classification of products and their components and materials into A, B, and C categories, and the rate work comprises the A products with their dedicated production lines and the B products with dedicated lines by product family.
	Together, the A and B products usually account for more than 90% of the total volume. The C products are the low-volume-high-mix response work. Scheduling A products is then simply a matter of adjusting the volume. For B products, it means sequencing the items through the production line with goals that may be maximizing output, minimizing work in process (WIP), or smoothing the flow of incoming materials. Orders for C products are treated like individual projects and made from scratch.
#2 Don't play priority games with WIP in rate work.	Even rate work first comes in in the form of customer orders, which can be shuffled every which way until they are released to production. Past this point, materials are committed and the work proceeds first-in-first-out until the complete order emerges from production.
	This is possible because lean engineering of the production process and the use of a pull system have made production lead times short for all orders. If the plant is fully booked, order lead times may be extended, but the waiting happens before production starts, not in mid-stream. Exception handling, by definition, is response work, done on resources or in time allocated for this purpose, and is not allowed to interfere with rate work.
#3 Avoid starting production with missing parts.	Performing partial assembly of goods with missing components creates stocks of units that are "99% complete" but still cannot be shipped, as well as complicated, error-prone catch-up operations. Short production lead times also enable the manufacturer, if not to terminate this practice altogether, at least to restrict it to brief shortages of non-safety-related parts that can be installed in an otherwise complete unit.
	On a car, a trunk lock satisfies these conditions, but a proportioning valve doesn't: it distributes brake fluid to the wheels, which is related to safety, and is mounted in a location that is not easily accessible. And indeed, when the Aisin Seiki plant in Kariya burned on February 1, 1997, depriving Toyota of 99% of its supply of proportioning valves in Japan, the Toyota assembly plants shut down within four hours rather than attempt to build cars with this part missing to add it later.
	Of course, validating a sequence of product units to build during a shift against available stock is technically feasible given an accurate database but, oddly, is not done by ERP systems but by advanced planning and scheduling (APS) systems.

Table 8.1 (continued)

	This validation, however, is insufficient, because product units may be built during the shift using parts that are not yet available at the time of the planning run. The parts delivered on a 10:00AM milk run, for example, can be assumed available for production by 12:00PM but are not in-hand at 6:30AM when the schedule is generated. To the best of our knowledge, this level of complexity is not handled by the software available as of this writing.
#4 Integrate production planning and scheduling with the pull system.	With a pull system, explicit scheduling of the work is needed only at the top of the supply chain —the start of final assembly in car making — with pull signals conveying the required information upstream.
	To the recipients of the pull signals, however, they constitute a demand, to which they may respond by explicitly scheduling their own production resources. The net result is not the elimination of the need to schedule but its decentralization.
	Not only is the problem of scheduling a cell of five workstations intrinsically easier than that of scheduling a plant with hundreds of machines and thousands of part items, but the detailed structure of a cell and the information about operator skills, process, and setup times can be better handled locally by a cell leader or a scheduler attached to a supervisor than globally by a central computer system.
	To the extent its discipline is followed, the pull system prevents local scheduling from pursuing goals that are not in the best interest of the plant as a whole, and the use of various forms of levelled sequencing, where applicable, dampens the bullwhip effect.
#5 Exchange information with suppliers.	In lean logistics, supplier communications go far beyond commercial transactions. The following paragraphs explain the key additional elements
#6 Use MRP for forecasting.	MRP, in the original sense of materials requirements planning, is performed in lean manufacturing as well as everywhere else. The difference is in the use of the output. In lean manufacturing, MRP is used strictly to translate forecasts of finished goods demand into forecasts of materials requirements, for suppliers to act upon as they see fit. While these forecasts are not orders, the agreements with suppliers usually include compensation for suppliers when consistently optimistic forecasts make them buy excess materials.
#7 Use EDI and kanbans as needed	Kanbans are recirculating physical tokens, most often cards, that serve as pull signals and have been used by Toyota as a means of issuing orders to suppliers for some items since 1949. Fifty-four years later, while most manufacturing companies have yet to master the logic of the kanban system, its implementers are challenged to take advantage of increasingly effective computer and communication technology.
	Human-readable tokens still need to be attached to containers but they must also be machine-readable through barcodes or RFID tags, and the pull signals issued based on the kanban system's replenishment logic using EDI technology

(Continued)

Table 8.1 (continued)

#8 Apply body-on-sequence as needed	In the automobile industry, some model and option dependent components made by local suppliers are ordered by electronically feeding them the exact start sequence of cars started on the first station of final assembly.
	The supplier then starts making the components, knowing that they must be delivered to the required station on the final assembly line within, say, 214 minutes. "Body-on-sequence" is the term used for this system at Toyota and NUMMI; Ford calls it "in-line vehicle sequencing."
#9 Use vendor-managed inventory and consignment/pay-per-build as needed.	At the opposite end of the parts spectrum are commodities like nuts, bolts, and washers, for which customers like to delegate as much responsibility as possible to suppliers. In vendor-managed inventory, the supplier is given access to the customer's inventory database and is allowed to initiate shipments when reorder points are crossed.
	Consignment arrangements delegate more responsibility, by letting the supplier own the stocks in the customer's plant until the parts are used, and, in the pay-per-build scheme, suppliers are paid based on the quantities of their parts incorporated in finished goods leaving the production line, per the bill of materials.

Collaborative Supplier/Customer Relationships

The relationships between suppliers and customers have received more attention in the press and the literature than the more technical aspects of lean logistics outlined above. The lean approach to managing supplier/customer relations, however, goes hand in hand with milk runs, pull systems, and the other approaches I have covered.

A lean supplier network has the following characteristics:

1 *A small number of direct suppliers with a tier structure.* Lean manufacturers rely on a tier structure allowing each large supplier to manage a group of smaller ones.
2 *Single sourcing.* Lean manufacturers do not use the strategy of sourcing the same item from multiple suppliers to assure supply. The single-source suppliers may make their own second-sourcing agreements but they retain sole responsibility for the supply of the item.
3 *Collaboration in product design.* The more complex a manufactured product is, the less sense it makes to treat its components like commodities. Instead, they are specific to the product and designed for it, and better, cheaper, and more manufacturable designs result when the engineering teams of suppliers and customers collaborate during design in target costing, value engineering, and *design for manufacturing and assembly* (DFMA).
4 *Collaboration in cost reduction during production.* During production, suppliers and customers work together to reduce costs through a process called *kaizen costing,* in which the customer provides technical assistance in exchange for price breaks.
5 *Collaboration in problem solving and emergency response.* Lean manufacturers do not look for suppliers who "never have any problems" but for suppliers who don't hide them and are diligent about solving them, particularly when they are emergencies. If a key piece of equipment breaks down and cannot be repaired right away, the supplier notifies the customer immediately. If the breakdown was due to human error, a mistake-proofing device is implemented within a week.

6   *A community*. The suppliers of a lean manufacturer are an organized community. Suppliers to NUMMI participate in the Golden State Automotive Manufacturers Association (GAMA); suppliers to Toyota in Kentucky, in the Bluegrass Automotive Manufacturers Association (BAMA); suppliers to Applied Materials, in its Lean Suppliers Association (LSA). These groups hold conferences, visit each other's plants, and, in the case of Toyota, contribute to each other's improvement projects through activities called *jishuken*.

This approach originated in the automobile industry, in which leadership and initiative rest with the car makers who assemble the final product. This is not a universal pattern. Computer industry companies, by contrast, follow the lead of software and chip suppliers for product design, and of chip suppliers—particularly microprocessors and memories—in logistics.

Conclusions

Since 2005, lean logistics has become a topic in its own right, and treated as if it were independent of the manufacturing activity it serves. It is, however, nothing of the kind, and pretending it is does not lead to success in implementing it. If you are pursuing lean in machining, fabrication, or assembly, then lean logistics is a necessary complement. Otherwise, there is no sense in pursuing it.

The technology of information changes much faster than the technology of materials handling, storage and retrieval, and transportation. When new technology is introduced in logistics, it automates existing methods and concepts. Later, it enables the development of new concepts. Barcodes took 30 years to become widespread as a means of automating basic warehouse management transactions; then it dawned on some users that they could be used to make shop floor objects self-identifying.

Today the *internet of things* (IoT) is seen as a means of taking it further. If these visions materialize, it will eventually lead to new concepts in logistics that may enhance or replace today's lean logistics, but I won't venture a prediction on how long this will take.

Case Study: From Forklifts to Small Trains

This happened in a 50-year old plant with about 1,000 employees, making large mechanical assemblies at the rate of about 100 units per day, involving thousands of parts and extensive customization. This plant is alive and well today.

Seven years ago, on the production shop floor, you saw traffic jams of forklifts, a sign that a plant is overusing this means of moving materials. The organization had no experience with any other method, with the forklifts delivering either pallets or pallet-sized, stackable bins, from which operators struggled to retrieve parts. The transportation aisles were not clearly marked and the forklifts penetrated the operators' workspace in the production area, causing frequent accidents.

It was like a city using taxis for mass transit. For millions of commuters making the same trips every day, trains and buses work better. The production lines consumed many of the same parts every day, at rates that did not vary massively from one day to the next. Rather than forklifts making unsolicited deliveries or calling for a forklift when running low, it would have been better to have deliveries at a regular pitch, in quantities that were just enough to feed the line until the next scheduled delivery. It required different equipment, like small trains and customized carts, and a higher level of organization and discipline. The key challenge was starting this transformation.

In this particular case, the plant manager had led a delegation on a tour of another plant and seen a small-train system in operation. He had then made the commitment to implement it back home. The *materials manager* in charge of in-plant transportation, however, was "too busy" to take on this project. This put the plant manager in a quandary. He could replace the materials manager, but he was a long-term employee whose contributions had, up to this point, been highly rated. Even if he was not fired, being removed from this position would not only be a blow to him, but would also affect the morale of the whole organization. On the other hand, if he were left in charge, nothing would happen.

However, the plant manager felt that the key was for the organization to gain experience with small trains and milk runs and he put production in charge of a pilot project, with help from the newly established kaizen office. For the target segment of the production line, materials management would still deliver pallets or large bins, but not to the line side. Instead, they were delivered to an area set aside for this purpose in one of the warehouses, where a team from production would pick parts from the bins and arrange them on a small train for delivery to the line.

As it added a step, it was not efficient, but it achieved the goal. The team bought a tugger and carts with connected axles to follow the tugger in turns, and a Creform starter kit to build structures on the carts. They chose to make a run every 30 minutes, not as a result of calculations but because it was the pitch they had seen used in their plant visit. They later adjusted it to the line's needs.

The inventory that cluttered the workspace around the target production line was removed. It not only made its operations visible, but it also enabled the production team to rearrange feeder operations into cells. The resulting improvements more than paid for the extra handling step. Five years later, most of the movements of materials inside the plant were through milk runs of small trains. Most of the forklift leases were terminated, but a few were retained. After all, even a city with a mass transit system still needs a few taxis.

References

Baudin, M. (2002). *Lean Assembly: The Nuts and Bolts of Making Assembly Operations Flow*, Portland, OR, Productivity Press.

Baudin, M. (2005). *Lean Logistics*, Portland, OR, Productivity Press.

Drucker, P. F. (2007). *Management Challenges for the 21st Century*, Amsterdam, Butterworth-Heinemann.

Frazelle, E. H. (2002). *Supply Chain Strategy*, New York, McGraw-Hill.

Fujimoto, T. (1999). *The Evolution of a Manufacturing System at Toyota*, Oxford, Oxford University Press.

Iyer, A., Seshadi, S. and Vasher, R. (2009) *Toyota Supply Chain Management*, New York, McGraw-Hill.

Louis, R. S. (1997) *Integrating Kanban with MRP-II*, Portland, OR, Productivity Press.

Sugimori, Y., Kusunoki, K., Cho, F. and Uchikawa, S. (1977). Toyota production system and Kanban system: Materialization of just-in-time and respect-for-human system. *International Journal of Production Research*, *15*(6), 553–564.

Further Reading

Ayers, James B. (2001). *Handbook of Supply Chain Management*, New York, The St. Lucie Press/APICS Series on Resource Management.

Bayles, Deborah L. (2001). *E-Commerce Logistics and Fulfillment: Delivering the Goods*, Upper Saddle River, NJ, Prentice Hall.

Bloomberg, David J., LeMay, Stephen A. and Hanna, Joe B. (2002). *Logistics*, Upper Saddle River, NJ, Prentice Hall.

Christopher, Martin (1998). *Logistics and Supply Chain Management*, London, Prentice Hall/Pearson Education.

Cooper, Robin and Slagmulder, Regine (1999). *Supply Chain Development for the Lean Enterprise: Interorganizational Cost Management*, Portland, OR, FAR/Productivity Press.

Frazelle, Edward H. (2002). *World-Class Warehousing and Material Handling*, New York, McGraw-Hill.

Harvard Business Review on Managing the Value Chain (2000). Boston, MA, Harvard Business School Press.

Hopp, Wallace J. and Spearman, Mark L. (1996). *Factory Physics*, Chicago, Il, Irwin.

Kulwiec, Raymond A. (ed.) (1985). *Materials Handling Handbook*, New York, Wiley-Interscience.

Lambert, Douglas M., Stock, James R. and Ellram, Lisa M. (1998). *Fundamentals of Logistics Management*, Boston, MA, Irwin/McGraw-Hill.

Liker, J. (ed.) (1994). *Engineered in Japan*, Oxford, Oxford University Press.

Monden, Y. (1993). *Toyota Production System*, North Carolina, IIE Press.

Mulcahy, David E. (1994). *Warehouse Distribution and Operations Handbook*, New York, McGraw-Hill.

NPW Promotion Division (2005). 実践日産生産方式キーワード２５ (25 keywords of the Nissan Production Way), Nikkankogyo.

O'Leary, Daniel (2000). *Enterprise Resource Planning,* Cambridge, UK, Cambridge University Press.

Piasecki, David J. (2003). *Inventory Accuracy*, Kenosha, WI, Ops Publishing.

Poirier, Charles C. and Reiter, Stephen E. (1996). *Supply Chain Optimization*, San Francisco, CA, Berret Kohler Publishers.

Productivity Press Development Team (2002). *Pull Production for the Shop Floor*, Shopfloor Series, Portland, OR, Productivity Press.

Simchi-Levy, David, Kaminsky, Philip and Simchi-Levi, Edith (2000). *Designing and Managing the Supply Chain*, Boston, MA, Irwin/McGraw-Hill.

Suri, Rajan (1999). *Quick Response Manufacturing*, Portland, OR, Productivity Press.

Wallace, Thomas F. (2000). *Sales and Operations Planning*, Cincinnatti, OH, T.F. Wallace & Co.

Wallace, Thomas F. and Kremzar, Michael H. (2001). *ERP: Making it Happen*, New York, John Wiley & Sons.

9

LEAN SAFETY

Robert B. Hafey

Introduction

Lean safety is an approach that utilizes both the lean philosophy and the lean tools to intentionally create a continuous improvement safety culture that engages the workforce and moves lean forward.

The management philosophy entitled lean has been in practice for more than 20 years and yet many or most companies that have attempted to make it a core principle in their business operations have struggled or failed in their attempts. Before we explore why that is the case, we must first understand the foundation, or building blocks, of lean. By knowing the definition and intent of lean we will be able to quickly see which parts have been neglected, misunderstood, or ignored by business leaders.

A very simple and broadly accepted definition of lean is reducing the cycle time of delivering products and services to customers by eliminating waste. If this definition is accepted, then it is obvious that the primary benefactors of a business's lean efforts are the customers of the business. It is the responsibility of business leaders to clearly state the definition and the purpose of the lean effort to ensure it is understood by everyone in their business. It is also their responsibility to define a lean implementation path that gives focus to all three pillars of lean as defined by the Toyota Production System. It is these three pillars, or focal points, that are the underlying foundation of lean. They are:

1   *Delivery or just-in-time:* Reducing the cycle times of every business process.
2   *Quality or jidoka:* Ensuring the delivery of quality products and services.
3   *Respect for people:* Trust building.

So why is such a seemingly simple concept so difficult to successfully implement? I believe it is because leaders deliver a very confusing message concerning the intent, focus, and purpose of their lean efforts. To state it another way, their purpose motive is not, either intentionally or unintentionally, clearly stated. They have too often focused their reports on one of the outcomes of lean—cost savings—rather than on the true north target of reducing cycle times to customers. Leaders understand that by reducing business process cycle times, labor hours can be dramatically reduced, which will, in turn, reduce their operating costs. There is no denying that lean can accomplish this, but that is an outcome rather than the goal of lean. When it becomes the stated goal of lean, both the communications and actions of management destroy trust in the workplace. This is problematic as lean is a trust-building, cultural change journey. These same leaders think lean is a set of tools rather than a philosophy and fail to see the need or lack the inner desire to spend the time on earning the trust of their workforce. They fail to recognize or care about the critical importance of the third pillar of lean—respect for people. This alone is responsible for most lean implementation failures.

The focus of leadership in this scenario is clearly on financial results rather than on their people who, if empowered and engaged, could have a dramatic impact on the financial results. They are dollar-centric rather than people-centric leaders. The cost savings purpose motive, when delivered by management, makes little or no sense to the workforce, for they envision the expected reduction in operating costs to result in layoffs or redundancies. Nobody will give their heart and mind to an effort that will result in the loss of their employment. Without trust, lean is a bust. Eventually management tires of pushing lean on an unreceptive, fearful workforce and their program dies. But it is not lean that fails, it is management: they have failed to impact their workplace culture by earning the trust of their employees.

These same management teams see the lean tools (5S, single-minute exchange of dies (SMED), kaizen blitz, process mapping, etc.) as a means to an end. Utilizing lean tools, for them, is an opportunity to expose waste in the business and reduce costs. During their relentless drive to reduce cycle times, stopwatches are used to record current state and future state cycle times to measure the gains. Eventually labor is freed up and management has to decide what to do next. They can redeploy the labor while growing the business or they can lay people off. If they choose the second option, they hide behind the belief that it is "management's responsibility" to lay off people to reduce costs. In this scenario the employee base remains unengaged and fearful of the outcomes related to continuous improvement activities. How can business leaders bridge this trust gap that exists between themselves and their workforce? How can they unify and redirect their work culture? By focusing on the one activity that everyone in the business will support without fail—safety.

What is Lean Safety?

Lean safety is a lean methodology that makes sense to all parties involved in the effort by providing an ethical, people-centric approach to lean implementation. It is the safe, trust-building path to lean. Lean safety differs from compliance safety in the fact that it is continuous improvement safety. The common focus of almost every safety program is compliance to regulatory agencies. Therefore, safety is most often a top-down "telling people what to do" activity. In lean terminology, safety is "pushed." As a result, safety professionals are often viewed as safety police—the enforcers of safety policies, rules, and regulations. A troublesome practice that is a direct result of top-down directive compliance safety programs is the use of discipline for safety infractions. This outdated practice, which relies on the use of fear and intimidation to drive safety compliance, is a trust killer. Current state safety programs therefore inhibit lean progress. Deming (1982), in his 14 key principles for management, clearly states the importance of driving fear from the workplace. Fear in the workplace is the opposite of trust and the importance of trust building while on a lean journey cannot be overstated for lean success is predicated upon it. The ability of leadership to redirect their work culture (how people think, act, and interact) is therefore the key to lean success.

The question that is begging is how or where to begin the trust-building journey required for lean success? When senior leaders are asked "what is the top priority in your operations?" they respond with "safety." When they state this priority they are close to understanding the easiest entry point to begin or recharge the lean efforts in any business. When change efforts such as lean are introduced into a work culture the question people ask themselves is "what's in it for me?" A cultural stalemate naturally occurs until the leaders of the business define an approach they can use to extend trust and engage the workforce in meaningful real continuous improvement activities that result in empowerment and ownership. Lean safety provides that approach and yields those results.

Unrelated to top-down, directive-compliance safety programs, lean safety utilizes both the lean philosophy and lean tools to intentionally create a continuous improvement culture that engages the workforce and moves a business's lean efforts forward. Leaders who embrace lean safety quickly recognize the many benefits that result. They include an improved safety culture, process cycle time gains, and a growth in trust that leads to an engaged workforce. Also note-worthy is the fact that lean safety will dissipate resistance to lean and will garner the support of management, unions, supervisors, and the workforce because it answers the critical all-important question of "what's in it for me?" for all stakeholders. Since the sole focus of lean safety is to *make work safer and easier*, it provides an ethical approach to lean implementation.

To address the issue of making work safer and easier, leaders are required to go to the *gemba*, where the work is performed, and engage their workforce. It is often stated in the lean community that the skills required to lead lean are 30 percent technical and 70 percent social. Therefore, these engagement opportunities require a change in management style. Those managers who historically have been skilled at telling people what to do, and were expected to do so, must change to a coaching style of leadership. They must now ask the right questions rather than have the right answers. It should be understood that when supervisors and managers tell people what to do it both perpetuates parent–child relationships and removes the responsibility of the employees to solve the customer service problems that exist in the business. A *lean safety gemba walk* provides leaders with the perfect opportunity to begin two-way, adult-to-adult conversations about continuous improvement with the initial questions all being safety related. Before beginning the gemba walk leaders should understand what to look for that will then allow them to ask the safety engagement questions. They are:

1   *Product flow*: Poor product and material flow increases the amount of material handling required. Material handling is a safety risk.
2   *Material handling methods*: Manual lifting (e.g. physical labor), forklifts, hoists, and cranes are just a few of the material handling methods used in industry and each comes with its own risks.
3   *Material storage containers*: Raw material and WIP (work in process) are received and stored in a variety of containers that provide opportunities for discussions about improvements.
4   *Work area layouts*: Ineffective layouts drive excess material handling and cause poor product flow.

With a good understanding of these and how each of them can physically impact an individual, a leader is ready to engage a worker in a safety discussion. After an initial introduction and an explanation of the intent of the observation, a leader should ask permission to observe the work being performed. Noteworthy is the fact that although the leader is observing an individual, it is being done to understand the impact of the work processes on the individual. Then by asking questions and actively listening, the leader can hold a dialogue based on any of the following observations:

•   *Body parts that are out of neutral.* Any work steps that require a worker to bend his or her back, twist his or her torso, or raise his or her arms, or which takes their shoulder out of neutral, is an opportunity for dialogue about work process change.

- *Straining to perform a task.* Strenuous pushing or pulling on anything is another chance to talk about change.
- *Lifting something that appears heavy.* Trying to decide if something is too heavy to lift is a fruitless exercise. Focus instead on eliminating lifting from work processes.
- *Performing repetitive tasks.* Many production operations have tasks that are repetitive. Engineering, human resources, and other opportunities exist to control or at least minimize exposure when performing these work tasks.

When leaders show they are greatly interested in someone's safety, and then follow up on their commitments to improve it, their actions are an honest and ethical trust-building approach to work culture change. Repeated lean safety gemba walks and the resulting improvements will begin to shift the culture and build trust.

Another lean tool easily adapted to use safety as the focus while engaging the workforce and building trust is the *safety kaizen blitz*. It differs from the lean safety gemba walk in that the targeted work area, department, or production process is larger in scope. A traditional kaizen blitz is a multi-day, cross-functional, team-based rapid continuous improvement event. A team of 6 to 10 members is chartered and challenged to improve the cycle time of a business process. A skilled facilitator guides the team members on their three- to four-day journey. The event concludes with the members presenting the results of their efforts to the senior leaders in a report out session. Since these events are hands-on and fun to participate in, the greatest value that results from a kaizen blitz is not the process that was improved—it is that mindsets have been changed. People think differently about continuous improvement after participating in just one event. The team almost always attains its cycle time improvement goals, using a stopwatch to measure those gains. The use of a stopwatch ensures everyone knows the team's goal is cycle time improvement. It also results in the fear, mentioned above, of full participation by the workforce. A safety kaizen blitz eliminates the stopwatch along with the fear, for the team is chartered to improve safety rather than cycle times. For instance, during a traditional kaizen blitz the goal might be to reduce a machine changeover time by 50 percent and a common safety kaizen blitz goal is to reduce the risk of soft tissue injuries. It is easy to understand why everyone will rally around the safety goal while the cycle time goal may cause angst for the hourly workforce.

In addition to the mentioned safety gemba walks and safety kaizen blitz events, there are other commonly used lean tools that help move a business forward. A few of them are 5S, process mapping, value stream mapping, SMED, kanban, and team building. In and of itself, tool usage does not qualify a company to call itself lean. Lean success is not gauged by the number of lean tools used but by the level of trust leadership has built. All lean tools allow leaders to extend trust with the hope of earning it in return. As trust grows engagement follows. The Gallup Organization, which recognizes workplaces with the Great Workplace Award, notes that employee engagement is a force that drives real business outcomes (Gallup, 2015).

So, if trust is the true path to engagement then trust paves the path to lean business success. By removing the stopwatches, and the ever-present focus on cycle times, and instead focusing on safety during their lean journey, leaders illuminate the ethical path toward meaningful business outcomes.

Challenges and Opportunities

The greatest challenge to a broader acceptance of lean safety is a lack of people-centric leaders. They are leaders who truly believe in the value of their workforce and are willing to invest their time and energy in the multi-year culture change journey that true lean requires. Another challenge is the inability of people to see and recognize the value of continuous improvement of safety. When they see book titles about lean safety or lean safety gemba walks, they assume the topic is related to compliance safety. Compliance-based safety programs are so ingrained in industry it is hard for those involved in managing those efforts to see beyond them. Leaders and many safety professionals are so focused on compliance, they fall into the trap of using top-down directive management methods in an attempt to maintain compliance. These actions create fear in the workplace and trust building stalls or retreats.

Another compliance safety program that adds a level of confusion to a clear understanding of lean safety is a long-standing safety methodology entitled *behavior-based safety* (BBS) (e.g. Geller, 2004). A frequently asked question is, "is lean safety like BBS?" Based only on the word "behavior," the answer is no. That word implies that BBS is about observing the behaviors of individuals and then providing feedback on whether or not the behavior exhibited was acceptable (safe) or unacceptable (unsafe). BBS programs focus on people as opposed to process and are saddled with a long history of finding fault with people. As the individuals who perform the work are the ones who are most frequently injured, BBS proponents define their behaviors as the root cause of the safety problems in a facility. Behavior-based safety is directly tied to top-down, directive-compliance safety and therefore is a policing methodology that does not build trust. High injury rates, rather than a focus on continuous improvement, drive the use of BBS and therefore reducing injuries is the target of BBS activity. So how does this approach differ from lean safety?

Lean safety is a process-focused methodology. All lean thinkers understand and accept the oft-cited statement that "the process is the problem, not the person." Therefore, rather than critiquing a singular individual performing a work task (the BBS approach), lean safety observes an individual performing a work task in order to understand and improve the underlying work process problems. The types of problems identified have to do with layouts, material handling equipment, and other things that are under the ownership of the management team. The root cause of people getting injured while rushing to get work done or bypassing a safety guard by applying tape over an interlocked door switch is identified as a worker behavior problem by BBS. A lean safety proponent would drill deeper by asking "why?" five times to get to the real root cause. The root cause is most often a management problem brought on by an incessant push for more productivity. In the eyes of the workers, management has set a safety culture where productivity trumps everything else, including safety. Since BBS programs are sold to management teams struggling with injury issues it is very difficult for the BBS consultants to point out that management is the real root cause problem. BBS fails to get to the real cultural root cause of a poor safety culture. BBS will reduce injuries in the short term, based solely on the amount of time and energy committed to the effort, but it can have no long-term positive cultural impact because no trust building occurs. There is much debate and discussion concerning the pros and cons of BBS. The individuals who should select either the BBS or lean safety approach should be those who do the work. Simply ask them if they want someone to observe them to assess if their behaviors are safe or if they would instead like someone to observe them working so the work tasks can be made safer and easier for them and anyone else who performs the same work tasks. Both BBS and lean safety can add some value to a workplace, but it should be very clear that lean safety is unrelated to BBS. Lean safety builds trust, which leads to engagement and long-term culture change.

Opportunities linked to the understanding and uses of the lean safety approach to work culture changes are numerous. First, lean safety is an educational opportunity for safety professionals. The numerous formal training and education programs that they have mastered prepare them well for the compliance safety world. When they begin their work careers, they are slotted into a career path that is a compliance management role. In addition to safety, they are often given responsibility for health and environmental compliance management. When company-wide initiatives such as lean are introduced to a work culture, those responsible for compliance safety are usually left on the sidelines wondering what is going on and worrying that those efforts may somehow impact compliance. Management mistakenly views compliance safety as something separate and unrelated to operational improvement efforts. Lean safety can open their eyes to continuous improvement safety and provide opportunities for safety professionals to move out of their compliance-policing role. By nature, they really care about people and can be trained to effectively lead safety gemba walks and safety kaizen events. In this way they can add value to the business beyond their compliance expertise.

Another opportunity is the ability of lean safety to dramatically change the safety culture within a business. An effective lean safety effort is intended to engage as many company employees as possible in managing different pieces of the company safety program. It can start with hourly employee safety committees quickly followed by sub-teams that manage personal protective equipment training and compliance, Lockout-Tagout (LOTO) training and compliance, and many other parts of a comprehensive safety program. Until management extends trust and invites hourly employees to take ownership of the company safety program, safety will always be "management's program."

Lean safety also provides the opportunity to move lean forward in a business. It has this ability because it is an honest trust-building effort. It allows managers to be seen in a different light. If they choose the lean safety path they can be viewed as people-centric leaders rather than people who are only concerned about the financials. Lean safety helps those leaders understand you can have both improved safety and reduced cycle times just by using safety as the entry point for your business continuous improvement efforts.

And finally, the greatest opportunity provided by the lean safety philosophy is making work safer and easier for people all over the world, while at the same time making the world a more productive place.

The Future of Lean Safety

Lean safety should be part of the curriculum for undergraduate safety professionals, operations management professionals and MBA program students. All of these programs give focus to financial management but fail to educate future leaders on the value of an engaged workforce. This is because those current programs see labor as a cost that can be increased or decreased by hiring or laying off staff. Lean will never be broadly successful and become ingrained in business life unless leaders understand the requirement to extend trust and develop different relationships with their workforce. Lean safety provides a proven path to begin the dialogue so that leaders start to see their staff as more than an expense.

> The idea of recognizing safety risks as opportunities for lean improvement is unique. By making a work activity safer we also make the work more productive. I think most lean practitioners do the reverse—they look for waste in the production cycle, fix that, and then trust that the process improvement also makes the work safer. But having a worker-centric point of view makes the whole lean improvement idea more personal and grounded in ethics, which makes sense to me.
>
> *Mike Abuls, COO, CGSchmidt (Hafey, 2014)*

Lean safety will continue to impact the compliance safety community, which for too long has been viewed as the enforcer of the rules and regulations. This is a role compliance safety professionals do not like or seek and from which they now have an exit strategy. Lean safety gives them a set of tools and techniques that will allow them to change how they are viewed by others. Some of these same safety professionals will be switched on by lean safety, expanding and adding to the body of knowledge of this relatively new topic. Lean safety will live on, not just because it is good for business, but because is good for people.

Case Study: Lean Safety at KSO Metalfab—Streamwood, Illinois, USA

The intent of using safety as the entry point to begin or restart discussions about continuous improvement is to engage the workforce while at the same time providing an answer to their question, "what's in it for me?" When the leaders at KSO asked me to provide lean basic training for their lead people, I understood I would use this approach but the business owners did not. They expected the lean training to take place in a classroom and focus on just cycle time gains. That is not how I like to spend my time—I like to take trainees to the gemba and allow them to learn by doing. People, like them, who work in manufacturing plants, do not like to sit in meetings or training classes. They are mechanically inclined hands-on learners. I wanted to provide them the opportunity to quickly make a tangible difference in their business. Over nine days the six trainees were exposed to the hands-on experience of implementing 5S, set-up reduction, plant/cell layout changes, process mapping, workflow improvements, a kaizen blitz event, and, of course, the opportunity to make work safer and easier for themselves and their co-workers. During our time together each trainee was immersed in their own personal lean discovery journey that challenged not just their work processes but each of them as individuals.

Out of all the training and experiential learning that occurred the most meaningful, to the people who performed the work, was the redesign of an electrical cabinet assembly process. One of the trainees was the lead person in the assembly area. During my initial visit to KSO I had been given a plant tour by the business owner. At that time, I remember seeing her and the other assemblers in a variety of unnatural and uncomfortable positions, including sitting or kneeling on the concrete floor, while they installed components into electrical cabinets (see Figure 9.1).

The trainee's final project was to tackle this final assembly work-center and improve the flow to customer of a large electrical cabinet. This required them to clearly define the steps of the assembly process and then design a new layout that would support that defined flow. All of their design work was driven by the requirement to keep the assemblers standing and in neutral positions to reduce the risk of soft tissue injuries. The results were amazing. They designed and built an assembly bench, with a hinged sloping end, on to which the assemblers could lay down, build, and then easily remove a cabinet. Components that were previously individually assembled inside the cabinet were now sub-assembled on a workbench and then inserted into the horizontal cabinet as one complete unit. Components and tools required during assembly were located on a rolling tool board/cart and positioned at point of use. This final project required them to apply all the lessons learned in their earlier training—process mapping, layout design, 5S, reducing cycle times, one-piece flow—while focusing on the safety of their associates during the new assembly cell design and build. When the new assembly cell was completed the first cabinet was built and they beamed with pride at their collective success.

Around two years later, because I was in the area, I called the owner and asked if I could stop in for a short visit. I was greeted warmly and given a verbal update on their lean progress before we headed to the gemba. As we walked into the shop, the assembly area lead saw me and said, "Just this morning

Figure 9.1 An obvious lean safety opportunity

as I was performing a new work task I asked myself, what would Bob think about this?" This meant she was looking for a safer and easier way to perform the work task. Her comment summed up the value and power of lean safety. She was exploring her options to reduce the cycle times of a new assembly process by making the work safer and easier to perform. She was engaged, empowered, and motivated because lean safety had provided the answer to the "what's in it for me" question. She was a lean thinker who has journeyed down the safe path to lean understanding and acceptance.

References

Deming, W. E. (1982). *Out of the Crisis*, Cambridge, MA, MIT Center for Advanced Engineering Studies.

Gallup (2015). *Gallup Great Workplace Award*. Gallup.com. Available at: www.gallup.com/events/178847/gallup-great-workplace-award.aspx (accessed August 22, 2015).

Geller, E. S. (2004). Behavior-based safety: A solution to injury prevention: Behavior-based safety "empowers" employees and addresses the dynamics of injury prevention. *Risk & Insurance*, 15(12), 66.

Hafey, R. B. (2014). *Lean Safety Gemba Walks: A Methodology for Workforce Engagement and Culture Change*, Boca Raton, FL, CRC Press.

10

LEAN TEAMS

Desirée H. Van Dun and Celeste P. M. Wilderom

Introduction

The success of a lean organization can, to a large extent, be traced back to its primary production units: teams at the lowest hierarchical level do a substantial amount of "value-added work" (e.g. at Toyota, see Liker and Convis, 2012, p. 144). Continuous process improvement within an organization is difficult to achieve without the smooth cooperation between non-managerial team members and their leaders. Despite this insight, an insufficient amount of research attention has been paid to the dynamics of leading *effective lean teams* (e.g. Van Dun and Wilderom, 2012). *Operations management* (OM) scholars emphasize the various bundles of lean tools in relation to high lean performance (Shah and Ward, 2003). However, these typically non-human tools are used by humans, who must function effectively in teams. Team human dynamics were long seen as an add-on instead of a key to lean's success; they have been analyzed by some other scholars under the relatively small rubric of "self-directed work teams" within human resource management (Shah and Ward, 2003). This may explain in part why so few *organizational-behavior* (OB) studies have dealt with lean teams' success and/or the implications for durably healthy lean work units or cultures (see, e.g., Shook, 2010). Without such OB-type knowledge, the unnecessary failures of lean initiatives will not be curbed.

This chapter summarizes the current behavioral findings on effective lean team dynamics and delineates new areas and OB-type approaches for future investigations. Lean practitioners may also benefit from these insights. It may improve their efforts in accommodating healthy lean contexts, especially now that lean is increasingly being embraced by efficiency-seeking managers worldwide. The chapter ends with an illustrative case, three years into the life of a continuously high-performing lean team.

What are Lean Teams?

We define a *"lean team"* as a more-or-less permanent work floor unit within a larger organizing context, which subscribes to lean's philosophy and uses tools to improve its own processes through the implementation of (non-managerial) workers' ideas. Lean team members, including their team leader, are typically responsible for producing or (pre)assembling goods or delivering (internal or external) services. Hence, we are *not* focusing here on the (often centralized) lean change teams of experts, named by some people as "lean teams."

Bridging the Lean and Team-effectiveness Literatures

Lean does *not* yet play a role in the generic team-effectiveness literature (which is a sizable part of the OB subdiscipline of business administration). We foresee a lot of useful room for OB-types of lean team studies (Bendoly et al., 2010). In our opinion, lean team effectiveness entails a desirable constellation of effective human team dynamics that are facilitated by specific enablers. Simply reversing this reasoning, by assuming that the human dynamics in and around lean teams are identical or similar to otherwise effective teams, does not seem to hold. Lean teams stand out from other types of effective teams because they adhere to different (sometimes experienced as counterintuitive) production principles such as pull, single-piece flow, and just-in-time (JIT) production. Moreover, lean teams are commonly seen as being "self-directed" or "self-managed teams" (Shah and Ward, 2003), which is different to top-down hierarchically organized teams that have much less autonomy. Hence, the human dynamics within and surrounding lean teams are worthy of close examination.

A structured review of the available empirical lean team studies to date distilled nine affective, behavioral, and cognitive intra-team dynamics in effective lean teams and four contextual enablers (see Figure 10.1, reprinted from Van Dun and Wilderom, 2012, p. 142). We will show how this linear *input-process-output* (IPO) type of model may be sketched more dynamically, based on a recent longitudinal study of five carefully selected, highly performing lean teams (Van Dun and Wilderom, 2015). First, however, we will review the so-called *input-mediator-output-input* (IMOI) model. This latter generic team model connects lean to the up-to-date generic team-effectiveness literature.

IMOI is different from the linear-stage models that have been most often presented in lean or continuous-improvement studies (see, e.g., Bessant et al., 2001; Hines et al., 2004); real (lean) teams are more dynamic social systems (Hackman, 2012; Humphrey and Aime, 2014; Salas et al., 2015). At the micro-level, teams and their leaders show behavioral patterns consisting of dynamical elements, such as the ones displayed in Figure 10.1. In addition, in the more realistic, recursive IMOI models, feedback loops are incorporated. A team's performance level may reinforce the continuance of input factors such as higher-level leaders' support for lean. Nevertheless, the "black-box" of effective (lean) teamwork has often been studied as a static phenomenon, with relatively "simple cause-effect models" (Hackman, 2012, p. 430). However,

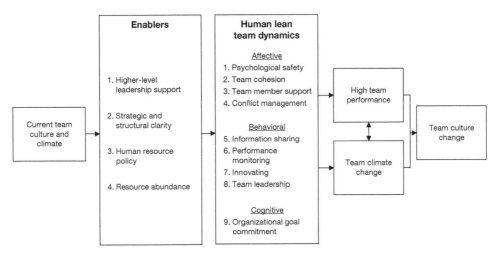

Figure 10.1 Model of behaviors in and around lean teams

in line with the IMOI model, performance outputs fuel the inputs, and, in turn, the evolution of mediating team processes. Hence, as lean is built upon the principle of continuous improvement, effective lean teams are seen to (re)organize (or reconstitute) themselves continuously (Humphrey and Aime, 2014). Consequently, "recent research has begun to match internal team behaviors with external contingencies, capturing at least part of the multilevel nature" of lean work floor teams (Humphrey and Aime, 2014, p. 464).

We will now describe the "internal workings" of effective lean teams (i.e. the middle column of Figure 10.1), and then discuss the enablers of these human lean team dynamics. Such internal workings of a lean work floor unit can be depicted from many different angles; we focus on the effective behaviors of both the members of lean teams and their higher-level internal stakeholders. The rationale for this focus is the need to know more about the (mundane) behaviors of people involved in lean work floor initiatives which enhance the overall effectiveness, including the efficiency of their own efforts.

Human Dynamics in Lean Teams

The nine dynamics displayed in Figure 10.1 reinforce each other in a delicately balanced way, as we will describe next. Central to this figure are four *affective* dynamics that pave the way for the improvement of a team's processes.

1   Team members' *psychological safety* (see, e.g., Edmondson, 1999; Salas et al., 2015) is a springboard for continuous improvement and cooperation. Without such safety, members will restrain the sharing of their criticisms, ideas, and suggestions, resulting in fewer process improvements. Furthermore, once those ideas are transformed into successful process improvements, the level of team psychological safety is likely to go up.
2   *Team cohesion* will help to establish or reinforce a safe climate for effective improvements. Of course, only up to a point because *very* highly cohesive teams risk social loafing, groupthink, or contentment with the status quo. The moment lean teams attain high performance, through their cohesive, collaborative process-improvement efforts, it is likely the level of team bonding will be strengthened (Mathieu et al., 2015, p. 727). There is thus "a mutual reciprocal relationship between cohesion and performance."
3   Team members must be willing and able to *support colleagues* or provide backup when needed, for instance after a worker pulls the andon cord. When such help is demonstrable in a team's performance figures or is appraised by management, it will spur members to stand in for their colleagues, up to a point where helping is the team's norm (Raver et al., 2012).
4   In order to challenge current work processes effectively and to curb the potential waste involved, team members must argue with each other constructively and *manage conflicts*. If a conflict between two or more team members is not brought to a close, it may inevitably damage both team members' psychological safety and team cohesion, and thus the level of overall lean team performance (see, for instance, Humphrey and Aime, 2014; Salas et al., 2015; Van Dun and Wilderom, 2015). Moreover, the lower a team's performance, the more it is likely that a conflict will emerge within the team (Peterson and Behfar, 2003).

Together, the four affective dynamics propel lean team members to engage in four lean *behavioral* dynamics:

5   When lean team members feel psychologically safe, members of effective lean teams customarily *share ideas and information* about, for instance, work standards, and tactical and

strategic developments. This sharing of information during meetings points to the non-wasting importance of effective lean team meetings. Our survey study among 25 lean teams showed that when team members shared more factual information, they scored significantly higher on team effectiveness (Van Dun and Wilderom, 2014). The implied direction of causality here is likely to work both ways, although this still needs to be established.

6   In addition to factual informing, effective lean teams are supposed to engage in continuous team- and individual-level *performance monitoring*. Team members are expected to know, discuss, and improve their individual as well as their team's performance by overcoming hiccups together. Members of effective lean teams use lean tools such as visual management, performance dashboards, and daily start-up meetings to enable and learn from such performance monitoring, to enhance their group's further progress or improvement.

7   Another behavioral dynamic within effective lean teams pertains to their so-called *innovating* efforts. The information, ideas, and data that effective lean team members share while monitoring their team performance are actually transformed by them into concrete, small process improvements or proposals for larger production process adjustments. In turn, team members' monitoring of their team performance level enables the evaluation of the effectiveness of those solutions and to what extent new process innovations are required.

8   A related dynamic is *supportive team leadership*. Formal as well as informal team leaders must guide and facilitate the continuous improvement processes, assist workers when problems occur (Shook, 2010), and also foster a psychologically safe and cohesively performing team climate. Indeed, our longitudinal study found leader support to be a key dynamic of effective lean teams. This is expressed through a behavioral pattern consisting of frequent active listening, informing, providing individual consideration, and infrequent task monitoring. The same longitudinal study showed that team leaders' behavioral pattern is handed over, gradually, to the team-member level, whereby workers engage in task self-monitoring, providing backup and information sharing, and are innovating. The leaders' personal value constellation also seems to play a role here. If lean team leaders endorse mainly self-transcendence types of values, their team members adopt more information-sharing behavior, resulting in a higher level of lean team effectiveness (Van Dun and Wilderom, 2014).

The final lean team dynamic is members' degree of *cognitive commitment* to lean:

9   Members of effective lean teams focus, often passionately, on achieving organizational-level lean objectives. At the very least, they must be willing to engage in continuous process improvement (Angelis et al., 2011). Members of effective lean teams are able to explain and pursue the organization's strategy, and can demonstrate well how their own work leads to achieving those goals. Such shared goal commitment is seen to enhance team cohesion (Salas et al., 2015). Thus, several interrelations can be assumed among the nine factors displayed in Figure 10.1. Moreover, it is better according to the IMOI model if the horizontal arrows in this hypothetical model are bidirectional.

Enablers of High-performing Lean Teams

Effective human dynamics in lean teams are fueled by four contextual enablers: visible *higher-level leader support*, *strategic and structural clarity*, a lean-supportive *human resource policy*, and *resource abundance* (see Figure 10.1). All these factors and their presumed linkages merit large-scale empirical testing in the field, also in recursive ways.

1   Higher-level leaders, i.e. *top and middle managers*, play particular roles in initiating and sustaining lean on their work floors (Beer, 2003; Soltani and Wilkinson, 2010; Marodin and Saurin, 2013; Netland and Ferdows, 2014). Specifically, the extent to which top managers show their true commitment to lean, for instance by frequently visiting the workplace, is likely to improve a lean team's effectiveness in the longer term (Netland and Ferdows, 2014; Van Dun and Wilderom, 2015). This type of top-leader behavior must be guided by work values that are focused on respect, teamwork, and the challenge of continuous improvement by aiming for a deeper understanding (Liker and Convis, 2012). Similarly, an exploratory empirical study of the precise behaviors and underlying value constellations of the middle managers who report to those top managers showed they support their teams with tactful, relations-oriented behaviors such as active listening and agreeing (Van Dun et al., 2010). Compared with non-lean middle managers, they adopted significantly fewer behaviors that tend to dampen the energy level within staff meetings such as task monitoring, providing negative feedback, and defending one's own position. Higher-level leaders enact their visible support for lean by showing tact or consideration for the feelings of their followers; they tend to listen actively to workers' ideas. As was found at the *team leader* level, the relations-oriented behavioral pattern of effective lean middle managers coincided predominantly with a self-transcendent type of value constellation and openness to change. In other words, various empirical studies on effective lean teams point towards a constellation of self-transcendent values and predominantly (but not only) to relations-oriented behaviors, thereby revealing the cascading effect of lean leadership: from the top and middle manager level to team leaders and team members (Van Dun and Wilderom, 2015). Effective lean managers are especially relations-oriented when coaching and developing their subordinates (Liker and Convis, 2012), by also adopting some *task-oriented behaviors* (e.g. structuring) and *change-oriented behaviors* (e.g. providing a vision) (Van Dun et al., 2010).

2   Another important enabler of lean team effectiveness constitutes top managers' provision of strategic and structural clarity. Beer (2003) noted that unclear organizational strategy and priorities are major barriers to lean (team) success. In line with that, Marodin and Saurin (2013) see "strategies and performance measures consistent with lean" as a factor that positively affects lean adoption. In order for members to mentally commit themselves to organizational goals, it is of course essential for work floor personnel to have strategic clarity. When lean team members know how to translate the organization's strategy to their team level, it becomes much easier for them to monitor and improve their team performance in line with that strategy. Moreover, perceived stability in terms of organizational strategy and structure is likely to boost team members' psychological safety: team members' psychological safety is difficult to achieve if they fear that their jobs might be cut. Consistent with this, our longitudinal study found that temporary destabilization, through formal reorganizations, negatively affects team members' commitment toward lean.

3   Human resource policy was noted as another lean enabler by Marodin and Saurin (2013). The focus of their study was on lean's organizational alignment of reward and bonus systems as well as job security. Other empirical lean studies have found that education and training is common practice in most effective lean teams (Bamber et al., 2014; Netland and Ferdows, 2014) (see also the illustrative case at the end of this chapter). It is known that Toyota leaders continuously train their leaders and workers in lean methods, enabling them to improve their work standards effectively (Liker and Convis, 2012).

4   Related to those human resource types of enablers is what we generally call organizational
     resource abundance; Marodin and Saurin (2013) list the "availability of financial and human
     resources." Shook (2010) noted the need for lean firms to provide their workers with
     necessary "tools" to successfully do their jobs. In order to improve (or innovate) processes
     and performance, lean team members need not only time, but also a dedicated performance-
     monitoring workspace on their work floors, access to higher-level leaders who function as a
     change or improvement sponsor, a reasonable budget for realizing small-scale improve-
     ments, and, from time to time, access to external help. Additionally, the availability of
     financial means has been shown to be a particularly challenging enabler of lean teams;
     firms may struggle to continue their investment in lean development when team perform-
     ance levels drop during a difficult economic tide (see, also, Netland and Ferdows, 2014; Van
     Dun and Wilderom, 2015).

Challenges and Opportunities for Effective Lean Teams: A Future Research Agenda

With the recently increased scholarly attention to human dynamics and enablers of effective lean
teams, we can sketch more opportunities for new lean team research. Even though the toils of
lean implementation in the lower-level organizational echelons have been described amply in the
form of OM types of case studies, few of them have taken a behavioral perspective. New academic studies of lean teams ought to integrate the wealth of non-lean team knowledge that is
already available in the field of OB. Future studies will then benefit from more cross-pollination
among both research areas. Considering that team effectiveness is a long-established field, it
would be fascinating, and important, to compare the content of effective lean teams and their
leaders with equivalent non-lean teams and their leaders. Several OB theories may be explored for
this purpose, including those on small groups, team learning, innovation, psychologically safe
team climate, voice behavior, and team identity. Follow-up studies should start by including
matching non-lean control groups as well as field experimentation (Marodin and Saurin, 2013).
Given that lean team studies have, to date, been mainly case-based, i.e. small in scope, it is high
time large-scale empirical studies are instigated that compare the dynamics and enablers of highly
effective with less effective teams across large lean organizations. Far too often lean scholars apply
the case study method without clearly accounting for *how* and *why* these studies were performed;
the same pertains to the predominantly *perceptual*, survey-based measures. Overcoming research
issues creatively such as arranging access to various behavioral field data is of importance here.
This will undoubtedly lead to more (theoretical and practical) knowledge of effective lean team
dynamics and enablers than described in this chapter.

   An opportunity for longitudinal field study entails the exploration of the precise links between
the contextual enablers and human dynamics in building effective lean teams: which enablers
should come first, and which human dynamics could fuel other effective dynamics? That of
course depends on the specific lean context. It is worthwhile to explore such multi-level and
recursive linkages over time. Especially, how higher-level managers, through their behavior,
enable the evolution of a team-level behavioral pattern. Then, through that, how enhanced team
performance may reinforce leaders' supportive behaviors. In line with the IMOI literature, an
empirical study of the dynamic evolvement of lean teams does justice to the "organizing nature of
teams" (Humphrey and Aime, 2014, p. 489). OM/OB scholars might benefit from such recursive
insights and use them to enhance their research designs so that they are able to capture more of
the dynamic (and not only static) reality of organizational life in work teams or settings aimed
at client-driven, continuous improvement. Also, since psychological safety has been noted as

enabling the open sharing of ideas and information (Edmondson, 1999), and thus lean teams' effectiveness, lean team leaders (or their superiors) will facilitate the development of such safe work climates (Salas et al., 2015). Interesting questions for new longitudinal follow-up research are: how much of the feeling of safety is needed (as a "tipping point") in lean work environments so that it fosters real-time performance tracking and transparent information sharing? Additionally, how (much) can such safety levels fluctuate? The cascade effect of leadership, which was revealed in our longitudinal study (Van Dun and Wilderom, 2015), also shows the importance of lean team leaders in empowering their team members. How the apparent transmission of what was once seen as *leader* behavior toward blue-collar workers/followers takes place precisely is another interesting line of study, i.e. how are lean team members learning to work effectively, monitor their own and team tasks, share information, and improve their work processes (see Liker and Convis, 2012)? Such new research is necessary for improving effective lean team development in practice (Scherrer-Rathje et al., 2009).

Following on from Figure 10.1, future research must also uncover more of the content of effective lean team climates/cultures, including subcultures. Schein's model of specific layers of culture (i.e. cultural artifacts, behaviors, norms, values, and basic assumptions) may aid in the unraveling of lean-specific cultural content (see also Shook, 2010, p. 66). Cultures are seen to gradually evolve over long periods of time. It is more likely that a team's work climate, which is much more situation dependent, will first change into a more improvement-focused climate. Also, if lean team dynamics have shown to be profitable, over a longer period of time, this may support the culture change toward lean although it may be particularly difficult to change an existing (team) culture toward a lean culture (Angelis et al., 2011). Notably, scholars need to disentangle specific and observable behaviors better from attitudes and underlying, motivational values, which to date often lack precision (see, for an overview, Van Dun et al., 2010). It would be worthwhile to include human value variables in follow-up studies of lean's human dynamics as they have not surfaced a lot in the lean literature and it is likely that leaders' values play important roles in the development of healthy lean team cultures. Video-based ethnographic studies may enable more detailed behavioral analysis, including the quality and timing of their behavior, because the recent video-based studies were aimed at exploring the frequency and patterns of lean team leader and member behaviors. Further examinations of lean team members' values and behaviors, at different levels of organizational hierarchies and effectiveness, and in different work situations, could increase our understanding and aid in offering more effective help in situations where lean initiatives would otherwise fail. Moreover, human team dynamics are, in practice, quite interrelated. Most lean team studies have tended to focus around only a few of them. There is a need for integral lean team studies connected to credible team-effectiveness measures.

Besides a further examination of the content of effective lean team dynamics and those of their leaders, the internal and external support roles in developing lean teams and their leaders deserve additional research attention. Consultants are often hired to aid or challenge managers to improve their processes, their leadership styles, and lean team dynamics (Scherrer-Rathje et al., 2009). Moreover, strategic human resource specialists co-determine the selection of and promotion criteria for (middle) managers; implementing lean within teams will probably make a demand on *human resource management* (HRM) to adjust those criteria. Hence, in line with Bamber et al. (2014), we encourage further integration of lean within the fields of change management, management consulting, organizational development, OB, and HRM.

In sum, more longitudinal and quantitative empirical studies of lean teams are needed. Specific theorizing within the fields of change management, human resource development, and small-group development as well as the ethnography literature must be used to prepare those examinations. Closely observing and codifying how a team's climate or culture evolves during a lean journey, perhaps also via informants' (video-)diaries, is relevant for those carrying out the empirical part. It would also be informative for those in charge of organizations that are contemplating starting with lean, enabling them to preview or to plan better effective trajectories in those organizations (see, e.g., Scherrer-Rathje et al., 2009). Eventually, we need to know how each of the lean team's contextual enablers (as shown in Figure 10.1) are linked to the various lean team dynamics. Given that continuously improving the efficiency of a work floor team toward the increasingly changing needs of customers is prototypical for effective lean teams, non-lean work floor teams may also learn from the results of such recommended research. We welcome all efforts as they will teach us how to enhance a team's efficiency while, at the same time, producing healthy lean human dynamics. This, in turn, would be a source for true progress for people and societies at large.

The Future of Lean Teams

This chapter highlights the content of lean team human dynamics and their enablers, as important social mechanisms within lean organizations. These insights may guide managers and others alike who envision a lean transformation on their work floors. While effective lean teams are often regarded as self-managed work teams, we found that top or higher-level managers play key roles in training and developing lean team members and their leaders (Liker and Convis, 2012). Managers showcase their desired behavioral patterns to their followers by exemplary role modeling relations-oriented behavior, and airing their self-transcendence and openness-to-change type values. In this way, higher-leader behavior is cascaded to the lowest organizational level, so that each organizational work floor member is focused on and committed to achieving optimal customer value through continuous process improvement and respect for people. Also, higher-level managers' guidance and clarity in terms of organizational strategy and structure, as well as aligned investment in lean and people development, is shown to facilitate lean team performance. In other words, despite frequent calls to simply "scrap" middle management, a remark often heard on work floors during initial attempts to implement lean, if such managers are good at translating organizational strategy to their (lean) teams, they will not become obsolete: "reducing management does grant autonomy, but it is undirected autonomy without leadership" (Liker and Convis, 2012, p. 146). This "state-of-the-art" presentation shows that, in lean organizations, middle or higher-level managers need to show their "leadership" by enacting valuable roles toward work floor employees. Lean practice may thus require a rethink of the standard (middle) managerial roles: instead of (middle) managers fixing problems themselves, their followers should be more enabled to come to them with problems, solutions, and improvement suggestions. Followers should not be commanded by them under normal lean circumstances (Liker and Convis, 2012; Salas et al., 2015).

Further, those who advise lean teams and their leaders (including internal and external consultants as well as HR officers) may benefit from the recent behavioral insights in order to craft increasingly effective lean teams. On the basis of the state-of-the-art knowledge on lean-team effectiveness, their interventions can be sharpened so that they become more focused, creative, and cost-effective. Their interventions should be directed more at leader behavioral development, instead of merely "rolling out" a predetermined set of lean tools such as value stream mapping, 5S, or kanban. Such leader coaching could take place on the basis of mapping personal value constellations (e.g. through a card sorting technique used by Van Dun et al., 2010) and subsequent reflection upon how their own values influence their own behaviors. This enables (lean) leaders to display specific, needed behaviors (Salas et al., 2015), e.g. more active listening. Another practical new option could be to get leaders to evaluate their own team in terms of the extent to which the human dynamics, as displayed in Figure 10.1, apply to their team. Based on our own try-outs of this approach with several team leaders during practitioner-oriented conferences, such a self-rating exercise could also be used to discuss their reflections on the current state of their team's human dynamics with their peers and followers. Moreover, leader coaching might entail giving feedback on visible behaviors in the workplace, perhaps after video registration of actual behaviors. From our own practical experiences, regular observations of particular behaviors in meeting or work floor settings, and feeding them back, have been shown to be an effective approach to developing "lean leaders" over time. This is likely to enhance managers' behavioral awareness and open up their eyes to higher-performing behavioral alternatives. Whether the longitudinal effects of such an inter-ventionist approach on actual team performance are significant is worth following up. Initial practical experiences certainly point to such practical behavior–performance relationships (and could be extended to their underlying work values). Linking leader behavioral development to actual performance targets, and discussing those targets in PDCA-oriented meetings, may assist leaders to improve their own lean or efficiency-related behaviors, as well as those of their followers.

Furthermore, those who select, train, and promote leaders may feel the need to enrich their leader profiles with the values and behaviors reported in this chapter. Whereas managers are often selected based on their past work experiences, it is worthwhile to also discuss their value con-stellations with them, especially because values may be difficult to change over time. Such a values-based selection process is advised for leaders who have to function in highly visible roles in any lean enterprise. Also, HR officers might create leader developmental programs that include elements of "training-on-the-gemba," in order to create more leader consciousness of own values, attitudes, and behaviors (as illustrated in the case at the end of this chapter). When leaders become more aware of their, in part, subconscious values, they might be able to convey their messages more strongly toward their colleagues and followers. Such programs may also help to develop a psychologically safe setting at the (team) leader level.

In sum, the insights drawn from this chapter are demonstrably useful in guiding managers of lean initiatives at various hierarchical levels. Our longitudinal study found lean work floor dynamics to be potentially cost-saving and there is much more evidence for this claim:

> When lean companies experience difficulties, they should not invest more resources to increase the level of hard practice implementation; instead, the companies should accurately analyze their context in terms of OC [organizational culture] and invest effort in soft practices.
>
> *(Bortolotti et al., 2015, p. 194)*

More studies on those human dynamics of lean are thus a wise research investment. Preventing human and other waste associated with day-to-day work floor production is the aim. With the knowledge derived from the lean (team) literature to date, it is likely that many more lean teams will succeed in becoming lean or sustaining lean effectively. We also hope that more effective lean team organizing leads to *more* respect for non-managerial employees, who are unique and often still underrated resources for substantial work process improvement. Improved team and organizational performance will follow when more people excel at work.

Case Study: Lean Teams in a Truck Facility

In the mid-1990s, a well-known multinational truck manufacturer implemented lean principles. A team of 11 at their largest production facility was studied over three years. It assembles a specific part of a truck, for which each one of the predominantly male members performs a particular task on the production line. During this period, the team significantly improved its actual performance, as measured in terms of its own defect ratio, the number of costly "line stops," and backlogs. Members' satisfaction grew from 5.10 (on a 7-point scale) to 5.63 three years later. Members' own effectiveness rating increased from 4.93 to 5.44. Sickness absence figures drastically decreased from 17.32% to only 3.82%. At the beginning of year 3, production was doubled and the team was divided into two smaller-sized morning and evening shifts. Below we describe the truck team's enablers and intra-team dynamics. Figure 10.1's elements are in italics.

Truck Team's Enablers

The 2008 crisis resulted in the unavoidable letting go of the temporary staff, while the permanent staff retained their jobs. *Higher-level leader support* was felt by these workers. During the study the leaders adopted own standard operating procedures so that they could spend more time with their work floor teams. Higher-level leaders even helped out when major problems occurred (i.e. in the case of a line stop). Despite substantially fewer orders coming in, the higher-level leaders held on to their clear, *long-term strategic priority toward lean*. They even intensified their investment in lean by upscaling their workers' skills, improving work standards, and streamlining the factory layout. Moreover, the human resource policy was fully aligned with the strategic company-level lean goals, and financial resources were made available to spend on those goals. Lean leadership development (in terms of values, attitudes, and behaviors) was part and parcel of the team-leader training course. Both permanent and temporary new staff members were sent on an obligatory two-day in-company lean course. In other words, the truck firm invested considerable *financial resources* in lean.

Manifestation of Effective Intra-team Dynamics in the Truck Team

During the course of the study, the team members *solved conflicts* that arose in a constructive manner, without the intervention of their team leader. Moreover, they often *backed each other up*, by fixing mistakes caused by one of their co-workers. By stepping in occasionally, they made sure production ran smoothly. Team members also actively engaged in *team-performance monitoring* and *information sharing*. Real-time performance figures were displayed and discussed during daily start-up meetings around a team board. Every now and then, team members pulled the andon cord and asked for help to prevent quality defects. The team leader openly discussed the defects that had occurred the day before with the members during the daily start-up meetings, as well as any corrective actions taken. This *psychologically safe* climate was nurtured by the *supportive team leader* who was constantly present on the work floor. He also gave compliments and socialized with team members, he frequently assisted workers, and even brought them coffee. This leader's relations orientation was evident in the behavioral pattern of active listening, informing, individualized consideration, some agreeing, task-performance monitoring, and little self-defensive behavior. Over time, team members mimicked his behavior with each other. They increased the *team's cohesion* by showing greater individualized consideration and active listening as well as informing and agreeing with ideas, and task-performance monitoring.

With regard to *innovating* behavior, two team members were assigned to develop a new set of standard operating procedures and an accompanying training program in preparation for a change in the factory's layout. Also, members participated in weekly kaizen events in order to eliminate any further process waste. The other members shared their improvement ideas mainly during formal team meetings, thereby showing their cognitive focus on and *commitment to the firm's strategic lean goals*. For instance, team members automatically explained the "why" of standard operating procedures to newcomers.

Conclusion

As illustrated by this case, effective lean work floor dynamics involve a delicate balance of almost invisible or tacit behavioral factors. Strong support from top management for lean enables the emergence of healthy lean team dynamics, which leads to improved team performance. Despite the fact that this team's leadership changed regularly, (positive) leader behaviors cascaded to and were absorbed at the team member level. In other words, such role modeling is advisable for managers who want to make a difference through lean.

Source: This case study is a more elaborate version of the first of the five case studies reported in our longitudinal study: Van Dun and Wilderom (2015)—awarded best paper, based on a dissertation, in AoM's Operations Management Division.

References

Angelis, J., Conti, R., Cooper, C. and Gill, C. (2011). Building a high-commitment lean culture. *Journal of Manufacturing Technology Management*, 22(5), 569–586.

Bamber, G. J., Stanton, P., Bartram, T. and Ballardie, R. (2014). Human resource management, lean processes and outcomes for employees: Towards a research agenda. *International Journal of Human Resource Management*, 25(21), 2881–2891.

Beer, M. (2003). Why total quality management programs do not persist: The role of management quality and implications for leading a TQM transformation. *Decision Sciences*, 34(4), 623–642.

Bendoly, E., Croson, R., Goncalves, P. and Schultz, K. (2010). Bodies of knowledge for research in behavioral operations. *Production and Operations Management*, 19(4), 434–452.

Bessant, J., Caffyn, S. and Gallagher, M. (2001). An evolutionary model of continuous improvement behaviour. *Technovation*, 21(2), 67–77.

Bortolotti, T., Boscari, S. and Danese, P. (2015). Successful lean implementation: Organizational culture and soft lean practices. *International Journal of Production Economics*, 160, 182–201.

Edmondson, A. (1999). Psychological safety and learning behavior in work teams. *Administrative Science Quarterly*, 44(2), 350–383.

Hackman, J. R. (2012). From causes to conditions in group research. *Journal of Organizational Behavior*, 33(3), 428–444.

Hines, P., Holweg, M. and Rich, N. (2004). Learning to evolve: A review of contemporary lean thinking. *International Journal of Operations & Production Management*, 24(10), 994–1011.

Humphrey, S. E. and Aime, F. (2014). Team microdynamics: Toward an organizing approach to teamwork. *The Academy of Management Annals*, 8(1), 443–503.

Liker, J. and Convis, G. L. (2012). *The Toyota Way to Lean Leadership: Achieving and Sustaining Excellence through Leadership Development*, New York, McGraw-Hill Education.

Marodin, G. A. and Saurin, T. A. (2013). Implementing lean production systems: Research areas and opportunities for future studies. *International Journal of Production Research*, 51(22), 6663–6680.

Mathieu, J. E., Kukenberger, M. R., D'Innocenzo, L. and Reilly, G. (2015). Modeling reciprocal team cohesion–performance relationships, as impacted by shared leadership and members' competence. *Journal of Applied Psychology*, 100(3), 713–734.

Netland, T. and Ferdows, K. (2014). What to expect from corporate lean programs. *MIT Sloan Management Review*, 55(4), 83–89.

Peterson, R. S. and Behfar, K. J. (2003). The dynamic relationship between performance feedback, trust, and conflict in groups: A longitudinal study. *Organizational Behavior and Human Decision Processes*, 92(1), 102–112.

Raver, J. L., Ehrhart, M. G. and Chadwick, I. C. (2012). The emergence of team helping norms: Foundations within members' attributes and behavior. *Journal of Organizational Behavior*, *33*(5), 616–637.

Salas, E., Shuffler, M. L., Thayer, A. L., Bedwell, W. L. and Lazzara, E. H. (2015). Understanding and improving teamwork in organizations: A scientifically based practical guide. *Human Resource Management*, *54*(4), 599–622.

Scherrer-Rathje, M., Boyle, T. A. and Deflorin, P. (2009). Lean, take two! Reflections from the second attempt at lean implementation. *Business Horizons*, *52*(1), 79–88.

Shah, R. and Ward, P. T. (2003). Lean manufacturing: Context, practice bundles, and performance. *Journal of Operations Management*, *21*(2), 129–149.

Shook, J. (2010). How to change a culture: Lessons from NUMMI. *MIT Sloan Management Review*, *51*(2), 42–51.

Soltani, E. and Wilkinson, A. (2010). Stuck in the middle with you: The effects of incongruency of senior and middle managers' orientations on TQM programmes. *International Journal of Operations & Production Management*, *30*(4), 365–397.

Van Dun, D. H. and Wilderom, C. P. (2012). Human dynamics and enablers of effective lean team cultures and climates. *International Review of Industrial and Organizational Psychology*, *27*, 115–152.

Van Dun, D. H. and Wilderom, C. P. M. (2014). Leader values, followers' information sharing, and team effectiveness: Advancing lean team cultures, *74th Annual Meeting of the Academy of Management*. Philadelphia, PA.

Van Dun, D. H. and Wilderom, C. P. M. (2015). Governing highly performing lean team behaviors: A mixed-methods longitudinal study. *Proceedings of the 75th Annual Meeting of the Academy of Management*. Vancouver, August 7–11.

Van Dun, D. H., Hicks, J. N. and Wilderom, C. P. M. (2010). What are the values and behaviors of highly effective lean middle managers? *70th Annual Meeting of the Academy of Management*. Montreal, Canada.

11

LEAN IT

Pär Åhlström, Ryusuke Kosuge, and Magnus Mähring

Introduction

To put it simply, *lean IT* is the application of information technology (IT) solutions to further the positive effects of adopting lean management principles. Separately, the application of lean management principles and the use of IT are undoubtedly two of the most powerful ways to improve organizations. Hence the importance of IT in operations management has escalated over the years and there is a strong interest in lean IT in both manufacturing and services. However, these two avenues for organizational improvement are often not well attuned. Although combining lean management with extensive use of IT in operations may seem to be an attractive option for achieving operational excellence, it is definitely a challenging one. Consider the following example taken from our research into a manufacturing company well known for its highly mature and developed lean practices:

In this company, one of the core practices is the involvement of production workers in continuous improvement. When identifying an opportunity to improve assembly routines, production workers pull an *andon cord* to stop the line and then gather the team at the assembly station to observe the problem and discuss possible solutions. When a solution is identified and decided upon, it is typically documented and implemented immediately, and the assembly process restarted. One such improvement cycle might take 15 minutes to complete.

In contrast, however, when the same team identifies an improvement opportunity requiring a modification to an information system which supports the production processes, an entirely different process takes place. Rather than pulling the andon cord, a team member brings the matter to the attention of the team and the team leader at a regular improvement meeting. If the team decides that a modification of the information system is necessary to improve assembly, the team leader writes up and submits a formal change request, which includes a required assessment of the potential monetary benefits of changing the production information system. The internal IT department receives the request, assesses it (and may even reject it due to budget restrictions or priority considerations), and then enters the change request into a queue to be submitted to an external IT service provider responsible for implementing the modification. This provider then implements the received modification requests in sequence and invoices the company.

Typically, this process takes between six and nine months to complete, and during this time period, other improvement efforts might be held up while waiting for the new IT functionality.

Not surprisingly, we learned that continuous improvement activities routinely include "work-arounds" (Boudreau and Robey, 2005) that enable improvements to be made without necessitating changes to the information system. When such workarounds cannot be introduced, production teams might refrain from implementing improvements that require changes to the information system. In effect, the company is an industry leader in lean management only when the IT infrastructure, applications, and services are not involved in the improvement efforts.

This tale of two very different improvement processes (the andon cord pull and the IT change request) illustrates a deeper-lying phenomenon, indicative of the often-conflicting nature of the relationship between lean management and IT. As such, the example illustrates the challenges of lean IT. A fundamentally important principle of lean management is continuous improvement, which implies *in situ* identification, assessment, and resolution of problems. In contrast, the use of IT typically leads to automation of processes through taking a moldable technology and fusing it together with physical and social processes in a way that—paradoxically—creates a stable "compound" (Lee, 1999). This compound is a sociotechnical system where procedures and activity sequences are partly embedded in the deployed technology in intricate and highly specified ways, which typically require extensive time and effort to change.

In this chapter, we discuss critical issues associated with lean IT by summarizing underlying reasons for the complex relationship between lean management and IT, as well as outlining some potential avenues for creating a more productive symbiosis between them. We do so by describing key attributes and principles underlying organizational improvement efforts based on lean management, and on IT deployment, respectively; discussing how these attributes can lead to conflicts between lean management and the use of IT in operations, and hence create the challenges of lean IT; and outline ways in which these conflicts might be resolved in order to succeed with lean IT.

Lean IT: From a Conflicting to a Supporting Relationship

Succeeding with lean IT involves finding a productive symbiosis between lean management and the application of IT. The literature on lean IT has over time changed its view on the relationship between lean management and IT, from viewing the relationship as conflicting toward viewing it as potentially supporting.

The research regarding lean IT can be traced back to Sugimori et al. (1977), who argued that using kanban is more advantageous than using computerized systems for organizing production logistics in terms of cost, acquisition of facts, and responsiveness. Whereas lean management emphasizes simplicity, IT tends to add unnecessary complexity. The argument has also been made that the push logic of material requirements planning (MRP) or enterprise resource planning (ERP) systems conflicts with the customer demand-driven (pull) characteristic of lean manufacturing (Olhager and Östlund, 1990). IT systems also encourage workarounds instead of fixing the root cause, and remove control from the plant, centralize it, and create a disconnect between the reality and the abstract information generated by information systems. This view advocates the need to understand and protect the unique nature of lean management and stresses the need to use IT in a way that follows lean principles (Bruun and Mefford, 2004; Hicks, 2007).

However, particularly since the 2000s, there has been a view that ERP systems can support lean production (Riezebos et al., 2009). The main argument is that ERP systems, as higher-level planning systems, support the implementation of lean principles at the shop floor. For example, based on a survey, Ward and Zhou (2006) state that IT integration, such as IT embodied in ERP systems, facilitates the implementation and use of effective lean/JIT (just-in-time) practices. More recently, based on case studies of small and medium-sized enterprises, Powell et al. (2013b) showed that ERP systems have the ability to support pull production practices. ERP systems may also help in automating repetitive tasks, and thereby enabling workers to have more time to engage in continuous improvement (Powell et al., 2013a). The systems may also be used to visualize important information which can be used in the work of continuous improvement (Bell, 2006).

Consequently, based on a critical review of the literature on lean IT, Powell (2013) proposes the concept "ERP-enabled lean." The main idea is that synergies could be realized by combining ERP systems with lean production principles. Since ERP systems share many attributes with other types of information systems, it seems reasonable to assume these and/or similar arguments could be applied more generally to combining extensive IT use with successful application of lean management principles.

Lean IT: Our Conceptual Basis

Before going into the details of the challenges involved in lean IT, it is necessary that we clarify our conceptual basis. This particularly concerns how we view IT and what we see as the core of lean management. It is through explicating these two concepts that we are in a position to understand what contributes to the challenges of lean IT, and how these challenges might be overcome.

Information Technology

So far, the debate on lean IT has focused primarily on specific types of information systems. While it is of interest to consider specific types of information systems, such as ERP systems (Powell, 2013) or *manufacturing execution systems* (MES) (Cottyn et al., 2011), it is important for our purposes to take a broader view and also include organizational practices related to IT.

Just as lean management consists not only of specific tools, but also of principles and values, so does the use of IT. For example, in our introductory case above, we could see that a modification to an information system required the team leader to make an estimate of the benefits beforehand. The effort was then assessed in relation to a specific IT budget, while such hurdles or control mechanisms were absent in situations when the andon cord was pulled. In other words, it is not only the characteristics of IT artifacts that contribute to rigidity, but also common organizing practices related to IT (Beath and Orlikowski, 1994; Boudreau and Robey, 1996).

Hence, in order to capture the areas where lean management and the use of IT potentially conflict, and to understand the challenges of lean IT, we find it important to take a broad view of IT. In IT we therefore include the infrastructure (hardware, communication and operating systems) and applications that are part of value-adding operative activities (information systems supporting value-adding processes). However, we also take into account IT development activities that have the purpose of implementing information systems into these environments, the IT maintenance activities that provide the service of modifying existing systems, and the IT governance arrangements related to controlling how these activities are carried out.

While novel ways to conduct IT activities continuously emerge, including variants of lean and agile software development that emphasize iterative development with frequent user input (Conboy, 2009), the practices from the past few decades remain dominant, particularly in large organizations (e.g. Gregory et al., 2015). Furthermore, while most companies routinely outsource some of their IT activities, including operations and development work, and this places a commercial vendor as the supplier of IT services, this does not necessarily create a more flexible supply of services (Choudhury and Sabherwal, 2003; Anderson and Dekker, 2005). As our initial example shows, an external vendor typically requires formal control means and specified procedures that might further increase bureaucracy and reduce responsiveness in IT service delivery.

Continuous Improvement: The Cornerstone of Lean Management

To understand the challenges of lean IT, it is particularly necessary to focus on the mechanism of continuous improvement that forms one of the cornerstones of lean management. In doing so, we see lean management as closely associated with the Toyota Production System (TPS), essentially a bundle of complex routines that originally emerged through trial and error (Fujimoto, 1999). Lean management can be seen as a flow-focused operations strategy, consisting of values, principles, methods, and tools that are also applicable in non-manufacturing environments (Modig and Åhlström, 2012). The principles can be summarized into JIT and jidoka, the two pillars of the TPS.

In order to create a smooth flow of value toward the customer, Toyota puts a focus on JIT and jidoka (Ohno, 1988). JIT aims to create and regulate flow based on actual customer demand. Jidoka aims to improve and ensure the quality of the flow through visible control, implying that problems should be identified and addressed on the spot. Through creating a tension around the streamlined flow, the two principles continuously challenge workers to engage in continuous improvement (Ohno, 1988).

It should be noted here that this continuous improvement builds on an evidence-based, systematic scientific inquiry (Spear and Bowen, 1999). Consequently, process improvement rests on developing and using human capability, rather than technology. This is the core idea behind Toyota's value of "respect for people" (Sugimori et al., 1977). In essence, what lies at the core of lean management is flow-focused continuous improvement underpinned by developing and making use of human capability. Ultimately, continuous improvement may lead to an evolutionary capability, which has enabled Toyota to learn from any experience including unexpected failures (Fujimoto, 1999). It is this dynamic nature of lean management that we believe can be in conflict with IT.

The Challenges of Lean IT

To better understand the challenges of lean IT, we believe that it is necessary to take a step back and look at the underlying assumptions of lean management and of IT deployment and use. On a philosophical level, lean management and IT build on fundamentally different logics. To a considerable extent, the established ways to deploy IT in organizations are at odds with the fundamental principles of lean management. Table 11.1 illustrates some of the underlying assumptions about or approaches to organizational improvement underlying lean management and IT respectively.

Table 11.1 illustrates fundamental differences in the assumptions underlying improvement work based on lean management and IT, respectively. In essence, lean management builds on continuous, local, and often small-scale change and improvement based on human capability. On the contrary, IT deployment regularly builds on large-scale initiatives aimed at automation of defined processes. Once implemented, IT tends to make processes rigid and difficult to change. Lean management is about making continuous improvements; this means that entire systems and databases need to be updated frequently, quickly, and accurately, and this is extremely difficult to achieve with most information systems.

This difficulty has partly to do with the fundamental attributes of IT. IT is an extremely malleable technology before it is implemented. Under development, IT can be molded in

Table 11.1 Underlying assumptions about or approach to organizational change and process improvement

	Assumptions and values typical to lean management	Assumptions and values typical to IT deployment and use
Processes	Processes are a source of competitive advantage and deserve attention and focus of improvement work	Efficient operations often require that processes are adapted to what standard application packages can do, which means that they become more generic
Improvement work	Continuous activity built into organizational culture and work processes	A planned activity taking place as part of IT projects
Operational excellence	Something you work toward every day	Something achieved through intelligent design of clever IT tools that support, and extensively automate, well-designed processes
Organizational change	Continuous change; planned change is an exception when processes have been neglected for too long or when there are fundamental problems with overall process design	Planned change organized and executed through projects
Information technology	IT is often useful for solving specific tasks, but can potentially rigidify processes	IT makes companies more competitive
Responsibility	Rests with production teams and is integrated into line functions	Assigned to project team by management when improvement is deemed necessary
Competence	The people doing the work are best equipped to improve their processes	Experts, such as management consultants and IT professionals, are essential for designing and implementing new processes and IT tools
Learning and competence development	Continuous learning and competence development related to process execution and improvement is essential for the development of each individual and the whole organization	It is not efficient or possible to educate all personnel in IT development; even the role of and training for a user representative needs to be selectively assigned
People	People are the origin and drivers of process improvement	The key to improvement is often to automate processes and thus remove people and labor costs; people are often a hindrance to radical IT-based solutions due to organizational politics, self-interest, and "not-invented-here" syndrome

almost any conceivable way. When implemented, however, IT "gels" with business processes in a way that conserves the processes that the information system is designed to support and/or execute. Operative processes and information systems together form a "compound" that tends to be difficult and time consuming to modify. ERP systems and production and control systems, for example, can be understood as examples of "recalcitrant technologies" with a rigidly defined hierarchy of components and operations bound together by a set of rules determining both their functional dependence and temporal sequence (Elbanna, 2006). It is highly unlikely that this IT/process compound will allow itself to be modified as frequently and rapidly as required when working along lean principles. Consequently, the best-established ways to acquire and deploy IT in organizations are more or less conflicting with fundamental principles of lean management.

Furthermore, many methodologies for IT development commonly build on what can be called a "*systems engineering mindset*" which includes the assumption that an "optimal" information system should be designed, built, and implemented. The idea that systems should be built to be continually modified after implementation is not well developed in the IT development literature. IT systems tend to induce inertia by automating the status quo, freezing the organization into patterns of behavior and operations that resist change (Allen and Boynton, 1991). The inertia induced by IT systems can also be attributed to capabilities, cognition, and culture developed around the existing technology. They constrain the organization's future behavior in that learning tends to be premised on local processes of search (Tripsas and Gavetti, 2000).

Different Approaches to the Successful Achievement of Lean IT

Given the fundamental differences between assumptions underlying lean management and IT, what can companies do to resolve the conflicts between the two? As both approaches to improve organizations have great potential, we believe that finding ways to combine lean principles for organizational improvement with the use of IT will become essential for organizations. In practice, some companies that excel in lean management are finding ways to resolve the conflicts and use IT to further the positive effects of adopting lean management principles. There are understandably different approaches to take, depending on the characteristics of processes, competencies, products and services produced, customer interaction patterns, and other key elements of value creation. Below, we briefly outline three different approaches and illustrate each with an example from our own ongoing research. Together, these examples show that fusing lean principles with IT can take very different forms.

Evidence-based Lean IT

This is a careful and stepwise approach that uses small, reversible investments and experimentation upon identification of improvement potential related to new IT at a production site. Our example here is the Global Manufacturing Company, a benchmark in lean management, which has elected to develop and maintain most of its production-related information systems in-house. It has developed an approach where production facilities around the world are allowed to develop local IT solutions to specific problems. These local solutions are subsequently evaluated by the central IT function and considered for inclusion into a subsequent release of the core production information systems. Locally, the principle for new IT tools is to always begin with the simplest solutions—often an Excel spreadsheet—to ensure that substantial experimentation and related process development has been conducted before an IT project is initiated. Bridging of perspectives and shared learning is also achieved by furthering cross-disciplinary knowledge of IT among the production staff and about production among the IT staff, respectively. The company eschews the standard procedure of initiating feasibility studies and subsequently full-scale IT projects early after problem/opportunity identification. Instead, it initiates this only after conducting reversible proof-of-concept experiments in operations. Only in a second step, if and when a viable and value-adding solution (i.e. an IT-supported or IT-based process) has materialized and stabilized, is a "regular" IT project initiated. Finally, the practice of centrally evaluating and including locally developed IT applications in the core information systems provided across the organization further emphasizes learning and continuous improvement. The practice of cross-disciplinary learning also helps build a lean culture that integrates IT challenges and IT professionals.

Customer Value-focused Lean IT

Another approach is to direct IT deployment efforts to those aspects of service delivery where customers perceive clearly visible benefits. For example, the Private General Hospital takes such a customer-centric and value-adding approach to IT, using IT tools to improve patient experience with healthcare services. It also predominantly relies on in-house development of IT tools rather than standard application packages to attune functionality closely to patient needs and care processes. An IT-based access system makes it possible for admitted patients to receive visits from relatives and close friends at all hours. Patients can select their food from a personal bedside monitor and learn about surgical procedures, treatments, and rehabilitation procedures from the system at their own leisure. While the ever-increasing demands of patients drive in-house development of IT tools, we can also see in this example that IT applications do not necessarily automate whole operative processes, but rather provide delineated and specific services that can be managed and improved separately from core medical and care-taking procedures, or as service modules that contribute to core processes without enmeshing deeply into them. For example, an automated access system for relatives does not materially affect how operative healthcare processes are conducted, but increases patient well-being and reduces manual administrative workload. Similarly, helping patients become better informed ahead of physicians' visits empowers patients and improves the perceived quality of care. Thus, IT either simplifies or improves patient–physician dialogue, without necessitating major changes in core processes.

People-centered Lean IT

Finally, a third approach is to tie IT development and deployment intimately with operations and develop new IT capabilities in a collaborative and iterative fashion with operational staff. Our example here is Kanagawa Toyota (see also the separate case study), a major car dealership company in Japan affiliated with Toyota Motor Corporation. Kanagawa Toyota learned from experience that IT could hinder, rather than support, the realization of JIT customer contact: contacting each customer at the right time and in a manner the customer appreciates. In their initial attempts to utilize advanced IT tools to improve customer management, Kanagawa Toyota relied on a purchased *customer relationship management* (CRM) system that calculated the "right" time for each salesperson to contact their allocated customers in a standardized manner. However, the system's lack of ability to flexibly adjust the timing parameter became an obstacle and, consequently, Kanagawa Toyota decided not to rely solely on IT but instead to follow the "respect for people" philosophy. After investing in developing skills and the mindsets of salespersons as well as IT personnel, Kanagawa Toyota focused on in-house development of a new generation CRM system. This system is continuously modified based on daily dialogue between salespersons and IT personnel. This approach also builds on iteratively adapting IT applications to retain and improve their fit with continuously improving processes, but does so through partly different organizational arrangements than the previous examples. Here, the focus is on establishing a close dialogue and collaborative partnership between the in-house IT unit and salespeople.

The Future of Lean IT

The three examples above and the different approaches to lean IT that they represent are of course neither mutually exclusive nor collectively exhaustive. However, they do illustrate that lean IT can take different forms, and above all that lean IT can be achieved in spite of the traditionally often contradictory assumptions and approaches of lean management and established practices of IT deployment and use.

Based on these three examples, as well as other ongoing research, we would like to propose a few principles for successfully marrying IT solutions with operative processes and with continuous improvement efforts to further leverage the positive effects of adopting lean management. The principles relate to the approaches introduced previously, but are articulated in a way that is more general and allows for additional approaches or new combinations of approaches to be employed.

Increasing Flexibility of IT Systems and Services

The first principle is to increase the flexibility of the IT systems and services. This could be achieved, for instance, by using a presentation layer separate from core systems and databases. In this way, flexibility can be increased as only the presentation layer has to be modified instead of the core ERP system or similar systems. This allows the complexity of core systems to be "hidden" or black-boxed. It also opens up the possibility for front-line personnel to take an active role in modifying the presentation layer, which is a practice used by Kanagawa Toyota. The increased use of cloud computing (e.g. Bharadwaj et al., 2013) is likely to open up new opportunities for creating IT applications that can be flexibly tailored to fit the need of core operations.

Increasing the flexibility of IT can also be achieved by choosing in-house developed proprietary information systems for functions where continuous development is crucial, such as when systems support core processes. For systems supporting core processes, continuous improvement directly affects competitiveness. This may require building in-house IT competencies with extensive first-hand knowledge of core processes, partly through job-rotation and recruiting IT staff from operative personnel. It may also require organizing IT development processes to support process innovation (such as in the Global Manufacturing Company example in the section on evidence-based lean IT).

Rethinking IT Development Practices

Organizations that wish to productively combine lean management and IT also need to learn to look for small and simple solutions rather than complete and ostensibly "ideal" solutions (as supported by all three of the examples above). There is a need to develop a continuous improvement approach to IT implementation that goes beyond iterative systems development (which still has an end goal). The improvements should expand IT implementation to include iterations between use and development involving the use of minimum viable systems, and the joint development of these systems and the processes they support together with operative personnel. This will focus on local learning in practice as a means for gaining knowledge of how processes should be supported.

Rethinking Responsibility for Integrated Process and IT Development

Not only do the IT development practices need rethinking, but also the division of responsibilities between IT development activities and core operations. As IT becomes more central to core processes, IT systems cannot be viewed as beyond the influence of operative personnel involved in continuous improvement (cf. the initial example in this chapter). IT development needs to become more integrated with other continuous improvement practices. This requires the competencies of operative personnel to include sufficient knowledge of IT tools such that these personnel can take an active and guiding part in developing and modifying IT tools to further improve processes. This is one of the principles behind Kanagawa Toyota's approach to lean IT (see the case study at the end of the chapter).

Developing a Joint Lean Culture that Includes and Integrates IT Professionals

Finally, as discussed in depth by Mary Poppendieck in Chapter 34 of this book ("Lean Software Development"), IT development practices need to evolve along the lines of lean principles. However, while lean and agile practices are beneficial for the efficiency of IT operations there is still a risk that IT processes are viewed as separate from core operations processes. Thus, as illustrated in our example from the Global Manufacturing Company, there is a need for the development of a joint lean culture encompassing IT personnel. The focus of the development should not be on improving IT development or IT operations per se, but rather on collaborative efforts involving operative and IT personnel in lean activities targeting core processes of the organization. In essence, this implies a weakening of the boundaries between IT services and processes, and core value-adding processes of the firm.

As these boundaries become blurred, it is likely that all organizations will become more similar to IT-based organizations, embracing digitalization as a core part of lean activities. Meanwhile, IT personnel will be challenged to take joint responsibility for operations rather than IT processes only. Further, they will be challenged by working in mixed teams and perhaps letting go of their belonging to a separate IT profession in favor of belonging, and bringing a core specialty, to integrated improvement teams.

Case Study: Lean IT in Kanagawa Toyota Motor Co., Ltd

Background: Lean Transformation and Just-in-time Customer Contact

In 2000, Kanagawa Toyota Motor Co., Ltd., a Japanese car dealership company affiliated with Toyota Motor Corporation, initiated a lean transformation program aiming to apply the tools and philosophies of Toyota Production System in order to eliminate waste and increase customer value. One of the major problems facing Kanagawa Toyota at that time was a lack of a consistent customer relationship strategy. Traditionally, each salesperson had their own portfolio of existing customers. They were supposed to contact the customers to promote various maintenance services, as well as build long-term relationships that would hopefully lead to repeat purchases of cars. In reality, however, salespeople were mostly inclined to achieve short-term sales results due to competitive peer pressure as well as monetary incentives. In fact, it was up to each salesperson to decide how and when to contact which customer. With the lack of process control at the company level, the inevitable consequence was a shrinking customer base and sales volume in the long run.

With the help of Toyota Motor Corporation, Kanagawa Toyota sought to address the problem by developing a process for contacting each customer at the right time and in a manner that the customer would appreciate. This was essentially an application of JIT to customer contact.

Learning from a Failure

Initially, the goal of the JIT customer contact was to simply remind customers of the maintenance services required by law, and the existing customer database came to play a key role here. The customer database was utilized to provide information regarding when to contact a customer to offer regular maintenance services. The simple CRM system calculated the "right" time for each salesperson to contact their share of customers in a standardized manner (e.g., 45, 30, and 20 days before the required date). The contact timings were visualized using printed "*follow-up cards*" and were stored on a shelf (see Figure 11.1).

However, it soon became clear that the CRM system was rigid in that it lacked the ability to flexibly adjust the timing parameter according to each customer's situation. This meant that customer contact was bounded by the system's constraints. In fact, many of the salespersons perceived it as a hindrance rather than a helpful tool to realize JIT customer contact. Consequently, management decided to abandon the IT part of the CRM system, emphasizing that what matters most is to take the customer's perspective in each contact situation. In fact, the attempt to realize JIT customer contact resulted in a perception of IT as controlling rather than supporting operative processes.

This experience made Kanagawa Toyota cautious about developing and using IT for customer contact purposes. Unlike many other companies that still sought to purchase advanced CRM

Figure 11.1 Visualization of customer contact tasks

systems, Kanagawa Toyota's attitude was that IT should always be able to meet the needs of the salespeople who actually interact with customers. In essence, Kanagawa Toyota started to follow the "respect for people" philosophy instead of relying on the capability of IT to automate processes. The core of the new policy was to shift the focus of IT initiatives to the in-house development of an extensive customer database that could support the work of identifying customer needs. The intention was to facilitate IT personnel to closely collaborate with salespersons to make IT more user-friendly and accessible.

Continuous Improvement of Both Processes and IT Applications

Kanagawa Toyota's renewed efforts bore fruit with the arrival of a next generation CRM system. Presently, a new CRM application is introduced to users when roughly one-third of the configuration and specification work has been completed, and small-scale, local experiments are conducted to modify the functions. What distinguishes Kanagawa Toyota's approach is that, because of the initiative being based on "respect for people," users become able to recognize and voice their own needs, i.e. what information they want in what manner in order to realize JIT customer contact. To sense and respond to the emerging needs, IT personnel frequently visit sales sites and have a constructive dialogue with users. Consequently, an IT application that enables salespersons to achieve JIT customer contact has been developed. Specifically, salespeople can develop a sales scenario based on information about the customer's life situation and past relationship with the company that is summarized in the application. The application also enables jidoka, as managers can see the customer contact process and, if there is a concern for quality, can provide a salesperson with on-the-job training regarding how to develop a sales scenario utilizing available information. In sum, continuous improvement is now facilitated by IT, which in turn drives IT development.

Kanagawa Toyota is now recognized as one of the leading car dealership companies in terms of using IT in harmony with lean principles and values. The next step on the journey is to further develop a customer-focused, joint lean culture that includes and integrates IT personnel, as well as everyone else in the company, so that JIT customer contact can be realized across multiple channels in a coordinated manner.

References

Allen, B. R. and Boynton, A. C. (1991). Information architecture: In search of efficient flexibility. *MIS Quarterly*, *15*(4), 435–445.

Anderson, S. W. and Dekker, H. C. (2005). Management control for market transactions: The relation between transaction characteristics, incomplete contract design, and subsequent performance. *Management Science*, *51*(12), 1734–1752.

Beath, C. M. and Orlikowski, W. J. (1994). The contradictory structure of systems development methodologies: Deconstructing the IS–user relationship in information engineering. *Information Systems Research*, *5*(4), 350–377.

Bell, S. (2006), *Lean Enterprise Systems: Using IT for Continuous Improvement*, Hoboken, NJ, John Wiley and Sons.

Bharadwaj, A., ElSawy, O. A., Pavlou, P. A. and Venkatraman, N. (2013). Digital business strategy: Toward a next generation of insights. *MIS Quarterly*, *37*(2), 471–482.

Boudreau, M. C. and Robey, D. (1996). Coping with contradictions in business process re-engineering. *Information Technology & People*, *9*(4), 40–57.

Boudreau, M. C. and Robey, D. (2005). Enacting integrated information technology: A human agency perspective. *Organization Science, 16*(1), 3–18.

Bruun, P. and Mefford, R. N. (2004). Lean production and the Internet. *International Journal of Production Economics, 89*(3), 247–260.

Choudhury, V. and Sabherwal, R. (2003). Portfolios of control in outsourced software development projects. *Information Systems Research, 14*(3), 291–314.

Conboy, K. (2009). Agility from first principles: Reconstructing the concept of agility in information systems development. *Information Systems Research, 20*(3), 329–354.

Cottyn, J., Van Landeghem, H., Stockman, K. and Derammelaere, S. (2011). A method to align a manufacturing execution system with lean objectives. *International Journal of Production Research, 49*(14), 4397–4413.

Elbanna, A. R. (2006). The validity of the improvisation argument in the implementation of rigid technology: The case of ERP systems. *Journal of Information Technology, 21*(3), 165–175.

Fujimoto, T. (1999), *The Evolution of a Manufacturing System at Toyota*, New York, Oxford University Press.

Gregory, R.W., Keil, M., Muntermann, J. and Mähring, M. (2015). Paradoxes and the nature of ambidexterity in IT transformation programs. *Information Systems Research, 26*(1), 57–80.

Hicks, B. J. (2007). Lean information management: Understanding and eliminating waste. *International Journal of Information Management, 27*(4), 233–249.

Lee, A. S. (1999). Researching MIS. In: Galliers, B. and Currie, W. L. (eds), *Rethinking Management Information Systems*, Oxford, Oxford University Press, pp. 7–27.

Modig, N. and Åhlström, P. (2012). *This is Lean: Resolving the Efficiency Paradox*, Stockholm, Rheologica Publishing.

Ohno, T. (1988). *Toyota Production System: Beyond Large-Scale Production*, Portland, OR, Productivity Press.

Olhager, J. and Östlund, B. (1990). An integrated push-pull manufacturing strategy. *European Journal of Operational Research, 45*(2–3), 135–142.

Powell, D. (2013). ERP systems in lean production: New insights from a review of lean and ERP literature. *International Journal of Operations & Production Management, 33*(11–12), 1490–1510.

Powell, D., Alfnes, E., Dreyer, H. C. and Strandhagen, J. O. (2013a). The concurrent application of lean production and ERP: Towards an ERP-based lean implementation process. *Computers in Industry, 64*(3), 324–335.

Powell, D., Riezebos, J. and Strandhagen, J. O. (2013b). Lean production and ERP systems in small- and medium-sized enterprises: ERP support for pull production. *International Journal of Production Research, 51*(2), 395–409.

Riezebos, J., Klingenberg, W. and Hicks, C. (2009). Lean production and information technology: Connection or contradiction? *Computers in Industry, 60*(4), 237–247.

Spear, S. and Bowen, H. K. (1999). Decoding the DNA of the Toyota Production System. *Harvard Business Review, 77*(5), 96–108.

Sugimori, Y., Kusunoki, K., Cho, F. and Uchikawa, S. (1977). Toyota production system and kanban system: Materialization of just-in-time and respect-for-human system. *International Journal of Production Research, 15*(6), 553–564.

Tripsas, M. and Gavetti, G. (2000). Capabilities, cognition and inertia: Evidence from digital imaging. *Strategic Management Journal, 21*(10–11), 1147–1161.

Ward, P. and Zhou, H. (2006). Impact of information technology integration and lean/just-in-time practices on lead-time performance. *Decision Sciences, 37*(2), 177–203.

12

LEAN SALES AND MARKETING

Brent Wahba

Introduction

In the late 1800s, John Wanamaker opened a number of department stores bearing his surname. A pioneer in leveraging the power of advertising, he is often quoted as stating: "Half the money I spend on advertising is wasted; the trouble is, I don't know which half." Unfortunately for Wanamaker's, the chain was unable to capitalize on this very early *lean sales and marketing* thinking and was slowly displaced by larger, more efficient retailers (with more effective advertising) (Wikipedia, 2016).

When the concept of lean sales and marketing is mentioned, most lean practitioners envision an assembly line-like "sales factory" where prospects are precisely moved through a sales funnel and somehow transformed into paying customers. While this creates an easy-to-communicate vision, it is grossly inadequate in capturing the complexities of the real work of sales and marketing. Real sales and marketing must deliver multiple physical and informational work products, to multiple external and internal customers, in multiple markets, across multiple interacting value streams. Further, it almost always has to do so with imperfect information and conflicting priorities. The factory analogy also makes the topic of lean much less engaging to sales and marketing professionals as they develop new ways of thinking and working while leveraging the constantly advancing scientific fields of consumer psychology, behavioral economics, and competitive strategy. There is nothing wrong with factory work; however, it is simply not a motivational comparison for these knowledge workers who are new customers of lean.

Sales and marketing therefore is (or at least should be) intimately involved in determining the organization's purpose, as well as leading the required problem solving necessary to make achieving that purpose more effective and efficient across the entire enterprise. Complexity makes applying lean in this discipline more challenging, but also more critical to uncovering viable new customer value creation and delivery opportunities, and the profitable growth that follows with proper execution.

What is Lean Sales and Marketing?

In setting the context of this chapter, lean is defined as engaging everybody, at all levels, every day, in solving problems and improving their own work to create more value, utilize fewer resources, and ultimately achieve the organization's purpose. This is accomplished while simultaneously helping customers solve their own problems to achieve their own purpose. When we create more value overall, the proverbial "pie" gets bigger and there are more rewards to share across customers, employees, investors, and supply chain partners.

The Work of Sales and Marketing

In most organizations, sales and marketing are often distinct functions with different processes, objectives, and performance measurements. But, since the working delineation of each varies greatly across organizations, I am combining the two into "sales and marketing" both for brevity and also to promote the concept of working in value streams instead of silos. As a result, sales and marketing fits into a complex network of multiple interacting value streams with external buyers, internal customers, and external influencers. Sales and marketing therefore impacts everyone's value and flow, as shown in Figure 12.1.

Sales and marketing processes span the entire timeline from a customer's first exposure to a need, desire, problem, or brand to the end when they can possibly influence someone else to buy from a vendor. Since customer value is such an important lean concept, the focus on understanding constantly evolving customer needs (stated and latent, technical, and emotional) and then developing and aligning corporate strategies to meet those needs is of utmost importance in creating alignment and preventing the enterprise-wide waste of bringing inadequate or uncompetitive products and services to market. Throughout this timeline, sales and marketing is tasked with gathering, interpreting, and then distributing useful customer needs information to different value streams within the corporation. This is done so that the total organizational system

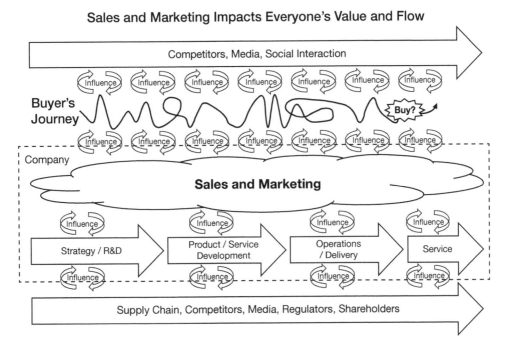

Figure 12.1 The role of sales and marketing

Source: Wahba (2012).

can create and deliver valuable and competitive solutions to customer problems. It is further used to communicate those solutions back to customers, facilitate the trial-buying-decision-purchase-delivery-feedback-satisfaction processes to please those customers, and then encourage customers to both repeat their purchases and say positive things to other potential customers. In addition, through advertising and public relations, sales and marketing is engaged in brand building and strategic influence to friends, family, co-workers, competitors, media, regulators, governing bodies, and standards bodies. All of these affect how customers and the market define value and the pricing that naturally follows.

Serving internal customers does not stop with defining value, however. Operations, engineering, research and development (R&D), strategy, purchasing, service, etc. all require critical customer/market/economic/competitor information and forecasts for managing their own processes. For instance, operations and supply chain cannot adequately plan capacity and resources, or level workflow without a lean method of understanding customer demand combined with a sale or order "pull signal" to trigger fulfillment. The work of sales and marketing is consequently quite broad as there is obviously no single input or output. Unlike manufacturing, often the work is non-deterministic (if we follow the standard sales process will we always meet our quotas or create the next social media sensation?), thus constant learning and improvement through hypothesis testing and feedback—plan, do, check, act (PDCA)—are a necessity.

Lean Improvement Techniques

There are many potential improvement opportunities within sales and marketing (not to mention helping to improve the other internal and external value streams). Often the best first step is to leverage strategy deployment, which is often referred to as "*hoshin kanri*." This assists in choosing the business's most important gaps, targeting the necessary improvement outcomes, engaging the workforce in problem solving, and then putting in place defined PDCA loops to help manage the improvement projects.

For those unfamiliar with the methodology, hoshin is a process of translating a select few strategic "business-changing" goals for an organization into a series of specific, measurable short-, medium-, and long-term improvement projects (Bechtell, 1995). The "whats" (as in, "What specifically do we need to accomplish?") are cascaded down into the organization. The "hows" (as in, "How are we going to accomplish that target by solving what specific problems and achieving what results?") are rolled back up through an activity called "catchball." Catchball is designed to increase ownership and engagement throughout every level of the organization by helping define the organization's strategic problems in the context of the higher-level goals, but not forcing any particular (and often misguided) solution down from above. Problems are thus solved where the best information and best ability to impact them resides. When all the projects are completed properly and on time, the results are combined and rolled up to the top and the original cross-organizational goals are met. The process continues forever with new or expanded goals.

Hoshin is very powerful in that it aligns the entire organization behind its most important goals while giving each individual, team, department, or division a better sense of how their contributions lead to overall success. PDCA is heavily leveraged in hoshin to make sure that the projects at each level are on track or to highlight where intervention may be required to address improvement project gaps. There should never be any surprises at the end of the planning through execution cycles (see Figure 12.2 for more details).

Hoshin and PDCA can also be very useful in managing ongoing work such as sales quota attainment, projects/campaigns, or market penetration (see Figure 12.3 for more details).

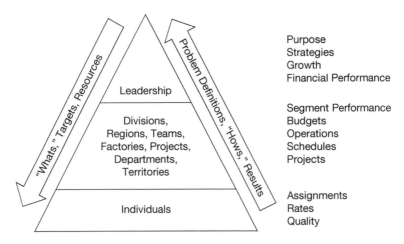

Purpose
Strategies
Growth
Financial Performance

Segment Performance
Budgets
Operations
Schedules
Projects

Assignments
Rates
Quality

Figure 12.2 Strategy deployment (hoshin kanri)

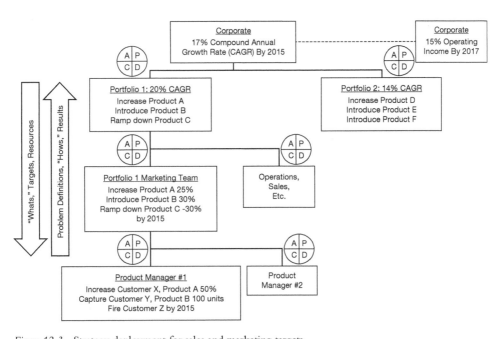

Figure 12.3 Strategy deployment for sales and marketing targets

While many other common lean tools and techniques can also be utilized in sales and marketing, it is important to understand their limitations and adjust accordingly to the nature of the specific work being improved:

- *Transactional* (repetitive, standardizable, and often administrative tasks): Since work like processing sales orders, preparing email campaigns, and replying to customer requests is transactional in nature, many lean manufacturing/lean office techniques can be applied successfully without much modification (Keyte and Locher, 2004).

- *Learning/creative* (relatively new each time and requires learning/inventiveness to narrow many possible solutions to an optimal choice): While some standardization is possible, work such as new market research, advertising, new product/service development, strategic planning, and interactive prospecting all require gathering or creating new knowledge through market observation, fast learning cycles, and experiments. These techniques plus lean project/campaign management methods are often similar to those utilized in lean product development or in lean start-ups (Ward, 2007; Ries, 2011).

- *Influence* (changing others' behaviors utilizing consumer psychology, behavioral economics, and complexity theory): A large part of sales and marketing work is geared toward influencing both external and internal customers to change their behavior to achieve a particular outcome such as pursuing a new market, enabling a novel marketing strategy, or closing a specific deal. Nobody woke up one day and out of the blue craved an iPhone, but rather consumers were educated and influenced over time to desire one because iPhones became perceived as more valuable through some combination of branding, features, and social envy. There is no doubt that Steve Jobs himself was influenced through many formal and informal processes to decide to put Apple's resources behind creating the iPhone in the first place. Influence processes such as social media marketing, relationship building, and needs creation rely more heavily on fast learning cycles and experiments as well as behavioral science (Sutherland, 2008).

Waste

While we want to be cautious so that our lean sales and marketing improvement activities strike the right balance between waste reduction and increased customer value creation, understanding the basic nature of waste through targeted examples of the traditional "seven wastes" can be useful, as shown in Table 12.1.

Value Stream Mapping

Value stream mapping (VSM) can be a very useful tool for identifying sales and marketing improvement opportunities. However, care must be taken, as it may be applied in a manner that will likely seem odd at first to both conventional lean practitioners and sales process improvement experts. Conventional VSM tends to be very internally and waste focused. Sure, the customers and their needs are captured in conventional VSM, but most of the analysis is related to improving internal operations with the (sometimes, incorrect) assumption that those improvements will benefit customers (Womack and Jones, 2005). "Customer journey mapping" (Boag, 2015), on the other hand, mainly focuses on the customer journey—each step a customer takes along the needs-through-purchase path, and where he or she gains or loses value through interaction both with the seller's company and through social means. A parallel lean sales and marketing mapping approach (with two or more simultaneous value streams being documented and improved), however, aids in capturing the interactions between customers and internal operations from both perspectives. It therefore yields both more insight and strategic improvement opportunities. It also changes the improvement focus to simultaneously increasing value while reducing waste instead of a natural bias toward one or the other.

A3 Problem Solving

A3s are useful problem-solving and communication tools in sales and marketing. However, it must be kept in mind that there are not always simple cause-and-effect problems and solutions

Table 12.1 Seven forms of waste in sales and marketing

Overproduction	Making more or sooner than customers need	• Spamming customers with email • Trying to close a sale too early • Too detailed proposals • Making a sale when there is no available delivery capacity
Waiting/delays	Process is stopped until an upstream process delivers	• "Why is it taking so long to talk to a salesperson?" • "Where is my quote?" • "Where are those sales leads?" • "We need more orders—our operation is running at half capacity"
Motion and transportation	Unnecessary people, material, or information movement	• "Do I really have to fill out this long form just to get a catalog?" • "How many webpages do I need to go through to find your phone number?" • "The quote requires *how many* approval signatures?"
Over-processing	Doing more work than is necessary	• "The quote requires *how many* approval signatures?" • Too many features or functions • "I surveyed other markets just in case"
Inventory	Material or information sits idle	• "Did we send that quote back to the customer yet?" • "Do you think that color trends study we did five years ago is still good?"
Defects	Material or information does not meet customer needs	• Fluff • "That's not what I ordered!" • "Your graphics ideas are great, but seriously, we *really* need to know how far the plane can fly before refueling"
Underutilized people	Not getting the most out of people (wasting their time)	• "No, I didn't call the customer yet—I spent all morning on my internal presentation"

when it comes to customers, competitors, or organizational behavior. People are not always rational or consistent and thus experiments like market testing are often necessary.

Other Lean Tools and Techniques

Visual management, standard work, workload leveling, pull systems, and other conventional lean methods have all found very successful applications within sales and marketing organizations. To prevent too steep a learning curve, however, tools should be "pulled" to solve specific problems rather than blindly taught or forced in application.

Challenges and Opportunities

Getting Started and Coaching Improvement

Two of the most common questions in adopting lean sales and marketing are "how do we get started?" and "won't the sales and marketing people resist?" While not to suggest that sales and marketing practitioners are unwilling to learn new methods, the changes required are often a greater transformation in thinking than in other disciplines. Selling, in particular, is often described as an "art," so discussion around creating more process and adding more discipline often seems counterproductive at first. To combat this resistance, it must be acknowledged as early as possible that great salespeople and marketers already follow a process—even if it is an unconscious mental process. Their techniques and embedded knowledge would be more useful if captured and disseminated throughout the entire organization. In addition, most of the major formalized sales methodologies (situation-problem-implication-need (SPIN), Sandler, consultative selling, solution selling, etc.) utilize some type of cyclical learning loop/influence process that leads to more customer value, efficiency, and effectiveness. More specifically, each model outlines a specific series of steps that salespeople can take to build customer rapport, uncover customer needs/pain points/fears, craft a solution, and then close the sale. Organizations that already utilize a formal selling methodology can therefore leverage it as a current state and make improvements based on their own and their customers' specific problems/needs. This is, however, not a requirement if no such formal methodology exists. Nevertheless, it is important to remember that these formal methods are very generic and are no substitute for uncovering and solving one's own organization's unique and prioritized problems.

Many coaches or "*senseis*" who do not have a sales and marketing background will struggle to help lead a transformation in this area because their lean manufacturing or even lean office examples help reinforce the misbelief that "lean is great for them, but cannot work for us" or that somehow lean will turn them into mindless, Japanese-speaking, sales robots. It is thus critical to quickly engage practitioners in applying lean to solve their very specific and important problems like solving customer problems, creating products and services that customers really want to buy, making their own work and selling lives easier, meeting quota, improving their interface with other parts of the organization, etc. Furthermore, it is vital that the future state process design is determined by the practitioners and their own derived best practices. As more and more problems are solved with lean thinking, the culture will naturally become more scientific and performance oriented. Lean must be part of the daily work itself and viewed as the solution to sales and marketing problems—not just another good-to-do thing lumped on top of everyone's day jobs.

Sales Funnels Versus Pipes

When beginning continuous improvement, sales organizations frequently look at two often misunderstood problems in their sales funnels: 1) trying to push more prospects into the mouth (with hopes that more customers will pop out the other end), and 2) trying to prevent more potential customers from leaking out along the way to a sales conversion. Somehow, it becomes sales' job alone to manage those customers through that funnel as if they were herding cattle to slaughter. A lean approach, however, would lead to a more holistic, enterprise-wide solution. We would better understand how our unique and beneficial capabilities would provide more value to the right customers, only pursue the right customers, and create a constant learning process along the strategy/product development/selling/delivery/service value streams so that we fine-tune our value proposition while simultaneously educating and influencing our customers. When we get to the end of something that looks more like a wide pipe than a funnel, there would be fewer surprises so we would have much higher forecast confidence and less unevenness and overburden in our production and delivery requirements. We would also know what elements of value have the most leverage for customer satisfaction and repeat purchase, thus allowing for improving them and not the things that customers do not care about or are unwilling to pay more to obtain. When we finally become more skilled at this than our competitors, our customers will actually transform into our extended salesforce and help spread the word for us. This is called "flipping the funnel" in the social media world—one customer enters the process and many more exit based on positive word of mouth or earned exposure (Jaffe, 2010).

Measurement Systems

Measuring the impact of outbound marketing (advertising, promotion, etc.) using metrics such as message "impressions" (customer exposure to a brand, product, or idea) has proven to be quite difficult for sales and marketing practitioners. Unfortunately, this is a commonly used gauge of sales and marketing effectiveness. Lead time between action and result, correlation versus causality, and several uncontrollable market variables often make measuring the impact of sales and marketing improvement activities very problematic. "Did my new sales technique not work very well or was my customer just having a bad day?" Even predicting whether a very well-tested and well-liked commercial will lead to increased sales is an incomplete science as companies still spend millions on humorous but ineffective ads. The key challenge and related opportunity still remain—how do we access customers' unconscious minds to determine how best to influence their analysis and decision-making processes? Evolving techniques range from asking indirect questions ("how likely are you to recommend this product to a friend or colleague?") (Reichheld, 2006) to measuring brain activity with functional MRI machines as commercials are being viewed by target customers (Lindstrom, 2008). Not everything important can be measured well yet, and sometimes we have to defer to running more market experiments to prove or disprove hypotheses.

Customer Behavior

As sophisticated as they are, human brains are not always as logical as a lean practitioner would predict, and there is a lot of danger when someone in a workshop proclaims, "well, if I was the customer, I would want. . . ." Technically speaking, it is impossible for one's conscious mind to predict how someone else's unconscious mind will make a purchase decision—much more the complex and constantly changing mental equation used to assign value. Packaged coffee has over 100 different attributes, yet only six have statistical significance in the buying decision. The science exists to make such determinations, yet many companies still have not adopted or even recognized this fact, and instead rely on personal experience, "gut feel," or rudimentary (and often misleading) surveys. Customers frequently state that they prefer one thing (like heathier fast food menu choices) and then purchase another (fries and milkshakes) or else spend more time in a less "efficient" buying process that they claim they hate, but in reality makes them feel better about themselves. Sophisticated website designers know that there are proven techniques for designing webpages for maximum response and these are not always the most timesaving for the customer. Many consumers actually enjoy the seemingly wasteful journey or "hunt" when purchasing certain types of products like luxury goods. Depending on the culture, different negotiation processes will result in different levels of customer transaction satisfaction—even with the same resulting price (Zaltman et al., 2003; Underhill, 2004; Cusick, 2009). It is therefore necessary for the sales and marketing organization to bring this science to the table as new products, services, and their related value streams are being designed and implemented so that the organization has more and better options for profitably satisfying customers.

The Future of Lean Sales and Marketing

Sales and marketing techniques are changing rapidly as the science behind them becomes better understood, better defined, more accepted, and more user-friendly. We now have the opportunity to use lean as the catalyst for driving the scientific method further into organizations as we create learning and problem-solving sales and marketing cultures. In doing so, we open up more sales opportunities and strengthen our ability to react to more rapidly evolving market demands. Specifically:

- *Corporate purchasing* is becoming more strategic and process focused while relying less and less on personal relationships. Supply chain location, quality, and agility are being weighed more and more as part of the total cost of doing business with any supplier, and as such, companies must do a better job of defining and delivering all aspects of product/service value—not just features, benefits, and price.
- *Lean itself is becoming a strong value proposition* as it signals to potential customers that a well-managed, high-quality process stands behind all of the promises.
- *The social nature of brands is increasing across the buyer population* which means that less and less buying is habitual while more and more is influenced by network communication and real user experience. Understanding the social value of products and services (even business-to-business (B2B) industrial products) and the communication paths between customers and influencers has become a necessity in order to rapidly react to changing information and perceptions as well as proactively promote the correct narrative.
- *Due to the mental overload from so many brands and advertising messages, customers are using traditional brand decision shortcuts less and less.* In other words, there are too many messages bombarding customers, and even non-competitor advertising is preventing both the building of strong brands that customers default to and, indeed, the basic ability to communicate timely, useful messages. This means that marketers need to: 1) sharpen their value propositions even more, 2) understand their customers' decision and purchase processes even better, 3) test their advertising more and more to prevent brand meaning dilution (Lindstrom, 2011), and 4) find the optimal times, locations, and methods to present appropriate advertising messages.
- *More comprehensive and timely determinations of constantly evolving customer value* help the entire extended enterprise (from strategic planning through the supply chain) to prioritize and manage their own work while preventing waste.
- *More and more customers are engaging in mass customization, co-creation, crowdsourcing, and branding* which means that new learning and influence processes are required from sales and marketing.
- *Sales and operations planning (S&OP—an information sharing process between sales and operations) is evolving and gaining importance* as a result of needing to support tighter lead times, improved responsiveness to customer demands, and less value stream inventory. From a lean perspective, this opens new doors for proactively leveling workload, preventing overburden, and creating flow. A sales and marketing organization has many levers (such as pricing, discounts, product rollouts, advertising, bundling, etc.) to help manage and level demand. This has to be well coordinated with operations to prevent stock-outs, late deliveries, quality problems, or high inventory from a demand imbalance with capacity.
- *More, better, and faster market experiments* are needed to help reduce the unacceptably high number of new product/service failures. It is estimated that between 80 and 90 percent of new products and services fail to meet their market objectives. As the complexities of sales and marketing science are revealing themselves, sometimes the most cost-effective method to prove or disprove a hypothesis is to run a simple, fast experiment like A/B testing of a new versus old website, logo, or tag line, but in other circumstances, much more sophisticated testing is required (Lindstrom, 2008). Sales and marketing practitioners therefore need to

be better versed in a multitude of tools so that the right ones can be leveraged for any particular problem.

Finally, why does nearly every organization only attempt to apply lean to sales and marketing after all of the other functions—if they even do it at all (Shizaka, 2009)? If we started our lean journey in sales and marketing, we would not only improve that work, but our advances would immediately lead to less waste in the other processes like planning, R&D, finance, operations, quality, and customer service—thus giving their value stream owners and team members more capacity to perform their own improvement work. Sales and marketing frequently has a more comprehensive view of what needs to change both strategically and to better satisfy new and existing customers, and this is very crucial to aligning a lean transformation with the business's real needs. There can be a lot of new waste generated in applying lean across an enterprise, and we can accomplish a more efficient and effective transformation if we just put in a little more upfront thought and planning into starting lean where it makes the most sense and will have the highest impact.

Case Study: Lean Sales and Marketing in Acme Auto Parts

When Acme Auto Parts was spun-off from its diversified parent company, it had a very pressing need to expand both its customer base and target markets. More aggressively priced and technologically advanced competition had led Acme's leaders to believe its current book of business was going to decrease rapidly. It therefore had to quickly find ways to offset those losses before it could even consider growth again. A simultaneous global economic downturn made capital even scarcer, and automotive suppliers were near the bottom of the list of viable investments. Since there was no singular solution to Acme's problems, each individual product line was left to determine its own path to success . . . or elimination.

The *transmission capacitor product line* started its improvement path by aggressively approaching many, many potential customers, and despite a lot of hard work it failed spectacularly to win new business. Its sales techniques were antiquated and its products lacked the world-class quality that all of Toyota's automaker competitors were demanding. Since these capacitors were 10 percent more expensive than their rival's to begin with, they had little hope of displacing their competition for any new customers who also required an additional 10 percent price reduction as an enticement to cover the switching costs like testing and validation, software reprogramming, and government certification. Transmission capacitors were in even worse shape than many of Acme's other products, and its management team realized it needed to be even more aggressive in holistically improving the entire global business.

Thankfully, Acme had begun its lean journey a few years earlier and had made some noticeable progress in both manufacturing and logistics. Even though the basics of lean were well understood, it was still unclear if lean could be applied successfully outside of operations and if so, what kind of gains could be realized. Faced with little choice, the transmission capacitor management team decided to take an enterprise-wide lean approach, but felt the biggest gains could be achieved by simultaneously focusing on *sales and marketing* and *new product development*.

Initially, capacitors needed a better strategy because improvement without a clear sense of direction often leads to more confusion, misalignment, counteracting changes, and general waste. They began their process by visiting each of their global regions for some intense problem solving. Instead of trying to work with every automaker, they decided to concentrate their efforts on three new customers per region, in addition to determining new ways to rescue their existing customer business through better quality—a key differentiator. Once their target customers were chosen, the *regional sales teams* worked to understand their specific needs in not just product quality, performance, and price, but also manufacturing and supply chain footprints in order to take advantage of faster deliveries, lower inventory, and reduced import duties. Holes in the product portfolio were identified and new customer-specific products developed and validated using both *lean project management* and a *workload-leveled portfolio management process*. Project workload leveling helped increase capacity by reducing the overburden of too many simultaneous projects. Fewer projects were active at any given time, but since they could be completed faster, overall project throughput increased by 25 percent. Corresponding lean manufacturing systems and associated value streams were developed to supply customers from a new regional hub-and-spoke production footprint. Regional suppliers were also brought on board and developed to a higher quality standard.

A big part of the lean sales and marketing effort revolved around the creation of detailed *value propositions*. Specific to a given customer opportunity, a value proposition captured performance, quality, durability, and manufacturing delivery needs, and then compared the Acme offering with what was known about the competition—both good and bad. Customers reacted very favorably to this openness and honesty, and actually helped supply critical competitive analysis data. Value propositions also included continuous improvement plans/*product roadmaps* so customers knew exactly how a given product would evolve over its life cycle. This helped improve supplier–customer coordination while reducing overall vehicle development cost. Over time, value propositions became a big part of an improved *learning cycle-based selling methodology*. Salespeople identified and bridged customer knowledge gaps and simultaneously implemented influence plans for specific customer decision makers.

The traditional automotive component industry had long development cycles and it typically required over four years to move from a proven design concept to production. Since transmission capacitors needed to move much faster, its leaders sought non-automotive opportunities, such as marine and motorcycle manufacturer programs, to be able to study and implement *lean product development* while simultaneously accelerating the lean manufacturing learning curve. In doing so, Acme was able to cut its development lead time in half to soundly beat all industry benchmarks for transmission capacitors, while reducing development costs by 40 percent. The positive press from applying new technologies in older but still high-profile industries also helped improve Acme's image as more of a technology leader.

Transmission capacitors' entire lean program was managed using a lite version of *strategy deployment/hoshin kanri*. Growth (measured as *compound annual growth rate* (CAGR)) and profit (*operating income*) were the two major overall goals. These cascaded throughout the organization as various teams were asked to develop and implement the supporting lean solutions. As an example, one combined sales and engineering team leveraged value stream mapping to reduce quotation preparation and approval lead time by 80 percent while simultaneously improving customer responsiveness and reducing rework. Another team utilized standard work in costing to reduce investment and pricing study effort by 30 percent.

The PDCA cadence within the strategy deployment process consisted of weekly, monthly, and yearly check and correction cycles for various level goals. One very significant outcome of using this methodology was that everyone in the 2,000-person organization could hold up their one-page business plan and speak specifically to where and how they were supporting the achievement of important and measureable business objectives (see Acme's strategy deployment model in Figure 12.4).

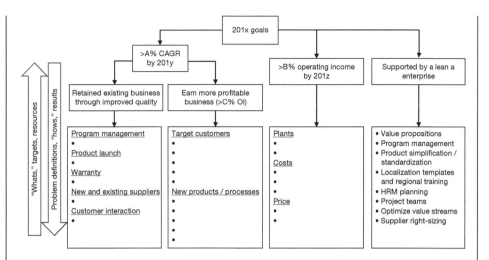

Figure 12.4 Strategy deployment in ACME Auto Parts' transmission capacitor product line

As lean spread throughout transmission capacitors, positive results and synergies began to compound. Since the product development lead time was cut in half, the product and related manufacturing process portfolios doubled in size. These portfolios were instrumental to capturing 10 of 10 target customers in seven of seven target markets—all while leveraging previously underutilized production capacity to minimize capital investment.

In the end, the lean sales and marketing and lean product development initiatives, coordinated with a continued focus on lean manufacturing and later *lean purchasing*, led to an increase in overall revenue and a 15 point operating income improvement. It was also accomplished with one less management layer and 25 percent fewer resources (achieved through retirements and normal attrition—not layoffs). Key to Acme's success was applying lean as a coordinated, cross-functional effort to improve the total business system. In doing so, transmission capacitors avoided the conflicting priorities and negative interactions in more common siloed functional group-focused improvement initiatives. Counter to many lean transformations, sales and marketing took a strong leadership role and that greatly aided in choosing and constantly refining the improvement path. Also, it never stopped learning how to better satisfy its customers as it simultaneously focused on both waste reduction and value improvement.

References

Bechtell, M. (1995). *The management compass*. AMA Management Briefing, New York, American Management Association.

Boag, P. (2015). All you need to know about customer journey mapping. *Smashing Magazine*. Available at: www.smashingmagazine.com/2015/01/all-about-customer-journey-mapping/ (accessed July 2016).

Cusick, W. J. (2009). *All Customers Are Irrational: Understanding What They Think, What They Feel, and What Keeps Them Coming Back*, AMACOM Division, American Management Association.

Jaffe, J. (2010). *Flip the Funnel. How to Use Existing Customers to Gain New Ones*, Hoboken, NJ, John Wiley & Sons.

Keyte, B. and Locher, D. (2004). *The Complete Lean Enterprise*, New York, Productivity Press.

Lindstrom, M. (2008). *Buy-ology: Truth and Lies about Why We Buy*, New York, Doubleday.

Lindstrom, M. (2011). *Brandwashed: Tricks Companies Use to Manipulate our Minds and Persuade us to Buy*, New York, Crown Business.

Reichheld, F. F. (2006). *The Ultimate Question: Driving Good Profits and True Growth*, Boston, MA, Harvard Business Press.

Ries, E. (2011). *The Lean Startup*, New York, Crown Business.

Shizaka, Y. (2009). *The Toyota Way in Sales and Marketing*, Bellingham, WA, Enna.

Sutherland, M. (2008). *Advertising and the Mind of the Consumer: What Works, What Doesn't, and Why*, revised 3rd international edition, Crows Nest, Australia, Allen & Unwin.

Underhill, P. (2004). *Call of the Mall: How We Shop*, New York, Simon & Schuster.

Wahba, B. (2012). *The Fluff Cycle*, CreateSpace.

Ward, A. C. (2007). *Lean Product and Process Development*, Cambridge, MA, Lean Enterprise Institute.

Wikipedia (2016). *John Wanamaker*. Available at: https://en.wikipedia.org/wiki/John_Wanamaker (accessed July 2016).

Womack, J. P., and Jones, D. T. (2005). *Lean Solutions: How Companies and Customers Can Create Value and Wealth Together*, New York, Simon & Schuster.

Zaltman, G., Dotlich, D. L. and Cairo, P. C. (2003). *How Customers Think*, Audio-Tech Business Book Summaries.

13

LEAN BRANDING

Laura Busche

Introduction

Lean principles have changed how we create, sustain, and recreate brands. Thanks to the internet, consumers located anywhere on Earth can form die-hard perceptions about a brand's offerings with the click of a mouse. In such an interconnected world, it is essential to recognize the impact that branding has in business success. Designing and sending the right brand message is now a strategic business endeavor, and it involves stakeholders at every level in the organization.

Trends that only used to affect small groups are now easily spread through omnipresent media channels. The speedy diffusion of innovation has the potential to shift behavior patterns, creating an unstable market where the only sound strategy is to place consumer research at the forefront. This emphasis on listening has become crucial because consumers' ideas of who they are and what they want are inevitably modified by changing patterns outside of their control.

In this environment, static brands—those that fight to preserve a given set of symbols, story, and strategy—are no longer viable. Rather than holding on to obsolete principles, brands are better off listening to market changes and learning from them. Lean branding brings about a much-needed middle ground between agility and consistency. Throughout this chapter, you will learn what lean branding is about, and how it can improve the way a product's value creation story is conceived and shared.

What is Branding?

Branding has awakened the interest of academics and practitioners from a wide array of fields. As a word, "brand" was first found in the Germanic languages that preceded Old English *c*.1000 (Stern, 2006). It finally made it to the marketing field in 1922, when it took the form of "brand name." At the time, it was being defined as a "trade or proprietary name," pointing to its intellectual property connotation. However, researchers like Stern (2006) claim that there is confusion around the actual *definition* of the term, which has hurt academic projects that attempt to study its effects.

Throughout its history, researchers have defined a *brand* as a group of mental associations or visual symbols stored in memory, while some have focused on its legal implications as a trademark. For the purposes of this chapter, and as described in *Lean Branding* (Busche, 2014), a brand is the unique story that consumers recall when they think about a specific business entity (individual, product, or service). This story associates the entity's product with the consumer's personal stories, a particular personality, what the entity promises to solve, and its position in relation to competitors. A brand is represented by visual symbols, and feeds from conversations taking place across multiple mediums.

Branding, then, is the practice of developing, extending, and maintaining this brand story in the marketplace. As a science, it involves continuous research into your target market's consumption behaviors and acute forecasting about emerging trends that might affect them. As an art, branding requires the integration of disciplines as diverse as design, marketing, and psychology to create resonant messages that can steer these behaviors in the desired direction. Branding is thus a strategic business function that should permeate the efforts of every single business area, going from customer support to product development. Gone are the days when we could leave brand development in the hands of the marketing department.

For decades, many marketers have been introducing brand development as a "soft" science, to the point where many believe that branding is ornamental or a second-class concern. This is because many haven't realized that brand development should be evidence based, and that our branding efforts can actually be matched to the returns that they generate. Lean branding sees brands much like you would see the items in a production line: as the result of a process that must be optimized to avoid inconsistency, waste, and overwork.

What is Lean Branding?

The business model canvas and the *build-measure-learn* (BML) loop described by Eric Ries (2011) in *The Lean Startup* have undoubtedly impacted the way in which practitioners build and sustain brands. In Ries' words, "the only way to win is to learn faster than anyone else." Based on the agile innovation cycle proposed in Toyota's production system, *The Lean Startup* translates lean production principles into a language that makes sense for today's fast-paced entrepreneurs. Like Toyota's approach to lean, the lean start-up method relies on the idea that organizations (and brands) exist in order to generate value for consumers, and investments that do not contribute to such value are seen as wasteful.

In lean branding, we continuously test hypotheses about a brand's symbols, story, and strategy to determine which version of them works best to generate conversion. Just like lean production aims to minimize waste, improve continuously, and prevent quality issues, lean branding practitioners learn to allocate resources strategically, engage in constant hypothesis testing, and build more informed brand components from the onset to avoid future expenses.

From 2012 to 2014, I mentored 97 early stage tech start-ups in Latin America as they built salable brands over the course of eight weeks. After working with over 300 entrepreneurs in the implementation of this methodology, I realized that those who went on to perform successfully in demo days, investor meetings, and client acquisition were those who had managed to build dynamic brands. These brands generated traction, interest, and positioned themselves more effectively in consumers' minds. We saw start-ups lose opportunities to others with simpler *MVPs* (minimum viable products) but a deeper sense of what their brand meant.

While the layperson's understanding of branding points to a product's visual identity (logo, color palette, packaging, and the like), these workshops focused on providing the tools to enable entrepreneurs to build compelling brands based on the understanding that there are three parts to the process (Figure 13.1):

1   Developing a *value creation story* that answers the consumer's "what's in it for me?" question.
2   Designing a set of *visual symbols* that represent that story in the marketplace.
3   Implementing a high-conversion *growth strategy* that can share this story and set of symbols with the right audience.

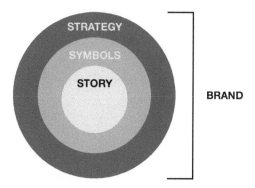

Figure 13.1 The three-layered nature of brands

As a result of these workshops, my team and I detected the tactics and tools that worked best for these ventures. We analyzed how they were implementing brand development alongside lean start-up principles and realized that it was time for lean branding to emerge both as a field of study and as a best practice. It became evident that the experimentation and continual hypothesis testing that these teams were implementing for product design were equally applicable to brand assumptions.

Lean branding is about building brands that adapt to consumers' ever-changing needs and desires. There's no use in standing still in the marketplace when consumers' ideas of who they are change continuously. To home in on these evolving ideas, lean brands have conversations, not monologues. They embrace the fact that their mission is to help consumers get closer to who they want to be. They're comfortable with the fact that this "who they want to be" is always evolving. So they evolve too: iterating continuously in endless cycles of building, measuring, and learning.

Lean branding is an evidence-based process to develop high-conversion brands while minimizing waste. In doing so, it is inevitably linked to continuous improvement. In 1986, W. Edwards Deming described a plan to foster continuous quality improvement within organizations. He named it the Shewhart Cycle, after Walter A. Shewhart's ideas in the 1939 classic *Statistical Method from the Viewpoint of Quality Control*. Today, we know this method as PDCA (plan, do, check, act) and it has been widely implemented in lean production cycles at companies like Toyota.

There is a close relationship between that continuous improvement cycle and the iteration process suggested in lean branding (see Figure 13.2). The "plan" and "do" phases come together in a single "build" stage, where minimally viable brand components are created. An initial set of visual symbols, a value creation story, and growth strategy are built to form the base of our iteration process. The "check" phase, which becomes "measure" in the BML cycle, introduces a series of methods to test out the validity and effectiveness of the previously built components in light of how much value they add for customers. The brand's visual identity, resonance, and traction are all evaluated based on actionable metrics. Finally, the "act" or "adjust" phase in PDCA becomes "learn." In lean branding, learning involves rebranding, repositioning, or rechanneling based on the feedback that one has obtained from the measurement stage. Just like in PDCA, the BML cycle repeats in order to guarantee continuous improvement.

Challenges and Opportunities

Implementing lean branding successfully doesn't come without its fair share of obstacles. Most of the challenges associated with this leaner approach to brand development are found in the

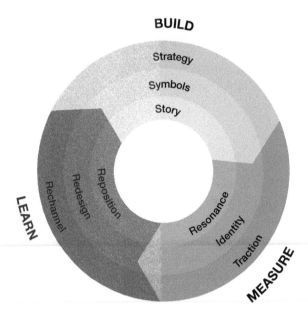

Figure 13.2 Lean branding merges the build-measure-learn loop in the lean start-up with the brand development process

"measure" and "learn" phases described above. While agencies, designers, and brand strategists are used to building, and even doing so under tight time constraints, they are often unfamiliar with the idea of experimentation.

The main struggles that most teams face when creating an iterative brand can be grouped in five categories.

The Cost of Experimenting and Testing

Testing two or more versions of a single brand component to determine which works best involves actually *designing* those alternative versions. Traditionally, the decision to incorporate certain elements in a brand's story, symbols, or strategy has remained in the hands of a few. With lean branding, hypotheses must be carefully formulated and tested with audiences that go beyond the brand's core team. Finding those testers, developing a set of alternative versions, and acquiring the tools to conduct the experiment are all common difficulties businesses face in this process. Fortunately, this challenge is offset by the opportunity brought about by simpler and cheaper prototyping tools, as will be explained in the forthcoming section.

To fully leverage the advantages of testing and experimentation, brands also need to be supported by a functional team focused on growth. Regardless of how user-friendly testing tools become, the basic principles and logic related to experimentation require a specific skillset found in individuals known as *growth hackers*. A relatively new term, *growth hacker* was coined by start-up advisor Sean Ellis in 2010. He defined this strategist as a "person whose true north is growth. Everything they do is scrutinized by its potential impact on scalable growth" (Ellis, 2010).

A growth hacker's agenda is focused on generating *conversion*, a goal that each brand defines differently. For some, conversion implies an acquired subscriber, client, or follower. For others, conversion is measured in terms of direct revenues generated from a certain activity. In any case, *conversion* is a desired action path that we expect a consumer to follow. This path is inextricably connected to the company's goals, business model, and survival. When building A/B tests, the conversion act becomes a growth hacker's true thermometer. Lean branding requires the existence of such individuals, since they are uniquely positioned to determine how effective certain brand components are in terms of the metrics that matter for the business.

The Threat to Consistency

Every brand asset that you have displayed in the past (think about your logo, imagery, messaging, color palette, and the like) has formed meaningful associations in consumers' minds. The idea of consistency, then, becomes crucial to stimulate desired behaviors by leveraging those lasting associations.

In this respect, two researchers have defined brands pointing to associations stored in the consumer's memory. Keller (1993) explained that brand knowledge consists of a special node in memory to which a variety of associations are linked. This idea of "node" is borrowed from the *Associative Network Memory Model* (Anderson, 1983), which views consumer memory as a set of interconnected nodes and links. In this cognitive model, nodes are units of information storage and links represent how strongly different nodes are connected to one another. Snickers, for example, has spent years positioning the connection between *hunger* and their brand (hence the message *"Hungry? Grab a Snickers"*). Aaker (1991) also defined a brand in terms of its ability to form and protect associations over time. In fact, he suggested 11 common types of associations that brands can hold in memory: *product attributes, intangibles, benefits, relative price, use/application, user/customer, celebrity/person, lifestyle/personality, product class, competitors, and country/geographic area* (Aaker, 1991).

Changing a given brand's visual symbols, value story, or growth strategy can shift these associations and threaten consistency. Consider the last time you heard that a company engaged in a rebranding project due to a merger, or due to the launch of a low-cost product line. Some brands detect new trends in their audience's lifestyle choices that transform the way in which their product or service is consumed. Faced with shifting market conditions, they launch a *brand redesign, repositioning,* or *rechanneling* project that shatters existing consumer beliefs about their offer. Long-standing associations like benefits, use/application, user/customer, and lifestyle/personality are inevitably modified—not without a fair share of temporary confusion.

Understanding existing associations, and how iterating can affect them, is a crucial consideration when embracing lean branding. Consistency is crucial because it helps us establish our brand's message in the marketplace, and strengthens the right associations that consumers use to recognize us. The consumer learning process involves a series of affirmative moments where our brand is proven to stand for certain values, ideas, and features. Over time, some of these associations become die-hard notions that largely determine our relationship with the consumer. A consistency obsession, on the other hand, can trap us in a strategy where little or no brand learning is taking place.

Brand Friction: Resistance to Change

One of the key problems with iterating, evolving, and learning as your brand grows is something I call *brand friction*. You've been carrying around a fixed set of assets (files, messaging, symbols) for so long that the mere thought of changing them seems frightening—to say the least. You are not alone: the resistance to change is a pervasive corporate challenge. No matter how large or experienced your team is, you will have to generate internal buy-in for brand changes.

The following questions are symptoms that you've undergone or are going through a period of brand friction:

- Will the market see me as "inconsistent"?
- Will I confuse the press? How can I pass on the news?
- Will customers be completely unable to recognize my brand after the change?
- How will I communicate this change to all of my team members?
- How can I communicate this change to existing and new customers?
- How can I share the new assets (story, symbols, strategy) with as little trauma as possible?

These questions will arise from different functional areas within your company, and being prepared to answer them is essential. If your experiments, measurements, and market listening activities indicate that a change in direction is necessary, make sure that you can articulate objective data in support of this decision. To strengthen the case for a brand redesign (visual symbols iteration), repositioning (brand story change), or rechanneling (brand strategy shift), devise a strategy for each of the questions above.

To avoid confusing the press, for example, your brand redesign project might include an event to announce your new set of symbols to a number of relevant media professionals in your space. Similarly, designing a campaign to educate consumers about your new identity would solve question three. *Yes,* your customers *will* be able to recognize your brand because you *took the time* to walk them through the change.

Finding Agile Design, Copywriting, and Growth Partners

Most of the principles embedded in lean branding require quick, responsive design skills that can be nurtured in-house or outsourced. In order to adapt to changing market conditions, or test alternative versions of brand symbols, your team will need to find an individual or company that can deliver design projects rapidly and efficiently. While the story and strategy components of the brand are often managed internally, it is also beneficial to invest in agile copywriting and growth services.

Your team must be able to incorporate market signals swiftly. Whether your value story needs to be repositioned, your visual symbols redesigned, or your growth strategy rechanneled, no innovation can happen unless your team has the bandwidth to move forward with the changes. Detecting the need to pivot is a necessary first step, but it won't be sufficient to bring meaningful change.

The Threat of Similarity: What Happens When Everyone is Lean?

It is tempting for individuals and teams to replicate successful brand development strategies exactly as they worked out for others. Instead of looking outside for imitation, browse around for inspiration. Those are two entirely different goals: while the first results in a mass-produced marketplace full of "me-too" brands, the second has the potential to power genuine innovation. Analyze competing brands' successes as a starting point—rather than perfect tracing, watch out for interesting strokes and add your own variations.

When working on a brand redesign project, where visual symbols are transformed to represent new business realities, companies often look at industry case studies for reference. The danger in designing (or rather, redesigning) your visual identity based on others' processes is that certain trends may start to subconsciously generate a bandwagon effect. Throughout 2015, for example, several tech brands including Google, Verizon, and Lenovo all changed their logos to feature some variation of a minimal sans-serif wordmark and flat (or nonexistent) symbol. In their effort to evolve with the times, many felt that these brands had fallen for the similarity trap. Such is also the case of the airline industry, where it seems like many brands have converged into a similar aesthetic approach.

As more brands move in the direction of lean development, the challenge is to remain differentiable, unique, and original. The fact that certain market changes call for iteration shouldn't lead to sacrificing a brand's singularities to favor convention.

Opportunities

Just as there are many challenges involved in implementing lean branding, new areas of opportunity continue to emerge for practitioners. On one hand, lowered web development costs and the boom of the tech start-up space have resulted in the creation of incredibly useful measurement tools. On the other hand, the same phenomenon has opened up interesting new channels for brand communications with lower barriers to entry. The following are some of the most outstanding opportunities available to lean branders.

More Sophisticated and Accessible A/B Testing and Measurement Tools

Testing tools that allow you to gauge the impact of one version (of a brand component) against the next are becoming both more sophisticated and commonplace. A/B testing, the practice of experimenting with two versions of a single component to optimize efficiency, is an essential tool for lean brand development.

It is normal to have "a hunch" or general impression that a given variation of your brand symbols will resonate better with your audience. If you've been in a particular industry for enough time, your judgment has probably evolved to a point where you can make educated predictions about buyer behavior. However, it is of the utmost importance to recognize that these hunches and impressions *are not data*. As much as we'd like to believe that we are in possession of an inner compass regarding what brand story, symbols and strategy will work best, this conception is simply not true. A/B testing helps validate ideas, gather evidence to support or deny hypotheses, and make informed brand decisions based on objective market signals.

Because more practitioners are adopting lean start-up and lean branding principles, the competitive landscape for testing tools has crowded relatively quickly. Software developers are interested in building applications that help business strategists make sense of big data, user behavior, and preferences. There's a growing emphasis on helping non-technical founders and marketers build experiments that would otherwise require a specialized development team. A/B testing is slowly becoming a standard skill in the competitive marketer's toolkit.

As the supply continues to rise, users will demand increasingly advanced features. You can now test one brand symbol (like a logo), a brand strategy asset (like a landing page), or a brand story message (like ad copy) against several other versions to figure out which is most successful. As more developers join this space, not only will our instruments improve, but prices will drop, making it significantly easier to get started with testing. Some examples of companies building efficient measurement tools for lean branding include Zurb (VerifyApp), UsabilityHub (5 Second Test), Pickfu, Ask Your Target Market, Optimizely, and Google (Content Experiments).

Simpler and More Accessible Design Tools

There is a generalized effort to make design software more accessible. In 2012, Adobe® switched to a SaaS (Software as a Service) model, serving its entire Creative Cloud™ design suite in exchange for low monthly payments that any type of individual or agency could easily commit to. In 2013, an Australian company called Canva vowed to revolutionize the graphic design industry with an easy to use drag-and-drop interface that requires no software downloads at all. Creative Cloud^{TM} now boasts over 4.6 million paid users (Adobe, 2015), while 4.7 million people are designing using Canva (Canva, 2016). Other competitors are quickly emerging in the low-cost design application space.

As developers continue to improve the efficiency of our tools, they'll help amplify our internal capabilities and those of our brand-building partners. The shift toward templatizing, what-you-see-is-what-you-get (WYSIWYG) interfaces, and low-cost design assets are all strong drivers of the advent of agile design. Templates, on one hand, make it easier to replicate brand assets without having to start with a blank canvas. WYSIWYG, on the other hand, provides visual tools that allow individuals with little or no technical knowledge to build assets online. Finally, low-cost resources like graphic kits, plugins, and fonts will continue to facilitate the fast design cycles that reactive brands need. With time, our design team's lead times will become much shorter, opening the door for continuous experimentation and improvement based on testing. A more visual future, with rapidly generated brand imagery, awaits.

Emerging Massive, Low-cost Communication Channels

Sharing a brand story using mass media used to be a privilege of large, established organizations. Back in the 1960s, a brand's communication options were limited to expensive radio, TV, or print spots. Small players tried tedious snail mail, phone calls, and trade show booths. Getting significant reach for brand messages was everything but democratic. Back then, engaging in a full-fledged brand redesign project would imply an unreasonable set of costs.

Fortunately, the emergence of low-cost channels like social media, email, blogs, and websites has leveled the playing field. Besides offering the opportunity to "earn" and "own" your channels, these mediums also provide a platform for paid exposure. The prices are significantly lower than those stipulated by traditional media. In opening new spaces for brands to establish conversations around their story, these emerging low-cost channels represent a disruptive opportunity.

Brands wishing to experiment with subtle design iterations or message changes today can simply use social media and other online channels as sandboxes to gauge their audience's reaction before rolling out a widespread change. The real-time feedback provided by online audiences can be an instrumental asset in validating new brand ideas. Over time, growing their reach in these channels leaves the company with an invaluable resource to tap into for market validation. Hence, we often use the term *owned media* to refer to these channels under the brand's control.

New Instruments for Consumer Listening

Aside from the measurement tools discussed in the first part of this section, developers are creating innovative widgets and apps to collect user feedback in real time. Instead of testing, these tools aim to open genuine conversations around the issues that matter for consumers and the brands they use. New instruments are now available to build customer support communities, initiate instant conversations with site visitors, and ask pertinent questions during specific points in the user experience. These are all crucial brand touchpoints that, until now, had gone completely under the radar. Some of the companies driving innovation in this space include Intercom, Zendesk, and UserVoice.

The Future of Lean Branding

What are your customer's first thoughts when they think about you? This can be a scary question to consider. Throughout this chapter, we learned how lean branding helps optimize your brand's value creation story, visual symbols, and growth strategy based on their effectiveness at generating conversion. Furthermore, you saw how this methodology requires that everyone within your organization aligns around the creation, measurement, and iteration of these ingredients to maximize growth.

In the near future, the evolution of tools and communication channels available to brand strategists will continue to change the game. The scientific side of branding will strengthen with more precise return-on-investment (ROI) measurement tools, defeating the outdated conception that brand development is a "soft science." Thanks to these tools, consumer behavior will be tracked in unexpected ways to facilitate retargeting and smarter brand campaigns.

Armed with new instruments, brands will pivot faster and become more agile at reacting to market changes. Even iconic products and services will finally forego the brand friction that they've dragged on and iterate after decades of stagnation. The future of branding is bright, and it is time for you and your team to start shaping it.

Case Study: Lean Branding at Starbucks

In 1971, two coffee-loving entrepreneurs decided to turn their passion into one of the "world's finest fresh-roasted whole bean coffees" (Starbucks, 2015). At the time, however, these two co-founders faced the same questions and extreme uncertainties that most entrepreneurs fight in their early stages. *Would people like this new concept? Would they grow fast enough to scale? Which image could help transmit the brand's values in the marketplace? Would they outgrow their competitors in time?*

To help them answer these questions, and come up with a name and visual identity that could represent their dream, founders Gordon Bowker, Jerry Baldwin, and Zev Siegl hired Terry Heckler's branding agency. Heckler and his associates sketched a logo based on a 16th-century woodcut of a two-tailed siren. The symbol was a metaphor for the "siren song of coffee that lures us cupside," as both founders and creatives wanted to associate Starbucks with Seattle's strong seaport roots. Old marine books were very popular at the time, and the team was trying to capture the "seafaring history of coffee" (Murray, 2011). The siren marked the beginning of a long history of brand building, iteration, and growth.

Incorporating Existing Associations: Women and Exposure

Soon after the original brand identity was launched, Starbucks began rolling out delivery trucks for its growing number of stores. The siren started to appear in streets across the United States, and women were not happy about it. As it expanded, women started sending letters complaining about the siren's racy demeanor and excessive exposure. The Starbucks brand was suddenly being associated with indecency—at least in the eyes of that demographic. Listening to those emerging associations, the team reacted, redrawing the siren's hair to cover her up more, as well as zooming into her face to reduce the focus on her body (Heckler Associates, 2014).

Adapting to female consumers' concerns about exposure was a by-product of listening, and it allowed the Starbucks brand to iterate to a visual identity that strengthened desired associations. Market listening was a prerequisite for many of the successful moves that moved the brand much closer to its audience in the early 2000s. This corporate practice continues to lie at the cornerstone of the Starbucks brand experience, and facilitates pivots that strengthen its privileged market position.

Reacting to Market Changes: Brand Extensions

By 2011 Starbucks had made a strategic business shift to sell much more than coffee. Espresso beverages, seasonal drinks, teas, Frappuccino™, and even bagels were now part of the menu. In reaction to the move beyond the realm of coffee, the brand's identity iterated once again to go from a combination mark (words and symbols) to an iconic or symbolic brandmark. The wordmark "Starbucks Coffee" was dropped, and the siren became the center of attention.

CEO Howard Schultz recognized the beginning of a new chapter full of brand extensions, and summarized a new brand identity change as "a small but meaningful update to ensure that the Starbucks brand continues to embrace our heritage in ways that are true to our core values and that also ensure we remain relevant and poised for future growth" (Schultz, 2011).

Preparing to Pivot Quickly: Assembling a Reactive Global Creative Team

Lean branding requires finding agile design, copywriting, and growth partners. In order to become more reactive to market changes, Starbucks decided to create, train, and grow its own team of brand creatives. This in-house team, known as Starbucks Global Creative, is in charge of various brand strategy initiatives that range from retail experience to messaging to packaging. Allowing the team to adapt to market changes quickly, Starbucks Global Creative may well be the engine that keeps the brand's continuous improvement cycle going.

References

Aaker, D. A. (1991). *Managing Brand Equity: Capitalizing on the Value of a Brand Name*, New York, The Free Press.

Adobe Systems (2015). Adobe Systems Investor Relations Data Sheet.

Anderson, J. R. (1983). *The Architecture of Cognition*, Cambridge, MA, Harvard University Press.

Busche, L. (2014). *Lean Branding: Creating Dynamic Brands to Generate Conversion*, Sebastopol, CA, O'Reilly.

Canva (2016). *The Canva Story*. Available at: https://about.canva.com/our-story/ (accessed July 2016).

Deming, W. E. (1986). *Out of the Crisis*, Cambridge, MA, MIT Center for Advanced Engineering Studies.

Ellis, S. (2010). Find a growth hacker for your startup. *Startup Marketing*. Available at: www.startup-marketing.com/where-are-all-the-growth-hackers/ (accessed July 2016).

Heckler Associates (2014). Brand stories: Starbucks. *Heckler Associates*. Available at: http://hecklerassociates.com/brand-stories/starbucks/ (accessed July 2016).

Keller, K. L. (1993). Conceptualizing, measuring, and managing customer-based brand equity. *Journal of Marketing*, 57(1), 1–22.

Murray, S. (2011). So, Who is the Siren? Starbucks Coffee Company. Available at: www.starbucks.com/blog/so-who-is-the-siren (accessed July 2016).

Ries, E. (2011). *The Lean Startup: How Today's Entrepreneurs Use Continuous Innovation to Create Radically Successful Businesses*, New York, Random House LLC.

Schultz, H. (2011). *Looking Forward to Starbucks Next Chapter*. Available at: www.starbucks.com/blog/looking-forward-to-starbucks-next-chapter/643 (accessed July 2016).

Starbucks Coffee Company (2015). *Company Information*. Available at: www.starbucks.com/about-us/company-information (accessed July 2016).

Stern, B. B. (2006), What does brand mean? Historical-analysis method and construct definition. *Journal of the Academy of Marketing Science*, 34(2), 216–223.

14

LEAN ACCOUNTING

Brian H. Maskell

Introduction

Companies seriously introducing lean methods throughout their organizations soon bump up against their accounting systems. Traditional accounting methods are actively anti-lean (Åhlström and Karlsson, 1996; Maskell et al., 2011). This does not mean those systems are bad and wrong; it just means that they were developed in the 1920s to support high volume, mass production-style management.

The purpose of *lean accounting* is to provide a complete operational and financial management system that is consistent with, and motivates, lean thinking throughout the organization. The thinking and methods of lean management are in many ways the opposite of traditional operational methods (Åhlström and Karlsson, 1996; Maskell and Kennedy, 2007; Kennedy and Widener, 2008). In order for lean companies to thrive, they need accounting, control, measurements, and decision-making processes that actively motivate lean change and lean thinking, and require a lot less wasteful work.

The Challenges of Traditional Accounting in Lean Environments

There are a number of ways that traditional financial and management accounting undermines lean progress within organizations.

First, conventional accounting is usually reported monthly and often several days after month-end. This cadence is too late to take appropriate action to solve problems and improve processes.

Second, the reports contain complex accounting methods like allocations, absorption, and variances. Very few people in the company understand these methods. For people to make effective use of financial reports, the reports must be timely and immediately understandable to everybody.

Third, the traditional financial and operational measurements actively push back against the thinking and methods of lean. Traditional accounting undermines lean because it is designed for high-volume operations with few variations, and focuses on maximizing the efficiency of the people and the equipment. For example, a very potent anti-lean measurement is the "overhead absorption variance." This measurement focuses company managers and employees on efficiency instead of customer value. This leads to large batches, long lead times, high inventory, shortages, expediting, and crisis management. Lean has different objectives, and focuses on single-piece flow, customer value, and the productivity of the entire value stream. A recent academic study by Krishnan et al. (2011) showed that the 2008 bankruptcies of General Motors and Chrysler Corporation were impacted badly by overhead absorption measures. The car plants continued to manufacture "economic" order quantities, spending huge amounts of money, and making thousands of cars that nobody wanted to buy, until the companies eventually ran out of cash.

Fourth, the use of standard product costing to make decisions inevitably leads to poor decisions. A standard cost is not a "real" number. It is a collection of allocations and assumptions, and cannot be seen as representing the ever-changing operational processes and costs. The true cost of a product varies according to any particular day's volume, product or service mix, available capacity, and the current issues and problems within the organization. Standard cost decision making leads to poor pricing, wrong make-buy, the impeding of lean improvement, and inappropriate capital purchases, outsourcing, etc. because the actual financial impact of the decision is obscured by the spurious allocation of unrelated overheads.

Fifth, conventional costing tracks people's "actual" work time and efficiency. This information is reported through a series of cost variances. These measurements drive behaviors incompatible with lean because they focus on the individual products and production jobs instead of seeing the real financial impact on the whole value stream. In addition to the complex and opaque information, this reporting leads to thousands or millions of wasteful transactions, reports, meetings, reconciliations, and anti-lean leadership.

Sixth, traditional accounting does of course fully comply with all the internal and external reporting rules. However, the month-end close requires many adjustments to match the standard cost information to the actual costs and inventory valuation required by these reporting rules.

Finally, conventional accounting requires a great deal of work for the accountants, the managers, and operations people. In most companies, the accountants are not able to use their skills to support the business operation or strategic decision making because their time is largely spent on bookkeeping and financial reporting. Similarly, managers, supervisors, and support staff are required to waste a lot of time grappling with financial reports that are inapplicable to the lean methods of business.

What is Lean Accounting?

Lean accounting is two-sided (IMA, 2006). On the one hand, companies can apply the lean principles to the accounting work itself, with the purpose of driving out waste in the accounting processes. On the other hand, the accounting function should be organized and managed in a way that supports the lean enterprise. This chapter is mostly addressing the latter.

Applying Lean to the Accounting Processes

A good starting point for lean accounting is to apply regular lean methods to the company's current accounting processes. This eliminates waste in the accounting and finance areas and it frees up people's time to work on the introduction of more significant lean accounting methods. Applying lean to the company's current accounting processes also enables the financial people to learn lean thinking and methods in a practical way within their own area.

The usual places to apply lean improvement in the accounting processes are month-end close, accounts payable, accounts receivable, inventory management, purchasing, payroll, etc. These improvements and time saved enable the accounting and finance people to address the more fundamental changes required by lean accounting.

Lean-enabling Operational and Financial Controls

Instead of using the traditional financial controls like variance analysis, overhead absorption, etc., lean accounting strengthens the operational controls within the company's business processes (Carnes and Hedin, 2005; Maskell et al., 2011; Fullerton et al., 2013). This is done through a careful selection and design of the performance measurement system. Attributes of good performance measures aligned to lean accounting are as follows:

- Having focused measurements at every level of the organization: senior management level, value stream level, and cell/process level.
- Linking all selected measurements at every level to the company's strategies. It is typical to have measurements at the company level, the value stream level, and the front-line cells and processes where the operational and support work is done.
- Minimizing the measurements to the "vital few" so as to provide clarity of purpose and exposure of problems, waste, and improvement opportunities.
- Using measurements that are simple and straightforward so there is no ambiguity or confusion. Unlike traditional financial statements, lean accounting statements are designed so that everybody in the company can immediately understand them. The information is straightforward and on a single page.
- Presenting all measurements visually, because this is the best way for people to recognize issues, understand causes, and take action. Visual measurements also enable team leaders, managers, and executives to see and understand the current performance of the business. This is particularly important when senior people are engaged in gemba walks.

Furthermore, companies should use visual management to show the reasons for problems and what actions are being taken to resolve them, or improve the process. At the cell/process level, these will be the immediate, current issues and their resolutions. At the value stream level, these will show the actions required to continuously improve the value stream's performance. At the company level, the measurements show how well the strategies are being achieved.

Value Stream Accounting

Value stream accounting is the primary financial reporting within lean accounting. Most companies using lean accounting have their primary financial reporting at the value stream level. The value streams for a lean business are mini companies within the company. They are typically focused on a family of products or services with similar flows. The value stream manager is fully responsible and accountable for the success and profitability of these products or services. Value streams can also be focused on particular markets rather than product families.

A lean accounting firm has frequent income statements for the value streams. These financial reports enable the value stream manager and his/her team to control their costs, revenues, and profits, and to take action quickly when financial problems arise. In order to control the processes and continuously improve, the value stream teams need to understand three things: the operational measurements, the use of their capacity, and the financial results of their work.

The income statement for each value stream is created (typically) weekly and shows the revenues, costs, profitability, and other relevant information like inventory value and return-on-sales, for example. This financial information is gathered directly from the company's financial systems and shows the real revenue and spending for that week. There are a number of different ways to show the information. For example, some companies want to show the value of materials *used* that week, while others want to see cost of what was *purchased* this week.

The income statements are typically reviewed within the value streams each week at a stand-up style meeting. A short, focused, standardized meeting where the value stream revenues and costs are reviewed and problems identified. These problems can then be resolved short term and/or long term. In addition, potential improvements and opportunities are brought to light, prioritized, and put into action. Further, the value stream managers within the company come together for a second meeting to review each other's income statements, and initiate activities across multiple value streams, or to help each other make progress.

It is common for the income statement to show, for example, 13 weeks of information so that the value stream managers and their teams can see trends, seasonality, and abnormalities in the financial results. It is common for the value stream income statement information to be supported with graphs or other visualization of the results.

For month-end close, the weekly financial statements for all value streams are summed across the whole company and for the number of days in the month (see Figure 14.1 for an example of four value streams reported at month-end close in a typical manufacturing company). This same information is used for the month-end financial reports, both internal and external. These lean accounting financial reports comply fully with *generally accepted accounting principles* (GAAP) and other external requirements. There are some adjustments required. For example, corporate overheads may be added, exchange rate gains/losses, etc.

When value stream accounting is first used, it is common for the financial numbers to be highly variable from one week to the next. The first task for the value stream team is to work to stabilize and control the spending, and then work to improve the revenues, costs, and profitability. It is the frequent reporting and the clear information that enables the value stream team to achieve exceptional results.

	OEM VALUE STREAM	SYSTEMS VALUE STREAM	SPARE PARTS VALUE STREAM	NEW PRODUCT DEVELPMENT	SUPPORT	TOTAL
REVENUE	$1,039,440	$1,009,246	$346,690	$0	$0	$2,395,376
Materials	$424,763	$339,810	$100,449	$84,953		$949,975
Direct Labor	$189,336	$123,648	$15,622			$328,606
Support Labor	$87,662	$67,616	$8,299	$40,772	$53,056	$257,405
Machines	$88,800	$27,750	$12,500			$129,050
Outside Process	$36,571	$17,731	$0	$12,588		$66,890
Facilities	$15,450	$10,300	$25,422	$3,090	$9,270	$63,532
Other Costs	$1,933	$2,899	$5,512	$483	$1,933	$12,760
TOTAL COSTS	$844,515	$589,754	$167,804	$141,886	$64,259	$1,808,218
VALUE STREAM PROFIT	$194,925	$419,492	$178,886	–$141,886	–$64,259	$587,158
Return on Sales	19%	42%	52%	0%	0%	25%

Opening Inventory	$1,186,035
Closing Inventory	$963,148
Inventory Adjustment	–$222,887
Corporate Overhead	$83,838
Exchange Rate Gain/Loss	–$3,220
NET PROFIT	$277,213
Return on Sales	11.6%

Figure 14.1 Example of income statement for four value streams at month-end close

Box Score and Decision Making

The *box score* is a primary document for lean accounting (see example of a box score used for tracking kaizen effects in Figure 14.2). The box score is used for reporting the performance of the value streams, calculating the financial impact of lean (and other) improvements, and for decision making. The decision making ranges from sales quotes to make/buy, sourcing, product and service rationalization, capital purchases, selecting which new products to design and launch, etc.

There are three parts to the box score: the value stream performance measurements, a summary of the value stream income statement, and the value stream capacity analysis. When these three are put together, you have a clear understanding of the value stream's performance and potential. The operational performance measurements show how well the value stream is serving the customer, flowing the primary processes, achieving good quality, etc. The capacity analysis shows if the value stream is making good use of the people's time and/or the machines and equipment time. The summary financial statement shows the financial outcome of the value stream.

When making lean accounting decisions we do *not* look at the cost of individual products or services. All decisions are made by assessing the impact on the entire value stream. The impact includes the changes to the operational results, the financial results, and the capacity usage within the value stream. From a financial point of view, decision making shows how much money will go into the bank as a result of the various options being considered.

The routine decision making is standardized so that the decisions are always made the same way. This ensures that the box score format and data are always accurate, and that good decisions can be made by the people closest to the issue at hand. This leads to better decisions and frees up time for the company's senior leaders because the decisions are made at a lower level in the organization.

As with most things in lean accounting, using the box score is quite simple and understandable. People can focus on the issues relating to the decisions because the format and numbers on the box score are familiar and trusted.

Product Costing

Lean accounting does not have much need to calculate product or service costs. All of the reporting, analysis, improvement, and decision making are made from the impact on the value stream as a whole, not the individual product or service. The reason is that the concept of a product/service cost is misleading and in some ways dangerous. A standard cost is largely a series of allocations that do not give any real or useful information about the cost or profitability of the product, other than for valuing inventory.

If a company sells a product for $100 and the standard cost is $80, is it making $20 profit? No. The allocated costs will be wrong (that's why they show up on variance reports) and the amount of money going in the bank will not be $20. If the company has immediate capacity to make the product or provide the service, then much more than $20 goes in the bank. Alternatively, if there is no capacity and the product or service requires extra people, overtime, outsourcing, or other methods then much less money goes in the bank. In lean accounting, we show the true "cash-in-the-bank" financial impact. It is done quickly and easily.

Many companies recognize the shortcomings of their accounting systems and reports. Some companies that are not lean-thinking use *activity-based costing* (ABC) to calculate product costs in a more precise way. There may be some benefit in the ABC approach but it does not match to lean thinking. The outcome is still a number of allocations and there will still be variance reports

		CURRENT STATE	EXPECTED KAIZEN IMPROVEMENT	AFTER KAIZEN IMPROVEMENT	ONE MONTH LATER	THREE MONTHS LATER	SIX MONTHS LATER
VALUE STREAM PERFORMANCE MEASUREMENTS	Productivity (Hrs Worked/Census)	4.89	3.92	3.67	4		
	Quality (Defects/Patient Day)	3.2	2.92	2.5	3		
	Average Length of Stay	5.7	4.2	4.2	4.2		
	Patient Satisfaction (0–5)	2.7	3.5	3.5	2.9		
	Average Cost per Patient Day	$192.69	$167.74	$167.55	$171.08		
VALUE STREAM CAPACITY	Productive time	41.90%	52.40%	52.40%	52%		
	Non-Productive time	21.70%	27.10%	27.10%	27%		
	Available Capacity	36.40%	20.50%	20.50%	20.50%		
VALUE STREAM FINANCIAL RESULTS	REVENUE	$332,630	$352,630	$346,111	$372,443		
	Supplies & Drugs	$154,582	$154,582	$154,090	$152,582		
	Salaries, Wages, & Benefits	$154,285	$109,428	$109,428	$113,428		
	Professional & Contracted Services	$0	$0	$0	$0		
	Equipment & Facilities	$23,752	$23,752	$23,752	$23,752		
	TOTAL COSTS	$332,619	$287,762	$287,270	$289,762		
	PROFIT	$11	$64,868	$58,841	$82,681		
	RETURN ON REVENUES	0.00%	18.40%	17.00%	22.20%		
20%	Hurdle Rate	-20%	-2%	-3%	2%		

Figure 14.2   Example of using a box score in a medical company

showing the differences. The ABC method is even more complicated than standard costing and therefore does not fill the need for people in the company to understand the financial reports. In fact, ABC is often 10 times more complex than even standard costing because it calculates costs using many "cost drivers."

Having said this, there are times when it is necessary to calculate product costs. The most important example of this is international customs requirements for product costs of imports and exports. When these product costs are needed, they can be calculated ad hoc using standard cost methods or they can be provided using a "features and characteristics" (F&C) method. The F&C method is a simpler way to calculate a product cost and provides a little more accuracy than standard costs. However, it should never be used for any decision making or financial reporting (Maskell et al., 2011).

Role of Lean Accounting in Tracking Improvement Activities

Motivating and tracking improvement is a very important aspect of lean accounting. Four broad types of improvement can be differentiated:

1 breakthrough improvement,
2 continuous improvement,
3 just-do-it improvement, and
4 target costing.

The first type of improvement is what I call "breakthrough improvement." It is largely driven by strategic needs and large investments. Box scores are used to evaluate the operational, capacity, and financial impact of the various options to achieve these changes. This is not "justifying" the decisions. It is analyzing the true impact of the options, and showing the most appropriate courses of action. Lean accounting is used to calculate the financial benefits of breakthrough improvement as the strategic plans are established.

The second type of improvement, "continuous improvement" (CI), is largely driven from weekly value stream performance boards. These visual boards contain the operational measurements and financial results both visually and on the value stream box scores. The purpose of the boards is not so much reporting the results, but understanding the results so the value stream process can be changed and improved. The CI processes are driven from the weekly "board meeting." The weekly value stream boards have Pareto charts showing the frequency of the various issues within the value stream. They also show the current CI projects and the status of the projects. When a project is completed, the team chooses another CI project to start the next week. The value stream team works out how many of these CI projects can be in action at all times. When a project is completed, a new project is initiated. This ensures *continuous* improvement. Box scores are used to evaluate the operational and financial impact of the various CI projects that the team is planning. This enables the team to decide which CI projects give the biggest financial gain. The box score is also used to monitor the improvements after the event so as to ensure they are being sustained over time.

The third type of improvement can be called "just-do-it improvements." These improvements are done daily by the people working in the processes. Just-do-it improvements are either driven from problems that occurred within the cell or departments, or improvement opportunities the team members have identified. The improvements are done by the people working in the area and are largely self-initiated and executed. As a part of the CI selection process the value stream box score is used to understand the operational and financial impact of the various available projects. While there are other issues to take into account, the box score is used to show which projects provide the largest financial and operational benefit. There is generally no need to do a financial analysis for just-do-it improvements. It is more important that the number of just-do-it improvements is measured and that everybody in the value stream is active in these small but cumulative changes. Over time, just-do-it improvements create significant change, improvement, and engagement of the team members.

A fourth type of improvement is "target costing." Target costing is a different kind of improvement that is driven through lean accounting to enhance the sales and profitability of the value stream. There are four ways to improve the profitability of a value stream: sell more products/services, increase prices, reduce spending, and introduce more desirable products/ services. Target costing is done by occasional analysis to understand the economics of a value stream. The purpose is to understand sales quantities, market share, and the price elasticity. An outcome of this is to identify the appropriate product/service prices for each primary market the value stream addresses. After the prices are known the value stream team identifies the amount of profit required to maintain the business, grow the company, and fund future products and growth. The outcome is a lean initiative to bring down the average cost of the value stream products so that the required profits and cash are achieved. These improvement measures do not address the "margins" of individual products or product families. The operational and financial improvements are achieved throughout the value stream as a whole.

Transaction Simplification and Elimination

When lean thinking and methods take root in a company, the operations throughout the organization come under much better control. This applies from sales through purchasing, product/service customization, production or execution, inventory control, delivery, cash collection and payment, new product/service development, and other primary processes. Traditional companies use complex management systems like enterprise resource planning (ERP) to track their processes so as to create a secondary electronic control system with thousands (or millions) of computer transactions. This is a perfectly good way to manage a traditional business, but lean companies have the advantage that they build effective controls into their operational processes through visual management, standardized work, single-piece flow, low inventories, frequent supplier deliveries, and highly trained and cross-trained employees. When the processes are well controlled operationally, there is no longer a need for the complex control systems that traditional companies use.

There are many advantages of removing the unneeded transactions, but much of it boils down to eliminating wasteful computer transactions together with the reports, reconciliations, meetings, and phone calls from senior managers. This considerable waste elimination frees up the time of operations people, support people, accounting people, and senior leadership. The operations people can use this time to provide more value to more customers, and grow the business. The accounting and senior staff can use the time freed up to focus on more strategic activities that will build a successful future business, and greatly increase the value, sales, profits, and cash.

Some companies reach the "gold standard" of transaction elimination where there are no transactions required within the operational areas. They need transactions to receive materials and to ship products, but everything else is better controlled visually. This level of simplification is not immediately possible or desirable for many companies, but is a long-term aim.

The big pay-off for eliminating waste in these areas is that it opens up one to three days per week for the accounting staff. These financial professionals can now engage in more strategic activities that will lead to higher sales, closer customer relationships, lower costs, and higher profits. There is a win–win when financial professionals can work in the value streams to help grow the business, the market share, and the cash flow. A goal of lean accounting is to move the senior leader focus from largely tactical to largely strategic.

Planning with Lean Accounting

The role of lean accounting in the planning process revolves around strategic planning and medium-term planning. The role of lean accounting in strategic planning is to quickly provide valid financial forecasts associated with each of the strategic plans, and all the variations resulting from the consensus-building process. This way, the financial aspects of the strategic planning process can be simply and readily assessed.

The medium-term planning is achieved using *sales*, *operations*, and *financial planning* (SOFP). SOFP is a monthly collaborative process within each value stream bringing together sales/marketing, purchasing, operations, logistics, new product development, quality, finance, and other key people to create, for example, an 18-month plan. There are five primary steps to the SOFP process:

- demand forecasting,
- capacity forecasting,
- balancing demand and supply,
- financial forecasting, and
- executive review and authorization.

Financial forecasts are developed for sales, expenses, projects and capital changes, and the resulting expected profits and cash flow. These forecasts are not done from scratch; they are modified and updated each month. Advanced lean companies extend this monthly financial forecasting so as to eliminate the time-wasting and flawed annual budget process used by most companies. Budgeting is replaced by rolling financial forecasts that are up to date and dynamic.

Conclusions

When companies transform to a lean enterprise, their traditional accounting, control, and measurement systems also need to change. The traditional accounting systems were designed for completely different control logics than that of lean production. In fact, traditional accounting systems can hinder the transition to a lean state, because they incentivize anti-lean behaviors. Therefore, lean accounting methods are designed to support the lean journey.

The vision for lean accounting can be summarized as follows:

1 Accurate, timely, and clearly understandable financial and operational information.
2 Financial and operational analysis that motivates and enables the value stream teams to maximize the value for the customer and financial benefits for the company.
3 Decision-making methods that provide relevant and understandable information leading to better decisions, better customer service, higher revenues, lower costs, and higher profits.
4 Rigorous operational and financial controls leading to orderly and predictable outcomes. These enable the controls to be focused in the operational processes, and thereby simplify the financial control system.
5 Full compliance with GAAP, external regulations, and internal reporting and audit requirements.

6   Freeing up people's time by systematically and continuously eliminating waste from the company's accounting, control, measurement, and decision-making methods. It is common for 20–50 percent of time to be freed up for financial controllers. Similar waste elimination frees up the time of operations people and support teams. Senior leaders can then focus more of their time on strategic activities because much of the tactical analysis and actions move to lower levels in the organization.

Case Study: Lean Accounting in the Watlow Electric Manufacturing Company

Watlow is a medium-sized, privately held, multinational company that designs and manufactures industrial heaters, temperature sensors, controllers, and supporting software. Since 1922, Watlow has grown in product capability, market experience, and global reach. The company holds more than 450 patents and has 2,000+ employees working in nine manufacturing facilities and three technology centers in the United States, Mexico, Europe, and Asia. Watlow also has sales offices in 16 countries around the world. The company continues to grow, while the commitment remains the same: to provide its customers with superior products and services for their individual needs.

For this case study, I asked Mr. Steve Desloge, the company's chief financial officer, to explain Watlow's approach to lean accounting:

The Beginning

In January 2005, we kicked off our company-wide lean transformation, covering all facilities. We went to it with a high level of vigor and energy, and we began value stream assessments at each of our sites and set about a series of seven-week kaizen events where our teams came together to work on improvement activities.

It became clear to us in finance that if we were to support our lean operations and get in the leading edge of the lean transformation, we were going to have to learn what finance can do to support this lean strategy. We did some research and came across the inaugural Lean Accounting Summit Conference in Detroit, MI. We took all the finance leaders to the conference and we were astonished and excited to learn about lean accounting.

Creating a First Pilot

Our first step was to select a model value stream that was fairly well along in its knowledge and implementation of lean principles and practices, and the goal was to create a model for value stream management including lean accounting. We concurrently learned what we needed to change at the enterprise level in terms of accounting policies, practices, and techniques, accounting systems and planning that would support value stream management. It was a dual effort to see what we can do at the value stream and at the enterprise level to develop a model that can be employed across the whole company.

As a result of this initiative, we developed a value stream management system that essentially replaced our current operational system (based on MRPII) which provided operational control and created a lot of accounting information, but which few people really understood. We created a new set of measurements that are linked to the enterprise and business unit strategies that showed the right targets to be achieved, and which needles we had to move in order to prosper that value stream.

We focused ourselves on the box score showing the operational performance and the financial performance of our model value stream. This created a regular weekly plan, do, check, act cadence as our standardized work for accounting, control, and measurement. We set up a process so that the teams themselves populate their own box scores (with little assistance from the financial people) so they can get their results as quickly and easily as possible. It soon became clear that no one in the value stream wanted to go back to the old way. Lean accounting was providing them with much better information to support their sales, production, customer service, and to drive the objectives of our lean transformation.

Changing the Enterprise Financials

On the enterprise side, we had to learn how to get rid of financial information on our statements that did not make any sense. We learned how to produce financial information without using allocations or other methods to spread costs around the business. This represented nirvana to us in terms of the finance teams being able to provide financial information to make better decisions and understand the impact of those decisions on the financial results in the context of the entire company's operation. It was very clear to us that this was a much better way to run the business, and it did not take much of a push to get the whole finance team behind lean accounting.

We were able to very quickly go to lean operational statements: clear, "plain English" information with no allocations, no overheads, no strange capital depreciations from the enterprise level all the way down to individual value streams. At the same time, we eliminated the reliance on standard costs together with all the calculations, all the maintenance and waste we were putting in each year to update those labor routings, overheads, volume assumptions, which did nothing but create confusion and ongoing waste. We replaced it with much simpler operational and financial reporting, and box-score decision making.

Eight Years on

We have been using lean accounting as an integral part of our business and our lean progress for eight years now. We continuously refine our processes using lean thinking and methods. We have added a number of more advanced lean accounting methods like the SOFP planning and budgeting, applying lean accounting in new product development, and better ways to address international financials. We have developed training methods so that people new to lean and lean accounting can quickly understand and use these rather simple methods.

There have been several occasions when we have made successful decisions in the company, and we have recognized that the decision would likely have gone the other way if we still had the standard costing. The simple clarity of lean accounting has led to some much better decisions being made.

We recently hired a new corporate controller who has a strong background in standard costing. He was skeptical of lean accounting during the interview stages and when he first came on board with us. Asked now if he would like to go back to standard costing, he will vociferously support lean accounting as the best way to go. His job as corporate controller is a much more strategic role than before because the regular bookkeeping and financial reporting does not take up all of his time. In addition, much of the analysis and decision making is now done by the people in business units and value streams.

Lean accounting has been a great contribution to Watlow's lean success and business success, although we realize that we still have a lot further to go in our lean journey.

References

Åhlström, P. and Karlsson, C. (1996). Change processes towards lean production: The role of the management accounting system. *International Journal of Operations & Production Management*, 6(11), 42–56.

Carnes, K. and Hedin, S. (2005). Accounting for lean manufacturing: Another missed opportunity? *Management Accounting Quarterly*, 7(1), 28.

Fullerton, R. R., Kennedy, F. A. and Widener, S. K. (2013). Management accounting and control practices in a lean manufacturing environment. *Accounting, Organizations and Society*, 38(1), 50–71.

IMA (2006). *Accounting for the Lean Enterprise: Major Changes to the Accounting Paradigm Statements on Management Accounting*, Montvale, NJ, Institute of Management Accountants.

Kennedy, F. A. and Widener, S. K. (2008). A control framework: Insights from evidence on lean accounting. *Management Accounting Research*, 19(4), 301–323.

Krishnan R., Brüggen, A. and Sedatole, K. (2011) Drivers and consequences of short-term production decisions: Evidence from the auto industry. *Contemporary Accounting Research*, 28(1), 83–123.

Maskell, B. H. and Kennedy, F. A. (2007). Why do we need lean accounting and how does it work? *Journal of Corporate Accounting & Finance*, 18(3), 59–73.

Maskell, B. H., Baggaley, B. and Grasso, L. (2011). *Practical Lean Accounting: A Proven System for Measuring and Managing the Lean Enterprise*, Boca Raton, FL, CRC Press.

15
LEAN AUDITING

James C. Paterson

Introduction

This chapter is adapted from my recent book *Lean Auditing*, published by John Wiley & Sons (cf. Paterson, 2015). The chapter is written for a non-audit audience and covers some key general points about auditing, external auditing and then internal auditing, as well as more specific insights about lean internal auditing. It also offers some wider reflections about lean ways of working, particularly in relation to some of the cultural and behavioral challenges that need to be recognized and managed.

What is Auditing and External Auditing, and How is External Auditing Different from Internal Auditing?

The origin of the word audit is actually from the Latin "to listen," as auditors would listen to accounts being read out to them and seek to establish if these accounts could be relied upon. Since then, auditing has developed into a term covering a range of activities typically concerned with carrying out a systematic and independent assessment of an area under scrutiny in order to establish whether it meets certain standards.

External auditing is principally concerned with validating that the financial accounts of an organization present a true and fair account of the financial performance and status of an organization to management and other external stakeholders. Readers will also be aware of numerous accounting scandals (Enron, WorldCom, etc.) that have led to an increasing scrutiny of the external auditing profession, seeking to ensure that the external audit opinion is providing a genuine assurance on the accuracy of the controls over financial reporting and the associated disclosures in the financial statements (see Sarbanes–Oxley US, the ACCA (2014) on auditor skepticism, and various publications by the Financial Reporting Council UK, e.g. Financial Reporting Council, 2015).

Internal auditing was formally created as an independent profession different from external audit in the 1940s. It was initially concerned with financial control matters that were below the radar screen of the external auditor. However, over a period of decades the profession developed a broader scope: looking at compliance with laws and regulations, IT controls, and the effectiveness of operational controls. In the past 20 years the internal audit profession has increasingly looked at risk management and governance (with the phrase "risk-based auditing" a commonly

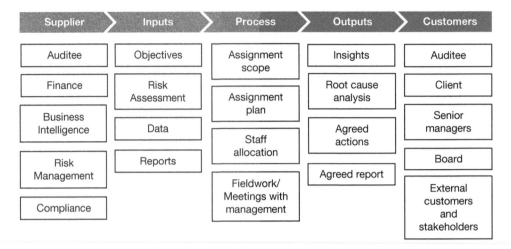

Supplier	Inputs	Process	Outputs	Customers
Auditee	Objectives	Assignment scope	Insights	Auditee
Finance	Risk Assessment	Assignment plan	Root cause analysis	Client
Business Intelligence	Data	Staff allocation	Agreed actions	Senior managers
Risk Management	Reports	Fieldwork/ Meetings with management	Agreed report	Board
Compliance				External customers and stakeholders

Figure 15.1　Internal audit process overview based on the lean SIPOC framework

heard term in audit circles). More recently still, following the 2007–2008 financial crisis, the profession has become more interested in questions concerning risk culture and looking at the effectiveness of customer interactions (particularly in UK financial services since the publication of a key report in July 2013). Auditing risk culture and customer interactions is by no means mainstream in internal audit at the time of writing this chapter, but, as we will see, adopting lean principles in the practice of internal auditing naturally leads internal auditors in this direction.

A brief overview of the internal audit process is outlined in Figure 15.1 using the lean SIPOC framework.

What is Lean Auditing?

After 15 years working in a range of finance roles, I was appointed as the chief audit executive (CAE) of the group internal audit (GIA) function of AstraZeneca PLC in 2002. My role was to assist in upgrading the contribution of the function: helping to develop its remit from mostly checking compliance and financial controls to a more proactive function, looking to contribute to the success of business initiatives as well as reviewing the management of high-profile risk areas. By 2005 we had made progress on a number of fronts. However, it was clear that pressure on costs would increase. As a result, the audit management team and I decided that we should engage with the cost agenda in a proactive manner: "Better to work on efficiency and effectiveness ourselves than have someone else do it for us."

At the suggestion of one of the GIA audit directors, we decided to work with colleagues in AstraZeneca's manufacturing function, who specialized in lean manufacturing techniques. After obtaining help in understanding lean ways of working, we developed a number of new approaches to our audit work. What impressed me was just how quickly and easily the lean techniques could be implemented and the scale of the efficiency gains achieved. Subsequently, I was impressed with the way lean principles informed much of what we were trying to do on the agenda of adding value (especially for a "back office" function) and the way lean ways of working improved our effectiveness as well as our efficiency. Lean ways of working led to changes in the way that we planned our work, engaged with stakeholders, carried out testing, and even the way we reported the results of our audit work.

The lean audit approach we developed also offered a positive way of thinking about the role of internal audit and the value it could deliver that was appreciated by senior managers, the board, and audit staff; and notably it challenged the convention that a "support function" should simply be regarded as an overhead whose costs must simply be reduced. In addition, our new approach to internal audit planning, and the ways that we had changed our executive and board reporting, gained recognition within the internal audit profession (by the UK Institute of Internal Auditors (IIA), as well as the Audit Director Roundtable of the Corporate Executive Board).

After seven years as CAE, I started my own consulting practice in 2010 and have been able to develop, refine, and learn about lean auditing practices across a range of organizations. This experience led me to write the book *Lean Auditing* during 2014, which was published in 2015.

Lean auditing refers to the practice of internal auditing as informed and enhanced by lean principles, tools, and techniques, based on my consulting work. Additionally, it has been informed by interviews with a number of CAEs in the UK, Europe, the US, and Asia Pacific, alongside various thought leaders in the internal audit profession. Captured in the book is a discussion about an evolving "family" of progressive practices and principles. Some of these were directly inspired by lean ways of working and others were arrived at independently as audit functions have faced cost management pressures and increasing demands from stakeholders to enhance value and reduce waste. This means that concepts from Six Sigma, agile and systems thinking have also been incorporated in the family of progressive, lean auditing practices. I am currently a firm believer in a pluralistic, evolutionary approach to the development of lean auditing practices. As far as I am concerned, if it delivers results, it is worth pursuing. Netland (2013) makes an equivalent point in a manufacturing context.

It is also worth saying that lean internal audit offers some interesting insights in relation to the extent to which wider organizational processes and procedures align with lean principles and practices (which might also be called lean auditing). This will be discussed further toward the end of this chapter. In any event, in the context of lean as applied to internal auditing, it has been striking to see how much progress internal audit functions have made with relatively limited training in lean. I think this is due to three key factors: 1) a close affinity between internal audit and lean (where notions of *gemba*, process excellence, and root cause analysis are also important to many in the audit profession), 2) the way in which lean offers a coherent and "back to basics" way of thinking about productivity, and 3) the fact that lean can offer a more constructive and positive way of looking at efficiency and effectiveness than conventional cost reduction and benchmarking reviews.

It is worth noting that the lean auditing approaches I have been promoting have been supported by influential figures in the internal audit profession, notably the current President of the Global IIA, Richard Chambers, and the former technical director of the UK IIA, Chris Baker. This has been very encouraging to me since some lean ways of working challenge traditional internal audit practices. However, at this stage, a number of internal audit professionals support lean ways of working and advocate that lean auditing can, and should, be compatible with the formal standards of the internal auditing profession. Furthermore, these professionals believe that the adoption of lean principles and practices would help to address various "hot topic" improvement areas identified by the profession. I will expand on this further toward the end of this chapter.

Lean Auditing: Achievements and Opportunities

Even Internal Audit has a Value-adding Role

Readers unfamiliar with internal audit may be interested to learn that the professional standards of the IIA state that: "The CAE must effectively manage the internal audit activity to ensure it adds value to the organization." IIA standards (IIA, 2013a) go on to say that internal audit "adds value to the organization . . . when it provides objective and relevant assurance, and contributes to the effectiveness and efficiency of governance, risk management, and control processes." At first glance these references to value adding are a helpful alignment toward lean principles. However, is it true to say that by simply doing internal audits, auditors will add value? The work I have done has revealed that the true picture "on the ground" is not as straightforward as the IIA standards would like to suggest.

First of all, *managers within an organization can have widely differing views on what adds value*. Senior managers often value audit when it carries out advisory or supportive tasks "to move the business forward," while non-executive directors often value assurance and audit work "to check everyone is doing their job properly." In addition, I have found that there can be problematic, even irrational, views held by some managers in relation to what adds value, divorced from true external customer value. In particular, it is not unusual to find managers who want to use internal audit to look at known or suspected areas of concern not simply to identify root causes, but to "prove" points for the purposes of internal politics (which was the topic of an article I wrote for the IIA US).

Second is *the need to encourage a mindset (for managers, as well as many internal auditors) that recognizes that internal audit can contribute to customer value-add as much as a "front-line" function*. John Earley (Partner, Smart Chain International) explains:

> Let's consider the internal audit function of a company; does the customer really care? Superficially, no, because they're still going to get a product or service tomorrow. However, let's look a bit beyond the here and now and look further into the future and start thinking, well, if internal audit didn't exist maybe some of the controls and check points that actually end up ensuring that the organization does the right thing by its customers could be lost. There may not be a direct impact on what the customer sees as value, but there may be an indirect one. You may not be on the main through route delivering what the customer values, but the aim should be to be a contributing factor. So long as you can trace the link between what you are doing and what the external customer would value, you cease to be a backwater. You are a tributary, not a backwater or a lost lake.

Making the link between audit work and what would add value in the eyes of external customers and stakeholders is a key focus for lean internal auditing. This perspective acts as a useful "north star" when trying to arbitrate between competing internal demands regarding what the audit function should spend its time on.

Third, *there are a lot of important insights that can be gained by looking at research in relation to where value is gained and lost (e.g. Dann et al. 2012)*. Much of this research has found that significant value has been lost due to the mismanagement of strategic risks (e.g. issues encountered when moving into a new market, the failure to create an attractive new product, or difficulties managing projects to time, budget, and quality etc.). Indeed, the research suggests that more value is lost in the strategic arena than through operational or compliance-related problems (illustrated in Figure 15.2). From my perspective, this challenges the idea that operational processes should be the prime area for the attention of lean ways of working. Rather, it suggests that in order to be truly lean, close attention also needs to be paid to ways of working in strategic areas as well. This is precisely the shift that needs to be made when thinking about more progressive internal auditing. Auditing operational processes can add value when there is a connection between this work and what the customer would want, but sometimes even more value can be added by reviewing the processes and information flows leading to key strategic decisions, and/or the management of key projects.

Figure 15.2 Illustration of the main sources of value destruction

How Variety Can be a Key Source of Added Value

It is understandable that lean ways of working might encourage greater standardization (when this is sought from an external customer perspective), and for a support function such as internal audit there is an important place for standardized and automated activities. However, my work in the lean audit arena suggests that standardization must not become such a cultural norm that the place for bespoke services is lost. Indeed, part of the challenge of being a lean audit function is learning how to balance lower-cost standard audits alongside higher-cost, tailored, assignments on higher value issues.

One CAE of a FTSE company explained their perspective on the value-adding mindset:

> Before you start an audit, you've got to ask yourself, when you come out the other end, what might be the particular outcomes from this audit? Look at that and say, will anyone care? For example, if you've issued a red report and everyone goes "so what?," you should ask yourself: why did we look at that? Finding a risk that is not well controlled is not adding value if the risk doesn't really matter to the organization. The question to ask is—if we come up with a finding will it be a unit level issue, a regional issue, or a group issue?
>
> If you know at the start it's unlikely to be more than a business unit issue you should think hard about whether the audit is worthwhile and properly scoped. It might add value to a particular unit's management, but is it right for the group as a whole, in terms of resource allocation? It's all about understanding internal audit's role in assessing the control environment at the correct level. There may still be a valid reason to go and audit a unit level issue, perhaps to do some root cause analysis and share that more

broadly. So the value of this assignment is going to be greater than addressing specific issues in that location.

Thus, taking a lean, value-adding perspective asks us to think carefully about questions of management "risk appetite" (cf. HM Treasury, 2006)—whether this "risk appetite" is explicitly stated or not. If management is not concerned by the results of an audit this *could* reveal that the audit is looking at areas that an end customer would not be concerned about. However, a lack of interest by managers in certain areas might reveal a culture of complacency is developing, and at its worst, a distancing between management and an end customer value orientation. If this is the case, audit may need to think carefully about the sorts of assignments it carries out since doing another standard audit assignment may simply result in more of the "so what" reactions from management! To be truly lean, an audit function must pay close attention to repeating issues and signs of cultural complacency. To do this a progressive audit function must be able to carry out robust trend analysis, impactful reporting, and have an ability to see and name behavioral and cultural issues. Encouragingly, more and more progressive internal audit functions are recognizing the crucial role of working on these topics in order to add value: identifying root causes that could be holding back their organization from properly adding value in the eyes of the customer. An awareness of issues with the risk culture of third-party suppliers can also be a powerful leading indicator of potential issues that might arise from them. However, to effectively operate in the domain of risk culture requires that the CAE should have a high degree of political savvy.

In more tangible terms concerning productivity, internal audit functions that adopt lean ways of working often develop an even wider range of assignment types than they did before. Jonathan Kidd (CAE, UK Met Office) describes the changes he saw:

> In relation to scheduling the audit plan, the number of days we scheduled for an assignment has changed a lot. It used to be done through a range of standard types, for example a 15-day audit, 25-day audit, 35-day audit and so on. As we adopted lean ways of working it became more dynamic so, where before it would have been 20 days, now it's going to be 16 or 17.
>
> As a result, the number of audits that were able to be done went up quite dramatically. So dramatically that I had questions from management. I heard a senior manager saying to me "Are you driving your team too hard?" However, they were working the same hours, nobody was doing overtime, and they were able to do more audits. The stuff that was not worthwhile and taking up time was not being done any more.

Thus, an important shift in mindset for a lean audit team is to be clear about the reasons for an audit assignment, to carefully judge an appropriate breadth and depth for each assignment based on its purpose and the value to be derived from it, rather than simply following a standard work program (and standard resource allocation) slavishly.

The Importance of Role Clarity and a Helpful Model for Audit

Developing the theme of ensuring that audit is working on truly value-adding areas, my experience has been that adopting lean ways of working pushes internal audit to think carefully about its role in the organization as well as the roles of others. Alongside this the Global IIA has recently developed guidance in relation to risk and assurance roles in its paper *The Three Lines of Defense in Effective Risk Management and Control* (IIA, 2013b).

The risk and assurance roles in the "*three lines of defense*" are (Figure 15.3):

- *In the first line of defense*: Management and staff should manage risks and opportunities on a day-to-day basis, in line with policies, processes, and standards as required.
- *In the second line of defense*: Compliance, policy, and oversight functions, such as finance, legal, and purchasing, who should help create the policies, processes, and standards that inform management and staff as to what is expected, and should be available to support them with answers to questions and some monitoring of the performance of the organization in meeting these standards.
- *In the third line of defense*: Internal audit (or other independent assurance and advisory roles) who should advise and assure whether the other two lines of defense are working properly.

The IIA (2013b) paper explains that in order to be truly effective, organizations need to be clear about the different roles that deliver effective performance and the robust management of risks and controls. It goes on to explain that while there should be sharing of information, and coordination between these lines of defense: "lines of defense should not be combined or coordinated in a manner that compromises their effectiveness" (p. 7).

This drive for role clarity is important from the perspective of lean auditing since very often problems with processes, controls, and risk management can stem from a lack of clarity about roles and responsibilities. One case in point that reinforces the importance of role clarity can be found in the UK's National Health Service (NHS). Between 2007 and 2008, there were some serious incidents in relation to patient care in some locations. Various reviews took place to identify key lessons. The UK Audit Commission (which has now been dissolved, for reasons unrelated to this discussion) was asked to examine how the patient care issues could arise when there had been a range of assurance statements signed off by managers and auditors during the years in which the issues arose. The results are contained in the report *Taking it on Trust* (Audit Commission, 2009). Numerous causes for the shortcomings were uncovered, including fundamental points about what management assurances were being sought and the robustness of those assurances (see also "How assured am I?", Paterson, 2013). In addition, the report included learning points

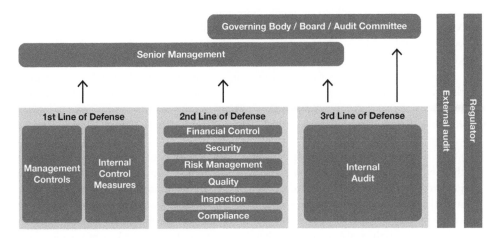

Figure 15.3   The three lines of defense model

Source: Adapted from ECIIA/FERMA *Guidance on the 8th EU Company Law Directive, article 41.*

concerning the role and focus of internal audit. One important conclusion was that: "Greater attention needed to be paid to compliance mechanisms, and these needed to be more clearly distinguished from internal audit, which should review the effectiveness of the compliance framework and not be a substitute for it" (p. 55).

Thus, when audit starts substituting for management (first-line) or functional (second-line) activities, this can create a culture in which control and quality cease to be part of the day-to-day activities of first line and second line, risking the chance of errors in day-to-day operations and/or requiring the need for rework. In addition, when internal audit carries out routine checking it may lose its independence and cease to be able to act as a safety net, increasing the chances of a problem that could lead to customer or stakeholder dissatisfaction.

The "Taking it on Trust" report also made another important point that is of relevance to the lean auditing debate, namely: "use of internal audit could be improved, with greater emphasis given to the quality of assurance derived from it rather than cost minimization." In addition, the report highlighted that the use of internal audit "should be placed in a wider framework of review, as there are alternatives to internal audit in many cases" (p. 55).

In conclusion, truly lean, value-adding internal auditing is about a lot more than simply doing auditing efficiently, it is also about audit pursuing opportunities to encourage others in the organization to take up their roles effectively, building quality control into day-to-day tasks: complying with the hallmarks of any truly lean organization.

A Selection of Lean Audit Ways of Working

The following areas highlight some of the key ways in which the practice of internal auditing develops when adopting lean ways of working.

Scheduling and Planning Assignments

- *Recognize that the timing of assignments is an important source of value-add*: Traditional internal auditing can sometimes be characterized as a rather plodding profession, with no strong sense of urgency. However, a lean auditing approach recognizes the value of providing "just-in-time" some advice or insight ahead of a key decision or customer interaction. This encourages internal audit to be much more interested in current risks and challenges. Marcin Godyn, CAE of USP Zdrowie, Poland explains: "If management isn't involving you in everything that's going on, how can you build the right audit plan and work on the key issues that *right now* may need to be better managed?"

  Needless to say, in line with having a more up-to-date understanding of the organization, the lean internal audit approach demands a more flexible and dynamic audit planning process.

- *Recognize the importance of the proper planning of assignments over immediate action*: In my experience many audit functions that try to become more productive without a solid understanding of lean principles can easily equate being efficient with being busy, a culture in which there is "no time to be wasted on research or preparation." In my experience one of the powerful things about lean ways of working is the way it supports certain counterintuitive steps that are crucial to developing more productive ways of working. In this context the counterintuitive step is to slow down and think through precisely why an audit is being sought ("what is the real exam question here?"), and to understand the key information and/or data that may need to be reviewed to make a robust judgment about the issues area under review, or their root causes.

Audit Execution

- *Have direct access to data and documents and use data analytics*: Many years ago the practice of internal auditing would involve reviewing a range of paper files and records. More recently IT systems have required auditors to be able to understand the information contained therein, asking for information to be extracted from these systems. However, this can sometimes result in a time-consuming "to-and-fro" of requests for data and documents, followed by delays and then additional requests for data and documents.

  The progressive, lean auditing approach demands that audit functions should obtain direct access to data and documents within systems. As well as by passing the delays that can arise from information requests to managers, it also gives audit an insight into the gemba of information storage "in the wild." This approach overcomes the risk that management will "tidy up" documents ahead of an audit, or, more seriously, "window dress" what is provided to the audit function.

  More recently there has been a significant increase in the use of data mining and data analytics to help audit identify and then zoom in on anomalies and key areas of risk. However, the use of these techniques must be thoughtfully managed, otherwise the audit function can be at the mercy of individual auditors who like to use this capability to focus on "pet topic" areas of personal interest, rather than properly focusing on the most important risk- and value-related issues.

- *Adopt an agile project mindset to assignment delivery*: A traditional approach to the delivery of internal audit assignments typically requires a shift in mindset for many audit functions that often find assignment delivery "dragging on" as findings are disputed and the contents of an audit report is negotiated. Greg Coleman, a former CAE of various UK plcs, explains:

  > I favor having very clear structure for most assignments, particularly an agreed date for the closing meeting and then the final report. We put proposed dates into people's diaries quite early on in the planning of an assignment. They are then told that they will get a draft of the report 24–48 hours before the meeting, and they are encouraged to make sure they have time to review it.
  >
  > Occasionally we do have to move this closing meeting, but it's rare. Generally speaking, we're able to hit the deadline. It does mean sometimes that the audit team has to work quite hard in the two or three days prior to the meeting, to make sure that the draft report is ready for the deadline. But I don't think that's a bad thing, and I think it keeps people focused on the key areas. In previous organizations where there was no firm assignment plan, in addition to audit scope creep, it was common to see meetings slipping since people weren't always available if you tried to book them at the last minute, and you can end up in a situation where audits just drag on.

It is worth commenting on the notion of "cycle time" at this juncture. Many CAEs have remarked to me that for audit assignments at overseas units, it is relatively straightforward to deliver an assignment within two or three weeks, albeit that a draft report might then take another two to three weeks to issue, and then several weeks more to finalize. However, there is often a reasonable sense of momentum and speed because the audit function had to organize travel, is only booked to be there for a fixed amount of time, and management in the overseas location would typically want to know what audit has found (and perhaps rebut it) before audit leaves the location! In contrast, CAEs dealing with assignments in "head office" areas often complain about the long time it takes to carry out assignments and how the reporting process can be even lengthier. It seems to me that when this happens we are observing some interesting differences in the natural pace of working (akin to "cycle time" or "*takt* time") between local units and head office functions. This may point to significant efficiency opportunities for both audit and the wider organization (e.g. "Why do things take so much longer in our headquarters?")

Build Quality Checks throughout the Assignment Process

A common mindset for more traditionally minded audit functions is to carry out an audit assignment, then to write a draft report, and then to have the draft report and associated working papers reviewed. This results in either additional testing at the end of the audit assignment, or amendments to the report before it is issued. Readers familiar with lean ways of working will appreciate that lean encourages a culture of building quality into each step of the process, and so lean auditing seeks to avoid reviewing working papers at the end of an assignment. The lean culture is about building a focus on value and efficiency on an ongoing basis, sometimes by creating "pit stops" as an audit assignment progresses. The "pit stops" are not just looking at whether or not there is the right audit documentation on file. They also help the auditors think about whether the key "exam questions" that prompted the audit assignment have been answered, as well as considering whether audit resources are being focused appropriately at each stage of the assignment (because of the tendency of some to focus on "pet topics" discussed earlier).

In addition, effective quality control in the audit assignment should also help auditors look for the underlying root causes for what they are finding. This has been an interesting "spin-off" area of my current consulting as an increasing number of internal auditors have gained an interest in this field and in understanding various root cause analysis methodologies, many of which originate from lean ways of working.

Outputs from the Audit Process

Recognize the Source of Value is not Always an Audit Report

While an audit report is a commonly accepted output from an audit assignment, lean ways of working challenge internal auditors to begin to think that this should be the main focus of their activities. Norman Marks, a thought leader in the auditing world, offers the following insights:

> If [audit] is going to be successful, just putting something in somebody's inbox is not going to get them to listen, to think about what audit has said, to understand it and move forward. Not nearly as well or sympathetically as if you sit down with them and talk about what you have found, why any change is necessary, what's in it for them and how it will help them and the organization to succeed. It comes down to what is the product. The product is not the memo. The product is to generate change, or to provide assurance.

Where a report is appropriate, then the advice of Phil Gerard, CAE of Rolls-Royce plc, is reflective of a lean audit approach:

> Assume the reader is a reluctant reader, is how I'd phrase it. The readers of most audit reports are senior people. They don't have a lot of time. So just psychologically if they see 20 or 30 pages land on their desk or inbox, it won't be encouraging for them to read.

Keep it concise, to the point; it needs to join the dots for the reader so the business impact of issues is clear.

Shagen Ganason (CAE, Department of Conservation, New Zealand) continues the theme:

A report is only valuable when management and the board use it and see that it helps them. If they briefly look at it and then put it aside, then it is basically useless in my view. On the other hand, if they look at the report and say "yes, this is something I think will help me manage my business" or if they discuss the contents of the report with other parts of the business, then it is a good sign. My measurement of the value of an audit report is not about the contents or the number of issues raised but by how management and the board use it to manage their business.

In addition, lean ways of working promote the development of audit reports over time. Jonathan Kidd (CAE, UK Met Office) explains:

I would expect to see a regular feedback process from stakeholders, and this should cover assignment reporting. As a result of this I would expect to see things gradually change. Six months ago we were doing this report, we don't do that anymore because that's no longer necessary.

Lean Auditing: Challenges

Perceptions about What Lean is

In the world I came from, and the world of many of my clients, "lean" is one of those terms that is recognized, and is "something about efficiency," but that few understand in any detail. Those who have encountered lean can have a range of impressions and these are not always either 1) accurate (e.g. "It's all about cost savings isn't it?") or 2) favorable (e.g. "An audit team I know had a terrible time with a lean consultant appointed by the CFO who tried to minimize and standardize most things that audit did"). Some auditors are curious about what lean has to offer, but tend to expect lean ways of working to lead to a more standardized, limited, even austere, way of operating. Indeed, one of the most common things that I hear is a sense of apprehension about becoming lean, with a view that being lean will mean that things will be more efficient, but certainly at the expense of quality. Of course, this is the opposite of my own experience of lean ways of working, but it represents a significant hurdle to getting going with lean auditing. I wonder how much of a barrier it represents in other industries and "back office" functions?

Not Everyone Wants to "Raise the Bar"

The next challenge to being lean arises when key stakeholders feel content with the current performance of internal audit, perhaps thinking that broadly favorable benchmarking results mean that the function can rest on its laurels. John Earley (Partner, Smart Chain International) observes: "If you're satisfied with the way things are, you're not there. Your head is in the wrong place." Indeed, some CAEs I have worked with have only expressed an interest in lean ways of working after they have had a "jolt" around some aspect of the performance of the audit function. This is often in relation to productivity or assignment delivery issues that have come as a surprise.

In my experience, another challenge for audit can arise when stakeholders realize that lean ways of working will not simply result in cost savings, but will also raise questions about the areas that audit should look at, and also how audit makes sense of what it is finding (through more robust root cause analysis, for example). This challenge is not simply about a resistance to lean ways of working per se, but about the problem of managers being really open to being challenged by audit on matters that are close to their own daily ways of working.

Finally, it is worth saying that even when a CAE seeks to implement lean ways of working, improving the approach to planning and enhancing the audit methodology to incorporate them, operating with a lean mindset can be a significant challenge for some auditors, who have a more step-by-step compliance mindset in relation to their work. Norman Marks, an internal audit thought leader, offers the following reflection:

> When you hire people you need to train them. Not only do you have to train them to think, but you have to break the shackles that bind them. They are actually weighed down and handcuffed and chained to stop them from thinking for themselves, and exercising their own judgment. We've got to tackle this as an internal audit profession.

Sometimes Staffing Changes are Needed

It should therefore not be a surprise for readers to learn that when implementing a lean internal audit approach, it is sometimes necessary to go beyond training and coaching to refresh the staffing of the audit function, since not everyone finds lean ways of working to their liking. This can mean, as it did with the GIA function of AstraZeneca, recruiting a number of non-audit staff into the internal audit function in order to create a more multidisciplinary approach to audit work. This approach helps to make audit work more relevant and impactful in a wider business context.

The Future of Lean Auditing

I personally regard the adoption of lean ways of working by members of the internal audit profession to be a sensible development for auditors seeking to add value and deliver more for less. Likewise, for lean practitioners, I regard the extension of lean ways of working into this activity to be a natural extension of lean ways of working to another "back office" area (such as lean finance or lean administration). Thus the dynamic we should see will hopefully be a "pull" from internal audit wanting to improve its value/productivity balance, alongside a "push" from general management and lean practitioners interested in expanding the benefits of lean ways of working into audit and other governance, control, and compliance activities.

However, at present I do not see any *systematic* uptake by the whole auditing profession of lean ways of working. This is partly due to the perception, mindset, and staffing challenges discussed earlier, as well as the fact that the internal audit profession is in very different stages of its evolution across different parts of the world (impacted by history, culture, and the presence of cost pressures (or not) and significant regulatory scrutiny (or not)).

However, I will conclude by saying that I hope to see lean professionals taking a greater interest in internal auditing. I think internal audit can offer some powerful perspectives on the way organizations operate from a gemba perspective. Additionally, at its best, internal audit can offer some very powerful value-adding insights to managers and lean practitioners when 1) working on high-profile, strategic, risk, and value areas, and 2) there is robust root cause analysis of the underlying reasons for performance shortcomings. Here I must close this chapter with the reflection that even if it is true that lean has an image problem within the internal audit profession at present, I must accept that internal audit probably has an even greater image problem—and not just with lean professionals! However, I hope that, in some small way, this chapter has helped to make a contribution to shifting readers' perspectives about what internal auditing is—or at least what it might be!

Case Study: Lean Audit Reporting at AstraZeneca

AstraZeneca plc is a leading biopharmaceuticals company created in 2000 when the Swedish company Astra merged with the UK company Zeneca plc. It is a UK listed company and has had an internal audit function since it was founded.

At the time of the lean audit initiative (in 2005) a range of new ways of working were put in place, notably an enhanced approach to audit planning (looking at risk and assurance requirements), a streamlined audit methodology, and shorter, more impactful reporting to managers and senior stakeholders.

Beyond simply streamlining internal audit reports, consultation with key stakeholders (under-pinned by kano analysis) revealed that there was more to be done to ensure that, from an overall perspective, the results of internal audits could be more easily digested and acted on.

After consultation with senior executives and board members, this led to a change in the way audit results were rated, as well as the way they were presented in digest form.

In the past a process that was judged as "poor" by internal audit would be rated "red," whereas a process that "required improvement" might be rated "amber." This would lead to many discussions about audit reports that were rated red and relatively fewer for the amber-rated audit results. However, the red-rated issue might actually be of lesser organizational significance than the amber issue.

As a result, the internal audit team agreed with stakeholders that audit results should be differentiated between 1) the severity of the issues that had been found in terms of process/control effectiveness (e.g. "how bad?") and 2) the organizational impact of the area in question (e.g. "how big?").

As a result of this change a weak purchasing process, for example, could be rated as a "poor" (with the color code red), but nonetheless be rated as "medium" impact because of, for example, limited impact on the organization as a whole, or on customer relationships. In contrast an assignment might uncover that a processes or project that was only in need of development (with an amber rating), might still receive a "high" impact assessment because of the importance of the area in question. A high impact area might concern a customer service process, the progress of a strategic project, or an issue with reputational implications.

The new rating approach of both "how big?" and "how bad?" ensured that 1) high impact issues were always discussed as a priority whether they were rated red or amber, and 2) poorly controlled (red-rated) issues were judged by impact as well. This meant that a poorly controlled process would still be rated as red, even if it was not of high organizational importance. This had the spin-off benefit of meaning that a poorly controlled issue of lesser overall organizational impact would not have its rating "diluted" simply because it did not have a high organizational impact. This was particularly helpful when looking at trends across units.

This new approach to reporting was featured as one of the audit best practices in its publication *Business Partnership Redefined* by the Audit Director Roundtable of the Corporate Executive Board in 2007. It has gained increasing interest from internal audit functions that want to ensure senior stakeholders can properly judge what they should and should not be concerned about in business impact terms and not simply through audit ratings.

References

ACCA (2014). *ACCA Commentary on ISA 200 Professional Skepticism.*

Audit Commission (2009). *Taking it on Trust*, UK Audit Commission. Available at: http://archive. auditcommission.gov.uk/auditcommission/subwebs/publications/studies/studyPDF/3523.pdf (accessed July 2016).

Audit Director Roundtable (2007). *Business Partnership Redefined,* Audit Director Roundtable, Corporate Executive Board.

Dann, C., Le Merle, M. and Pencavel, C. (2012). *The Root Causes of Value Destruction: How Strategic Resiliency Can Help*, Booz & Co. Available at: http://static1.squarespace.com/static/5481bc79e4b01c4bf3ceed80/t/54e5009de4b0f2941442ff1a/1424294045993/BoozCo_The-Root-Causes-of-Value-Destruction.pdf (accessed July 2016).

Financial Reporting Council (2015). *Promoting Audit Quality*. Available at: https://frc.org.uk/Promoting-audit-quality.aspx (accessed July 2016).

HM Treasury (2006). Thinking about risk: Managing your risk appetite. A practitioner's guide. Available at: www.gov.uk/government/uploads/system/uploads/attachment_data/file/191520/Managing_your_risk_appetite_a_practitioners_guide.pdf (accessed July 2016).

IIA (2013a). *International Standards for the Professional Practice of Internal Auditing (Standards)*, The Institute of Internal Auditors. Available at: https://na.theiia.org/standards-guidance/Public%20Documents/IPPF%202013%20English.pdf (accessed July 2016).

IIA (2013b). *IIA Position Paper: The Three Lines of Defense in Effective Risk Management and Control*, The Institute of Internal Auditors. Available at: https://na.theiia.org/standards-guidance/Public%20Documents/PP%20The%20Three%20Lines%20of%20Defense%20in%20Effective%20Risk%20Management%20and%20Control.pdf (accessed July 2016).

Netland, T. H. (2013). Exploring the phenomenon of company-specific production systems: One-best-way or own-best-way? *International Journal of Production Research, 51*(4), 1084–1097.

Paterson, J. (2013). How assured am I? Available at: http://accaiabulletin.newsweaver.co.uk/accaiabulletin/18ra51rsuag?opc=false&s= (accessed July 2016).

Paterson, J. (2015). *Lean Auditing*, Hoboken, NJ, John Wiley & Sons.

16

LEAN REMANUFACTURING

Elzbieta Pawlik, Winifred Ijomah, and Jonathan Corney

Introduction

"How do I apply lean methods in my remanufacturing organization?" is a question many executives and managers ask themselves. Since the literature on using lean tools in production environments is usually focused on original equipment manufacturers (OEMs), its application in commercial remanufacturing is often unreported. This chapter fills a gap in the literature with a brief overview of how remanufacturers can translate manufacturing-oriented lean tools and principles into their processes. The authors also discuss the challenges and opportunities that are peculiar to lean remanufacturing operations.

What is Remanufacturing?

Continued strains on the planet's resources, limited sites for product disposal, and the introduction of new environmental legislation have resulted in a growing interest in material and product recovery options. One of the most promising and cost-effective options for establishing a low-carbon, circular economy is remanufacturing, which can bring back end-of-life products to an as-good-as-new condition in terms of quality, performance, and warranty (Ijomah et al., 2007). Usually, the process starts from the initial cleaning of used products (called cores), which are often dirty, to allow accurate assessment of their condition (Ijomah et al., 1999). Then, cores are disassembled so that individual components are obtained, cleaned, and carefully inspected to verify that they meet the required quality standards. Very often inspection is not a separate operation but rather carried out during the disassembly step. Those that do not meet expectations can be reprocessed via remanufacturing. Remanufacture of the components includes all activities that would bring worn parts to at least the original OEM specification (for example, surface grinding, welding, etc.). If this is not possible due to technological issues, economic reasons, or safety restrictions, the substandard components are put toward other product recovery options—i.e. recycling—and are replaced with new parts. When all required components are collected (including remanufactured parts and new components), the product can be reassembled. The entire product must then pass a final test to ensure that quality is at least equal to a newly manufactured, equivalent product. Figure 16.1 represents the remanufacturing process.

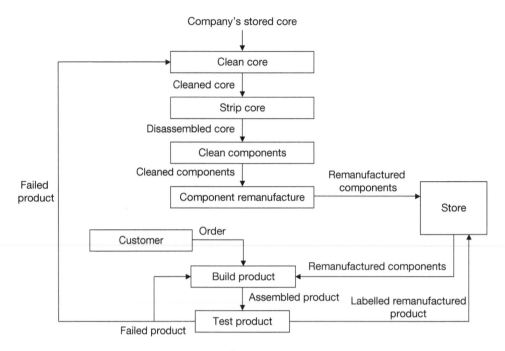

Figure 16.1 Generic remanufacturing process chart

Source: Ijomah (2002).

The remanufacturing process differs from conventional manufacturing. Thus, remanufacturers face different challenges from those experienced by conventional manufacturers. As such, Guide (2000) distinguishes the major challenges that influence and complicate production planning and control activities within the remanufacturing industry. These are explained below.

Uncertainty in the Timing and the Quantity of Returns

The product returns are highly uncertain in terms of time and quantity of available cores for remanufacturing, which is mainly caused by the uncertain nature of the life of the products. The fact that the numbers and delivery times of returned cores cannot be controlled by remanufacturers forces them to keep a higher level of inventory to protect against the variability in supply and demand.

Need to Balance Returns with Demand

To avoid excessive inventory, which generates costs, while simultaneously having sufficient stock to meet customer expectations, remanufacturers have to balance returns and demand rate. It requires extra effort that includes not only core acquisition (which includes identifying the potential source of cores, establishing preferences, etc.), but also coordination in the purchasing of replacement parts that are dependent on the expected volume and condition of cores. Moreover, all of the production decisions regarding resource planning also depend on core acquisition and timing.

Disassembly of Returned Products

Returned product has to be disassembled first, before being handed to the next remanufacturing operation. The result of this stage impacts on many activities such as purchasing new components, scheduling and resource planning. It becomes even more difficult when the products have not been designed with disassembly in mind, as components can be damaged or destroyed during disassembly. This leads to less predictable material recovery rates and generates more waste. Moreover, as there is no evidence that existing automated techniques can be used during disassembly, this also makes this task very labor intensive with highly variable processing times.

Uncertainty in Materials Recovered from Returned Items

The remanufacturers have to acquire the replacements for parts that cannot be reused from cores. The process is further complicated because it is difficult to predict the rate of material recovery before the product is disassembled. For example, two identically returned items may contain very different sets of parts that are either currently in the expected condition or can be returned to it.

Requirement for Reverse Logistics Network

This challenge addresses the requirements regarding the collection and movement of goods from end users to remanufacturers. A number of decisions have to be made that involve the number and location of take-back centers, the transportation method, etc.

Complication of Material-matching Restrictions

Complicated material-matching requirements define the situation whereby some products have their own unique serial and part number, and it is important to reassemble the same components. Moreover, sometimes products remain in the possession of customers who require the same unit to be returned. This complicates resource planning, shop floor control, and material management.

Routing Uncertainty and Processing Time Uncertainty

This is a consequence of the different condition of cores. The same components taken from different products might require different processes to be recovered and even different degrees of treatment for these operations. The condition of the components is dependent on both user habits and the repair, remanufacture, or reconditioning history. Very often, such activities are carried out without adhering to a specification, which results in mistakes such as wrongly painted surfaces. The consequential effect is more operations and time required to correct the mistakes.

These make the remanufacturing process less stable and less predictable than conventional manufacturing and require high levels of inspection and testing to achieve high quality products. This can lead to higher costs and longer remanufacturing lead times (Pawlik et al., 2013). Despite the existing challenges, remanufacturing has experienced rapid development during the past decade.

Lean Remanufacturing

The application of the lean manufacturing approach within a remanufacturing context—termed "lean remanufacturing"—has only recently gained the attention of researchers and practitioners (Pawlik et al., 2013). However, although slim, the reported work does suggest that the combination of remanufacturing and lean principles offers a good opportunity to increase process efficiencies within the remanufacturing industry (Kucner, 2008). A significant component of lean is the concept of value. Therefore, it is important to reconsider the commonly held paradigms of the value-added and non-value-added activities with regard to the remanufacturing context. There is a need to take a bigger-picture view of the value of waste, as what might be considered waste by a customer is actually valuable for the remanufacturing business. Remanufacturing is clearly adding value to the products, which were meant to be discarded in terms of life cycle value. However, it is important to look closely into the inefficiencies that occur during the process.

Excess inventory is one of the most significant wastes in remanufacturing. Indeed, most remanufacturers report that they struggle with the excess inventory of cores, work in process (WIP), and remanufactured products. Remanufacturers do not have influence over when a product will be returned to the facility, therefore forcing them to keep a higher level of the inventory against the variability in supply and demand (Guide, 2000). In many instances, the remanufacturers don't examine and refresh their inventories to remove the obsolete products. They want to keep them "just in case." Moreover, because the quality of the components can only be uncovered when the product is disassembled, remanufacturers prefer to do that early in the remanufacturing process which results in high WIP (Kucner, 2008). In addition, the uncertain quality of the components results in imprecise estimates of the times required to carry out operations. As a strategic buffer against this variability, many remanufacturers maintain significant-level inventories between operations.

In remanufacturing, some of the operations do not add value. Indeed, it has been observed that a higher percentage of operations that transform the product (but do not add value for the final customer) occur in remanufacturing than in conventional manufacturing. For example *inspection*, being a crucial stage for the remanufacturing process (Errington and Childe, 2013), has been identified as adding no value (Kucner, 2008). This is unfortunate because remanufacturing always requires 100 percent inspection, in contrast to conventional manufacturing where sampling methods are often used (Brent and Steinhilper, 2004). Another essential step in the remanufacturing process, *disassembly,* has been identified as an operation that is not adding value for the final customer and indeed might even be seen as a reduction of the inherent value of used products (Kucner, 2008).

Compared with the literature on conventional manufacturing, there is relatively little in the academic literature relating to the application of lean to remanufacturing. The first reported study of lean remanufacturing was presented by Amezquita and Bras (1996), which focused on an independent automotive remanufacturer of automobile clutches. This research compared a remanufacturing process that contains traditional craft and mass production practices with lean remanufacturing practices. One major benefit observed was the elimination of the non-value-added operations, resulting in enormous cost savings. Indeed, this research shows that the effectiveness of the remanufacturing process can be improved through the development of lean automation techniques.

Kucner (2008) claims that lean production tools and techniques can be applied to remanufacturing; however, there is not a single "best" lean solution. Specific solutions must be tailored to particular remanufacturing contexts. He examined four types of remanufacturing process, ranging from high product variability to low product variability. In each of these case studies the implementation of lean methods significantly improved performance, particularly in developing internal process stability, built-in quality, and just-in-time production. Fargher (2007) and Pawlik et al. (2013) also confirmed that the application of lean manufacturing within remanufacturing operations can bring significant benefits including a reduction in lead time, reduced WIP, improved on-time shipments, increased utilization of floor space, improved quality, and increased production control (Pawlik et al., 2013).

Sundin (2006) used the "rapid plant assessment" tool—a unique assessment tool used to assess plant performance, which helps to identify where the opportunities for improvement are—to conduct case studies in five companies (from different remanufacturing sectors). The results of this work showed that the investigated remanufacturers performed well in the following categories: "customer satisfaction," "people teamwork," "skill level and motivation," "ability to manage complexity and variability," and "quality system development." He identified also that, in most companies, categories such as "visual management deployment," "product flow," "space use," "material movements," together with "inventory and WIP level," presented below-average or poor performance and needed to be improved to make the company more "lean."

With regard to material flow, Hunter and Black (2007) investigated cellular layout in remanufacturing. They proposed a cellular layout for the recovery of product environment and claim that this solution can help to achieve a higher level of productivity and increased quality of remanufactured products. However, to maintain the flow and be able to use cellular layouts in remanufacturing, it is important to supply sufficient volume and frequency of return products (one of the remanufacturing challenges). Other researchers have also noticed existing restrictions and difficulties with the application of established lean tools and methods within the remanufacturing environment. Pawlik et al. (2013) identified that in the automotive sector, the uncertainties involved with incoming cores are a key issue influencing the probability of successful implementation. A similar conclusion was reported by Östlin and Ekholm (2007) regarding a toner cartridge remanufacturer. It was observed that the variable processing time and uncertainties in materials recovered limited the implementation of lean approaches. Moreover, Amezquita and Bras (1996) noticed that because of the stochastic nature of returned products, traditional remanufacturing processes are difficult to standardize.

Although there is relatively little in the academic literature relating to the application of lean philosophies to remanufacturing, practitioners do appear to be exploiting the concepts where possible. Indeed, some of the companies, particularly OEMs, are obligated to introduce lean within their facilities according to corporation policies and procedures.

Challenges and Opportunities

The main aim is to focus on challenges and opportunities within the processes and areas where a different view is required compared with conventional manufacturing. A more complete picture is presented, briefly discussing the similarities between different areas. Many people perceive lean as a set of tools and principles for eliminating waste, forgetting that "people are at the center of the Toyota Production System house" (Liker et al., 2008). Engaging all individuals is crucial in driving continuous improvement. Creating a lean culture in the organization requires strong leadership with managers who understand the lean concept, coupled with the will and capability to move forward. Within a remanufacturing environment, it was frequently observed that managers believe the lean concept is applicable only to conventional manufacturing. Consequently, the diverse problems arising in remanufacturing environments (described earlier in this chapter) coupled with a lack of, or at least limited, knowledge of the opportunities for application of lean in their operations discourage managers from beginning lean initiatives. However, this is an unnecessarily negative view. The following section reviews the challenges and opportunities of applying lean tools in remanufacturing operations.

The 5S method is often a starting point for that journey (Petersson et al., 2010). This is a process that allows managers to create a well-organized and functional workplace where there is a *place for everything and everything in its place*. The primary purpose of the first "S" is to sort the tools and materials within the workplace in order to separate those frequently used from those rarely or never used. However, in remanufacturing where there is a higher variety of products compared with conventional manufacturing, this approach results in a need to keep many different tools in the workplace. Reducing the number of tools can cause *waste in motion* as a result of frequently needing to pick up tools from the store when required (Pawlik et al., 2013). Uncertainty in the quality of incoming cores causes difficulty in producing consistent results over time. In conventional manufacturing, managers remove as much variation as possible from the process. However, in remanufacturing, managers will need to deal with a certain level of variation. The variety does not, however, render lean tools inapplicable. For example, value stream mapping is a diagrammatic technique which illustrates all the activities required to bring a product from order to delivery. It aids understanding of the inherent complexities involved with the process and highlights waste. Similarly, a *current-state map* is a team effort that is carried out by the people who are involved in the process to characterize the current conditions. The *future-state map* introduces the opportunities for improvement recognized in the current-state map and represents a shared vision of a lean future state (Lean Enterprise Institute, 2003). Remanufacturing, strongly affected by variations in products and their quality, is much more complex than conventional manufacturing and, consequently, it is much more difficult to create a map. Depending on a component's condition, different operations are needed. The associated map might therefore be one of several variants available for each product family depending on the condition of cores/components.

Remanufactured products often add their own unique serial and part numbers. To ensure parts will not be mixed during the process, remanufacturers build *kits*. In these kits are individually separated components that are related to the same unit which are kept together in the same basket. Introducing the standardization of kits appears to be an advantageous opportunity for remanufacturers. Defining standards in terms of the work required to remanufacture as light, medium, and heavy also helps to reduce levels of uncertainty involved with the different conditions of products/components. Even though it is difficult to cover all aspects relating to existing variations, some sort of standardization can be achieved in the remanufacturing process. *All operations, no matter how creative or unpredictable, include a large amount of repetitive activities* (Petersson et al., 2010).

So, despite the variety encountered in remanufacturing, there is still an amount of repetitive work that presents opportunities for standardization. Even if not all possibilities can be covered, it still contributes to reducing variations in the system. When something is outside the standard, it provides information about the extremes of the process. Standards describe the best currently known way to perform an activity, which means that the workforce shares the knowledge that also contributes to learning. This is particularly important as remanufacturing relies heavily on human experiences compared with conventional manufacturing. According to Graupp and Wrona (2006), 5 to 10 percent of every work task embodies tackling "tricky parts" which require "know-how" skills gained through years of experience. Within the remanufacturing environment, this percentage might be substantially higher because of the high variability of the condition of cores. Indeed, it has been observed that the inspection process can only be carried out by skilled and experienced employees. In other words, identifying the condition of a component as "good enough" to be remanufactured needs years of experience.

The *Training Within Industry* (TWI) methods are a series of training programs developed during World War II allowing US companies to hire and train huge numbers of new employees to replace those who had gone to war. The TWI methods describe *standard work instructions* that should consist of not only major steps which are common-sense reminders of what is essential to do the work correctly, safely, and conscientiously, but also key points (illustrated by pictures or drawings) and reasons for them (Graupp and Wrona, 2006). They are called "key points" as they are essential pieces of information that make the work easy to do. Even though TWI methods describe standard work instructions as being effective during the teaching process, in the remanufacturing environment it was noticed that they might be successfully used in daily operations. Skills required in the remanufacturing environment are developed over time by employees, which shows the importance of taking part during the developmental processes of creating standard work instructions. Identifying the so-called "tricks" would perhaps be the most important and difficult task because employees very often don't want to share their knowledge and experiences. In addition, standardized work instructions in the remanufacturing environment often also cover acceptability criteria for the components, which are used to direct the operators on how to do the job. This can help in the decision-making process, especially for inexperienced employees or when new products are introduced to the facility.

Given the above, there is no doubt that the lean philosophy can be implemented within the remanufacturing environment; however, the question that inevitably arises is concerned with the improvement of that application. To be most effective, what is essential is a clear understanding of the underlying differences between lean remanufacturing and lean manufacturing.

Case Study: Lean Remanufacturing in Caterpillar

Caterpillar is both an OEM and successful remanufacturer with more than 30 years of expertise. The company as a whole recycles and remanufactures over 50,000 tons of used products per year (around 2.2 million end-of-life products). The operations are spread all over the world, amounting to 17 remanufacturing facilities that undertake remanufacture of medium- to heavy-duty machinery. As an OEM remanufacturer Caterpillar has access to the technical information on each and every component, and controls the aftermarket and intellectual property. The UK-based facility employs around 300 employees who are dedicated to remanufacturing. Within this facility, engines (mostly diesel), transmissions, gearboxes, oil pumps, water pumps, cylinder heads, cylinder packs, and individual engine components are remanufactured. Once a returned core arrives at the facility, it is disassembled so components are separated, losing their original identity. Usually, used products are very dirty, and so it is important to clean components to facilitate accurate assessment. Each element is inspected against strict engineering specifications to determine if it can be effectively salvaged. Accepted components are then reprocessed through advanced salvage techniques or directly reused. Those assessed as having satisfactory functionality move on to the reassembly area where new components are delivered as well. Here, products are reassembled, with each product having to pass a final inspection. If the required specification is matched, the product can be painted and shipped to the customer with an as-new warranty. The product is packaged in a way that clearly identifies it as remanufactured and not "new," where the term "new" describes newly manufactured using all virgin components (i.e. conventionally manufactured). The overview of the remanufacturing process is presented in Figure 16.2.

Lean manufacturing methods were first introduced into the company in 2005. Since then the principles and tools have been gradually implemented on a broader scale. Introducing value stream mapping was one of the first tasks undertaken by the lean team. It provided a good starting point for the company to describe and understand the inherent complexities involved with the remanufacturing process and highlighted wastes. The current-state map was the first map that was created within the facility. It showed all the processes, inventory, flow of information, etc., within the remanufacturing facility. As soon as the managers started to be more aware of the actual flow of material and information through the process, they saw numerous examples of waste and opportunities for improvements. As a result, the plant's layout was significantly changed.

Standard work instructions are of particular importance for the company during the visual inspection process. According to Errington and Childe (2013), the inspection step is crucial for

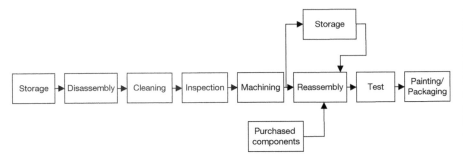

Figure 16.2   An overview of the remanufacturing process within Caterpillar

remanufacturing. The incorrect assessment of a core, or component, can cause unnecessary additional operational costs. As remanufacturing is strongly affected by variation in products and their quality, those tasked with assessment require precise knowledge of each variation. Standard work instructions are placed at the workstations and display sample components with given visual and written descriptions of the critical areas for inspecting as well as the acceptable criteria. They are located near to the inspection, machining, and assembly areas. This means that if an operator is unsure of whether the component he or she receives is good enough to remanufacture, he or she can check it at the work instruction. This also serves to remind operators of the importance of quality.

Caterpillar also implemented visual management displays and controls within the facility's most critical areas. It provides clear information on how the most critical areas operate. The visual display boards introduced included section boards (display metrics specific to the section in which they are located) and facility boards (display metrics for the whole facility) to measure, communicate, and control the following metrics: people (largely safety and training); quality (warranty to sales, test rejects, etc.); speed (on-time delivery, performance to *takt* time, etc.); and cost (unplanned overtime, etc.). The top 10 most common defects are also presented on the section metrics boards. All of these visual displays are used to aid the machine operator in the lean process and act as a reminder of the most prevalent quality issues as part of general communications. They make problems visible and allow all employees to quickly notice if a condition is in a normal or abnormal state. Employees have a meeting with managers every day, in which they discuss the previous day's production and the coming day's production, and disseminate any local or corporate information such as visits to the factory. There is also the opportunity for employees to voice comments and give feedback to their manager. Each identified problem is investigated and resolved by using the Ishikawa diagram, five whys, and histograms.

The interviews with managers also identified that Caterpillar has implemented standard work for all remanufacturing operations—some general (for example, for cleaning and inspecting bolts) and some specific to a particular product (for example, remanufacturing a cylinder head). They also have *standardized work* for other processes such as machine maintenance and daily operator checks. This means they can give a standard to the operator but if additional salvage/activities are required they cannot always cover it in the documentation. For example, a part might need additional (and not necessarily cost-effective) work because it is not possible to buy new parts (the engine is not in current production) or because the lead time for the new part is too long. In such a case, sometimes other similar used parts are adapted to make the part that is required.

To make sure that every machine is able to perform when required, Caterpillar has implemented *total productive maintenance* (TPM) for critical machines. Consequently, all employees, in a systematic way, are involved in maintenance routine, improvement projects, and simple repairs. To evaluate how effectively this equipment is used, the *overall equipment effectiveness* (OEE) is measured.

All these activities have improved the operations within Caterpillar by:

- Reducing work in process,
- Increasing production control, and
- Providing better service (to increase ability to meet deadlines).

Despite the advantages gained from implementing lean manufacturing tools and principles, it was detected that individual processes are unstable due to the uncertain condition of cores. It is also difficult to determine cycle time—the time required to produce a part or complete a process, as timed by actual measurement—for each operation. Components have to go through different operations to meet the required specification. Some of them need more time to pass each step and in some cases some operations are omitted. Additionally, sometimes there is a need to wait for a new component, which causes a delay in a reassembly step, thereby causing waste in waiting and unnecessary transportation. The pull system within operations is difficult to apply because of the high variability and low repeatability of products.

It was observed that there was a high inventory level of used products. This is a result of the uncertainty in the quantity and timing of incoming cores, i.e. difficulties in predicting the types of cores and when they will arrive at the facility. During the interviews it was found that implementation of 5S is also difficult, since operations on various components are carried out at the same workplace. As a result, there is a need to keep many different tools at a workstation, not all of which are required regularly. However, reducing the number of tools can cause waste in motion as a result of continuously picking up tools from the store when required. Returned products are usually dirty, making it difficult to keep workplaces clean.

Caterpillar has benefited widely from the application of lean within the remanufacturing environment. Following the idea that small, continuous improvements create long-lasting results, the company will implement a *kaizen* program, where, on an everyday basis, employees will be able to introduce improvements. In addition to the tangible benefits, employees will become more engaged with the wider culture and company as a whole.

References

Amezquita, T. and Bras, B. (1996). Lean remanufacture of an automobile clutch. In: *Proceedings of First International Working Seminar on Reuse*, Eindhoven, The Netherlands, p. 6.

Brent, A. C. and Steinhilper, R. (2004). Opportunities for remanufactured electronic products from developing countries: Hypotheses to characterise the perspectives of a global remanufacturing industry. In: *AFRICON, 2004. 7th AFRICON Conference in Africa, 2*, IEEE, pp. 891–896.

Errington, M. and Childe, S. (2013). A business process model of inspection in remanufacturing. *Journal of Remanufacturing, 3*(1), 1–22.

Fargher, J. S. W., Jr. (2007). *Lean Manufacturing and Remanufacturing Implementation Tools*, Rolla, University of Missouri.

Graupp, P. and Wrona, R. J. (2006). *The TWI Workbook: Essential Skills of Supervisors*, New York, Productivity Press.

Guide, V. D. R., Jr. (2000). Production planning and control for remanufacturing: Industry practice and research needs. *Journal of Operations Management, 18*(4), 467–483.

Hunter, S. L. and Black, J. T. (2007). Lean remanufacturing: A cellular case study. *Journal of Advanced Manufacturing Systems, 6*(2), 129–144.

Ijomah, W. L. (2002). A Model-based Definition of the Generic Remanufacturing Business Process. Ph.D. dissertation, University of Plymouth, UK.

Ijomah, W. L., Bennett, J. P. and Pearce, J. (1999). Remanufacturing: Evidence of environmentally conscious business practice in the UK. In: Yoshikawa, H., Yamamoto, R., Kimura, F., Suga, T. and Umeda, Y. (eds), *Proceedings of the First International Symposium on Environmentally Conscious Design and Inverse Manufacturing*, Tokyo, Japan, February 1–3, 1999, pp. 192–196.

Ijomah, W. L., McMahon, C. A., Hammond, G. P. and Newman, S. T. (2007). Development of design for remanufacturing guidelines to support sustainable manufacturing. *Robotics and Computer-Integrated Manufacturing, 23*(6), 712–719.

Kucner, R. J. (2008). A Socio-technical Study of Lean Manufacturing Deployment in the Remanufacturing Context, Ph.D. dissertation, University of Michigan.

Lean Enterprise Institute (2003). *Lean Lexicon: A Graphical Glossary for Lean Thinkers*, Brookline, MA, Lean Enterprise Institute.

Liker, J. K. and Hoseus, M. (2008). *Toyota Culture: The Heart and Soul of the Toyota Way*, New York, McGraw-Hill.

Östlin, J. and Ekholm, H. (2007). Lean production principles in remanufacturing: A case study at a toner cartridge remanufacturer. In: *Proceedings of the 2007 IEEE International Symposium on Electronics & the Environment,* IEEE, pp. 216–221.

Pawlik, E., Ijomah, W. and Corney, J. (2013). Current state and future perspective research on lean remanufacturing: Focusing on the automotive industry. In: Emmanouilidis, C., Taisch, M. and Kiritsis, D. (eds), *Advances in Production Management Systems. Competitive Manufacturing for Innovative Products and Services SE-54.* IFIP Advances in Information and Communication Technology, Berlin and Heidelberg, Springer, pp. 429–436.

Petersson, P., Johansson O., Broman, M., Blucher, D. and Alsterman, H. (2010). *Lean: Turn Deviations into Success!* Bromma, Sweden, Part Development AB.

Sundin, E. (2006). How can remanufacturing processes become leaner? In: *CIRP International Conference on Life Cycle Engineering*, Leuven, *31*, pp. 429–434.

17

LEAN AND GREEN

Keivan Zokaei, Ioannis Manikas, and Hunter Lovins

Introduction

Lean often focuses on waste (non-value-adding processes) reduction from the system, which leads to cost minimization. It also strives for continuous process improvement to achieve level scheduling and economy of scale in the operation. This enables organizations to augment the quality of the product and improved services by transforming the traditional batch and queue production system (Larson and Greenwood, 2004). On the other hand, the green supply chain emphasizes sustaining the organization, people, and future generations. This is based on 3Ps— people, profit, and planet—and strives for reduction in the use of natural resources and CO_2 emissions and for recycling used products; it also applies the reduction of environmental risks and improving ecological efficiency (Carvalho and Cruz-Machado, 2009).

Lean refers to "nimble" or "with less fat" and is a Western interpretation of the Toyota Production System and the Toyota Way. The Toyota Production System is generally associated with the elimination of all types of waste from a process in order to increase the throughput of the whole system. Womack and Jones (1996) further elaborated the idea by discussing how lean thinking can be applied beyond the automotive sector.

The lean supply chain is about lean time reduction and value enhancement for customers; it follows the principles of just-in-time (JIT) and also strives for "zero inventory," although, as Grunwald and Fortuin (1992) pointed out, it is unrealistic to have zero inventory as this simply means zero output. Some inventory would still remain at different stages of the supply chain such as the production and distribution systems. Supply chains should therefore push forward to set up *minimum reasonable inventory* (MRI). However, Simons and Taylor (2007) showed how the UK red meat industry failed to achieve leanness in the system due to the lack of deep supplier relationships ("*kiertsu*" in Japanese). They also brought forward the idea of extensive supplier relations to implement effective leanness in the supply chain.

The lean supply chain also promotes a pull system, for example by means of visual signaling systems such as *kanban*. In order to create a pull system, it is necessary to reach a smooth and predictable demand with low variety, and to strive for "continuous improvement" in the system (Naylor et al., 1999).

The concept of a sustainable supply chain is also known as the "triple bottom line" where three aspects are considered: people, profit, and planet. None of them is subject to compromise.

Therefore, supply chain strategies should reflect concerns with social issues like working conditions, human rights, and health conditions, and other environmental issues like usage of natural resources, energy, water, air, and the natural habitat and ecosystem, and most importantly maintain economic profitability and growth (Rao and Goldsby, 2009; Christopher and Holweg, 2011).

Integrating lean management with environmental sustainability practices is an idea that came to light recently, although both paradigms developed separately decades ago and have been in practice successfully in many organizations. Originally developed by the Toyota Motor Corporation, lean management strives to eliminate the waste (non-value-adding tasks, like overproduction and over processing, and waiting in terms of idle staff and machinery, etc.) from the system and is based upon the idea of JIT production. At the operational level it includes some mechanisms such as kanban (production starts with a "pull" signal), *takt* time (the rate of production matches the rate of sales in the market), 5S system (shop floor housekeeping), poke-yoke (error-free production), and SMED ("single-minute exchange of the dies" which is a changeover technique in the production system). All these mechanisms contribute to make the *lean supply chain* (Carvalho and Cruz-Machado, 2009; Stone, 2012). On the other hand, sustainability is based upon the 3Ps, people, profit, and planet, where reducing the environmental risk and improving ecological efficiency of organizations and other partners in the supply chain is the prime motive. Environmental sustainability involves reduction in CO_2 emissions at every stage of the supply chain and reduction in the consumption of natural resources such as water, land, or natural gas. Moreover, at the operational level it includes various concepts like sustainable design (product design), sustainable source (procurement from a sustainable source), sustainable production (fewer raw materials, by-product treatment etc.), sustainable delivery (local source, less carbon mileage), and sustainable return (end-of-product-life treatment, reverse logistics). It also incorporates practices like the 3Rs (reduce, reuse, and recycle), 5Rs (3Rs, redesign, and re imagine), and carbon and water footprint reduction from the upstream to the downstream components of the supply chain (Vermeulen and Seuring, 2009; Walker and Jones, 2012).

There could potentially be a clash between the two paradigms as lean is based upon the JIT system where small batch production and frequent delivery of raw materials are the norm, whereas the green supply chain emphasizes less transportation and fewer CO_2 emissions. Economic and environmental continuous improvements are usually located in separate organizational silos and sometimes are even in conflict with each other. Integrating them could be the biggest opportunity missed across most industries. There is a lot that the environmental movement can learn from the lean and quality community about people engagement, structures, and methods. Equally importantly, the lean community can find a new purpose and once again lead the continuous improvement of their organizations using environmental waste as a proxy for identifying key areas for economic progress. Hines (2010) argued that lean thinking must be green as it emphasizes waste reduction and reduces the amount of energy use and by-product waste. Therefore, it acts as a green chain. He also proposed a generic model to combine these two conflicting paradigms. Yet *greening* the supply chain does not necessarily involve only CO_2 reduction. However, some organizations try to "*green-wash*" it by only reducing the CO_2 emissions in the transportation stage, instead of investing in product innovation and green product design if the product (for example, an automobile) is going to produce high amounts of CO_2 emissions during its lifetime. The trade-offs and the boundaries of lean and green should therefore be analyzed and clearly marked (Dües et al., 2011).

Lean and Green Integration: A Governance Shift

Jonathon Porritt, founder of the Forum for the Future, argues that a governance shift is occurring in the field of sustainability, where governments are stepping back and businesses stepping forward to lead the change (Zokaei et al., 2013). Prior to the 2008 financial crisis, environmental policies of the US and the EU had an influence in the formulation of the strategic planning of several large companies, where, for example, political, economic, social, and technological (PEST) analysis was systematically used for business macro-environment analysis (OECD, 2011). In the post-crisis world fewer governments demonstrate real appetite for transformative economic policy of the sort necessary to reduce the risk of climate disruption. Nor do they demonstrate efforts to ensure that the billions of developing country residents get an equitable shot at sustainable prosperity, despite rhetorical concern for future generations, typically expressed by imposing austerity to reduce debt (Lovins and Cohen, 2012). For example, policy makers failed to make binding commitments at the Rio+20 Summit, resulting in the lowest common denominator consensus delivering few scalable benefits. In 2010, the UK Sustainable Development Commission (SDC) was axed as part of cutting down expenses. In the US, Republican energies to defund the entire Environmental Protection Agency risk even deeper structural shifts.

Simultaneously, private sector companies are cutting carbon emissions to enhance profitability, signing declarations to account for the value of nature, and safeguarding jobs by making their businesses more sustainable and more profitable. The proactive approach of leading-edge companies that put sustainability at the heart of what they do is inspiring. Greater sustainability has become a key economic driver for firms such as Toyota, Walmart, DuPont, Volvo, Sainsbury's, Tesco, Unilever, Marks & Spencer, General Electric (GE), Adnams, and Worldwide Fruit. All of these firms have invested heavily in greening their products and processes over the past few years.

On the other hand, small and medium enterprises (SMEs) are considered as central contributors to sustainable development. Sustainability strategies in SMEs have recently been investigated in the context of value creation and increase of innovation capacity (Moore and Manring, 2009; Klewitz et al., 2014). According to Lloyds corporate research (Lloyds, 2014), 25 percent of SMEs in the UK placed sustainability high on their list of priorities for 2014, and 30 percent of them expect to increase their investment in sustainable business practices over the next five years while still focusing on traditional green activities such as energy saving and recycling rather than broader areas such as supply chain management and purchasing. Consider the following examples:

- *DuPont*, one of the early leaders, committed itself to a 65 percent reduction in greenhouse gas emissions in the 10 years prior to 2010. By 2007, DuPont was saving $2.2 billion a year through energy efficiency, almost equivalent to its total declared profits for the same year (Russel, 2011).
- One of today's leaders, *Unilever*, plans to double its revenue over the next 10 years while halving the environmental impact of its products.
- *GE* is on track to reduce the energy intensity of its operations by 50 percent by 2015. Its Eco-magination project, if a separate company, would be Fortune 130.
- *Tesco* has announced that it will reduce emissions from stores and distribution centers by half by 2020 and that it will become an altogether zero-carbon business by 2050.
- *Walmart*, aiming at *zero waste*, claims to have diverted more than 80 percent of trash generated in its US operations from landfill. In 2010, Walmart announced it would cut total carbon emissions by 20 million metric tons by 2015 (Walmart, 2013).
- In the UK, *Sainsbury's* announced the "20×20 Sustainability Plan" as a cornerstone of its business strategy. So far it is on track against the plan. In April 2013, for example, it had already beaten a self-imposed target to reduce water consumption by 50 percent (Osborn, 2013).

- *Toyota*, in its Fifth Environmental Action Plan, committed to improve average fuel efficiency of its vehicles by 25 percent in all regions by 2015 compared with 2005. In production, it had already cut emissions per vehicle by 37 percent between 2001 and 2012 (Daihatsu, 2013; Toyota Motor Corporation, 2013; Pagliarella, 2014).

Since none of these companies joined Greenpeace, one may question why they show such a level of commitment to sustainable development. Their secret is in a simple yet powerful realization that their environmental and economic footprints are aligned. When physical waste is prevented, energy efficiency is increased and resource productivity is improved; this is when money is saved, profitability is improved, and competitiveness is enhanced. They are correcting decades of neglect to capture huge "quick win" opportunities, discovering that environmental wastes are a proxy for economic savings.

A Parallel Story from Quality Management

Lean thinkers discovered precisely this about the lean wastes of variation, overburden, over-production, and inventory: that they are key substitutes for economic development. The "greening industry" movement now stands where the "quality movement" was 40 years ago. Since then, the industry realized that quality can be improved through cheaper means. The quality movement, variably referred to as total quality management, Six Sigma, lean sigma, or just lean, found that there is no intrinsic dilemma between quality and cost.

When quality gurus Deming and Juran went to Japan in late 1940s and 1950s to help rebuild the war-torn economy, they were being overlooked in the triumphant West. In a devastated economy they started an industrial regeneration that allowed companies such as Toyota to become a benchmark for lean management. By the 1970s, as the West faced rising oil prices, the work of the quality gurus started gaining interest, mainly due to the constant growth and prosperity that the Japanese companies continued to achieve in spite of the oil crisis. During this period, European and US companies, seeking a way to regain profitability, found that the somewhat hazy know-how of the East was best distilled in the work of Phil Crosby. He not only contributed greatly to the promotion of the total quality movement with his accessible style and plain speech, but in his 1979 bestseller *Quality is Free* famously claimed that "quality is not a gift, but it is free" (Crosby, 1979).

Crosby, and the other quality gurus, defied conventional wisdom of the time that it must cost exponentially more to get to the highest levels of quality because each increment of quality has its own price. They pointed out that poor quality creates hidden costs, including the need for inspection, rework, scrap, delivery delays to the customer, and potential costs during product use. These typically dwarf what it might cost to implement systems and training to prevent defects in the first place. Thus enhanced quality had to be achieved. The costs to do so saved so much money by implementing more cost-effective production systems that the resulting quality was effectively free.

Equally, "the environment is free." Implementing more sustainable methods to make products and services reduces environmental impact as, counterintuitively, it brings lower costs. The reasons are the same ones that reinforced the "quality movement" of the 1960s to 1970s: low-quality products or services result in wasting time, energy, and resources. Making it right the first time is much more cost-effective and guarantees better customer satisfaction. In the same way, sustainable business means saving resources and energy, which in turn means better quality and much more cost-effective products. Waste generation and harmful emissions are eventually outcomes a company actually pays to incur, but from which, by all means, no benefit derives. These outputs should be better named as "unsalable production" (Lovins et al., 1999).

192

However, the environment is not a gift. As with the quality movement, prevailing paradigms that see environmental protection as a cost prevent executives from capturing better performance and lower costs. Just like the quality movement, the reasons behind leading-edge companies' attention to the environment is not the environment per se, but rather the business competitiveness that the new paradigm of sustainable business offers. The companies that move fastest to adopt "the environment is free" outlook will be the billionaires of tomorrow. *Greening your business is not just a "nice to have"—it is a "must have,"* just as lean and total quality have become a necessity for most businesses for decades.

More important, the benefits are additive. Businesses can implement more sustainable practices in combination with lean techniques. Recently one of us worked with the largest sandwich factory in the world. A team of great managers and shop floor staff set out to reduce waste. They used simple lean tools and techniques such as value stream mapping and A3 problem solving. They cut 1,000 tons of waste in just a few weeks in a very mature industry. They also saved nine million liters of water from going down the drain every year, and dramatically increased profits. The financial benefits were even more staggering.

However, there are several deeper paradigms that must be transformed before you can reap the benefits of combining lean and green. We have come across lean practitioners who have an unfortunate tendency to see environmental programs as a threat. Operational researchers came to a similar conclusion when they highlighted that complexity, measurability, and the social character of environmental problems may impose barriers to the interaction between operations and environmental management (Bloemhof-Ruwaard et al., 1995). Martínez-Jurado and Moyano-Fuentes (2014) identified a significant gap in research on social sustainability, especially in the area of *lean supply chain management.* This is pointless. Lean means doing more with less. Lean thinking supports green thinking and vice versa. So why are economic and environmental continuous improvements located in separate organizational silos and sometimes even in conflict with each other? Integrating them could be the biggest opportunity missed across most industries. There is much that the environmental movement can learn from the lean and quality community about people engagement, structures, and methods. Equally importantly, the lean community can find a new purpose and once again lead the continuous improvement of their organizations using environmental waste as a proxy for identifying key areas for economic progress.

What's the Size of the Opportunity for Realizing "the Environment is Free"?

Western manufacturers have made enormous productivity gains over the past two decades and continue to draw on lean methods for doing more with less and to counter the sharp productivity decline in the late 1980s and claims that, at the time, all manufacturing jobs would soon be off-shored to cheaper labor economies. According to the US Bureau for Labor Statistics, the manufacturing sector's indexed productivity doubled between 1992 and 2012 in terms of real output per hour of labor. According to BLS, the manufacturing sector's productivity in 1992 was 57.47 rising to 114.7 in 2012 in the United States (indexed to 2005). The manufacturing industry safeguarded millions of jobs by means of lean thinking, by adopting the new quality paradigm, and through the appropriate use of modern technologies to lower costs while enhancing value.

The macro- and microeconomic impacts of lean and the quality movement in preserving jobs and enhancing competitiveness are undeniable. However, the task is not complete. The "environment is free" movement offers huge opportunities to protect jobs against the continuing outsourcing trend, to fend off the more recent "robo-sourcing" trend (as termed by Al Gore in *The Future,* 2013), and to address critical challenges such as climate disruption. The "3% Report" published recently by the World Wildlife Fund and Carbon Disclosure Project (2013) shows that the economic prize for curbing carbon emissions in just the US economy is $780 billion between now and 2020 (net present value), rising to $190 billion a year by 2020. It puts the return on investment (ROI) for lean and green interventions at 233 percent. In the authors' own experience, this is conservative. Most organizations can achieve ROI of 1,000 percent or even higher when adopting the right behavioral and managerial changes.

McKinsey & Co. (Choi Granade et al., 2009) showed that energy efficiency is the single largest source of energy in the US, worth $130 billion per year. Some 47 studies from the likes of the Economist Intelligence Unit, Goldman Sachs, AT Kearney, Deloitte, MIT Sloan, and others show that companies that commit to such aspirational goals as zero waste, zero harmful emissions, and zero use of non-renewable resources are financially outperforming their competitors. Conversely, the DARA Group found that climate disruption is already costing $1.2 trillion annually, cutting global GDP by 1.6 percent. Unaddressed, this will double by 2030 (DARA, 2012).

Nonetheless, far too many companies still delay creating lean and green business systems, arguing that it will cost money or require hefty capital investments. They remain stuck in the "environment is cost" era.

Creating a Lean and Green Enterprise

In order to create a lean and green business system, there needs to be orchestration across all levels of managing an organization in order to balance efficiency gains and environmental friendliness in operations and products (Garza-Reyes, 2015). There is much more to creating a lean and green business system than just drawing upon a set of tools and techniques. Figure 17.1 demonstrates various aspects of creating a lean and green enterprise: strategy deployment, process management, supply chain collaboration, and leadership and people engagement. In what follows we discuss each area of the model through a short case study.

Toyota proved "quality is free." Can it prove that "the environment is free" too? The publication of *The Machine that Changed the World* in 1990 (Womack et al., 1990) was a wake-up

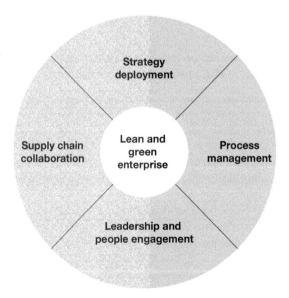

Figure 17.1   Creating a lean and green enterprise

call for most Western manufacturers. It benchmarked Japanese automakers against the rest of the world, showcasing Toyota's immense efficiency and quality lead over such Western car makers as GM and Ford. Toyota took only half as long as GM to manufacture a similar size vehicle, with a fraction of the inventory and a third of the defects (see Table 17.1). The term "lean," which was first popularized in the book, refers to Toyota's ability to do a lot more with substantially less. The Japanese had put "quality is free" into practice with ample proof that better quality did not cost more. In fact, it was far cheaper for the manufacturer, better appreciated by the customers and much more fulfilling for the employees. According to Kurdve et al. (2014), who investigated the integration between Toyota's specific lean-based improvement programs, such as the Toyota Production System (TPS), and formal management systems concerning the environment (EMS), quality (QMS), and occupational health and safety (OHS), incorporating environmental management systems into a company-specific production system (XPS) is an effective way towards continuous improvement, resulting in a holistic understanding and improved organizational performance.

More than 20 years after the publication of *The Machine that Changed the World*, we investigated if the cheapest and most efficient car manufacturers are also the "greenest." Responsible for 14 percent of all greenhouse gas (GHG) emissions worldwide (Stern, 2006), the transport industry has been pressed more than most other sectors of the economy to shift towards Kyoto Protocol target levels. Our research showed that Toyota—the holy grail of economic efficiency for decades—tops the green charts too (Zokaei et al., 2013). Industry benchmarks (Harbour Report, 2012) show that Toyota stays on the top of the economic performance charts for the same year (2012) in terms of productivity and quality. Table 17.2 illustrates a summary of our findings using

Table 17.1 Benchmarking of Toyota proved that quality is free

	GM Framingham, USA	NUMMI (Joint venture between Toyota and GM in Fremont, USA)	Toyota Takaoka, Japan
Assembly productivity (hours/car)	31	19	16
Assembly quality (defects/car)	135	45	45
Average inventory of parts (measure of delivery)	2 weeks	2 days	2 hours

Source: Womack et al. (1990, p. 83).

Table 17.2 Benchmarking Toyota's environmental performance vs main competitors

Year 2010	No. of staff	Revenue in $m	No. vehicles produced	Tons CO_2-e	Tons CO_2/ vehicle produced	Tons CO_2/ $m sale
Toyota	320,808	222,000	8,557,351	7,334,000	0.86	33.0
GM	209,000	135,592	8,476,192	7,863,406	0.93	58.0
Fiat S.P.A.	190,014	72,200	2,716,286	2,663,645	0.98	36.9
Volkswagen	399,381	162,851	7,341,065	7,700,000	1.05	47.3
Ford	164,000	128,954	4,988,031	5,300,000	1.06	41.1
Honda	181,876	120,270	3,643,057	4,000,000	1.10	33.3
Daimler (Mercedes)	260,100	130,900	2,410,021	3,699,102	1.53	28.3

Source: Zokaei et al. (2013, p. 90).

different "key indicators" for benchmarking. We benchmarked the environmental performance of various incumbents in the industry from different perspectives. Clearly, there are various sources of GHG emissions during the end-to-end life cycle of an automobile and it is hard to measure any given company's environmental performance, especially in an industry as complex as automotive.

Toyota has consistently reduced its total emissions, setting itself a target to cut emissions per unit of sales globally by 20 percent by 2010 against 2001 levels, and delivering 23 percent reduction from 2001 levels and 51 percent reduction from 1990 (Toyota Motor Corporation, 2011b).

No one familiar with the company is surprised. These improvements are rooted in its *kaizen* (continuous improvement) mentality. The day-to-day kaizen in Toyota is guided and driven by "five-year environmental action plans" that set tangible goals for all areas including production, facilities, transport, and offices, as well as specific regional targets for various plants. These targets are integrated into the company's "strategy deployment" mechanism or "*hoshin*" planning, which aligns the organization from top to bottom.

Toyota believes that managers must delegate as much authority as possible:

> That is the way to establish respect for humanity as your management philosophy. [Hoshin] is a management system in which all employees participate, from the top down and from the bottom up, and humanity is fully respected.

These are the words of Professor Kaoru Ishikawa, father of hoshin planning, in his book, *What is Total Quality? The Japanese Way* (1985, p. xiv).

Hoshin planning ensures that environmental goals are integrated into everyone's working life. Across all Toyota plants, there are cascading measures in place at all levels, from the top board to operators, to discern the correct direction. As stated in an interview with Steve Hope, general manager of Environmental Affairs and Corporate Citizenship, Toyota Motor Europe in Zokaei et al. (2013), when opportunities are identified Toyota employees apply five key performance indicator (KPI) criteria which are, in order of priority: safety, environment, quality, production, and cost. Hoshin planning is so deeply rooted in the notion of "respect for people" that Toyota members often exceed their targets and deliver results which are much more sustainable than in any organization in which targets are enacted by means of control or even bonuses.

As shown in Table 17.2, Toyota emits the lowest "tons of CO_2 per vehicle manufactured"— certainly a key measure for benchmarking environmental performance across the automotive sector. Toyota also tops the ranking in terms of "tons of CO_2 per dollar revenue," when Daimler (Mercedes), which predominantly assembles luxury vehicles sold at premium prices, is discounted. In this category, Toyota is closely rivaled by Honda and Fiat (which also owns luxury brands such as Ferrari, Maserati, and Alfa Romeo).

Toyota's leanness and greenness stem from the same corporate values. In an interview with a Toyota executive, Steve Hope told us:

> We have a role to exercise in relation to the society. We don't think we can manufacture what we want to manufacture independently of the impacts on the wider society. Our philosophy is that we are an integral part of the environment and we are fulfilling a need of society which is the desire for personal transportation.

Toyota's Guiding Principles, established in 1992 and available on Toyota's corporate website (www.toyota-global.com), are also clear: "pursue growth in harmony with the global community through innovative management."

Toyota's fifth Five Year Environmental Action Plan, the cornerstone of its sustainability commitment, begins with the following statement of purpose: "*Contributing to growth of sustainable society and earth through monozukuri, co-existing with the global environment, making cars and offering quality products and services*" (Toyota Motor Corporation, 2011a).

Monozukuri captures the true spirit of Toyota in relation to the concept of sustainability. The literal meaning of the word is "production." *Mono* is the thing which is made and *zukuri* means the act of making, but monozukuri implies more than simply making things. It can be best compared to the word "craftsmanship" in English, although in craftsmanship, the emphasis is on the craftsperson, whereas in monozukuri the person doing the making is de-emphasized and the attention is on the "thing" being made.

This subtle difference reflects the Japanese sense of responsibility for using "things" in production and their respect for the world around them, both animate and inanimate. In the Japanese tradition of monozukuri, the craftsperson takes great care using resources so as not to be wasteful. When an item or human effort is taken into use, there needs to be a benefit for the society as a result while, at the same time, the balance between production, resources, and society should be maintained.

Monozukuri is also about deeply respecting the individuals who do the job. As in craftsmanship, in monozukuri, workers "bring their mind to work" and are fully empowered and trained to deal with different situations, creating an elevated sense of ownership. There is no mindless repetition in monozukuri. Within Toyota, it is crucial for all workers not to be robbed of their right to "pride of workmanship" and to gain intrinsic satisfaction in what they do. In this concept, making products (or monozukuri) is also making people (or *hitozukuri*) because they are instilled with pride and passion for their jobs. Toyota's green vehicle technologies and other lean and green initiatives will not work without the full engagement of its people. Mutual trust, authority, empowerment, skills to make quality products, lifetime employment, and the inquisitive culture of *genchi genbutsu* (go see at workplace) are all tenets through which Toyota respects its people.

Monozukuri, therefore, is manufacturing that is in harmony with nature and is value-adding for the society. *You could even say monozukuri is the older sister of sustainable manufacturing.* Toyota's official website says:

> Toyota has always sought to contribute to society through the monozukuri philosophy—an all-encompassing approach to manufacturing. In its application of monozukuri to the production of automobiles, Toyota has pursued a sustainable method of making its cars ever more safe, environmentally friendly, reliable and comfortable.
>
> *(Toyota Global, 2015)*

Toyota's environmental performance is driven far more by its profound commitment to harmonious manufacturing (monozukuri) and its role in society as a value-adding corporate citizen, dating back to the precepts of the founding father, Sakichi Toyoda, than by environmental regulations. Derived from the founding fathers of Toyota, the company's core values stress a sense of duty to contribute to the development and the welfare of society at large rather than seeing the company just as a money-making machine. Compare this with the present day's banking culture!

Conclusion

The starting point for creating a lean and green business system is the mindset of senior managers. It is hard to deliver the type of results we have seen from leading-edge organizations such as

Toyota, Marks & Spencer, Tesco, and Adnams without executive commitment to integrating these two approaches to achieve the dual benefit of improved economic and environmental performance.

A starting point is the understanding that there is no trade-off between lean and green, that lean and green should be brought together in a symbiosis, as Toyota has done with its mono-zukuri approach. The next step is to create a whole business approach that focuses on the needs of customers, the business, the employees, and wider society, all at the same time. In achieving this integration, there is a great deal we can learn from a similar paradigm shift that occurred during the 1960s and 1970s across the Western world as managers came to realize that there was no trade-off between quality and cost, i.e. the *total quality movement*.

This requires a coherent strategy that is well developed and well deployed across all levels of the business. It also requires that continuous improvement is seen to be about the reduction of not just the classic economic wastes but also environmental wastes such as pollutants, landfill, and excess resource usage. This will mean bringing lean people together with environmental teams in a common function and improvement process.

The bottom line remains that the environment is free; but it is not a gift.

Case Study: Lean and Green in Adnams plc

Leadership and *people engagement* are the building block of creating a lean and green business system. Adnams plc, a UK-based brewery with a turnover of only around $80 million, is a great example of putting lean and green leadership and people engagement at the heart of business. The Adnams story proves the central role that committed, inspirational leadership can play in making fundamental changes to business operations through engaging staff and facilitating a genuinely bottom-up approach. The company engenders an enviable and widespread dedication and commitment to sustainable business at all levels. Across the company, team members lend their support willingly because they see top management's thorough commitment to the vision of building a more sustainable company for the long term.

The company has a long-standing history of putting a strong set of social and environmental values at its heart. These values, combined with ongoing innovation, have not only enabled substantial improvements in terms of environmental performance, but also generated quantitative and qualitative business benefits, principally in the form of cost savings and brand development. For example, while the UK beer market remains in long-term decline, Adnams has almost doubled its beer volumes produced since starting its lean and green journey in 1999. In 2011 and 2012, Adnams grew volumes by 7 percent and 4 percent respectively. In terms of people engagement, the business received an 88 percent response rate to its last staff opinion survey. Of this 88 percent, some 92 percent of respondents said they were either proud or very proud to work for the company. 92 percent rated sustainability as the company's most important value and some 94 percent were clear or very clear about what is expected of them in their role.

The business does not specifically talk about *corporate responsibility* (CR) or *corporate social responsibility* (CSR) and holds the view that if these acronyms need to be used any organization is treating such matters as an adjunct and is not truly embedding the approach within its operations. Over the past decade the company has been an outstanding example of green business activity, considerably reducing its impact on the wider physical environment and increasing its positive social and economic returns. The business sequestered in excess of 500 tons of CO_2 by using crops in the design and construction of its distribution center which boasts a green roof. The use of food waste as an energy source within its anaerobic digestion facility means that the business diverts 69,700 tons of CO_2 equivalent from landfill. In 2013, Adnams was on track to reduce its CO_2 emissions a further 6 percent. These and other environmental measures are reported to the main board of the company on a monthly basis.

Using innovative cutting-edge green technologies, Adnams has installed one of the most energy- and raw material-efficient breweries in Europe and constructed an eco-efficient distribution center (with the green roof described above); its anaerobic digester takes food waste from brewing, retailing, pubs, and hotels and turns it into bio-gas for injection into the national grid. The savings generated from not having to run any mechanical heating or cooling in its warehousing operation saves the business in the region of $160,000 per year and the commercial anaerobic digestion facilities should generate revenues of around $300,000. The joint venture company Adnams Bio Energy invested £1m (approx. $1.5m), so a straight payback was expected to be about 3.3 years. The facility cost more than this, with the additional monies being provided by European Regional Development Fund (ERDF) providing grants of around £1.1m ($1.65m) and the now defunct East of England Regional Development Agency (EEDA) providing a grant from its single pot of £900,000 ($1.35m). The total project cost has been £3m (approx. $4.5m).

It is the human element that drives the application of these ideas. The culture of the company encompasses value-based decision making from a deep conviction that long-term thinking and sustainability pays off. This has led to positive staff engagement in the whole process and a corporate-wide tenacity and determination to succeed. In 2012 the company won its second consecutive Queens Award for Sustainable Development in the United Kingdom. In 2013 it won the First Woman Award, a national competition run by the Confederation of British Industry (CBI), that recognized Adnams for the way it develops and progresses female careers. The person who collected this award on behalf of the company was Karen Hester. Currently the operations director for the organization, Karen used her skill, determination, and tenacity to progress from office cleaner to the boardroom during her tenure at Adnams, a further example of a progressive culture alive and well at Adnams that is working for the long term. According to the company CEO, the five principles of lean and green leadership at Adnams can be summarized as *value-based decision making, tenacity, challenge, proximity to workplace, and staff engagement.*

References

Bloemhof-Ruwaard, J. M., van Beek, P., Hordijk, L. and van Wassenhove, L. (1995). Interactions between operational research and environmental management. *European Journal of Operational Research, 85,* 229–243.

Carvalho, H. and Cruz-Machado, V. (2009). Integrating Lean, Agile, Resilience and Green Paradigms in Supply Chain Management (LARG_SCM), *Proceedings of the Third International Conference on Management Science and Engineering Management,* 3–14.

Choi Granade, H., Creyts, J., Derkach, A., Farese, P., Nyquist, S. and Ostrowski, K. (2009) *Unlocking Energy Efficiency in the US Economy,* McKinsey and Company. Available at: www.mckinsey.com/ ~/media/mckinsey/dotcom/client_service/epng/pdfs/unlocking%20energy%20efficiency/us_energy_ efficiency_exc_summary.ashx (accessed July 2016).

Christopher, M. and Holweg, M. (2011). Supply Chain 2.0: Managing supply chains in the era of turbulence. *International Journal of Physical Distribution & Logistics Management, 41*(1), 63–82.

Crosby, P. (1979). *Quality is Free,* New York, McGraw-Hill.

Daihatsu (2013). *The Fifth Daihatsu Environmental Action Plan FY2011–FY2015,* Environmental Affairs Department, Daihatsu Motors Co. Ltd.

DARA and the Climate Vulnerable Forum (2012). *Climate Vulnerability Monitor, 2nd edition. A Guide to the Cold Calculus of a Hot Planet,* Fundación DARA Internacional.

Dües, C. M., Tan K. H. and Lim M. (2011). Green as the new lean: How to use lean practices as a catalyst to greening your supply chain. *Journal of Cleaner Production, 40*, 93–100.

Garza-Reyes, J. A. (2015). Lean and green—A systematic review of the state of the art literature. *Journal of Cleaner Production, 102*, 18–29.

Gore, A. (2013). *The Future: Six Drivers of Global Change*, New York, Random House.

Grunwald, H. T. and Fortuin, L. (1992). Many steps towards zero inventory. *European Journal of Operational Research, 59*, 359–369.

Harbour Report (2012). *Oliver Wyman's The Harbour Report*. Available at: www.theharbourreport.com (accessed November 2015).

Hines, P. (2010). How to create and sustain a lean culture. *Training Journal*, June, 28–32.

Ishikawa, K. (1985). *What is Total Quality? The Japanese Way*, Englewood Cliffs, NJ, Prentice-Hall.

Klewitz, J. and Hansen, E. G. (2014). Sustainability-oriented innovation of SMEs: A systematic review. *Journal of Cleaner Production, 65*, 57–75.

Kurdve, M., Zackrisson, M., Wiktorsson, M. and Harlin, U. (2014). Lean and green integration into production system models—Experiences from Swedish industry. *Journal of Cleaner Production, 85*, 180–190.

Larson, T. and Greenwood, R. (2004). Perfect complements: Synergies between lean production and eco-sustainability initiatives. *Environmental Quality Management, 13*(4), 27–36.

Lloyds Banking Group (2014). Supporting UK Businesses. Report, October. Available at: www.lloydsbankinggroup.com/globalassets/documents/media/press-releases/lloyds-banking-group/2014/141028-lloyds-sme-factsheet-q3.pdf (accessed July 2016).

Lovins, H. and Cohen, B. (2012). *The Way Out: Kick-starting Capitalism to Save Our Economic Ass*, New York, Hill and Wang Publishing.

Lovins, A. B., Lovins, H. L. and Hawken, P. (1999). A roadmap for natural capitalism. *Harvard Business Review*, May–June, 144–158.

Martínez-Jurado, P. J. and Moyano-Fuentes, J. (2014). Lean management, supply chain management and sustainability: A literature review. *Journal of Cleaner Production, 85*, 134–150.

Moore, S. B. and Manring, S. L. (2009). Strategy development in small and medium sized enterprises for sustainability and increased value creation. *Journal of Cleaner Production, 17*, 276–282.

Naylor, J. B., Naim, M. M. and Berry, D. (1999) Leagility: Interfacing the lean and agile manufacturing paradigm in the total supply chain. *International Journal of Production Economics, 62*, 107–118.

OECD (2011). *Towards Green Growth*, Paris, OECD Publishing.

Osborn, P. (2013). *Sainsbury's 20x20 Sustainability Plan: Energy, Efficiency, Store Generation Technologies. 5th Smart Grids & Cleanpower Conference*, June 5, 2013, Cambridge.

Pagliarella, R. M. (2014). Carbon challenges and charging infrastructure. *2014 Australian Energy Storage Conference*, Melbourne, Australia.

Rao, S. and Goldsby, T. J. (2009). Supply chain risks: a review and typology. *International Journal of Logistics Management, 20*(1), 97–123.

Russel, G. (2011). Socially responsible investing. In: Andreas, F. M., Cooperman E. S., Gifford B. and Russel, G. (eds), *A Simple Path to Sustainability: Green Business Strategies for Small and Medium-Sized Businesses*, Santa Barbara, CA, Greenwood Publishing Group.

Simons, D. and Taylor, D. (2007). Lean thinking in the UK red meat industry: A systems and contingency approach. *International Journal of Production Economics, 106*(1), 70–81.

Stone, K. B. (2012). Four decades of lean: A systematic literature review. *International Journal of Lean Six Sigma, 3*(2), 112–132.

Stern, N. (2006). *Stern Review on the Economics of Climate Change*. London, HM Treasury.

Toyota Global (2015). *Toyota's Social Contribution Activities*. Available at: www.toyota-global.com/sustainability/social_contribution/vision/pdf/citizenship.pdf (accessed July 2016).

Toyota Motor Corporation (2011a). *Fifth Five Year Environmental Action Plan*. Available at: www.toyota-global.com/sustainability/environment/plan/fifth_plan/ (accessed November 2015).

Toyota Motor Corporation (2011b). Toyota Environmental Report. Toyota Motor Corporation. Available at: www.toyota.com/usa/environmentreport2011/ (accessed November 2015)

Toyota Motor Corporation (2013). *Sustainability Report 2013*. Toyota Motor Corporation.

Vermeulen, W. J. V. and Seuring, S. (2009), Sustainability through the market—The impacts of sustainable supply chain management: introduction. *Sustainable Development, 17*(5), 269–273.

Walmart (2013). Global Responsibility Report. Available at: https://cdn.corporate.walmart.com/39/97/81c4b26546b3913979b260ea0a74/updated-2013-global-responsibility-report_130113953638624649.pdf (accessed July 2016).

Walker, H. and Jones, N. (2012). Sustainable supply chain management across the UK private sector. *Supply Chain Management: An International Journal*, 17(1), 15–28.

Womack, J. P. and Jones, D. T. (1996). *Lean Thinking: Banish Waste and Create Wealth in Your Corporation*, New York, Simon & Schuster.

Womack, J. P., Jones, D. T. and Roos, D. (1990). *The Machine that Changed the World*, London, Simon & Schuster.

Zokaei, K., Lovins, H., Wood, A. and Hines, P. (2013). *Creating a Lean and Green Business System: Techniques for Improving Profits and Sustainability*, London and New York, CRC Press.

18

LEAN PURCHASING

Tim Torvatn, Ann-Charlott Pedersen, and Elsebeth Holmen

Introduction

Lean purchasing is the introduction of lean principles into the purchasing function. It covers two important, but separate, areas of professional practice. One is to use lean principles in the governance of the purchasing department itself. The other involves the purchasing personnel's use of their professional knowledge in handling suppliers to help the company in its efforts to build lean supply chains and networks. The first area is in many ways easier, as the purchasing personnel exercise a fair amount of control over their own procedures and, consequently, can decide to manage their department according to lean principles. Usually, this would happen within the context of an already established lean initiative at the company or division level. The second area is more challenging to handle as it involves other organizations and thus cannot be decided solely by the purchasing personnel or top managers within a company. Instead, a collaborating process must be applied, where the purchasing personnel and managers from a company work with the personnel of one or more suppliers to create the framework for cooperation. This framework for cooperation should implement lean principles at the supplier, supply chain, and supply network levels, thus benefiting all companies involved. This chapter discusses these two different areas of lean purchasing.

Applying Lean Principles in a Purchasing Department

Many production companies that have started a lean initiative have found the lean principles easier to apply to the actual production processes than to supporting departments, such as sales and marketing, research and development, and purchasing. Nevertheless, the principles remain useful even for these kinds of supporting activities. However, these principles need to be reinterpreted to fit with the different settings of the relevant departments. In this section, we examine a reasonable interpretation of the five main principles that work well for purchasing departments and should be applied as follows (Womack and Jones, 2003):

1 Specify value
2 Identify the value stream
3 Flow
4 Pull
5 Seek perfection.

Principle 1: Specify Value

This principle is often challenging for purchasing personnel, who are frequently organized at an operative level and whose usual task is to procure whatever is determined necessary by the production department (Gadde and Håkansson, 1993). This practice is harmful to companies since the purchasing department would clearly benefit from knowing the target customers for a product or service, the customers' criteria for judging quality, and which parts of the product or service are particularly important for them. After all, the economic value of purchased goods and services is frequently 60 percent or higher (Gadde and Håkansson, 1993; van Weele, 1994). Thus, suppliers and their deliverables are clearly important for the quality and cost of the end product/service. The purchasing department and its purchasers are the key to obtaining the maximum value from the suppliers. We also understand from work–life science that the possibility of knowing about end customers and their requirements, thus learning how the work of purchasing personnel fits into a larger whole, is an important motivator for any type of personnel as well as for purchasers (Wilton, 2013).

Therefore, if contact with customers is imperative for purchasing personnel, what can a typical company do to enable its purchasing personnel to meet with customers and understand their needs? One necessary, although insufficient criterion, is to deal with the purchasing department as a strategically important sector within the company. Its top-level managers should occupy high-level positions in the organization, and the strategic decisions about purchasing and supply chain management should be treated at least as crucially as sales and production decisions. This will bring senior purchasing managers into frequent contact with other top-level managers and thus with the customers and their concerns. For lower-level personnel, the use of cross-functional teams (Sethi et al., 2001) linked to a customer order can be a good solution. Such structures allow purchasers to interact with personnel from the production, sales and marketing, and research and development departments, as well as with customer representatives. Purchasers can then bring customer concerns to their department's attention. As an added bonus, the interactions will also provide information about other internal departments' concerns regarding the customer requirements. A more direct way is to arrange for visits to customers where purchasing personnel can observe how their products/services are used at the customer sites and thus discover the relevant customer concerns.

In some cases, particularly for companies situated far upstream in a value chain and mostly producing raw materials and/or standardized components, knowledge about the end users may not be relevant as the products delivered have passed through many intermediate stages before arriving at their final destination. In this regard, top management should carefully designate which intermediate customers are relevant and consider them those whom they should "understand" properly.

Finally, purchasing personnel should also find out about their nearest internal customer, usually the production department, and be knowledgeable about its requirements and how it uses the supplies procured by the purchasing department. Such a "work-unit analysis," where a work unit interviews the counterpart that takes over its deliverables in an attempt to find out the requirements set by the latter, is useful for any kind of department, purchasing included.

Principle 2: Identify the Value Stream

Similar to all the other departments, the purchasing department needs to work on the description and analysis of its main activities. Central processes, such as ordering (including follow-up, expediting, and invoicing), supplier selection, supplier evaluation, supplier development, strategic decisions (involving setting and measuring key performance indicators), and internal improvement and change (van Weele, 1994) should be broken down into separate activities.

This will allow purchasing managers and personnel to analyze the activities and decide on how they can focus more on value adding and eliminate or reduce activities that do not add value.

Value stream mapping (Rother and Shook, 2003) is a well-developed technique that will also work well for the purchasing department. In addition to evaluating internal activities, a company-wide value stream map will contribute to a shared understanding of the purchasing department's efforts, as well as help the purchasing staff understand and appreciate the value-adding activities in other departments. This work will become easier and more efficient if policies are already implemented to ensure that purchasing personnel are well informed about the preferences of their (end) customers and of the internal work units to which they hand over their deliverables (see Principle 1).

Principle 3: Flow

Flow means ensuring that the production process is continuous and not hampered by functional or physical borders within the company. Ideally, this should also stretch to suppliers and inter-mediate customers.

For a support function such as purchasing, one of the central ways of helping with flow is to avoid waste. This can be achieved by doing only value-adding activities as much as possible. This presupposes that the department has performed a value stream mapping or a similar type of activity mapping (see Principle 2). Given that such an analysis has been done, the department can simplify or simply remove activities that do not contribute to customer value.

The purchasing department is also in some sense a logistics provider as all purchased materials and components usually pass through it on their way to production lines. Simplifying this logistics trail, especially reducing the waste of time and resources in storage, is almost as important as minimizing non-value-adding activities. Even when steps have been taken to ensure that the company employs the pull principle (see Principle 4), waste can still occur. This may happen because the purchasing department is unable to coordinate deliveries, storage space, and handoff to the production and/or sales departments to achieve a stream of materials and supplies that enters production as close to just-in-time as possible (Monden, 2011). Cross-docking, coordination of transport to and from the production site, and optimization of incoming transportation routes may also be relevant to eliminate waste. If, for some reason, the company is unable to buy everything based on orders only, the purchasing department must assume the additional task of handling storage space and ensuring that minimal waste occurs there. Most purchasers have been trained in the relevant techniques, such as economic order quantity and optimum storage size and placement (Bailey et al., 1994). The company may also have information technology (IT) systems that can help in obtaining the information necessary to create and compute optimization solutions.

Waste can also result from the necessary documentation and money trail associated with ordering materials and supplies. Here, the purchasing department can make certain that ordering and payment routines are simplified and, where possible, coordinated so that they take a mini-mum of resources to perform.

Even in the management of the human resources of the purchasing department, actions can be taken to reduce waste. Using value stream mapping, a matrix can be used to show all the skills and competencies necessary to perform these activities. This matrix can then illustrate the compe-tencies that the department needs to possess and at what levels. This information can in turn be fed back to the human resources department to help with recruiting and staffing. It should also be used by managers in the purchasing department to decide what courses their staff should take and what competencies need to be developed. The information should also allow managers to ensure that all existing competencies are used to the maximum.

However, some of the most promising possibilities for reducing waste are not related to internal procedures but to how the company interacts with its suppliers. How this can help reduce waste is further discussed in the second part of this chapter.

Another important way for the purchasing department to ensure flow is to stay constantly updated on production plans and schedules, including sales orders and forecasts. Such internal information should always be open across departments so that purchasers can anticipate the demand for certain raw materials and components, instead of waiting until the production department has sent official requests for materials.

Principle 4: Pull

Pull systems are lean because they only produce as a result of consumption. Production is thus a function of knowing that the actual product will be consumed by an end user. If the company is lucky, this can be a result of a direct customer order. Otherwise, the company must either be very good at knowing where and how much the consumers will buy or have short production and distribution cycles and be quick to respond to consumer demands.

Purchasing departments usually work based on derived demand (van Weele, 1994), whether it comes directly from a customer order or from internal "customers" (usually the production department, but sometimes the sales department when goods bought by the purchasing department are sold directly to customers without going through internal production stages). Thus, if the company itself buys on order, then so will the purchasing department in most cases. Two central processes are used in purchasing to produce for derived demand. One is soliciting competitive bids to procure the necessary products/services. The other is to base the buying company's purchases on agreements (usually frame agreements) or long-term purchases from strategic partners.

The purchasing department is a gateway to external suppliers and can in some cases experience a mismatch between the internal order time and external delivery cycles. In other words, a supplier may need more time producing a component to sell to the buying company than the buying company's available time before the customer wants his or her finished product/service delivered. In such cases, the purchasing department needs to take action. The best situation is where the purchasing department can bring the two cycle times in congruence by eliminating or improving internal activities (for example, by eliminating non-value-adding internal activities). If this is not possible or wanted, purchasing personnel can attempt negotiations with suppliers to help them make changes to reduce their cycle time and thus enable better congruence. If none of these options is workable, purchasing personnel should discuss with key suppliers that encounter these challenges to seek other solutions that may reduce the problem. Modularization of purchased items can be a possible solution, as can better coordination and information systems between companies. A supply chain management (Lamming, 1993; Wincel, 2004) and/or supply networks (Gadde and Håkansson, 2001) perspective is useful here, where the larger needs of the supply chain are in focus, and individual challenges and problems can be discussed and possibly solved.

In the end, if none of these alternatives can arrive at solutions, some form of scheduling and prognosis-based purchasing must be implemented. However, this should be a last resort, and thus implemented only after every other possibility has been exploited.

Principle 5: Seek Perfection

In the context of this discussion, perfection means that systems and people in the purchasing department need to constantly improve their own competencies, as well as the systems and routines in how they work.

Central to working with continuous improvement is a system where the measures of important value-adding activities are developed and used to keep track of existing procedures and practices (Netland et al., 2015). The value-adding activities are uncovered with value stream mapping or similar activities (see Principle 2). The measures to keep track of the performance of these activities are necessary to help with improvement. Typical measures that may be useful can be divided into the following categories:

1   activities and process measurements (for example, how many orders an employee can handle within a specific time period),
2   price measurements (for example, the price of a particular commodity tracked over time),
3   quality measurements (for example, how many errors occur in a product in a particular period or how often a late delivery from a supplier occurs), and
4   cycle time measurements (for example, how long it takes from the order to the arrival of purchased goods, or how long a typical material stays in raw material storage).

The purchasing department needs to employ several such measurements and track them over time. A relatively small number of measurements should be tracked at any given time; when one measurement shows promising development, it should be replaced by another. Measurements need to be displayed openly so that all employees in the department can check their status and improvement at any given time. Measurements should also be coordinated with the production department (and perhaps other departments as well) so that the two departments do not pick measurements that counteract each other. Moreover, it is important to choose measurements related to the activities that the employees can actually affect. "Bad" measurements in terms of improvement constitute any measurement relying on and/or derived from external factors, such as raw material global prices.

All employees should also be constantly challenged to improve their performance and to test whether their improvements actually work. It is important that employees are continuously involved in improvement activities so that they acquire the habit of constantly thinking about improvements.

Lean Supply Chains and Networks

The purchasing department has gained increased attention in recent years. One reason for this is that companies are increasingly outsourcing, downsizing, and focusing on their core competencies. Consequently, they often spend 60–75 percent of total revenues on purchasing materials, components, and services from suppliers (Lamming, 1993; Cusumano, 1994; Dyer, 2000; Gadde and Håkansson, 2001). With a larger purchasing bill, companies have become increasingly reliant on their suppliers to improve both their quality and delivery performance, as well as to develop new products and technologies (Cusumano, 1994; Gadde and Håkansson, 2001; Liker and Choi, 2004). Therefore, competitive advantages and disadvantages of an individual firm are often perceived as linked to the supply chains and networks in which the firm is embedded (Håkansson and Snehota, 1995; Dyer, 2000).

Following this line of thought, enterprises such as Toyota and Honda have developed lean practices aimed at managing internal matters, diffusing lean production through the supply chain, and creating lean suppliers (Lamming, 1993; MacDuffie and Helper, 1997; Cusumano and Nobeoka, 1998). Furthermore, striving for an extended lean enterprise, Toyota and Honda have each developed a set of practices for creating high-performance, knowledge-sharing supplier networks and *Kyoryoku Kai* (Supplier Association) (see Hines, 1994; Dyer and Nobeoka, 2000).

These supply network practices include initiating and developing partnerships with individual suppliers, as well as developing joint learning and continuous improvement among the suppliers involved in the networks to utilize the strength of specialist players in the company environment (Dyer, 2000).

One way to organize and develop lean thinking among key suppliers is the stepwise process of involving and educating them. Several authors have discussed how to manage complex business networks (see, e.g., Möller and Halinen, 1999; Ritter et al., 2004). In the following, we use the four-level model introduced by Ritter et al. (2004) to discuss lean supply in relation to the suppliers:

1   manage dyads or single business relationships,
2   manage a portfolio of relationships,
3   manage connected relationships, and
4   manage in business networks.

The first step is to manage dyads or single business relationships viewed in isolation. This implies focusing on how to interact in supplier relationships, how to build trust and mutual orientation, how the two parties involved can engage in adaptations, what types of dependencies and interdependencies are created, and so on (Gadde and Håkansson, 2001). To develop lean suppliers, the firm must start by focusing on lean supply base management, i.e. evaluating the supplier base. According to Dyer (2000), building deep supplier relationships often requires supply base reduction and consolidation. Thus, the buying firm needs to assess its key suppliers with regard to price, total cost, quality, delivery performance, and so on, as well as to take into account the suppliers' experience with lean management (Harris and Streeter, 2010). After the supplier base has been reduced, the buying firm may need to develop the remaining key suppliers through some sort of lean supplier relationship development program. According to Sako (2004), who has studied supplier development at Honda, Nissan, and Toyota over several decades, the development of lean suppliers requires that the buying firm's internal lean practices be transferred to and replicated by the suppliers. The goal of this supplier development process is to develop the suppliers into partners and to create mutually beneficial relationships that provide efficient and consistent values to end customers (Harris and Streeter, 2010).

The second step is to examine the portfolio of relationships; that is, to perform portfolio management of a set of relationships seen together. According to Ritter et al. (2004), focusing on the simultaneous management of several relationships and handling the interconnection among these relationships have often been neglected in management literature. The literature on supply chain management pays attention to different types of purchasing and supplier portfolio models, classifying either the purchased goods or different suppliers into 2x2 matrixes (see Kraljic, 1983; Bensaou, 1999). This approach to the portfolio of relationships has also been explained with regard to lean suppliers. Drake et al. (2013) discuss lean suppliers in relation to agile suppliers in a portfolio model. Nonetheless, very few of these models handle or consider the interdependencies among the different supplier relationships.

The third step is to manage connected relationships where the buying firm is not directly involved in all the relationships; for example, with suppliers' suppliers and customers' custo-mers in a supply chain. According to Ritter et al. (2004, p. 179), "the management problem here involves dealing with the indirect effects of management action in one relationship on other relationships . . . including responding to opportunities and problems arising from action taking place in connected relationships." This is also relevant when we discuss lean supply chain management. Moyano-Fuentes and Sacristán-Diaz (2012) claim that it is important to extend the lean principles to the value/supply chain by eliminating waste, improving quality, reducing costs, and increasing flexibility at all stages in the chain. To accomplish this, the buying firm must not only work with its direct suppliers but also encourage them to start their own lean supplier development processes to educate and develop their sub-suppliers while also ensuring that these changes are creating value for the end customer.

The fourth and last step involves managing in business networks or managing part of a business network; for example, a strategic net or a supply network. In the supply management literature, the creation, development, and management of supply networks have constituted an important topic (see, e.g., Holmen et al., 2003; Harland et al., 2004). Furthermore, some articles have discussed how suppliers can react to a buying firm that is trying to orchestrate a supply network (Johnsen and Ford, 2005; Holmen and Pedersen, 2010). Relating this to lean supply, Dyer and Nobeoka (2000) introduced a method for creating high-performance, knowledge-sharing supplier networks. Such supply network practices include initiating and developing partnerships with individual suppliers, as well as developing joint learning and continuous improvement among the suppliers involved in the supplier networks to utilize the strength of specialist players in the company environment (Dyer, 2000). According to Liker and Choi (2004), the involved suppliers were often eager to become part of the supply network since it gave them the opportunity to be taught and to learn the philosophy and practices of world-class lean companies. The suppliers often gained benefits from the collaboration, which could be transferred to their other customer relationships.

The Future of Lean Purchasing

As discussed, we suggest two quite different ways in which purchasing managers can adopt lean thinking in their main function. One approach is directed (more) toward issues that are internal to the function and to the company; the other concerns working with the external environment, particularly with suppliers. We believe that companies that truly want to become lean should plan for and work with both options. This is not a question of mutual exclusivity or of one way being better than the other.

However, we stress that the possibilities for introducing the approaches are not necessarily equal. Establishing lean practices together with suppliers may be considerably more difficult and require more resources than setting up lean practices internally. Furthermore, the two routes require different competencies from purchasing managers and personnel.

Establishing lean practices with suppliers may require the company to have established lean practices internally, for several reasons. First, to inspire, guide, and support the suppliers' journey toward lean practices, the company should have amassed experiences and built up lean competencies. Second, the company's development of lean experiences and competencies may be a prerequisite for gaining the suppliers' respect for and trust in it as a capable company from which the suppliers will accept directions on their lean journey.

Consequently, we suggest that purchasing managers facing a company in its early stages of lean practices can benefit from introducing lean principles internally, especially if the company is operating in an industry dominated by arms-length relationships with suppliers. Working with suppliers also requires that the top management be committed to taking a long-term perspective on them. Additionally, to ensure continuity in the efforts to develop lean suppliers, it will be beneficial if the purchasing department is suitably positioned to influence the company's strategy. It will be advantageous as well if the purchasing managers are used to working in a cross-functional manner since this will assist the efforts to link the production and product development functions in their own company with similar functions within their suppliers.

Finally, competence development, in terms of understanding the main business processes, key steps, and challenges in the company's production processes, is necessary to enable purchasing managers and personnel to participate in lean development, both inside and outside the organizational boundaries.

Case Study: Lean Purchasing at NAMMO AS

In 2011, the Norwegian University of Science and Technology launched a large research project called Lean Operations. As part of this project, research partners have cooperated with seven companies to implement and develop their lean initiatives. One of the companies participating in this development work was NAMMO, which (among other initiatives) chose to start applying lean principles in its purchasing work. The authors of this case were involved in this development work and are thus in a position to report on the efforts made and their effects. The readers should be aware that the initiative is still ongoing; as such, several themes have not been covered yet. However, we think it is interesting to show how a company can become lean, rather than adding more stories about successful examples of lean companies.

NAMMO is a medium-sized Norwegian company in the defense sector, producing ammunition for professional use. The production division at Raufoss has worked with lean principles for a long time. Lean processes were originally introduced to the company as a requirement of one of its customers but had mainly been applied in the production departments. NAMMO wanted to spread the implementation of lean processes to other internal departments, and the newly appointed supply chain manager decided on this as a way of developing better routines and procedures within the purchasing department. The researchers contributed to this development by suggesting models, tools, and the relevant literature to support the steps that the manager wanted to take. In this way, the process involved fruitful interactions between the researchers and the business managers.

The first step taken was to commission a master's thesis where students examined how purchasing work was performed in the company. They ended this work with a status report suggesting six areas of improvement. The manager chose to start with one of these suggestions and mapped the purchasing processes, describing each major purchasing activity and the different roles connected to it. This project represented an early form of value stream mapping and helped the company in assigning roles to the purchasing personnel and others to clarify their respective responsibilities and to avoid overlaps between activities and areas of responsibility. Now this project helps the company fulfill two of the five lean principles—to identify the value stream throughout the company and to avoid waste.

The next main activity was to create a map of the competencies needed in the purchasing department. The map also included useful books and articles, and courses that could be taken to improve the individual purchasers' core competencies. More general competencies, such as IT skills and business economics, are also included in the map but without a similar list of books, articles, and courses. This competence map allows the manager and the purchasing employees to gain a better understanding of how individual competencies match the mentioned roles and fit together to create a competence profile for the entire department. This again is a useful tool for discussing and prioritizing competence development within the department and is also valuable for recruitment. Job offers can provide more precise information about the required competencies, and the applicants' competencies can be compared directly with those that are existing or lacking in the department. This helps the company fit its competence profile better to the tasks and activities that need to be performed, thus improving the value stream. It also reduces the waste by tailoring competencies more clearly to roles and activities.

The third improvement project aimed to evaluate how cross-functional teams could work in the NAMMO context. The production and development teams were already linked to the different product groups. Therefore the improvement project concentrated on how the purchasers could become regular members of these teams and what roles they could play in such teams. The results from this project are still unfolding. Nonetheless, a successful implementation is expected to make improvements along all five lean principles since early involvement in cross-functional teams increases the possibility for the purchasers to know the customers and their requirements. Moreover, better coordination with the production department allows concentration on value-adding activities, avoiding waste, and producing based on the actual orders.

In the spring of 2015, the researchers also contributed to an external evaluation of possible supplier relationship management (SRM) software. The company wanted to determine whether such a system could help it improve its relation to its suppliers. This is the most recent project, and the results have not yet been revealed, but the information is expected to help the company find an SRM system that can further support the focus on value-creating activities. Additionally, the system can tie into existing production management systems to give more accurate information about who can supply the parts needed in production, thus improving the chance for production to always be strongly related to actual orders rather than relying on prognosis.

Finally, the whole process of the improvement projects described in this case can be considered an application of the fifth lean principle of perfection. The supply chain manager at NAMMO has persisted in improving how the purchasing department works through the implementation of the results of these projects. In this way, the department is currently much closer to operating on lean principles than it was when the process started in January 2012.

The next step for the company is to "export" the solutions to other purchasing departments within the larger company group (the division where we worked is only one of four divisions, each having multiple production sites with separate purchasing departments). Furthermore, the purchasing department will start developing lean supply chains. This last part is the focus of another research project being conducted from 2015 to 2017 to continue the productive interactions between the researchers and the company personnel.

References

Bailey, P., Farmer, D., Jessop, D. and Jones, D. (1994). *Purchasing Principles and Management*, London, Pitman Publishing.
Bensaou, B. M. (1999). Portfolios of buyer–supplier relationships. *Sloan Management Review*, Summer, 35–44.
Cusumano, M. A. (1994). The limits of "lean." *Sloan Management Review*, 35(4), 27–32.
Cusumano, M. A. and Nobeoka, K. (1998). *Thinking Beyond Lean*, New York, The Free Press.
Drake, P. R., Lee, D. M. and Hussain, M. (2013). The lean and agile purchasing portfolio model. *Supply Chain Management: An International Journal*, 18(1), 3–20.
Dyer, J. H. (2000). *Collaborative Advantage: Winning through Extended Enterprise Supplier Networks*, New York, Oxford University Press.
Dyer, J. H. and Nobeoka, K. (2000). Creating and managing a high-performance knowledge-sharing network: The Toyota case. *Strategic Management Journal*, 21, 345–367.
Gadde, L.-E. and Håkansson, H. (1993). *Professional Purchasing*, London, Routledge.
Gadde, L.-E. and Håkansson, H. (2001). *Supply Network Strategies*, Chichester, John Wiley & Sons.

Håkansson, H. and Snehota, I. (1995). *Developing Relationships in Business Networks*, London, Routledge.

Harland, C., Zheng, J., Johnsen, T. and Lamming, R. C. (2004). A conceptual model for researching the creation and operation of supply networks. *British Journal of Management*, *15*, 1–21.

Harris, C. and Streeter, C. (2010). A new purchasing philosophy. *Industrial Engineer*, *42*(9), 42–46.

Hines, P. (1994). Internationalization and localization of the Kyoryoku Kai: The spread of best practice supplier development. *International Journal of Logistics Management*, *5*(1), 67–72.

Holmen, E. and Pedersen, A.-C. (2010). How do suppliers strategise in relation to a customer's supply network initiative? *Journal of Purchasing & Supply Management*, *16*, 264–278.

Holmen, E., Håkansson, H. and Pedersen, A.-C. (2003). Framing as a means to manage a supply network. *Journal of Customer Behaviour*, *2*, 385–407.

Johnsen, T. and Ford, D. (2005). At the receiving end of supply network intervention: The view from an automotive first-tier supplier. *Journal of Purchasing & Supply Management*, *11*, 183–192.

Kraljic, P. (1983). Purchasing must become supply management. *Harvard Business Review*, September–October, 109–117.

Lamming, R. C. (1993). *Beyond Partnership: Strategies for Innovation and Lean Supply*, London, Prentice Hall.

Liker, J. K. and Choi, T. Y. (2004). Building deep supplier relationships. *Harvard Business Review*, December, 2–10.

MacDuffie, J. P. and Helper, S. (1997). Creating lean suppliers: Diffusing lean production through the supply chain. *California Management Review*, *39*(4), 118–151.

Möller, K. and Halinen, A. (1999). Business relationships and networks: Managerial challenge of network era. *Industrial Marketing Management*, *28*, 413–427.

Monden, Y. (2011). *Toyota Production System—An Integrated Approach to Just-In-Time*, 4th edition, New York, CRC Press.

Moyano-Fuentes, J. and Sacristán-Diaz, M. (2012). Learning on lean: A review of thinking and research. *International Journal of Operations & Production Management*, *32*(5), 551–582.

Netland, T. H., Schloetzer, J. D. and Ferdows, K. (2015). Implementing corporate lean programs: The effect of management control practices. *Journal of Operations Management*, *36*(0), 90–102.

Ritter, T., Wilkinson, I. F. and Johnston, W. J. (2004). Managing in complex business networks. *Industrial Marketing Management*, *33*, 175–183.

Rother, M. and Shook, J. (2003). *Learning to See*, Cambridge, MA, Lean Enterprise Institute.

Sako, M. (2004). Supplier development at Honda, Nissan and Toyota: Comparative case studies of organizational capability enhancement. *Industrial and Corporate Change*, *13*(2), 281–308.

Sethi, R., Smith, D. C. and Whan Park, C. (2001). Cross-functional product development teams, creativity and the innovativeness of new consumer products. *Journal of Marketing Research*, *38*(1), 73–85.

Van Weele, A. J. (1994). *Purchasing Management*, London, Chapman & Hall.

Wilton, N. (2013). *An Introduction to Human Resource Management*, London, Sage Publications.

Wincel, J. (2004). *Lean Supply Chain Management*, Boca Raton, FL, CRC Press.

Womack, J. P. and Jones, D. T. (2003). *Lean Thinking: Banish Waste and Create Wealth in Your Corporation*. London, Simon & Schuster.

19

LEAN SUPPLY CHAINS

Jonathan Gosling, Maneesh Kumar, and Mohamed Naim

Introduction

The idea that supply chains compete against each other, rather than individual firms or brands, has been written about extensively (Christopher, 2005). Similarly, lean thinkers have for some time encouraged us to think beyond the "door to door" of our factory to the extended value stream (Jones and Womack, 2002). Lean principles and practices when adopted and spread among supply chain members effectively will derive potential benefits for all concerned (Hines et al., 2004; Shah and Ward, 2007). Very often the main focus of *lean supply chain initiatives* is the reduction of waste, the elimination of non-value-adding activities, the reduction of costs, and increasing flexibility from order placement to order delivery processes to the end customer (Womack and Jones, 1996; Mollenkopf, et al., 2010; So and Sun, 2010; Martinez-Jurado and Moyano-Fuentes, 2014). The overall aim is to optimize activities along the supply chain from the final customer's point of view (Martínez-Jurado and Moyano-Fuentes, 2014).

Japanese approaches have had a large impact on how many firms consider the role of suppliers in optimizing supply chain performance. This includes the rationalization of the supply base, and a focus on active development of suppliers (Aoki and Kumar, 2014; Gosling et al. 2015). In order to describe characteristics of *lean supply chains*, this chapter explores the experiences of three different companies in three very different sectors—a tale of three lean supply chains. We show how market sector and the underlying structure of the supply chain created different conditions for the implementation of lean concepts. For each case, we give some general background to the context and nature of products, as well as describing sourcing approaches and strategy. We then give an overview of the lean supply chain initiatives implemented, giving some insight into the impact, then we explain the challenges and the lessons learned. The chapter then reflects on a number of questions: How are the case studies different? What are lean supply chains? How are the case studies similar? What are the "levers" of change? We then close by considering the future of lean supply chains.

The concept of the decoupling point is useful as an underlying structure for comparing lean supply chains. The decoupling point describes the way in which orders penetrate the "basic structure" of a supply chain (Hoekstra and Romme, 1992), and provides a buffer between fluctuating customer orders and smooth production output (Naylor et al., 1999). Upstream of the decoupling point, activities are typically speculative, aggregated, and standardized. Downstream of the decoupling point, activities are typically non-speculative and attached to known orders.

Figure 19.1 illustrates how these points relate to different parts of the supply chain. Using the decoupling point concept, a range of structures can be defined to give a simplified classification of supply chain types, including engineer-to-order (ETO), make-to-order (MTO), assemble-to-order (ATO), and make-to-stock (MTS).

This underlying structure defines the basic conditions for how the customer engages and interacts with a supply chain and, in turn, affects the types of practices that are appropriate (Naylor et al., 1999). Throughout this chapter, we use this as a basis for comparing and discussing lean supply chain initiatives. We explore an ETO supply chain from the construction industry, an ATO supply chain from the electronics sector, and a hybrid MTO and MTS supply chain in the automotive industry.

Lean Supply Chain Case 1: Construction

Case Study Background, Context, and Products

Our first case study documents the lean improvement initiatives in a global construction and consultancy organization. The MACE Group has approximately 4,700 employees (3,300 in the UK) at the time of writing, with a turnover of £1.5bn. It operates in a range of sectors, such as infrastructure, education, retail, leisure, and residential building sectors. In this case study we will focus on the unique challenges of delivering one-off iconic commercial and residential buildings in the UK. These are primarily based in London, and include projects such as the Shard, the London Eye, and a range of company headquarters buildings, such as that of Merrill Lynch. Projects might range from one year to, in some cases, up to five years in length. The sector is challenging, since designs tend to be unique architectural showpieces. Hence it is difficult to engage the same supply chain from one project to the next, and those suppliers that are selected often have to work around new design specifications. Applying lean concepts in such a setting is far from easy.

Sourcing and Strategy

The supply base of the company has been rationalized over the past two decades or so. Operating on the Pareto principle, the company has made efforts to focus on less than 20 percent of suppliers

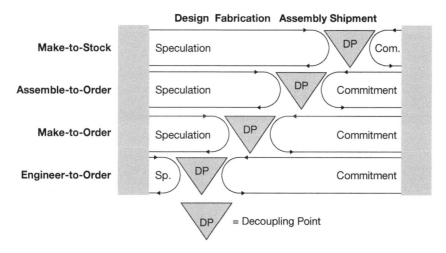

Figure 19.1   Family of supply chain structures

Source: Adapted from Wikner and Rudberg (2005).

that deliver up to 80 percent of the work, and to increasingly reward those companies. This has resulted in a structured supply base consisting of approved suppliers, preferred suppliers, and strategic partners for each business sector. While the company has many suppliers in its complete supply chain, within the specific subsector of interest there are currently 98 suppliers, of which 13 are long-term strategic partners, 33 are preferred suppliers, and 52 are approved suppliers. As will be described later, development initiatives are tailored to the different categories. In terms of the decoupling point, the company operates in an ETO environment, where clients and designers co-create the products. The company holds no material stocks, and sources materials and services on a project-by-project basis.

Lean Supply Chain Initiatives Implemented

The company began a significant supply chain improvement program in the early 2000s, incorporating lean concepts. Importantly, a physical base was established to collate best practice. By 2006, the Mace Business School was established, a first of its kind in the industry. This was a response to the increasing complexity of projects and the interfaces between different parts of the supply chain, and recognition of the importance of the role of active supply chain management. The decision was therefore made to share expertise through learning and knowledge sharing with its supply chain.

This internal "business school" aims to develop and implement training schemes, and gather and undertake supply chain data and intelligence, as well as implement best practice across the organization and supply chain. Training is delivered to the supply chain by senior managers and directors with the relevant expertise. This represented a significant step forward, and a pioneering approach within the industry. Among other things the business school has been responsible for the following:

- executive briefing workshops for suppliers to give information about upcoming projects and work that may be available in the coming months, allowing the supply chain to forecast and gain a better understanding of market outlook;
- "head start" and cluster management workshops to help groups of suppliers work together more effectively, and consider likely interfacing issues at an earlier point;
- leadership coaching and passport training programs to upskill and educate suppliers;
- establishing collaboration with research institutions, such as Cardiff and Reading universities, to foster new thinking and innovative ideas;
- implementing performance management and accreditation systems for suppliers;
- streamlining of the sourcing process, including standard bid templates to reduce workload and lead times;
- incentivizing good performance through awards and accreditations.

The business school has also played a proactive role in developing IT systems to support supply chain management. Industry lead times are monitored through a "foresite" system, a custom web-based system designed to monitor lead times, and project management systems have been implemented allowing suppliers to see up-to-date project plans and drawings. A system has also been developed to provide real-time information to manage risk around performance, financial status and compliance, and to assist in capacity forecasting. The company is committed to developing *building information modeling* (BIM) capabilities, systems that help to visualize and manage design information, both internally and throughout the supply chain. In addition, an internal logistics consultancy was set up. This internal department, as well as taking on external engagement, advises site teams, designers, and clients on logistics and material management issues in advance of the site phase of a project. This includes the encouragement of JIT systems with suppliers to synchronize deliveries with site progress, as well as lean flows of materials as a site develops.

The company has been at the forefront of promoting and adopting modular design principles, such as offsite pre-assembly to reduce process times. All projects are now required to complete a prefabrication and offsite assembly strategy review as early as possible in order to evaluate potential options, and an innovations director has been appointed to promote this strategy. Current examples of this include prefabricated plant rooms and bathroom pods as well as roof structure and membrane. Co-location, where supplier and contractors work together in a central site location, is also regularly used to facilitate information exchange and collaborative working. The latest development at the company is that a *lean construction* expert has been employed to work across a number of projects, and the company has formal ties with the Lean Construction Institute. These efforts have led to multiple awards for its supply chain practices, including *Building* magazine's "Supply Chain Management of the Year Award."

Challenges and Lessons Learned

It is interesting to consider this case in the context of the ETO environment in which it operates. Implementing lean in a production environment that lacks regularity is difficult, and many standard lean concepts may need to be adapted. Capturing project-specific learning is a challenge, since it is not clear if and how lessons will carry over to future projects. At the firm level, the establishment of a department within the organization, including a physical base to support it, has been key to ensuring that knowledge is shared from one project to the next. In addition, the training programs have played a significant role in upskilling and communicating effectively with suppliers.

Lean Supply Chain Case 2: Personal Computers

Case Study Background, Context, and Products

The second case study is of a global personal computer (PC) supply chain, originally owned by IBM but transferred to Lenovo in 2004. The case describes an evolution of a supply chain, from a mass production system through to a lean and agile mass customization-oriented approach (Berry and Naim, 1996, Naylor et al., 1999). That latter state is synonymous with the Dell business model.

At the time of the study IBM had a high degree of vertical ownership of the supply chain involved in marketing and manufacturing as well as research and development of PCs. The supply chain was in fact a large complex network. As well as the company's own sales and marketing outlets and manufacturing plants spread throughout the world it also had a global vendor base.

Production was defined at three main levels—basic components (e.g. microchips, boards, hard disks), sub-assemblies (e.g. keyboards, screens, "boxes"), and finished goods (the PC itself). Intermediate products are sold to sister plants, finished products are sold to sales and marketing, with the latter selling to end customers such as organizations or, via retailers, to consumers.

Sourcing and Strategy

Originally the in-house supply chain was established to be totally self-reliant with sufficient capacity to meet most demand. The company had four different final assembly plants, three sub-assembly plants and four components plants. There were 10 distribution centers and tens of thousands of retail outlets that the company owned. To account for peaks in demand, an external vendor base, at the component and sub-assembly levels, was sourced primarily based on price with multiple vendors procured on a "just in case" basis. While there were "primary" vendors—five printed circuit board suppliers and a hard disk provider at the sub-assembly level, and hundreds of component suppliers—at any time the company could source from thousands of different vendors.

Typically, the cumulative physical lead time from component level through to end customers was 32 weeks. Hence, for consumers who wanted an "off-the-shelf" PC, this meant a speculative MTS strategy was adopted. Despite the vertical ownership business model each unit in the company was a self-contained cost center with its own planning and forecasting systems. Adversarial relationships had developed within the company and also with the external vendor base. The supply chain suffered from classic symptoms found in mass production systems—high levels of waste in the form of scrap rates; product returns; non-value-added lead times; duplicated, excessive, and redundant stock; and poor customer service levels and lack of information transparency.

Lean Supply Chain Initiatives Implemented

With the aim of reducing in-plant lead times and enhancing quality, via the elimination of waste in all its forms, what we now might term lean manufacturing tools and techniques were implemented in the company's own plants in the early 1980s. A major education program was developed for the manufacturing workforce with respect to developing a total quality management culture combined with total productive maintenance and JIT techniques and disciplines, including:

- batch size reduction,
- set-up reduction,
- group technology layout,
- workstation ownership,
- individual quality responsibility, and
- multiskilling.

By 1990 this initiative saw in-house manufacturing lead times and inventory reduced by 50 percent.

Despite the considerable advance in time compression of manufacturing lead times, they were still greater than the time the end customer would be prepared to wait if products were to be fully customized to their requirements. In preparation for developing a totally new approach to satisfying customers, which ultimately led to an ATO-based approach to mass customization, the second phase of the program led to substantive initiatives.

In the early 1980s materials planning was undertaken at individual plant levels. This meant that there were sequential plans from the material requirements planning (MRP) system that led to what we now term the "bullwhip effect." In coping with "bullwhip," plants built up inventory, and duplicated inventory, at the interfaces. To mitigate the "bullwhip effect" the company developed an integrated approach to information flow and materials control. Taking a global approach, the company considered the manufacturing plants across the three levels as a single pipeline entity. Hence a collaborative planning forecast and replenishment (CPFR) system was established that included:

- the creation of a global MRP, that applied MRP logic for subassembly and component requirements;
- shared and agreed forecasts of end demand;

- visibility of stocks and work in process (WIP) throughout the "manufacturing pipeline"; and
- the use of electronic data interchange (EDI) for simultaneous transmission of demand at all manufacturing levels.

While planning was undertaken globally the manufacturing plants still had local autonomy for the execution of the plans. This global planning initiative saw information delays reduced by 70 percent.

In parallel with the development of CPFR there was a reassessment of the global vendor base strategy. The company moved away from an adversarial approach to sourcing and toward a more "partnering" approach that procured suppliers' services as well as goods. This reorientation selected suppliers not just on price but also on capabilities, which included their ability to deliver goods according to other criteria such as quality and lead time. Further, it also included their ability to work with the company such as in new product development. This led to fewer but "better" suppliers in the vendor base.

Tied in with the in-house manufacturing changes in phase 1 and with the CPFR implementation, the vendors were linked to the EDI network, got better longer-term visibility of daily requirements, provided information on their stock and WIP levels, and hence they delivered JIT to the company's plants.

With the previously described initiative as a platform, the company was able to radically rethink its approach to delivering better value to the end customer. While the previous initiatives were very much focused on the manufacturing function the final phase of change was concerned with impacting the "front" and "back" ends of the supply chain. At the "front end" there was the move toward greater interaction with the end customer. Retailer outlets were passed by, allowing customers to place orders directly with the company via the internet and the company delivering directly to the customer.

At the same time, at the "back end" concurrent engineering meant that PCs were designed for manufacturability. However, it also allowed for adoption of greater standardization at the component and sub-assembly levels while offering choice of the finished assembled product. This required an ATO strategy so that assembly of PCs was not finalized and shipped until a direct customer order was received. Hence, strategic stocks of standardized sub-assemblies were required. These were made to an aggregate forecast, but the stock was used for final assembly.

This final phase was the fruition of 10 years of change that meant that end customers had a degree of choice and only had to wait a few days for their PC at a price that was competitive.

Challenges and Lessons Learned

Covering a 10-year span of change requires considerable foresight and vision in terms of an end point. Predicting customers' likely wants and needs, and likely future manufacturing capabilities to fulfill them, over such a period of time suggests a high degree of uncertainty. Therefore, there is a need to articulate a clear vision of the long-term corporate strategy and develop manufacturing and marketing strategies that are strongly aligned. At the end of the change program there was an ATO system that could accommodate the trade-off between increased customer choice and a quick response to their orders while maintaining a degree of efficiency that ensured that any premium paid by the customer was minimized.

The supply chain reengineering program also required multiple considerations regarding the levers for change at different stages. Central to the changes is the buy-in of a culture shift that regarded quality as paramount. This could only be achieved via a holistic and long-term view that required cooperation rather than competition internal to the supply chain.

Lean Supply Chain Case 3: Automotive

Case Study Background, Context, and Products

The last comparative case presented in this chapter is a well-known Japanese automotive *original equipment manufacturer* (OEM), similar to Nissan or Toyota, that has a production facility in India. This OEM started its India operation in the 1990s and provided employment to over 6,000 employees in 2015. The decision to have production facilities in India was influenced by several factors such as:

- the liberalization of the Indian automobile industry and concurrent induction of foreign players changed the market dynamics, with the majority of the leading automotive manufacturers in the world establishing their presence in the Indian market;
- improvement in living standards and the increase in purchase capacity of the Indian middle class due to strong economic growth in the past decade, which has attracted the major automobile manufacturers, including the OEM, to the Indian market;
- the availability of trained manpower at competitive cost was another reason for the OEM to enter the Indian market.

The OEM manufactures more than seven car models with many variants or combinations in its Indian plants. It is leading the automotive industry in terms of volume, high-quality reliable cars, and customer satisfaction and service. This enviable reputation has been built in the past 30 years by closely working with the company's supply network including suppliers, distributors, and dealers in every country it operates or has production facilities in. In India, more than 65 percent of the passenger car market share is captured by segment "A" and "B," where the OEM has little presence. The company witnessed growth of more than 15 percent in February 2015 compared with the same month the year before. This could be attributed to the launch of a new model in category "B."

Sourcing and Strategy

The supply chain structure is very stable with more than 90 percent of material sourced from local suppliers that are either within 50–60 km radius, in the same city, or co-located inside the plant. At the time of data collection, the organization had 111 local first-tier suppliers. Most of the important and large locally procured parts, such as radiators, air-conditioners, seats, bumpers, instrument panels, and body shell parts, were supplied from within the same city—most by their *keiretsu* suppliers, i.e. the same Japanese-owned suppliers. These suppliers have supplied the OEM in Japan for more than 30 years and are now co-located near the OEM plant in India. The remaining suppliers were Indian and other foreign-owned companies, such as American and German, with production facilities in India. Following the Japanese philosophy, the OEM involves all 111 suppliers, instead of only a few strategic suppliers, in the supplier development activities with the aim of improving on suppliers' performance on KPIs related to safety, quality, production, delivery, environment, and costs.

The decoupling point in the automotive industry is very different from that in the construction and electronics industries. In complex industries such as automobile manufacturing, it is harder to implement an ATO approach as seen in the electronics industry. As per statistics, as little as 5 percent of cars manufactured in the United States are MTO. For the upstream operations in the OEM supply chain, MTO is the most prominent system, followed by the majority of first-tier suppliers. An example of an MTO system in our case is a seat supplier which supplies seats just in time in the correct sequence to match the OEM's final assembly schedule. This has helped to address efficiency issues at the supplier and OEM end—limited finished goods of seats at the supplier's plant and limited seats in raw material at the OEM's plants. This was managed by having real-time information exchange between the OEM and its suppliers using technologies like EDI to generate work orders. The downstream operation including distribution center and dealers follows a hybrid system of MTO and MTS. In the hybrid approach, the OEM makes stable high-volume product specifications to forecast (MTS) and build specifications to order less frequently (MTO). The final assembled product is stored either at the OEM's distribution center or at the dealer's end to manage the stock level between the two locations.

Lean Supply Chain Initiatives Implemented

The OEM is an established player in the automotive industry and is known for high-quality and reliable cars. The OEM is considered as an exemplar case for promoting lean initiatives across its supply chain and building collaborative supplier relationships including both horizontal and vertical relationships. The three key activities discussed below have helped its suppliers to become more efficient and effective.

The first is the supplier association that is called *Kyoryoku Kai* in Japan. The OEM has established a supplier association through which network norms and knowledge are shared among community members, which contributes to the improvement of quality and safety in suppliers. The second is suppler consulting through which OEM provides suppliers with on-site assistance as well as education and training on lean and other production systems that can help them to operate more efficiently. This type of support aims to develop suppliers' capability to implement lean initiatives in a learning-by-doing manner. The third is mutual learning activities in which the OEM jointly conducts lean projects at suppliers' plants through which best practices are shared not only between the OEM and its first-tier supplier but also among first-tier suppliers. The main purpose of this activity is to share knowledge in both vertical buyer–supplier relationships and horizontal supplier–supplier relationships. This is achieved by forming vol-untary study groups, termed *jishuken* in Japan, in which five to eight suppliers jointly try to improve on quality, production, delivery, safety, and cost-related issues using lean or Japanese production systems in one of these suppliers' plants. Almost 100 such projects are running every year, helping suppliers to learn from each other and the OEM in a learning-by-doing manner.

The OEM organized four to five joint kaizen conventions, such as a quality circle convention, in which only 40–50 strategic first-tier suppliers actively participated. However, all of the 111 first-tier suppliers participated in a general supplier meeting conducted annually. There was an award ceremony organized every year for recognizing best performing suppliers in each area of quality, delivery, cost, new project, and safety and environment. Suppliers' performance across different KPIs was also monitored on a monthly basis and the supplier development team worked with the underperforming supplier(s) to address issues critical to OEM performance. The OEM had a supplier support center to enhance suppliers' capabilities in the areas of safety, quality, production, costs, and *gemba kaizen*. One of the two main roles of the center was to train employees from the supplier end for one year; these employees were in charge of kaizen initiatives in the supplier plant. The center had already trained 50–60 suppliers in 2013, and planned to train all the local suppliers by the end of 2015. The other key role of the center was to support suppliers requesting assistance from the OEM by allocating and sending one or more support personnel from a group of 25 to the supplier's plant. In this case the suppliers had to cover the costs of support. This support was provided not only to the production lines of the OEM supply network, but also to other producers. The head of the supplier support center noted that this activity aimed to improve suppliers' capability.

Challenges and Lessons Learned

Unlike the other two cases included in this chapter, this OEM faced a different set of challenges when operating in the developing economy of India. The biggest challenge faced by the Japanese OEM operating in India was managing labor union and strike issues; the company had a lockdown in the past that significantly affected its production. The other challenge of operating in a developing country is infrastructure voids, i.e. the lack of a good road network, rail network, or shipping network, human resource voids, and managing cordial relationships with local and national government. The OEM is still importing some critical parts from Japan at relatively high costs due to currency fluctuations. The vision is to develop a 100 percent supplier base in India to minimize the effect of currency fluctuations. Developing the skills of the employees at its own plant and the suppliers' plants has helped maintain similar quality to that seen in the mother plant in Japan.

Cross Comparison of the Case Studies

How are the Case Studies Different?

The decoupling points across the three sectors are very different; ETO in construction, ATS in electronic, and hybrid MTO and MTS in the case of the automotive sector. Therefore the way in which the companies engage with the customer is different, as is the nature of work activities. In the construction sector case study, the contractor works closely with clients to co-design unique building solutions. Many manufactured products are heavy, bulky, and difficult to transport, so there is a tendency toward national supply arrangements. One-off projects make the standardization agenda promoted in lean very difficult to pursue, so techniques have to be adapted. Due to a more standard product range in the electronics and automotive sectors, it is easier to apply lean principles at the plant level. These sectors tend to operate globally.

What is a Lean Supply Chain? How are the Cases Similar?

To describe common characteristics of lean supply chains, we look at similarities across the three cases, as given in Table 19.1. All three sectors face challenges of complexity at the design, production, and supply chain level, though they all have a different approach in addressing these challenges. In each case there is also recognition that there is a dependence on suppliers' performance to meet the end goal of delivering the quality product on time and in full. Hence, each company has been prepared to lead change and play an active role in the development of individual suppliers, clusters of suppliers, and, in some cases, the whole network of suppliers. This endeavor is often longitudinal in nature with significant attitudinal change required. All three case studies place emphasis on moving toward more collaborative models of working, as well as rationalizing the number of suppliers in order to promote longer-term partnerships. Working closely with strategic suppliers, all three cases have managed to reduce complexity in delivery practices by adopting modular approaches and greater use of sub-assemblies and pre-assembly. On a final note, the three sectors all seem to be facing similar pressure from regulatory and government bodies to design more environmental friendly products to meet the needs of future generations.

It is also worth noting that the journeys described in the case examples take different starting points and trajectories, encountering slightly different issues. The electronics industry gives insight into a long history of industrial engineering improvements in the 1980s and through to

Table 19.1 Comparing lean supply chain initiatives across the case companies

Initiatives	Case Study 1 Construction	Case Study 2 PC	Case Study 3 Automotive
Rationalization of supply base	Pareto and strategic partners	Tiered structure with primary vendors	Keiretsu suppliers
Communication management and leadership	Executive briefings, head-start workshops, cluster meetings, colocation. Lean champion, affiliations with lean bodies	CPFR, shared forecasts, active WIP management	Supplier associations (Kyoryoku Kai), supplier support center, co-location
Performance management	KPIs, accreditations and supplier awards		KPIs and supplier awards
Training	Leadership training schemes, passport program	Large education program	Joint lean projects (jishuken), in-house, and gemba-based training for supplier
Knowledge exchange, and technical support	Physical base for best practice, logistics consultancy		Consultancy; on-site problem solving; jishuken
Delivery practices	Modular approaches and greater use of pre-assembly	Greater use of sub-assemblies, industrial engineering initiatives	Modular approaches for critical parts such as dashboard; just-in-sequence supply of engine from inside the plant; JIT delivery from local suppliers
Joint time compression	Lead time monitoring and management through "foresite" system	Active lead time reduction	Joint supplier activities promoted to achieve lead time reduction targets
Quality initiatives	Fostering a culture of continuous improvement	TQM, TPM	Japanese Production System; awards for best 5S, kaizen, and quality circle projects for the suppliers
Supplier participation in design and engineering activities	Strategic partners contribute to tenders and bids	Limited involvement of suppliers	Suppliers and customers involved in design and engineering activities

lean supply chain developments. The automotive example explains that even for a pioneer of lean concepts experienced in the application of lean thinking, opening a new plant in the emerging market of India creates significant challenges.

What are the "Levers" of Change?

The substantive levers of change may be categorized as technological, organizational, and attitudinal (Towill, 1997). The first may include specific manufacturing technologies such as machine tools but also information and communication technologies (ICT). Organizational factors may include changes associated with processes and procedures. The last category encompasses human factors and includes the development of relationships intra- and inter-organizationally.

The dominant lever in the three cases studies presented is attitudinal. All three case studies highlight the need for developing new ways of working that require buy-in from individuals within a specific organization but also with suppliers. It should be noted that all three case studies take as their focal point a dominant customer perspective and hence new relationships are instigated upstream in the supply chain from the focal company. Each of the case studies also suggests an internal focus prior to instigating external change. This has a lot in common with seminal work on supply chain management by Stevens (1989) who suggested a model for supply chain change. In that model, companies bring about internal change before widening the scope first to the supply base and only then to the customer end of the business.

A key lesson is the development of closer collaborative arrangements between the focal company and the supply base. This necessitates visibility of supplier operational capabilities, which may be facilitated by ICT. However, this requires willingness by the suppliers to expose them to detailed scrutiny in the form of monitoring of key performance indices. The potential payback for the suppliers is greater transparency of demand, support by the focal company in enhancing capabilities, and the promise of continued business if they do perform to set standards.

The Future of Lean Supply Chains

The case studies above cover a period of time spanning from the 1980s to the present. In each example, we find commonalities and differences with respect to the actual initiatives developed and implemented and the outcomes. This suggests the continuous evolution, and perhaps occasional revolution, of supply chain strategies and/or contextual adaptations.

As Hines et al. (2004) suggest, lean now encompasses all "good" things related to operations management, including agile production, theory of constraints, Six Sigma, and production planning and control systems such as MRP and ERP. Thus we find that there is no single unified lean supply chain management approach, with Vamshi et al. (2015) identifying 30 different existing frameworks.

A plethora of approaches to lean supply chain management potentially could result in confusion as well as the provision of opportunities. The former may result in practitioners seeking distinctiveness that does not exist in lean supply chains, the latter in having a strategic suite of options from which to choose and to evolve in the spirit of continuous improvement.

We suggest that there is a need to return to some basic principles of which the family of supply chain structures provides the foundations. Research has been undertaken in defining the characteristics of the processes downstream and upstream of the decoupling points (see Olhager, 2003; Wikner and Rudberg, 2005; Gosling and Naim, 2009), yielding "leagility," i.e. exploitation of lean and agile facets in a holistic approach to managing supply chains (Naylor et al., 1999) and networks (Purvis et al., 2014).

Another strand in the lean supply chain research could focus on the triadic buyer–supplier–supplier relationship and how such relationships promote knowledge sharing and mutual learning among network members (Dyer and Nobeoka, 2000; Wu and Choi, 2005; Wilhelm, 2011; Aoki and Kumar, 2014). Here focus could be on cooperation and competition among network suppliers and how that affects knowledge acquisition and learning (Wilhelm, 2011; Aoki and Kumar, 2014).

There is considerable discourse on the ongoing viability of lean supply chains in delivering value and ensuring resilience to ongoing and growing challenges such as climate change and humanitarian crises. The former requires more sustainable approaches to supply chain management while the latter may need redundancy in the form of capacity and stock holding, "just in case."

Determining the right mix of efficiency and effectiveness in the supply chain is a future research endeavor. By taking a contingent approach we can ensure that right solutions are selected for each and every problem we face in the supply chain. Further, we can ensure that we capitalize on new and emerging technologies, such as additive layer manufacturing and the internet of things, to facilitate the delivery of value to all stakeholders, such as customers, employees, suppliers, and wider society.

References

Aoki, K. and Kumar, M. (2014). Kaizen initiative through vertical supply networks in emerging economies. *Academy of Management Proceedings, 2014*(1), 1–40.

Berry, D. and Naim, M. M. (1996). Quantifying the relative improvements of redesign strategies in a PC supply chain. *International Journal of Production Economics, 46*, 181–196.

Christopher, M. (2005). *Logistics and Supply Chain Management: Creating Value-Adding Networks*, Harlow, UK, Financial Times Prentice Hall.

Dyer, J. H. and Nobeoka, K. (2000). Creating and managing a high-performance knowledge-sharing network: The Toyota case. *Strategic Management Journal, 21*(3), 345–367.

Gosling, J. and Naim, M. M. (2009). Engineer-to-order supply chain management: A literature review and research agenda. *International Journal of Production Economics, 122*(2), 741–754.

Gosling, J., Naim, M., Towill, D., Abouarghoub, W. and Moone, B. (2015). Supplier development initiatives and their impact on the consistency of project performance. *Construction Management and Economics, 33*(5–6), 390–403.

Hines, P., Holweg, M., and Rich, N. (2004). Learning to evolve: A review of contemporary lean thinking. *International Journal of Operations and Production Management, 24*(10), 994–1011.

Hoekstra, S. and Romme, J. (1992). *Integral Logistics Structures: Developing Customer Oriented Goods Flow*, London, McGraw-Hill.

Jones, D. T. and Womack, J. P., (2002). *Seeing the Whole: Mapping the Extended Value Stream*, Cambridge, MA, Lean Enterprise Institute.

Martínez-Jurado, P. J. and Moyano-Fuentes, J. (2014). Lean management, supply chain management and sustainability: A literature review. *Journal of Cleaner Production, 85*, 134–150.

Mollenkopf, D., Stolze, H., Tate, W. L. and Ueltschy, M. (2010). Green, lean, and global supply chains. *International Journal of Physical Distribution and Logistics Management, 40* (1/2), 14–41.

Naylor, J. B., Naim, M. M. and Berry, D. (1999). Leagility: Integrating the lean and agile manufacturing paradigms in the total supply chain. *International Journal of Production Economics, 62*(1), 107–118.

Olhager, J. (2003). Strategic positioning of the order penetration point. *International Journal of Production Economics, 85*, 319–329.

Purvis, L., Gosling, J. and Naim, M. M. (2014). The development of a lean, agile and leagile supply network taxonomy based on differing types of flexibility. *International Journal of Production Economics, 151*, 100–111.

Shah, R. and Ward, P. T. (2007). Defining and developing measures of lean production. *Journal of Operations Management, 25*(4), 785–805.

So, S. C. K., and Sun, H. Y. (2010). Supplier integration strategy for lean manufacturing adoption in electronic-enabled supply chains. *Supply Chain Management: An International Journal, 15*(6), 474–487.

Stevens, G. C. (1989). Integrating the supply chain. *International Journal of Physical Distribution and Materials Management, 19*, 3–8.

Towill, D. R. (1997). The seamless supply chain—The predator's strategic advantage. *International Journal of Technology Management, 13*(1), 37–56.

Vamshi, N., Jasti, K. and Kodali, R. (2015). A critical review of lean supply chain management frameworks: Proposed framework. *Production Planning and Control, 26*(13), 1051–1068.

Wikner, J. and Rudberg, M. (2005). Integrating production and engineering perspectives on the customer order decoupling point. *International Journal of Operations and Production Management, 25*(7–8), 623–641.

Wilhelm, M. M. (2011). Managing coopetition through horizontal supply chain relations: Linking dyadic and network levels of analysis. *Journal of Operations Management, 29,* 663–676.

Womack, J. P. and Jones, D. T. (1996). *Lean Thinking: Banish Waste and Create Wealth in Your Corporation,* New York, Simon & Schuster.

Wu, Z. and Choi, T. Y. (2005). Supplier–supplier relationships in the buyer–supplier triad: building theories from eight case studies. *Journal of Operations Management, 24*(1), 27–54.

20

LEAN DISTRIBUTION[1]

Matthias Holweg and Andreas Reichhart

Introduction

Despite the fact that the benefits of lean production have been documented across many industry settings, firms find it difficult to extend lean principles downstream into their distribution systems. The application of lean to downstream or distribution operations has been scarce. This has been recognized by manufacturers, including Toyota itself. At the Detroit Motor Show in 2000, Toyota's president Fujio Cho—who incidentally co-authored the first article written in English on the Toyota Production System (TPS) (see Sugimori et al., 1977)—announced that it was now "time to apply Toyota's mastery in Just-in-Time production to its distribution and marketing operations" (Andrews, 2000).

Lean distribution is essentially the extension of the demand-driven "pull" signal downstream from the factory to the final customer, in order to build products only when the customer demands them. However, extending lean beyond the factory and component supply system into distribution operations results in a potential conflict: lean production is based on the principle of level scheduling, which by reducing schedule variability enables the tightly synchronized *kanban* links between processes, and even companies. The resulting need for long-term stable production schedules conflicts with the often volatile demand in the marketplace, which a *lean distribution system* cannot buffer against. In the light of this conflict between *lean production* and *lean distribution*, vehicle manufacturers have traditionally decided in favor of the former by producing large proportions of vehicles to forecast, ensuring a high capacity utilization (Holweg and Pil, 2004). Interestingly, Toyota conducted several experiments with more responsive ordering systems in the 1970s to significantly increase the proportion of cars built to customer order, yet later abandoned the system in favor of a less responsive order amendment system (Shioji, 2000).

Lean thinking has been applied across manufacturing and component supply echelons in a wide range of industry sectors, leading to unequivocal performance improvements. However, these accounts stand in stark contrast to the few studies and cases that have been reported on the adoption of lean strategies in distribution. It would appear that adopting a lean distribution strategy presents an equal leap of faith to the one that lean production posed when it was introduced to the Western world three decades ago. To quote a senior executive from an OEM we have worked with: "If we had had to quantify the net benefits from lean distribution before going down that path, we would not have done it, yet we are glad we did."

What is Lean Distribution?

The concept of lean distribution can be defined as a logical extension of the lean production approach. Lean distribution, similar to the concept of *lean supply* (Lamming, 1993; Hines, 1994; MacDuffie and Helper, 1997), should in our view be regarded not as a novel concept in its own right, but as a logical and consequent extension of lean principles into the distribution system downstream from the final manufacturing facility. As such, the distribution echelon in the supply chain only started to receive attention quite late in the lean debate. While the principles of lean production began to evolve in the 1950s and were extended to supplier operations from the 1970s onwards, the distribution function only started to attract mainstream academic attention from the late 1980s (see Figure 20.1) (Davis, 1993; Fisher et al., 1994; Lowson et al., 1999). However, in many supply chains the main focus still rests on the manufacturing operation (Kiff, 1997; Holweg and Pil, 2004).

In this respect, discussing lean distribution—as distinct from lean production—is fraught with difficulty in defining the boundaries of the (sub)system in question. The philosophy of contemporary *lean thinking* can be summarized as maximizing the relative value delivered (considering varying consumer preferences) by reducing waste and thus operational costs. Accordingly, we define lean distribution as *minimizing waste in the downstream supply chain, while making the right product available to the end customer at the right time and location.*

In line with the principles of TPS and lean thinking, this can best be achieved by the end customer "pulling" products from the factory instead of the factory "pushing" products into the market. This is a simple extension of the JIT concept by executing production only once products are pulled by the subsequent process, i.e. the customer. That way, "our worst enemy" (Ohno, 1988)—overproduction—is averted, and the company essentially produces or replenishes its goods against customer orders. Such a definition of lean distribution applies to all types of supply chains, although its implementation will depend on various product- and market-related factors.

The Importance of the P:D Ratio for Lean Distribution

While for some products, such as cars and personal computers, build-to-order supply chains have been suggested (Hertz et al., 2001; Holweg and Pil, 2001; Kapuscinski et al., 2004), other products, such as fashion or sports apparel and groceries, may require inventory-based, yet responsive supply chains and manufacturing techniques (Fisher et al., 1994; Lowson et al., 1999; Christopher, 2000). This has a direct impact on the strategies that can be pursued to minimize distribution costs by eliminating waste.

The main product characteristics that determine the applicability of any order fulfillment strategy are product variety and related differences in demand uncertainty (Fisher, 1997)

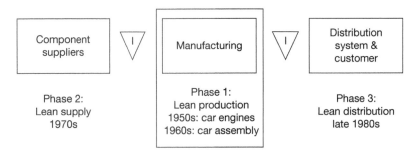

Figure 20.1 Expansion of lean concepts in the value chain

Table 20.1 Distribution scenarios

Scenario	D=0	D>0 and P>D	D>0 and P≤D
Explanation	Customers require instant gratification at the location of their choice (commonly retail outlets). In this case *P* is almost irrelevant, because inventory will always be required.	Customers are willing to wait but the combined production and distribution time is longer than they are willing to wait.	Customers are willing to wait and the combined production and distribution time is less than they are willing to wait.
Characteristics of necessary inventory	Decentralized inventory is required; the decoupling point must be in retail outlets.	Inventory is required in the distribution system. However, the location of the decoupling point depends on various factors.	No inventory is required in the distribution system.
Industry examples	Fast-moving consumer goods, groceries	Furniture, printers, most automotive spare parts	Traditional project work

combined with the *P:D* ratio. In the *P:D* model, *P* stands for a product's production lead time and *D* for the delivery lead time a customer is willing to wait for a product after placing an order (Mather, 1988; Shingo, 1989). While the *P:D* ratio determines whether distribution systems are generally capable of delivering products without the need for inventory, one of the most significant wastes (Womack and Jones, 1996; Jones et al., 1997; Lowson et al., 1999), the amount of inventory required to satisfy customer needs in inventory-based systems depends primarily on the product variety offered and partially related demand characteristics. Table 20.1 summarizes the characteristics of the three generic distribution strategies depending on a product's *P:D* ratio.

Although the first aim should be to reduce the production lead time *P* to avoid stock altogether (Shingo, 1989; Monden, 1998), the important point to make here is that lean distribution cannot simply be defined as stockless distribution or build-to-order (BTO). This is because there will always be products for which customers are not willing to wait as long as it takes to produce them. A wide range of contributions exist about supply chains requiring instant gratification (i.e. where *D=0*), such as food and groceries (Womack and Jones, 1996; Lowson et al., 1999), and textiles (Fisher et al., 1994; Christopher, 1998; Lowson et al., 1999) as well as supply chains with a *P:D* ratio of much greater than one, such as furniture (Lowson et al., 1999), automotive spare parts (Womack and Jones, 1996), and printers (Davis, 1993). Lean distribution in these supply chains has often been covered under the "quick response" initiative that started in the textile industry in the mid-1980s (Lowson et al., 1999), or as part of the "agile" supply chain literature (Christopher, 2000).

Womack et al. (1990) and Kiff (2000) have previously examined characteristics of lean distribution in the automotive supply chain. They illustrate how under lean distribution a change in the relationship between customer and vehicle manufacturer would allow the manufacturer to increase its profits over the life cycle of a car and secure customer loyalty, to leverage its knowledge of customer preferences in the product development process, and to improve its production forecast based on improved market understanding. While a number of the techniques mentioned, such as the segmentation of dealerships by car size/type, arguably serve marketing and sales purposes, a close relationship with the end customer can reduce flexibility requirements on manufacturing operations. Not only will sales forecasts improve with an improved understanding of customer needs, but customer expectations can also be managed better to smooth the order flow and reduce variability in demand before it occurs (Womack et al., 1990). However, a detailed account of the operational and organizational difficulties of extending pull beyond the factory is still lacking. This is a particular shortcoming, as even the "lean" Japanese vehicle manufacturers have not achieved the lean transformation of their distribution systems (Andrews, 2000; Shioji, 2000). In this respect, reportedly high percentages of BTO production for the Japanese market (Womack et al., 1990; Shioji, 2000) may have to be re-evaluated, given large vehicle exports into less demanding overseas markets that act as buffers (Holweg and Pil, 2004), and a lower product variety in combination with a less responsive order amendment system (Shioji, 2000; Pil and Holweg, 2004).

Finally, supply chains with a *P:D* ratio of smaller or exactly equal to one, such as traditional one-off engineering projects (like large construction projects), are arguably less interesting from a distribution point of view. However, products with a *P:D* ratio of close to one featuring potentially strong variations between different customer segments pose a significant problem for distribution systems. This has yet to be covered sufficiently in the literature. Such supply chains may have to rely on some form of inventory in the distribution system for some but not all customers. The car industry provides a good example for such distribution systems (Fisher, 1997; Holweg and Pil, 2004).

Challenges with Lean Distribution

Various authors have investigated the general conflicts between a firm's manufacturing and sales, distribution and/or marketing functions (Shapiro, 1977; Karmarkar, 1996; Malhotra and Sharma, 2002). While few contributions discuss the specific conflicts between *lean manufacturing* and *lean distribution*, some similar conflict areas, such as the cost of manufacturing flexibility (manufacturing) versus the need to respond to changing customer requirements (sales and marketing), have been highlighted (Shapiro, 1977; Karmarkar, 1996; Mukhopadhyay and Gupta, 1998). One of the main causes for the conflicts between manufacturing and marketing is that each function has a different focus. Cost is the focus in the manufacturing department while revenue is the focus in the sales department, while both departments fail to see the overall goal of maximizing profitability (Shapiro, 1977; Mukhopadhyay and Gupta, 1998).

A specific feature of the Toyota Production System, and in particular the kanban production control system, is that it requires a level, or smoothed, production schedule (also referred to as "*heijunka*") (Sugimori et al., 1977; Shingo, 1989; Monden, 1998). Smoothed production schedules minimize the variations between two consecutive periods (day-to-day changes as well as week-to-week changes) to minimize costs through otherwise required capacity or inventory buffers (Shingo, 1989). Market demand, however, is seldom smooth and even aggregated demand over multiple products can vary significantly on a day-by-day basis, let alone the demand for individual products.

The resulting rigidity or inflexibility of lean production schedules has been a major point of criticism (Naylor et al., 1999; Christopher, 2000; Mason-Jones et al., 2000). Hines et al. (2004) argue that a lot of this criticism is based on an overly narrow understanding of the wider lean approach. On the contrary, Towill and Christopher (2002) suggest that the lean (i.e. inventory-based distribution) and agile (i.e. responsive distribution) concepts can be integrated into a combined supply chain strategy, as long as they remain separated by space and/or time. Separation by space is given, for example, when one product is manufactured in a lean plant, while a different product is produced in an agile plant. Separation by time means that the same supply chain can be lean or responsive at different times (e.g. agile during summer and lean during winter). However, problems remain when lean production and lean distribution are to be truly combined for the same product and at the same time. The earlier quoted statement by Fujio Cho provides further support for such a conflict between lean production and lean distribution. Fujimoto (2006) recently revealed that Toyota was still looking for ways to implement a "stress-free" BTO system, i.e. without any adversarial impacts on their lean production processes.

So far, the main coping mechanisms are inventory buffers in the distribution system, which vehicle manufacturers implicitly favor over capacity buffers in their final assembly plants, because of the large investments in plant and machinery required in vehicle assembly. Commonly, this has resulted in a decoupling of production from the distribution function through considerable buffers of unsold vehicles in the market (averages of two months' worth of on-hand inventory have been reported (see Kiff, 1997; Holweg and Pil, 2004)). We see this decoupling as the most visible indication of the conflict between lean production and lean distribution. In many ways holding inventory at this point in the system is the worst possible scenario, as not only is the value of the product the highest (and it is thus the most costly point at which to hold stock), but also the product is fully configured here. This leads to high levels of alternative specification discounts (Williams, 2005).

In general, such localized approaches to managing the supply chain will invariably lead to "islands of excellence" within otherwise inefficient value chains (Womack and Jones, 1996; Holweg and Pil, 2004). Equally, the implementation of lean distribution without the consideration of the wider system will not facilitate an overall lean supply chain, as the savings made in distribution must be weighed against potential adversarial impacts in other parts of the value chain, such as manufacturing. Thus, the implementation of lean distribution must entail the understanding and management of the trade-offs between the sometimes conflicting manufacturing and distribution requirements. The latter argument is well illustrated with the following quote from an automobile company which implemented lean distribution:

> Ten years ago, we thought 100 percent build-to-order was the right approach. Now we have achieved this capability but see that the market and especially our growth strategy require a balanced mix between build-to-order and make-to-forecast production.

The Future of Lean Distribution

The challenge for the future will be to keep the operational capabilities to produce customer specific orders with short lead times and high precision (for those customers who value individuality), while at the same time leveraging the stability that a managed make-to-forecast (MTF) production (for those customers who want instant gratification and a cheap deal) can add in order to reduce operational costs. Such an approach is likely to include at least some of the following characteristics and processes:

- *An increased build-to-order content facilitates lean distribution.* Our findings from research in the automobile industry show that an increase in BTO production by 1 percent can reduce finished goods inventories by an average of 0.67 days of demand.
- *Extending frozen horizons facilitates lean distribution.* The main reason for short frozen horizons is the fear of unused capacities in times of low customer demand. In a setting with managed supply, the frozen horizon can be extended, because a certain percentage of cars are supposed to be produced to stock. This will save costs in the upstream supply chain by providing more reliable planning information to suppliers.
- *Conducting Pareto analysis of customer demand facilitates lean distribution.* Considering large product variety, cars produced to stock are unlikely to meet a specific end customer's wishes.

Therefore, a Pareto analysis of customer demand must be carried out to only produce cars to stock that have a high chance of finding a customer afterwards. Even if a number of vehicle manufacturers claim that they never build the same car twice, given millions of possible option combinations the chances of finding at least a close match can be increased by Pareto techniques.

- *Centralizing inventory facilitates lean distribution.* A number of vehicle manufacturers have already established central holding compounds for cars in order to increase the availability of cars produced to stock without incurring costly dealer transfers. While central holding compounds can reduce the costs of distributing MTF cars, it needs to be investigated whether such a strategy has any advantages over BTO production when it comes to the customer's desire for instant gratification.

- *Producing customer orders before stock orders facilitates lean distribution.* In order to ensure short lead times for customer orders, they must be given priority over stock orders. Otherwise, customers will be discouraged from ordering BTO cars.

Conclusions

In this chapter we have argued that the slow adoption of lean thinking in distribution is due to an inherent conflict between lean manufacturing techniques (related to production smoothing and kanban systems that cannot cope with high levels of variability) and the need to link the production pull signal to variable demand in the marketplace. We concede that quantifying the trade-off between the cost of coping with flexibility in manufacturing and the cost-saving potential due to reduced finished goods inventory and incentives is complex. In the light of Simon's work on bounded rationality (Simon, 1982), it should therefore be hardly surprising that many manufacturers have opted to optimize their manufacturing operations. This requires considerable capital investment and incurs large operating expenses. Thus, the distribution system has been considered only as a secondary concern.

Considering the efforts that firms need to invest in order to achieve comparative reductions in component stock in their manufacturing plants, it is surprising to see so few firms adopt lean distribution strategies. However, the organizational dynamics and barriers that need to be overcome in order to manage the cross-functional trade-offs in the organization can pose considerable obstacles. This is further amplified by misaligned performance metrics, short-termism induced by artificial reporting periods, and the difficulty in quantifying the operational cost savings a priori. Considering this, we believe there is a great unrealized potential in applying lean distribution.

Case Study: Implementing *Douki-Seisan* at Nissan

Nissan Motor Company was established in 1933, and rapidly grew in the post-war years under the guidance of the Japanese Ministry for Trade and Industry (MITI) to become one of the world's top car manufacturers. In the 1990s, however, the company entered a period of poor profitability, and the often-lauded strong interlinkage with its *kereitsu* (conglomerate) partners became a financial liability rather than a source of strength (see Figure 20.2).

Many root causes for the crisis were at play, but one of the obvious failures was a drastic overstocking situation of finished vehicles in the marketplace (see Figure 20.3). Producing ahead of demand and selling cars from inventory clearly was no longer a viable strategy. It locked up large

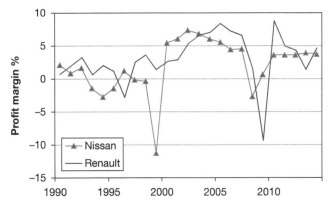

Figure 20.2 Pre-tax profit margins at Nissan and Renault, 1990–2014

Source: Holweg and Oliver (2016).

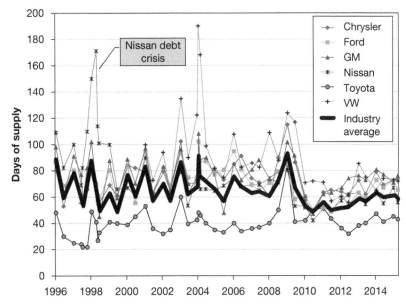

Figure 20.3 Finished vehicle inventory levels in the US market, 1996–2015

Source: Holweg and Oliver (2016).

sums of capital, led to considerable financial losses due to rebates and discounts needed to shift the metal, and often left the customer with a vehicle that did not meet his or her needs (Holweg and Pil, 2004).

In the wake of the merger with Renault, Nissan decided to meet this challenge by implementing "*douki-seisan*" (which literally translates as "the customer leads the way"), a strategic initiative that would extend the lean manufacturing logic to the distribution arm. Key objectives were to raise the build-to-order content, thereby reducing inventory levels as well as sales incentives needed to shift aging stock or to persuade customers to take vehicles that did not meet the required specification.

Operationally, two main changes were implemented. First, a "D-6" (day minus 6) approach was implemented, which saw orders only being "frozen" six days before production. Up to this point unsold vehicles could be amended to meet a customer's needs. Second, unsold stock was merged into national distribution centers (operated by Nissan itself), which allowed all dealers to access these vehicles freely (thereby avoiding costly dealer transfers of individual cars).

The outcomes were impressive, especially in Europe where the shift from MTF to BTO was the most pronounced. Average savings for vehicles built to order, as compared with those made to forecast and sold from stock, ranged in the order of several hundred euros. Nissan observed a significant drop in both inventory and rebates needed to sell its vehicles across all major markets.

More recently, Nissan is further improving its BTO initiative by developing an open order pipeline, which seamlessly integrates all available options for order fulfillment into one system available to the dealer. The boundaries between true build-to-order, order amendment, and fulfillment from central or dealer stock thus blur into one coherent approach to fulfilling customer needs in the shortest possible time, while minimizing inventories and incentives needed in distribution.

Acknowledgments

We would like to thank Philip Wade and Jonathan Brown for their kind support.

Note

1 This chapter is a shortened and updated version of the paper "Lean distribution: Concepts, contributions, conflicts," published in the *International Journal of Production Research*, 2004, *45*(16), 3699–3722.

References

Andrews, F. (2000, January 26). Dell, it turns out, has a better idea than Ford. *The New York Times*.

Christopher, M. (1998). *Logistics and Supply Chain Management*, Harlow, UK, Pearson.

Christopher, M. (2000). The agile supply chain—Competing in volatile markets. *Industrial Marketing Management*, *29*(1), 37–44.

Davis, T. (1993). Effective supply chain management. *Sloan Management Review*, *34*(4), 35–46.

Fisher, M. L. (1997). What is the right supply chain for your product? *Harvard Business Review*, *75*(2), 105–116.

Fisher, M. L., Hammond, J. H., Obermeyer, W. R. and Raman, A. (1994). Making supply meet demand in an uncertain world. *Harvard Business Review*, *72*(3), 83–93.

Fujimoto, T. (2006). Toyota and its evolution since "The Machine." *IMVP and WZB Sponsor Industry Workshop*, Berlin.

Hertz, S., Johansson, J. K. and De Jager, F. (2001). Customer-oriented cost cutting: Process management at Volvo. *Supply Chain Management: An International Journal*, *6*(3), 128–141.

Hines, P. (1994). *Creating World Class Suppliers: Unlocking Mutual Competitive Advantage*, London, Pitman Publishing.

Hines, P., Holweg, M. and Rich, N. (2004). Learning to evolve—A review of contemporary lean thinking. *International Journal of Operations & Production Management*, *24*(10), 994–1011.

Holweg, M. and Pil, F. K. (2001). Successful build-to-order strategies start with the customer. *MIT Sloan Management Review*, *43*(1), 74–83.

Holweg, M. and Pil, F. K. (2004). *The Second Century: Reconnecting Customer and Value Chain through Build-to-Order*, Cambridge, MA, and London, MIT Press.

Holweg, M. and Oliver, N. (2016). *Crisis, Resilience and Survival: Lessons from the Global Auto Industry*. Cambridge, Cambridge University Press.

Jones, D. T., Hines, P. and Rich, N. (1997). Lean logistics. *International Journal of Physical Distribution & Logistics Management*, 27(3/4), 153–173.

Kapuscinski, R., Zhang, R. Q., Carbonneau, P., Moore, R. and Reeves, B. (2004). Inventory decisions in Dell's supply chain. *Interfaces*, 34(3), 191–205.

Karmarkar, U. S. (1996). Integrative research in marketing and operations management. *Journal of Marketing Research*, 33(2), 125–133.

Kiff, J. S. (1997). Supply and stocking systems in the UK car market. *International Journal of Physical Distribution & Logistics Management*, 27(3/4), 226–243.

Kiff, J. S. (2000). The lean dealership—A vision for the future: "From hunting to farming". *Marketing Intelligence & Planning*, 18(3), 112–126.

Lamming, R. (1993). *Beyond Partnership: Strategies for Innovation and Lean Supply*, New York, Prentice Hall.

Lowson, B., King, R. and Hunter, A. (1999). *Quick Response*, Chichester, Wiley.

MacDuffie, J. P. and Helper, S. (1997). Creating lean suppliers: Diffusing lean production through the supply chain. *California Management Review*, 39(4), 118–151.

Malhotra, M. K. and Sharma, S. (2002). Spanning the continuum between marketing and operations. *Journal of Operations Management*, 20(3), 209–219.

Mason-Jones, R., Naylor, J. B. and Towill, D. R. (2000). Lean, agile or leagile? Matching your supply chain to the marketplace. *International Journal of Production Research*, 38(17), 4061–4070.

Mather, H. (1988). *Competitive Manufacturing*, Englewood Cliffs, NJ, Prentice Hall.

Monden, Y. (1998). *Toyota Production System*, Norcross, Engineering & Management Press.

Mukhopadhyay, S. K. and Gupta, A. V. (1998). Interfaces for resolving marketing, manufacturing and design conflicts. *European Journal of Marketing*, 32(1/2), 101–124.

Naylor, J. B., Naim, M. M. and Berry, D. (1999). Leagility: Integrating the lean and agile manufacturing paradigms in the total supply chain. *International Journal of Production Economics*, 62(1/2), 107–118.

Ohno, T. (1988). *Toyota Production System: Beyond Large-Scale Production*, New York, Productivity Press.

Pil, F. K. and Holweg, M. (2004). Linking product variety to order-fulfillment strategies. *Interfaces*, 34(5), 394–403.

Shapiro, B. P. (1977). Can marketing and manufacturing coexist? *Harvard Business Review*, 55(5), 104–114.

Shingo, S. (1989). *A Study of the Toyota Production System from an Industrial Engineering Viewpoint*, New York, Productivity Press.

Shioji, H. (2000). The order entry system in Japan. *International Symposium on Logistics*, Morioka, Japan.

Simon, H. A. (1982). *Models of Bounded Rationality*, Cambridge, MA, MIT Press.

Sugimori, Y., Kusunoki, K., Cho, F. and Uchikawa, S. (1977). Toyota Production System and kanban system: Materialization of just-in-time and respect-for-human system. *International Journal of Production Research*, 15(6), 553–564.

Towill, D. R. and Christopher, M. (2002). The supply chain strategy conundrum: To be lean or agile or to be lean and agile? *International Journal of Logistics: Research and Applications*, 5(3), 299–309.

Williams, G. (2005). Does customer pull work in a recession? *New Vehicle Supply Workshop*, International Car Distribution Programme, February 24, Solihull, UK.

Womack, J. P. and Jones, D. T. (1996). *Lean Thinking: Banish Waste and Create Wealth in Your Corporation*, London, Simon & Schuster.

Womack, J. P., Jones, D. T. and Roos, D. (1990). *The Machine that Changed the World: A Story of Lean Production*, New York, HarperCollins.

21

LEAN AFTER-SALES SERVICES

Barbara Resta, Paolo Gaiardelli, Stefano Dotti, and Dario Luise

Introduction

Lean principles were originally developed in industrial manufacturing operations and were operationalized as a set of tools and practices that managers and workers could use to eliminate waste and inefficiency from production systems—reducing costs, improving quality and reliability, and speeding up cycle times.

The recent transformation of manufacturing organizations toward the development of differentiation strategies founded on a product-service paradigm, well known as "*servitization of manufacturing*" (Vandermerwe and Rada, 1989), has encouraged scholars and practitioners to extend their discussions on lean production principles' portability in the light of this changing manufacturing setting. Researchers have started to explore the linkage between the adoption of lean thinking and product-service design, development, and management and delivery through the analysis of how the deployment of the lean philosophy: 1) enables the alignment of value-adding activities with the customer value stream (Hines et al., 2011), 2) supports enterprise knowledge transfer through exploiting the capabilities of those involved, 3) increases the communication across functional boundaries (Tracey and Flinchbaugh, 2006), and 4) decentralizes the decision-making process, fostering a dynamic process of change to ensure a robust, flexible, adaptive, and responsive enterprise (Bozdogan et al., 2000).

In particular, managerial and practical studies have focused on understanding how lean initiatives can help organizations dealing with the first level of servitization (Oliva and Kallenberg, 2003), also called after-sales services, to improve and differentiate themselves while lowering costs and capital investments. Indeed, as a consolidated business strategy adopted by the majority of Western manufacturing companies, after-sales services require new ways and approaches to significantly increase operations performance. A lean approach can support companies to move in this direction.

On these premises, this chapter introduces an overview of the application of lean thinking philosophy in after-sales services. Through real examples and a case study, the chapter explores how lean principles, methods, and tools can advance both efficiency and effectiveness of after-sales service processes, underlining strengths and weaknesses, as well as opening issues and challenges in the adoption of lean thinking in the after-sales area.

After-Sales Services

After-sales services represent the activities that support products after they are sold and delivered to customers. Created to guarantee functionality and durability of a product, and support customers during the middle and end-of-life phases of a product life cycle, after-sales services can be grouped into four main categories (Legnani et al., 2013):

1 services provided during the process of transferring the ownership of the product to the customer to make it work, such as product installation, training, product documentation, or financial or insurance services as well as extension or customization of the warranty,
2 services provided to facilitate and improve the procedures for efficient use of the product by the user as well as to periodically assess any unforeseen issues that may arise, such as customer care, upgrades, and product check-up,
3 services associated with the recovery of product functions, such as maintenance and repair of products, and replacement of defective parts, and
4 services associated with product disposal, dismissal, or recovery at the end of its lifespan.

The relevance of after-sales services is demonstrated by the several advantages achievable by companies in terms of higher profit margins, more stable source of profits, and lower cash flow vulnerability. For instance, in the automotive industry, while the average sales profitability for car manufacturers and their dealer networks ranges between 0 and 2 percent, the after-sales business accounts for up to 23 percent of revenues and 50 percent of profits (SupplierBusiness, 2009), generating at least three times the turnover of the original purchase. Moreover, the huge number of vehicles in circulation can secure important and stable revenues over time. In addition, in a context of global competition and decreasing profits from product sales, the after-sales service is not only a profit source. It also becomes a key differentiator for manufacturing companies, supporting them in building up barriers to entry, and making market penetration by potential new competitors more difficult. Through long-term warranties, service contracts, or mandatory maintenances to preserve warranty rights, after-sales services represent a powerful marketing force for establishing durable customer loyalty and promoting the company brand image. Finally, data gathered from the field are a topical input for an effective undertaking of new product and service development, sales and promotion, as well as marketing and customer relationship management activities.

Nevertheless, escalating challenges characterizing the current after-sales market call modern organizations to rethink their after-sales operations processes and activities. Examples of such challenges include rising customer expectations (in terms of new and challenging levels of perfection, response time, and convenience), revenue, regulatory and competitive pressures, and increasing expenses requested to sustain the proliferation of complex and high-technological product-service offerings. In such a context, translating lean production philosophy to the management of after-sales processes may represent a valid managerial solution to enable organizations to meet their customers' expectations and sustain competitive advantage and growth.

What are Lean After-Sales Services?

Adapting the lean production definition provided by Shah and Ward (2007) to the after-sales domain, it can be stated that "Lean after-sales services are an integrated socio-technical system focused on the definition and the creation of successful and profitable after-sale value streams by eliminating waste and concurrently reducing or minimizing supplier, customer, and internal variability." By focusing on the value creation concept, a lean after-sales service approach supports companies in meeting the challenges and the additional complexities that are introduced when services are integrated into a product, notably (Pawar et al., 2009):

- defining the value proposition that will satisfy the customer,
- designing the operational system to deliver the value proposition, and
- delivering the value through a network of partners.

In particular, lean after-sales service is related to the revision and application of lean production principles, as defined by Womack and Jones (1996), that organized production work as an uninterrupted flow proceeding through all processes at a steady pace without rework, backflow, or inventories, for the flexible delivery of quality products in the shortest possible time and at minimum cost.

Principle 1: Specify After-sales Service Value

Identify what customers really want. In lean thinking, the value of a product or service is defined exclusively by the end-use customer. The product or service must meet the customer's needs at both a specific time and price. Similarly, in after-sales the customer becomes an integral part of the process (value co-creator) and the consumption experience defines what is valuable to a customer (Smith et al., 2014). In particular, value tends to focus on product availability and performance, along with risk and reward sharing between customer and after-sales service provider (Baines et al., 2009). Therefore, the application of a lean production approach can create a powerful methodology for defining and designing the value proposition that will satisfy individual customer expectations over time. Thus, it will also create a powerful methodology for identifying the related value co-creation process.

Principle 2: Identify the After-sales Service Value Stream

Identifying the value co-creation stream means to understand all the activities required to provide an after-sales service, and then to optimize the whole process from the view of the end-use customer. The customer's standpoint is fundamental for identifying activities that: 1) add value from waste, 2) add no value but are essential under current conditions (type 1 *muda*), and 3) add no value and thus can be eliminated immediately (type 2 *muda*). In after-sales, eight waste areas can be identified:

1   *Transportation*: Unnecessary, wrong, or slow movement of materials and/or information between employees and departments results in variable time being wasted. For example, the rejection of a loan to finance a product sale or expensive after-sale repair due to incorrect income calculations goes through multiple handoffs and approvals before it is corrected. Unnecessary transportation includes not only documents and materials, but also moving customers to different offices and desks to complete a process.
2   *Inventory*: The traditional manufacturing concept of inventory does not exist in after-sales services, since services cannot be kept in stock. However, poor balancing of workloads, particularly when work is processed in large batches, suboptimal housekeeping (for example, poor filing or record-keeping, or lost documents) and insufficient communication may cause excess items or supplies, activities backlogs, or, conversely, stock-out events.

3   *Motion*: Inefficient work routines caused by high levels of bureaucracy and/or unproductive and unstructured layouts involve the creation of unnecessary movements not required for performing a service activity. This implies an inefficient management of the service level promised to customers.

4   *Waiting*: Unbalanced workload among employees, too few office machines and working stations, lack of a clear process, and quality problems cause delays with customers waiting for service delivery.

5   *Over-processing*: Unclear communication with customers generates too much information. This creates unnecessary duplication of service activities (e.g. re-entering data) that, in turn, implies confusion among the employees, who get stressed and start to make mistakes.

6   *Overproduction*: A poor understanding of customers' true needs or failing to design the results of processes that conform to customer requirements generates the provision of unnecessary or non-added-value after-sales solutions. Moreover, any rework takes up effort that actually should be going into a fresh transaction. For example, a misdelivered spare part results in extra pick-up from and delivery to the destination.

7   *Defects*: Low-quality service delivery or a lost opportunity to retain or win customers by ignoring them, unfriendliness, or similar could result in a real adverse and very costly event that, unlike in manufacturing, can not be rectified. For example, the rework on an engine has no impact on the customer as long as the final product meets the specifications. Conversely, the wrong answer provided in a call center will leave a bad feeling with the customer even after the mistake is corrected.

8   *Employees*: Making insufficient use of employee creativity and commitment as well as customers' abilities causes underutilization of service delivery capacity. Underutilization also occurs when organizations fail to make full use of available knowledge, skills, and abilities, e.g. using highly trained professionals to perform tasks that could be performed by someone with less training.

Identifying the value stream means identifying the components of the after-sales service activities which add value to customers. However, customer expectations may vary both between customers and for individual customers over time. Therefore, identifying the adding-value activities is not a simple task. There is the risk that what some customers may see as waste, other customers see as adding value to their experience and hence to the whole system. Moreover, activities that may be considered waste in a manufacturing setting may create value in after-sales. For example, a technician illustrating product conditions after completing product diagnosis tasks may appear a non-added-value task from a manufacturing point of view, depleting highly expensive resources. In an after-sales service setting, however, information transparency achieved through such activities results in a fundamental increase in customer trust and thus improves their satisfaction.

Principle 3: Create the After-sales Service Flow

Get the activities that add value to flow without interruption. Flow can potentially improve both efficiency and customer satisfaction by minimizing provision delays or stoppages for after-sales services in which diversity of demand and customers' disposition to participate are low. This is particularly true for service activities that are evaluated by customers on technical quality determinants, like timeliness, responsiveness, and reliability (as with repair maintenance and spare parts delivery). However, when the customer participates to a greater extent with their own efforts and resources (e.g. in front-office activities), the application of the flow principle is more difficult. The customer helps create the service instead of being a flow-brick in the provider's process, potentially resulting in reduced customer satisfaction. Indeed, actively pushing the customer through a standardized flow may negatively affect the customer's emotional experience (Carlborg et al., 2013).

Moreover, since after-sales value is mostly delivered through a network of partners, it is fundamental that flow identification and optimization encompasses the entire value chain. This means it includes all parts of the organization involved in value co-creation, as well as the external suppliers, partners, and stakeholders.

Principle 4: Establish Pull

The pull principle is typically embedded in the characteristics of after-sales services and, in general, of pure services, because they cannot be kept in stock or be produced before a customer's order is placed. However, the firm must constantly forecast after-sales service demand in order to have the right competencies and quantities of resources available (equipment, personnel, spare parts, etc.) to satisfy customers. The workflow must be simplified for everyone and the service team has to work to continuously improve the process with scientific methods like PDCA (plan, do, check, act) standards.

Principle 5: Pursuit of Perfection

Lean is a journey of continuous improvement rather than a destination, where value is constantly identified and waste eliminated. While perfection will never be achieved, it is a goal worth striving for because it helps maintain a constant guard against waste. Indeed, on the road of excellence every step must be scrupulously considered. This means that every company pursuing perfection in after-sales services must apply a high level of attention to everything it does, at all levels of its service network, from planning to execution.

Lean Operations in After-Sales Services

To grasp the lean after-sales service approach in an after-sales service provider, managers must focus on eliminating non-value activities from processes by applying a robust set of approaches, and emphasize excellence in operations to deliver superior customer service. Nevertheless, even though some current lean production methodologies are suitable for manufacturing as well as for the majority of after-sales service settings (process mapping methodologies dealing with work-flow and from which the information flow can be identified), other methodologies can be more appropriate in specific circumstances. For example, standardization of procedures is a fundamental step in implementing every lean after-sales service. The standardization of processes is appropriate only for highly repeatable services with low customer involvement, such as back-office (planning and administration) and preventive maintenance activities. Such an approach is less suitable in the case of front-office activities that require stronger customer involvement and participation (such as help-desk support) and that are characterized by a lower repeatability (as in repair activities). On these premises, configuring lean strategies into after-sales services operations requires considering both structural and infrastructural characteristics. This is summarized by Resta et al. (2015) and briefly discussed in Table 21.1.

Lean After-Sales Services: Challenges and Opportunities

Benefits achievable from lean implementation in the after-sales business can be outstanding (see Figure 21.1). A survey carried out by Politecnico of Milan in 2010 on a sample of 100 manufacturing

Table 21.1 Lean after-sales service—structural and infrastructural characteristics

Characteristic	Description
Structural	
Process and technology	Lean after-sales services tend to utilize standardized procedures and simple, proven technologies as a way of reducing waste and non-value-adding activities (type 1 muda). Conversely, advanced technologies are avoided due to possible negative effects of the use of "black-box" solutions, and should only be applied once they have been sufficiently proven in practice. However, technology is seldom a substitute for people in after-sales services, but should rather be used as support instead of as a replacement ("automation with human intelligence" or "after-sales service autonomation"). Thus, this will balance the overt need to provide users with a responsive service with the internal drivers of operational efficiency and budgetary constraints. This fundamental difference leads to a search for a methodology that first maps information flow. This would allow for identification of the components of the process rather than the opposite, as prescribed by the value stream mapping approach.
Capacity	Lean after-sales services tend to aim for spare capacity for flexibility to avoid delays which result from over utilization of resources. They tend also to create load balancing and a level schedule (through *heijunka boxes*) to support continuous material flow and reduce costs while still meeting customer expectations. Extra workers are added to the system to reduce *takt* time only if full capacity is reached.
Facilities	After-sales service facilities tend to be distributed and located optimally with the needs of the customer in mind. Inventories and warehouses tend to remain more centralized with effective and regular distribution in mind. Internally, the implementation of workplace organization programs (such as 5S, re-layout, *kamishibai*, or standard work procedures) as well as material flow analysis and optimization (such as *kanban*, water spider), facilitates the synchronization of processes, increases capacity utilization, and reduces idle times.
Supply chain positioning	Lean after-sales services tend to maintain both vertical and horizontal integration. In order to assure an efficient and effective lean operation system, the headquarters design and apply the same organizational model in the subsidiaries and the network. Every function in the subsidiaries and network has to pursue the goal of customer retention in the whole product life cycle. The management of processes is standardized according to the headquarters' guidelines. Internal lean production structure is replicated outside the manufacturing process in terms of lean procurement, distribution, and partnership. Multifunctional teams are responsible for supervisory tasks, while vertical integration systems relying on direct information flow are made available to the relevant decision makers, allowing for rapid feedback and corrective action. Long-term relationships with suppliers and supplier development are also fundamental.
Planning and control	Lean after-sales services tend to aim for product availability, first by reducing lead times, and then by increasing reliability of the product through high service levels (high customer orientation). However, if standardized activities cannot be applied, after-sales cycle time could vary and it is difficult to determine prior to service. By using balancing operation tools

(Continued)

Table 21.1 (continued)

Characteristic	Description
	(heijunka box), companies improve buying from suppliers and the use of equipment and team planning, leading to efficient use of resources, inventory reduction, and downtime and costs elimination, hence directing the creation of flexibility of processes.
Infrastructural	
Human resources	Compared with manufacturing operations, the after-sales area depends on human factors to a larger extent. On the one hand, human resources are responsible for the prospection, execution, and delivery of service to the customer, especially in contact-intensive activities where the crucial role of employees in delivering value to customers creates a permeable border between them and customers. This condition implies creating a core team of multi skilled and multi tasked operatives. This applies both in-house and in-field, and requires good product knowledge and understanding of customer value creation, including both technical and relational competences. The workforce is also involved in small improvement projects through work teams, but responsibility rests with after-sales managers in order to create a win–win and closed-loop relationship between workforce and management. Therefore, manpower is one of the most relevant and costly factors in doing the job. Functional analysis tools support the evaluation of employees by skill levels, competence areas, and activities to identify excessive worker divisions and diluted worker skill base. On the other hand, the customer is often an active participant to service creation and provision with their own efforts and resources.
Quality control	Lean after-sales services tend to maintain a system of quality control whereby measures are taken to guarantee service process quality in production, as well as during operation in the hands of the customer, and considering both technical and functional perspectives. Technical perspectives include those service determinants that refer to the results or outcomes of a service (i.e. what the customer is actually receiving). Examples include service flexibility, availability, timeliness and responsiveness, accessibility and comfort, reliability, technical competence, cleanliness and tidiness. Functional perspective relates to the manner or the process by which a service is provided (i.e. how the service is delivered). Examples include service customer care, attentiveness/helpfulness, friendliness and courtesy, information, communication, integrity, security, and commitment. In general, data and information quality becomes a key area of both strategic and operations management. It plays a superior role compared with manufacturing settings, where machines, automation, and quality of workflow are more important.
Product/service range	Lean after-sales services tend to offer standardized yet customizable products (mass-customization) with a variety of choices of supporting services, where efforts are made to reduce variation.
New product/service introduction	Lean after-sales services tend to have a core cross-functional team that is responsible for the development of new products and supporting services, with input from the customer and key suppliers.
Performance measurement	In manufacturing settings, the performance of workers is easier to measure. In contrast to measuring the effectiveness of after-sales professionals, dealing with various complexities during operation processes is much more

Table 21.1 (continued)

Characteristic	Description
	difficult. Therefore, lean after-sales services tend to address after-sales services at different levels, from business to process, activity, and development/innovation. This emphasizes both efficiency and effectiveness performance, and considers both internal and customer-oriented measures. In other words, a core set of balanced multi-layered and multi-levelled measures (e.g. a lean product-service system (PSS) balanced scorecard approach), that emphasizes system effectiveness and that is aligned with the strategy of the business, is used. Moreover, activities are coordinated and evaluated by the flow through the team or plant, not by individual departmental targets, to: 1) capture the discrepancies in emphasis and metrics among performance measurement systems adopted by different actors involved; 2) align the strategy and the management practices with those of the supply chain; 3) define and reconfigure the performance measurement system by aligning the new strategic vision and goals with the tactical and operational objectives; and 4) identify the impact of the specific performance results obtained by each actor on the overall after-sales service supply chain performance at any level.
Supplier relations	Lean after-sales services tend to work closely with suppliers in order to reduce supplier lead times and increase supplier quality, e.g. supplier development. Long-term supplier relationships are deployed. As such, suppliers are an integral part of the lean after-sales service operations. For example, supplier kanban programs with spare parts suppliers could ensure fast-fit repair services to customers.
Customer relations	Lean after-sales services tend to focus on customer value, which requires close contact with customers. Wasteful (non-value-adding) activities are systematically identified and eliminated. Customer-focused value creation is the main criterion for lean after-sales service. Customers are an integral part of lean after-sales service operations.

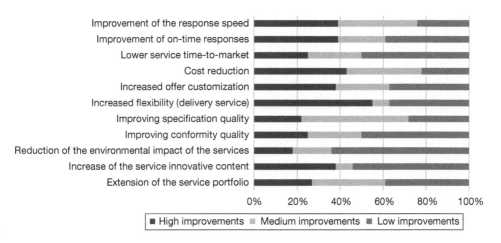

Figure 21.1   Lean after-sales service benefits

Source: Corti et al. (2011).

companies providing after-sales services underlined that the main benefits resulting from the application of lean philosophy principles to after-sales services refer to time, cost, and flexibility (Corti et al., 2011).

Despite the high benefits achievable through the application of lean thinking to after-sales processes, the level of adoption is still low. Indeed, lean implementation can be quite challenging. While the principles and learnings from lean manufacturing are conceptually applicable to after-sales, lean implementation needs to be tailored to the different contexts under which service processes operate.

Key challenges that make lean implementation a difficult proposition can be summarized as follows:

- *After-sales processes are not visible*: In a manufacturing context, waste is visible and, consequently, can be identified relatively easily. In the case of after-sales service, processes are not visible and commonly result in waste that is more challenging to pinpoint. Similarly, some activities seen as waste from a "manufacturing angle" should be treated as added-value processes due to their impact on customer satisfaction. Therefore, after-sales services require a high degree of skills and competences to distinguish what is really important from what is not. Tools such as the *lean opportunity questionnaire* and value stream maps can enhance such ability.
- *After-sales processes are complex and not standardizable*: In after-sales processes, some activities can be easily standardized, others cannot because they require the individual handling of the executor of the process. In addition, the task's sequence could be unclear or more than one employee could be involved in the process. The complexity of processes also causes difficulties in defining suitable performance indicators that need to be aligned with the new specific lean target.
- *After-sales processes are multi-functional and multi-organizational*: In after-sales organizations, part or whole of an end-to-end process flows through several corporate functions and often requires the participation of external partners. In such a context, aligning external companies to the operational excellence target could be difficult. It requires a high level of commitment from all the actors involved in process engineering and execution, as well as integrated systems for coordination and performance measurement.
- *After-sales processes are people-intensive*: Aligning all individuals directly or indirectly associated with the process according to the improvement goals is a key aspect. Moreover, lean implementation for after-sales service processes should include improvement targets having both tangible and intangible components. The intangible elements depend on moods: how people are feeling at different points of time. This is also valid for people outside the organization, including the partners providing products or competences, as well as the customers receiving the service.
- *Specific knowledge on lean after-sales service is unavailable*: Lack of knowledge in after-sales implies a low level of commitment from management and staff. The usual reaction is that people and customers are not things. However, when training is provided, the staff gradually understand that there is a great amount of waste in their processes and applying lean principles could provide great benefits. Moreover, unlike manufacturing, only a few studies and analyses are available to support lean adoption in after-sales. Therefore educators need to be hired from the manufacturing sector. Unfortunately, they often talk manufacturing language and lack relevant examples from after-sales. This makes it more difficult for staff to accept the ideas of lean, and longer assimilation periods are requested. Moreover, when lean projects are carried

out, managers and practitioners usually have to translate lean production competencies and experiences into after-sales. This risks the adoption of non-adequate tools and methodologies.

Lean after-sales service enabling factors do not seem different from enablers of any other change initiative. There are three key factors that contribute to its successful implementation:

1   *Employees' full commitment and participation in the improvement processes*: Employees are experts at performing their work. Their full participation enables their professional competences, skills and experience to be used for corporate growth. Empowered staff are keener to realize their ideas and suggestions as opposed to an unenthusiastic staff feeling forced to carry out top-down process improvements. It is therefore crucial that staff feel the ownership and the control of lean initiatives.
2   *Focus on empowering people before developing organization*: It is crucial to provide training and give responsibility to employees, so they will be able to take improvement initiatives on their own. Training activities should be focused not only on theoretically teaching lean tools and methods, but also on empirically learning a new approach to thinking. This will allow employees to feel that they can make use of their skills and creativity, take initiative, and make things happen.
3   *Support from managers at all levels*: Top-level managers must show a genuine interest in the lean implementation work, pay attention to the results, and provide necessary resources. Managers at lower levels, leading units implementing lean, need to take ownership and responsibility of the change, and actively support their employees in the improvement process.

The Future of Lean After-Sales Services

The future of lean after-sales services is strongly related to the servitization of the manufacturing phenomenon. This is defined as the evolution of companies' business models from a "pure-product" orientation toward integrated *product-service systems* (PSSs) based on the provision of integrated bundles consisting of both physical goods and services. After-sales services can be placed at the first stage of the "servitization continuum," which can be described by the following dimensions (Gaiardelli et al., 2014):

- product-service ownership orientation, where the focus changes from product-oriented to use- and result-oriented services and the ownership of the product is shifted from the customer to the product-service provider,
- product-service process orientation, where the focus changes from the product to the process, measured in terms of relationship intensity and level of customization, and
- product-service interaction orientation, where the nature of the interaction between the customer and the product-service provider is characterized by different price policies and risk levels.

Moving along the first dimension, the decision-making power and process control is progressively transferred from the customer to the product-service provider. Consequently, the lean after-sales service approach should be enlarged to consider the entire product life cycle. It should include all the life cycle phases of a product-service solution, from PSS design and engineering, through PSS provision and delivery, up to PSS end-of-life management. Further, it should expand a lean approach in all directions, between departments, divisions, and network partners. Applying lean principles to these new insights arising at the interface of marketing, product and service development, and multi-partner operations could enable manufacturing companies to embark on an efficient and effective servitization journey.

Considering the second dimension, the value moves from the physical product to the entire ecosystem. This requires new models and approaches to understand how product-service attributes contribute to customer value. Thus it stresses the importance of cross-functional and cross-partner problem solving to eliminate anything that does not contribute to customer-defined value.

When the nature of interaction between the customer and the product-service provider moves from transaction-based to relationship-based, digital and information technology becomes incrementally important. It improves the manufacturers' visibility of the assets in the field, increasing the ability to handle greater risk in asset performance, reliability, and availability implied by the provision of advanced services, such as revenue sharing, pay-per-use, availability contracts, etc. The convergence of data availability and information processing technology requires a redesign and a standardization of operating processes, which could be supported by introducing a lean thinking approach.

In the future the lean after-sales service approach will flow into a lean product-service system approach, where all the changes required by servitization transformation along its three dimensions will be included in an integrated lean system. This integrated lean system will encompass engineering, manufacturing, delivery, sales and after-sales, financial, and risk management activities managed by different actors operating in a product-service ecosystem. Nevertheless, the most important role of lean in servitization will be related to its ability to enable a cultural change; this represents the strongest challenge that manufacturing companies have to cope with in their servitization transformation.

Conclusions

Theoretical and industrial experiences show that lean initiatives appear very helpful for companies embarking on an after-sales strategy, due to their inclination toward making processes efficient. Moreover, such principles can help boost customer satisfaction measurably and sustainably through the adoption of several change management methods and efficient learning processes. These learning processes should support a shift of mindset that any organization embarking on a service transformation is called to interiorize. Moreover, the success of any lean initiative in after-sales, as in manufacturing, is achieved not just through applying good operational methods and approaches, but also through establishing a clear vision and strategy. In other words, management must be highly committed in adopting adequate methods to communicate the lean strategy, as well as implement necessary mechanisms to support the development and the diffusion of a lean culture across the overall organization. Nevertheless, operating in a context requiring more customer-intensive knowledge and more complex, multifunctional, and multi-organizational people-intensive processes makes lean principles in after-sales even more important than in manufacturing.

Case Study: Lean After-sales Services in DAF Veicoli Industriali

DAF Veicoli Industriali is the Italian subsidiary of an international group leader in the development, manufacture, and sales of a vast range of medium and heavy trucks. The product

---

offering is complemented by a range of financial and after-sales services, provided by the company either directly or through its technical assistance network. Despite the strategic importance played by after-sales services within DAF Veicoli Industriali's business, the profitability within this area has progressively shrunk. This is due to the harsh crisis that the Italian market has been experiencing since 2008. This situation has encouraged the management of DAF Veicoli Industriali to research, develop, and implement new approaches, methodologies, and tools to support the improvement of after-sales service productivity and effectiveness. On these premises, a lean project was launched to improve the existing after-sales management in the assistance network through new effective and efficient procedures. The project was carried out in a pilot case study in 2010 and then replicated during 2011–2012 at a few dealers. The main characteristics of each project, built upon five main stages, are briefly described below:

1   *Team definition*: First of all, a lean project team was created. The team was made up of two representatives of DAF Veicoli Industriali, acting as project manager and project sponsor, namely the service manager and the network development manager, and a lean consultant team made up of specialized practitioners in after-sales management. The dealer owner was also involved to establish internal commitment.

2   *Understanding customer value*: A preliminary market analysis underlined that customers were mainly interested in receiving services supporting high levels of truck availability over time. Such a consideration was in line with the main result of a gap analysis carried out to detect the main differences between customer expectation and perception for main value attributes. These attributes included both technical (e.g. timeliness, responsiveness, flexibility, promptness, reliability) and relational (e.g. attentiveness, courtesy, frankness, integrity) aspects.

3   *Setting the direction*: Brainstorming was carried out to complete a SWOT analysis aiming at identifying strengths, weaknesses, opportunities, and threats in after-sales business. It also developed a list of critical success factors. Of course, the results achieved in each SWOT analysis depended on the specific characteristics of the involved companies. Afterwards, matching the main results of the strategic assessment with the gap analysis allowed for the identification of what the key value stream should focus on. Two key processes emerged as critical: spare parts and warehouse management, and maintenance and repair management. Eventually, a list of relevant KPIs dealing with the selected key processes was created and the relative targets were defined.

4   *Detailed mapping and definition of improvement plans*: A detailed value stream mapping of the key value processes was carried out to depict the current state. A gap analysis followed to identify the main actions to be taken to improve selected processes. For each action, project responsibilities, the project plan, and timetable, as well as the main intended lean tools, were identified. Table 21.2 summarizes the list of the adopted lean tools together with the main value attributes involved in each single lean project.

5   *Develop improvement actions*: Each lean project was then carried out through the application of a lean process-oriented approach called PDCA (*plan, do, check, act*). This was followed by a standardization cycle called SDCA (*standardize, do, check, act*). Lean approaches, such as 3G (*gemba, genbutsu, genjitsu*), 5 whys, and Ishikawa causal diagrams, were adopted to enable participation and collaboration among people. A very high priority was placed on the human factor, because of the decisive role individual behavior plays in making service processes successful.

Table 21.2 Lean projects in DAF Veicoli Industriali

Project	Value attributes involved	Adopted lean tool
Mapping and development of technical and relational competences and skills	• Service capacity • Service flexibility • Service attentiveness and courtesy	• Skill matrix • Empowerment boundaries
Reception desk area re-layout and process reorganization	• Service delivery time • Service reliability	• Spaghetti chart • 5S and workplace organization
Reorganization of maintenance booking and planning activities	• Service capacity • Service delivery time • Service flexibility	• Muda/muri/mura analysis • Visual management tools • Heijunka box
Reorganization of spare parts and warehousing management	• Spare parts availability • Spare parts delivery time • Service delivery time	• Muda/muri/mura analysis • Kamishibai (work standards) • Water spider (mizosumashi)
Reorganization of the control process	• Service efficiency • Service productivity	• Kamishibai (work standards)

Table 21.3 Results achieved from the implementation of lean after-sales service

Main result	Initial value	Final value	Achieved result
Customer satisfaction index	81.6	87.6	+7.3%
After-sales service productivity	106.3%	130.5%	+24.3%
After-sales service capacity saturation	87.5%	88.9%	+1.4%

As summarized in Table 21.3, which reports the relevant results coming from the application of lean projects, the implementation of lean thinking principles allowed for the maximization of efficiency, improvement of quality, elimination of unnecessary motion and inventory, and the saving of time and resources.

References

Baines, T., Lightfoot, H., Peppard, J., Johnson, M., Tiwari, A., Shehab, E. and Swink, M. (2009). Towards an operations strategy for product-centric servitization. *International Journal of Operations & Production Management, 29*(5), 494–519.

Bozdogan, K., Milauskas, R. and Nightingale, D. (2000). *Transition to a Lean Enterprise. A Guide for Leaders, 1.* Cambridge, MA, Massachusetts Institute of Technology.

Carlborg, P., Kindström, D. and Kowalkowski, C. (2013). A lean approach for service productivity improvements: Synergy or oxymoron? *Managing Service Quality: An International Journal, 23*(4), 291–304.

Corti, D., Tantardini, M. and Roscio S. (2011). *Utilizzo dell'operational excellence per la gestione dei servizi: Il caso dei servizi post-Vendita.* Report Indagine 2011, ASAP Service Management Forum.

Gaiardelli, P., Resta, B., Martinez, V., Pinto, R. and Albores, P. (2014). A classification model for product-service offerings. *Journal of Cleaner Production, 66,* 507–519.

Hines, P., Found, P., Griffiths, G. and Harrison, R. (2011). *Staying Lean: Thriving, Not Just Surviving,* Cardiff, Lean Enterprise Research Centre, Cardiff University.

Legnani, E., Cavalieri S. and Gaiardelli, P. (2013). Modelling and measuring after-sales service delivery processes. In: Borangiu, T. Trentesaux, D. and Thomas, A. (eds), *Service Orientation in Holonic and Multi-Agent Manufacturing and Robotics.* Studies in Computational Intelligence Book Series, *472,* London, Springer, pp. 71–84.

Oliva, R. and Kallenberg, R. (2003). Managing the transition from products to services. *International Journal of Service Industry Management, 14*(2), 160–172.

Pawar, K. S., Beltagui, A. and Riedel, J. C. (2009). The PSO triangle: designing product, service and organisation to create value. *International Journal of Operations & Production Management, 29*(5), 468–493.

Resta, B., Powell, D., Gaiardelli, P. and Dotti, S. (2015). Towards a framework for lean operations in product-oriented product service systems. *CIRP Journal of Manufacturing Science and Technology, 9,* 12–22.

Shah, R. and Ward, P. T. (2007). Defining and developing measures of lean production. *Journal of Operations Management, 25*(4), 785–805.

Smith, L., Maull, R. and Ng, I. C. L. (2014). Servitization and operations management: A service dominant-logic approach. *International Journal of Operations & Production Management, 34*(2), 242–269.

SupplierBusiness Ltd (2009). The European aftermarket report. *EPP.* Available at: www.pricingplatform. eu/index.php?option=com_jdownloads&Itemid=6&view=view.download&catid=4&cid=1041&lang= en (accessed July 2016).

Tracey, M. and Flinchbaugh, J. (2006). HR's role in the lean organizational journey. *World at Work Journal, 15*(4), 49–58.

Vandermerwe, S. and Rada, J. (1989). Servitization of business: Adding value by adding services. *European Management Journal, 6*(4), 314–324.

Womack, J. P. and Jones, D. T. (1996). *Lean Thinking: Banish Waste and Create Wealth in Your Corporation,* New York, The Free Press.

22

LEAN GLOBAL CORPORATIONS

Torbjørn H. Netland

Introduction

If implementing a "lean" program at a single site is a challenge, imagine doing it in a network of sites. Multinational corporations are always looking for ways to improve the productivity of their operations. To that end, a popular strategy is to develop and deploy *corporate lean programs* in their networks. Instead of leaving every subsidiary to solve its own improvement issues, they offer a corporate template for the sites to implement. Today, companies spend billions of dollars to develop, deploy, manage, and maintain corporate lean programs. There is evidence that the programs can be very effective if implemented correctly, but the experiences in many corporations vary.

Corporate lean programs can take different forms. The most successful ones are tailored to the needs and characteristics of the firm (Womack and Jones, 1996, 2007). Rather than copying the programs of other companies, or buying a standard lean program from an external consultancy, the firm should invest time and money to develop something that fits its purpose. Inspired by Toyota's successful Toyota Production System (TPS), many firms develop their own "company-specific production systems" (or "XPS," where X stands for the company name, and PS for production system) (Feggeler and Neuhaus, 2002; Clarke, 2005; Netland, 2013). A few good examples of reportedly successful XPSs include the Alcoa Business System, Boeing Production System, Bosch Production System, Caterpillar Production System, Electrolux Manufacturing System, Nissan Production Way, Scania Production System, and Wiremold Production System. In practical terms, these examples are all corporate lean programs.

The Rise of Corporate Lean Programs

Developing and deploying corporate lean programs is an ongoing trend that is spreading far beyond its origin in manufacturing. The start of this trend coincided with seminal publications on lean production which appeared about 25 years ago (e.g. Krafcik, 1988; Womack et al., 1990). During the early 1990s, automobile companies realized that they needed a more holistic and company-wide approach to lean programs than the scattered, ad hoc, and project-based attempts of implementing "just-in-time," which they had attempted since the 1980s (Barthel and Korge, 2002). For example, Chrysler's introduction of the Chrysler Operating System in 1994 was one of the early corporate lean programs developed for a multi-site network (Clarke, 2005). Almost all automobile OEMs developed their own tailored lean programs in the 1990s, and many suppliers to the car manufacturers soon followed. In the 2000s, the trend spread to companies in process industries and to manufacturers of mechanical and electrical equipment. During that decade, corporate lean programs became more and more common among global firms in industries that produce high-volume physical products: furniture makers, home and office appliance manufacturers, the food and retail industry, publishing houses, and so on. Since 2010, corporate lean programs have also become popular in the construction industry, in various service industries (banks, insurance companies, law firms, etc.), and in public service and healthcare firms. The increasing spread of lean programs beyond discrete production hints that they are effective.

Why do more and more firms develop corporate lean programs? A primary objective of such programs is that they *put improvement into a system*. Whereas companies have always had systems in place for creating value for customers (admittedly to varying degrees), they have traditionally lacked structured systems for creating *more* value for their customers tomorrow than they do today. Improvement has been left to scattered initiatives and chance. The ability to make continuous improvements is what really sets Toyota apart from its competitors (Spear and Bowen, 1999; Liker, 2004). Having a corporate lean program sets a direction and provides marching orders for the improvement of all sites in the network.

A second objective of corporate lean programs is to align improvement activities across different sites and departments. Organic growth, and mergers and acquisitions are resulting in larger and more complex companies with manufacturing facilities and service offices spread across the globe. A result is often varying performance levels and uncoordinated ad hoc improvement projects. A shared corporate lean program can effectively help control, coordinate, and align the improvement efforts in big firms. For example, DaimlerChrysler developed its common DCPS immediately after merging in 1999 in order to align its production methods. Another example is the Volvo Group. After acquiring majority shares in Mack Trucks in the US, Renault Truck in France, Nissan Diesel in Japan, and some other firms, the Group launched the Volvo Production System in 2007 with the purpose of streamlining operations and improving productivity on a global scale (Hill, 2006). By codifying improvement principles and practices, a corporate lean program is helpful for effectively sharing knowledge about productivity improvement across sites, cultures, and borders.

Yet many firms have yet to take advantage of the benefits a corporate lean program can provide. In industries with widespread implementation of lean programs, simply having one is arguably necessary for achieving competitive parity (Netland and Aspelund, 2013). In industries that are new to lean thinking (e.g. healthcare and low-volume engineer-to-order industries), early starters can take advantage of a temporary competitive advantage. Late starters in any industry can achieve a competitive advantage if they develop a better lean program than their competitors develop, and/or if they implement it at a faster speed than their competitors implement it. This does not mean that a lean program is the answer to every problem. It is not. It only posits that if a company uses its own corporate lean program to put improvement into a system, it will probably be more productive than if it did not have a program. For that reason, I believe we will see the trend of corporate lean programs continue to grow in the future.

What is a Corporate Lean Program?

A corporate lean program is a productivity improvement program developed specifically for a corporation. Importantly, it differs from improvement projects in its intention of being permanent. In multinational companies, it is a shared system for all sites. A corporate lean program is often manifested in a company-specific production system. The use of the company's name and corporate design shows that the system is "ours," in the same way that the TPS is Toyota's system. A graphic model often summarizes the chosen principles (e.g. a house at Toyota, a temple at Chrysler, or a pyramid at Volvo).

When developing their own lean programs, multinational companies choose and adapt principles from available production improvement templates, such as total quality management (Deming, 1982), just-in-time production (Sugimori et al., 1977; Ohno, 1988), the theory of constraints (Goldratt and Cox, 1984), world-class manufacturing (Schonberger, 1986), business process reengineering (Hammer and Champy, 1995), mass customization (Pine, 1993), Six Sigma (Pande et al., 2000), and, most notably, lean production (Womack et al., 1990). There is no doubt that the famous TPS has been an inspiration for other firms.

An analysis of the company-specific production systems of 30 renowned multinational firms found that key principles of TPS and lean production were common among all the programs (Netland, 2013). That study found that the most common principles were "standardization," "continuous improvement/kaizen," "quality focus," "pull production," "flow/value stream/ customer orientation," "employee involvement," "visualization," "stable processes," and "workplace organization." All of these are well-established lean principles (Womack and Jones, 1996; Liker, 2004). Other studies confirm that companies' different systems and "houses" are essentially corporate lean programs (Hofman, 2000; Feggeler and Neuhaus, 2002; Clarke, 2005; Lay and Neuhaus, 2005; Lee and Jo, 2007). Companies seem to develop their corporate lean programs by choosing the principles that best suit their needs from a broad palette of proven lean production principles.

Although lean programs in different firms may look like exact copies, very few corporate lean programs do in fact contain the same principles. Even if the principles stem from the same templates, tailoring to the unique needs of the firm takes place when the program is developed. Not all firms choose all the technical principles found in lean literature. The argument is that not all lean principles suit all companies. The strength of developing a unique corporate lean program is that it allows for this specific adaptation.

A firm can (and should) include company-specific elements when it develops its lean program. For example, Volvo, which is known for its focus on attractive workplaces and on teamwork, has emphasized these elements with a "teamwork" principle in its Volvo Production System; Electrolux, which competes in the fast-cycling household appliances business, includes "design for manufacturing" in its Electrolux Manufacturing System; and Virginia Mason, a pioneering hospital in Seattle, includes "service (creating an extraordinary patient experience)" in its Virginia Mason Production System. These adaptations of the TPS principles to the situation at hand are critical for the success of the corporate lean program.

The Effect of Corporate Lean Programs

A big question is whether corporate lean programs are effective and whether they provide a positive return on investment. Borrowing a quote from Shiego Shingo, one of the key influencers of the TPS, my answer to the question is as follows: "The medicine works . . . but only if the patient takes it." There is a staggering amount of research into the effect of implementing lean and related improvement practices. Empirical studies have evaluated the effect on performance of implementing just-in-time, total quality management, total productivity maintenance, Six Sigma, and corporate lean programs. The research evidence is clear—companies that succeed in implementing these programs and practices outperform their peers in terms of operational performance.

Many practitioners are not always convinced by the research: "OK, on average, the corporate lean programs seem to help the companies that have been studied, but that does not mean this would work for us!" Pointing to unique characteristics of their companies, markets, or strategies, they believe they need something "smarter" or more exclusive. However, the ongoing migration of lean thinking across industries shows that lean can be useful under a wide variety of circumstances. It is not likely that lean would have continued its growth and spread over the past three decades if it was a faddish trend. There is an abundance of anecdotal evidence from companies across many different industries that lean programs help improve performance, both from the companies' own reports and in the popular literature.

An in-depth study of the implementation of the Volvo Production System in 67 plants in the global Volvo Group revealed that as a plant progresses in its implementation of lean, its operational performance improves slowly at first, then grows rapidly, and finally tapers off—essentially following the shape of an S-curve (Netland and Ferdows, 2014, 2016). The initial stage can be characterized by "exploration," during which the plant is discovering and experimenting with lean principles, and the later stages by "exploitation," during which the plant is realizing their benefits (see Figure 22.1). The exploration phase does not lead to radical performance improvements at the plant level (although good results can be achieved quickly in pilot areas); thus, organizations must be patient when they launch a lean program. At Volvo, we observed that plants that were "beginners" to lean needed a minimum of two years to move to the "in transition" stage where benefits could be reaped (later, the plant could progress to the "advanced" and "cutting-edge" stages). Our findings support the opinion of Womack and Jones (1996, p. 148), who wrote: "Three years is about the minimum time required to put the rudiments of a lean system fully in place, and two more years may be required to teach enough employees to see that the system becomes self-sustaining."

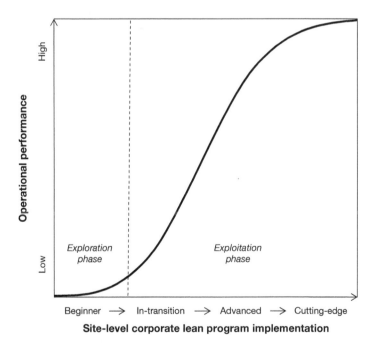

Figure 22.1 The S-curve effect of implementing corporate lean programs

Source: Netland and Ferdows (2016, p. 1114).

Implementing Corporate Lean Programs

Of course, just having a lean program and a "house" described in presentations and strategy documents does not improve anything. Without implementation, strategies are not really adding value. Perhaps a note on the word "implementation" is useful here. Many lean authors and practitioners argue that the word "implementation" gives the wrong impression. Lean cannot be "implemented," they claim, because lean is not like software or technology, but rather is "a journey" or "a way of living." Although I see the point and agree that there is no end point to lean, I believe the word "implementation" is useful for companies that are looking for ways to improve their operations. When I use "implementation" in this chapter, I refer to all activities related to improving operations using lean philosophies, principles, and practices.

In research that I have conducted at several multinational corporations, I have investigated which *specific managerial actions* assist in the implementation of a corporate lean program (some results are reported in Netland et al., 2015). Managers encounter a number of questions in their lean journeys that call for decisions and actions. This chapter does not intend to address all of these questions, but rather touch on a few topics that always seem to pop up. They are:

- What type of leadership is needed?
- How should the organization be trained in the lean program?
- Is there a need for local lean coordinators and "lean teams"?
- How can progress be tracked and monitored using corporate lean assessments?
- Can implementation be facilitated using local top-down or bottom-up reporting structures?
- Can financial or non-financial incentives assist in implementation?
- To what degree is corporate governance needed?

Lean Leadership

Developing a corporate lean program is the easy part; the hard part is implementing and sustaining it. Luckily, after 25 years of trial and error in many firms, we now know quite a bit about what it takes to succeed. On the downside, however, it is not a quick fix. First and foremost, it takes a particular form of *leadership* (Spear, 2004; Liker and Convis, 2011; Ballé and Ballé, 2014). Leaders must not only stay committed to the corporate lean program for a long time, they often also need to change behaviors to reflect a more supportive style. Why? Leaders cannot implement a lean program alone; success is fully dependent on the participation of the front-line employees. The primary job of a lean manager is to motivate and enable the workforce to integrate lean thinking and continuous improvement in their jobs. There are a number of recent books on lean leadership (see, for example, Ballé and Ballé, 2009, 2014; Rother, 2010; Liker and Convis, 2011; Liker and Trachilis, 2014; Mann, 2014), so I will not go into further detail here.

Training Programs

One of the first questions managers have after launching a new lean initiative is how to spread "the knowledge." Training must start in the boardroom, because if top management is not aware of the purpose and basics of the program, they are not likely to stay committed to it beyond the kick-off event. Ideally, the knowledge should spread in the organization via an on-the-job, train-the-trainer model. However, this model is admittedly slow, and most organizations therefore launch corporate training programs. Good training programs consist of a mix of eLearning, classroom training (including simulations and games), project assignments, and on-the-job training.

To motivate employees to undergo training, some organizations have adopted the "belt" programs that are commonplace in the Six Sigma methodology. Employees progress through a hierarchy of yellow belt, green belt, black belt, and master black belt. This practice has led to an attractive business model in consultancy; many firms offer training programs, certifications, and accreditation services in lean, Six Sigma, and the like. Although belt programs and accreditations can create motivation, there is also a risk of creating a non-value-adding bureaucracy that does not contribute sufficiently to the true objective of the lean program: process improvement.

Local Lean Coordinators and Teams

In our research, we found that lean teams and coordinators play an important role in the implementation of a corporate lean program. The usual criticism of them is that they disconnect the rest of the employees from engaging in the lean program. Instead, we found that the teams serve a coordinating role. They help employees learn about lean principles, and they support them in improvement activities. Lean teams can employ experts with deep knowledge of lean methods such as value stream mapping, problem-solving tools, and workplace organization ("5S"), which is necessary in lean transformations.

There is admittedly a risk that lean teams could turn into bureaucratic, non-value-adding departments that mainly report lean implementation upwards for compliance reasons (many plants have seen that happen). To avoid this risk, managers must carefully consider the size and composition of their lean teams. A rule-of-thumb is one member per 150 factory employees. However, more important than the number of members is the competence, people skills, and drive of those employed. Also, managers should carefully consider the lean implementation stage that the plant is currently in. In the beginner stage of a lean journey, the team—supported by the leadership—is the "driver" for implementation. As the plant progresses to the in-transition stage, the team should take the role of a "trainer," and as the plant matures in its journey into the advanced stage, the role changes again into that of a "facilitator." Finally, if the plant gets to the cutting-edge stage, the team's role should be to "mentor."

Corporate Lean Assessments

Lean assessments are a central part of many corporate lean programs. Their purpose is to evaluate the degree to which lean is "implemented" in a business unit, and thereby identify areas for further improvement. On a corporate level, assessments gauge the overall lean implementation progress. There is little doubt that lean assessments can be useful, but managers should not take a quick approach to them. Few aspects of corporate lean programs create as much frustration and unfruitful discussion as lean assessments. These assessments often backfire. Poorly designed and performed assessments are upsetting and demotivating, rather than energizing and motivating.

There are many ways to design and conduct lean assessments, ranging from simple self-assessment templates to extensive audits carried out by a professional third party. A typical middle ground is the "corporate lean assessment," where a corporate team of experts, external to the units assessed but internal to the organization, carry out the assessment. A corporate lean assessment uses a detailed scoring card to assess the level of implementation of the lean program in a unit. It is usually a spreadsheet table with lean practices in the rows and scoring levels in the columns. The most common scoring scheme is to use five levels ranging from "not implemented in any areas," to "fully implemented in all areas," with or without detailed explanations of each level of maturity. An individual assessor or a team of assessors performs the assessments. Multinational corporations often have a dedicated team of expert assessors that travels to the units and performs

Table 22.1 Pros and cons of corporate lean assessments

Pros	Cons
+ Check implementation progress	− Cost of assessment
+ Create motivation	− Added bureaucracy
+ Provide a roadmap for implementation	− Management of assessment
+ Communicate importance	− Risk of compliance focus
+ Create learning opportunities	− Lack of relevance
+ Collect success stories	− Risk of bias toward assessment-friendly aspects of lean
+ Create opportunities for celebration	(tools and techniques)
+ Assimilate lean implementation among sites	− Lack of local ownership
	− Risk of demotivation (not-invented-here)

assessments at regular intervals (ranging from 6 to 36 months). The assessment typically lasts one day or up to five days, depending on the preparations, depth of assessment, and size of the unit. In between the regular corporate lean assessments, the units can use the scoring scheme for self-assessments to track and push local implementation.

Corporate lean assessments have two major purposes: on the one hand, the assessment assists corporate managers in keeping track of their progress in lean implementation across multiple units. On the other hand, assessments should create motivation—and offer assistance—for further implementation in the units. An assessment also has other benefits. It communicates the importance of the program. It provides an excellent opportunity for learning, collecting success stories, and celebrating achievements. It also helps assimilate lean implementation among sites and thereby ease communication and sharing of standards and best practices. There are clearly many benefits to assessments, but often the disadvantages outnumber the benefits. The corporate lean program office should not be carried away by the opportunity to "travel the world and 'manage' the implementation of lean in distributed sites" by conducting assessments. Table 22.1 summarizes the main pros and cons of corporate lean assessments.

Top-down and Bottom-up Performance Reporting

To check the implementation progress at the local site, many managers employ different forms of top-down audits. The most common example is the 5S audit, which is a checklist of elements that should be implemented in an area for each of the five "Ss": sort, set-in-order, shine, standardize, and sustain. In our research, we found that such audits *do not* have a motivating effect on the further implementation of the lean program (Netland et al., 2015). Audits may be useful for knowing where you are (which is a prerequisite for improvement), and can help maintain attention to the lean program, but managers should not expect audits to advance the lean implementation in a specific area. An exception was plants that were in the beginner phase, for which the audits had two major advantages: first, managers who were visible on the shop floor during the audits showed commitment, and second, the audits were helpful for employees who needed to learn the elements of the lean program. The need for top-down audits signals that the plant has not achieved a self-sustaining improvement culture. The following quote from a manager captures this idea well: "We need to go from a *push-based* implementation to a *pull-based* implementation" (c.f. Netland et al., 2015).

Different from top-down performance reporting, bottom-up daily operations meetings have a positive effect on lean program implementation. The meetings focus on a balanced set of performance measures and are conducted regularly as part of the daily operations. They are held on the shop floor, performed standing up, and do not take longer than 5 to 10 minutes. These short meetings help everyone in the unit to be up-to-date on the latest progress and problems, every day. These meetings can create a "pull" for implementation. It is not enough, however, to call for short meetings in front of visual boards every morning; there is a huge amount of variance in how these meetings are conducted and in how effective they are. The best practice is when every employee comes prepared and contributes to solve problems. At the other end of the scale are the meetings where a manager stands at the board and dictates the work plan of the day. The best way to create effective bottom-up performance reviews is to start holding meetings, and continually improve them using the Deming PDSA cycle (plan, do, study, act).

Incentives for Implementation

A usual practice in any change program is to offer incentives for implementation. Financial rewards, or "pay for performance," are some of the strongest incentive mechanisms that exist in the business world. Many managers strongly believe that they can motivate employees to "implement lean" by offering financial rewards in the form of money or expensive goods and services. These managers, however, rarely succeed with their programs. The problem with using financial rewards is not that it does not work; it does. The problem is that it only has a temporary effect. After a while, people take the "extra money" for granted, and it loses its motivational power. Any reduction in the rewards can have a destructive effect on the lean program. Financial reward programs also have other negative side effects: people argue fiercely about the way the rewards are calculated and distributed, and the added bureaucracy is not creating value for the customer. Of course, management should share the financial gains from the lean program with all employees, but not by connecting financial rewards to the lean program. Rather, they should share the gains through investments in the site (e.g. in the canteen, changing facilities, and equipment), end-of-year bonuses, or a general increase in salaries.

Another type of incentive system is non-financial rewards. Non-financial rewards can be any positive attention that does not involve a substantial monetary element. Some examples are praise and recognition from a senior manager or peers, a diploma, a free lunch, or a simple prize such as flowers. Nearly every employee appreciates being seen and recognized for good performance. For example, when workers bring home flowers and explain to their spouse and children that the gift was given to acknowledge extraordinary performance, the goodwill that is generated is likely to have a positive effect on the lean program implementation. Companies can also foster friendly competition among different areas by using non-financial rewards. One particularly effective form of recognition is when senior managers come to the shop floor to learn from front-line personnel and acknowledge their improvements. By linking some form of non-financial reward to the lean program, managers communicate the importance of the program and encourage employees to pay attention to it.

Local Autonomy Versus Global Coordination

A recurrent question in discussions about improvement programs is the balance between global control and coordination versus local autonomy (Prahalad and Doz, 1987; Netland and Aspelund, 2014). Plant managers may fear that something they do not need is being imposed from above, and corporate managers believe the plants will not improve efficiently without a coordinating program. Obviously, there is no fixed point on the continuum from full local autonomy to full corporate control that is right for all sites, at all times, in a network.

Companies need both control and autonomy, and they can coexist. For example, Colotla et al. (2015) described how Procter & Gamble differentiates between "hard" and "soft" points for implementation of its program. The hard points are mandatory for all sites. The soft points are guidelines and recommended practices, but they are not mandatory. A practical example is the daily operations meeting on the shop floor. While the meetings and a few important key performance indicators (KPIs) are hard points, how the meetings are conducted, which other KPIs should be tracked, and which tools to use (whiteboard or computer) are soft points.

The Future of Corporate Lean Programs

Corporate lean programs can be an effective way to spread lean thinking in a multinational company. Their purpose is to improve productivity across all sites, and both research and practice show that companies can indeed achieve substantial improvements through these lean programs. Just as value-creating activities are codified and standardized, improvement of the same activities cannot be left to chance and random initiatives.

Importantly, corporate lean programs are intended not as one-off projects, but rather as lasting strategic initiatives. Many firms carry out countless ad hoc and temporary production improvement projects that do not lead to sustained performance improvement. In contrast, the corporate lean program has no end point. It sustains the emphasis and focus on lean thinking across the global network for a long period. Since a significant investment is required to develop a lean program, it must come with managerial support and attention from the corporate level. Lean initiatives that do not have the same support from the top are not likely to be sustained. Corporate lean programs also have other benefits. They are tailored to the needs of the corporation and create a common "improvement language."

Whether a specific corporate lean program in a company will be successful or not, however, is a different story. A corporate lean program is a serious investment that pays off if done correctly, but it is not easy. If there is one factor that decides whether a company makes it or breaks it, it is leadership.

Case Study: Corporate Lean Program at Jotun AS

Jotun is a multinational manufacturer of decorative, marine, protective, and powder coatings. Jotun's global operations network consists of close to 10,000 people, 36 factories, and 68 companies. Jotun products are available in more than 90 countries. It is a family-owned company headquartered in Sandefjord, Norway. The company has delivered strong financial results over several years and is still expanding through organic growth. Jotun is a market-driven firm that offers high-quality products.

Strong growth combined with sharpened competition over the past several years caused Jotun to embark on a corporate lean journey in 2007. Before 2007, there were several pockets of lean experimentation in the group, and some plants had already made a successful lean transformation. The benefits of a common lean program were clear: more standardization, more competence, more sharing of good practices between plants, and ultimately, improved competitiveness. Jotun has worked with lean production in its sites, and has patiently developed the Jotun Operations System (JOS) over several years. A global launch of an updated JOS took place in 2014. By including the main manufacturing processes for paint, JOS is a corporate lean program tailored to the needs of the industry. The JOS "house" is shown in Figure 22.2.

The JOS house consists of four key components: fundamental operations principles, best practice process management, two pillars of development, and at the top, the expected results. The purpose of JOS is to improve the productivity of all Jotun plants worldwide. Two of the fundamental principles—"Health, safety, and environment" and "Maintenance"—are of particular importance for Jotun as a chemical processing company.

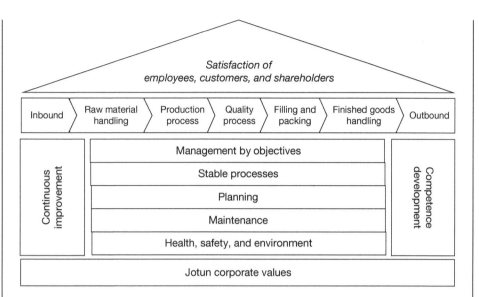

Figure 22.2 Illustration of the Jotun Operations System house

Source: Jotun AS.

To assist and govern the implementation of JOS in the global production network, Jotun has established a corporate department. Lean experts in this department have traveled to sites and assisted with specific improvement projects. In parallel, a special focus has been to increase the general knowledge level in both technical operations and lean thinking. As a result, in 2007 Jotun created the Jotun Operations Academy, which features courses and qualifications for all employees worldwide. Although Jotun recognizes that it still has room for growth when it comes to productivity improvements, positive results from the lean efforts in some sites are substantial. To support the growth, the top management at Jotun believes that JOS is key for future competitiveness.

References

Ballé, M. and Ballé, F. (2009). *The Lean Manager: A Novel of Lean Transformation*, Cambridge, MA, Lean Enterprise Institute.

Ballé, M. and Ballé, F. (2014). *Lead with Respect: A Novel of Lean Practice*, Cambridge, MA, Lean Enterprise Institute.

Barthel, J. and Korge, A. (2002). Implementierung Ganzheilicher Produktionssysteme als Aufgabe des Managements—Ergebnisse einer Studie in Brownfield-Werken der Automobilindustries. In: Feggeler, A. and Neuhaus, R. (eds), *Ganzheitliche Produktionssysteme—Gestaltungsprinzipien und deren Verknüpfung*. Cologne, Wirtschaftsverlag Bachem.

Clarke, C. (2005). *Automotive Production Systems and Standardisation: From Ford to the Case of Mercedes-Benz*, Heidelberg, Physica-Verlag.

Colotla, I., Keenan, P. and Spindelndreier, D. (2015). The power of production systems: Unlocking lean in decentralized organizations. *BCG*. Available at: www.bcgperspectives.com/content/articles/lean-manufacturing-lean-services-unlocking-lean-decentralized-organizations/ (accessed July 2016).

Deming, W. E. (1982). *Out of the Crisis*, Boston, MA, Massachusetts Institute of Technology.

Feggeler, A. and Neuhaus, R. (eds) (2002). *Ganzheitliche Produktionssysteme—Gestaltungsprinzipien und deren Verknüpfung*, Cologne, Wirtschaftsverlag Bachem.

Goldratt, E. M. and Cox, J. (1984). *The Goal: Excellence in Manufacturing*, Croton-on-Hudson, NY, North River Press.

Hammer, M. and Champy, J. (1995). *Reengineering the Corporation: A Manifesto for Business Revolution*, London, Nicholas Brealey.

Hill, B. (2006). *The Volvo Production Systems Pre-study Results* [Online]. Gothenburg: Volvo Technology. Available at: http://goo.gl/1mmZc (accessed April 4, 2010).

Hofman, A. (ed.) (2000). *Arbeitsorganisation in der Automobilindustrie—Stand und Ausblick*, Cologne, Wirtschaftsverlag Bachem.

Krafcik, J. F. (1988). Triumph of the lean production system. *Sloan Management Review*, *30*(1), 41–51.

Lay, G. and Neuhaus, R. (2005). Ganzheitliche Produktionssysteme (GPS)—Fortführung von Lean Production? *Angewandte Arbeitswissenschaft*, *42*(185), 32–47.

Lee, B. H. and Jo, H. J. (2007). The mutation of the Toyota Production System: Adapting the TPS at Hyundai Motor Company. *International Journal of Production Research*, *45*(16), 3665–3679.

Liker, J. K. (2004). *The Toyota Way: 14 Management Principles from the World's Greatest Manufacturer*, New York, McGraw-Hill.

Liker, J. and Convis, G. L. (2011). *The Toyota Way to Lean Leadership: Achieving and Sustaining Excellence through Leadership Development*, New York, McGraw-Hill.

Liker, J. K. and Trachilis, G. (2014). *Developing Lean Leaders at all Levels: A Practical Guide*, Winnipeg, Manitoba, Lean Leadership Institute Publications.

Mann, D. (2014). *Creating a Lean Culture: Tools to Sustain Lean Conversions*, Boca Raton, FL, CRC Press.

Netland, T. H. (2013). Exploring the phenomenon of company-specific production systems: One-best-way or own-best-way? *International Journal of Production Research*, *51*(4), 1084–1097.

Netland, T. H. and Aspelund, A. (2013). Company-specific production systems and competitive advantage: A resource-based view on the Volvo Production System. *International Journal of Operations & Production Management*, *33*(11/12), 1511–1531.

Netland, T. H. and Aspelund, A. (2014). Multi-plant improvement programmes: A literature review and research agenda. *International Journal of Operations & Production Management*, *34*(3), 390–418.

Netland, T. H. and Ferdows, K. (2014). What to expect from a corporate lean program. *MIT Sloan Management Review*, *55*(3), 83–89.

Netland, T. H. and Ferdows, K. (2016). The S-curve effect of lean implementation. *Production and Operations Management*, *25*(6), 1106–1120.

Netland, T. H., Schloetzer, J. D. and Ferdows, K. (2015). Implementing corporate lean programs: The effect of management control practices. *Journal of Operations Management*, *36*(0), 90–102.

Ohno, T. (1988). *Toyota Production System: Beyond Large-Scale Production*, New York, Productivity Press.

Pande, P. S., Neuman, R. P. and Cavanagh, R. R. (2000). *The Six Sigma Way: How GE, Motorola, and Other Top Companies are Honing their Performance*, New York, McGraw-Hill.

Pine, B. J. (1993). *Mass Customization: The New Frontier in Business Competition*, Boston, MA, Harvard Business School Press.

Prahalad, C. K. and Doz, Y. (1987). *The Multinational Mission: Balancing Local Demands and Global Vision*, New York, The Free Press.

Rother, M. (2010). *Toyota Kata: Managing People for Continuous Improvement and Superior Results*, New York, McGraw-Hill Professional.

Schonberger, R. J. (1986). *World Class Manufacturing: The Lessons of Simplicity Applied*, Milwaukee, WI, ASQ Quality Press.

Spear, S. (2004). Learning to lead at Toyota. *Harvard Business Review*, *82*(5), 78–86.

Spear, S. and Bowen, H. K. (1999). Decoding the DNA of Toyota Production System. *Harvard Business Review*, *77*(5) 95–106.

Sugimori, Y., Kusunoki, K., Cho, F. and Uchikawa, S. (1977). Toyota Production System and kanban system: Materialization of just-in-time and respect-for-human system. *International Journal of Production Research*, *15*(6), 553–564.

Womack, J. P. and Jones, D. T. (1996). *Lean Thinking: Banish Waste and Create Wealth in Your Corporation*, New York, The Free Press.

Womack, J. P. and Jones, D. T. (2007). *Lean Solutions: How Companies and Customers can Create Value and Wealth Together*, London, Simon & Schuster.

Womack, J. P., Jones, D. T. and Roos, D. (1990). *The Machine that Changed the World*, New York, Rawson Associates.

PART II

Lean across Industries

23

LEAN HEALTHCARE

Daniel T. Jones

Introduction

In the advanced economies, healthcare providers face two problems. First, they need to recognize that the quality of healthcare has fallen behind other products and services. This has led to thousands of unnecessary deaths and injuries, as summarized in Allen (2013). Second, aging populations and less healthy urban lifestyles are resulting in a more rapid increase in demand for healthcare than can be paid for by both income and tax revenue growth in the squeezed middle classes. The situation is particularly challenging in the USA, which has some of the best hospitals in the world, but at the same time spends twice as much per head relative to other advanced countries to achieve similar outcomes.

The Institute for Healthcare Improvement (IHI, www.ihi.org) was established in the USA in 1991 to address the quality challenges facing healthcare. This became a global initiative with a large annual conference, many improvement activities, and research collaboration. It was led by Don Berwick, whose annual speeches are collected in Berwick (2014). It became apparent that the sustainability of improved medical practices needed to be embedded in improved processes for delivering care to patients. This has resulted in a growing interest in the potential of lean to simultaneously address both quality and costs issues.

What is Lean Healthcare?

Although lean was born in Toyota in the 1950s and 1960s (see Womack and Jones, 1996; Liker, 2004) it was not until after 2000 that the first hospitals in the USA, Europe, and Australia began to explore the use of lean. These pioneers came together to share their stories at the first Global Lean Halthcare Summit in the UK in 2007 and at a conference of healthcare leaders organized by the Lean Enterprise Institute (LEI, www.lean.org) in the USA in 2008. These conferences triggered many more experiments around the world, new training programs, and an army of consultants offering to help in return for learning how lean works in healthcare. ThedaCare established the *healthcare value network* for hospitals interested in lean (www.createvalue.org). Interest has grown rapidly over the past decade, with a growing literature collection, including Jimmerson (2007), Graban (2008), Baker and Taylor (2009), Toussaint (2010), and Barnas (2014), to mention a few.

It is now clear that lean can deliver better quality (and safety) and a better patient experience (fewer queues and less rework) while simultaneously making better use of existing resources (to treat more patients) and improving the work experience of staff (less frustration and stress). Although it is true that "we don't make cars," the operational challenges hospitals face are actually not so very different from those in manufacturing or service delivery. The language is certainly different and the patient directly experiences the process of solving their problem. However, what is common is not the tools but the evidence-based methodology that is central to lean. Lean uses the same scientific method to diagnose and treat organizational problems as doctors use to diagnose and treat medical problems.

There are all kinds of examples where lean has made a significant difference in healthcare, varying from clinics and departments through to whole hospitals and even whole healthcare systems. However, not all of the initial experiments were successful or were sustained. Additionally, we are still a long way from lean being the way of working across healthcare. So what lessons can we learn from the first decade of lean in healthcare?

Challenges and Opportunities

What distinguishes lean from other process improvement methodologies is its focus on developing the capabilities of the front-line teams (doctors, nurses, and support staff) to manage and continuously improve their work. This begins as teams learn to create stability and standardize their work as a baseline for improvement. It deepens as teams practice using the scientific approach in addressing the issues that interrupt and distract them from caring for patients. Repeated practice in solving problems enhances their ability to see and to solve tomorrow's problems, which leads to a virtuous circle of continuous improvement (Jimmerson, 2007; Shook 2010). It also results in highly motivated employees who feel a strong sense of ownership of "their" improvements.

The use of a common problem-solving framework, such as Toyota's A3 process based on Deming's plan, do, check, act (PDCA) sequence, is the foundation for using the scientific, evidence-based approach to solving problems. Daily practice of solving local problems builds the capabilities of teams to address and solve larger problems, like in Figure 23.1 which designs an improved patient journey.

Individual and team-based learning is therefore the key focus of lean. We now know that these problem-solving skills are learnt through daily practice and not just from classroom training in lean tools or occasional kaizen workshops. These skills are best nurtured and sustained by team leaders and line managers supported by coaches and therefore not by delegating the implementation of lean to external or internal consultants. Improvement teams often end up extinguishing fires for top management, which reignite soon after they go off to fight the next fire.

To significantly improve the experience of patients and to deliver better hospital performance, these islands of improvement need to be joined together along the patient journey from admission to discharge and beyond. As we map patient flows through healthcare systems, we see all the handoffs and delays and interactions with support services that need to work together to enable the patient to move to the next step in their treatment journey. It also allows managers to see, for instance, that unless attention is paid to the timely discharge of patients, improving the admission process will only lead to longer queues waiting for beds. It also highlights the need for primary care and hospitals to work more closely with rehabilitation and social care in the community (see, for example, Baker and Taylor, 2009; Worth et al., 2012).

Value stream maps are initially used to help teams understand the flow of tests, records, patients, and so forth through their area or department. These are later used by cross-departmental and management teams to understand the handovers and bottlenecks between departments along

What is the problem?

Patients' length of stay (LOS) is the big problem and is having an adverse effect on our other Big 4

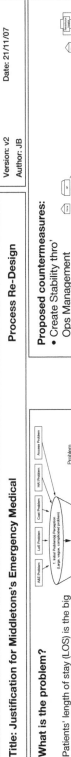

Current condition:

1571 minutes (15%) Treatment Time

V's

9,415 minutes (85%) Waiting Time

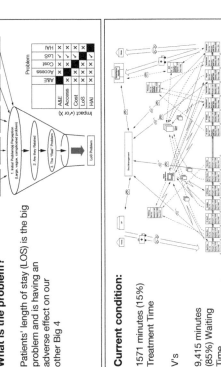

Target condition: Reduce Waiting Time by 64%, therefore reduce average LoS for Medical Patients By 4.94 days

Root Cause Analysis:

- No real plan for patients (hence no actual)
- Departmental working hours are not synchronized
- Capacity (staff) not calculated to meet Demand
- Frequency of interventions not designed to meet Demand

Responsible: JB Team members: BW/NE/JE/ML/HW

Proposed countermeasures:

- Create Stability thro' Ops Management
- Place "offline" services "online" & get them operating to takt
- Create Continuous Flow
- Introduce Buffers where we cannot Flow
- Create a Single Point of Schedule (Pacemaker)

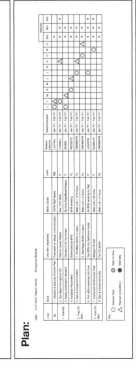

Plan:

Follow Up:

- Conflicting Cost Improvement Initiatives in departments & divisions
- Who will do this work?
- How will we know if the actions have the impact needed?

Agreed by: MT   **Date:** 08/11/07

Figure 23.1   Example of A3 in a hospital

the patient journey from door to door, as in Figure 23.2. Later still they can be used by teams from primary, secondary, and tertiary care to map the entire patient journey from beginning to end.

The key to managing patient flows is to make the work and patient flows visible. This begins on admission as the team establishes a plan for all the expected steps right through to discharge for each patient. Displaying this on a whiteboard (rather than hiding it on a computer) helps the team to see whether the planned steps were completed on time and thus captures the reason for potential delays. Action can then be taken to get back on track. However, recurring interruptions signal the need for the team to diagnose and address the root causes of the problem rather than jumping to a solution and blaming others. Collecting the status of patients who are nearly ready to go home every two hours on a central *visual hospital* board helps to trigger the necessary actions to ensure they go home on time in order to free up enough beds for incoming patients (Baker and Taylor, 2009). Management at all levels can also see the current status of the hospital at a glance.

Visual planning boards, built upon a *plan for every patient*, are created on admission and revised on a regular basis, detailing all the work to be done through to a planned discharge date. *Patient planning boards* in each department are used to track planned versus actual work at intervals each day, to highlight delays and their causes. Visual hospital boards like the one in Figure 23.3 are updated frequently to review the status of all the hospital beds and unblock issues that might delay discharge.

It has become clear that supporting front-line improvement activity and the visual management of patient flows presents new challenges for senior management. Managers need to spend time on the front line understanding the issues, eliminating obstacles, challenging teams, and coaching problem solving. Perhaps the biggest challenge is learning how to manage by asking questions rather than telling subordinates what to do, which takes the responsibility for learning what could be done away from them. In this way managers learn to see the bigger, underlying issues by helping the front line learn to solve problems on their own.

The lean way to free up managers' time is to use a visual strategy planning process to establish the key objectives for the organization and to conduct a structured dialogue up and down the organization on proposed actions to achieve them (that is, "strategy deployment") (Dennis, 2009). As a result, resources and energies are focused and aligned through a visual process reaching right down to the front line. Using the same visual system for monitoring progress and managing deviations gives management the confidence that these vital few objectives will be achieved. This, in turn, dramatically cuts the number of projects and meetings that waste so much of managers' time. Building this visual management system and the very different behaviors that go with it is a long process.

Strategy or *policy deployment* is a framework for prioritizing actions to close the key performance gaps and for aligning all the improvement activities to achieve them. It is also used to track progress so the team can address the causes of delays in a timely manner. It can be used at the whole hospital or trust level, as in Figure 23.4, at department level, and in planning each improvement project.

Transforming a Healthcare Organization

There are several approaches to transforming a healthcare organization. A good example is Thedacare's six-step process described in Toussaint (2015):

1   *Laying the foundation.* Leaders should understand the potential of lean through visiting other lean organizations and training. This gives them a clear idea of their role in leading a lean transformation. They also need to be clear about the desired direction and objectives.
2   *Creating a model cell.* This can be done so that the team can create standard work and visualize plan versus action as a basis for making improvements. The team builds experience in making

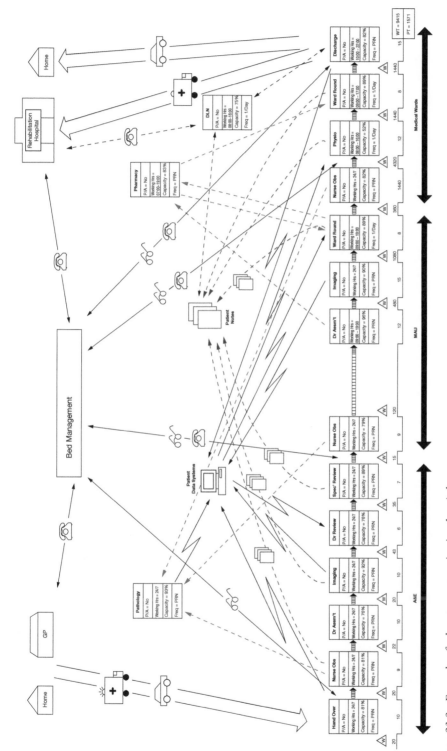

Figure 23.2   Example of value stream mapping in a hospital

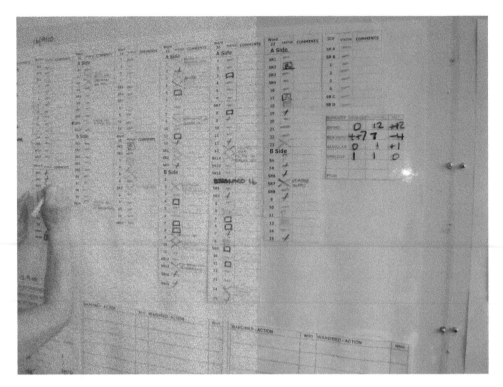

Figure 23.3   Example of a visual planning board in a hospital

step-by-step improvements toward challenging performance goals. In addition, others can learn from their experiences.

3   *Establishing values and principles.* This includes, for example, "Patient first" and "Show respect for others," developing a consensus on expected behaviors and leadership, and making problems transparent in a no-blame culture.

4   *Creating a central lean or improvement team.* This can be implemented to facilitate lean activities while teaching lean concepts and developing future leaders.

5   *Building a daily management system.* This management system should include start of shift meetings, bed management meetings, and departmental progress meetings right through to board meetings. At each level management reviews the actual situation and discusses how obstacles to planned progress can be removed. At the same time they coach their teams in problem solving.

6   *Spreading lean across departments.* Teams should be engaged to begin using lean to solve problems in their areas. They should be provided with the necessary support and coaching. Challenges and results should be communicated across the organization.

A full description of a lean hospital management system can be found in Barnas (2014).

The Future of Lean Healthcare

We have certainly come a long way in learning how lean can help healthcare. Many of these lessons are common to other activities. However, we are still at the beginning of a long journey to

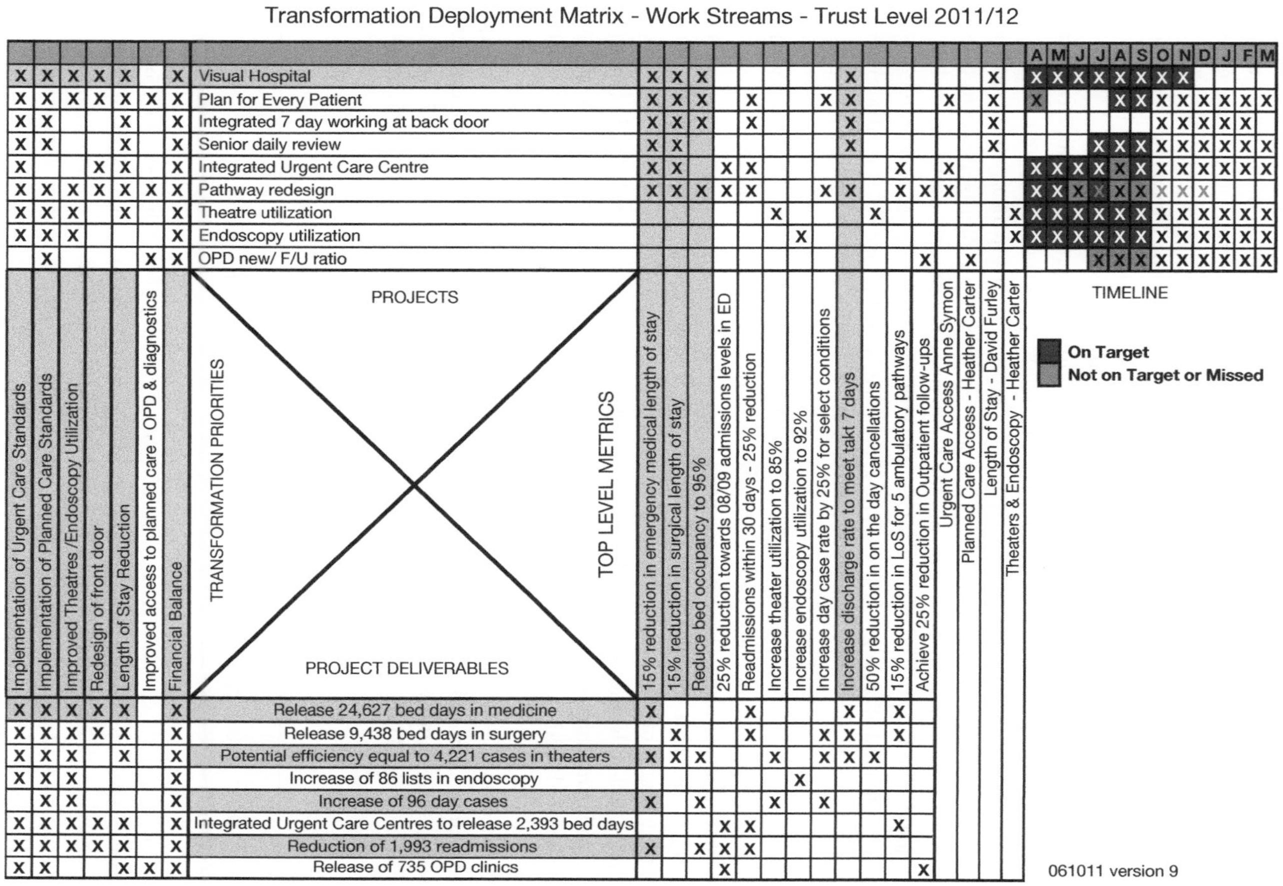

Transformation Deployment Matrix - Work Streams - Trust Level 2011/12

PROJECTS (Visual Hospital)
- Plan for Every Patient
- Integrated 7 day working at back door
- Senior daily review
- Integrated Urgent Care Centre
- Pathway redesign
- Theatre utilization
- Endoscopy utilization
- OPD new/ F/U ratio

TOP LEVEL METRICS
- 15% reduction in emergency medical length of stay
- 15% reduction in surgical length of stay
- Reduce bed occupancy to 95%
- 25% reduction towards 08/09 admissions levels in ED
- Readmissions within 30 days - 25% reduction
- Increase theater utilization to 85%
- Increase endoscopy utilization to 92%
- Increase day case rate by 25% for select conditions
- Increase discharge rate to meet takt 7 days
- 50% reduction in on the day cancellations
- 15% reduction in LoS for 5 ambulatory pathways
- Achieve 25% reduction in Outpatient follow-ups
- Urgent Care Access — Anne Symon
- Planned Care Access — Heather Carter
- Length of Stay — David Furey
- Theaters & Endoscopy — Heather Carter

TRANSFORMATION PRIORITIES
- Financial Balance
- Improved access to planned care - OPD & diagnostics
- Length of Stay Reduction
- Redesign of front door
- Improved Theatres /Endoscopy Utilization
- Implementation of Planned Care Standards
- Implementation of Urgent Care Standards

PROJECT DELIVERABLES
- Release 24,627 bed days in medicine
- Release 9,438 bed days in surgery
- Potential efficiency equal to 4,221 cases in theaters
- Increase of 86 lists in endoscopy
- Increase of 96 day cases
- Integrated Urgent Care Centres to release 2,393 bed days
- Reduction of 1,993 readmissions
- Release of 735 OPD clinics

TIMELINE: A M J J A S O N D J F M

Legend:
- On Target
- Not on Target or Missed

061011 version 9

Figure 23.4 Example of policy deployment matrix at a hospital

realize the full potential of lean as a management system and as a framework for designing healthcare delivery systems for the future.

So far we can distinguish between four different approaches to lean healthcare. First, numerous experiments in different departments, from admissions to operating rooms and imaging to pathology, where teams have learned to see the flow of their work differently using a lean perspective (see Jarvis, 2015). There have also been several experiments in joining these together along the patient journey (see Baker and Taylor, 2009).

Second, whole hospital examples, notably Thedacare and Virginia Mason (see Toussaint, 2010; Kenney, 2011), which have developed a comprehensive management system throughout the hospital and associated primary care units, described above.

Third, big experiments in state-wide healthcare transformation programs, modeled on the Virginia Mason experience, most notably in Saskatchewan in Canada (see Florizone, 2015).

The fourth model is a much simpler do-it-yourself approach where top management seeds and supports problem solving across the hospital, and actively links these improvements to deliver hospital-wide results. Instead of relying on outside or internal consulting support, lean is taken up by front-line staff and top management is advised and challenged by *senseis* or advisors with deep experience in asking challenging questions. This approach is being followed by several hospitals in Barcelona, Spain (see the case study below; Adalid, 2014; Pardos, 2014; Sanchez and Suarez, 2015).

Improving the performance of existing hospitals and healthcare systems is also the foundation for designing next-generation lean healthcare systems. Interesting experiments are underway in Saskatchewan, Canada using the lean *production preparation process* (3P) to design new hospitals (Florizone, 2015). This involves teams of front-line staff and patients mapping all the flows through the hospital (of patients, doctors, tests, drugs, etc.) in order to design an ideal room layout and to build full-scale mock-ups of key rooms. Once this process knowledge is captured, architects and contractors can then work out exactly how to build the new hospital. As a result, they will not only reduce the footprint and capital cost of the new hospital but also cut the running cost over the 40-year life of the building significantly.

What is striking about lean is its ability to touch people and give them hope that they can improve their work in caring for patients. When they describe with real pride the problems they have already solved and what problems they plan to tackle next, you know they will continue down this journey. The challenge for management is mobilizing and supporting this army of problem solvers.

Case Study: Lean Healthcare in Consorci Sanitari Del Garraf

Consorci Sanitari Del Garraf is a 440-bed public hospital with 961 employees located south of Barcelona in Spain. It was formed in a merger of three hospitals in 2009 and the new CEO, Josep Lluis Ibanez Pardos, was faced with a 17 percent cut in the budget for the hospital. While the first two years were spent integrating the operations and systems of the three hospitals, he was also determined to address the crisis by transforming the culture instead of just pursuing short-term cost savings. In previous assignments he witnessed the limitations of two external consultant-driven lean projects which did not last and was determined to lead this one himself.

In 2011, he took his management team to a lean practitioner training workshop run by the Instituto Lean Management in Barcelona, and later hired them as coaches and teachers for his team. Following the workshop, they learned to diagnose their situation and they developed a plan. The focus of this plan was to build the capabilities of employees in order to improve the core processes in the hospital. The basic thinking was to teach the use of data-driven analysis to establish stability, to teach scientific problem solving (PDCA) to make improvements, to focus on reducing time, and to communicate and share the results across the hospital.

Rosa Simon was appointed lean manager, supported by five staff. They developed their own training course for the hospital staff from pilot areas and helped them make their work visual, address the causes of variation, and use A3 for problem solving. While the staff from each area selected the problems to tackle, supported by the lean team, top management was always available to support and unblock issues they encountered. In many cases they tried experiments with alternative potential solutions to see which worked best. The experience of solving their own problems quickly built engagement, pride, and ownership, which was communicated across the hospital. They went on to identify the next problems they wanted to address.

Over the next three years, projects were conducted in many different areas. They streamlined the admission process at the front door to reduce waiting times and direct people to the right location, something that was visible to everyone visiting the hospital. In the operating room (OR) they reduced the time between operations from over an hour to 35 minutes, so they could carry out one additional procedure a day per OR. On the wards, they made the work visible so everything was done on time, response times were faster, and it took less time to prepare rooms and beds for the next patient. They also worked very hard to discharge a majority of patients before midday, freeing up beds for patients coming from the OR and the emergency department (ED). In the ED they reorganized the work sequence and the response times from imaging and blood tests so that waiting times and length of stay in the ED were cut in half.

Linking these improvements is making a big difference to patient experience and simplifying the work for staff as patients move through the hospital without delays and the hospital is able to treat more patients while meeting the reduced budget. These improvements were recognized as it became one of the top 20 hospitals for quality in Spain, and later won the award for best hospital in Spain in 2013. Visiting the hospital today gives the impression of a calm situation well in control. The staff are strongly committed to continuing their problem solving on into the future. As a result, they have inspired several other hospitals, large and small, in the Barcelona area to follow their example.

References

Adalid, C. F. (2014). *A Healing Organisation*. Available at: http://planet-lean.com/model-hospital-working-with-lean-healthcare-in-a-bad-economy (accessed July 2016).

Allen, M. (2013). *How Many Die from Medical Mistakes in US Hospitals?* ProPublica.

Baker, M. and Taylor, I. (2009). *Making Hospitals Work*, Goodrich, UK, Lean Enterprise Academy.

Barnas, K. (2014). *Beyond Heroes*, Appleton, WI, Thedacare Center for Healthcare Value.

Berwick, D. (2014). *Promising Care*, New York, Jossey Bass.

Dennis, P. (2009). *Getting the Right Things Done*, Cambridge, MA, Lean Enterprise Institute.

Florizone, D. (2015). *Saskatchewan: A Lean Government Lab*. Available at: http://planet-lean.com/implementing-lean-management-principles-across-government (accessed July 2016).

Graban, M. (2008). *Lean Hospitals*, New York, Productivity Press.

Jarvis, P. (2015). *A Better Emergency Department*. Available at: http://planet-lean.com/lean-healthcare-improving-emergency-departments-in-the-uk (accessed July 2016).

Jimmerson, C. (2007). *A3 Problem Solving for Healthcare*, New York, Productivity Press.

Kenney, C. (2011). *Transforming Health Care*, New York, Productivity Press.

Liker, J. (2004). *The Toyota Way*, New York, McGraw-Hill.

Pardos, J. L. I. (2014). *My Lean Story No. 3*. Available at: http://planet-lean.com/my-lean-story-3 (accessed July 2016).

Sanchez, M. and Suarez, M. (2015). *Lean Hospitals? Do It Yourself.* Available at: http://planet-lean.com/diy-lean-transformation-at-barcelona-s-hospital-clinic (accessed July 2016).

Shook, J. (2010). *Managing to Learn*, Cambridge, MA, Lean Enterprise Institute.

Toussaint, J. (2010). *On the Mend*, Cambridge, MA, Lean Enterprise Institute.

Toussaint, J. (2015). *Management on the Mend*, Appleton, WI, Thedacare Center for Healthcare Value.

Womack, J. and Jones, D. (1996). *Lean Thinking: Banish Waste and Create Wealth in Your Corporation*, New York, Rawson Associates.

Worth, J., Shuker, T., Keyte, B., Ohaus, K., Luckman, J., Verble, D., et al. *(2012). Perfecting Patient Journeys*, Cambridge, MA, Lean Enterprise Institute.

24

LEAN CONSTRUCTION

Glenn Ballard

Introduction

Lean came into the construction industry in 1993 with the formation of the International Group for Lean Construction (www.iglc.net), followed in 1997 by the Lean Construction Institute (LCI) in the United States (www.leanconstruction.org), and the Egan Report in the United Kingdom in 1998 (Egan, 1998). Two primary drivers can be identified, one external and the other internal to the construction industry. The external driver was the superior performance of Japanese motor vehicle manufacturers discovered in MIT's International Motor Vehicle Program and reported in *The Machine that Changed the World* (Womack et al., 1990). The internal driver was widespread dissatisfaction with construction industry performance. These two drivers coincided in the Egan Report's call to apply lean manufacturing methods to the construction industry to radically reduce cost, time to market, defects, and accidents.

Some, but not all, of the principles and methods used in manufacturing have been applied to construction without adaptation to the differences between these two types of production. Others have been adapted or invented to fit with the peculiarities of construction as a type of project production system. This chapter describes what is unique about *lean construction,* its current state of the art, and future challenges and opportunities.

What is Lean Construction?

To understand how lean applies to the construction industry it is important to understand the industry's special characteristics. All artifacts are first designed and made in project production systems. Construction is one type of project production system. Project production systems also include new product development, software engineering, air and sea shipbuilding, and performing arts productions. Construction is differentiated from other forms of project production by, at least, the following set of characteristics:

- First, its products are rooted in the earth. All products are designed for the conditions in which they will be used. Design of construction's products is constrained by the locations in which the products are to be placed. Location variables can include: meteorological, geological (e.g. seismic, substructure requirements), cultural, regulatory, availability of materials, and availability of resources.

- Second, during the process of assembly, product components become too large to be moved through workstations, so workstations must be moved through the components. This is the defining characteristic of fixed position manufacturing, of which construction is one type (Schmenner, 1993).

- Third, construction's customers are individuals, not types. When products are produced prior to sale, the buyer cannot fully participate in the production process. Construction's products are typically produced in response to an order; hence there is someone speaking for the buyer. One consequence is the need to understand exactly what *this* customer wants, what constraints define the design space in which to search, and what preferences should be used to select from design alternatives within the constrained space. A second consequence of individuals as customers is the need for the customer to maintain an active role during the production (designing and making) process. This ranges at minimum from approval of design as it develops through stages to direct participation in generation, evaluation, and selection from design alternatives when the project is more complex and uncertain.

Lean differs in construction in consequence of this *set* of characteristics. Some characteristics are shared with other types of project production. For example, shipbuilding is also a type of fixed position manufacturing. However, its products are not rooted in the earth, but rather float. As a result, ships are designed for different conditions of use than are products of construction, such as buildings or bridges. Like construction, software engineering may be produced in response to a customer order, but its products are, like shipbuilding, not rooted in the earth. Product development faces the same challenges of designing and making products fit for purpose within constraints, with features responsive to the preferences of different customer groups. However, they are designing products for customer types, not for individuals, and consequently customers are not involved in the design process. Products of the performing arts are not fixed in the earth, and are not instances of fixed position manufacturing. Further, its customers are not typically involved in product design.

How lean differs in construction can be seen in the different principles employed to pursue the lean ideal, and in the methods developed to implement lean principles. The lean ideal is to deliver value to customers with no waste. Value in this case is instrumental value, having value which enables customers to accomplish their objectives. Waste is anything with a cost of any kind (e.g. stress to personnel) that can be eliminated without reducing value delivered to customers. Customers include the paying customer (the immediate customer of those delivering the project), other project stakeholders, both internal and external, and arguably the human species, e.g. consider the environmental and esthetic impacts of projects (Ballard et al., 2001).

A Few Examples of Principles and Methods Employed in Lean Construction

Optimize the Project, not the Piece

All projects use some means to align the commercial interests of the specialist companies on the project team. The more complex and uncertain the project, the greater the risk that fixed links between work scope and compensation will fracture with changes in what's to be made and how to make it. In those conditions, the principle used in construction (which may also apply else-where) is: "*Allow money and resources to move across contractual and organizational boundaries in search of the best project-level investment.*" This principle will be revisited when we discuss the state of the art below, and also in the case study.

Last Planner System of Production Planning and Control

Since construction crews must eventually move through the components being assembled, some means of coordinating the activities of specialists is required to replace the direction and timing provided by moving assembly lines (more generally, by machine-paced line flow). *The Last Planner® system* of production planning and control was developed to provide this coordination (Ballard, 2000). Last Planner functions appear to be broadly applicable to project-based production and include:

- collaborative planning to specify what *should* be done when,
- making ready what *should* be done so it *can* be done when needed,
- increasing the match between *did* and *should* through shielding and reliable promising, and
- learning from plan failures.

The development of *Last Planner®* was inspired by the discovery, in the early 1990s, that workflow reliability was chronically low in construction projects. The percentage of tasks completed on weekly work plans was found to range roughly from 35 percent to 70 percent (Ballard and Howell, 1998). This phenomenon is not detected by traditional project management measures of progress or cost, but has been found to be a fundamental driver of progress and cost. An example is given in Figure 24.1, showing a correlation analysis of "percent planned tasks completed" (PPC) and labor productivity. The causal explanation for this correlation is that low predictability of near-term workload discourages planning and preparation, which in turn reduces productivity (see Figure 24.1). It is apparent that the same cause-effect mechanism operates to reduce all aspects of performance: safety, quality, time, and cost.

Substituting values for PPC in the equation of the line of best fit in Figure 24.1, we can forecast labor productivity as shown in Table 24.1.

A PPC of 50 percent corresponds very nearly to budget productivity, with only 4 percent difference. This implies that productivity was budgeted from historical data generated on projects

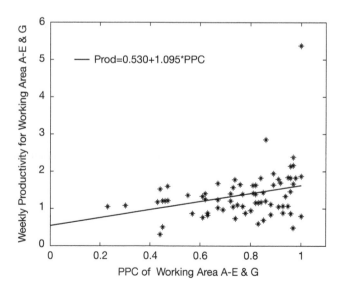

Figure 24.1 Correlation between labor productivity and PPC

Source: From Liu et al. (2010).

273

Table 24.1 Forecast productivity for various PPC values

Percentage planned completed (PPC)	Percentage actual productivity will be below budget
50%	4%
60%	16%
70%	23%
80%	29%

where PPC was approximately 50 percent. A PPC of 80 percent, which is now quite common on projects delivered using Last Planner, corresponds to a labor productivity 29 percent better than budget.

Target Value Design

In response to the uniqueness of construction's customers, target value design (Zimina et al., 2012) has been adapted from the target costing practiced by manufacturing's product development (Cooper and Slagmulder, 1997).

Target costing makes cost a driver of design, as opposed to an outcome of design. Its adaptation in construction makes explicit the primary objective; namely, to deliver value to the customer, where cost is less often a value than a constraint on realization of value from the constructed asset. Hence the centrality of the allowable cost: what a customer is willing and able to pay to get what they want. Target value design is a complex method that begins with determining customer *ends, constraints*, and *preferences* in order to assess feasibility of their alignment, and if feasible, to set the task for designing and making. As previously noted, constraints limit the solution space to be searched for designs that are fit for purpose and best enable realization of preferences. Targets are set for functionality, capacity, sustainability—whatever qualifies the asset as fit for purpose. Targets are also set for constraints, which usually include cost and time.

Figure 24.2 provides a bit more detail about the project definition process in target value design, understood on the model of a conversation intended to align *ends, means*, and *constraints*.

This conversation may start with the customer voicing what they want: for example, a bridge across the river, a two-bedroom flat near downtown, etc. However, what's needed is to work back to customer purpose. What are they trying to accomplish? What do they intend to do with the flat, bridge, factory? If purpose is understood, then it is possible to determine what features of the product are valuable; i.e. what features are means for realizing that purpose. In order to incorporate those values into the product, it is necessary to translate from the voice of the customer into the voice of the engineer. That involves moving from "I want to be able to hear a pin dropped on stage from any seat in the balcony" to specification in decibels of the sound at specific locations in the facility. Both of these linkages are difficult and critical: linking purposes and values, and linking values and engineering specifications/design criteria.

That is one set of motions, entirely within ends. A second motion occurs within means. If it is true that the fitness for purpose of hospitals, schools, factories, and other means of production is a function of their design, then for at least those product types it is necessary to first design how the product will be used before designing the product (facility) itself. In some cases, prior analysis of facility operations reveals ways to improve an existing facility and avoid the cost and time of new building.

Finally, there is the conversation between ends, means, and constraints. As ends are more clearly defined and translated into *design criteria* (specifications), and as the design-for-use of the

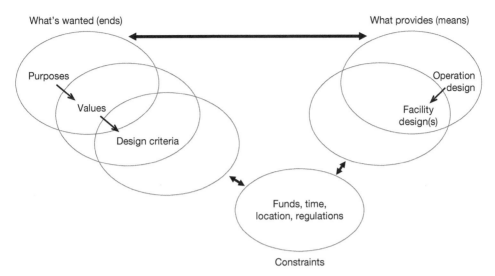

Figure 24.2 Project definition process

Source: Ballard (2008).

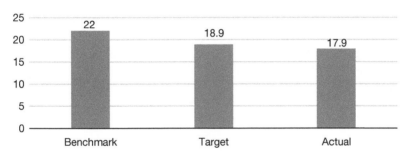

Figure 24.3 Benchmark, target, and actual cost, Sutter Fairfield Medical office building (figures in million US dollars)

facility emerges, constraints are also better defined. What are you able and willing to spend? When do you need to have the facility for your use? What are the implications of alternative locations for geotechnical, meteorological, cultural, and regulatory conditions? Cultural criteria link projects and buildings to the communities in which they are located, and to the values and interests of that set of stakeholders. Ends, means, and constraints are mutually determined and so become clearer as each is progressively determined in alignment with the others.

The next steps are to design to targets, then to build to targets. The final step is for the customer to realize the target value through use of the constructed asset.

Figure 24.3 shows the various costs for Sutter Health's Fairfield Medical office building, one of its first target value design projects. The market benchmark cost was $22 million, the target cost was $18.9 million, and the cost at completion was $17.9 million. The target was set 14 percent below market and the actual cost was 19 percent below market.

Figure 24.4 shows how the expected cost changed during design and construction. Normally, as design becomes more detailed, the expected cost increases. Here we see the opposite. Expected

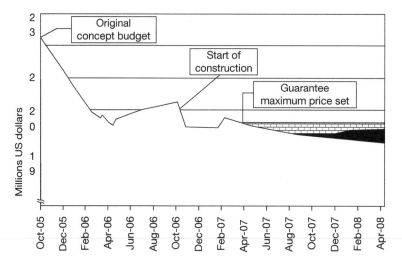

Figure 24.4   Sutter Fairfield Medical office building project: expected vs target cost over time

Source: From The Boldt Company (2008).

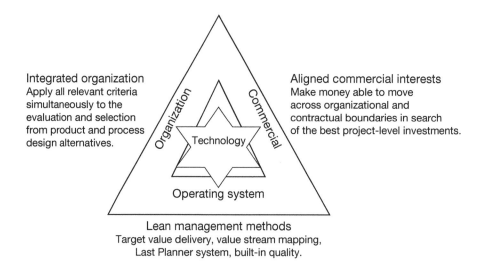

Integrated organization
Apply all relevant criteria
simultaneously to the
evaluation and selection
from product and process
design alternatives.

Aligned commercial interests
Make money able to move
across organizational and
contractual boundaries in search
of the best project-level investments.

Lean management methods
Target value delivery, value stream mapping,
Last Planner system, built-in quality.

Figure 24.5   The LCI triangle

Source: Adapted from Thomsen et al. (2010).

cost declined as the project team worked to deliver target scope within target cost, and was reduced yet more during construction, enabling additional value-added scope (shown in black in Figure 24.4), while reducing cost below target.

Current State of the Art

The current state of the art of lean in construction is best presented in terms of the LCI triangle (Thomsen et al., 2010) as shown in Figure 24.5.

All projects have:

- commercial terms that engage the various companies involved in project delivery,
- an organizational structure (perhaps different in different phases) and methods of project governance, and
- an operating system consisting of management principles and methods.

Projects vary along a spectrum between simple and certain on one end and complex and uncertain on the other. Complex and uncertain projects have the best chance at successful execution when commercial interests are aligned by means of shared risk and reward, the organization is integrated (upstream players in downstream processes and vice versa), and the project "operating system" is based on the lean philosophy, principles, and methods.

As projects approach the dynamic end of the spectrum, it becomes ever more necessary to link compensation to achievement of the owner's objectives for the project. Designers and constructors are engaged to help the owner solve a problem not yet fully understood, as opposed to being engaged to provide the means the owner thinks she needs. Traditionally, commercial terms have been structured in terms of compensation for delivery of an agreed product, whether as fixed price or, when quantities are indefinite, as a mark-up on costs. Due to uncertainty and complexity making it unlikely that project ends or means will remain stable throughout, separate commercial interests dependent upon fixed scopes of work are no longer useful.

This method of aligning commercial interests enables money to move across contractual and organizational boundaries in search of the best project-level investments. Relational contracts are needed, as opposed to only transactional. Macneil (1980), head of the Law School at Northwestern University until his retirement, argues against the classical legal theory that understands contracts as entirely transactional, without regard to the relationships between the parties. He proposes that all contracts can be located on a continuum between fully transactional and fully relational, and that no contract is exclusively one or the other. He uses the marriage vow to illustrate a relational contract because the commitment is to sustaining and developing a relationship in expectation of turmoil, as opposed to simply specifying a transaction. For an example of a relational contract in the construction industry, see Lichtig (2006).

Organizational integration is driven by the need to apply all relevant design criteria simultaneously to the evaluation and selection from design alternatives, whether of product or process. It is apparent that the way buildings and other assets are designed impacts how they are constructed: fabrication, installation, assembly, and disassembly processes. Consequently, one of the lean principles is to design together both what is to be built and how it is to be built. That requires collaboration between designers and builders, corresponding to the degree of project complexity and uncertainty, because innovation is needed to solve problems for which old solutions are inadequate. Downstream players (fabricators and constructors) are needed in the upstream design phase, and vice versa. However, the penalty for sequential processing (the opposite of organizational integration) is less for projects that are simpler and more certain. For example, when the assets to be constructed are similar to others previously produced, the same product and process designs may be used, even if not optimum. Consequently, toward the stodgy end of the spectrum, design-bid-build can be successful.

Traditional, non-lean project management typically strives to reduce the time or cost of each contract or purchase. However, this strategy delivers the least cost/least duration project only if the contracts and purchases are independent. Even though independence of project components is never fully achieved, when complexity is low it is more closely approximated. When complexity and interdependence are high, traditional local optimization does not work.

Even the "operating system" for a project can vary with its location on the stodgy–dynamic spectrum. Lean promotes learning, develops people, and pursues continuous improvement. Obviously, these are valuable in any circumstances, but become critical when projects pose unprecedented challenges that demand new solutions.

Even though traditional commercial terms, organizational structures, and management methods can work for less dynamic projects, it is important to understand that the penalty is less, but nonetheless exists. Further, waste (avoidable costs) tends to remain and even grow when construction projects and companies are managed traditionally, as opposed to the lean operating system's striving for continuous improvement.

For criticism of non-lean project management theories and practice, see Koskela and Howell (2002). For criticism of the theoretical foundations of production as a whole, see Koskela (2000, 2011), and Koskela and Ballard (2012).

A last important consideration is that the delivery system for dynamic projects also works for stodgy projects, but the reverse is not true. When there is uncertainty about the dynamic character of projects, it is prudent to use the lean construction operating system. Likewise, when you want to further improve the performance of slower and simpler projects, it is prudent to use the lean construction operating system.

Future Opportunities and Challenges

There are many opportunities for advancing lean in the construction industry, as well as some formidable challenges. Opportunities include:

Compete through Supply Chains

One important opportunity is to extend lean beyond projects and individual organizations to the networks through which value is produced in the industry. It is well understood in manufacturing that it is no longer sufficient to be the best at what you do, but you must be a member of the best supply chain (Ketchen and Giunipero, 2004). The focus of optimization and improvement must be on the entire supply chain, not on its individual companies. That is not so well understood in construction, which has struggled to understand exactly how competition is supply chain vs supply chain, as opposed to one bidder against another bidder. However, a moment's reflection reveals that the performance of a company, whether architectural, engineering, or contracting, is greatly influenced by the capabilities of its suppliers. This means that improving that performance requires improving supplier capabilities—both through selection and through development. A big step in that direction has been taken by Skanska Nordic in Sweden, Norway, and Finland (Elfving and Ballard, 2013).

Simplify Site Installation to Final Assembly and Commissioning

There is also an opportunity to apply lean management methods and new technologies to simplify site construction to final assembly and commissioning. Prefabrication and modularization can increase concurrency, thus reducing project durations. They can also improve productivity from working in shop conditions, from increased mechanization, from repetition, and from applying lean manufacturing principles and methods to fabrication shops.

The quality and timely delivery of engineered-to-order (ETO) and made-to-order (MTO) products often make or break construction projects. Fabricators are the link between construction and manufacturing and are ideal candidates for the application of more traditional lean manufacturing methods. An example is found in Ballard et al. (2002), which describes the restructuring of a precast concrete factory into production cells. Production cells are used when demand for similar products (product families) warrants dedicating resources to their production. That approach was first applied to the production of precast concrete shear walls in the case study factory and the fabrication process was restructured to approximate continuous flow. The result was an improvement in production from 3.2 to 9 walls per day with the same labor force and equipment. As shown in Figure 24.6, when the entire factory was reorganized into production cells, revenues increased 250 percent, again with no change in labor or equipment.

Application of lean methods to job shops that cannot be structured in production cells because of variations in workload composition was explored in Brink and Ballard (2005). In a different precast concrete shop, also doing wet cast products, cost was reduced 27 percent and productivity was improved 67 percent, as a result of applying 5S, total productive maintenance, pull (as opposed to push as a mechanism for assigning workload), value stream mapping, and more—all of them standard lean methods from manufacturing.

Use TAKT *Time Planning*

Site assembly can benefit from the application of *takt* time planning (Frandsen et al., 2014), which likewise increases concurrency and substantially improves the reliability of release of work between trades, measured by *percent plan complete* (PPC), which reduce project duration and cost (cf. Figure 24.1 for correlation between PPC and productivity).

Takt time planning is a way of structuring the various types of work involved in the construction phase of projects. It is a type of location-based planning, which divides the work to be done into locations such as rooms of a hotel. It also allows each trade the same amount of time to complete its work in each room. This approach has been used for some time on highly repetitive projects such as pipelines, highways, and high-rise commercial buildings, the most famous example of which is the Empire State Building (Sacks and Partouche, 2009). More recently, attempts have been made to accommodate less repetition by using equal amounts of labor time to define takt locations (Linnik et al., 2013).

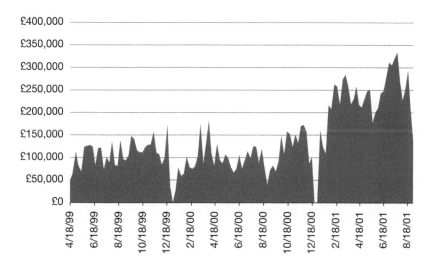

Figure 24.6 Increase in revenue-malling precast products

Source: Ballard et al. (2002).

Increased predictability of work release facilitates logistics and just-in-time (JIT) delivery. When a trade knows with a high degree of certainty what information, materials, tools, and equipment will be needed x weeks in the future, it becomes feasible to kit and deliver work packages to construction sites just when needed. Two last planner system metrics, *tasks made ready* (TMR) and *tasks anticipated* (TA), measure the performance of the look ahead process, which has the job of making scheduled tasks ready to be performed. This is done by identifying and removing constraints on scheduled tasks, by breaking tasks down into operations (e.g. "install the piping in isometric drawing #101," as opposed to "install piping in area A"), and collaboratively planning operations with those who are to perform them (Ballard et al., 2009).

Target Net Benefits in Use

Target value design has been applied very successfully in the construction industry, enabling the delivery of constructed assets for less capital cost (Conwell, 2012). That same approach can be used to target and deliver greater benefits in use of constructed assets. Evans et al. (1998) showed that if the cost to construct an asset is set at 1.0, the cost of design is approximately 0.1, so the capital cost of the project is represented by 1.1. Operating and maintaining the physical asset might be a 4.3 over 20 years, and business costs might be a 4.2. All these costs summed together must be less than the benefits in use; otherwise, the project is not economically viable.

The problem is how to best estimate longer-term costs and benefits, and how to relate them to the capital cost of the construction project. In the target value design method, the allowable cost for a project is defined as the most the owner is willing and able to spend to acquire use of the asset to be constructed. Willingness to spend is a function of the expected worth of the asset, i.e. net benefits in use. Assuming availability of funds, the higher the worth of the asset the greater the allowable cost. One possibility worth exploring is to link computer product models to operations cost models to evaluate the impact of alternative designs on whole life costs and benefits of the assets being constructed. Operations cost models could generate estimates of costs and benefits in use, and also generate design requirements for the asset. If we learn how to "clash" the computer model of the building or bridge against the operations model, we can better evaluate the fitness for use of alternative designs. This opportunity has been exploited to some extent, but limited both in the types of constructed assets (principally industrial) and the completeness of the operations models (e.g. in healthcare).

Learn from Other Types of Production Systems

There is opportunity for construction to learn from other types of production systems that share the same characteristics. For example, since construction and shipbuilding are both types of fixed position manufacturing, construction could benefit from understanding how ships of different types are built, e.g. modularization. Software engineering's Scrum methodology has been found especially beneficial in construction because both types of project production system produce custom products, and share the problem of how to best understand or develop customer requirements (Blokpoel et al., 2005). More exploration is likely to find additional useful methods applicable to both systems. Study of performing arts productions may yield useful insights into construction production planning and control. Christin Egebjerg's ". . .and Action!" (Egebjerg, 2012) is an excellent example. Study of manufacturing's product development has already produced concepts and practices that have been applied to construction projects, e.g. concurrent engineering (Tommelein, 2002). Further study may yield additional useful insights into project organization and delivery.

Apply Lean to the Triple Bottom Line

Sustainability is now commonly understood in terms of the triple bottom line: social, environmental, and economic. Lean has historically been focused on economic outcomes, but may also be effective in achieving all elements of sustainability. Some work has already been done to show the correlation between lean practices and environmental outcomes, e.g. reductions in solid waste and noxious emissions from construction sites (Nahmens, 2009). Less has been done to exploit lean's potential for improving the quality of working life (social at the level of the individual) and employment opportunities (social at the national and international level).

Enable Just-in-Time Delivery of Fabricated Products

Increase the number of fabricated products that can be pulled from production to site by extending the window of reliability (improve the extent to which the state of construction projects can be accurately forecast) or reducing the lead time for fabricated products. The percentage of planned tasks completed (PPC) measures the extent to which we do what we say we're going to do one week ahead. When PPC is 85 percent, the forecast accuracy two weeks ahead is typically below 40 percent, making JIT delivery of fabricated products infeasible for those with lead times greater than one week. Takt time work structuring is one way to increase the window of reliability.

Challenges

Embracing Lean Leadership to Enable Sustainability

Lean advocates (e.g. Rother, 2010; Mann, 2014) argue persuasively that sustaining lean in any type of production system requires a change in leadership behaviors, both at the top of organizations and by everyone with supervisory responsibility over others. Essential to that change is that bosses become teachers and coaches, pursuing the lean principle to respect people by challenging and helping them to develop their capabilities (Liker, 2010). This change will be more difficult where the culture is one of knowing, not learning.

Learning from Failure

A related challenge lies in the inevitability of poorly performing lean projects. Lean is not magic; it is sound engineering and management in pursuit of increasing customer value and eliminating waste. Projects may fail to achieve their targets even when well engineered and managed. The industry must be prepared to learn from such failures, and not view them as reasons to give up pursuit of the lean ideal.

Self-imposing Necessity

Developing the mindset and discipline to self-impose necessity is both opportunity and challenge for those pursuing the lean ideal in construction. Lean organizations have the wisdom to impose necessity upon themselves, without waiting for demands from customers or challenges from competitors. They also have the discipline to treat that necessity as if it were externally imposed. This capability, at the heart of continuous improvement, is well expressed in Taiichi Ohno's popular advice to "lower the river to reveal the rocks." Following Ohno's advice means that we should systematically attack causes of variation and waste, then reduce the buffers of time, capacity, and inventory in our production systems to match the lower levels of variation. Broken promises, defects and errors, and accidents and illnesses are opportunities for learning, and for reducing costs no longer needed for delivering value.

An example: In the Last Planner system, daily and weekly work plans are understood as promises between interdependent players. Broken promises are analyzed to find opportunities for countermeasures to prevent reoccurrence. Reducing interruptions and delays increases the actual capability of workers. Consequently, as the percentage of promises kept (PPC) approaches 100 percent, the amount of output expected from weekly work plan tasks can be increased without increasing the risk of accident or defective work. Figure 24.7 is the first Last Planner weekly work plan produced by Phillip, a pipefitter foreman for a mechanical contractor working on a wafer fabrication plant for Texas Instruments in Dallas, Texas, in 1996.

Presumably Phillip has followed the Last Planner rule to only include on weekly work plans tasks that are well defined for the performers, sound, properly sequenced, and sized to the capability of performers. To do that, Phillip would have checked that everything that the workers will need to perform each task is available, and that each task is done in the right sequence, so later penalties are avoided. Phillip would also have sized the amount of work to be done based on his knowledge of individuals' capabilities. Soundness, sequence, and size can be assessed after the fact, but definition is evident from the work plan itself. Each sub-crew (e.g. Sylvano, Modesto, and Terry) can determine what, where, and when for each of their assigned tasks (e.g. install 48 hangers for gas and fuel oil lines from the ceiling of Building K on Monday and Tuesday).

To further assess the performance of the planning system, at the end of the plan week Phillip noted whether or not the task was completed as planned, and if not completed, why. Continuing with the first task as our example, the workers did not complete installation of pipe hangers because the elevation of the prefabricated hangers had been changed by engineering without notifying construction. This plan failure was first analyzed by Phillip in discussion with Sylvano, Modesto, and Terry, who explained that they had constructed a scaffold in order to reach the

PROJECT: Pilot ACTIVITY			**1 WEEK PLAN**							FOREMAN: PHILLIP DATE: 9/20/96	
	Est	Act	Mon	Tu	Wed	Thurs	Fri	Sat	Sun	PPC	REASON FOR VARIANCES
Gas/F.O. hangers O/H "K" (48 hangers)			XXXX Sylvano,	XXXX Modesto, Terry						No	Owner stopped work (changing elevations)
Gas/F.O. risers to O/H "K" (3 risers)				XXXX Sylvano.	XXXX Modesto,	XXXX Terry	XXXX			No	Same as above-worked on backlog & boiler blowdown
36" cond water "K" 42' 2-45 deg 1-90 deg			XXXX Charlie,	XXXX Rick,	XXXX Ben					Yes	
Chiller risers (2 chillers wk.)						XXXX Charlie,	XXXX Rick,	XXXX Ben		No	Matl from shop rcvd late Thurs. Grooved couplings shipped late.
Hang H/W O/H "J" (240'-14")			XXXX Mark M.,	XXXX Mike	XXXX	XXXX	XXXX	XXXX		Yes	
Cooling Tower10" tie-ins (steel) (2 towers per day)			XXXX Steve ,	XXXX Chris,	XXXX Mark W.	XXXX	XXXX	XXXX		Yes	
Weld out CHW pump headers "J" mezz. (18)			XXXX Luke	XXXX	XXXX	XXXX	XXXX	XXXX		Yes	
Weld out cooling towers (12 towers)			XXXX Jeff	XXXX	XXXX	XXXX	XXXX	XXXX		No	Eye injury. Lost 2 days welding time
F.R.P. tie-in to E.T. (9 towers) 50%			XXXX Firt, Packy, Tom	XXXX	XXXX	XXXX	XXXX	XXXX		Yes	
WORKABLE BACKLOG Boiler blowdown-gas vents -rupture disks											

Figure 24.7 Last Planner weekly work plan

Source: Ballard (1997).

ceiling, had pulled a compressor hose to the location to operate air hammers for drilling bolt holes in the ceiling, and had begun to work when a design engineer happened to walk by and told them the pipe hanger elevations had been changed. Phillip's project manager further analyzed the plan failure in discussion with the design engineers, who said they had been thinking about this change for six weeks and had made the decision to change two weeks earlier. The agreed countermeasure was to integrate the work plans for design engineering and for construction, so foremen like Phillip could see when changes were being considered or had been made that affected their tasks.

It is important to note that Last Planner is concerned to improve the planning system. A plan failure does not signal retribution, but rather investigation and learning. With rare exceptions, whose fault it was is irrelevant. What matters is preventing reoccurrence. That makes everyone better.

Case Study: Lean Construction in Sutter Health

Sutter Health is the largest healthcare company in Northern California, with more than 25 hospitals and 4,900 physicians. In April 2004, Sutter Health held a lean conference with 250 people from the design, engineering, and construction firms in its supplier community. Sutter Health committed to delivering its capital program using lean principles and methods, and invited suppliers to help make that happen. This commitment was a response to a twofold crisis. Sutter Health projects had experienced increasing delays, cost overruns, and claims. In addition, it was in competition with other healthcare companies for scarce design and construction resources, all of them struggling to meet the deadline for upgrading acute care hospitals to remain operational during and after major earthquakes. Sutter Health embraced lean in hopes of improving project performance and of becoming a preferred customer of architects, engineers, and constructors.

Sutter Health's commitment to lean project delivery was a breakthrough event for lean in the Northern California construction industry. Suddenly, lean became a business imperative for companies that wanted to work on Sutter Health projects. Moreover, it was not long before other healthcare companies, both in and outside California, followed its lead. The Sutter Health lean initiative spawned the first Lean Construction Institute community of practice and the formation of the Project Production Systems Laboratory at the University of California, Berkeley. Ten years later, there were more than 25 LCI communities of practice in the United States.

A new form of contract, the Integrated Form of Agreement (IFOA), was developed by Will Lichtig, Sutter Health's outside counsel. The IFOA featured a multi-party agreement between all key members of project teams, including the client. It also incorporated gain- and pain-sharing and organizational integration (downstream players involved in upstream processes, and vice versa), and required the use of lean management principles and methods. Included in those principles was the previously mentioned "allow money to move across organizational and contractual boundaries in search of the best project-level investment." Given shared risk and reward commercial terms, owners of the various companies participating in projects tend to release their employees to collaborate with other companies. This is precisely because that is the way to increase their profits. This collaboration is the key to innovation and creativity in the design of product and process. The performance of Sutter Health's projects is evidence of the effectiveness of this lean principle in practice.

In August 2012, Dan Conwell, Sutter Health's chief architect and planner, reported that Sutter Health had completed 22 lean projects each above $10 million, with no projects over budget or schedule, with no loss of functionality or quality (see Conwell, 2012). Market cost benchmarks had been done on half those projects. Comparing cost at completion with these benchmarks revealed that Sutter Health projects were completed on average 15 percent under market. Even this may understate the extent of improvement because Sutter Health modified its estimating standards as it achieved ever-more ambitious cost outcomes.

References

Ballard, G. (1997). Lookahead planning. *Proceedings of the 5th Annual Conference of the International Group for Lean Construction*, July 16–17, Gold Coast, Australia.

Ballard, G. (2000). The Last Planner System of Production Control. Ph.D. Dissertation, Civil Engineering, University of Birmingham.

Ballard, G. (2008). The lean project delivery system: An update. *Lean Construction Journal*, 4(1), 1–19.

Ballard, G. and Howell, G. (1998). Shielding production: Essential step in production control. *Journal of Construction Engineering and Management*, 124(1), 11–17.

Ballard, G., Koskela. L., Howell, G. H. and Zabelle, T. (2001). Production system design in construction. *Proceedings of the 9th Annual Conference of the International Group for Lean Construction*, August 6–8, Singapore.

Ballard, G., Harper, N. and Zabelle, T. (2002). Learning to see work flow: An application of lean concepts to precast concrete fabrication. *Proceedings of the 10th Annual Conference of the International Group for Lean Construction*, August 6–8, Gramado, Brazil.

Ballard, G., Hammond, J. and Nickerson, R. (2009). Production control principles. *Proceedings of the 17th Annual Conference of the International Group for Lean Construction*, July 15–17, Taipei, Japan.

Blokpoel, S. B., Reymen, I. M. M. J. and Dewulf, G. P. M. R. (2005). Uncertainty management in real estate development: Studying the potential of the SCRUM design methodology. *Proceedings of the 3rd International Conference on Innovation in Architecture, Engineering and Construction—AEC2005*, June 5–7, Rotterdam.

The Boldt Company (2008). *Sutter Health Fairfield Medical Office Building*. Self-published.

Brink, T. and Ballard, G. (2005). SLAM—a case study in applying lean to job shops. *Proceedings of the American Society of Civil Engineers Construction Research Congress*, April 5–7, San Diego, CA.

Conwell, D. (2012). Sutter Health's lean/integrated delivery model. Presentation at a University of California Berkeley's Project Production Systems Laboratory workshop, *August 29, Berkeley, CA.*

Cooper, R. and Slagmulder, R. (1997). *Target Costing and Value Engineering*, New York, Productivity Press.

Egan, J. (1998). The Egan Report: Rethinking Construction. *Report of the Construction Industry Task Force to the Deputy Prime Minister*. London.

Egebjerg, C. (2012). . . . and Action! Ph.D. dissertation, Department of Management Engineering, Technical University of Denmark.

Elfving, J. and Ballard, G. (2013). In search of lean suppliers—Reporting on first steps in supplier development. *Proceedings of the 21st Annual Conference of the International Group for Lean Construction*, July 29–August 2, Fortaleza, Brazil.

Evans, R., Haryott, T. R., Haste, N. and Jones, A. (1998). *The Long-Term Costs of Owning and Using Buildings*, London, Royal Academy of Engineering.

Frandsen, A. Berghede, K. and Tommelein, I. T. (2014). Takt time planning and the Last Planner. *Proceedings of the 22nd Annual Conference of the International Group for Lean Construction*, July 22–24, Oslo, Norway.

Ketchen, D. J., Jr, and Giunipero, L. (2004). The intersection of strategic management and supply chain management. *Industrial Marketing Management*, 33(1), 51–56.

Koskela, L. (2000). *An Exploration towards a Production Theory and its Application to Construction*, VTT Technical Research Centre of Finland.

Koskela, L. (2011). Fifty years of irrelevance: The wild goose chase of management science. *Proceedings of the 19th Annual Conference of the International Group for Lean Construction*, July 13–15, Lima, Peru.

Koskela, L. and Howell, G. (2002). The underlying theory of project management is obsolete. *Proceedings of the PMI Research Conference*, July 14–17, Seattle, WA.

Koskela, L. and Ballard, G. (2012). Is production outside management? Building research & information. Available at: http://dx.doi.org/10.1080/09613218.2012.709373.

Lichtig, W. A. (2006). The integrated agreement for lean project delivery. In: Kagioglou, M. and Tzortzopoulos, P. (eds), *Improving Healthcare through Built Environment Infrastructure*, Oxford, Wiley-Blackwell. doi: 10.1002/9781444319675.ch6.

Liker, J. K. (2010). *The Toyota Way,* New York, McGraw-Hill.

Linnik, M., Berghede, K. and Ballard, G. (2013). An experiment in takt-time planning applied to non-repetitive work. *Proceedings of the 21st Annual Conference of the International Group for Lean Construction*, July 29–August 2, Fortaleza, Brazil.

Liu, M., Ballard, G. and Ibbs, W. (2010). Work flow variation and labor productivity: Case study. *Journal of Management in Engineering, 27*(4), 236–242.

Macneil, I. R. (1980). *The New Social Contract: An Inquiry into Modern Contractual Relations*, New Haven, Yale University Press.

Mann, D. (2014). *Creating a Lean Culture: Tools to Sustain Lean Conversions*, Boca Raton, FL, CRC Press.

Nahmens, I. (2009). From lean to green: A natural extension. *Proceedings of the American Society of Civil Engineers Construction Research Congress*, April 5–7, Seattle, WA.

Rother, M. (2010). *Toyota Kata: Managing People for Improvement, Adaptiveness, and Superior Results*, New York, McGraw-Hill.

Sacks, R. and Partouche, R. (2009). Empire State Building project: Archetype of "mass construction." *Journal of Construction Engineering and Management, 136*(6), 702–710.

Schmenner, R. W. (1993). *Production/Operations Management: From the Inside Out*, New York, Macmillan College.

Thomsen, C., Darrington, J., Dunne, D. and Lichtig, W. (2010). Managing integrated project delivery. *Construction Management Association of America*. Available at: https://cmaanet.org/files/shared/IPD_White_Paper_1.pdf (accessed July 2016).

Tommelein, I. D. (ed.) (2002). Concurrent engineering in construction. *Proceedings of the 3rd International Conference on Concurrent Engineering in Construction*, July 1–3, Berkeley, CA.

Womack, J. P., Jones, D. T. and Roos, D. (1990). *The Machine that Changed the World*, New York, Simon & Schuster.

Zimina, D., Ballard, G. and Pasquire, C. (2012). Target value design: Using collaboration and a lean approach to reduce construction cost. *Construction Management and Economics, 30*(5), 383–398.

25

LEAN ENGINEER-TO-ORDER MANUFACTURING

Daryl J. Powell and Aldert van der Stoel

Introduction

Engineer-to-order (ETO) is a type of manufacturing that is inherently different from mass production. It refers to a strategy by which design, engineering, and production do not commence until after a customer order has been received. ETO as a manufacturing approach is typically characterized by a high variety of customized products produced in low volumes (often one-of-a-kind), a series of complex, non-repetitive, labor-intensive processes (often demanding highly skilled labor), and long lead times due to the additional elements of engineering lead time and procurement lead time in addition to production and delivery lead times.

ETO can be described using a concept called the customer order decoupling point (CODP), which is often used to distinguish between ETO and other manufacturing approaches, namely make-to-order (MTO), assemble-to-order (ATO), and make-to-stock (MTS). As illustrated in Figure 25.1, the CODP separates the part of the supply chain that responds directly to customer demand from the part that relies on forecasts and speculation.

Due to the uncertainties in both the supply and demand perspectives of ETO, ETO manufacturers can neither produce to stock nor purchase materials based on forecast, which significantly pushes the CODP upstream, lengthening the supply lead time. Though MTO producers can also experience the problems associated with delivering high-variety products in low volume, this chapter primarily focuses on ETO environments, where lengthy purchasing, production, and delivery lead times are also accompanied by significant engineering lead times.

Where lean production has traditionally been very effective in eliminating variability through standardization of both product and process, in ETO the very core of the value proposition is based on designing and producing a customer-specific product, which inherently introduces a degree of variability into the production system. The result is that ETO producers struggle to improve their performance adequately using the standard Toyota Production System (TPS) lean toolbox.

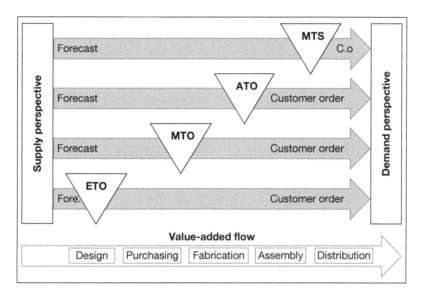

Figure 25.1   The CODP

Source: Adapted from Rudberg and Wikner (2004).

What is Lean ETO?

Taiichi Ohno, one of the chief architects of TPS, is often quoted as saying:

> All we are doing is looking at the time line, from the moment the customer gives us an order to the point when we collect the cash. And we are reducing the time line by reducing the non-value adding wastes.

> *(Ohno, 1988, p. ix)*

He goes on to say that one of the primary goals of TPS, or indeed the phenomenon we now know today as lean production, is to reduce the customer delivery lead time. Due to the inherently long lead times in ETO, the principles and practices of lean production have therefore recently become a very interesting concept for increasing the competitiveness of the sector, where the importance of shortening lead times is a stringent requirement for remaining competitive. However, Ohno (1988) also describes lean production as an alternative way of organizing mass production, suggesting that large volumes are intrinsically associated with the lean production paradigm, at least in the traditional sense. This leads to subsequent problems when attempting to apply lean production to ETO. For example, the basic principles of mass and flow production state that a) mass production demands mass consumption, and b) flow production requires continuity of demand (Woollard, 1954). ETO manufacturers exhibit neither of these traits; thus an alternative approach to "traditional" lean production is required for lean ETO.

Pavnaskar et al. (2003) suggest that a headlong rush into becoming lean has resulted in many misapplications of lean tools, often due to an inadequate understanding of them. After all, the traditional lean production tools were initially developed in order to pursue lean in a given context—the Toyota Production System. In the case of manufacturers in other types of industry, particularly in ETO, the relevance of the original toolbox must be reconsidered. Matt and Rauch

(2014) support this notion by suggesting that the suitability of certain lean methods, such as value stream mapping or kanban, is limited in ETO, while the more basic lean practices such as 5S and continuous improvement can indeed still generate significant improvement in any given situation. Though basic lean tools such as 5S are seemingly universally applicable, alternative methods are required to realize the greatest benefits from a lean transformation in ETO. This requires a fundamental re-examination of lean as both a management philosophy and a set of guiding principles, rather than simply attempting to make the existing tools fit in the new application area by adopting a "square peg, round hole" approach. Forcing a square peg into a round hole will only lead to inferior performance.

We suggest the following as a formal definition of lean ETO: *the adoption and deployment of lean principles in high-variety, low-volume manufacturing and project-based production environments*. We suggest that the ideal starting point for evaluating lean principles in the context of ETO producers is Womack and Jones' (1996) five lean principles: precisely specify *value* by specific product; identify the *value stream* for each product; make value *flow* without interruptions; let the customer *pull* value from the producer; and pursue *perfection*.

Value

One of the major reasons for the requirement of an alternative approach for lean in ETO is the way in which customer value is defined, with particular reference to the idea of variability. In traditional lean production, one of the goals is to eliminate all forms of variability through rigid standardization of product and process such that continuous flow production is achieved. This has often been accomplished through demand and production leveling, a concept known as "*heijunka*" (a Japanese term for "steady wave"). However, heijunka has itself been criticized as making lean production too inflexible and not applicable in more volatile markets, such as in ETO (Holweg, 2005). For example, where it is always desirable to reduce and eliminate dysfunctional variability in ETO, customer value propositions are built on the very idea of exploiting strategic variability. As such, customization and bespoke product offerings are recognized as a strategic advantage in ETO manufacturers; thus the elimination of this type of variability is not desirable.

Value Stream

The second lean principle in Womack and Jones (1996) is the identification of all value streams for products/product families. A value stream consists of all actions (both value added and non-value added) that are currently required to bring a product from raw material into the arms of the customer, from concept to launch (Rother and Shook, 1999). The logical starting point in identifying value streams is value stream mapping (VSM). VSM is a very useful tool, but, like many of the lean tools, should not be treated as a one-size-fits-all solution. For example, systems without a highly linear material and information flow are unlikely to benefit from this approach. ETO environments are dynamic environments in that they encounter many product variants, often with non-linear material flows with iterative cycles through similar process stages. This presents difficulties with regard to the use of VSM. The requirement to deliver one-of-a-kind products also makes VSM difficult to apply, due to several underlying circumstances (see also Alves et al., 2005):

- *Takt time*: The definition of *takt* time is contingent upon a certain and consistent demand. Thus, if demand is not known or constant, neither is the takt time.

- *Every part, every. . . (EPE)*: Again, where there is no constancy of demand, it is difficult to achieve a steady-state EPE. The actual loading of the production system as well as the demand for each product/product family typically varies from one period to the next in ETO.
- *Batch sizes*: Though batch sizes in ETO can be in the order of one, production orders in an ETO environment do have the likelihood of varying largely in terms of number of units (e.g. anything from one-offs upwards) and work content (from minutes to days). Therefore, the definition of a batch size that keeps a smooth flow of work and matches the takt time is a challenge in ETO.
- *Pacemaker*: The absence of a takt time and existence of complex production routings makes the implementation of a pacemaker hard to achieve in ETO.
- *FIFO*: Establishing FIFO (first-in-first-out) lanes is hard to achieve in ETO, for example where products must return to previous operations as part of the defined production routing. These items should not go to the back of the FIFO queue, as this simply lengthens the throughput time in the system.

As an alternative to VSM, swim lane diagrams are a visual management tool that can be used to visualize value streams in ETO and take into account non-linear and returning material and information flows.

Besides these challenges, ETO manufacturers must still attempt to segregate products based on similar characteristics as well as frequency of occurrence, for example, a "runners, repeaters and strangers" type classification. In this respect it may be possible to establish flow lines for the "runners" (the more regular, higher volume articles) and flexible cells for repeaters/strangers with similar characteristics. This type of classification often leads to a trade-off between a focus on the power of time (Suri, 2010) and increasing flow efficiency (Modig and Åhlström, 2012), and a focus on high capacity utilization through economies-of-scale thinking. Suri (2010) suggests that the huge impact time reduction can have on a manufacturing operation is unknown to most managers. Suri's quick response manufacturing (QRM) concept focuses on reducing the lead times for all tasks in the entire enterprise through emphasizing the power of time. As an alternative to (or more precisely an enhancement of) value stream mapping, Suri suggests manufacturing critical-path time (MCT) mapping as a simplified tool for understanding high-variety, low-volume environments. MCT mapping distinguishes touch time (value-added time) from white space (non-value-added time), where "touch time typically accounts for less than 5% of total lead time" (Suri, 2010, p. 9).

Flow

A central tenet of lean production has been improving the flow of material and information throughout a product's value stream. In their discussion of *flow efficiency*, Modig and Åhlström (2012) suggest three laws that should be adhered to in order to realize efficient flow:

1   *Little's law*: Basic queueing theory states that a reduction in work-in-process (WIP), for example a reduction in the number of flow units in the system, will result in a reduction of throughput time, given a constant cycle time (Little and Graves, 2008). Hence the recommendation for reducing the number of flow units and enforcing a WIP cap on the system (Hopp and Spearman, 2004).
2   *Law of effect of utilization and variability on lead time*: Theory of queueing systems also states that the greater the variation in the process, the longer the resulting throughput time, especially

with a high level of resource utilization (e.g. Kingman, 1961). Thus the recommendation of planning to operate at a maximum of 80 percent or even 70 percent capacity in ETO environments, particularly on critical resources (Suri, 1998).

3   *Law of bottlenecks*: Basic queueing theory also states that the throughput time in a process is primarily affected by the stage in the process that has the longest cycle time, therefore the recommendation is to subordinate the non-bottleneck (non-constraint) resources in order to protect the bottleneck (Cox and Goldratt, 1984).

Central to flow thinking is the choice of buffer that an enterprise uses to manage day-to-day variations in demand. The choices available are time, capacity, and inventory, or indeed a mixture of all of these. In high-volume environments where economies of scale and a high level of capacity utilization is desired, buffers are often found in the form of inventories, e.g. semi-finished and finished goods. However, in an ETO situation, where it makes little sense to buffer against variation with inventory due to the customized nature of products, and where it makes little sense to add extra time buffers to already lengthy lead times, capacity buffers are the only real solution (see the second law, above). This means that the traditional focus on achieving 100 percent capacity utilization and keeping machines running as much as possible must be replaced with a focus on achieving the greatest flow efficiency through reducing batch sizes, WIP, and throughput time. Where flow efficiency becomes the new goal, production operations and those responsible for them must not be measured on resource utilization, at least in the immediate term. Spare capacity becomes essential in order to achieve a satisfactory level of flow in light of high product and process variation (Kingman, 1962).

Pull

Once the value stream has been identified and products begin to flow, Womack and Jones (1996) suggest that the next step is to let the customer pull value from the producer. This is achieved by deploying pull systems throughout the value stream. The fundamental difference between pull systems such as the kanban system (e.g. Sugimori et al., 1977) and push systems such as material requirements planning (MRP) is that push systems schedule releases, while pull systems authorize them (Hopp and Roof, 1998). Rother and Shook (1999) suggest that where continuous process flow cannot be achieved, pull systems should be established to help support and maintain the flow. However, the concept of supermarket-based pull systems raises some issues in the context of ETO. Powell and Arica (2014) suggest that although the term pull has become a cornerstone of modern manufacturing operations, there seem to be mixed views and interpretations of the pull concept across different contexts. Exploring the various interpretations, they go on to propose three context-dependent definitions of pull (Table 25.1).

In the case of ETO, one could say that production would always be in response to demand pull, as production occurs after the CODP. However, production pull, for example the traditional kanban system with its associated supermarkets and product-specific kanban cards as described in Sugimori et al. (1977), is difficult to apply in ETO due to the requirement of min-max inventories of standardized components, sub-assemblies, and finished goods (e.g. the two-bin system). On the other hand, plan pull would almost always be a suitable pull mechanism for production control in lean ETO, whereby the number of flow items (or items of work in process) are limited and a system of constraint management is used to control and reduce flow time, regardless of product type or configuration. *Constant work-in-process* (CONWIP) or *paired-cell overlapping loops of cards with authorization* (POLCA) (e.g. Spearman et al., 1990; Riezebos, 2010) are two common examples of this type of hybrid push-pull system. We also consider *Scrum*

Table 25.1 Context-dependent definitions of pull

Context	Definition
Demand pull	Value-adding activities only take place in response to real customer demand (however, production can still be either pull-based or push-based).
Production pull	Value-adding activities take place in response to a specific withdrawal from an explicitly limited inventory buffer or supermarket. The direction of information flow is the reverse direction of material flow, and production takes place in order to replenish an exact amount of consumed products and/or components.
Plan pull	Value-adding activities take place based on a priority rule such as earliest due date (EDD) and constraint management.

Source: Powell and Arica (2014).

(Sutherland, 2014) to fit this classification. And indeed, when we consider kanban in the literal sense (kanban in fact means "to look closely at the wooden board"), kanban "boards" are also a suitable workflow control mechanism (see, for example, Kniberg and Skarin, 2010). Therefore, in this chapter, we adopt the terminology kanban to mean visual board, and maintain that this is just one part of Toyota's kanban system, which also uses supermarkets and product-specific kanban cards as a material control system (as described in Sugimori et al., 1977).

Perfection

Continuous incremental improvement, or *kaizen*, is perhaps the most universally applicable of the original lean production principles in terms of the ways in which it is applied, for example through the use of what one might refer to as traditional lean production practices. If continuous process flow is the goal of the lean system, the involvement of everybody in daily continuous improvement activities and team-based problem solving is the substance by which this can be accomplished. Here, continuous experimentation and reflection is the key, through the adoption of a plan-do-check-act (PDCA) problem-solving approach. PDCA is of course just as applicable in one-of-a-kind ETO as it is in high-volume production environments. This approach to continuous improvement, otherwise known as the scientific method (Spear and Bowen, 1999), helps to create common understanding among all involved parties. The A3 process, as used by Toyota and other lean exemplars, is a supporting visual approach that helps strengthen the focus on continuous improvement throughout the enterprise.

Challenges and Opportunities of Lean ETO

The obvious challenge in lean ETO lies in creating a common understanding among employees in this sector that lean thinking applies just as much in ETO as it does in mass production ATO/MTS environments. The "we're different" mentality is a common obstacle for lean transformations in ETO. A major contributor to this issue has been the all-too-common focus on tools and techniques rather than adopting a focus on purpose, process, and people. For example, Shook (2014) suggests that starting with the question *"what is our value-driven purpose?"* allows for a situational approach to lean transformation, where every given situation is different, and in many cases the result will be a rather different set of countermeasures, tools, and techniques. There is much more to lean ETO than simply dwelling on an already established set of tools and techniques that have been made famous by the overwhelming interest in the practices employed by the Toyota Production System.

A copy-and-paste, cookie-cutter approach to lean transformation should be avoided at all costs. A simplistic view of transferring proven tools and techniques from one context to another often leads to a number of challenges and essentially failure of the lean transformation. One issue in particular is that of the kanban system. As we know, kanban systems, with supermarkets of standard parts and product-specific kanban cards, have been proven to work very well as the production control mechanisms in the context of high-volume production of similar products and with fairly stable demand, reducing work-in-process (WIP), smoothing production, and improving quality (Hopp and Spearman, 2004). However, there are three fundamental issues that prevent the application of the traditional kanban system as a suitable control mechanism in ETO manufacturing (Suri 2010):

1 *The kanban system's reliance on takt time*: Though the kanban system creates a balanced flow through the shop floor given stable demand and regular takt, high-variety, low-volume project-based production environments encounter a high level of instability in processes, particularly processing times and capacity utilization. This renders the traditional kanban system ineffective in ETO manufacturing.
2 *Kanban system as a pull system*: With a kanban system, parts are replenished—pulled through the factory—as they are consumed in downstream operations. However, given a high variety of products with low annual demand, it does not make a lot of sense to have supermarkets of finished goods waiting to be pulled by the customer and semi-finished goods waiting to be pulled from an upstream operation.
3 *Difficulties with completely custom/bespoke products*: Finally, kanban systems are unable to manage custom-engineered parts and components. The success of the kanban system is highly dependent on the use of standard components and parts.

Even though the traditional kanban system is not necessarily suitable for ETO environments, this doesn't mean that the pull principle that first motivated the development of such a simple workload control system cannot be adopted in ETO (see Powell et al., 2013b for a description of workload control: job entry, job release, priority dispatching/WIP control). After all, an ETO producer is always acting in response to customer demand (i.e. demand pull). In this respect, no value-adding activity is carried out based on speculation, as little or no engineering, procurement, production, or assembly takes place before a customer order is received. This makes it necessary for an ETO producer to pay close attention to the way in which materials flow through the value-adding activities that make up the value stream. The real benefits of adopting the pull principle in ETO can only be achieved when we realize that increased customer service levels and reduced throughput times are achieved by adopting a focus on flow and explicitly limiting the amount of work-in-process (WIP) that can be released into the system (Hopp and Spearman, 2004). Some ways in which the pull principle can be deployed in ETO include the implementation of alternative pull systems such as CONWIP, POLCA, and Cobacabana. We suggest that Scrum and kanban (in the form of production control boards) can also be applied for workload control in order to reduce throughput times and improve flow in ETO environments.

CONWIP

The CONWIP system has been described in some detail in Spearman et al. (1990). In general, CONWIP reduces throughput time by explicitly limiting WIP levels on the shop floor. This is achieved by limiting the number of jobs that are released into a system, i.e. by defining a constant (max.) level of WIP. Slomp et al. (2009) identify CONWIP as one of three elements (CONWIP,

FIFO, and takt time control) for lean production control in make-to-order (MTO) job shops, where volumes are typically low and variety is high. Thus a CONWIP system of production control is a likely possibility for establishing pull also in ETO.

POLCA

Paired-cell overlapping loops of cards with authorization (POLCA) is a material control system designed for both make-to-order and engineer-to-order companies (Riezebos, 2010). It is the predominant production control system in quick response manufacturing (QRM). POLCA is a material control system that regulates the authorization of order progress on the shop floor in a cellular manufacturing environment (Powell et al., 2013b). As the name suggests, POLCA is dependent on the establishment of a cell-based layout as a prerequisite for its successful application. Again, by strictly limiting the amount of WIP between and in cells, POLCA aims to increase the flow efficiency of the system by speeding up job transfer and reducing imbalances in the system. Before work can begin on a production order, upstream capacity must be reserved through taking a POLCA card from each of the pair of cells next in sequence in the production routing. If either of the cards is not available, this is a sign that there is not sufficient available capacity at that particular cell, so the next job on the prioritized release list (backlog) for which there can be found an available pair of required cards should be released into production. Each time a production operation is complete, capacity must again be reserved at the next pair of cells, again by attaching the next available card to the work order/routing document. The previous card can be returned to the POLCA board to visualize available capacity at the respective operation. A detailed description of designing a POLCA system can be found in Riezebos (2010).

Cobacabana

As an alternative to both CONWIP and POLCA, *Control of balance by card-based navigation* (Cobacabana) is a simple card-based pull system for job-shop control (Land, 2009). Land suggests that the Cobacabana system has been specifically organized around the order acceptance and order release decisions in job-shop control. The system uses card loops consisting of color-coded cards between the planner performing the releases and all critical workstations (see Land, 2009 for a more detailed description). In essence, available cards authorize the planner to release a new order to a specific work center. The planner attaches the cards to a work order, and, on completion of the work, the cards are returned to the planner from the workstation to signal additional available capacity at the station. Each card represents a certain percentage of available capacity at a workstation, with the total number of cards adding up to 100 percent of a station's available capacity. Thus each order will normally require multiple cards.

Scrum and Kanban

Scrum was developed as an alternative to using the Waterfall method (Gantt charts) for managing projects, particularly in software development (Sutherland, 2014). It is often considered as an agile software development approach. This also goes for kanban, which in the agile development world is primarily defined in terms of its visual representation of work. When we consider the two Japanese characters that make up the word kanban, the visual nature of this approach becomes highly apparent (Figure 25.2).

The first character—Kan—is made up of the symbols for *hand* and *eye*. It represents a man shielding his brow in order to see clearly, and means *"to look at closely."* The second character—

Figure 25.2 Japanese characters for kanban

Ban—is made of the symbols for *tree*, *wood*, and *wall*. It represents a wooden board leaning against a wall, and literally means "*wooden board*." In essence, then, kanban means "*to look at the wooden board closely*." As such, kanban can simply be translated as board, and provides an effective form of visual management for development activities, project management, and production control.

Both Scrum and kanban use visual boards to show available work, work-in-process, and completed work (often under the headings "To-do," "Doing," and "Done"). Scrum and kanban encourage and promote team-based problem solving throughout the completion of prioritized tasks, and can be effectively adopted in both software and hardware development, as well as in project-based production environments, such as in ETO manufacturing.

In Scrum, tasks are selected from a prioritized backlog and posted under "To-do." The tasks that are selected are expected to be completed by the Scrum team during the *Sprint* that follows, which typically takes place over the next seven days to four weeks (Sprint duration is normally constant from one sprint to the next). Each day during the Sprint, all team members gather around the Scrum board in what's known as a stand-up meeting (typically maximum 15 minutes long). During the stand-up, the participants discuss what was achieved on the previous day, the plan for today, and the problems that were addressed/remain to be addressed such that the Sprint can be completed on time. On the first stand-up meeting, individuals will select and move "To-do" items to "Doing." Upon completion, these jobs will be moved to "Done." On the last day of the Sprint, team members should reflect on the Sprint in order to improve during the subsequent Sprint. In essence, Scrum constitutes a pull mechanism as the quantity of tasks that is released into each Sprint remains fixed for the duration of the Sprint. The quantity of tasks released is based on the amount of required capacity that is anticipated to complete each task during the Sprint. No further tasks will be released into the current Sprint unless there is a plausible exception, and only then by approval of the product owner.

Kanban is very similar to Scrum in that a visual board and daily stand-up team meetings are the mechanisms for success. However, the major difference is that a kanban board explicitly limits the amount of tasks that can be assigned to each stage of the operation. In the case of kanban, "Doing" is often segregated into separate operations, each with a visually defined limit of tasks that can be processed simultaneously in that operation. Tasks are still selected from a prioritized release list, as in Scrum (and indeed POLCA and CONWIP). Yet the fundamental difference between kanban and Scrum is that kanban can be more reactive to changes in requirements. This is due to the fact that tasks are not locked in for the duration of the Sprint (e.g. 7 to 28 days); the response time of a kanban team is the time it takes for capacity to become available after having completed a current task in process. This follows the general principle of one-out-one-in, as in CONWIP.

For example, in Figure 25.3, all items selected in the current iteration or Sprint (A–H) are locked for the duration of the Sprint, and must be completed before the next set of new jobs from the release list/backlog can be released. On the other hand, in Figure 25.4, as soon as one of the jobs C or D is completed, capacity becomes available to process one of the "To-do" jobs E–H, or, in kanban, an alternative job from the backlog replaces any one of the jobs E–H and subsequently becomes the next in the queue.

Besides the more common challenge of overcoming the "we are different" perception of ETO manufacturing personnel and the issues that result due to misplaced attempts to simply transfer lean tools and techniques from high-volume, low-variety production environments into ETO manufacturing, there are some more general challenges that should be highlighted when it comes to applying lean in ETO. These include:

- how to address the complex information flows and frequent delays (e.g. during the request-for-quotation (RFQ) phase right up to order confirmation),
- how to simplify the complex and unpredictable flow of materials,
- how to secure the supply of long-lead items,
- how to overcome frequent engineering change orders (ECOs), and
- how to prevent penalties for late delivery.

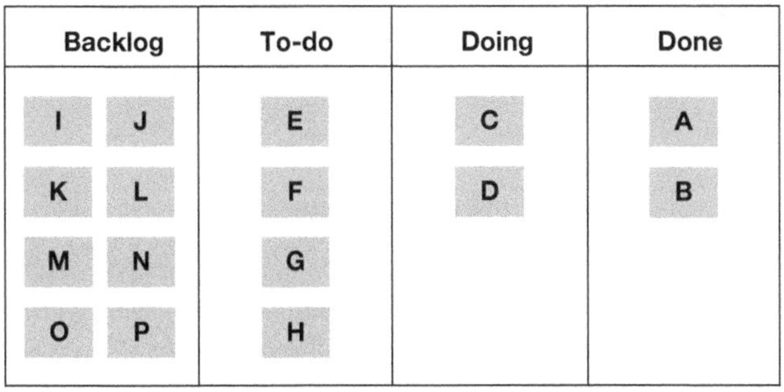

Backlog		To-do	Doing	Done
I	J	E	C	A
K	L	F	D	B
M	N	G		
O	P	H		

Figure 25.3 Scrum board (jobs A–H will be completed during current Sprint)

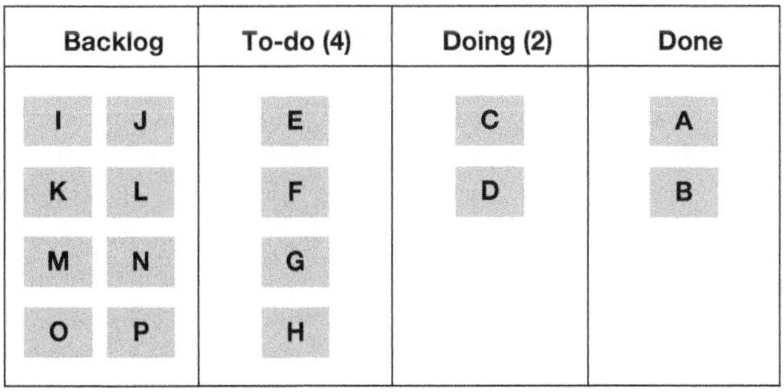

Backlog		To-do (4)	Doing (2)	Done
I	J	E	C	A
K	L	F	D	B
M	N	G		
O	P	H		

Figure 25.4 Kanban (notice maximum levels 4 (To-do) and 2 (Doing) respectively)

We suggest that such challenges can be addressed through the application of concepts such as "quick response office cell" (QROC), cellular manufacturing, pull production, and Scrum.

For example, QROCs are formed to cut through functional boundaries such that information flows can be simplified and accelerated. A QROC (pronounced queue-rock) is a closed loop, co-located, dedicated multifunctional, cross-trained team that is responsible for the office processing of all jobs belonging to a particular product family or value stream (Suri, 2010). QROCs use the same principles as those applied in the cellular manufacturing approach that is used to simplify material flows on the shop floor, only here we drastically simplify information flows in the supporting administrative tasks in addition. QROC would be a potential solution to the issue raised by Hicks et al. (2000), who suggest that the variety of work that is involved in ETO projects, e.g. designing and producing customized products while simultaneously addressing the underlying uncertainties of markets, indicates that procurement and marketing must be integrated with other processes, particularly tendering and design.

In an attempt to manage the supply of long-lead items, an ETO producer may well have to hold a minimum level of safety stock of these items in order to eliminate such lengthy procurement lead times. This of course encounters a cost that must be considered along with the cost of holding the inventory, in particular the cost of risk of obsolescence, seeing as we are perhaps dealing with one-of-a-kind products. However, as the success of lean ETO really is about realizing the power of time, there are few alternative options other than holding a small supermarket for long-lead items, if supplier agreements cannot be put in place to reduce these lead times in the first place. We suggest that best-practice supplier development and supplier collaboration are fundamental to addressing the problem of long-lead items in lean ETO.

A satisfactory system for managing ECOs must also be established in those ETO environments where regular, often unexpected, ECOs are the norm. A satisfactory way of following up and closing out ECOs could be the adoption of Scrum, for example, with regular week-long Sprints to address and deliver effective engineering changes through regular collaboration with the customer.

The Future of Lean ETO

The complexities associated with ETO make it very much a form of *advanced manufacturing*. Advanced manufacturing is not a static entity. Washington (2015) suggests that what was once considered advanced decades ago has now become traditional, and what is advanced today will be considered mainstream in the future. While the traditional production of high-volume, low-variety products with low profit margins may well have migrated to low-cost countries, the knowledge-based engineering and technological development involved in delivering customer-specific products and solutions to turbulent markets can be considered as the future of competitive manufacturing in high-cost regions. Most simply, Washington (2015) states that advanced manufacturing is about innovating products and processes in the manufacturing cycle to operate more productively. The future of ETO will therefore include the complete set of activities from the engineering and design stages all the way through production and assembly processes to the development of innovative after-sales services. We suggest that this makes lean ETO a strategic factor for the success of the future of manufacturing in high-cost countries. Furthermore, we also suggest that the real triumph of a lean transformation in ETO will depend on the adoption of ETO-specific tools and techniques in order to successfully deploy the fundamental lean principles. Powell et al. (2013a) suggest that a lean implementation process typically consists of three phases: a basic lean phase, an advanced lean phase, and a continuous improvement phase. Such a view on lean implementation is perhaps just as applicable in ETO manufacturing as it is in mass production. First, the basic lean phase involves the application of the more universally applicable lean practices such as 5S workplace organization and visual management. This prepares the workplace for what is to come in the second phase—the advanced phase. In this phase, ETO-specific lean tools are deployed, such as the alternative pull systems discussed previously. Finally, for the results to be sustainable, the third phase is continuous improvement, involving all personnel in ongoing incremental improvement activities, every day.

A final thought comes from Rajan Suri (2011, p. 3), who encourages us to realize that success in this area may have major impact on the way we look at our current business models:

> Many employees in developed countries live in fear of their operation being outsourced to low-wage countries, such as China. However, for a typical product made in a developed nation, direct labor accounts for only 10% of its cost. Moreover, in terms of the selling price of a product, the number is lower: less than 7% of the price to the customer is attributable to direct labor. Thus, if you use QRM methods to reduce cost by 25%, you wipe out the labor-cost advantage of low-wage countries. When you consider that overseas competitors need considerable lead-time for shipping, your short response time makes it impossible for them to compete on the same terms. You can compete against anyone, making products anywhere.

Case Study: Lean Engineer-to-order in Bosch Hinges and Metal

Bosch Hinges and Metal designs and manufactures high-quality metal bespoke hinges for industrial applications. At the start of 2004, the company was challenged with the need to adapt its strategy in order to survive the onset of increased competition. At that time, in light of low-cost competition, the company was in fact operating at loss. Today, with its 30 staff in the east of the Netherlands, Bosch Hinges and Metal is an example of a very successful lean engineer-to-order (ETO) manufacturer. The company has over 4,000 orders for approximately 600 different customers annually, with batch sizes ranging from 1 to 1,000 pieces and product sizes from just a few centimeters to 4 meters in length. On average, a production operator at Bosch Hinges and Metal (otherwise known as a hinge maker) is working on one particular order no longer than 30 minutes before starting on the next. Some of the operations needed to produce the company's customer-specific hinges include laser cutting, punching, sawing, rolling, folding, carving, bending, drilling, welding, grinding, and brushing. Products flow through these operations in many different routings. But even before production can begin, 10 employees in the office at Bosch Hinges and Metal carry out tasks for quoting (acquisition, calculation, and quotation), engineering, order preparation, and production and material planning.

Challenge

The primary reason for a change of strategy in 2004 was the fact that Bosch Hinges and Metal was confronted with a market that was demanding ever-smaller series and shorter lead times. This had led the company into the vicious circle of prioritizing and re-prioritizing "rush" orders, which led to an increased order backlog, increased work-in-process, and increased lead times. More and more new rush orders simply escalated this problem. A typical quoted delivery lead time in 2004 was six weeks, with actual delivery lead times of around eight weeks or more. At that time, planning, scheduling, and rescheduling was a time-consuming effort. The company typically used a one-week planning horizon, with detailed day-to-day planning and a separate backlog order planning. This demanded the full attention of one full-time employee. Delivery performance was poor and customer satisfaction suffered, which caused the company to lose some of its customers.

Journey

Bosch Hinges and Metal first attempted to apply traditional lean techniques but, like many ETO companies, failed to realize the expected results. Despite some initial success with 5S and single-minute exchange of dies (SMED), the company kept struggling with vast amounts of backorders, high amounts of WIP, and poor delivery performance (around 60 percent on-time delivery). It was not until 2007, when Godfried Kaanen, director and owner of the company, heard of Rajan Suri's work on *quick response manufacturing* (QRM), that he realized the importance of lead time reduction. From this moment, the company managed to realize breakthrough improvements. Examples of these include a reduction in delivery lead time from eight weeks to three weeks and an increased delivery performance from 60 percent to around 90 percent. Production planning, which was previously a full-time job, now takes no more than 1.5 hours per day. Quotation lead time was improved from 3–5 days to same-day delivery. Together, these improvements transformed the company from being unprofitable to turning a healthy profit. In the remainder of this case study, some of the specific practices that helped transform Bosch Hinges and Metal into a lean ETO exemplar are described.

Focused Sales

On a strategic level, Bosch Hinges and Metal adopted a new business model. Realizing that its primary customer value proposition was flexibility to offer unique hinges fast, the company began to focus on the delivery of bespoke hinge solutions. This meant refusing the occasional large order, as large orders lead to substantial disruption in the flow, consume large amounts of capacity, and offer relatively low margins compared with specialized, low-volume orders.

POLCA Cells in Production

Originally, the shop floor at Bosch Hinges and Metal was functionally organized in a traditional job-shop type layout. This was also the case in the office. MRP was used for production planning and control, which led to high WIP, low visualization, poor quality control, long lead times, and a large backlog of orders and the occurrence of many rush orders. In order to regain control of its production processes and reduce throughput times, the company implemented a POLCA system to improve and control order release and material flow. With the introduction of POLCA the shop floor was transformed into just a few production cells, which were also color coded (within the cells, floor marking, equipment, and operators' overalls correspond to the cell color). After an analysis of machine capacity, investments had to be made for spare capacity on some of the more highly utilized machines. The POLCA system creates an improved material flow by using POLCA cards to authorize production, in combination with a high-level MRP release list. The high-level MRP system back-schedules using fixed throughput times per cell to calculate the earliest release dates. The release list indicates the earliest allowed start dates of all orders in queue and prevents overproduction. The POLCA cards limit overall WIP and prioritize orders based on the next operation with the least work in the queue. Within-cell planning is carried out autonomously by the cell operators, using the predetermined conditions of the POLCA system. The prioritization of orders and strictly controlled WIP limits, together with the strategic choice to have spare capacity, creates a robust system with stable and predictable throughput times.

Quick Response Office Cells

Once the main problems in production were controlled and corrected, further opportunities for the reduction of lead times were found in the office processes. Three *quick response office cells* (QROCs) were formed in the office environment. The "commercial cell" consists of four full-time employees (FTEs) and is responsible for acquisition, calculation, and quotation. As a rule, potential customers now receive their quotation within 24 hours after first inquiry. The "engineering cell" (3 FTEs) is responsible for all required engineering, for order preparation, and for customer confirmation (which is needed before production is allowed to start). The third QROC is called "general affairs" (3.5 FTEs) and is responsible for daily management, administration, and human resources. Employees within the cells are all cross-trained and jointly responsible for continuously improving and reducing total lead time.

Future Outlook/Further Improvements

While the introduction of the POLCA system led to the needed breakthrough improvements, the company struggled with the day-to-day handling of the system. Additionally, since the introduction of the POLCA system the company grew, leading to larger distances between the cells. This hampered the effective use of the traditional POLCA card system. Also the physical nature of the cards lacked the capability to monitor the shop floor status in real-time. To overcome these issues, Bosch Hinges and Metal engaged the services of an external software development entrepreneur and developed the *production and POLCA operating system* (PROPOS), a company-specific manufacturing execution system (MES). In PROPOS, the physical cards and POLCA boards are replaced by touch screens at all cells. The PROPOS system shows the release list in order of earliest starting date and shows the availability of materials and cards for the next cells. The system gives the operators insight into which order to start first, what is to come, and what the current lead time performance is. To the engineering cell, PROPOS provides real-time insight into production flow, and highlights where issues may arise such that they can be anticipated as early as possible.

Godfried Kaanen, Director and Owner of Bosch Hinges and Metal, concludes that despite the huge success of the implementation so far, the company has only just begun—"In order to stay in front of the competition, we must understand that today's lead times are still too long for tomorrow." Time is on their side though; a relentless focus on lead time reduction gives Bosch Hinges and Metal a bright future in lean ETO.

References

Alves, T. C. L., Tommelein, I. D. and Ballard, G. (2005). Value stream mapping for make-to-order products in a job shop environment. *Construction Research Congress 2005*, San Diego, CA.

Cox, J. and Goldratt, E. M. (1984). *The Goal: A Process of Ongoing Improvement*, Croton-on-Hudson, NY, North River Press.

Hicks, C., McGovern, T. and Earl, C. F. (2000). Supply chain management: A strategic issue in engineer to order manufacturing. *International Journal of Production Economics*, *65*(2), 179–190.

Holweg, M. (2005). The three dimensions of responsiveness. *International Journal of Operations and Production Management*, *25*, 7–20.

Hopp, W. J. and Roof, M. L. (1998). Setting WIP levels with statistical throughput control (STC) in CONWIP production lines, *International Journal of Production Research*, *36*(4), 867–882.

Hopp, W. J. and Spearman, M. L (2004). To pull or not to pull: What is the question? *Manufacturing and Service Operations Management*, *6*(2), 133–148.

Kingman, J. (1961). The single server queue in heavy traffic. *Mathematical Proceedings of the Cambridge Philosophical Society*, *57*(4), 902.

Kingman, J. F. C. (1962) On queues in heavy traffic. *Journal of the Royal Statistical Society, Series B (Methodological)*, *24*(2), 383–392.

Kniberg, H. and Skarin, M. (2010). *Kanban and Scrum: Making the Most out of Both*, C4Media.

Land, M. J. (2009). Cobacabana (control of balance by card-based navigation): A card-based system for job shop control. *International Journal of Production Economics*, *117*(1), 97–103.

Little, J. D. C. and Graves, S. C. (2008). Little's law. In: Chhajed, D. and Lowe, T. J. (eds) *Building Intuition: Insights from Basic Operations Management Models and Principles*, Springer Science+Business Media.

Matt, D. T. and Rauch, E. (2014). Implementing lean in engineer-to-order manufacturing: Experiences from an ETO manufacturer. In: Modrak, V. and Semanco, P. (eds), *Design and Management of Lean Production Systems*, Hershey, PA, IGI Global, pp. 148–172.

Modig, N. and Åhlström, P. (2012). *This is Lean: Resolving the Efficiency Paradox*, Stockholm, Rhealogica Publishing.

Ohno, T. (1988). *Toyota Production System: Beyond Large-Scale Production*, Boca Raton, FL, CRC Press.

Pavnaskar, S., Gershenson, J. and Jambekar, A. (2003). A classification scheme for lean manufacturing tools. *International Journal of Production Research*, *41*, 13–15.

Powell, D. J. and Arica, E. (2014). To pull or not to pull: A concept lost in translation? *American Journal of Management*, *15*(2), 64–73.

Powell, D. J., Alfnes, E., Dreyer, H. C. and Strandhagen, J. O. (2013a). The concurrent application of lean production and ERP: Towards an ERP-based lean implementation process. *Computers in Industry*, *64*(3), 324–335.

Powell, D. J., Riezebos, J. and Strandhagen, J. O. (2013b). Lean production and ERP systems in small- and medium-sized enterprises: ERP support for pull production. *International Journal of Production Research*, *51*(2), 395–409.

Riezebos, J. (2010). Design of POLCA material control systems. *International Journal of Production Research*, *48*(5), 1455–1477.

Rother, M. and Shook, J. (1999). *Learning to See: Value Stream Mapping to Add Value and Eliminate MUDA*. Cambridge, MA, Lean Enterprise Institute.

Rudberg, M. and Wikner, J. (2004). Mass customization in terms of the customer order decoupling point. *Production Planning and Control*, *15*, 445–458.

Shook, J. (2014). *Transforming Transformation*. Available at: www.lean.org/shook/DisplayObject.cfm?o=2533 (accessed February 2016).

Slomp, J., Bokhorst, J. A. and Germs, R. (2009). A lean production control system for high-variety/low-volume environments: A case study implementation. *Production Planning and Control*, *20*(7), 586–595.

Spear, S. J. and Bowen, H. K. (1999). Decoding the DNA of the Toyota Production System. *Harvard Business Review*, *77*, 96–108.

Spearman, M. L., Woodruff, D. L. and Hopp, W. J. (1990). CONWIP: A pull alternative to kanban. *International Journal of Production Research*, *28*(5), 879–894.

Sugimori, Y., Kusunoki, K., Cho, F. and Uchikawa, S. (1977), Toyota Production System and kanban system: Materialization of just-in-time and respect-for-human system. *International Journal of Production Research*, *15*(6), 553–564.

Suri, R. (1998). *Quick Response Manufacturing: A Companywide Approach to Reducing Lead Times*, Boca Raton, FL, CRC Press.

Suri, R. (2010). *It's About Time: The Competitive Advantage of Quick Response Manufacturing*, Boca Raton, FL, CRC Press.

Suri, R. (2011). *Beyond Lean: It's About Time!* Available at: http://quickresponse-enterprise.com/wp-content/uploads/2013/10/Beyond-Lean-it-is-about-time-eng.pdf (accessed February 2016).

Sutherland, J. (2014). *SCRUM: The Art of Doing Twice the Work in Half the Time*, London, Random House.

Washington, L. (2015). The importance of advanced manufacturing to the changing global economy. Available at: www.cincom.com/blog/advanced-manufacturing/the-importance-of-advanced-manufacturing-to-the-changing-global-economy/ (accessed July 2016).

Womack, J. P. and Jones, D. T. (1996). *Lean Thinking: Banish Waste and Create Wealth in Your Corporation*, New York, Simon & Schuster.

Woollard, F. G. (1954). *Principles of Mass and Flow Production*, London, Iliffe and Sons.

26

LEAN MINING

Behzad Ghodrati, Seyed Hadi Hoseinie, and Uday Kumar

Introduction

Modern-day mining is mechanized, automated, and capital intensive. Systems are expected to be robust and reliable and to perform safely at a designated level most of the time or even around the clock. However, due to unforeseen events and processes, design deficiencies, or operational and environmental stresses, system performance may not meet production requirements.

Lean mining refers to the application of the concept of lean production, to the mining industry. Mining as a process industry has specific characteristics and uncertainties. It differs from other industries where everything is human-designed and deterministic. Due to the nature of a mine, most factors are unknown until they are discovered and dealt with. This causes uncertainties from the beginning of the process (mine exploration) to the end (exploitation and reclamation). Thus, minimizing or eliminating uncertainty is a goal in the mining industry.

Mining companies are looking for ways to improve productivity; for example, adapting proven techniques used in other industries to suit the needs of mining. The concept of lean production, formulated by John Krafcik (1988), has attracted the attention of the mining industry. A company applying lean production has the goal of achieving continuous production at minimum cost (Kumar et al., 2015). Lean production focuses on managing resources to identify and eliminate any factors that do not create value for the end customer (Liker, 2009). Mann (2005) says lean principles include discipline, daily practices, and tools to establish and maintain a persistent, intensive focus on processes. In lean systems, results certainly matter, but the approach to achieving them differs sharply from conventional management methods. Lean management systems differ from conventional ones as they focus on process in addition to results (Steinberg and De Tomi, 2010).

Over the past 25 years, the lean concept has penetrated many industries and is being implemented in such diverse sectors as aircraft manufacturing, office processes, construction, and oil well drilling. Given the success of this production strategy, it is appropriate to consider its possible application to the mining industry. In fact, some mining companies have already started to do so (Wijaya et al., 2009).

The mining industry is inherently heterogeneous because of the variety of products exploited, grades, markets, and, most importantly, the size of its companies. However, it contains similarities as well. For example, the industry as a whole intensively uses capital investments, working continuously within a high degree of financial leverage. It is also a high-risk activity, since a mine plan is based on estimates. Since mines operate under conditions of permanent uncertainty, they require specialized business planning and analysis; hence the interest in lean thinking.

Other reasons for the mining industry's interest in lean production include the decreased profitability and increased cost pressure associated with uncertainty, not to mention the social and environmental demands of sustainable development (Humphreys, 2001). Arguably, the need to be compensated by reducing production costs can be achieved via lean management.

Lean principles require more than simply adopting the tool, however; the work culture must be changed to create "a true culture of continuous improvement." Furthermore, as Morgan (2005) points out, lean thinking is based on a single principle: all forms of waste should be identified and eliminated. This seems simple; however it is not always easy to recognize waste.

This chapter discusses the concept of lean thinking and management in mining. It notes possible areas of application in the mining industry and suggests reasons for using the concept in mine production processes. It concludes by presenting a number of successful lean mining case studies.

Mining Process

Mining exploitation is divided into surface and underground mining. Although we more commonly think of mining as an underground operation, high shares of raw minerals are produced by surface mining worldwide (Hartman and Mutmansky, 2002; Yamatomi and Okubo, 2015). Surface mining in the form of open pit or open cast is usually employed for deposits that are near the surface, or deposits with a low stripping ratio. Although a large capital investment is generally required, the result is a good one: high productivity, low operating cost, and good safety conditions.

The unit operations of mining can be defined as the basic steps required to produce mineral from the ore deposit. The two main components of the production cycle are rock breakage and materials handling. Each can be broken down into unit operations. Breakage comprises drilling and blasting; handling includes loading, excavation, haulage, and occasionally hoisting. A basic production cycle, therefore, consists of four unit operations: drilling, blasting, loading, and hauling.

Traditionally, the various production operations have been separate, but the current trend is to eliminate and/or combine functions. Accordingly, a number of specialized machines have been designed. In modern surface mining, to remove consolidated rock, rotary or percussion drills are used to create blast holes of 3 to 15 in. (75 to 380 mm) in diameter; explosive charges are inserted into these holes and detonated to reduce the ore to a size suitable for excavation. Shovels, draglines, or wheel loaders are then used to load the ore fragments on to trucks or other haulage units. Some common unit operations in surface mining are shown in Figure 26.1.

Lean Principles' Requirements in Mining

Mine production systems are associated with a wide range of uncertainties. These uncertainties often result in unplanned non-value-adding activities, leading to a waste of resources. Implementing lean manufacturing principles in the mining processes may help eliminate waste, but the high degree of uncertainty makes it difficult to do so. Mining is dynamic in nature and somewhat unpredictable compared with manufacturing processes. Therefore it requires unique solutions.

To reduce the waste of resources and efforts, we need to predict the process behavior as accurately as possible to meet just-in-time (JIT) delivery with agreed-upon quality. At the same

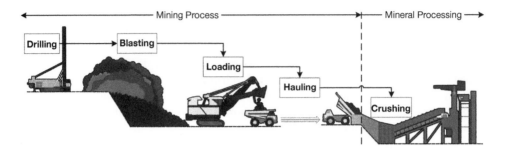

Figure 26.1 Typical unit operations in a surface mining process

Source: Adapted from Boliden AB (2012).

time, measures must be taken to remove uncertainty. To achieve a lean approach in mining, the entire mining chain needs to be considered, from mine exploration to mine planning, drilling, blasting, loading and transporting, ore dressing processes, reclamation, etc. Lean mining is not only dependent on mine production systems consisting of equipment and machines. It also depends on the quality and reliability of information flow in real time, generating action plans to achieve production goals and reduce waste. As in the manufacturing sector, reliability and maintenance preparedness have a major influence on the degree of waste generated. For example, if an ore body is not correctly delineated/characterized, if drilling operations are not performed correctly, or if the wrong charging process or the wrong loading process is used, resources are likely to be wasted.

The application of lean production to mining has two main objectives:

1   *Increasing productivity by eliminating waste and reducing cost*: Mine production processes are designed to meet customer needs and cost objectives. Lean mining recognizes that the marketplace, not the producer, sets the price of raw minerals, and better profitability can only be attained through cost reduction. Customer-oriented production is considered appropriate to meet profitability objectives, and the company continually seeks to reduce the production cost.

2   *Increasing safety*: Decreasing the cost of production should not result in a reduction in safety. Cost reduction generally affects safety issues in production. However, in lean mining we attempt to maintain costs, profit, and risk in an overall balance and at an acceptable level.

Mine exploitation is a cyclical series of activities, with one activity dependent on the next. Failure in one activity leads to many delays in the whole process. All activities are naturally subject to uncertainty (market, geological, operational, human, society, natural and rare events) (see Figure 26.2). On the operational level, uncertainty stems from the complex interaction between the ore body, the machinery, and the environmental parameters. This complexity results in the propagation of uncertainty which can be impossible to understand, realize, or control. Simply stated, the main concern in lean mining is the elimination of uncertainty.

Sources of Waste in Mine Operation

As mentioned earlier, waste elimination is one of the core issues tackled by the lean production concept. To implement lean thinking in mining, we must first define the sources of waste accurately.

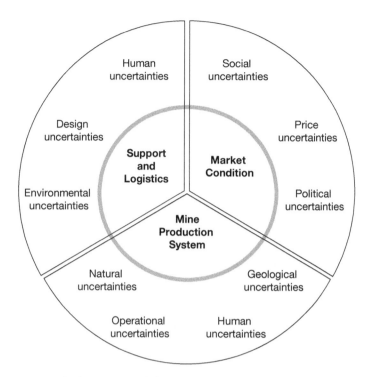

Figure 26.2 Actors involved in mining and their associated uncertainties

Based on the literature and the experience of the authors, we identify the main sources of waste in the mine production process as the following:

1 *Waiting*: Machines may have to wait to receive service/feed from each other in a production chain. For example, a shovel may wait for a truck or a load-haul-dump (LHD) machine might wait for a scaling machine.

2 *Overproduction*: This can be internal or external. Internal overproduction could represent producing more ore than the hauling or processing capacity in the mine. For instance, the mining capacity may outstrip the plant's ability to process ore, or the drum shearer might cut too much coal and overload the armored face conveyor (AFC). External overproduction could be producing more ore than market demand requires.

3 *Repair or rework*: Machinery might have to wait for repairs if there are large numbers of machines in a fleet, or they may take a long time to repair because of unskilled crews, complex machinery, or disorganized workshops. Finally, the support and logistics may be inefficient.

4 *Motion*: In large-scale operations, this represents operators' transportation to working faces or the transportation time of machines to the workshop.

5 *Over processing*: Ore may be processed to a better grade than the customer is willing to pay for (Dunstan et al., 2006).

6 *Inventory*: Too much inventory (capital blocking) or too little inventory (risk of shortage when it's needed) of material may be kept on site.

7 *Transportation*: Non-continuous transportation and low-capacity machinery.

To sum up, there is a wide range of waste in the mining industry, making it difficult to handle and having a destructive effect on mine production.

Flow, Stability, and Flexibility of Operation

Basically, the concept of flow in lean thinking may be expressed in terms of two ideals: 1) continuous flow, whereby products should flow continuously through value-added operations without delay, and 2) leveled production, whereby every product is produced in direct proportion to the demand for that product. In lean mining, continuous production is important to respond directly to demand, but leveled production is not applicable.

A high degree of stability is a prerequisite of flow because it minimizes operational disruptions, which are difficult to tolerate in continuous flow systems. In lean production systems, stability is achieved through such practices as consistent work and quality.

A key performance measure for achieving continuous and stable production is the availability of the production fleet during scheduled operational time. Here, the reliability and maintainability of the machinery play a key role. An optimal maintenance strategy, efficient spare part planning, effective logistics/support, and skilled personnel are crucial if lean mine production is to be achieved.

As mentioned, mine operation is cyclical, with specific machines set up in specific places at specific times. This procedure seriously reduces the utility of the mine fleet. A reduction of set-up time would significantly reduce idle time and increase productivity. A good strategy is to develop systems that increase the cycle duration and minimize the frequency of set-ups.

Flexibility is another feature of lean production. In mining, it can be attained through the use of flexible equipment (i.e. used for more than one task) and multi-workface (i.e. work in more than one location at one time). From a flexibility and production reliability point of view, several working faces with the same or different capacities would assure continuous and reliable throughput.

Case Studies

While lean production seems to be a new concept in mining, it has been indirectly used since 1975 when continuous mining was introduced into many mining methods, including longwall, and room and pillar. In addition, in the past 20 years, an impressive level of automation has been achieved. This has the potential to improve both safety and productivity. A holistic and lean view of the mine value chain and business has emerged more recently and continues to be developed. Applications of lean production in mining include long conveyor belts and *continuous material handling systems and machinery* such as huge bucket wheel excavators (Figure 26.3). These solutions avoid many problems associated with transportation (e.g. dump trucks) and discontinuity of operation.

Case Study 1: VALE Mining Company

VALE mining company has implemented the concept of lean in its iron ore mining and processing in Carajas mine in Brazil. To ensure the stable flow of goods along the mine production chain, VALE has designed its process with a *high degree of automation* (Steinberg and De Tomi, 2010). In addition, a high level of availability has been achieved for its mining machines by applying proper maintenance. Automation, along with continuous material handling, has resulted in good and reliable production.

(a) Continuous material handling system (conveyors) from underground to train loading station, Tabas Coal Complex, Iran (Photo: Authors)

(b) Continuous excavating and transporting of overburden and lignite by giant bucket wheel excavator in open pit mines in Hambach, Germany (Photo: Thyssenkrupp AG)

Figure 26.3   Continuous material handling systems

Table 26.1 Annual achievements of lean production in Carbon Bake Furnace

Criteria	Parameters and measures (2004–2006)	
Health and safety	Incidents (154 ↘ 67)	First aid (24 ↘ 0)
People commitment	Turnover (15.5% ↘ 9%)	Absenteeism (3.4% ↘ 1.8%)
Environment and communities	Odors (14 ↘ 2)	
Operational excellence	Carbon dust (20% ↘ 6%)	Net carbon ratio (0.431 ↘ 0.41)
Financial strength	Recycled >200 t coke valued at $386,867. New in-house coke screen saves $130,000. $2 million annual savings. $1.9 million gained by avoiding additional fan capacity. Delays of $1.2 million furnace rebuild.	

Source: Dunstan et al. (2006).

Case Study 2: Rio Tinto Mining Company

Rio Tinto is one of the best-known international mining companies. It has selected lean thinking to extend business improvements into the workplace. Its objective is to achieve *daily incremental improvements* at an operational level, engaging everyone in the process (Dunstan et al., 2006). Aware of the successful application of the lean concept in other aluminum business activities, Rio Tinto Aluminum (RTA) tried to implement it in its own aluminum mining, refining, and melting processes. Rio Tinto has also applied lean mining in its other mines, especially in coal mining in Northparkes Mines and Hunter Valley Mine in New South Wales, Australia. However, the best results have been achieved in Rio Tinto's Carbon Bake Furnace; the results are presented in Table 26.1. As shown in this table, for the five criteria (health and safety, people commitment, environment and communities, operational excellence, and financial strength), Rio Tinto has achieved considerable improvement (more than 200 percent in some cases).

Case Study 3: National Iranian Steel Company

National Iranian Steel Company is the owner of several coal and iron ore mines in Iran and has started to implement the lean concept in its mines. As a prerequisite, it sought *ISO certificates* for its mines. Tabas coal mine, a fully mechanized longwall mine, was the first Iranian mine to run the ISO-9001 and ISO-14001 standards in its operation and managerial systems. ISO-9001 describes how an organization should focus on customer needs and review internal working methods to reduce costs and increase efficiency and profitability. ISO-14001 is an internationally accepted standard, providing the basis for establishing environmental management in all types of organizations in all kinds of industries. The main goal of these standards is to minimize the waste in the whole production process. This, of course, is the main goal in lean production. As in the VALE experience, the implementation of ISO standards and lean thinking in the Tabas coal mine has resulted in daily improvements at an operational level, with everyone engaged in the process.

We should point out that these applications are not consistent with a holistic view of mining. Rather, the lean idea has been applied in certain individual operations in the mining process. The results are positive but cannot be considered holistic, largely because of the partial application of lean thinking.

Case Study 4: A Swedish Mining Company

The final case study is a Swedish open pit mine. It presents the results of a lean mining research project (2010–2014) in the Division of Operation and Maintenance Engineering at Luleå University of Technology, in combination with other research findings in Sweden (Yngstrom, 2012; Loow and Johansson, 2015). The mine in the case study is one of Europe's largest open pit mines. It produces copper, along with some gold and silver as by-products. The mine began production in 1968 with two million tons of annual ore production. Since then, production has gradually increased to 18 million tons per year. At the end of its current expansion projects, it could potentially produce 39 million tons.

Mining is an outdoor, large-scale, and harsh industry. The case study shows the difficulties involved in implementing the lean concept throughout the entire mining production process. It takes years to be successful. If lean thinking is partially implemented at the outset, this could lead to subsequent expansion throughout the whole system.

Defining subgoals and establishing a step-by-step procedure is an essential start to applying the lean concept in mining. The case study mine defines the following as its subgoals:

1   improving the reliability of production machinery,
2   creating a continuous mining process, and
3   improving the working environment to enhance quality.

The field analysis of the case study mine and the assessment of current operational conditions considering the basic principles of lean production show some weaknesses that need to be eliminated from the mining processes, as well as some strengths which should be extended. These are presented in Table 26.2.

When we take a close look at the weaknesses and strengths, we realize the case study mine could take a number of practical and managerial actions to improve the production system from a lean point of view. Suggested improvements include:

1   establishing better data collection and flow,
2   improving fleet availability,

Table 26.2 Strengths and weaknesses of mine production process from a lean concept point of view

Weaknesses	Strengths
• Insufficient data available	• Value added in all process steps
• Low machinery availability	• Partly standardized information flow
• Lack of standardized work	• Flexible production resources
• High level of uncertainty	• Several working places and high-capacity machinery
• Low integrity of production components	
• Inefficient use of batch	

Source: Adapted from Yngstrom (2012).

3   implementing advanced maintenance programs (e.g. eMaintenance),
4   implementing comprehensive decision support systems for different organizational levels,
5   implementing automated systems and machinery,
6   developing visual controls and mobile apps for continuous production monitoring, and
7   developing new standards and getting more standardized work orders in daily operation.

In addition, two lean metrics should be used to follow up the mine's lean initiative: total lead time and machine availability. Individual cycle times are important components of total lead time. The total lead time of ore production (time length of the exploitation process from drilling to delivery to crusher) is 33.6 days in the current state. According to the future-state map, the lead time could be lowered to 17.16 days by enhancing the fleet availability from the present average value of 78 percent to 90 percent (Yngstrom, 2012). This could be achieved by implementing the lean-based improvement techniques mentioned above, especially maintenance-related solutions and automation.

Findings from the case study suggest the lack of stability and standardization in the production process are the main challenges to lean mining. If standard approaches are developed in mining, companies will be able to adjust their specific cases to fit the benchmarks. Lean production will lead the way to a substantial improvement in efficiency.

Conclusions

The lean thinking approach involves the creation of continuous production flows based on customer demand. The use of lean thinking can increase a company's ability to satisfy its customer needs in delivery time, price, and quality, thus ensuring a higher level of profitability. These concepts apply in all types of industries, including mining.

With the emergence of less costly technologies, it is possible to enhance the accuracy of mining processes (e.g. correct delineation of ore body, elimination of hole-deviation, etc.) and reduce waste from the mining value chain. These new technologies facilitate real-time condition monitoring, eliminating unplanned stoppages and system idle time as a major cause of the loss of production capacity.

There are still many challenges to the full implementation of the lean concept in the mining industry:

1   Lean thinking must be culturally accepted by miners and mine managers. A prevailing mindset says "mines are different from Toyota." This may be true, but we should focus on the similarities and implement as many features of lean thinking as possible.

2   Due to the high degree of heterogeneity in mining and the many variations in logistic and support systems, it is challenging to establish a single standard process for all kinds of underground and surface mining methods. It may be best to partially apply the lean concept in the beginning and then gradually extend it.

3   Mining is associated with a wide range of uncertainties, making it a complex process to analyze and improve. Therefore, lean implementation should be considered at all levels of operation and in all aspects of mine design.

4   Companies using lean mining methods have been met with only partial success. That said, they have noted a considerable improvement in health and safety, environment, and operational excellence.

Acknowledgment

This chapter presents the results of an ongoing research project, "Lean Mining," at the Center for Advanced Mining and Metallurgy (CAMM), Luleå University of Technology, Sweden. The financial support of CAMM is acknowledged.

References

Boliden AB, (2012). *Welcome to Boliden Aitik.* Available at: www.boliden.com/Documents/Press/Publications/Broschures/Aitik_folder_eng_web.pdf (accessed July 2016).

Dunstan, K., Lavin, B. and Sanford, R. (2006). The application of lean manufacturing in a mining environment. *International Mine Management Conference*, October 16–18, Melbourne, Victoria.

Hartman, H. L. and Mutmansky J. M. (2002). *Introductory Mining Engineering*, 2nd edition, Hoboken, NJ, John Wiley and Sons.

Humphreys, D. (2001). Sustainable development: Can the mining industry afford it? *Resources Policy*, 27(1), 1–7.

Krafcik, J. F. (1988). Triumph of the lean production system. *Sloan Management Review*, 30(1), 41–52.

Kumar, U., Ghodrati, B. and Hosienie, S. H. (2015). Implementation of lean manufacturing principles in the mining sector: Benefits, issues and challenges. *International Mining Conference on Technological Innovations, Interventions and Collaborations for the Development of Mines and Minerals Industry*, November 19–22, Hyderabad, India.

Liker, J. (2009). *The Toyota Way*, Liber AB.

Loow, J. and Johansson, J. (2015). An overview of lean production and its application in mining. *Proceedings of International Conference on Mineral Resources and Mine Development*, Aachen, RWTH Aachen University, pp. 121–136.

Mann, D. (2005). *Creating a Lean Culture—Tools to Sustain Lean Conversions*, New York, Productivity Press.

Morgan, J. (2005). *Creating Lean Corporations—Reengineering from the Bottom Up to Eliminate Waste*, New York, Productivity Press.

Steinberg, J. G. and De Tomi, G. (2010). Lean mining: Principles for modelling and improving processes of mineral value chains. *International Journal of Logistics Systems and Management*, 6(3) 279–298.

Wijaya, A. R., Kumar, R. and Kumar, U. (2009). Implementing lean principle into mining industry issues and challenges. *International Symposium on Mine Planning and Equipment Selection*, November 16–19, Banff, Canada.

Yamatomi, J. and Okubo, S. (2015). Surface mining methods and equipment, civil engineering. In: Kiyoshi Horikawa (ed.), *Encyclopedia of Life Support Systems (EOLSS)*. Available at: www.eolss.net/sample-chapters/c05/e6-37-06-01.pdf (accessed July 2016).

Yngstrom, J. (2012). Lean production: adaptation to a case in the mining industry. Master's thesis, Divisions of Operation Management, Chalmers University of Technology, Goteborg, Sweden.

27

LEAN MAINTENANCE, REPAIR, AND OVERHAUL

Mandyam M. Srinivasan

Introduction

The *maintenance, repair, and overhaul* (MRO) industry presents a significant opportunity for the application of lean. According to a Standard & Poor's industry survey report published in 2011 (Tortoriello, 2011), the global MRO market generated $111 billion in estimated revenues from maintenance, repair, and overhaul of commercial and military aircraft in 2009. To put this number in perspective, data drawn from the International Monetary Fund reveals that about 70 percent of the countries in the world will have a GDP less than $111 billion in 2015. Moreover, this number, $111 billion, represents the annual global revenues for just the aircraft MRO industry. Many other industries, such as shipping, construction equipment, railroad, and manufacturing, have significant MRO expenditures. An article published in 2006 in the *Harvard Business Review* estimated that customers in the United States spend $1 trillion every year to maintain assets they already own (Cohen et al., 2006).

Organizations that provide MRO services—the suppliers—can thus realize large revenues and profits through efficient delivery of these services, regardless of whether they perform their own MRO work or provide MRO services to other organizations. Organizations requiring these services—the customers—can realize significant cost savings from good MRO practices. Managers in the MRO industry, both suppliers and customers, will benefit from an in-depth understanding of key concepts and principles for managing the MRO business more effectively.

What is Lean Maintenance, Repair, and Overhaul?

Before discussing how lean applies in this industry, let's first describe MRO since it can have multiple definitions. MRO is the set of all actions needed to restore equipment, a machine or a system to an "as-new" state, or at least to a state where it operates at its required level of performance. In this regard, MRO activity is also sometimes referred to as a type of *remanufacturing* (Kurilova-Palisaitiene and Sundin, 2014).

It is important to distinguish MRO from maintenance. Maintenance is typically an activity undertaken by an organization to maintain its own assets, an activity that is almost entirely performed in-house. MRO, on the other hand, is an activity typically performed by an outside organization that contracts to do the MRO activity, although in some cases it is performed in-house just like with maintenance. Thus a subtle, yet significant, difference between maintenance and MRO is that the organization performing maintenance on its own assets would typically like to *reduce* this activity. On the contrary, an organization offering MRO services would typically like to *grow* this activity by performing it better than its competitors are able to.

To set the following discussion in context, consider a typical MRO process carried out on an asset. The asset in question can be an aircraft, a locomotive, a ship, oil-drilling equipment, or some other equipment. Typically, the asset is disassembled and the structure and its components are inspected to determine the extent of the repair/overhaul. The inspection is typically followed by some structural repair work on the asset during which time some of the disassembled components are either routed to support shops (*back-shops*) for repair or are replaced with parts procured from outside vendors. Next, the build-up activity takes place after all these components are repaired or procured and the structure is repaired and ready for build-up. A primary purpose of the MRO activity is to restore the asset to as close to an "as-new" condition as possible. When the build-up activity is completed the asset is typically provided a fresh coat of paint and controlled by a functional test. Figure 27.1 provides a high-level schematic of the MRO process.

One important goal, arguably the primary objective in the MRO business, is reducing *flow time*, where flow time is the time that elapses between the start of the process and its completion. Flow time reduction is especially important in the MRO business because the asset is unavailable to perform its intended function while undergoing MRO and that translates as lost revenue. Consider, for instance, the aircraft MRO industry. Boeing states that a one-to-two-hour aircraft-on-ground delay costs an airline $10,000 in downtime with the actual costs of such delays running as high as $150,000, depending on the airplane model and the airline (Schleh, 2000). The international shipping organization DHL estimates the cost per day for a grounded A380 Airbus to be $1,250,000 (DHL, 2014). No doubt, the cost of an aircraft-on-ground can be determined using different assumptions, resulting in significantly different estimates. However, a lower limit on this cost may be determined simply by looking at the aircraft leasing cost, with other factors such as repair costs and lost revenue (an opportunity cost) contributing to the total cost. Numerous websites provide leasing rates for aircraft. One of these, Myairlease.com, indicated that the lease cost for a Boeing 777-300ER ranged from $675,000 to $1,250,000 per month in September 2015 (Myairlease.com, 2015).

A number of MRO organizations have seen improvements in their financial performance through lean implementations. However, many other organizations have implemented lean and experienced little or no improvement in financial performance. What factors help explain why some organizations find success with lean while others fail to do so? While a number of the lean techniques used in the manufacturing industry also apply in MRO, the unique challenges in MRO result in some of the lean tools either not being applicable or requiring adaptation to the

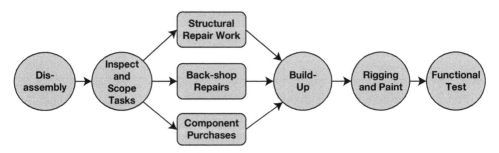

Figure 27.1 A high-level schematic of an MRO process

MRO environment. I have seen many examples of disappointing results where a lean template has been forced, without adaptation, on to MRO operations.

An article by Ayeni et al. (2011) surveyed the state of the art of lean in the aviation MRO industry and concluded that while there is a strong emphasis on the adoption of lean within the MRO industry, its actual adoption is difficult to determine. The report states that the paucity of literature on lean within the MRO industry serves as evidence of the industry's reluctance in its adoption, compared with other industrial sectors. It goes on to indicate that while lean is widely interpreted as a viable tool within the aviation industry, it is not sufficient by itself to realize all the goals set by organizations. Furthermore, the report finds that the focus of lean in the aviation MRO industry is predominantly directed toward waste reduction rather than the creation or enhancement of value.

In this regard, lean, in conjunction with a body of knowledge popularly known as the *theory of constraints* (TOC), offers a significant opportunity for improving the performance of MRO organizations. TOC adopts a perspective that has the objective of maximizing the organization goals and offers the tools and techniques for identifying the points of leverage that have maximum systemic impact. With its big-picture perspective, TOC guides organizational efforts on flow time reduction by focusing on the key constraints. Lean complements TOC by addressing waste reduction at these key constraints. This winning combination, simply termed lean/TOC, is the focus of this chapter.

Characteristics of MRO

To see how lean/TOC can help significantly improve the performance of MRO organizations, consider the characteristics of the MRO process. These characteristics include high demand variability, uncertainty in work scope and material requirements, unpredictable and complex flow paths, and limited technical data. Arguably, these challenges are also present in some manufacturing organizations. The classical job shop, which typically operates in a high-variety, low-volume environment, certainly must be prepared to deal with a high variation in demand. However, these challenges are relatively more severe for the MRO business. Thus, relative to high-volume manufacturing environments, in an MRO environment:

- the rate of demand and the mix of products are more variable;
- a significant portion of the work may be "over and above" work that is not part of the standard work package and is different for each item;
- much of the additional work scope and parts requirements is not known in advance but is only revealed during the course of the repair process;
- some parts have long and unpredictable flow times;
- after disassembly and inspection, a signification portion of the work is handed off to remote shared capacity support shops (back-shops) and/or external contractors;
- many different tasks compete for shared resources;
- *work in progress* (WIP) inventory represents not just inventory in the traditional sense, but a piece of the customer's equipment that is not generating revenue for the customer.

In particular, MRO operations have to contend with work scope variation in addition to process variation. Unlike a typical manufacturing process where the work content is determined by the product design well before production commences, work content definition in the MRO process often takes place within the context of the ongoing repair process. Such on-the-spot work content definition results in uncertain demands and schedules for the back-shops leading to

313

unpredictable response times. These back-shops often have to deal with unplanned repairs for which adequate tooling and work standards are unavailable. Lacking adequate checklists or work instructions for such unanticipated repairs, these shops often resort to trial and error techniques. Quite often, the shops have to share their resources across multiple requests from different facilities, which often leads to priority changes and multitasking at these resources.

It is clear that the characteristics of the MRO process present significant challenges. Aside from the challenges resulting from the unpredictable nature of the MRO business, MRO organizations also face a familiar challenge. This is the *cost world perspective*, a perspective prevalent in most organizations, which emphasizes cost reduction over throughput improvement.

The Cost World

One of the most important metrics used to measure performance is *return on investment* (ROI). Consider how this metric influences the decision-making process of the chief executive officer (CEO). The CEO is quite aware that if he does not deliver on this metric, someone else might be given the opportunity to do so. What will the CEO do in this situation?

If the CEO's job depended on improving ROI it is very likely he would choose to cut costs to improve financial performance. The cost world perspective presents a serious threat to the business because it offers a relatively quick and easy option to an organization that presents financial reports to its shareholders each quarter. A focus on cost control usually results in sub-optimal decisions. Such cost reduction programs often paradoxically increase costs and waste instead of increasing profitability. For example, a typical result of such cost reduction efforts is headcount reduction. What are the consequences of this cost reduction effort? Aside from the fact that the employees still remaining in the organization are now demoralized, anticipating the next round of cuts, they may also have to take on the workload of the canned employees. The increased workload also tends to affect their job output. Even though they might be more "productive" as measured by traditional metrics, the customer now suffers because it usually takes longer for these employees to complete the work with the increased workload.

The preceding discussion is not intended to suggest that organizations should abandon efforts to contain costs. The point is that cost containment should not be the driving focus for the CEO. There is a better way. This is the *throughput world perspective*, a perspective that focuses continuous improvement efforts toward a growth strategy. This perspective is discussed next in terms of the opportunities lean/TOC provides to organizations.

The Throughput World

The throughput world perspective often results in decisions that are very different from decisions made with a cost world perspective. Maintaining a throughput world perspective, however, requires a lot of courage and effort, since decisions made with this perspective do not produce tangible results immediately. Albert Einstein said, "Any intelligent fool can make things bigger, more complex, and more violent. It takes a touch of genius—and a lot of courage—to move in the opposite direction." The question is, how can an organization move to a throughput world perspective? TOC provides the answer, offering the tools and techniques for tackling complexity and for identifying the points of leverage that have maximum systemic impact. These leverage points are the system's constraints. TOC avoids the pitfalls of localized cost world thinking by adopting a perspective that has the objective of maximizing the organization's goals.

The developer of TOC, Eliyahu Goldratt, published the concepts and principles for TOC in *The Goal: Excellence in Manufacturing* (Goldratt and Cox, 1984). Goldratt notes that since the system's constraints determine the extent to which the goal is realized, the intent is to obtain the maximum productive output from the constraint(s) to ensure sustainable growth with stability. The implication is that not all changes will result in improvement toward the goal and may in fact jeopardize stability. The challenge is therefore to arrive at a reliable focusing mechanism that can tackle complex problems and can identify the points of leverage that have the maximum systemic impact.

As noted earlier, lean complements TOC by addressing waste reduction at the key leverage points identified by TOC. In its original incarnation, lean was viewed as a management philosophy that focused on *continuous improvement* (CI) through the elimination of *muda* or waste. Such a focus can be attributed in part to the book published by Womack and Jones (1996), in which it was stated that lean was "a powerful antidote to muda" and "provides a way to do more and more with less and less" (p. 15). While the true intent of that book was to present lean as a vehicle for CI, it was not interpreted that way. Instead, many organizations pursued lean efforts as a way to simply remove waste wherever possible.

In hindsight, such pursuits were narrow and inherently limiting in a number of ways. No doubt the tools provided by lean show how to eliminate waste from processes. By more efficient use of its floor space, equipment, and labor, an MRO facility can increase capacity and improve throughput without a significant increase in capital investment or labor costs. However, the quest for removing waste also promoted a tendency to reward managers for effecting *kaizen* or CI efforts that often led to local performance improvement without affecting organizational performance. That perspective has changed. Lean is now viewed as a CI philosophy aimed at creating a smooth flow of products. The focus is on having the CI team help the organization move from a current state to the next desired state using a pre-defined target condition. Such a redefined focus leads to a pleasant convergence with the TOC philosophy—lean/TOC.

The combination of lean/TOC is an organizational transformation that removes the organizational barriers to growth. These barriers are the written and unwritten rules of the organization (policies, measures, mindset, and methods). In essence, lean/TOC works as follows. The tools of lean prescribe the process changes needed to eliminate waste. TOC shows how and where to apply these tools to grow the business and to create the organizational transformation needed to achieve that growth. Some lean/TOC guidelines MRO organizations can adopt to achieve improved financial performance are as follows:

1   focus on the *intent* of lean, not on the techniques or tools themselves;
2   lay out processes to facilitate flow and minimize handoffs to other areas (process layout);
3   apply lean to reduce process variation and evolve a strategy to cope with work scope variation;
4   focus performance metrics on growing the business, not on cost reduction, and not on lean events; align the performance metrics with the big picture goal of growth;
5   focus improvement efforts on the constraint;
6   control the induction of work to match the processing capacity of the constraint;
7   develop clear rules for assigning priorities to tasks competing for shared resources; provide the information needed for implementation of these rules at the floor level.

The first two guidelines are intuitively clear. As far as the third guideline is concerned, process variation can be reduced using lean tools such as *standard work*, mistake-proofing, and the tools of Six Sigma. Work scope variation is managed using flexible, cross-trained workers, creating flex capacity in the form of overtime capacity especially at bottleneck machines, and by using inventory strategically. For instance, inventory can protect bottleneck resources.

The fourth guideline speaks to the differences between the cost world perspective and the throughput world perspective. Performance metrics should focus on growing the market while creating the capacity for growth by the elimination of waste. Focusing on local metrics, such as machine utilization, worker efficiencies, and earned hours, causes dysfunctional behaviors. Metrics related to cost reduction tend to be local. The cost saved may actually hurt performance in another area. In many cases the cost saving is actually an illusion created by the cost accounting system that fails to differentiate between fixed or sunk costs and costs that are truly variable.

The fifth guideline is fairly intuitive but, unfortunately, is often sidelined in practice. For example, it is a common practice to measure lean progress by the number of lean improvement events (or kaizen events) that have been conducted. These events, unfortunately, typically do not necessarily translate into improved financial performance. As noted earlier, improvement efforts should be focused on just a few leverage points in the system, namely at the constraints that limit business growth, whether they are physical capacity constraints, constraints resulting from poor policies, or a market constraint. Thus, if the constraint is a physical constraint, improvement efforts should aim at increasing its capacity of physical constraint since additional capacity at the physical constraint results in additional throughput. Improvement efforts on resources that are not constraints will not increase throughput. Similarly, if the constraint is the market then the improvement efforts should focus on improving those factors that will increase sales, such as shorter turnaround time.

The last two lean/TOC guidelines are achieved by a couple of TOC-based tools, the *drum-buffer-rope* (DBR) and *critical chain project management* (CCPM). These two tools are described in detail in the book *Lean MRO: Changing the Way You Do Business* (Srinivasan et al., 2014). In a typical MRO application, DBR is applied to handle the back-shop repairs while CCPM is applied to handle the rest of the process steps identified in Figure 27.1. To motivate the discussion of these two tools in this chapter, we visit an article that Goldratt published in 2008: "Standing on the shoulders of giants." This article, subsequently reprinted in the *Management & Production* magazine (Goldratt, 2009), applies some of the concepts and techniques used in high-volume production operations by Henry Ford and Taiichi Ohno—the "giants" in the article's title—to create and enable flow in a much more widespread setting. This article presents four key considerations:

1 Improving flow (or equivalently reducing flow time) is a primary objective of operations.
2 This primary objective should be translated into a practical mechanism that guides the operation in when not to produce (prevents overproduction).
3 Local efficiencies must be abolished.
4 A focusing process to balance flow must be in place.

The first key consideration emphasizes the importance of flow and its relationship to flow time. The lack of flow, or any flow imbalance, results in long flow times. Conversely, long flow times are symptomatic of poor flow and affect performance in a number of ways. By focusing on the constraint(s) in the system, organizations can significantly improve flow.

With respect to the second key consideration, Goldratt explains that lean and TOC combine to increase flow in the system by monitoring and improving those steps in the process that constrain flow. Henry Ford, for instance, created flow simply by limiting the space allowed for WIP between two work centers. In fact, the first flow lines in his assembly operations did not have any automated means of moving inventory from one work center to another. Ford thus used space to create flow. In contrast, Taiichi Ohno used inventory to control flow. The *kanban* mechanism put in place by Toyota used inventory between workstations. Each process would produce to replenish only the products that the downstream process selected. The kanban system thus became the practical mechanism that guided the operation in when not to produce (prevented overproduction). Ohno essentially adapted Ford's concepts by altering the mechanism that stopped overproduction from space to inventory.

While kanban systems can be used in MRO organizations, the primary mechanism for controlling and improving flow in these organizations is the DBR technique, a method to control the induction of work to match the processing capacity of the constraint. In essence, this is the sixth lean/TOC guideline for improved financial performance. If there is adequate work to keep the constraint busy, then inducting more work will not increase the rate of flow. On the contrary, inducting more work will only serve to increase waste. More work in progress only serves to increase the inventory to be managed, presents more opportunities to misallocate capacity, and increases workspace clutter.

Additionally, in facilities where flow times are long, there is a tendency to release work into the system as early as possible based on a mistaken notion that early induction will result in an early completion of the work. In fact, in capacity constrained systems the opposite is true. Inducting work at a rate exceeding the rate of the bottleneck increases flow time. This is because early induction creates waste that reduces the capacity of the system which in turn drives up flow times. It also causes the capacity to be spread across multiple items which will cause a longer flow time for all items. As an aside, it is noted that when too much work is inducted, it is often due to a performance measurement system that is focused on local measures of performance such as worker efficiencies and machine utilizations.

The seventh lean/TOC guideline is to provide clear rules for assigning priorities to tasks competing for shared resources, and to provide the information needed for implementation of these rules at the floor level. This prioritization mechanism is provided by CCPM. CCPM is used to coordinate activities across projects and to assign priorities in the back-shops among tasks competing for the same capacity.

Challenges and Opportunities

The challenges to implementing lean/TOC in the MRO industry stem directly from the characteristics of the MRO process described earlier, namely the uncertainty surrounding the process combined with the complexity of the repair and overhaul process. In particular, the variation in the demand, work scope, and material requirements makes application of lean in the MRO industry far more difficult than in the repetitive manufacturing industry. In addition, as with any other industry, the challenge of overcoming resistance to change is always present.

That said, there are a number of opportunities for applying lean/TOC, especially since the scope for improvement is very significant in the MRO industry, with a considerable amount of low-hanging fruit prospects. One repair facility I recently worked with used these techniques to reduce its flow time by more than 40 percent. Another engine repair facility applied these techniques to achieve a flow time of 15 days, a remarkable feat in an industry where flow time for engine repairs is typically around 45 to 60 days. A leading overseas manufacturer of regional jets, with maintenance facilities in the USA, applied concepts from our lean/TOC course to improve the turnaround times of its components by more than 50 percent in 2015. The case study presented at the end of the chapter describes the application of lean/TOC at a major military base in Albany, Georgia (Srinivasan et al., 2004) that reduced flow time for repair and overhaul of a major asset from an average of 167 days to an average of 58 days.

The Future of Lean Maintenance, Repair, and Overhaul

Lean/TOC, the combination of the theory of constraints and lean, provides a big opportunity for MRO organizations to gain a significant competitive advantage and grow their business. For example, with its big-picture perspective, TOC guides organizational efforts on flow time reduction by focusing on the key constraints. Lean complements TOC by addressing waste reduction at these key constraints. These two philosophies combine to leverage an organizational growth strategy focused on improving throughput.

The TOC methodology provides businesses with a systems perspective, allowing for a more strategic focus. Lean/TOC, the combination of TOC with lean, generates significant outcomes. We have used these tools and techniques to train participants from organizations that overhaul aircraft, locomotives, ships, and oil-drilling equipment.

Case Study

The Maintenance Center at the Marine Corps Logistics Base, Albany, Georgia, is responsible for the regeneration and reconstitution of the equipment required by the Marine Corps for combat readiness. The center undertakes complex maintenance operations that include rebuilding equipment to original manufacturers' specifications. It repairs and overhauls a wide variety of products that include small arms, amphibious vehicles, light armored vehicles, fuel tankers, trucks, earthmoving equipment, and logistics vehicle systems.

In 2001, the Maintenance Center was struggling to complete equipment repairs on time and was coping with an increasing backlog of work. Asking for "plus-ups," a request for additional time and resources to complete the work, had become a normal way of doing business.

One of the major assets the center repairs and overhauls is the MK-48, a heavy-duty hauler for the Marine Corps. In 2001, the center was struggling to repair and overhaul five MK-48s per month against a customer demand of ten MK-48s per month. The center dealt with apparent capacity shortages in virtually every department. The customer was dissatisfied and threatened to divert orders to the private sector in search of better service. Employee morale was low.

At that time, scheduling of maintenance operations was based on an MRP-II system that used a push system to load the resources at the center based on anticipated customer demand, resulting in frequent rescheduling and expediting of critical items. The center reviewed alternative approaches to schedule production, and eventually decided to implement a pilot project on the MK-48 vehicle that was based on TOC principles, in particular CCPM and DBR.

As a first step, the center sought input from its workforce on where bottlenecks were located. Opinions varied on what the bottleneck activities were, but every major activity in the center was believed to be an important bottleneck by at least someone in the facility. An analysis of the data collected revealed that, contrary to everyone's opinion, the facility had more than enough capacity to carry out the activities required to meet the demand for repair and overhaul of ten MK-48s per month. The root cause of the consistent shortfalls and high inventory levels appeared to be the MRP-II scheduling system in place that was pushing products out to the shop floor without regard for the status of the resources. The bottleneck was thus not a physical resource constraint. Rather, it was a *policy constraint* introduced by the scheduling process. To address the center's problems, the main shop where the products were first disassembled and subsequently reassembled was modeled as the *critical chain* in the CCPM implementation. The activities in the shops that processed components

Table 27.1 Results on the MK-48 and LAV-25 lines

Line	Average flow time (days)		WIP/Monthly demand	
	Before	After	Before	After
MK-48	167	58	5.5	1.4
LAV-25	212	119	4.3	3.1

removed from the main products were modeled by a variant of the DBR mechanism known as the *simplified drum-buffer-rope* mechanism.

The pilot project proved successful and the center began implementation plant-wide in April 2002. The implementation generated dramatic improvement in the center's performance. Flow times for the MK-48 were reduced by a factor of three, from an average of 167 days to an average of 58 days. The center was even able to repair and overhaul 23 MK-48s per month. For another asset repaired and overhauled at the center, the LAV-25, the corresponding flow days were 212 days and 119 days, before and after the implementation. The work in process levels (relative to demand) were also reduced significantly for both these units, as shown in Table 27.1. Other products showed similar reductions in flow times and work in process.

Some of the other results of the lean/TOC implementation included a 6-S activity that significantly increased available shop floor space. Hundreds of labor hours were saved and tools in excess of $200,000 were turned in for redistribution and future use. The process flows in production work centers were streamlined. A major benefit from the implementation was that it resulted in increased morale for the employees of the center. The workplace became cleaner, less cluttered, and safer.

The magnitude of culture change was greatest in the support shops through which disassembled parts are routed for repair. Holding disassembled parts for release caused great fear among the workforce, and resistance was substantial. This aspect of the implementation was the last part of the culture change accepted and accomplished by the maintenance center. As they saw significant improvement with every other aspect of the implementation, the workforce gained the courage to move forward.

References

Ayeni, P., Baines, T., Lightfoot, H. and Ball, P. (2011). State-of-the-art of "lean" in the aviation maintenance repair overhaul industry. *Proceedings of the Institution of Mechanical Engineers*, 225(11), 2108–2123.

Cohen, M. A., Agrawal, N. and Agrawal, V. (2006). Winning in the aftermarket. *Harvard Business Review*, 84(5), 129–138.

DHL (2014). Aircraft on ground: When speed matters most. *Delivered*, 1, 13. Available at: www.delivered.dhl.com/content/dam/delivered/master/issues/2014-1/pdf/delivered-issue-1-2014-web.pdf (accessed July 2016).

Goldratt, E. M. (2009). Standing on the shoulders of giants: Production concepts versus production applications. The Hitachi Tool Engineering example. *Gestão & produção (Management & Production Magazine)*, 16(3), 333–343.

Goldratt, E. M. and Cox, J. (1984). *The Goal: Excellence in Manufacturing*, Croton-on-Hudson, NY, North River Press.

Kurilova-Palisaitiene, J. and Sundin, E. (2014). Challenges and opportunities of lean remanufacturing. *International Journal of Automation Technology*, 8(5), 644–652.

Myairlease.com (2015). *FleetStatus*. Available at www.myairlease.com/resources/fleetstatus (accessed July 2016).

Schleh, D. (2000, July 27). *Boeing Rapid Response Center Proves its Worth in First Year*, Boeing.mediaroom. com. Available at: http://boeing.mediaroom.com/2000-07-27-Boeing-Rapid-Response-Center-Proves-Its-Worth-In-First-Year (accessed July 2016).

Srinivasan, M. M., Bowers, M. R. and Gilbert, K. (2014). *Lean MRO: Changing the Way You Do Business*, New York, McGraw-Hill.

Srinivasan, M. M., Jones, D. and Miller, A. (2004). Applying theory of constraints principles and lean thinking at the Marine Corps maintenance center. *Defense Acquisition Review Journal*. August–November, 134–145.

Tortoriello, R. (2011, February 10). *Standard & Poor's Industry Surveys: Aerospace & Defense*, New York.

Womack, J. P. and Jones, D. T. (1996). *Lean Thinking: Banish Waste and Create Wealth in Your Corporation*, New York, Simon & Schuster.

28

LEAN PUBLIC SERVICES

Zoe Radnor

Introduction

Public service reform has been on the political agenda since the late 1970s and has included such approaches as the 3Es (economy, efficiency, and effectiveness) through to *best value* and *new public management* (NPM) (Rashman and Radnor, 2005). More recently, "lean thinking" has become a prominent and popular approach to public service reform. In the current era of constrained and reduced public spending, it has promised to maintain service productivity, improve resource utilization, and maintain service quality. In short, it has been promoted as enabling public service providers to "do more, with less" (Radnor et al., 2012). This chapter will review the application of lean in public services, illustrating that to date there has been an over-focus on technical tools without an understanding of the principles and assumptions of lean, or the context in which it is being implemented. The chapter will conclude that to develop further there needs to be greater consideration of the underlying logic and theories of service management.

In the US and UK in 2005, the total outlay on public services as a percentage of National Gross Domestic Product (GDP) was 35.9 percent and 44.5 percent respectively (Pettigrew, 2005) rising from 12.7 percent and 24.0 percent in 2001 (Karwan and Markland, 2006). In 2011, the Index of Economic Freedom reported that government spending as a percentage of National GDP was 38.9 percent for the USA and 47.3 percent for the UK (Index of Economic Freedom, 2011). During this same period (2005–2011) both countries, as well as other countries such as Greece and Portugal, have experienced a profound recession leading to budgetary and spending cuts across the public sector. In England, for example, the Operational Efficiency Report (HM Treasury, 2009) in April 2009 stipulated that potential savings of around £10 billion a year should be sought over three years across public services.

This growing pressure on public services across the Western world has led to a focus on increased efficiency over and above the outcome measures of effectiveness and equity. Both public services, including health (Guthrie, 2006; Fillingham, 2008) and local government (Office of the Deputy Prime Minister, 2005; Krings et al., 2006), and central and federal government (Richard, 2008; Radnor and Bucci, 2010) have responded by implementing a range of business process improvement methodologies including lean thinking, Six Sigma, business process reengineering, continuous improvement, and total quality management. Tellingly, in the literature review presented in this chapter, focusing on the use of these methodologies in the public sector, 51 percent of publications focused on lean, with 35 percent of these within health services (Radnor, 2010a).

This research on lean has suggested it can offer significant impact related to quality, cost, time, and even the satisfaction of both staff and service users. Connecticut Department of Labor, for example, eliminated 33.5 staff hours in its work by the redesign of its processes, saving $500,000 in staff time over a year. Likewise, Solihull Borough Council produced a £135,000 saving in the postal costs for its fostering service, through a lean review (Radnor, 2010a). Other reported benefits have included the reduction of waiting time for public services and a reduction in service costs through a reduction in resource utilization (Silvester et al., 2004) as well as intangibles such as increased employee motivation and satisfaction and increased customer satisfaction (Radnor and Boaden, 2008).

This apparent success story marks the starting point of this chapter. Through exploration of the empirical literature, and referring to a large evaluation within the public sector (Radnor and Bucci, 2007), it will reflect on this success story. The chapter will argue that although lean appears to have had a successful impact within public services, the actuality has been one of easy successes and a lack of sustainability and resilience in the benefits achieved.

It could be argued the majority of studies about lean thinking in the public sector to date are not comparative or rigorous (Lilford et al., 2003). Carefully selected case studies have been used to promote benefits in public services without a balanced view of the negative aspects or consideration of the influence of other factors. Radnor and Boaden (2008) stated in an article that lean may be a panacea, because there is evidence indicating that it can support and help in addressing some of the inefficiencies in public services focused around processes and practices. However, it may also be a paradox, because many public service managers appear to be attempting to apply it without fully understanding its underlying principles, seeing it merely as another policy or set of tools. More recently Radnor and Osborne (2013) argued that lean could be a failed theory for public services, due to the easy successes but a lack of underpinning sustainability. They argue that lean does have the potential to have a substantial impact upon public services reform. To achieve this, however, it should not be treated as a theory in its own right. Rather it needs to be situated within *public service-dominant business logic* (Osborne et al., 2013) to achieve enduring benefits for public services and their users.

This chapter will unpack these views, suggesting that the current picture is that lean in the public sector has focused on tools and not on culture, and considering the consequences of why and what this means for its implementation. The chapter will consider the application of lean in public services through a literature review and an evaluation study in order to present a discussion of what has been introduced, examples of where it has been introduced, and what the relevant factors are for informing its understanding, application, and implementation. The chapter focuses on the empirical data from the UK due to the country's historic (Radnor and Bucci, 2007) and planned (HM Treasury, 2009) focus on lean.

Lean Thinking in the Context of the Public Sector

The implementation of lean is often described as "a journey," with the various stages of the implementation being landmarks of the total journey (Bicheno, 2004; Hines et al., 2008). This journey is described by some authors as about developing a lean philosophy, suggesting that organizations should aim to create "a lean lifestyle" (Hines et al., 2008). Hines et al. (2004) note that the framework of lean often exists at two levels: at a strategic level focusing on the principles and at an operational level focusing on the tools and techniques. In later publications, Hines et al. (2008) develop this concept with the aid of an iceberg model illustrating two main elements: below the waterline the enabling elements of strategy and alignment, leadership and behavior, and engagement, and above the waterline visible technology, tools and techniques, and process management.

This iceberg model (Hines et al., 2008) indicates that strategy should be the foundation, supported by decisive leadership and an engaged workforce, to understand the processes and then use a range of tools and techniques to improve the processes. A number of tools are used throughout the model, including policy deployment, visual management (making information visible), standardized work, 5S (housekeeping practices), and process mapping (Hines et al., 2008). The model illustrates the technical (above waterline) and culture (underwater) aspects of lean and supports the idea that lean is a journey which takes time, with people needing to engage with and embed ideas (Radnor and Walley, 2008). So, considering lean as a journey and that it needs to consist of two elements—tools and culture—then through evaluating its implementation in public services, to what degree have the two elements been embraced? However, before considering this let us understand the context of the public sector.

Table 28.1 summarizes the key differences between the private and public sectors. Often the accepted role of the private sector is to engage in commercial enterprise, for profit. Firms are generally free to engage or not engage, purchase inputs at the market price, and abandon activities at will. Principally accountable to their owners, businesses are held accountable by the market against several "hard" indicators, especially profitability (Steward and Walsh, 1994). Whereas the key purpose of public services is to undertake activities in areas where profit cannot be made, but the interests of society demand that the activities occur (Drucker, 1993; Box, 1999). Unlike the private sector, Smith (1995) argues public sector services must continue to operate however difficult the local environment, or even despite clients' inability to pay, sometimes delivering nationally and regionally.

Kelly et al. (2002) suggest that most public sector enterprises have multiple objectives with no single "bottom line." Even though financial indicators and ratios are widely used in the private sector with ratios permitting comparisons between choices and market accountability within the public sector, profit is an oxymoron (Johnson and Broms, 2000). Therefore, often financial indicators and ratios have limited application and receive little effective executive attention within government.

Comparing the two sectors, "from the bottom up" at a basic level, managerial requirements are similar between the two sectors, e.g. management of human resources, budget, project management, service delivery, etc. However, from a "top-down" perspective, democratic values, ministerial demands/politics, laws, and rights, etc., shape a very different picture of managerial requirements (Savoie, 2003; Good, 2004).

In summary, while public and private sectors require similar basic management functions, the differences in environment, context, and constraints do affect the managerial role and the way it is performed (Mintzberg and Bourgault, 2000). Public sector management is more complex, addressing key issues of equity, transparency, and probity, within a political context (Wilson, 1989; Osbourne and Gaebler, 1993; Pollitt, 2003). Due to these differences, it can be argued that simply adopting private management practices, including lean practices, into public management may not lead to the significant improvements expected and, in fact, what is needed is "adaptation" of the approach (Radnor and Boaden, 2008). The next section will consider this further through presentation of a case study in a large UK government department.

Case Study: Lean Public Services in HMRC

Her Majesty's Revenue and Customs (HMRC) was established in April 2005 and is a non-ministerial department, accountable to the Chancellor of the Exchequer. HMRC is responsible

Table 28.1 Key differences between the private and public sectors

Issue	Private sector	Public sector
Overall direction	• Profit • Some attention on future profit	• Government/minister establishes directions • Long term frequently limited to next election • Subject to contradictory pressures • Highly adversarial relations between political parties • Direction may be at policy not administrative level
Legislative and judicial	• Minimum set of law constraining all business (tax, environmental, employment, etc.)	• Citizen "rights" • Government managers must conform to legislation regardless of costs • Generally subject to scrutiny by legislative oversight groups or even judicial orders
Authority	• Authority is generally invested in one CEO • Can operate in any sector/market	• Authority is often shared between senior officers/managers and professional people (politicians, lawyers, doctors/surgeons, academics, etc.) • Limited authority to expand/contract "sphere of operations" and to disengage from activities which are not meeting current goals
Overall goal	• Profit • Application is also measured by increase/decrease in net returns on capital invested and shareholder/economic value added	• Create and sustain citizen satisfaction • Economic, efficient, and effective • Value for money • Ethical and equitable
General culture	• Profit based • Entrepreneurial • Managerial style matches business needs • Innovative • Quicker decision making	• Values based • Bureaucratic • Risk adverse
Accountability	• Through clear objectives • Owners, shareholders • Legal reporting requirement	• Central agencies, parliament/politicians, citizen • Information generally "acquirable" (e.g. access to information laws) • Role of media
Primary stakeholder	• Shareholder is dominant stakeholder	• Conflicting and shifting stakeholder interests and dominance • Potential for conflict with government policy • Public media opinions influence decision making

Table 28.1 (continued)

Issue	Private sector	Public sector
Role of information	• Most held internally and remains confidential	• Exposure to intense public scrutiny—"managing in a fishbowl" • *Access to Information Act*—managers must, and do, consider every memo, letter, briefing note, presentation, and email a public document • Consideration must always be given to public perception and the potential for political embarrassment, even for logical and sensible decisions
Budgets	• Flexible, based on expected profit, return on investment (ROI), economic value added (EVA) • Budgets subject to significant changes	• Relatively fixed, stable budgets • Frequently budget based on previous year plus inflationary adjustment

Source: Various authors, including Rainey et al. (1976), Dunlop (1979), Allison (1997), Box (1999), Larson (2002), and Kroeger and Heynen (2003).

for administering taxes (both direct and indirect), National Insurance contributions and Customs duties. HMRC also pays and administers tax credits, Child Benefit, and the Child Trust Fund.

At the time of the research, there were four types of business units in HMRC: operational units, product and process groups, customer units, and corporate functions. The operational units employed over 70,000 staff and focused on delivering the services such as processing, local compliance, and customer contact. This research focused on HMRC Processing which in April 2006 developed and began rolling out a change program, "Pacesetter." The four main elements of Pacesetter were defined as leadership development; operational management; lean; and workforce strategy and capacity management. The focus here is on the element of "lean."

Almost every UK individual and business is a direct customer of HMRC. HMRC has over 30 million individual customers and 4 million business customers due to taxes paid by UK citizens and businesses. Pacesetter was developed by HMRC Processing to improve efficiency and customer service by delivering a 30 percent improvement in productivity, reducing backlogs and inconsistencies, and ensuring that HMRC Processing was among the best UK processors, the UK government's processor of choice. Lean, one of the elements within Pacesetter, was designed to take a three-pronged approach by:

• redesigning service delivery processes to eliminate waste and variability and maximize flexibility, and to improve productivity and quality and reduce lead time;
• changing current management processes to create appropriate management infrastructure to sustain improvements;
• changing mindsets and behaviors of leaders and front-line staff to support the new systems and deliver continuous improvement.

Lean was being implemented in all HMRC Processing strategic sites. These were the larger sites that would incorporate the work of the smaller sites over a period of time and would use lean as the way of working. In order to implement lean across these sites, there were a number of dedicated *local lean experts* based in local offices. They were supported by dedicated *central lean experts* who rotated over three-month periods between sites. In addition, these internal HMRC staff were supported by external consultants since lean was originally trialed and implemented in 2004. Consultants involved with the lean implementation had included McKinsey Consultants, PA Consulting and since January 2006, the Unipart Group (Radnor, 2010a). During the period of the research, many sites still had Unipart consultants on site working with the central and local lean experts in order to transfer learning and good practice.

In order to undertake the evaluation of lean, 10 HMRC strategic sites were identified by the Pacesetter Program Office. The 10 sites included five large processing offices (LPO), two distributed processing offices (DPOs), and three national processing centers. There was also a visit to the Pacesetter Program Office in London, prior to starting the site visits.

The site visits were undertaken between January and May 2007. These site visits, with one exception, were undertaken over a two-day period. As well as collecting data and material from the sites, semi-structured interviews and focus groups were undertaken with nearly 300 personnel representing a broad range of individuals using an interview schedule that was tailored to the different grades of staff.

The purpose of the site visits was to gain an understanding of the following aspects of lean:

1   When did the lean implementation start and what proportion of the site had been affected by it?
2   What was the understanding by staff of Pacesetter and lean and the links between them?
3   What was the qualitative and quantitative impact of the lean implementation?
4   What problems had occurred or what had worked well during implementation?
5   What had changed as a result of the implementation in terms of individual roles, the processes, the interaction with the customer, and the working of individual teams?

Secondary data was also collected from the sites and the program offices to aid the evaluation including Pacesetter Program documents and the Lean Academy handbook. Further data collected from the sites included the organization chart for the site, current and future state maps for the processes concerned, and information on performance collated over a period to identify trends.

Notes were taken of all interviews and the majority were recorded on a digital recorder and then transcribed so a full record was available. At the end of each site visit, a site report was prepared by the visiting researcher. This report summarized the main responses to the questions asked during the interviews and focus groups and highlighted the site-specific reflective notes of the visiting researcher. These reports were amalgamated at the end of the evaluation and common issues were chunked together and coded so that the research team were aware of which sites had raised the issues. The chunked data was used to develop a final evaluation report, which was validated by senior HMRC personnel (see Radnor and Bucci, 2007 for the full report).

Implementation

The findings will focus on which lean methods and tools were implemented and their impact in HMRC. First, it is interesting to consider how the approach taken in HMRC relates to the principles set out by Womack and Jones. Table 28.2 identifies the approach and tools within HMRC, and maps them against the five lean principles.

Table 28.2 highlights that many of the activities and tools being used focus on the fifth principle followed by the third principle. In terms of implementation and operations there was

Table 28.2 Principles of lean related to HMRC lean

Lean principle	HMRC approach and tools
1 Specify the value desired by the customer	• Process mapping, value stream maps
2 Identify the value stream	• Diagnostic of current state
3 Develop a continuous flow	• Standard work
	• Visual management
	• Key performance indicators (KPIs) for quality and productivity
	• Line balancing
4 Introduce pull between all steps where continuous flow is impossible	• Flag system in the teams: visual small flags used by the member of staff to indicate that they were free to take on work
5 Manage toward perfection so that the number of steps and the amount of time and information needed to serve the customer continually falls	• Workplace assessment
	• 5S
	• Structured problem solving
	• Stretch targets and timings
	• Visual management/performance boards
	• 3Cs
	• Process hubs
	• Go and see

pressure to implement standard processes across the LPOs and DPOs based around the four key processes: *self-assessment, employee maintenance, open cases,* and *post*. There were "process owners" across a number of the strategic sites who both developed and managed the changes for a particular process. At each LPO/DPO there was a diagnostic stage which considered the "current state" and consisted of a location diagnostic for the whole site and a process diagnostic for each process. The location diagnostic considered the set-up of the teams and processes whereas the process diagnostic also included mapping (value stream) and considering the volumes/demand on the office. The next stage was to implement the future state, which had been designed by the process owners and included setting the targets to be achieved through the implementation of the standard process. The targets agreed between senior managers and directors were often "stretch" targets designed to increase performance. All these stages involved all grades of staff often with "pilot" teams within each process.

However, staff at the LPO/DPO sites later felt they had not had significant involvement in the development of the processes. There was considerable evidence that many of the staff felt that lean was imposed and that front-line staff had no real say in how it was implemented. A specific example of this is when standard work instructions appeared not to have always been explained to the staff. Staff stated that they were not "fit for purpose" and that when they tried to change them (through the appropriate procedure through the process owners) they were not successful. This led to some teams in some sites openly admitting that they were no longer following the standard instructions.

Unlike the LPO/DPO offices, the national processing centers developed and implemented their own standard processes through the diagnostic process. Within these diagnostic processes more flexibility was built in with teams being able to take time out for meetings and problem solving to reflect on the design and development of the new processes. The research team was informed that at these sites the senior management had been very firm with the program office with regard to the Pacesetter timescales for implementation. They had also been very determined, through the presentation of a business case, to keep Unipart consultants until there was no longer a need for them. This was so that the consultants could be involved in, as well as set up, "mini" program teams to manage and coordinate the roll-out of lean working with the local lean experts; the justification was that the involvement of Unipart and the full implementation of lean should be based upon business needs and not just led by an end date stipulated in a contract. At these sites, the level of "buy-in" and understanding among the staff was much more apparent and positive.

In terms of continuous improvement, from the interviews it became apparent that while attention has been paid to increasing productivity and the detection and prevention of errors, the focus on customer needs and staff motivation was sometimes lost in the pressure to achieve targets. Some sites did not achieve all their targets and some targets were viewed as unachievable. This was summed up in the Union documentation as lean "creating a divisive, unhappy working environment with low morale, no challenge, and bored employees." It is important to note that the way that the non-achievement of targets was treated differed across the sites. At two sites, teams were under pressure to achieve targets but were not criticized for not doing so. At other sites, the good performers in the team felt more pressure to hit the targets because they were compensating for the poorer performers. It seems that lean or team working had not motivated the poorer performers to raise their performance nor had lean allowed individuals to perceive that they were using their experience or knowledge.

Additionally, the lean teams were not always using the tools and techniques to generate and support improvement, too often focusing on poor performance (i.e. the tools were being used to ask "why not" rather than "how to"). The format of the daily meetings, which were described to and witnessed by the research team, were about discussing (or finding reasons for) non-achievement of targets (i.e. poor performance) rather than improvement. If daily meetings were carried out based on continuous improvement then they could be used to motivate teams, seek improvements, or praise improving performance. They would also not be seen as a "waste of time and resource when I could be getting on with some real work and meeting the targets." Only at two of the national processing sites and the model office was the focus less on the non-achievement of targets at the daily meetings. Here, fundamental reasons as to why targets were not achieved were looked for, good performance was praised, and training issues and problem solving discussed.

Supporting the implementation of lean there were a number of training activities. One at Unipart's office in Cowley where they were able to see lean in action, and another titled "Learning to Lead in a Lean Environment" which was held at various locations depending on the needs of the attendees. Senior managers who attended the courses stated how useful, they were particularly the second one, and how they had now been able to see the benefits and understand the components of a lean approach more clearly. At the other extreme, the staff training was described by one person "a day of playing games like being back at school." Some felt that the focus of the day was on what lean was and not how it was going to be implemented within HMRC, and nor was there any analysis of their skills in relation to the new lean work.

The central and local lean experts attended over a period of time three "*lean academies*" run by a combination of HMRC and Unipart. The training received by the lean experts was important due to the various backgrounds, skills, and experiences held by the experts. Many from within the business mentioned how they knew little about lean but became "experts" overnight. This meant often learning on the job and from the Unipart consultants. Some local experts felt that the central experts, who moved from site to site, had little ownership of the business and so only wished to be involved in elements that either interested them or helped to develop their career. However, the local experts are managed by the business, therefore often could not see where changes were needed nor were able to address difficult situations with senior management. The central experts met with the rest of the Pacesetter team twice a year as well as having a regular fortnightly teleconference, whereas the local experts had no formal mechanism to meet the local experts from other sites. As a result, there was limited opportunity for face-to-face contact between both sets of experts to discuss "hot issues," new developments, and good practice. The result of this was that frequently experts interpreted some of the standard practices in their own way, meaning that often practices were not standard.

Reflecting more broadly on which tools and techniques of lean were felt to be important, and which ones should remain and support sustainability, a variety of staff across the sites mentioned standardization, process management, team working, and continuous improvement. From the eight sites visited, the majority of the staff highlighted the use of performance boards and visual management as important to measure performance. The impact of using the performance boards to measure progress toward the targets was seen as significant at all sites.

> I think the boards are vital and they would be the last thing I want to get rid of. There is reluctance to complete them every hour but this is vital. Someone will challenge past performance, and we can refer to the information of that time to give a reason as to why performance was good or bad. Before lean, there was no record of past performance.

Workplace assessments were also seen as important and efforts were being made by the senior managers in five sites to ensure that they would be sustained. Interestingly, three sites that were initially skeptical about workplace assessment were beginning to see the benefit of this tool.

> I do checks every week. I can see the benefit of doing them. Already, things come up from the checks where you see inconsistencies between teams, so you can put that right.

Interviewees stated that they hoped problem solving would remain because staff were engaging in the process, although some staff highlighted that there was still likely to be resistance to problem solving until it was seen to be working.

> Problem solving is key to staff engagement. If staff are involved meaningfully in problem solving and they can actually change what they are doing, then they feel they have some control over what they do. We need to do more on this, but we are doing a lot better than we were.

Related to this it was mentioned that team working and the way that the teams were composed would continue to develop because, apart from anything, it would be too difficult to go back to the previous ways of working due to the new processes.

Challenges and Opportunities: Adaptation of Lean in Public Services?

The HMRC evaluation, taken together with other evaluations and a wider review of literature, identified significant challenges embedded in the implementation of lean in public services (Radnor and Bucci, 2007, 2010; Radnor, 2010a, 2010b). Many of these could be described as "common" for most change management initiatives and not specific to lean as such. These included a lack of commitment from senior management, change objectives that are not aligned to customer requirements, a lack of training for staff, and a poor selection of projects for implementation (Lucey et al., 2005; Radnor et al., 2006; Antony, 2007; Oakland and Tanner,

2007). However, four challenges can be identified that are particular to lean in public services. These are:

1   a focus and over-reliance on lean workshops: "rapid improvement events" (RIEs);
2   a toolkit-based approach to lean implementation, but without an understanding of the key principles or assumptions;
3   the impact of public sector culture and structures, and particularly the competing professional and managerial role in relation to lean implementation;
4   a lack of focus on the centrality of the customer (or service user) and understanding of the service process.

Challenge 1: A Focus and Over-reliance on Lean Workshops

There are two main approaches to lean implementation in public services. These are the use of discrete workshops or events taking place over a concentrated period of time, often known as RIEs, or a comprehensive implementation or program approach across the whole public sector organization (PSO). Both of these approaches often use the same tools but are different in the breadth, depth, and regularity of their use—with RIEs being short-to-medium term in focus and the programmatic approach being committed, at least in principle, to continuous improvement.

RIEs (sometimes called "kaizen" events) are workshops involving staff from across the organization, often with multiple functions, getting together to make small and quick changes. RIEs comprise three phases, beginning with a preparation period, followed by a five-day event to identify potential lean changes, and a three to four-week follow-up period when these changes are implemented. The approach is often favored by staff as it provides an apparently fast return for effort, is visible, and does not challenge existing management control styles (Radnor and Walley, 2008). However, in isolation this approach can be problematic. RIEs tend to be more focused on short-term outcomes than longer-term developmental issues (Radnor and Walley, 2008). Spear (2005) has noted that a series of such small-scale successful lean projects can have a dramatic impact in the longer term. However, he also notes that, in order to achieve this longer-term impact, it is important that these small-scale projects are all focused around a clear long-term improvement strategy. Currently, this appears not to be case in many public service RIE events (Radnor et al., 2012).

The full program approach requires the entire PSO to be engaged in the implementation of lean. RIEs may be used to change key areas or departments but fundamentally the program is focused on developing behaviors throughout the organization which continuously improve value, flow, and performance through the use of a range of lean tools. The tools include performance boards/visual management, daily meetings, workplace audits, problem solving, and experimentation (Spear and Bowen, 1999; Holweg, 2007). The key issue in such programs is not so much the application and use of these tools. Rather it is about building a more fundamental understanding of the underlying principles of lean through their application. They are a means to an end rather than the end itself (Shah and Ward, 2007). Although HMRC did claim to be carrying out a full programmatic approach, the evaluations revealed only pockets of short-term impact around RIEs rather than a systemic embedding of the principles of lean (Radnor and Bucci, 2007, 2010).

Challenge 2: A Toolkit-based Approach to Lean Implementation

Drawing from the extant literature, typical tools and techniques associated with lean include kaizen events, process mapping, 5S, value stream mapping, and visual management (Radnor, 2010a).

Assessing these tools, Radnor (2010a) has argued that they can be used for three purposes within PSOs as part of lean implementation. These purposes are:

1   *Assessment*: To assess service delivery processes at organizational level, e.g. value stream mapping, process mapping.
2   *Improvement*: To support and improve the processes of service delivery e.g. RIEs, 5S, structured problem solving.
3   *Monitoring*: To measure and monitor the impact of the processes and their improvement, e.g. control charts, visual management, benchmarking, work-place audits.

As discussed above, lean implementation in the HMRC began in April 2006 across a number of sites (Radnor and Bucci, 2007). It consisted of introducing revised processes in the four key customer-facing operations at each of the sites: performance boards which reflected the team's performance, resource planning mechanisms, targets, and problem solving. These operations were supported by daily meetings (10 minutes each morning) to motivate the staff to reflect upon the achievements of the previous day, to plan the coming day's work, and to resolve any outstanding problems or issues with the lean implementation process. Other tools were also introduced to support ongoing problem solving (Radnor, 2010b).

The HMRC case study demonstrates a preoccupation in public service lean programs with the tools of lean rather than the overarching approach itself. These tools may, and often did, lead to short-term success in improving the internal efficiency of the PSOs concerned. However, rarely, if ever, did they consider the issue that is actually at the heart of true lean implementation: the centrality of the customer and customer value to organizational effectiveness. This is returned to below.

Radnor (2010a) has stressed the importance of organizational readiness factors for the implementation of lean. These factors include an understanding of the processual nature of public services delivery, an appreciation of what "value" actually comprises within public services, an external orientation for the lean process and the PSO, the active engagement of staff in process redesign, and the centrality of co-production to effective lean (Radnor, 2010a). She has argued further that an absence of focus on these factors in lean implementation in public services has resulted in a lack of sustainability in the longer term for these lean initiatives (Radnor and Bucci, 2007; Radnor, 2010a). Tools have been focused on to the exclusion of strategic intent.

Challenge 3: The Impact of Public Sector Culture and Structure

McNulty (2003) notes that across PSOs as a whole, policy is invariably focused at the senior level and undertaken by managers, whereas practice occurs at the operational level and is undertaken by professionals (such as clinicians, teachers, or social workers). He describes, further, how professional work is broken down into specialties that very rarely cross departmental boundaries and that professionals control the flow of their work. Consequently, they can resist managerial attempts to make their work more predictable, transparent, and standardized.

Within healthcare in particular, it has been argued that this challenge can cause conflict. Clinical acceptance of change initiatives proposed by service managers can be difficult because of resistance to being told how to do things, because staff are uninterested in process improvements across departments that are apparently aimed at efficiency gain alone, and because they perceive these initiatives as in conflict with their professional values (Wysocki, 2004; Cauldwell et al., 2005). This has been especially so in the case of process redesign initiatives, such as lean (Woodard, 2005). Despite this opposition, clinical buy-in is critical to the success of the initiatives, as clinicians invariably have a strong power base within the health service and the power and credibility to convince colleagues that these initiatives can improve patient care—or not (Cauldwell et al., 2005; Massey and Williams, 2005; Guthrie, 2006).

Gulledge et al. (2002) point out that the mandates and structure of the implementation of these process improvement methodologies are based on the traditional "command and control" structures that will be found most commonly in private sector firms and that their implementation in PSOs has been predicated upon the existence of this model. Significantly, the research has revealed that many lean initiatives are actually top down, driven by policy and public spending necessities, rather than bottom up, based upon expressed need. This was found to be the case in the HMRC. These lean programs were decided upon and designed to the exclusion either of the tax officers or of legal staff, who would be responsible for their implementation, or of the service users, who were purportedly to benefit from these reform programs. Consequently, these lean initiatives became policy-, or finance-, facing rather than oriented to the benefits of the end users of services—a core element of true lean. As a consequence, both Gulledge et al. (2002) and Seddon and Caulkin (2007) have suggested that this has meant that lean can never achieve its potential in public services, precisely because it is policy- and finance-facing, rather than end-user facing. Front-line staff end up reacting to internal measures and targets rather than to external customers (i.e. their end users). This is an anathema to the true vision of lean.

Challenge 4: A Lack of Customer Focus and Understanding of the Service Process

Proudlove et al. (2008) argue that a key problem for lean in healthcare is "identifying customers and processes in a healthcare setting and the use of clear and appropriate terminology" (p. 33). Halachmi (1996) has also contended that it is hard to specify value in public service delivery because some organizational functions and procedures do not contribute directly to value, at least in the eyes of the customer (Halachmi, 1996).

Within a commercial organization, the definition and requirements of the customer are comparatively straightforward and directly impact upon turnover and profit. It therefore becomes easier to identify value and value-added activities. Within public services, though, the concept of a "customer" is not so straightforward and can be contested. It can include direct end users, unwilling or coerced users, multiple users of a service, citizens who indirectly benefit from a service, and future users of a service (Osborne et al., 2013). Moreover the terminology of "customer" or "consumer" is itself problematic, rooted as it is in the discourse of commercial and business firms. The concept of the end user is perhaps more appropriate. It does not assume the presence of a market exchange or commercial relationship—though it too suffers from some of the multiple meanings identified above. This issue of the centrality of external customer/end-user value to successful lean implementation is particularly important and is discussed further below.

Moving on to the issue of the role of "process" in successful lean implementation, Denison (1997) has described the ideal type of "process-organization" as one "wherein the primary issue of organizational design is creating value and organizing is understood not as a series of functional units or business units but as a collection of interrelated processes that create value" (p. 31). A key problem for lean in PSOs has been, in contrast, that it has focused upon internal departmental efficiency rather than external, service-user driven, value (Radnor et al., 2012).

Three brief examples will make this point. First, across HMRC, in response to the question "who is the customer?" the response was often "everyone!" When asked whether the require-ments of these customers were understood the answer was invariably "yes—high-quality quick information," but with little articulation as to what that meant in terms of standards and requirements. Therefore, there was no clear understanding either of who their end users were, or of what level of quality and timing of information would result in better service delivery processes and more satisfied end users (Radnor and Johnston, 2013).

Second, it is a truism within healthcare that the delivery of patient care is largely a human process and consequently that the causes of variability are often difficult to quantify. Walley et al. (2006) and Seddon (2005) have both argued that there is a need to better understand how demand varies across healthcare and to remove activities that do not add value to the patient or that create bottlenecks in the system. An example of such an improvement might be transferring patients from emergency departments to theaters more quickly by removing unnecessary paperwork, reducing the number of different staff involved in the process to minimize handover time, and/or improving the physical layout of hospitals (Lister, 2006; Walley et al., 2006). This is a classic lean approach—it seeks to reduce queues by managing the variation in process. All too often, though, the public service approach has been to focus on increasing the number of public goods provided, in a situation where demand is, literally, inexhaustible. Like de-marketing (Osborne and Kinder, 2011), lean approaches seek to control either the level of demand for value and/or the processes used to deliver it.

Finally, Seddon and Brand (2008) outline two different types of demand: value demand ("what we are here to provide," or mission-driven demand) and failure demand ("failure to do something or do something right for the customer"). They report that in local government departments in the UK, the level of failure demand can be as high as 80 percent, severely limiting the ability of such departments to deal with value, mission-driven, demand. Understanding this key distinction in types of demand is vital to PSOs. Yet the findings of the HMRC evaluations detailed above clearly indicated that the reform focus was not on how patterns of work could be changed to better meet the demands of service users but rather on how the demand could be moved around to fit with the existing work patterns of the organization. The organization was *capacity-led*, not demand-led. The result was an increase, not decrease, in failure demand. This is a failure of lean (Radnor and Bucci, 2007, 2010).

The Future of Lean Public Services

Earlier in the chapter the comparison between the private and public sector highlighted the similarities of the "bottom up" elements (i.e. the management around service delivery, human resources, etc.) whereas the "top down" perspective in terms of the complexities and structures of public services around the professional's roles and policy making is very different to that in the private sector. These complexities were also discussed as barriers to lean implementation. This distinction between bottom up and top down could explain the focus on tools, i.e. it is easier to implement lean into the management elements that are similar to those in the private sector. Even if this is the case there is a need to go beyond just isolated implementations of RIEs and to try, even if just in management areas, to develop a culture of improvement or consider elements "beneath the waterline."

Exploring organizational readiness, when asked participants claim to enjoy RIEs but they also often mention "frustration" at not being able to implement the changes agreed due to lack of management support, lack of time, or lack of resource which can lead to people becoming disengaged with the practice (Bateman, 2005; Radnor and Boaden, 2008). The lack of support, time, and resources themselves may be due to the lack of organizational readiness, making it difficult to encourage and implement the conditions for lean outside the RIE workshop environment. In terms of organizational readiness for lean, this includes elements such as having a process view, developing a culture focused on improvement, developing an understanding of demand and variation, of the customer, and the "value" within the process. These elements of readiness are critical as the foundation for process improvement as they provide a basis to which the tools can be applied (Bateman and Rich, 2003; Radnor et al., 2006; Bhatia and Drew, 2007; Hines et al., 2008). Without these elements it may be easy for people to go back to the "way it was before," for the change not to be implemented and so not sustain any improvements made (Cinite et al., 2009).

The extant literature clearly indicates that there are potential benefits from introducing lean approaches into public services delivery and that these benefits can add real value to the end users of these public services (see Radnor, 2010a, 2010b; Radnor and Johnston, 2013 for some examples across public services). First, it is true that PSOs have made some time and cost savings that have benefited the public purse. HMRC, for example, has saved £400m from the implementation of the Pacesetter initiative (National Audit Office, 2011). Arguably, though, these savings were primarily a product of addressing the prior poor design of these public services—what we have termed "picking the low hanging fruit (and windfalls!)" of public management reform (Radnor and Osborne, 2013, p. 275). This may be an important goal in its own right, but it is not the intent of lean. This intent is rather to improve the effective delivery of end outcomes to the external users of public services and to add value to their lives in doing so. To extend our metaphor, the challenge is therefore not how to pick more of the low hanging fruit, no matter how easy this may be. They are invariably the smallest and least tasty of the fruit on the tree. Rather it is to become more ambitious and seek to gather the real, substantive, harvest of public management reform.

Second, it is vital to its success to understand that lean is context dependent (Radnor et al., 2012). It derives originally from a private sector, manufacturing context (Toyota) and this context has affected, and limited, its early implementation in public services. However, it cannot be simply transferred across to a public service context, assuming that it can offer the same benefits. If this is the intent, then lean will indeed be a "failed theory" with little to offer public services beyond the correction of previous design faults. If lean is to go beyond this and to offer a genuine route to increased public service effectiveness and increased end-user value, then we need to develop a modified theory of lean suited to the public service context. The remainder of this chapter will sketch out the preliminary elements of such a theory of public service lean, based within a public service-dominant business logic.

Currently the focus of lean appears to be around the tools and not the culture. Where it is being implemented it appears to also be having significant impact. However, as argued, this could be due to the "newness" of the approach in that, by considering the process for the first time, many obvious wastes can be removed, e.g. reducing the number of forms to be filled in. This tools approach may be due to the early stage of the journey of lean within the public sector but it may also be due to the complexities within public services which mean that for lean to evolve beyond a management (to an organizational) philosophy may be more challenging.

An argument that has been presented is that much contemporary public management theory has been derived conceptually from prior "generic" management research conducted in the manufacturing rather than the services sector. This has generated a "fatal flaw" (Osborne and Brown, 2013) in public management theory that has viewed public services as manufacturing rather than as service processes—and as ones that are created by professional design and input and then delivered to the user even though the business of government is, by and large, not about delivering pre-manufactured products but to deliver services. Nor are most relationships between public service users and public service organizations characterized by a transactional or discrete nature as they are for such products (McLaughlin et al., 2009). On the contrary, the majority of "public goods" (whether provided by government, the non-profit and third sector, or the private sector) are in fact not "public products" but rather "public services" that are integrated into people's lives. Social work, healthcare, education, economic and business support services, community development, and regeneration, for example, are all services provided by service organizations rather than concrete products, in that they are intangible, process driven, and based upon a promise of what is to be delivered. Public services can of course include concrete elements (healthcare or communications technology, for example). However, these are not "public goods" in their own right; rather they are required to support and enable the delivery of intangible and process-driven public services.

This product-dominant flaw, we argue, has persisted despite the growth of a substantive body of services management and service operations management theory that challenges many of its fundamental tenets for the management of services (Normann, 1991; Gronroos, 2007; Johnston and Clark, 2008). This *service management theory* should inform our theoretical and conceptual understanding and analysis of the management and delivery of public services.

So should public sector organizations be investing in process improvement methodologies? The answer is probably yes as evidence indicates that lean is potentially a good framework for public services as the principles give managers something to "hang on to" with simple tools and techniques to use. However, it needs to be fully understood as a philosophy and seen as more than just a policy and a set of tools. It needs to be set within a service management context and logic.

Lean in a (Public) Service-dominant Context

This service management and service-dominant body of theory has profound implications for the implementation of lean in public services. For the first time it provides a meaningful context within which to operationalize the core philosophy of lean, rather than simply applying its tools in a mechanistic and product-dominant manner. As has been discussed above, the reasons for the apparent successes of lean as a public service reform strategy have not been based within the rigorous application of lean. Rather, the successes have derived from two other sources: that the processes and systems of PSOs were poorly designed initially and/or that little attention had been given previously to the inefficiencies of existing internal organizational processes.

By focusing attention, often for the first time, on the design of processes and systems within and across departments within PSOs it has actually been comparatively "easy" to identify and remove forms of waste stemming from such poor design—the "low hanging fruit" of public services reform we discussed above. Much of these early gains have been achieved primarily through focusing on lean workshops and RIEs. Such a reduction of waste, as long as it does not undermine mission-critical activity, is an important achievement in its own right. However, by itself it can only ever be a short-term objective of lean (Ballé and Regnier, 2007; Hines et al., 2008; Radnor and Walley, 2008).

Viewed in this context, lean has to date simply been a catalyst to address the prior poor design of the public service within and across PSOs. Once waste has been removed, however, the larger issue still remains of designing public services to meet the needs of end users and to add value to their lives. This is true effectiveness. This focus on the external end users of a public service is essential to the genuine application of lean to public services. To date, though, it has been absent, with the focus being upon internal customers and internal efficiency rather than external end users and external effectiveness. This has been the fatal flaw of the implementation of lean in public services and why, to date, it has been a failed theory of public services reform. Once the implementation and application of lean in public services moves away from being solely tool based and engages in the culture and service management paradigm to build a viable and effective theory of public service-dominant lean, then it can be "fit for purpose" to underpin and to drive forward the successful reform of public services delivery in the 21st century.

References

Allison, G. T. (1997). Public and private management: Are they fundamentally alike in all unimportant respects? In: Sharfritz, J. M. and Hyde, A. C. (eds), *Classics of Public Administration*, 4th edition, Chicago, IL, Dorsey Press, 384–401.

Antony, J. (2007). Is Six Sigma a management fad or fact? *Assembly Automation, 27*, 17–19.

Ballé, M. and Regnier, A. 2007. Lean as a learning system in a hospital ward. *Leadership in Health Services, 20*, 33–41.

Bateman, N. (2005). Sustainability: The elusive element of process improvement. *International Journal of Operations & Production Management, 25*(3), 261–276.

Bateman, N. and Rich, N. (2003). Companies' perceptions of inhibitors and enablers for process improvement activities. *International Journal of Operations & Production Management, 23*, 185–199.

Bhatia, N. and Drew, J. (2007). Applying lean production to the public sector. *McKinsey Quarterly*, 97–98.

Bicheno, J. (2004). *The New Lean Toolbox*, PICSIE Books.

Box, R. C. (1999). Running government like a business: Implications for public administration theory and practice. *American Review of Public Administration, 29*, 19–43.

Cauldwell, C., Brexler, J. and Gillem, T. (2005). Engaging physicians in lean Six Sigma. *Quality Progress, 38*, 42–46.

Cinite, I., Duxbury, L. E. and Higgins, C. (2009). Measurement of perceived organizational readiness for change in the public sector. *British Academy of Management, 20*, 265–277.

Denison, D. R. (1997). Towards a process based theory of organizational design: Can organizations be designed around value-chains and networks? *Advances in Strategic Management, 14*, 1–44.

Drucker, P. F. (1993). *Post-Capitalist Society*, New York, HarperBusiness.

Dunlop, J. T. (1979). Public management. Unpublished manuscript.

Fillingham, D. (2008). *Lean Healthcare: Improving the Patient's Experience*, Chichester, Kingsham Press.

Good, D. A. (2004). *The Politics of Public Management*, Toronto, IPAC.

Gronroos, C. (2007). *Service Management and Marketing*, Chichester, John Wiley & Sons.

Gulledge, R. T. R. Jr and Sommer, R. A. (2002). Business process management: Public sector implications. *Business Process Management Journal, 8*, 364–376.

Guthrie, J. (2006, June 22). The joys of a health service driven by Toyota. *Financial Times*.

Halachmi, A. (1996). Business process reengineering in the public sector: Trying to get another frog to fly. *National Productivity Review, 15*, 9–18.

Hines, P., Holweg, M. and Rich, N. (2004). Learning to evolve: A review of contemporary lean thinking. *International Journal of Operations & Production Management, 24*(10), 994–1011.

Hines, P., Found, P. and Harrison, R. (2008). *Staying Lean: Thriving, Not Just Surviving*, Cardiff, Lean Enterprise Research Centre, Cardiff University.

HM Treasury (2009). *Operational Efficiency Programme: Final Report*, London, HM Treasury.

Holweg, M. (2007). The genealogy of lean production. *Journal of Operations Management, 25*, 420–437.

Index of Economic Freedom. (2011). Heritage. *Wall Street Journal*. Available at: www.heritage.org/index (accessed May 22, 2011).

Johnson, H. T. and Broms, A. (2000). *Profit Beyond Measure*, New York, The Free Press.

Johnston, R. and Clark, G. (2008). *Service Operations Management*, Harlow, UK, FT/Prentice Hall.

Karwan, K. R. and Markland, R. E. (2006). Integrating service design principles and information technology to improve delivery and productivity in public sector operations: The case of South Carolina DMV. *Journal of Operations Management, 24*, 347–362.

Kelly, G., Mulgan, G. and Muers, S. (2002). *Creating Public Value—An Analytical Framework for Public Service Reform*, London, Cabinet Office.

Krings, D., Levine, D. and Wall, T. (2006). The use of "lean" in local government. *Public Management, 88*, 12–17.

Kroeger, A. and Heynen, J. (2003). *Making Transitions Work: Integrating External Executives into the Federal Public Service*, Ottawa, Canadian Centre for Management Development.

Larson, P. (2002). *Ten Tough Jobs*, Ottawa, Public Policy Forum.

Lilford, R. J., Dobbie, F., Warren, R., Braunholtz, D. and Boaden, R. (2003). Top rate business research: Has the emperor got any clothes? *Health Services Management Research, 16*, 147–154.

Lister, S. (2006, June 15). Bloated NHS is to receive the Tesco treatment. *The Times*.

Lucey, J., Bateman, N. and Hines, P. (2005). Why major lean transitions have not been sustained. *Management Services, 49*(2), 9–13.

McLaughlin, K., Osborne, S. and Chew, C. (2009). Developing the marketing function in UK public service organizations: The contribution of theory and practice. *Public Money and Management, 29,* 35–42.

McNulty, T. (2003). Redesigning public services: Challenges of practice for policy. *British Journal of Management, 14,* 31–45.

Massey, L. and Williams, S. (2005). CANDO: Implementing change in an NHS Trust. *International Journal of Public Sector Management, 18,* 330–349.

Mintzberg, H. and Bourgault, J. (2000). *Managing Publicly*, Ottawa, Institute of Public Administration of Canada.

National Audit Office (2011). *Pacesetter: HMRC Programme to Improve Business Operations*, London, National Audit Office.

Normann, R. (1991). *Service Management: Strategy and Leadership in Service Business*, New York, Wiley.

Oakland, J. S. and Tanner, S. J. (2007). *Lean in Government: Tips and Trips*, Oakland Consulting.

Office of the Deputy Prime Minister (2005). *A Systematic Approach to Service Improvement*, London, Office of the Deputy Prime Minister.

Osborne, S. P. and Brown, L. (eds) (2013). *Handbook of Innovation in Public Services*, Cheltenham, UK, Edward Elgar Publishing.

Osborne, S. P. and Kinder, T. (2011). Debate: "Want doesn't get"? Public management responses to the recession. *Public Money and Management, 31*(2), 85–88.

Osborne, S. P., Radnor, Z. and Nasi, G. (2013). A new theory for public service management? Toward a (public) service-dominant approach. *American Review of Public Administration, 43*(2), 135–158.

Osbourne, D. and Gaebler, T. (1993). *Reinventing Government: How the Entrepreneurial Spirit is Transforming the Public Sector*, Reading, MA, Addison-Wesley.

Pettigrew, A. (2005). The character and significance of management research on the public services. *Academy of Management Journal, 48,* 973–977.

Pollitt, C. (2003). New forms of public service: Issues in contemporary organizational design. In: Couchene, T. J. and Savoie, D. J. (eds), *Governance in a World without Frontiers*, Montreal, Institute for Research on Public Policy (IRPP), pp. 209–238.

Proudlove, N., Moxham, C. and Boaden, R. (2008). Lessons for lean in healthcare from using Six Sigma in the NHS. *Public Money and Management, 28,* 27–34.

Radnor, Z. J. (2010a). *Review of Business Process Improvement Methodologies in Public Services*, London, Advanced Institute of Management.

Radnor, Z. J. (2010b). Transferring lean into government. *Journal of Manufacturing Technology Management, 21,* 411–428.

Radnor, Z. J. and Bucci, G. (2007). *Evaluation of Pacesetter: Lean Senior Leadership and Operational Management, within HMRC Processing*, London, HM Revenue & Customs.

Radnor, Z. J. and Boaden, R. (2008). Lean in public services—Panacea or paradox? *Public Money and Management, 28,* 3–7.

Radnor, Z. and Walley, P. (2008). Learning to walk before we try to run: Adapting lean for the public sector. *Public Money and Management, 28,* 13–20.

Radnor, Z. J. and Bucci, G. (2010). *Evaluation of the Lean Programme in HMCS: Final Report*, London, HM Court Services.

Radnor, Z. J. and Johnston, R. (2013). Lean in UK government: Internal efficiency or customer service. *Production Planning and Control, 24,* 903–915.

Radnor, Z., and Osborne, S. P. (2013). Lean: A failed theory for public services? *Public Management Review, 15*(2), 265–287.

Radnor, Z. J., Walley, P., Stephens, A. and Bucci, G. (2006). *Evaluation of the Lean Approach to Business Management and its Use in the Public Sector*, Edinburgh, UK, Government Social Research.

Radnor, Z. J., Holweg, M. and Waring, J. (2012). Lean in healthcare: The unfilled promise? *Social Science and Medicine, 74,* 364–371.

Rainey, H. G., Backoff, R. W. and Levine, C. N. (1976). Comparing public and private organizations. *Public Administration Review*, March–April, 233–244.

Rashman, L. and Radnor, Z. (2005). Learning to improve: Approaches to improving local government services. *Public Money and Management, 25,* 19–26.

Richard, G. (2008). *Performance is the Best Politics: How to Create High-Performance Government Using Lean Six Sigma*, Fort Wayne, IN, HPG Press.

Savoie, D. J. (2003). *Breaking the Bargain*, Toronto, University of Toronto Press.

Seddon, J. (2005). *Watch Out for the Toolheads!* Available at: www.systemsthinkingmethod.com/downloads/watch_for_toolheads.pdf (accessed July 2016).

Seddon, J. and Caulkin, S. (2007). Systems thinking, lean production and action learning. *Action Learning: Research and Practice, 4*(1), 9–24.

Seddon, J. and Brand, C. (2008). Debate: Systems thinking and public sector performance. *Public Money and Management, 28*, 7–10.

Shah, R. and Ward, P. T. (2007). Defining and developing measures of lean production. *Journal of Operations Management, 25*, 785–805.

Silvester, K., Lendon, R., Bevan, H., Steyn, R. and Walley, P. (2004). Reducing waiting times in the NHS: Is lack of capacity the problem? *Clinician in Management, 12*, 105–111.

Smith, P. (1995). On the unintended consequences of publishing performance data in the public sector. *International Journal of Public Administration, 18*, 277–310.

Spear, S. (2005). Fixing health care from the inside. *Harvard Business Review, 83*, 78–91.

Spear, S. and Bowen, H. K. (1999). Decoding the DNA of the Toyota Production System. *Harvard Business Review*, September–October, 97–106.

Steward, J. and Walsh, K. (1994). Performance measurement: When performance can never be finally defined. *Public Money and Management, 14*, 45–49.

Walley, P., Silvester, K. and Steyn, R. (2006). Managing variation in demand: Lessons from the UK National Health Service. *Journal of Healthcare Management, 51*, 309–320.

Wilson J. Q. (1989). *Bureaucracy: What Government Agencies Do and Why They Do it*, New York, Basic Books.

Woodard, T. D. (2005). Addressing variation in hospital quality: Is Six Sigma the answer? *Journal of Healthcare Management, 50*, 226.

Wysocki, B. Jr (2004, April 9). Industrial strength: To fix health care, hospitals take tips from factory floor; Adopting Toyota techniques can cut costs, wait times; Ferreting out an infection; What Paul O'Neill's been up to. *Wall Street Journal* (Eastern edition).

29

LEAN ARMED FORCES

Nicola Bateman and Peter Hines

Introduction

This chapter outlines some of the unique challenges in applying lean in the armed forces and highlights other challenges that extend beyond the military, for example to other uniformed services, technical service and repair facilities, or other public sector services. It does not address the application of lean in the military supply chain, as this is well covered elsewhere. Rather, it addresses how suppliers to the armed forces interact with the military or form on-site partnerships. This chapter examines the major differences between military organizations and conventional organizations that effect lean implementation and goes on to explore the impact of these differences. A separate case study focuses on the Tornado Joint Integrated Project Team (JIPT), part of the British Royal Air Force.

This chapter engages with material from all military services; in most countries, this constitutes army, navy, and air force. There also exists an overlap in application of lean in other public services in terms of multiple stakeholders and the associated complexity of definition of value. This complexity of definition of value is also in common with some specific public services where the service user does not necessarily seek the service at all (such as the prison service and drug rehabilitation) as may be the case with those who engage with the military. Finally, additional subsectors of public services are the uniformed services such as the police and fire service where a hierarchical command structure echoes the military.

Challenges and Opportunities

The major differences between military organizations and conventional (high-volume, low to medium variety, and commercial) lean organizations are highlighted in Bateman et al. (2014) (the subject organization in that paper is summarized in the case study). The paper highlighted the principal differences as:

1   military hierarchical culture,
2   two-state demand pattern,
3   complex extended enterprise,
4   non-growth, and
5   service and repair.

The first of these differences is the hierarchical nature of military organization. This affects how lean is implemented at both the operational and strategic level. At the operational level continuous improvement (CI) activities (also known as rapid improvement or *kaizen* activities) are likely to be less consensual than is conventionally expected and more likely to follow the chain of command. Military organizations rely on the command structure (Feld, 1959) to function in conflict situations where challenge to the command structure is not appropriate. Thus, CI activities that rely on discussion and consensus (Laraia et al., 1999) may be disrupted by the hierarchical structure.

At a more strategic level, the typical two-year tour of duty for personnel is identified as an issue for lean implementation sustainability by Cullen et al. (2005) and from interaction with military personnel attending lean courses run by us, the authors. A tour of duty in the UK armed forces is essentially an individual's time in a particular job; previous and subsequent postings can be completely different in terms of role and location. Lean typically requires a long time span, five years or more according to Womack and Jones (2003). Thus, a change of direction due to changes in leadership can disrupt this. Further, although all organizations are subject to leadership alterations, the two-year tour of duty is widespread and enforced in many military organizations.

The second major difference is the need to cope with two states: peace-time state, which is largely predictable, based around training schedules and below capacity, and a combat or "surge" state which is essentially unpredictable (Hines and Samuel, 2005) but likely to be near, at, or above capacity (Godsell et al., 2006). While conventional lean organizations clearly have the need to change capacity, the combination of the change from planned to unpredictable with response imperative of a combat state combines to produce a challenging two-state environment for military organizations. Overlaid upon this is the desire to cut military budgets in a challenging public sector environment (Figure 29.1), thus providing an intolerance of excess capacity (equates to cost) in a peace-time state.

The third difference is the complex enterprise nature of the process. An example of this is shown in Figure 29.2 in the case study in this chapter. Three levels of the supply chain are shown. Strike command that trains and delivers air defense, the JIPT that services and maintains aircraft (at multiple sites), and DARA (Defence Aviation Repair Agency) and suppliers from industry that

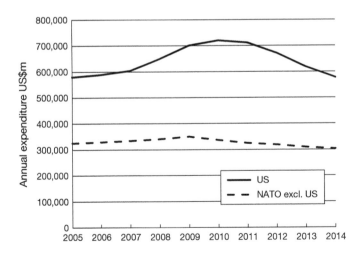

Figure 29.1   Annual military expenditure for all NATO (excluding US) and US

Source: Information from the Stockholm International Peace Research Institute (SIPRI) (2015).

provide spares and replacement parts. Alongside this supply chain is the governmental aspect of the military; in the UK this is the Ministry of Defence and in the US it is the Department of Defense. The role of these types of government organization is typified by the US Department of Defense mission: "The mission of the Department of Defense is to provide the military forces needed to deter war and to protect the security of our country" (Department of Defense, 2015). In the case of the Tornado aircraft in the case study, servicing and maintaining the aircraft is shared between a number of military and civil organizations in such a way that staff from different organizations are often co-located at either the RAF bases or supplier manufacturing and repair facilities.

This type of complexity is common in public sector organizations as highlighted by Boyne (2002) and can be strongly influenced by government policy. This political influence means that decisions about the design of the supply chain often have to take into account stakeholders from the wider community. For example, people who gain valued high-skill employment from military spares manufacture may strongly influence the retention of sites that are no longer in the best place for the supply chain in lean terms, as stated by Amicus (Manufacturing, technical and skilled persons' union) in 2004: "We need a UK defence procurement policy that works in tandem with our suppliers so these vital and high earning jobs can be safeguarded and the military can be supplied with the high quality apparatus they need." So the overall design of the supply chain cannot be solely based on a lean imperative; it is subject to military strategic requirements and political intervention.

The fourth difference is that the military in many major countries is not a growth environment. In NATO (excluding US) countries the military expenditure has been shrinking since 2009 with a peak of US$350,000 million, and US peaking in 2010 with US$720,220 million (SIPRI, 2015).

The consequence of this reducing budget is that resources liberated by lean improvements may not be redeployed. This affects military personnel and civil servants who could then be subject to redundancy, and suppliers to the military who face smaller future business contracts with the associated consequences of reduced profit and redundancy. Clearly reducing budgets are an issue faced by many public services. The impact of lean in the military will be similar in that the motivation to participate at either an individual or organizational level will be reduced if adverse consequences are likely.

The final difference relates to specific activities in the military that service and repair hardware in contrast to original manufacture where lean ideas were initially conceived. Our case study focuses on service and repair, along with many other studies on the application of lean in the military (Agripino et al., 2002; Cullen et al., 2005; DLO News, 2005; National Audit Office, 2007). The implication of a service and repair environment is that the main purpose of the function is to respond to incoming equipment for scheduled service or unscheduled repair, and overhaul it to achieve the required quality standard. The unpredictability of the incoming equipment to be serviced causes additional variability in the process that would not usually be present in lean manufacturing processes. An example could be an aircraft engine coming in for a regular service: while most of the processing requirements could be predicted, quality tests can highlight unexpected repairs known as "arisings." Arisings add additional load to the servicing team and can delay the return of the engine to the pool of spares.

Consideration of Lean Principles in the Armed Forces

These five differences result in the need to consider the impact on the principles of lean as laid out by Womack and Jones (2003): value, waste, flow, pull, and perfection.

The first lean principle is "value for the customer." This principle is mostly affected by the complexity of the extended enterprise and the different stakeholders in this enterprise including members of the military, defense-related civil servants, the defense ministry, governing politicians, the tax-paying public, and, beyond state borders, militarily allied countries. Designers of the military value stream need to take into account and reconcile what value is for this diverse range of stakeholders. This complexity of value to stakeholders is not unique to the military and reflects a problem common to public sector organizations (see Radnor et al., 2015).

The next principles of waste, and design of the value stream to enable flow, work well in the military within the limitations placed on the design by the multiple stakeholder environment. The two-state demand pattern can be challenging in terms of efficient design, but given the need to design to these two states, principles of waste and a value stream are well executed. However, the effect of service and repair affects the principle of a pull system. Service and repair to some extent does "pull" repaired equipment from the process. However, the main trigger to work is not from a demand signal at the end of the process as in conventional lean, but an input into the system in the form of equipment to be serviced. The idea of "pull" thus becomes a misnomer. A deeper consideration of the idea of "pull" is explored in Powell and Arica (2015) who conducted a literature review drawing from production management, project management, and supply chain management. Powell and Arica did not specifically consider a service and repair system, but did highlight the problem of oversimplification of the principle of pull in different situations and explored different interpretations of pull. In the case of military service and repair a better way of considering the signal to work and the system's ability to respond to it is the idea of "demand readiness" (Bateman et al., 2014).

The idea of demand readiness is that the service is ready to respond to demands placed on it. The signal of demand is *placed*, and this signal can be a pull, push, or other type of signal that meets the needs of the stakeholders. Demand readiness is about understanding demand patterns, both in terms of volume and nature, then ensuring the system is best placed to respond to these demands. This idea of demand readiness is not unique to military systems and is often required in patient-centered processes where the patient presents as a signal to work. For example, in emergency care the arrival of a patient not at a scheduled appointment is the signal placed on the healthcare system that there is demand to which the healthcare system needs to respond.

Finally, the principle of striving for perfection is most affected by the hierarchical nature of military organizations. Perfection as recommended by Womack and Jones (2003) is best pursued by "*radical and continuous improvement*" (p. 94); radical improvement is top down and continuous improvement is bottom up. Striving for perfection through top-down systems design could be enhanced by the military structure. This has, however, not been an area for which we have found evidence, but could perhaps form an area for further research. However, CI activities can be impeded by the command structure (Feld, 1959) inherent in military organizations as it does not necessarily sit well with the consensual nature of continuous improvement activities (Laraia et al., 1999; Kang and Apte, 2007).

The Future of Lean in the Armed Forces

Three main aspects influence the future for lean in the military: how lean matures as a general way of working, how military activities respond to their changing role, and how lean is applied in the public sector. This advances two main areas for applying lean in military organizations:

1   *How lean informs change in the military*: This change is likely to be derived from two sources, first the changing role of the military in our society and second from the reform of public sector organizations (Bateman et al., 2015). Lean could inform how these changes are

implemented but does not have to. The extent to which it does depends on the will and knowledge of key decision makers.

2 *How to mature lean in the military*: As military organizations change from being new to lean ways of working to being more experienced, military organizations need to decide how they want to apply lean. They could continue to apply lean in a traditional "improve the work" way. More significantly, they could evolve to seeing it as an improvement approach and use lean as a way of creating a cultural change in the thinking and behavior of all their people.

To some extent how lean matures as a subject and whether it remains regarded as a separate way of managing will affect how both of these areas develop. However, if the military follows other sectors then it is likely that there will be greater emphasis on lean as a "system of improvement" and the more strategic and human aspects of lean (Hines et al., 2011).

Case Study: Lean in the Royal Air Force's Tornado JIPT

This case focuses on the Royal Air Force's Tornado Joint Integrated Project Team (JIPT), part of the British Royal Air Force. The JIPT was a partnership between the Royal Air Force, BAE Systems, and Rolls-Royce. Its responsibility was to maintain the Tornado aircraft, the RAF's "all weather attack aircraft" (Royal Air Force, 2013) to provide a "fit for purpose" aircraft for RAF Strike Command (Figure 29.2).

The JIPT was supplied by DARA and other military commercial suppliers with spares and expertise regarding maintenance issues. The JIPT had decided to implement lean within its five

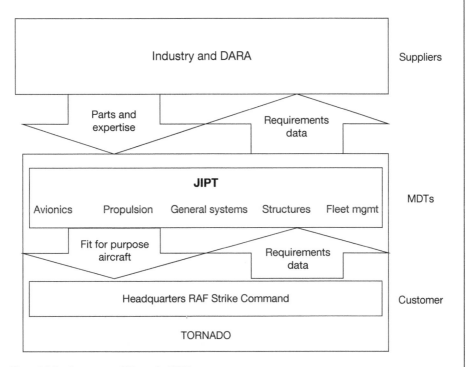

Figure 29.2 Structure of Tornado JIPT

multidisciplinary teams (MDTs) to support maintenance and repair of the Tornado aircraft. The authors of this chapter were commissioned to review critically the lean activities with the JIPT over a period of three-and-a-half years, specifically looking at four operational-level rapid improvement activities (RIAs) and 18-month implementation of performance measures for the JIPT within each MDT.

The review of the lean activities in the Tornado JIPT resulted in the differences identified in the main body of this chapter being recognized. In addition, common lean tools such as 5S, standard operations (SOP), and visual management were examined and were found to be useful in this environment and "robust in their applicability" (Bateman et al., 2014, p. 562).

In terms of the lean principles, an interesting variation on the idea of "pull" is where the Royal Air Force has adopted the concept of a "*pulse*" line. A pulse line responds when an aircraft needs servicing; it combines the idea of demand readiness with low volume and high technical complexity. It consists of a number of different stages (that act like manufacturing cells) that specialize in servicing part of the aircraft. The aircraft moves from stage to stage after each pulse and emerges having had a complete service. The pulse line at RAF Cottesmore had a throughput time of 60 days so although there is flow it is substantially slower than conventional lean and intermittent, hence the name pulse (Becker, 2003; DLO, 2005). Such a pulse line is highly applicable to a "runner" environment where demand is stable and predictable and the product is standard (as in the new build of aircraft). However, it becomes more problematic when applied to a "repeater" or "stranger" environment such as aircraft repair.

References

Agripino, M. Cathcart, T. and Mathaisel, D. (2002). A lean sustainment model for military systems. *Acquisition Review Quarterly, 9* (Fall), 275–296.

Bateman, N., Hines, P. and Davidson, P. (2014). Wider applications for lean: An examination of the fundamental principles within public sector organisations. *International Journal of Productivity and Performance Management, 63*(5), 550–568.

Bateman, N., Maher, J. and Randall, R. (2015) Drivers of change in the UK Fire Service: An operations management perspective. In: Radnor, Z., Bateman, N., Esain, A., Kumar, M., Williams, S. and Upton, D. (eds), *Public Service Operations Management: A Research Handbook*, London, Routledge, pp. 139–155.

Becker, D. (2003). *The Boeing 737/757 Lean Story*. Available at: www.nsrp.org/Industry_Initiatives/lean_shipbuilding_initiative/lean/presentations/4a.pdf. (accessed July 10, 2015).

Boyne, G. A. (2002). Public and private management: What's the difference? *Journal of Management Studies, 39*(1), 97–122.

Cullen, P. A., Hickman, R., Keast, J. and Valadez, M. (2005). The application of lean principles to in-service support: A comparison between construction and the aerospace defence sectors. *Lean Construction Journal, 2*(1), 87–104.

Department of Defense (2015). *Department of Defense*. Available at: www.defense.gov/about/ (accessed June 15, 2015).

DLO News (2005). How logistics have been transformed at RAF Cottesmore. Available at: www.mod.uk/linked_files/dlo/DLO_News_ISSUE_25_section2.pdf.

Feld, M. D. (1959). Information and authority: The structure of military organization. *American Sociological Review* (Feb.), 15–22.

Kang, K. and Apte, U. (2007). Lean Six Sigma implementation for military logistics to improve readiness, *4th Annual Acquisition Research Symposium, Thursday Sessions*, May 16–17. URL ADA493547.

Godsell, J., Harrison, A., Emberson, C. and Storey, J. (2006). Customer responsive supply chain strategy: An unnatural act? *International Journal of Logistics Research & Applications, 9*(1), 47–56.

Hines, P. and Samuel, D. (2005), Runners, repeaters & strangers: A contingent approach to lean thinking. Logistics Research Network, Plymouth University, September, *Conference Proceedings, Chartered Institute of Transport & Logistics*, pp. 179–184.

Hines, P., Found, P., Griffiths, G. and Harrison, R. (2011). *Staying Lean: Thriving, Not Just Surviving*, Boca Raton, FL, CRC Press.

Laraia, A. C., Moody, P. E. and Hall, R. W. (1999). *The Kaizen Blitz: Accelerating Breakthroughs in Productivity and Performance*, New York, John Wiley & Sons.

NAO – National Audit Office (2007). *Transforming Logistics Support for Fast Jets*, No. 0825 2006–07, London, The Stationery Office.

Powell, D. and Arica, E. (2015). To pull or not to pull: A concept lost in translation? *American Journal of Management*, *15*(2), 64–73.

Radnor, Z., Bateman, N., Esain, A., Kumar, M., Williams, S. and Upton, D. (eds) (2015). *Public Service Operations Management: A Research Handbook*, London, Routledge.

Royal Air Force (2013). Tornado GR4 website. Available at: www.raf.mod.uk/equipment/tornado.cfm (accessed August 2013).

SIPRI, Stockholm International Peace Research Institute (2015). SIPRI NATO Milex Data. Available at: www.sipri.org/research/armaments/milex/milex_database/nato-milex-data-1949–2014 (accessed June 15, 2015).

Womack, J. P. and Jones, D. T. (2003). *Lean Thinking: Banish Waste and Create Wealth in Your Corporation*, New York, Simon & Schuster.

30

LEAN POLICING

Harry Barton, Rupert L. Matthews, and Peter E. Marzec

Introduction

An effective and legitimate police service represents a fundamental cornerstone of a developed nation. However, such services need to be located within a new age of public sector finances that call for budgetary responsibility, greater levels of efficiency, and a need for the provision of value-for-money services (Radnor and Osborne, 2013). Such changes have been further accelerated by global economic changes in public sector finances. In the UK, this was evident in the government's comprehensive spending reviews of 2010 and 2015, which resulted in increased external pressures on previously protected public services to make tangible changes in service structure in order to deliver significant savings. In addition to reductions in central funding, service complexity has also placed significant pressure on public services and particularly the police forces in England and Wales due to the continuing evolution of the communities they serve. In addition to the not inconsequential task of providing similar services while making significant cost savings, there is also a need to radically reimagine what police forces deliver, what they look like, and how they operate (Barton, 2013). Similar transformations have taken place in the private sector, with the implementation of lean providing a potentially relevant framework with which to pursue such reform. However, traditional conceptualizations of lean have been identified as inappropriate for the public sector (Radnor and Osborne, 2013).

Barton (2013) presented the police as an expensive public service that had resisted previous attempts at reform. While possessing many similar characteristics to other public services, such as multiple stakeholders and complexity, difficulties in implementing police reform provide a unique context in which to research public service reform. Although Radnor and Osborne (2013) suggested that knowledge played a key role in revising public sector theory, Harvey et al. (2010) took an explicit knowledge-based approached to exploring performance improvement in public service operations. Specifically, they drew from absorptive capacity theory (Cohen and Levinthal, 1990) to illustrate the strengths of a knowledge-based perspective and how it could support the development of understanding of public services. Absorptive capacity provides a framework that acknowledges the need for organizations to actively develop internal capability that supports firms in acquiring, assimilating, and making use of knowledge that originates beyond firm boundaries.

This chapter therefore seeks to reconceptualize the implementation of traditional approaches to "lean" that often focus upon small-scale and rapid improvement activities. By taking a critical perspective on empirical observations of a successful lean implementation, new insight is developed on how to facilitate greater success in lean implementations. By taking a knowledge-based perspective, the critical deconstruction of "lean" aims to present it as a means of developing awareness of the need to change, the accumulation of understanding, and the motivation to deliver organizational change. This process will be interpreted through a revised absorptive capacity conceptual framework that builds upon the two-stage process presented by Zahra and George (2002). This conceptualization of *absorptive capacity* acknowledges there is a need for accepting information about the need to make changes as well as possessing internal capabilities to integrate knowledge into organizational processes, in order to realize organizational change.

What is Lean Policing?

Browning and Eppinger (2002, p. 428) state that "process improvement requires process understanding" where it is necessary for practitioners to explore operational processes in order to make appropriate changes that will deliver the desired improvements. Similarly, Radnor and Osborne (2013) highlight how improvement interventions were not about learning tools to make change; rather they were about supporting participants in building an understanding of what improvements aimed to achieve. From this perspective, while there may be a need for those implementing lean to learn about particular tools and techniques, emphasis needs to be given to the underlying principles of lean and how the tools can help develop new knowledge and understanding of operational practices.

The accumulation of knowledge has been identified as the key component of competitive advantage in a modern environment (Grant, 1996). Previous research in operations improvement initiatives has illustrated the critical role of knowledge as an outcome of improvement projects (Choo et al., 2007; Anand et al., 2010). Improvement activities can produce both explicit knowledge, in the form of operational procedures, and tacit knowledge, such as changes to individual values, mindsets, and beliefs. In combination, these help to capture and transfer the outputs of projects across the organization while promoting the acceptance of new operational procedures. Hines et al. (2004) applied the knowledge-based perspective specifically within lean by conceptualizing it as an organizational learning process. Drawing from Fiol and Lyles (1985, p. 803), they present lean as "a process of improving action through better knowledge and understanding." By focusing on lean as a framework for knowledge creation, Hines et al. (2004) demonstrated how the pursuit of lean provided firms with a sustainable competitive advantage.

This perspective on operational improvement and lean activities appreciates the mechanisms that require knowledge to change operational systems and reflect organizational requirements, a necessity within public service organizations (Betts and Holden, 2003). As a result, insight is provided on why the acquisition of information, knowledge, or external performance measurement data on their own may not initiate organizational change. Additionally, while there may be an awareness of a need to change, Fiol and Lyles (1985) illustrated that it may require the onset of an organizational crisis to accept new knowledge and discard accepted approaches to operating. Within the private sector, it was not until local manufacturers had experienced significant reductions in their market share that firms began to accept the merits of their international competitors.

In addition to an organization's willingness to accept externally originating information, in order to realize change knowledge has to be interpreted by the organization and disseminated in order to affect subsequent behavior (Crossan et al., 1999). March (1991) conceptualized this process in terms of organizations being able to adapt to account for the introduction of new organizational members. He stated that unless firms regularly introduced members (or new ways of operating) and adapted their processes to account for the new insight, they became unable to learn from new sources of information, instead favoring continuing to refine existing operational processes. Within the context of policing, such phenomena can be interpreted as an organization looking internally when making improvements, and developing operational practices, processes, institutions, and doctrine over significant periods of time. Even though recruits provide a regular source of new organizational members, they join the organization at lower ranks so are less likely to be able to realize significant organizational change. By developing and institutionalizing organizational codes of practice, through training biased toward socialization (Fiol and Lyles, 1985), the police are potentially less likely or able to accept new knowledge originating from external sources.

March's (1991) work appears pertinent to the police context, where attention is given to formalized roles and hierarchical structure, with seniority related to tenure. Unfortunately, when individuals have seniority, the length of tenure may result in them being unable to question existing practice or resisting changes to institutionalized processes. Absorptive capacity therefore both highlights this issue and provides a means for addressing it. In the foundational work on the theory, Cohen and Levinthal (1990, p. 133) presented this as rejecting knowledge that was "*not-invented-here*," which resulted from a lack of related knowledge or poor absorptive capacity. The lack of related knowledge is therefore a double-edged sword—it both prevents individuals and organizations from appreciating the value associated with acquired knowledge and prevents the integration of the newly acquired knowledge with existing knowledge in order to create new, organization-specific knowledge. Through the processes of learning about new acquired knowledge, firms can develop a greater absorptive capacity to engage in innovative behaviors, without necessarily coming up with the original idea.

This leads to the identification of two key learning processes that determine how organizations, and specifically police forces, engage in learning, organizational improvement, and ultimately innovative practices. First, how police forces identify the need to change and which sources of information they are able to make use of. Second, how they implement change to account for the information they acquire. This second process not only relies on the knowledge within the organization to motivate and make changes, but also the ability to absorb externally originating knowledge and resources if there is insufficient internal knowledge to make changes. Zahra and George (2002) conceptualized this learning process as a two-stage model of absorptive capacity: the need to access new knowledge and appreciate the value of it (potential absorptive capacity); and the implementation of change through the application of new knowledge (realized absorptive capacity). Both Harvey et al. (2010) and Hodgkinson et al. (2012) have illustrated that absorptive capacity represents an appropriate theoretical perspective for use within public sector research. Hodgkinson et al. (2012) illustrated the impact the increased complexity of public sector organizations has on the relationship between absorptive capacity and firm performance, illustrating the need for more conceptual development.

In addition to these two learning processes, Zahra and George (2002) also propose that the relationship between potential and realized absorptive capacity is moderated by social integration mechanisms. Within wider management, the characteristics of external connections and social integration (or social capital) have been identified as key determinants of organizations' ability to accept and create new knowledge (Nahapiet and Ghoshal, 1998). Social capital acknowledges that it is not only the presence of connections, but also the strength and type of connections that determine the benefits organizations are able to realize. With the police context tending to be focused upon internally developed knowledge, the nature of the connection between external sources is likely to have a notable impact on whether the information is accepted. However, it is not only whether the knowledge can be accepted but also whether change can be realized by mobilizing internal resources, highlighting that both internal and external social capital are critical for realizing benefits from external knowledge (Adler and Kwon, 2002).

Although Harvey et al. (2010) made a clear distinction between the learning and knowledge-based perspectives on public sector management, Sun and Anderson (2010) illustrated how Zahra and George's (2002) conceptualization of absorptive capacity was structurally consistent with the 4I (intuiting, interpreting, integrating, and institutionalizing) framework of organizational learning (Crossan et al., 1999). The key realization here is that knowledge is created at different organizational levels, from acceptance at an individual level to strategic renewal at an organizational level, and critically that there exist feed-forward and feedback processes between the resources present at different organizational levels (Crossan et al., 1999).

With the impact of established practices within the police force, combined with the hierarchical structure, appreciation of the role of power and politics in realizing organizational change is also critical. Lawrence et al. (2005) acknowledge the inherently political nature of organizations and extended this 4I framework of organizational learning by discussing the framework in relation to politics and power. Rather than the best ideas being selected and integrated into organizational processes, individuals with power, or knowledge of political processes, could integrate knowledge *they* consider important into organizational processes. Senior management may also be more attuned to information being presented by particular organizational members or relevant experts than other less credible sources. Lawrence et al. (2005) also stated that if new interpretations were forced on organizational members, changes were more likely to fail, meet with resistance, or involve high costs, all critical factors to consider when making organizational change.

In summary, these discussions identify elements of an overarching framework through which to view processes of organizational improvement, change, and knowledge within the context of policing. This leads to the development of a conceptual framework, informed by Zahra and George's (2002), but adapted for the requirements of the police context (Figure 30.1).

Explaining the Framework

Figure 30.1 provides a framework for analyzing organizational change processes that draws from a selection of influential theoretical perspectives. Within the framework, change is considered to be initiated by change stimulus (#1); in the case of policing, this was the reduction in central government funding and the increase in service complexity from the changing requirements of the public. Consistent with organizational learning, change may be initiated by identified opportunities or awareness of alternate, more effective, lean ways of working (Fiol and Lyles, 1985). Dependent on the nature of the connection, or the form of information (#2), it is likely to affect the organization in different ways. If the connection is with a trusted source or has considerable power (central government, for example), the information will motivate new learning behaviors (#3), such as learning more about what the impact of the acquired information may be. Conversely, if the source of the information is not known, trusted, and does not apply political pressure, while there may be an awareness of a need to change, no actual change may take place, potentially if it is considered that information "does not apply to us." Over-focus on the development of internally focused social capital (Adler and Kwon, 2002), a lack of new members (March, 1991), or lack of related knowledge (Cohen and Levinthal, 1990) can all impact the ability to accept externally originating information.

The exploration of newly acquired topics, concepts, and the need to change can help build what Zahra and George (2002) present as potential absorptive capacity. This effectively consists of

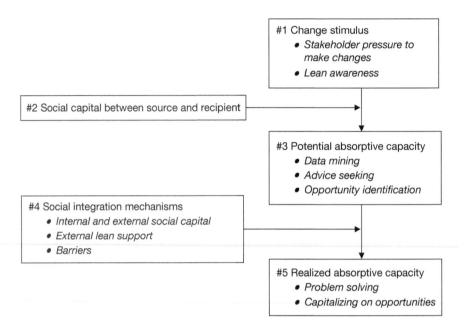

Figure 30.1 Conceptual framework of implementing lean in the police force

those in the organization building an understanding of the opportunity for improvement, a key factor in public sector lean implementation (Radnor and Osborne, 2013), or what we term opportunity recognition. Developing understanding can also help determine whether it is actually appropriate or necessary to react to the acquired information. In such cases, the scope of the change may fall within the level of absorptive capacity of the organization, therefore the change becomes obvious. If not, it might necessitate the need to search for confirmation and advice outside the organization, or what we term advice seeking. Finally, organizations may proactively search for opportunities for change, which is aligned with the "continuous pursuit of perfection" principle of lean. In such cases, this may manifest as the proactive searching and discovery of knowledge and change opportunities, or what we term data mining.

Following the development of potential absorptive capacity, it is necessary to translate the accumulated knowledge into changes in organizational behavior. To realize change, drawing from Lawrence et al. (2005) and Zahra and George (2002), it is necessary to overcome internal resistance to change and it may also be necessary to gain access to additional knowledge and resources to facilitate change. This process will thus require internal social capital in order to motivate organizational change activities, as well as external social capital to gain access to external resources that can be integrated into the organization (#4). Following the acceptance of the need to change and external resources, change activities that take the form of problem solving and capitalizing on opportunities will result in organizational change (#5). The case study provides an example of a successful change activity that is related to the different elements of the conceptual framework.

Discussion

The case illustration of the implementation of lean in a selection of UK police forces (see case study) provides insight on the relevance of the proposed framework (Figure 30.1) for implementing lean activities within the police. By giving emphasis to what initiates improvement, activities that take place within the force at multiple levels and involve multiple stakeholders, the framework highlights the complexity of operational improvement activities, particularly within the police context. By taking a much broader perspective of the implementation of lean, weight is given to viewing lean as more than simply the transfer of tools from the manufacturing context.

The tools did, however, provide two main functions, with an additional indirect function. Initially the problem-solving tools promoted the deconstruction of the existing processes, to identify sources of problems and direct potential changes that could be made. This supported unquestioned assumptions about organizational processes to be openly critiqued, in order to provide a foundation for new processes that built upon the knowledge that had been created. The second function of the lean tools was to help embed new operational processes, through the use of daily meetings and visual management to maintain changes and support the identification of further improvement opportunities. The indirect benefit was how group discussions that resulted from both sets of tools promoted the sharing of insight that supported individuals in changing their perceptions of operational processes. With policing practice historically based on social-ization activities, the elements of lean that support the changing of embedded and potentially tacit perceptions of how organizational processes work appear critical.

An additional enabling factor of lean in the police context was how the improvement was initiated that ensured that management were aware of the need for change and provided the necessary resources to realize change. Key within the hierarchically structured police context was the power to overcome any resistance of those involved in the improvement activities to ensure the necessary commitment to achieving results, and facilitate contributions from external part-ners. This ensured those with responsibility and knowledge about the poorly performing process were able to contribute to improvement activities, helping identify why the problem had occurred. Due to the external and formal nature of the audit within the Welsh force, it was necessary for force management to be actively involved in resolving the issues identified. The audit also provided focus for the improvement activity and a measurement framework against which success could be assessed. The second aspect, which led directly from the focus given to the initiative, was the provision of the support of external sources that provided lean knowledge, rather than instruction on how improvement activities should be carried out.

Finally, the level of engagement of those involved in the improvement activities promoted the use of procedures once they were implemented. By involving a range of parties, the revised procedures reduced complexity and removed activities that may have previously caused frus-tration and delay. By creating new knowledge that resulted in an improved process, individuals were motivated to use the revised procedure simply because it was better. Visual management tools then ensured the procedure was adhered to as well as demonstrating that they continued to achieve the original aims of the initiative, supporting the embedding of new practices. Complementing this element, formal metrics and key performance indicators helped illustrate to external stakeholders that the refined procedure was an improvement on the previous process. While providing validation for those involved in the initiative that their work had been suc-cessful, such measures of performance built support within management for further improvement activities and the resources that may be required. Reflecting back on the theoretical underpinning of the conceptual framework, this represents the development of managerial absorptive capacity that will more readily accept support, and deliver further change activities.

The Future of Lean Policing

The findings provide a broad picture of the practices and parties engaged in an initial application of lean within English and Welsh police forces, with particular emphasis on a more successful lean intervention. However, the activities reported in this chapter were related to initial improvement activities, or pilots, with either explicit or implicit attention given to determining whether a "lean" transformation was appropriate within the context of policing. This characteristic of the improvement activities is consistent with when the research was conducted. While the comprehensive spending review required initial cost savings, savings were not required for a considerable period of time or could be achieved without requiring significant change activities. Radnor and Osborne (2013, p. 275) spoke of this as realizing such cost savings by picking the "low hanging fruit (and windfalls!)" of existing process inefficiencies. Consequently, it was difficult for any of the case forces, even the Welsh force, to be viewed as having undertaken fundamental organizational change, a requirement of lean policing. Instead, improvements and learning outcomes were related to particular operational processes, building awareness of certain "lean" techniques.

As the second phase of the comprehensive spending reviews starts being implemented, police forces across England and Wales will be required to deliver considerable cost savings that may not be possible without considerable changes to their size and shape. Notwithstanding lean's focus on removing waste, with wages constituting the majority of police spending (around 80 percent) it is unlikely that all savings can be made by removing waste and redistributing resources. Consequently, to achieve significant cost savings, it is almost inevitable there will be redundancies. While there is potential to make savings by reducing recruitment, effectively not replacing those who retire, this can introduce further problems. Reflecting on March (1991), without a regular influx of new members, absorptive capacity may reduce further. Additionally, such an approach, if combined with limiting the promotion of those in the police force to control wage increases, may embed resistance or resentment in those who find themselves stuck in particular roles. This process has been defined as creating recalcitrant workers (Ackroyd and Thompson, 1999), who, while completing their work, actively resist involvement in organizational activities. With Barton and Barton (2011) stating the importance of involving the workforce in police reform, such issues are likely to cause further problems in the implementation of lean policing.

To achieve the requirements of the comprehensive review while avoiding potential problems, and maintaining the level of service, Barton (2013, p. 222) stated a need to "fundamentally review" existing police practices. Building upon Radnor and Osborne (2013), the implementation of lean may initially focus on achieving tangible cost savings by removing non-value-adding activities from existing processes. In comparison with the operational, process-level learning that took place within the illustrative case, attention also needs to be given to higher-level, strategic learning (Matthews et al., 2015). Womack and Jones (1996) stated that "*kaikaku,*" or radical improvement activities, were needed to realize the full benefits of lean. Furthermore, the seminal work on lean (Womack et al., 1990) also illustrates that the true achievement of lean is not realized through operational competence, but by integrating lean thinking into the nature of what is being delivered (whether products or services). Consequently, improvement frameworks that aim to completely change organizational structures may have value, by initially defining what the end user requires of a service and then reengineering accordingly (Hammer and Champy, 1993). The evidence from the illustrative case begins to suggest that lean techniques may provide a useful first step, on a longer road to transformation, by increasing awareness of the need for more fundamental change. Following implementation of such radical change, understanding of lean techniques may then support the refinement and improvement of reengineered processes, while also maintaining involvement of those affected.

The identified framework of absorptive capacity provides a broad framework for further research within this domain. The framework introduces a new theoretical perspective on lean policing, moving away from the relevance of traditional lean techniques to a new context.

Instead, the current research explores the role of knowledge acquisition, learning, and knowledge creation processes within the wider context of organizational change. Drawing from research work on the evolution of lean (Hines et al., 2004), the research suggests the need for the police to use lean and related improvement frameworks to develop their own context-specific improvement frameworks. Such a perspective gives greater attention to lean as a tool for knowledge creation, rather than a set of tools that were developed for use in a fundamentally different environment. The research also highlights the importance of carefully defining the aims of improvement activities in order to focus change activities in addition to validating the effectiveness of any changes that are made.

With over five years more experience of organizational change, police forces can be viewed as making progress on a "lean journey." While the improvements reported in this chapter may not provide examples of lean transformations, these pilots provide those affected with awareness of the potential for organizational change, helping them consider what lean policing may consist of. Reflecting on Hines et al. (2004), progress can be viewed as moving beyond a tools-based approach to lean, toward lean becoming part of police organizational culture. To complement a focus on the removal of waste, attention will also need to be given to comprehensively re-imagining what constitutes a "lean" police force. Further research is needed to explore the lean journey of how improvement interventions have been embedded into police organizations following on from the current research and the comprehensive spending review of 2015. Rather than looking at isolated improvement activities, the exploration of broader change activities could provide insight into changing organizational structures and the roles of external parties as well as collaboration across forces. This will help provide rich data through which to explore the relevance of our proposed absorptive capacity conceptual framework within the implementation of lean policing and policing reform, helping build a picture of what constitutes "lean policing." Further direction can then be provided to practice in terms of what forms of knowledge acquisition, learning, knowledge creation, and support are required to realize wholesale transformation of policing services.

Case Study: Lean Policing in a Welsh Police Force

The conceptual framework in Figure 30.1 was applied to a number of UK police forces involved in a variety of lean implementation initiatives. While elements of the framework were apparent within each of the cases, from various types of initiating information and support, the Welsh force in particular adhered to the framework consistently. While this case will provide the focus of the case discussion, other forces involved in the research project will be drawn from to provide counter-arguments.

The lean activity within the Welsh force was initiated by a critical audit of the arrest process that was sponsored by the Crown Prosecution Service that worked closely with the force. Irrespective of whether the force had sufficient knowledge of operational improvement approaches, the audits provided force-specific feedback that highlighted how the arrest process was not fit for purpose and required changing (#1). By introducing this information through senior management, it built commitment of those with access to the necessary resources to make the changes to improve the process (potential absorptive capacity (#3)). In combination with the organization that had carried out the audit, a multi-agency workshop investigated the identified problem (#4). This ensured that the focus of the improvement workshop was on developing an understanding of the issues identified by the audit.

The external support allowed the force to engage with, and apply, a number of the lean tools and techniques in order to explore and solve the issues (i.e. problem solving in realized absorptive capacity in the conceptual framework (#5)). Instead of training focusing on how to use the tools, the involvement of the external party facilitated the use of the tools to analyze and effectively deconstruct the arrest process. The tools, which included brainstorming and five whys, were used to explore the arrest process, and provided a foundation to construct value stream maps to illustrate how value was added to the end users (including the Crown Prosecution Service). The cross-functional nature of the workshops ensured that the developed process map reflected the combined knowledge of those involved, enabling the removal of duplicate activities, while giving greater attention to key activities. The cross-functional nature also ensured that any changes made to the arrest process could be considered in terms of their impact on all stakeholders involved.

Complementing the knowledge creation through cross-functional workshops, additional lean management practices were employed to establish the new knowledge within the force. By making changes to organizational processes, the improvement activity had tangible outputs in the form of changes to the arrest practice. The changes to practice provided evidence that addressed concerns raised by the audit, while also providing measures to illustrate some cost savings.

Although the immediate change to the process provided tangible improvements, the tacit knowledge created during the improvement activity was likely to play a key role in the acceptance of new practices (i.e. social capital developed during the improvement activity (#4)). However, to prevent practices reverting before they had become embedded, the Welsh force applied further lean tools. The force utilized visual management tools to ensure practices were maintained, while also illustrating the impact of changes to external parties. The force integrated visual management into daily team briefings, supporting the continued use of the revised process, helping embed revised perceptions of the process, while also creating new knowledge in those who may not have been involved in the original lean initiative (Anand et al., 2010). This ensured that the outcome of the improvement activities became embedded in the organization, and did not only affect those directly involved in the improvement workshop.

In comparison with the Welsh lean initiative, other forces involved in the research experienced a range of difficulties that resulted in limited benefits being realized from their lean implementations. Other improvements were initiated by imposed cost saving that appeared to provide insufficient motivation to make improvements, or lean was not considered by senior management as an appropriate means of making changes. Many of the forces received funding to support them in pursuing productivity and performance improvements; however, support and involvement of external parties were not focused on particular organizational issues. Combined with not engaging directly with force senior management, only small savings were realized that were not considered sufficient to justify the continued implementation of lean. The less successful cases illustrate important factors in implementing lean within the police context, such as building acceptance of the need to change at senior management level, providing resources to make changes, and integrating changes with existing processes. Such activities appear to ensure tangible changes were made that benefited end users and improvements could be validated and sustained over time.

The focus by the Welsh force on implementing lean within the arrest process appears to play a key role in sustaining change. This process ensured the learning that took place from involvement in the lean activities did not only take place at an individual level but led to changes at an organizational level, illustrating the link between absorptive capacity and organizational learning (Sun and Anderson, 2010). At an individual level, the processes ensured the new knowledge became part of individuals' perceptions of how practices should take place, developing favorable perceptions of engagement and support in any further lean activities. These changes in perceptions also included individual-level understanding of the role of other agencies, facilitating group-level, cross-agency work within existing and further lean activities. This was stated by those involved in the activities as resulting in changes in the culture of parts of the force.

Further benefits were also realized by the Welsh force that were a result of activities that focused not just internally. By linking the outcomes of the improvement initiative to the initial external audit, it was possible to effectively communicate key measurable outcomes to external stakeholders. This provided a means of demonstrating benefits that had been realized and illustrating the impact of any investment that had been made. Within the wider context of policing reform, both the involvement of external stakeholders in the activities and communication following the activities supported the development of understanding and motivation to engage in further improvement activities. With less adherence to the conceptual framework, the other forces involved in the research had much greater difficulty in realizing and demonstrating sustained changes from involvement in lean initiatives. However, due to the pilot nature of each of the initiatives, while improvements were not embedded in one case, the potential absorptive capacity part of the framework (see Figure 30.1, steps #1, #2, and #3) provided some insight. Rather than the improvement activities resulting in tangible change, they supported the development of understanding that itself built potential absorptive capacity. This led the chief constable of the force to view the activities as a success, and to review how services needed to be restructured. Such an increase in potential absorptive capacity could lead to follow-up improvement activities necessary for developing realized absorptive capacity.

References

Ackroyd, S. and Thompson, P. (1999). *Organizational Misbehaviour*, London, Sage Publications.

Adler, P. S. and Kwon, S. W. (2002). Social capital: Prospects for a new concept. *Academy of Management Review*, 27(1), 17–40.

Anand, G., Ward, P. T. and Tatikonda, M. V. (2010). Role of explicit and tacit knowledge in Six Sigma projects: An empirical examination of differential project success. *Journal of Operations Management*, 28(4), 303–315.

Barton, H. (2013). "Lean" policing? New approaches to business process improvement across the UK police service. *Public Money & Management*, 33(3), 221–224.

Barton, H. and Barton, L. C. (2011). Challenges, issues and change: What's the future for UK policing in the twenty-first century? *International Journal of Public Sector Management*, 24(2), 146–156.

Betts, J. and Holden, R. (2003). Organisational learning in a public sector organisation: A case study in muddled thinking. *Journal of Workplace Learning*, 15(6), 280–287.

Browning, T. R. and Eppinger, S. D. (2002). Modeling impacts of process architecture on cost and schedule risk in product development. *IEEE Transactions on Engineering Management*, 49(4), 428–442.

Choo, A. S., Linderman, K. W. and Schroeder, R. G. (2007). Method and psychological effects on learning behaviors and knowledge creation in quality improvement projects. *Management Science*, 53(3), 437–450.

Cohen, W. M. and Levinthal, D. A. (1990). Absorptive capacity: A new perspective on learning and innovation. *Administrative Science Quarterly*, 35(1), 128–152.

Crossan, M. M., Lane, H. W. and White, R. E. (1999). An organizational learning framework: From intuition to institution. *Academy of Management Review*, 24(3), 522–537.

Fiol, C. M. and Lyles, M. A. (1985). Organizational learning. *Academy of Management Review*, 10(4), 803–813.

Grant, R. M. (1996). Towards a knowledge-based theory of the firm. *Strategic Management Journal*, 17(S2), 109–122.

Hammer, M. and Champy, J. (1993). *Reengineering the Corporation: A Manifesto for Business Revolution*, London, Nicholas Brealey Publishing.

Harvey, G., Skelcher, C., Spencer, E., Jas, P. and Walshe, K. (2010). Absorptive capacity in a non-market environment: A knowledge-based approach to analysing the performance of sector organizations. *Public Management Review*, *12*(1), 77–97.

Hines, P., Holweg, M. and Rich, N. (2004). Learning to evolve: A review of contemporary lean thinking. *International Journal of Operations & Production Management*, *24*(10), 994–1011.

Hodgkinson, I. R., Hughes, P. and Hughes, M. (2012). Absorptive capacity and market orientation in public service provision. *Journal of Strategic Marketing*, *20*(3), 211–229.

Lawrence, T. B., Mauws, M. K., Dyck, B. and Kleysen, R. F. (2005). The politics of organizational learning: Integrating power into the 4I framework. *Academy of Management Review*, *30*(1), 180–191.

March, J. G. (1991). Exploration and exploitation in organizational learning. *Organization Science*, *2*(1), 71–87.

Matthews, R. L., Tan, K. H. and Marzec, P. E. (2015). Organisational ambidexterity within process improvement: An exploratory study of 4 project-oriented firms. *Journal of Manufacturing Technology Management*, *26*(4), 458–476.

Nahapiet, J. and Ghoshal, S. (1998). Social capital, intellectual capital, and the organizational advantage. *Academy of Management Review*, *23*(2), 242–266.

Radnor, Z. and Osborne, S. P. (2013). Lean: A failed theory for public services? *Public Management Review*, *15*(2), 265–287.

Sun, P. Y. T. and Anderson, M. H. (2010). An examination of the relationship between absorptive capacity and organizational learning, and a proposed integration. *International Journal of Management Reviews*, *12*(2), 130–150.

Womack, J. P. and Jones, D. T. (1996). *Lean Thinking: Banish Waste and Create Wealth in Your Corporation*, New York, Simon & Schuster.

Womack, J. P., Jones, D. T. and Roos, D. (1990). *The Machine that Changed the World*, New York, Rawson Associates.

Zahra, S. A. and George, G. (2002). Absorptive capacity: A review, reconceptualization, and extension. *Academy of Management Review*, *27*, 185–203.

31

LEAN JUSTICE

Ana Lúcia Martins, Isabell Storsjö, and Simone Zanoni

Introduction

Justice is a service provided to citizens by judicial bodies and other organizations in the public sphere, that is, courts, prosecutors, legal aid services, police, and prisons. The judicial system provides individuals and legal professionals with procedures for having disputes solved by a third party or having unlawful acts investigated and evaluated. Justice is also a societal value that encompasses legality, fairness, and equity.

Judicial bodies are, just like other public sector organizations, under pressure to become more efficient while simultaneously living up to citizens' expectations of being provided with high-quality and equitable services. Statistics on processing times and case backlogs show that much remains to be done to achieve efficient and effective justice. The right to a fair trial and the right to have one's case dealt with within a reasonable time have been the main issues in 43.13 percent of all violation judgments given by the European Court of Human Rights throughout its history (ECHR, 2015a) and were among the main issues for violation judgments in 2014 (ECHR, 2015b).

In the task of balancing efficiency with different quality dimensions in justice-making, lean thinking is a promising ideology for this setting. Lean has been widely applied, first in manufacturing systems and later in service contexts, to overcome problems, eliminate waste, and drive an organization to focus on customers and value creation. In this chapter, we elaborate on how lean can be applied in justice and how different wastes in this sector can be classified, and we identify unutilized opportunities to go leaner in this area.

What is Lean Justice?

The way in which legal (civil, criminal, or administrative) cases are dealt with and justice is "produced" is determined by regulations and traditions. Procedures are fairly standardized, and cases that fall within a certain category are processed in a similar way, no matter the scope or complexity of the case. The categories of disputes or crimes that can be taken up by a tribunal are predefined. The tribunal's task is to evaluate the arguments and evidence laid before it and to reach a conclusion that fulfills certain criteria. The full content and circumstances of a case and the final decision, however, are difficult to anticipate, and the amount and kind of resources (in terms of hours and special knowledge) required to reach a conclusion vary.

Justice-making is an information-processing service that is performed by legal professionals and other individuals with specific skills and training. Although public authorities are the main actors in the production of justice, legal processes often involve private actors such as law firms, postal services, transportation services, or consultants, in certain process stages and for particular activities. In order for justice to be achieved, the service process requires the involvement and input of different stakeholders; for example, citizens take part in legal processes in the role of claimants or victims, respondents or suspects, witnesses or jurors. The interests of some of these actors or stakeholders may conflict with the justice court processes' efficiency.

Judicial proceedings are co-produced processes that aim to re-establish social equilibrium after a disturbance occurs, by applying written or case-based norms that correspond to the social values of the community. There are a number of quality dimensions to consider, both regarding the outcome of the process and with respect to the case-handling process itself. These value dimensions include independence (of tribunals), trustworthiness, legal protection, rule of law, good governance, equity, and transparency. Speed and costs have also become important performance outcomes in legal processes due to budget constraints.

Following Womack and Jones' (2003) principles of lean, *lean justice* should be focused on value, processes, and the flow of cases through those processes. As such, it requires removing unnecessary steps in the legal process without losing sight of the quality of the decisions produced and the fundamental rights of each party involved. In other words, it is about reaching a fair decision within a timeline that fits the matter and uses resources in a rational way. The outcome of the proceedings, the final judgments, should be acceptable to both parties in the case and should be considered fair and correct by society as a whole.

From a legal perspective, quality can be assessed as the accuracy of the application of the norms and the wording of the verdict. From a lean perspective, the framing of the judgment might not create value. To be valuable, the final decision not only has to carry the assurance of quality, but it also needs to have been produced without undue delay and using resources proportional to the relevance of the case. This requires addressing waste in the judicial system.

Ohno (1988) proposed seven types of waste that can be found in manufacturing systems, and Maleyeff (2006) redefined these for a service system. Based on their classifications and the work by Mattsson (2014), Table 31.1 provides examples of corresponding waste that can be found in judicial systems.

The potentially non-value-adding activities are interrelated, and one type of waste might cause other types of waste. Whether or not the examples given in Table 31.1 can actually be seen as waste depends, according to Womack and Jones (2003), on the needs of the customer, but with reference to justice the definition of the customer is still a challenge that needs to be addressed.

Challenges

Adjusting justice to lean thinking involves revealing challenges that emerge from the fundamental principles of lean and from the distinctive features of the judicial system. Other challenges, such as the ones highlighted by Hines et al. (2008a) in their *lean iceberg model*, should also be addressed if sustainable change is to be achieved. The following topics analyze the challenges the judicial system is likely to face in attempting to become leaner.

The Challenge of Defining the Customer and Value

Johnston et al. (2012) differentiate between the customer, the payer, and the beneficiary of a service and conclude that all of them have to be considered in service delivery. In the justice

Table 31.1 Types of waste and their interpretations in judicial systems

Type of waste	Interpretation in judicial systems
Waiting/delays	Time goes by without activities being performed due to vacations, postponed hearings (e.g. because parties do not show up the first time and/or because of inflexible scheduling of hearing rooms), or a lack of balance of (human) resources between the different stages of the handling process (which creates queues in the process).
Inefficient use of resources	Technology is not used although available and allowed (from which follows more transportation of people and documents, which takes more time); shared court rooms stand empty while cases are waiting to be scheduled.
Overproduction	Imbalance between the effort put down in an activity in relation to the complexity of the case and the law.
Defects/mistakes	Procedural errors that lead to rework; decisions based on erroneous information.
Inspection	Preceding tasks are checked due to doubt that they have been performed correctly.
Transportation/ movement	Transportation or movement—of people and documents—due to poor layout or in circumstances where it would have been possible to use modern communication technology.
Unnecessary motion	Relates to ergonomics at work, but also switching between computer programs and documents due to complicated IT solutions and work tools.
Inappropriate processing	Some simple tasks could be performed by court employees other than judges; tools that would ease work are not used.
Duplication of activities	Unclear division of work tasks or different work routines in different locations causes work to be done twice; case files are read unnecessarily many times by court personnel due to disruptions in the work on the case.

system, activities that can be considered waste from one customer's perspective can be essential from another customer's standpoint (for instance, allowing additional time to provide evidence). At the same time, the parties do not support the full cost of the service. The society in which a dispute is brought for consideration in a tribunal wishes it to be decided with the use of the least amount of resources possible, as the cost of producing the decision will be covered (partly) through taxes. Subsequently, it is possible to define two levels of customers for the justice system service (Martins and Carvalho, 2005)—society as a whole and the parties involved—as well as two levels of payers and beneficiaries. These two levels have to be considered when defining the value created in the judicial system.

The exact value stream and activities required for each case are only known once the final decision is reached. As flexibility is required to assure fairness and equity, value varies not only from customer to customer but also from case to case.

The diversity of customers (users and beneficiaries, among others) of judicial services, together with the need to involve other actors and stakeholders in different stages of the judicial proceedings, leads to difficulties in defining value. In addition, balancing what each customer, payer, and beneficiary considers to be of value is a challenge the justice system has to continuously consider while producing its output and defining its value stream.

Challenges Relating to Strategy and Alignment

Management issues (namely the rational use of the resources available) are becoming strategic concerns of justice systems in addition to the traditional focus on fairness and legality.

The tendency to develop faster and more rational procedures that allow better use of available resources and deliver more value to customers may find some resistance in terms of one of the stakeholders of the judicial system—the lawyers. Developing more rational procedures, such as the European small claims procedure (ESCP), which can be used by individuals without the need of a legal counselor, may lead to a reduction in the demand for lawyers. This repositioning of legal procedures toward more efficient solutions may then face the external challenge of resistance from these professionals.

Measuring and monitoring are essential parts of strategy alignment, as they are what actually allow an understanding of whether the goals have been achieved throughout the system. Although changes can be seen at the top management level in the judicial systems, measurements remain as before (e.g. Pekkanen et al., 2009); that is, mostly focused on counting the number of entries and solved cases per year and the average time in the system for each type of case. No measures have yet been introduced to match the new concerns, which pose a major challenge if the alignment of a new and leaner approach is to be pursued (Hines et al., 2008a). The rigidity of the justice systems can also be seen as a concern for alignment, as it restrains the necessary adjustments. The fact that justice value streams are supported by and cross several entities poses an additional layer of challenge in aligning the overall strategy.

Challenges Relating to Leadership, Behavior, and Engagement

Resistance is to be expected when change is pursued. The engagement of the various entities involved is a way to help overcome that resistance. Implementing lean in the judicial system can be more or less challenging depending on the perspective it takes. Implementing it from the top of the system and imposing it upon the community (both final users and all those working through the process) does not create much room for engagement. Changes may end up not even pursuing actual value. However, approaching lean in the judicial system from the customers' perspective, that is from the perspective of the society being served by the procedures and of the parties involved, generates more commitment from those involved in the system and in change. Clients need to recognize the benefits from the lean intervention and the way it is addressing their needs. The ESCP is an example of a lean procedure developed to satisfy specific needs of speed and cost reduction for clients. If clients recognize the benefits from change, their behavior will positively influence the adoption of the process. In turn, this may even influence lawyers in the adoption of leaner legal procedures. Nonetheless, an eventual reduction of their volume of work may discourage them from engaging in this type of procedure.

In a broad approach to the judicial system, since the value streams can be long and can cross several entities and actors, it is the joint effort of these entities and actors that will allow the co-production of value. The challenge is to identify leaders (change agents) with the ability to overcome informal rules/routines that restrain the flow between the entities in the value stream and who are able to raise commitment among the actors involved and improve communication.

A major obstacle to overcome when adopting lean practices and procedures in the judicial system is the prevailing culture in courts and prosecution offices according to which judges' or prosecutors' work cannot be touched or intervened in. It is important that a verdict is arrived at on objective grounds by an independent tribunal, but the process and the outcome are often treated as inseparable units. This poses a major cultural challenge in the justice system.

The professional services in this context have distinctive features resulting from professional rules and ethics that can restrain acceptance of changes in leadership style and work routines. Judges, for instance, with their working values of independence and objectivity, may perceive teamwork as limiting those values. The same applies to other professionals in the system such as prosecutors, clerks, policemen, lawyers, etc. Pekkanen and Niemi (2013) noted that fixed roles and duties of different participants in the legal proceedings not only affect performance at the court level but also complicate the utilization of cooperation in the production process. Nonetheless, teamwork, in the context analyzed here, is related to making cases flow through the value stream so that value is enhanced. Thus those professional values are not jeopardized.

Hines et al. (2008a) identify reflection, observation, objectivity, and listening as examples of lean behavior. While performing their professional service, judges and prosecutors develop skills of observation, reflection, and objectivity as they analyze and decide on many different types of cases, each with specific requests. This is to say that these elements of the judicial system might be more prone to commit to a lean approach. The remaining staff, however, are used to a more routine job and a rigid environment, which can limit their initial engagement in change. Additional care should be provided to these professions in terms of training.

Challenges Relating to Process Management

Process management is one of the visible features of the implementation of lean. In judicial systems, the key "business" processes are supported by value streams that cross many different entities and actors and include the parties involved in the cases. Based on Hines et al. (2008a), Table 31.2 identifies and describes key business processes in the judicial system.

These processes are long and complex, with a multitude of entities and different ways of being performed. As argued by Hines et al. (2000), the lean value stream needs to be focused on the key processes, which is to say that it has to see beyond the perspective of the individual firms and departments. Managing such complex processes that cross several entities in each value stream, even for each profile of supply, is a major challenge judicial systems face.

Challenges Related to Technology, Tools, and Techniques

Technology, tools, and techniques are visible features of the implementation of lean. However, they will be of no consequence in the long term if a lean culture is not pursued. The judicial system has been known for its difficulties in embracing change. Some practices have been in use

Table 31.2 Key business processes in the judicial system

Key business process	Interpretation in the judicial system
Strategy and policy deployment	Strategic management of the judicial system and of each of the entities, focusing on change management and value.
Order fulfillment	Receiving the cases, taking them through the co-production process, scheduling, producing decisions, and assessing requests and documents, announcing decisions, payment management.
Supplier integration	Integrating other entities in the value stream to other key processes, procurement of suppliers (e.g. consultants, experts, police, or courts from other countries), managing relationships with suppliers.
Technology, space, and equipment management	Developing and maintaining equipment and IT solutions, sharing of databases from other entities, managing space in the judicial entities.
Human resources	Developing, managing, and maintaining employees, including training, recruitment, and retention.
Continuous improvement	Continuous, incremental, or radical improvement of key business processes.

for a long time, and adjustments are difficult to implement. An example of this situation can be found in the sharing of hearing rooms in Portugal; when predefined time slots of judges are not being used by their owners, the rooms are not made available to the other judges.

IT has a role in justice systems when it comes to simplifying, standardizing, and automating work and output. It reduces the time required to produce documents, prevents rework, reduces transportation and motion, and removes the option of multiple and arbitrary ways of performing the same activity. However, several IT solutions can be found in different entities inside the judicial system—for example, police, prosecutors, and courts may have their own IT solutions—and the incompatibility can make it more difficult to transfer information smoothly or even to access information. Making these divergent systems work in an integrated way is a major challenge still to be overcome.

Opportunities to Go Leaner in the Justice System

Despite many challenges, lean thinking offers a philosophy of process improvement that emphasizes the importance of creating value, here intended as customers' (in a broader sense, i.e. all stakeholders') satisfaction. The judicial system has just recently started being subject to operational and managerial change initiatives, and the improvement potential is large. Opportunities to improve judicial systems can be found at different levels. The following sections address opportunities that can be found at a more strategic level and at a tactical and operational level.

Opportunities on the Strategic Level

Many challenges relate to the deeply rooted structures, values, and traditions within the judicial context, and the first change attempt should be to rethink the way in which legal issues are dealt with. However, justice is governed by norms and values (developed through regulation and practice). Change, with lean in mind, must therefore be addressed at the strategic level through political decisions and policies and not only through reengineering or redesigning the processes.

The structure of some judicial systems assumes that regardless of the complexity of a case and its scope, the stream it has to go through is almost always the same. Under these conditions, variety is not addressed. Under a lean perspective, and expanding on Hines et al.'s (2008b) suggestion, there is room to divert cases of a similar scope to specialized courts, allowing the creation of different value streams. Inside these specialized courts, there are still different levels of complexity in terms of cases and the decisions required by the judges. The least complex or more routine ones should be addressed by less experienced judges or other court personnel. The more skilled judges could then focus on the more complex cases.

Besides the creation of different value streams, the capacity of the courtrooms remains a bottleneck in the justice system. Addressing it from a broader perspective is to remove demand from that resource, which requires creating alternative dispute resolution options in civil matters, for example mediation and conciliation. Examples of initiatives at this level have started to emerge. In Finland, for instance, judges actively encourage parties to reach a common understanding so that the case can be solved in the pretrial procedure. In Italy, for civil and commercial cases, the mediation steps became mandatory in 2013.

The value streams cross several entities, and aligning them is complex. Each entity is more focused on its own independent goals and is less focused on case continuity in the stream. Creating the position of value stream manager for each value stream, a job position requiring strong management skills, would facilitate an understanding of the flow of cases through the processes. His/her influence could be perceived not only inside the courts but also outside them, in the linking of the courts with the various other entities in the judicial system. Externally, these management-skilled professionals could facilitate information sharing and strengthen the link between the various entities in the judicial systems, while detecting and eliminating delays. Internally, their influence could be felt not only in terms of identifying the waste and signaling delays in the value streams, and enhancing flows, but also in terms of their being a facilitator of continuous improvement processes.

Decisions regarding information technologies can also be addressed at a strategic level. There is a clear trend in Europe to introduce new IT and digital solutions and move toward paper-free processes. These solutions can facilitate the quicker transfer of documents and more prompt (automated) procedures for certain types of cases (e.g. speeding tickets or parking fines). Nonetheless, developing new IT solutions to support the justice system does not lead to a leaner solution if these solutions are solely used for automating a current process. There must be simultaneous improvement efforts to make the process smoother, with less waste.

Opportunities on the Tactical and Operational Level

Value stream mapping, as suggested by Rother and Shook (2003), could be a starting-point tool to identify the value-adding and non-value-adding activities. This is an opportunity to take into consideration the variety of customers of the justice system. By using this tool, justice systems actors can examine the procedures to gain a better understanding of the flow of information and of the cases and can identify improvement areas.

The potentially wasteful activities presented above correspond to *muda*, but the judicial system also contains what could be seen as *muri* (overburden; that is, overload during some period of time) and *mura* (unevenness; that is, variability, for instance in the workload or behavior). An example of mura is that the Portuguese courts stop for several weeks at different moments during the year (when there is no reception of documents or decisions leaving the court), which in turn disturbs the flow of cases and leads to muri, overburden, when the court activities start again. The introduction of lean concepts such as *heijunka* (leveled workload attributed to each judge over time, without interruptions) could potentially contribute to overcoming this by allowing a smoother flow of cases.

There is an opportunity to use IT systems to assure similar workload distribution to each judge in order to prevent discrepancies in waiting times. Italy has implemented a solution at this level by allowing some courts to use software that automatically assigns cases to different departments and judges. The algorithm-based system helps in the balancing of the number and complexity of the cases assigned.

Opportunities to go leaner at a tactical level also emerge from the way resources are utilized. The sharing of resources such as courtrooms, instead of being based on oral agreements extending for long periods of time, could be based on IT systems, which would allow visibility of available time slots. This would lead to shorter overall waiting periods for hearings and therefore to reduced waste in terms of both the use of resources and the cases' waiting time in the system.

The flow of cases could also be improved by addressing the concept of *kanban*. The reduction of the size of the batch of cases that is sent to the judge for analysis would increase the number of kanbans through the day (the number of times batches of cases are sent to the judge's office and solved cases are collected from it), which in turn would allow those cases to flow sooner to the subsequent activity in the process.

Workers in the judicial system are trained for their specific technical functions, but they lack management training and awareness of lean issues. This presents a major improvement opportunity not only to enhance the flow but also to engage workers in change and improvement. In parallel, agents of change must be appointed to facilitate improvement. Judges with proper training in lean awareness could be agents of change and flow facilitators (Martins and Carvalho, 2013). From the same perspective, court administrators could work as leaders to manage the courts under leaner principles and to act as value stream managers/flow facilitators.

Scheduling issues also present lean improvement opportunities. Regardless of the implementation of specialized courts, judges from the same court analyze a wide range of cases, leading to long set-up times between cases. Without reducing fairness and equity—that is, while still allowing cases to be distributed to a pool of judges—these could be organized in smaller pools, each with a specialized profile. This would lead to set-up time reduction and faster evolution in the learning curve.

In terms of lean tools and techniques, such as PDCA (plan, do, check, act), 5S, visual management, kaizen blitz, and continuous improvement, these can be used inside the separate entities and activities for improving management and the flow of cases within the entity and through the value stream.

The Future of Lean Justice

The pressure on the public sector to become more effective and efficient is translating to new practices and changes throughout the sector, including the justice system. The way in which legal cases are dealt with is being developed on international, national, and local levels, and the legal sector is starting to implement performance measurement practices to assist management in improving judicial services. It also supports taking measures to move toward a digital case-handling process.

The lean philosophy contains all elements needed to continue improving the kind of justice that is delivered to citizens and how it is delivered. Just as the lean concept resulted from a dynamic learning process in the automotive industry (Holweg, 2007), in justice systems, lean must result from a learning process of adaptation and change in strategy and alignment, leadership development, and commitment from those involved in the lean journey (Hines et al., 2008a). The professional culture is likely to cause internal resistance in the judicial system. Leaders of change and motivators are fundamental elements for creating environments where change is accepted and the remaining members of the team consider themselves engaged and committed to change and to the new procedures. According to Ohno (1988), it is teamwork within and across areas that will allow a smooth flow.

Making justice leaner requires the recognition of lean thinking (including a focus on value, pull, flow, and continuous improvement) on the policy level, so the long lean journey therefore must start at the level of Ministries of Justice and as part of a *hoshin kanri* process (i.e. a process of setting the direction for the organization). Lean tools can be helpful in improving specific subprocesses and activities. However, an overall perspective is necessary in order to achieve sustainability in a smooth case flow and value for the many different customers involved.

Case Study: Lean Justice in the European Small Claims Procedure

Countries in the European Union have developed simplified civil procedures for small claims throughout the years. These disputes were traditionally dealt with in procedures designed for more complex claims, which led to delays and the inefficient use of resources. These small claims all require similar paths, and these countries were in search of standardization as a means to reach faster and less expensive outputs. Nonetheless, disputes between parties from different countries increased complexity in national procedures, even if small amounts of money were involved. These court customers were dissatisfied and in need of a faster and more cost-efficient procedure; that is, a procedure that would provide more value. This was the context that led the European Parliament and the European Council to develop a European procedure for small claims, the ESCP established by Regulation (EC) No. 861/2007.

The ESCP is an alternative to national civil claims processes and aims at simplifying and speeding court cases through the procedure while reducing costs and assuring fairness in cross-border disputes where the value of the claim does not exceed 2,000 euros. It is a written procedure in which parties submit arguments using standard forms available online. The exception to the written principle is the possible need for an oral hearing. This standardization of forms provides the reduction of inappropriate processing and a reduction of possible overproduction as complexity is reduced.

The ESCP comprises three phases (illustrated in Figure 31.1). In the first phase, the *commencement* phase, the claim is received and assessed in terms of the information provided. Only claims that are within the scope of the regulation and which contain sufficient information are allowed to continue to the next phase, the *conduct* phase. This second phase begins with the court calling the defendant to the case. The path the claim will follow during this phase depends on the type of reply provided by the defendant. There are only three reply possibilities from the defendant (parallel streams represented by boxes with dotted borders in the middle part of Figure 31.1): either a claim for higher value, a counterclaim, or neither of these. Whatever the reply is, the claimant is informed and can also reply. If there is a counterclaim or a claim for higher value, the court reassesses the monetary value of the claim. It will only remain in the ESCP if the court concludes that it is still within the scope of this procedure. The third phase, *conclusion*, starts with the court assessing the sufficiency of information for concluding the case. If there is not enough information, the court can request further information, schedule an oral hearing or take evidence (parallel streams represented by boxes with dotted borders in the lower part of Figure 31.1).

The ESCP is a clear example of the use of a lean approach to justice to allow outputs to be reached more quickly and to require fewer resources while assuring the fairness of the output. The procedure is standardized and can only be applied to requests that fit a specific scope. This alone allows the filtering of demand, only considering claims with similar procedural requirements, that is, claims that can follow a similar value stream. The procedure allows the use of modern technology. Its standard forms are available online, which in turn allows cases to flow more quickly and with less transportation through the procedure, making better use of available resources than in the traditional civil procedures of many EU member states. The ESCP considers flexibility at some points, specifically in the conduct and the conclusion phases, by allowing alternative predefined paths in the procedure to better fit the specific characteristics of each claim. Although aiming for a leaner approach, the ESCP adds flexibility to the dispute resolution process without losing sight of its purpose—providing faster and adjusted solutions with a more rational use of the resources.

This procedure took effect on January 1, 2009. However, the deployment of the procedure in member states has remained at a low level, according to the Special Eurobarometer 395 (TNS Opinion and Social, 2013), due to a lack of awareness among citizens and judges of its existence (among other reasons). The European Parliament and Council have decided to revise the regulation. Reforming EU regulations is a time-consuming political process, but the continuous development of

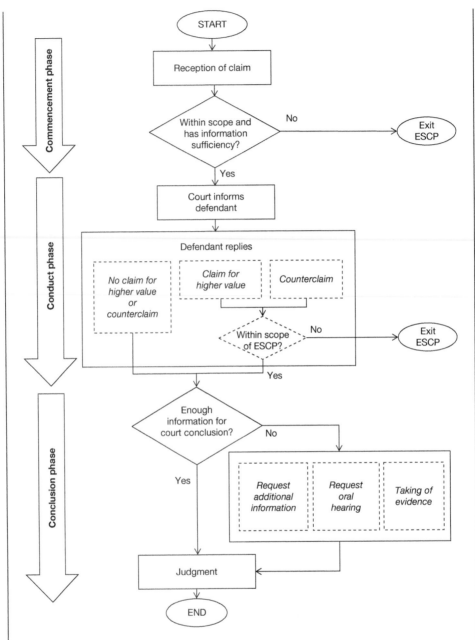

Figure 31.1   The main phases and decision points in the European small claims procedure

the law in striving for the best adjusted rules and solutions for value provision—in the case of the ESCP, striving to achieve a simpler, prompter, and less expensive procedure—is in line with the lean thinking principles of continuous improvement and striving for perfection.

References

ECHR (2015a). *Overview 1959–2014 ECHR*. Strasbourg, European Court of Human Rights/Council of Europe. Available at www.echr.coe.int/Documents/Overview_19592014_ENG.pdf. (accessed September 1, 2015).

ECHR (2015b). *Violations by Article and by State—2014*. European Court of Human Rights. Available at www.echr.coe.int/Documents/Stats_violation_2014_ENG.pdf (accessed September 1, 2015).

Hines, P., Lamming, R., Jones, D., Cousins, P. and Rich, N. (2000). *Value Stream Management—Strategy and Excellence in the Supply Chain*, Harlow, Financial Times/Prentice Hall.

Hines, P., Found, P., Griffiths, G. and Harrison, R. (2008a). *Staying Lean: Thriving, Not Just Surviving*, Cardiff, Lean Enterprise Research Centre.

Hines, P., Martins, A. L. and Beale, J. (2008b). Testing the boundaries of lean thinking: Observations from the legal public sector. *Public Money & Management*, 28(1), 35–40.

Holweg, M. (2007). The genealogy of lean production. *Journal of Operations Management*, 25(2), 420–437.

Johnston, R., Clark, G. and Shulver, M. (2012). *Service Operations Management—Improving Service*, 4th edition, Harlow, Pearson.

Maleyeff, J. (2006). Exploration of internal services systems using lean principles. *Management Decision*, 44(5), 674–689.

Martins, A. L. and Carvalho, J. C. (2005). Creating value in a services supply chain. In: Pawar, K., Lalwani, C., Carvalho, J. C. and Muffato, M. (eds), *Proceedings of the 10th International Symposium in Logistics*, 708–713.

Martins, A. L. and Carvalho, J. C. (2013). Slimming lead times in courts of law—A case study. *International Journal of Industrial Engineering and Management*, 4(3), 123–130.

Mattsson, I. (2014). Spill och onödigheter i finska straffprocessen. *Tidskrift för juridiska föreningen i Finland*, 150(1–2), 73–93.

Ohno, T. (1988). *Toyota Production System: Beyond Large-Scale Production*, New York, Productivity Press.

Pekkanen, P. and Niemi, P. (2013). Process performance improvement in justice organizations—Pitfalls of performance measurement. *International Journal of Production Economics*, 142(2), 605–611.

Pekkanen, P., Karppinen, H. and Pirttilä, T. (2009). What causes prolonged lead-times in courts of law? In: Reiner, G. (ed.), *Rapid Modelling for Increasing Competitiveness*, London, Springer, pp. 221–231.

Rother, M. and Shook, J. (2003). *Learning to See: Value Stream Mapping to Create Value and Eliminate Muda*, Brookline, MA, Lean Enterprise Institute.

TNS Opinion and Social (2013). European Small Claims Procedure. Special Eurobarometer 395, Wave EB78.2. Brussels, European Commission.

Womack, J. P. and Jones, D. T. (2003). *Lean Thinking: Banish Waste and Create Wealth in Your Corporation*, London, The Free Press.

32

LEAN PUBLIC WATER SUPPLY

Kirstin Scholten, Benjamin Ward, and Dirk Pieter van Donk

Introduction

The quantity and quality of water delivered and used by households is an important aspect of domestic water supplies, influencing hygiene and thus public health (Howard and Bartram, 2003). Fresh, clean water is commonly taken for granted as a basic commodity in most European countries. Typically, the primary goal of public water supply organizations, e.g. in the Netherlands, Ireland, or Sweden, is to achieve consumer satisfaction through high service levels. Service level is indicated by the amount of downtime (lack of water) experienced by customers. Downtime in water supply can occur due to several foreseen (e.g. scheduled maintenance work) or unforeseen reasons due to disruptions (e.g. quality issues, but usually pipe breakages). Organizations use proactive planning to try to avoid unforeseen disruptions by employing redundant resources (additional pipelines, pumps, water sources, employees, etc.). This prevents disturbances from reaching the final customer. In addition, maintenance activities are used to detect possible weaknesses in the system in advance. Yet not all events can be proactively planned for. A variety of restrictions hinder the ability of the water supply organization to engage in proactive maintenance activities to try to avoid unforeseeable disruptions, e.g. the relative inaccessibility of the distribution network due to its underground location.

Consequently, to be able to deal with disturbances in the most effective and efficient way, water supply organizations need to strive not only for robustness via proactive planning (e.g. design of the system) and redundant resources, but also for agility to be able to respond to unforeseen events; they need to be resilient. At the same time, however, keeping costs low to satisfy the demands of public authorities is increasingly an issue for public services at large. This has made lean a popular concept in this sector. Yet to keep the required redundancies for resilience identified proactively and to be agile is relatively costly. Seemingly, striving for low cost using lean principles while simultaneously being sufficiently responsive to maintain service levels as high as 99.99 percent delivery reliability is contradictory. Investigating possible incompatibilities or synergies in this context is the main aim of this chapter.

Both lean and resilience have received considerable attention in the literature. Resilient supply chains have the adaptive capacity to prepare for, respond to, and recover from supply chain disturbances (Ponomarov and Holcomb, 2009), often enabled by the (necessary) expense of adding redundancy or "slack" in a supply chain (Sheffi and Rice, 2005). As indicated, the public sector focuses on reducing costs in response to pressure to improve performance (Radnor and Walley, 2008). Aspects of lean have been implemented in these settings as a possible means to achieve cost reductions (Radnor et al., 2012). At a basic level, lean and resilience appear to be conflicting ideas in a supply chain context owing to lean advocating the reduction of waste (Holweg, 2007; Shah and Ward, 2007). In addition, resilience is often enabled by the addition of redundancies (Sheffi and Rice, 2005). Simultaneously, authors have acknowledged that a focus on applying lean philosophies to supply chains has increased the risk of disturbances (see, e.g., Christopher and Peck, 2004; Ponomarov and Holcomb, 2009; Blackhurst et al., 2011). It follows, therefore, that *lean supply chains also require a level of resilience*, as no supply chain is immune to disturbances. It is unclear in literature whether striving for lean and resilience is mutually beneficial or counterproductive: incompatible or synergistic. The empirical context of the water supply sector is specifically interesting, as this sector needs to be able to achieve high customer service levels while keeping costs low for society.

This chapter sets out to explore the compatibility of supply chain resilience and *total productive maintenance* (TPM), an important facet of the lean philosophy and an approach to ensure reliability in a system (Ahuja and Khamba, 2008). First, we will give an overview of TPM in the context of lean. Subsequently, challenges and future opportunities of TPM in relation to supply chain resilience will be discussed. We will conclude with suggestions for future directions of TPM and resilience, and briefly address consequences for managers.

Total Productive Maintenance in the Water Supply Industry

Lean can be seen as a philosophy, as a rule-driven system or as a congregation of tools and techniques. The latter level of aggregation considers lean as a multidimensional approach that incorporates a wide variety of management practices such as just-in-time (JIT), total quality management (TQM), human resource management, and aspects of maintenance, which work together synergistically to seamlessly produce finished products in line with customer demand with little or no waste (Shah and Ward, 2003). Lean supposes, among other things, reduction (if not elimination) of intermediate inventories. This means that if a machine breaks down, it will eventually stop all the following downstream and upstream flows. Therefore, inadequate and inefficient maintenance can affect the profitability, product quality, and survival of an organization (Min et al., 2011), especially if the organization is truly lean. Thus TPM can offer the robustness needed for implementing lean practices. Despite Cua et al. (2001) relating TPM to some key tenets of lean, such as JIT and TQM, in general TPM and lean are often treated as two different and non-integrated philosophies. This is rather surprising as dependable and effective equipment is an essential prerequisite for implementing lean manufacturing initiatives such as pull, JIT, single-minute exchange of dies (SMED), and continuous improvement (CI).

While lean thinking has always sought reliable processes, TPM provides the route map to zero breakdowns and continuous improvement in equipment optimization (McCarthy and Rich, 2004). TPM has been accepted as the most promising strategy for improving maintenance performance in organizations aiming to achieve a reliable manufacturing system (Ahuja and Khamba, 2008). Similar to other methods associated with lean, the fundamental goals of TPM are waste reduction and CI (Cua et al., 2001), especially of product quality, operational efficiency, and capacity assurance (Chan et al., 2005). In particular, TPM strives to continually maintain, improve, and maximize the condition and effectiveness of equipment (mostly indicated and measured as *overall equipment effectiveness* (OEE)) (Ireland and Dale, 2006). In anticipation of breakdowns, it is a proactive planning approach applied in supply systems, networks, and organizations. While lean thinking aims to improve the design *efficiency* of transformation processes, providing the potential to deliver greater customer value with less effort, TPM allows for greater *effectiveness* of the transformation process (i.e. dealing with the reasons why things go wrong) (McCarthy and Rich, 2004).

In the water supply industry, implementing lean, as discussed in the introduction, has been stimulated through a pressure to reduce the costs of water supply. Given the very nature of water supply, it seems natural to aim for TPM as a means to reduce costs, as a basis for further lean initiatives, and mainly because of the dependability and reliance on the (underground) infra-structure as the main production means. In other words, TPM can help to improve the effective maintenance of kilometers of underground piping, as well as numerous pumps and valves. Successful maintenance of these elements is paramount to ensuring uninterrupted delivery of water to consumers.

Key tenets of TPM are often found to be either actions or philosophies, for example building profitable operations through reduction of breakdowns; practicing "prevention is better than cure"; bringing equipment to its ideal state; involving all organizational members through par-ticipatory management; creating a self-sustaining cycle in the workplace based around culture and management (Nakajima, 1988). The distinction between actions and philosophies lies in the fact that actions are directly contributing to TPM implementation, whereas philosophies can be referred to as guiding principles (Shah and Ward, 2007). While it can conceptually be important to consider both of these when studying TPM, the actions and philosophies can overlap. In practice, this will easily be grouped under a few key components or building blocks of TPM. For this reason, we unify the philosophies and actions leading to TPM found in literature into three primary components of TPM in line with Wang (2006). In the next sections, we further explore these three components and briefly discuss their performance implications:

1   increasing reliability;
2   preparing contingencies for disruptions; and
3   ensuring participation in maintenance management (continuous improvement).

Increasing Reliability

TPM aids in improving maintenance in operations management by focusing on reliability (Prabhuswamy et al., 2013). Maintaining equipment in an ideal state is the best preparation for disruptions. At the same time, it is easier to respond to disruptions with reliable equipment. Reliability can be increased through prevention of equipment failure (Kleindorfer and Saad, 2005), and through the managing of equipment performance and technology (Prabhuswamy et al., 2013). Accordingly, maintenance should be managed and carried out before it is required (McKone and Weiss, 1998), ensuring profitable operations through the reduction of avoidable breakdowns (Ahuja and Khamba, 2008). Reliability of the different parts, machines, and equipment will increase the robustness of the overall organization, laying the foundation for effective and lean operations.

Preparing Contingencies for Disruptions

While TPM is arguably proactive and aims to minimize the effect of breakdowns via increased equipment reliability, it is inevitable that disruptions occur. For this reason, the implementation of TPM should also enable the system or network to respond adequately to the breakdown (Cua et al., 2001). Therefore, it is important to establish contingencies. TPM enables a deeper understanding of the equipment as it supports the establishment of strategies while strategically planning for the useful life of the equipment, its limitations, and capabilities during normal operation as well as during disturbances (Chan et al., 2005). It allows for long-term planning and preparation for a wider range of disruptions through the incorporation of additional organizational members. While a lean philosophy would in general state that a disruption would be waste (as valuable time for production will be lost), at the same time this TPM component will reduce such waste as much as possible and therefore help to enable lean practices.

Ensuring Participation in Maintenance Management (Continuous Improvement)

Arguably the most "familiar" element of any lean philosophy is continuous improvement (Holweg, 2007). Categorized here as participation in maintenance management, involving organizational members in TPM initiatives is commonly found in literature. It is important that application of TPM be all-encompassing in an organization, including all departments and staff and, further, through the creation of group activities to highlight to organizational members the importance of TPM (Nakajima, 1988). This ensures participation in TPM is both a top-down and a bottom-up process. As the onus of coping with disturbances lies as much in operators and other organizational decision makers as with the equipment itself, involving employees in employee training enables a quicker response to maintenance-related disturbances (Ahuja and Khamba, 2008). This point also stresses that maintenance is not the responsibility of the maintenance department, but needs to be a part of the task of all organizational members at all levels.

Besides the benefits of TPM in contributing to organizational performance, maintenance is seen by many as having a poor rate of return due to the lack of a direct relationship between cost and profit or quality (Ahuja and Khamba, 2008; Marais and Saleh, 2009). Equipment maintenance represents a large portion of cost for a variety of organizations (Ahuja and Khamba, 2008). In this chapter, we use the concept of *supply chain resilience* to shift the focus from cost to value of maintenance. As argued, there is an ongoing debate about whether the implementation of the two concepts is mutually beneficial or contradictory, as resilience often is based on redundancies and TPM as a concept of lean strives for waste reduction and efficiency. The next section will explore the challenges and opportunities that emerge from their joint usage in a water supply network.

TPM and Supply Chain Resilience: Challenges and Opportunities

Before we explore challenges and opportunities, we briefly introduce the concept of supply chain resilience. Supply chain disruptions are inevitable (Tang, 2006) and often result in decreased performance due to factors such as underestimated risk, inability to manage supply chain risk, and increased exposure to risk due to the "leaning" of supply chains (Kleindorfer and Saad, 2005; Tang, 2006). As a result, various factors to overcome or prevent these disturbances have been investigated by academics to provide insight into supply chain resilience (see, e.g., Christopher and Peck, 2004; Blackhurst et al., 2011; Wieland and Wallenburg, 2012). Research on resilience mostly agrees that resilience itself has a proactive and a reactive phase. In particular, Wieland and Wallenburg (2012) argue that resilience is composed of two antecedents—robustness (proactive) and agility (reactive)—which will guide our further discussion.

TPM as an Enabler of Robustness

Wieland and Wallenburg (2012) conceptualize robustness as anticipation and preparedness. Anticipation, the actions taken to predict potential future events and to identify potential incidents, can be improved through information sharing about changes prior to their occurrence. Preparedness, or "readiness," directly contributes to resilience (Ponomarov and Holcomb, 2009), and encompasses all actions taken to prepare for the events identified in the "anticipation" stage. Preparedness is based on the ability to prepare an effective and efficient response to change. It enhances resilience by increasing robustness through lowering the likelihood of a disturbance affecting the entire system.

In classical TPM literature, TPM increases the reliability of a system (Ahuja and Khamba, 2008), prepares contingencies to better react to disruptions (McKone et al., 1999), and ensures the participation of employees in maintenance management (Nakajima, 1988). Considering TPM as an enabler of robustness in preparing contingencies for disruptions should enable the system to respond adequately (Cua et al., 2001). Thus it indicates parallels to anticipation. This is particularly linked to the need for information and knowledge, e.g. information and knowledge on the system layout, materials, age of infrastructure and machines, and context disturbances. This is outlined in the case study. Meanwhile, historical data can help measure reliability and prepare contingencies. However, it only gains value through interpretation by employees and specifically by the operators who have in-depth knowledge and expertise in dealing with these materials (employee involvement). This combination of information and knowledge can be used to estimate the likely lifespan of equipment, enabling the organization to anticipate failures. Therefore, preparing contingencies in anticipation of future requirements is based on a concerted effort to gather data and expertise. Further employee involvement needs to be utilized during the establishment of working standards and operating procedures both in practice and through initiatives aiming to classify and take stock of the workers' knowledge. These initiatives help to define the skill level and training of each worker for recourse when future disturbances call for specific expertise, enabling a more efficient response to disturbances.

Preparedness in a network can be achieved through the placement of specific parts and tools as close as possible to areas most likely to require them, as well as periodical checking of materials to ensure they are fit for use. Such activities are reinforced by TPM factors. This might concern periodically inspecting equipment and materials, judging the reliability of both, and so prompting an increase in preparedness. The placing of tools and parts at strategic points throughout the network prepares it for contingencies. Hence, the contribution of preparedness to robustness and preparing contingencies for disruptions as defined in TPM are equivalent. Additionally, both are strongly influenced by information and knowledge gathered and acted upon in the anticipation phase. The outcome is that in order to enhance both anticipation and preparedness (and thus, robustness), visibility is required. Robustness is increased if good basic information and knowledge of what is in stock is available. Blackhurst et al. (2011) propose that visibility in a supply chain reveals risk, location of resources, and how disruptions propagate. It can therefore be considered a prerequisite to build anticipation and preparedness. This becomes clear from the case study in this chapter. In summary, from an information management point of view, both anticipation and contingency planning hinge on the gathering and interpreting of data. This data can then be used to build a unified view of future potential disruptions in a system, which then enables the development of preparedness.

TPM as an Enabler of Agility

Agility is "the ability to respond rapidly to unpredictable changes" (Christopher and Peck, 2004, p. 18) which is enabled by visibility and velocity (speed) (Wieland and Wallenburg, 2012). Visibility, according to Jüttner and Maklan (2011), is the extent to which supply chain members have access to, or share in a timely way, information about supply chain operations, other actors, and management. Visibility allows for a transparent view of inventories, supply and demand conditions, the status of other supply chain actors, and so on throughout the supply chain. Velocity is the second antecedent to supply chain agility. Velocity refers to the ability to quickly respond to market changes or events (Christopher and Peck, 2004) while attempting to improve the speed of recovery from disruptions (Jüttner and Maklan, 2011; Wieland and Wallenburg, 2012).

Although it can be argued that TPM has a strong effect on robustness, due to the procedural nature of preparedness and, to some degree, anticipation, neither is readily achievable without increased visibility. This has already been highlighted in relation to robustness. However, visibility can be attributed to two main factors, both concerned with information and knowledge. The first considers the physical properties of the distribution network and the availability of knowledge regarding it, that is, the accuracy of the information in the system in relation to the parts and components physically laid out. The second factor reviews information pertaining to stocks, inventory, and the movements of parts, tools, and people within the network. As reflected in the case study in this chapter, the reliability of both the network and the processes revolving around the network and its maintenance are dependent upon these factors. Increasing the reliability of the information available to workers can be facilitated by investments in technologies such as the deployment of smartphones, tablets, and dedicated applications through which workers at work sites can add information, images, and update technical drawings as they encounter issues and execute repairs.

The concept of velocity determines how quickly an equipment disruption can be resolved. In practice, this often relates to how rapidly an occurrence is detected and how fast maintenance staff can repair the malfunctioning equipment. On the other hand, to singularly focus on speed as a result of physical factors, such as driving time, is limiting. Velocity can also be improved in the supply network through other factors. One way is to improve the coordination both within and outside the supply network. This can be done, for example, through the multiskilling of employees that leads to higher versatility and higher likelihood of an efficient and effective repair, or through improving the linkages with other members of the wider supply chain. Hence, the contribution to speed could be separated into two main aspect types. The first aspects are those that stem from physical layout of facilities, the tangible factors. The second aspects are those related to visibility and resilience, such as the use of standard procedures developed through anticipating disruptions and from greater visibility in the supply network. These allow for more effective use of resources.

Conclusions: Future Role of TPM for Supply Chain Resilience in the Water Supply Sector

The discussion above has shown that resilience is composed of robustness and agility. Further, TPM actions and philosophies have been aggregated into three components. These three components highlight ways in which TPM contributes to increased reliability, prepares for disruption, and ensures participation in maintenance management. From the outset, it seemed that a concept based on the lean philosophy, aiming to reduce waste, and the concept of resilience, often enabled by additional redundancies, are incompatible. However, aligning TPM with the study of resilience suggests TPM can aid resilience by enhancing robustness and agility, as TPM contains both proactive and reactive elements. Owing to the strong need for information and knowledge for TPM practices, visibility is increased. This increases robustness as well as agility, thus increasing resilience. These findings are summarized in Figure 32.1.

The issue of cost reduction and efficiency is of increasing importance in the public sector. There is a trend of privatization of public utilities, such as the water supply in France, the UK,

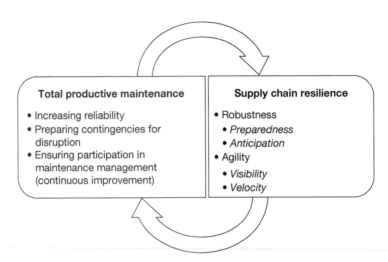

Figure 32.1 TPM and supply chain resilience: synergetic concepts

and USA. Hence, public utility organizations need to find ways to remain competitive. This is often maintained by applying lean principles. Equipment maintenance represents a large portion of cost for a variety of organizations. However, this equipment ensures that the water supply companies can achieve the required high service levels. Consequently, cutting costs in maintenance activities might not be the way forward. This chapter shows that one way of shifting the focus from costs to value of maintenance is through the synergy of TPM and supply chain resilience, two—at first sight—seemingly incompatible concepts. TPM was shown to have the potential to enable resilience, with the caveat that visibility is the driving factor in enabling resilience in a supply network. Although it can be argued that TPM has a strong effect on robustness due to the procedural nature of preparedness and, to some degree, anticipation, neither is readily achievable without increased visibility. As a matter of fact, in the context of water supply organizations, visibility transpires to be the key antecedent of resilience, and one that would enable improvements in robustness and agility. Therefore, the requirement is to enhance resilience using TPM while shifting the focus from cost to the value of maintenance information for visibility.

At a more philosophical and general level this contributes to the discussion on lean and agility. Often these are seen as opposing or even incompatible to some extent. From the above discussion, and also supported by the findings in our case study, it can be concluded that at least TPM, an important pillar of lean, might contribute not only to robustness as expected but also to agility. This finding may shed new light on the discussion in scientific literature. Additionally, it might be an indicator that, in fact, lean and agile can, like TPM and agile, be mutually supportive and synergetic to some degree. Furthermore, TPM has the potential to evolve from a maintenance management methodology used in manufacturing to reduce instances of breakdowns and finesse production equipment to introspectively analyze decision-making processes with regard to resilience in a supply network. In this sense, it is not unlike the Six Sigma methodology that evolved from a methodology used to reduce the instances of defects in mass production environments to a change management process used to improve measurable processes in organizations (Schroeder et al., 2008).

Managers attempting to enhance resilience using TPM will quickly find that information is required to do so. It is therefore advised they start the process by identifying available information regarding their network and gather an understanding of additional information required. Furthermore, it is also important to remember that actors in the supply network (employees) are often those best placed to provide input regarding these processes. Managers should therefore involve employees from across the organization in resilience initiatives.

Case Study: Lean Public Water Supply in the Waterbedrijf Groningen[1]

The water utility company in this case is based in Groningen, the Netherlands. The company is currently considering changes to the physical layout of the maintenance network (number and location of warehouses and satellite warehouses) and how this would influence the ability of the organization to carry out maintenance work while staying true to high service levels (resilience). In the Netherlands, utility companies need to meet the requirements placed on them by law, namely the seamless supply of water all day, every day of the year. The main goals of utility companies are maintaining and improving the quality and reliability of service (termed here as the service level) while keeping costs low. This differs from private businesses as their focus is on increasing profit. However, due to the necessity of retaining redundancy in the supply and maintenance network (see Figure 32.2) as required through legislation, aligning resilience via redundancies and applying lean principles poses an inherent challenge.

Interestingly, while investigating the effect of the redesign considerations on maintenance practices, TPM was found to be not only a tool that could be applied to the supply network to improve resilience, but also a tool to diagnose shortcomings of the network in its current state. It was found that the considered redesign of the maintenance network would most likely have an effect on the resilience of the organization in the form of on-time materials at work sites, reduced variability in lead times in the supply chain and the network, decreased response time for repairs from initial awareness, and reduction of stock-outs and duplicate orders within the network.

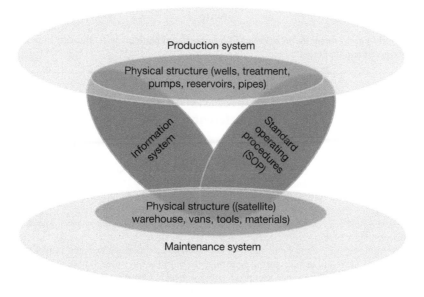

Figure 32.2 System set-up in the Waterbedrijf Groningen

Due to its very nature, the organization contains large amounts of redundancies, which cannot be removed (as, for example, they were required by law for the safety of drinking water). Therefore, the robustness of the network requiring preparation and anticipation could be maintained through knowledge and information regarding the physical system layout (pipes underground), materials, age of infrastructure, and machines not affected by the redesign considerations. Yet, at the same time, the effect of changes in other parts of the organization need to be understood. Visibility became a placeholder for more than end-to-end communication in the supply chain. It also entailed understanding the knowledge which is contained in the system in the form of the people, and the knowledge that is considered part of the organization itself. This knowledge has a fundamental effect on the resilience of the organization as it allows the Waterbedrijf Groningen to be specifically prepared and able to cope with disruptions specific to the network. Examples of disruptions include drilling operations or settling of ground related to traffic load. Such implicit knowledge combined with the explicit knowledge contained within the organization contributes to visibility in such a way that the organization is able to apply itself to maintenance, which has a positive effect on resilience. Additionally, it became apparent that many small actions could have a profound effect on visibility (and thus on resilience), with very little cost. For example, the implementation of a kanban system can be used to manage the stock of parts kept in vehicles, which would streamline stock-keeping and purchasing activities, leading to a more level loading of both departments and facilities.

Furthermore, the redesign of the maintenance network was found to have a profound effect on agility, which is required to respond to any disturbances due to the main metrics used to quantify the service level of the distribution network—customer minutes lost. In practice, this relates to the speed at which operators can reach the location of a disruption (driving time and distance). Therefore, speed is most affected by the design of the supply network such as number of warehouses, amount of inventory in warehouses, stock kept in maintenance vans, or a separate logistics team with the sole role of supporting workers in the field in delivering tools and parts, etc.

Note

1 We would like to thank the Waterbedrijf Groningen and particularly Ir. Bernard Enthoven for their support and comments.

References

Ahuja, I. P. S. and Khamba, J. S. (2008). Total productive maintenance: Literature review and directions. *International Journal of Quality & Reliability Management, 25*(7), 709–756.

Blackhurst, J., Dunn, K. S. and Craighead, C. W. (2011). An empirically derived framework of global supply resiliency. *Journal of Business Logistics, 32*(4), 374–391.

Chan, F. T. S., Lau, H. C. W., Ip, R. W. L., Chan, H. K. and Kong, S. (2005). Implementation of total productive maintenance: A case study. *International Journal of Production Economics, 95*(1), 71–94.

Christopher, M. and Peck, H. (2004). Building the resilient supply chain. *International Journal of Logistics Management, 15*(2), 1–13.

Cua, K. O., McKone, K. E. and Schroeder, R. G. (2001). Relationships between implementation of TQM, JIT, and TPM and manufacturing performance. *Journal of Operations Management, 9*(6), 675–694.

Holweg, M. (2007). The genealogy of lean production. *Journal of Operations Management, 25*(2), 420–437.

Howard, G. and Bartram, J. (2003). *Domestic Water Quantity, Service Level and Health.* Available at: www.who.int/water_sanitation_health/diseases/en/WSH0302.pdf (accessed February 2016).

Ireland, F. and Dale, B. G. (2006). Total productive maintenance: Criteria for sucess. *International Journal of Productivity and Quality Management*, *1*(3), 207–223.

Jüttner, U. and Maklan, S. (2011). Supply chain resilience in the global financial crisis: An empirical study. *Supply Chain Management: An International Journal*, *16*(4), 246–259.

Kleindorfer, P. R. and Saad, G. H. (2005). Managing disruption risks in supply chain. *Production and Operations Management*, *14*(1), 53–68.

McCarthy, D. and Rich, N. (2004). *Lean TPM: A Blueprint for Change*, Oxford, Elsevier.

McKone, E. and Weiss, N. (1998). TPM: Planned and autonomous maintenance: Bridging the gap between practice and research. *Production and Operations Management*, *7*(4), 335–351.

McKone, K. E., Schroeder, R. G. and Cua, K. O. (1999). Total productive maintenance: A contextual view. *Journal of Operations Management*, *17*(2), 123–144.

Marais, K. B. and Saleh, J. H. (2009). Beyond its cost, the value of maintenance: An analytical framework for capturing its net present value. *Reliability Engineering and System Safety*, *94*(2), 644–657.

Min, C. S., Ahmad, R., Kamaruddin, S. and Azid, I. A. (2011). Development of autonomous maintenance implementation framework for semiconductor industries. *International Journal of Industrial Systems Engineering*, *9*(3), 268–297.

Nakajima, S. (1988). *TPM Development Program: Implementing Total Productive Maintenance*, Portland, OR, Taylor & Francis Group.

Ponomarov, S. Y. and Holcomb, M. C. (2009). Understanding the concept of supply chain resilience. *International Journal of Logistics Management*, *20*(1), 124–143.

Prabhuswamy, M. S., Nagesh, P. and Ravikumar, K. P. (2013). Statistical analysis and reliability estimation of total productive maintenance. *IUP Journal of Operations Management*, *12*(1), 7–20.

Radnor, Z. and Walley, P. (2008). Learning to walk before we try to run: Adapting lean for the public sector. *Public Money & Management*, *28*(1), 13–20.

Radnor, Z. J., Holweg, M. and Waring, J. (2012). Lean in healthcare: The unfilled promise? *Social Science and Medicine*, *74*(3), 364–371.

Schroeder, R. G., Linderman, K., Liedtke, C. and Choo, A. S. (2008). Six Sigma: Definition and underlying theory. *Journal of Operations Management*, *26*(4), 536–554.

Shah, R. and Ward, P. T. (2003). Lean manufacturing: Context, practice bundles, and performance. *Journal of Operations Management*, *21*(2), 129–149.

Shah, R. and Ward, P. T. (2007). Defining and developing measures of lean production. *Journal of Operations Management*, *25*(4), 785–805.

Sheffi, Y. and Rice, J. B. (2005). A supply chain view of the resilient enterprise. *Sloan Management Review*, *47*(1), 40–49.

Tang, C. (2006). Robust strategies for mitigating supply chain disruptions. *International Journal of Logistics Research and Application*, *9*(1), 33–45.

Wang, F. K. (2006). Evaluating the efficiency of implementing total productive maintenance. *Total Quality Management & Business Excellence*, *17*(5), 655–667.

Wieland, A. and Wallenburg, C. M. (2012). Dealing with supply chain risks: Linking risk management practices and strategies to performance. *International Journal of Physical Distribution & Logistics Management*, *42*(10), 887–905.

33

LEAN DEALERSHIPS

David Brunt

Introduction

It is 25 years since *The Machine that Changed the World* (Womack et al., 1990) first described an alternative logic for running a business and showed how Toyota was doing this. While many people look to the chapters on lean production and the coordination of the supply chain, there were equally important sections that covered the development of new products and how the automakers dealt with customers and managed their dealers. It was this last subject area that led to our research into applying lean to the areas of sales and service.

Our research in this area has a long history. After *The Machine* was written, Dan Jones played a key role in creating the International Car Distribution Program (ICDP) to explore these ideas further. Initially we recognized the true significance of Toyota's *parts distribution system*—delivering exactly the right parts to dealers with much less human effort and a tenth of the inventories in the pipeline. These insights were widely published, most notably in *Lean Thinking* (Womack and Jones, 1996).

The missing link between the parts operations and the end consumer was the application of lean in the car dealership. Early adopters included Pedro Simao and Ricardo Lopes from Grupo Fernando Simao in Portugal. Triggered by my regular visits in the late 1990s and early 2000s they transformed their dealerships by implementing lean principles and practices in the sales and service of vehicles and the parts distribution to each of their branded sites, and applied the same logic to their body repair facilities. Their success was reported in the *Harvard Business Review* article "Lean consumption" (Womack and Jones, 2005a) and in Womack and Jones' (2005b) book *Lean Solutions*.

In 2007, we decided to publish our findings in greater detail. *Creating Lean Dealers* (Brunt and Kiff, 2007) was developed as a workbook to help dealers on their lean journey. The book concentrated mainly upon the after-sales (service and repair) activities in a dealer to illustrate the principles and practices required to implement lean in this environment. The insights in the book, alongside regular coaching and mentoring, have inspired a number of dealers to embark on their lean journey. Most notable are the early efforts at Grupo Fernando Simao in Portugal; Jaeger (a family-owned group of Toyota dealers headquartered in Bergen, Norway); and the Halfway Group (a South African group where implementation started in their Toyota dealers).

What is Lean Dealership?

Applying lean to the processes that occur closest to the customer—the dealer operations—is still in its infancy. This seems more surprising when one considers the first principle of lean thinking—specify value through the eyes of the customer—and the competitive advantage that can be gained from implementing lean.

Lean thinkers have a structured way of thinking about an organization. First, we think about customer purpose—"what do your customers want that you are not currently able to supply?"— as well as organizational purpose: "what does your organization need to survive and even to prosper?" Second, we think about process: in particular, the process providing the value the customer is seeking. We call these processes value streams. Third, we think about people: "does every important process in your organization have someone responsible for continually evaluating that value stream in terms of purpose?" "Is everyone touching the value stream actively engaged in operating it correctly and continually improving it to address your purposes better?" PDCA (plan, do, check, act) (A3 thinking) ties *purpose, process,* and *people* together. Do you have a structured methodology for: defining and refining purpose; managing, sustaining, and improving the processes; and engaging and developing the people? We need purpose, process, and people in order to develop a lean organization.

This framework can be applied to the sales and service activities in a car dealer. First, what is the purpose of a customer getting a car? While we cannot argue that value is a complex issue and that customers have cars for lots of reasons (including image, prestige, and the utility of the product for their circumstances), all of us who drive actually want cars for the purpose of mobility. When we acquire a car, customer purpose is to have the right car (quality) in the right place at the right time (delivery) at the right price (cost). Quite simply, we want to be able to go where we want to, when we want to. We want the car to start at the beginning of the journey and switch off at the end of the journey and to be no trouble in between. To be able to use the vehicle up to now we have had to accept that the car will need maintaining from time to time. For this maintenance task to go as smoothly as possible (and so we can continue to use our car for its intended purpose) at the most basic level we want the relevant work to be completed right, first time (quality), on time, every time (delivery), at the right price (cost). After a period of running a car, we will decide whether we need or want to replace it by acquiring another one.

Customer purpose for both sales and service follows the simple definition that lean is about "Providing the most value from the customer's perspective, while consuming the fewest resources and utilizing the talents of the people who do the work."

Challenges and Opportunities

The dealers that think through the dimensions of customer purpose quickly find gaps to close. It turns out that dealers never measure customer fulfillment. When selling the car, customer fulfillment is the ability of the dealer to provide the right car (quality), in the right place, at the right time (delivery), at the right price (cost). When completing the relevant service and/or repair work, customer fulfillment is the ability to do it right the first time (quality), on time, every time (delivery), and at the right price (cost). In brief, this is the ability of the dealer to meet the customer purpose. Instead (like many industries), the retail motor industry is obsessed with customer satisfaction and is taught that customer satisfaction leads to loyalty. This is questionable as it can be argued that it is not customer satisfaction that leads to loyalty but customer dissatisfaction that leads to customers not being loyal. Each of the dealers that have successfully been implementing lean have recognized the need to measure and improve customer fulfillment.

In our early studies (prior to a dealer implementing lean) we found that the average customer fulfillment was 56 percent, one in two cars being fixed right first time, on time. This shocked us more than it did the dealers and manufacturer head office personnel—imagine a first-tier automotive supplier being able to remain in business with that level of right first time! While each dealer's customer fulfillment and hence problems are unique, when most dealers start to implement lean this is often the problem that needs to be solved: how to improve customer fulfillment—the ability to be able to provide the right vehicle or service and/or repair a vehicle right, first time, on time.

Having defined the high-level problem to solve or the gap(s) to close we need to develop problem-solving capability to be able to establish the root cause(s) of the reasons for failure to fulfill. To do this we look at what work needs to be done, what is being done, and the process by which it is being done. This is where we think about process: in particular, the process providing the value the customer is seeking—defining the value streams that are important for the customer and the organization. For each customer in each value stream we need the dealer to assess what happens to cause an error. There are a whole host of reasons that could be clustered into a series of categories: issues concerned with parts, planning, communication, front- and back-office errors, and technical issues. Confronted with so many issues, it helps to have a visual overview of the process that currently exists when selling, servicing, or repairing a car so that we can design how value should flow to the customer. This is principle number two from *Lean Thinking* (Womack and Jones, 1996): mapping the value stream from conception of requirement through to receipt of the product.

We have tried a number of experiments over the years to engage dealer management and team members to look at their value streams. As the end customer is a key part of both the sales and service value streams, we found it useful to map how they see things (see Figure 33.1). The consumption map (Womack and Jones, 2005a) looks at the value stream from the consumer's point of view. This helps the team understand the difference between value-creating time, necessary non-value-creating time, and waste.

We have also found it useful to help the dealer construct value stream maps of their internal processes. However, we frequently hit a stumbling block as we are told that dealers are not like manufacturing companies. Dealers tell me that "every job in the workshop is different" or "every interaction to sell a car to a customer is unique." With so much apparent variety, it is difficult to see the process and produce a value stream map that is representative of all the work for either the sales or service value stream. Therefore, we need a way to categorize the work, essentially putting it into product families. One of the ways to do this is by using a tool called the Glenday Sieve (Glenday, 2005). It becomes clear that work contains patterns. For example, in a dealer's workshop, a few types of jobs occur frequently and so Juran's concept of the "vital few" or Pareto principle is evident. In addition, by sorting the work by time we find that up to 80 percent of the work in a dealer's workshop takes less than two hours to complete. A further sort reveals that work can be categorized as either predictable work or unpredictable work. Examples include a simple service or a known recall that has a predictable duration, whereas repair work that involves diagnosis has an unpredictable total time (at the outset of starting the work we do not know how long it will take to complete).

Having these insights allows the dealer to create a value stream map for frequently carried out work (for example, a simple service that is dropped off and picked up by a customer) in order to understand how to get these jobs to flow (see Figure 33.2).

Mapping the value stream involves obtaining customer information (demand and customer fulfillment), understanding the physical flow of the product (the vehicle), understanding the information flow, and producing a summary of what we see. Figure 33.2 shows that the physical

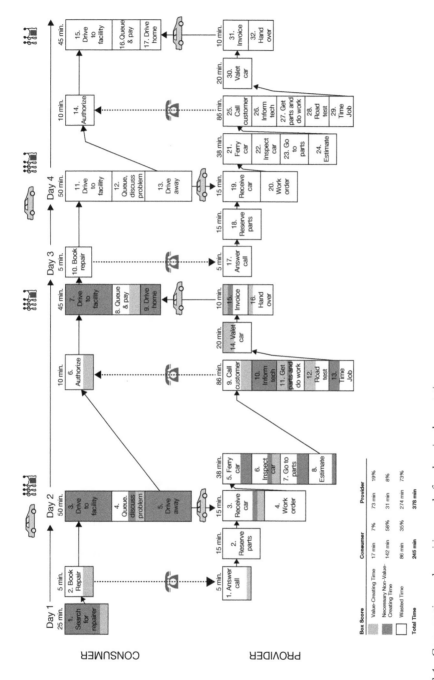

Figure 33.1 Consumption and provision map before lean implementation

Source: Brunt and Kiff (2007, p. 10).

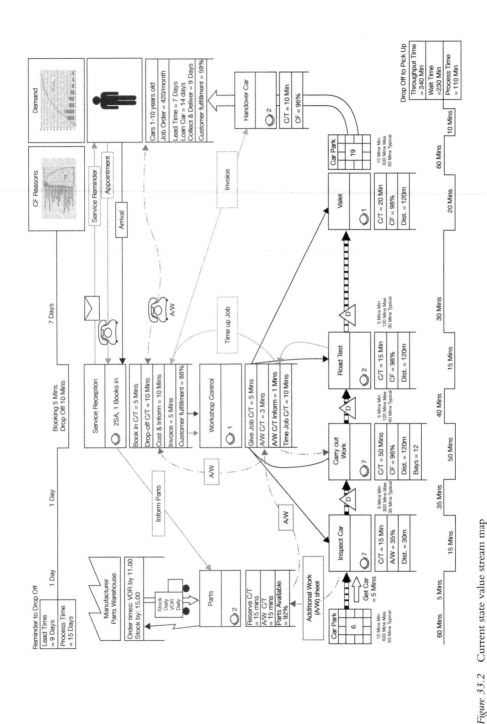

Figure 33.2 Current state value stream map

Source: Brunt and Kiff (2007, p. 26).

steps required for a simple service involve inspecting the vehicle, carrying out the work, conducting a road test, and valeting (washing and vacuuming) the vehicle.

By mapping the information flow, we see how each person in the process knows what to work on next. We see the flow of information from the customer order through all the people involved through to handover of the vehicle. We can see that the instruction of what to work on travels from the service advisor via the workshop controller to the technician. Once the technician starts the work and finds additional work, there is further information flow back to the customer in order to check parts availability, price up the additional work, and inform the customer.

The final step in completing the current state value stream map is to add a timeline to the process so that we can see when the activities take place, right from the time the customer placed the order. The time taken for the whole process (the throughput time) is important because the shorter the throughput time (for all the cars we sell or service/repair) the shorter the time between receiving the vehicle, doing work on it, and getting paid by the customer. Cash to cash is particularly important where we are supplying new cars built to an individual customer order or where we are selling used cars. For service and repair, time is important because the amount of space we need is proportional to the amount of time the car is on the dealer's site.

In addition, we can separate out the process time (the time spent carrying out the activities in a process box) from the waiting time. When we do this, we see that the process time is a small proportion of the total lead time. Generally, the process-time activities are operations (both value added and non-value added) while the lead time is almost always non-value added. The delays between the process boxes only add cost not value (e.g. the cost of having the vehicle on-site as stock). Our summary shows that the time taken from a customer ringing to book an appointment through to the car (and the parts required) being on-site takes nine days' lead time and 15 minutes' process time. Once the car is on-site, the wait time is 230 minutes and 110 minutes of process time.

By walking a value stream, it becomes obvious that there are opportunities to deliver more value to customers—better quality, on time while reducing waste (non-value-creating steps) and hence cost. Referring back to the purpose, process, people PDCA framework there is an opportunity to redesign the technical aspects of the process (value stream) so it better meets the customer purpose. However, to sustain and continuously improve performance it is also essential to engage people in improving the way they provide value for customers.

On the technical side, a lean organization focuses on compressing the time taken for each value stream and each activity. This focus on time helps us to bring to the surface the waste inherent in a process so we can go about eliminating it. To compress time so that a value stream flows reliably and consistently, it is necessary to ensure that each step in the process is valuable (to the customer), capable (can be conducted with the exact same result each time to produce good quality), available (whenever it is needed), adequate (in terms of having the capacity to perform exactly when needed), and flexible (to be able to change over without compromising capability, availability, and adequacy) (Womack, 2003).

Each of the dealers we have worked with has implemented improvements by designing a *future state* value stream. The design of the value stream uses the following principles and technical good habits. Each dealer:

- defines value and measures customer fulfillment, understanding the causes of failure to fulfill;
- understands demand for their products and services—separating predictable and unpredictable work in planning their operations;
- understands where and how work can be flowed;
- where work cannot be flowed, pulls work rather than pushing it to the next process;

- makes efforts to improve the upfront planning as this enables flow to occur in the value stream;
- uses visual management in the operation, for example, in the daily scheduling of the work to be done and in the highlighting of problems;
- levels as much work as possible, avoiding end-of-period rushes, which are a push-and-prevent flow.

In our example, compared with the current state the total lead time for the redesigned future state is down 30 percent from 340 minutes to 235 minutes (see Figure 33.3). Most of the improvement comes from eliminating delays rather than having people speed up their work. Crucially customer fulfillment improves to 92 percent

While value stream mapping serves to highlight the potential and gain agreement to improve the processes that provide value for customers, it is equally important to focus attention on people during a lean implementation. Brilliant processes do not just happen. People play an intrinsic part in the creation of a lean organization (one could argue they are the organization). One of the factors that differentiate a truly excellent lean organization from an organization that is just using lean tools and techniques is the deep engagement and involvement of people at all levels of the organization in continuous improvement of all processes. A key aspect to implementation is ensuring that every important process in the organization has someone responsible for continually evaluating that value stream in terms of purpose and actively engaging each worker in operating it correctly and continually improving it to better address purposes. For example, Toyota has "Respect for People" as one of the key aspects of the Toyota Way (2001) document. Respect for people is about mutual respect—for managers, employees, and between people in each team. Mutual respect means that leaders and managers must be aware that the people closest to the work know most about it. However, the team member must also understand the role of the leader in developing the creativity and problem-solving ability in each team member. Each person can be helped and coached (through a common problem-solving method) to identify problems and develop countermeasures at their level in the organization, then true learning can take place.

It can be argued that the role of leadership in implementing lean also follows the purpose, process, people, problem-solving framework. In terms of purpose, it is a leader's role to set alignment around the vision. Second, it is the leader's role to design and support processes that create/provide value to customers (value streams). Third, it is the leader's role to develop people to take personal responsibility for problem solving.

Where we have witnessed successful lean transformations take place in sales and service the leadership component has been a key differentiator. Leaders of sustainable lean transformations display two essential components. John Shook suggests that they:

1   get each person to take initiative to solve problems and improve his or her job;
2   ensure that each person's job is aligned to provide value for the customer and prosperity for the company.

Lean leadership is about getting the work done and developing your people at the same time. The $64,000 question is "how" do we do that? Fujio Cho suggests there are three keys to lean leadership:

1   "Go see": Management must spend time on the front lines.
2   Ask "Why?": Use the technique daily.
3   Show respect.

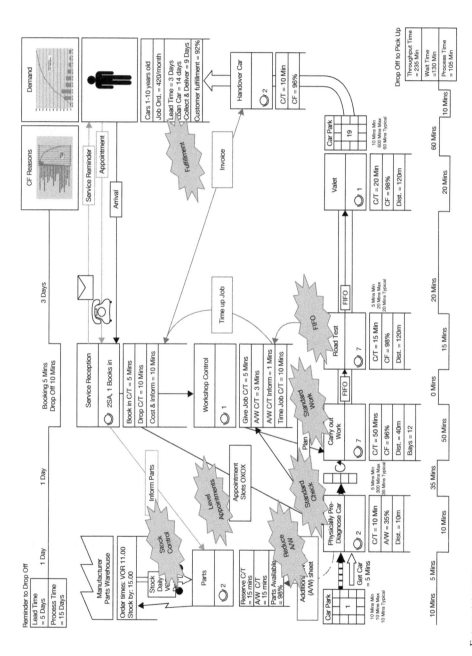

Figure 33.3 Future state map

Source: Brunt and Kiff (2007, p. 52).

If PDCA is the engine that drives lean leadership, how do we build a culture of PDCA? Firstly, it is necessary to break with the stereotype that "having a problem is bad." It is natural that there are some problems in our workplaces. If we reinforce the view that having a problem is bad, some team members may not inform their supervisor or manager of problems. It is therefore imperative that we make abnormal from normal visible immediately. This helps workers do their jobs better, it helps workers know when to ask for help, and it helps management know what questions to ask. In addition, we need to practice. We must solve real business problems (based on need) and make improvements in the way work is performed: at each level of the company, in each activity of the company, in real time, at the root cause—at the real place, to see the real thing and to understand the real fact, to address real problems. Finding problems and taking countermeasures to eliminate them will lead to continuous improvement.

Of course, leaders can set alignment around the vision (purpose), they can design and support processes that create/provide value to customers (process), and they can try to develop people (people) to take personal responsibility for problem solving (problem solving.) However, the leadership style and behaviors (the way leaders act) are also a key factor in determining whether they will be successful. There are many different leadership styles, but the lean style is neither the old dictator style of "do it my way," nor is it the empowerment style "do it your way." Instead, lean leadership is about "follow me . . . and we'll figure this out together." Leadership styles and behaviors are a key factor in determining the success a leader has when developing and implementing lean. Thus it is necessary to develop experiments that help leaders understand their underlying values and beliefs so they can reflect on whether there are differences between them and the underlying values and beliefs that are required to develop a sustainable lean transformation.

The Future of Lean Dealership

As outlined at the beginning of this chapter, applying lean to the processes that occur closest to the automotive customer—the dealer operations—is still in its infancy. This is not only true for the automotive sector but also for sales and service in both "business-to-consumer" and "business-to-business" environments. While this is surprising to anyone who knows about the benefits lean thinking can bring to an organization, one also has to think about the situation each organization finds itself in and the issues affecting it.

Being a car dealer is not easy. The business is complex. It operates with high levels of competition and in an environment where customer expectations have increased over the years. In a number of mature markets, consolidation of dealer businesses has occurred with groups representing a number of competing brands. It can be argued that interest in process has been less prevalent in businesses where profit can be made by additional deals. The environment coupled with the short-term nature of many sales organizations contributes to the lean approach being off the radar for many dealers.

Of course, manufacturers know about lean thinking. Many have implemented their versions of lean production and use lean in product development. However, when manufacturers are talking to dealers they are mostly working with a network of organizations external to their organization. In contrast to the supermarkets that started to apply lean to their supply chains in the 1990s the auto manufacturers don't typically operate the processes closest to the customer. However, as the brand in the value stream, they have increasingly sought to tighten the standards they expect of their retailers and deploy programs to improve the performance of their dealers. The focus is often therefore concerned with improving poorer-performing businesses rather than making a step change in performance. All manufacturers benchmark their networks, identifying the gaps between upper- and lower-quartile performers. The limitation with this approach is that the few dealers using the lean approach appear as outliers and that as competition at dealer level is local and not global (as it is in automotive design and manufacture) each dealer only has to be slightly better than their local competition.

There is no doubt that applying lean to sales and service is on the agenda of some manufacturers. Indeed, a number have programs that help dealers in this area. However, many attempts have been proof-of-concept experiments followed by a rollout to a number of other sites. Experiences from the Halfway Group in South Africa have shown that the rollout approach is limited. Such an approach misses what is really at the heart of lean thinking: the integration of purpose, process, people, and PDCA to problem solving and the fact that when used most successfully lean is a mechanism for people to learn.

Instead of attempting to roll solutions out, the future direction for lean in sales and service needs to be situational—aligning organizational purpose to create more value for customers while developing people at the same time—to the organization in question. Rather than applying a series of predetermined answers, we should think about the questions we need to ask in order to carry out lean transformations that are sustainable. In January 2014, John Shook shared what we at the time called the *lean transformation model* (now understood to be a framework rather than a model). This is the framework we have been developing to guide transformations. It is also the framework we have used at the Halfway Group in South Africa.

The Lean Transformation Framework

To explain lean transformation, we have borrowed the house metaphor from Toyota (Figure 33.4). The house comprises foundations, two pillars, and a roof. Of course, many organizations are aware of Toyota's production system house—and many firms have tried to emulate or build their own versions, often by copying the elements. However, the transformation framework is very different in its intent. Instead of listing the tools and techniques used, or even the principles of "*jidoka*" (production leveling) and just-in-time, we are seeking a way to communicate the questions one needs to think about when embarking on a *lean transformation*. What we have learned over the years is that each company's circumstances are unique and therefore we need a situational approach to the transformation. However, we must remember that it is built around the lean approach and therefore a distinctive feature is that we need to understand value from the perspective of the customer. We have called this "value-driven purpose"—here we are asking, "what is the purpose of the organization?" More specifically, "what problem are you trying to solve?"

Next, we turn our attention to the first of our two pillars. We have called this operational or "process improvement." This is the second distinct piece to lean. What we are doing here is focusing on the work that creates value for customers. This is often where many lean folks are most comfortable, and what many people see as being lean. However, it is really only one element of the system. What is distinct about the approach used when asking the questions in the framework is that it becomes apparent that the people who manage the work must learn to improve it (in order to sustain the transformation). Improvement is part of the management system.

We have called the second pillar "capability development." It is all about how we develop people. Here our target condition is to build capability so people can do more and improve themselves. By using a typical skills matrix we can look at ability from level 1—having "knowledge" through understanding, being capable, being able to do a job well through to being able to do, teach, and improve the job. Interestingly it is really only knowledge of work that is suitable to teach in an off-the-job classroom training. Levels 2 through 5 are taught better with actual problems and situations on the job with mentoring from capable superiors. You cannot

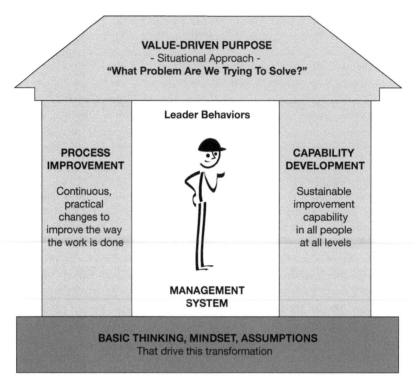

Figure 33.4   The lean transformation framework

Source: Shook (2014).

develop skill just by sitting in a classroom—you have to practice. So to build capability we need to design processes that develop people "on the job." Developing people needs to be explicit. It is actually each leader's job. To develop people, we have to develop experiments. We must begin from the need and aim the training a level above what the current organizational need is, in order to "stretch" people and the organization. The engine for such experiments is the scientific method using PDCA. Beginning with the real need means solving real problems that help close our performance gaps.

In the center of the house, the focus is on leadership and management. In particular, we think about what management system we need and the leadership behaviors that are required to drive the transformation. This is tricky, because there are elements of these dimensions within the transformation that are not as easy to see as perhaps understanding and improving the actual work to be done. However, some elements of this are well known. One example is the process for developing and deploying strategy using "*hoshin kanri*" (policy deployment) (Dennis, 2006) within the management system. A second example would be managing teams using processes such as daily team meetings or managing projects using *obeya* rooms. It is also possible to define what leadership behaviors we need. What's more difficult to do is to understand how well this is being done on a daily basis.

For the foundations of the house, we refer to the basic thinking—the assumptions and mindset—that underlies the entire system and drives the transformation itself. This is really about the basic beliefs we, as individuals, have about the way the transformation works. These beliefs and mindset constitute the culture of the organization. To use a practical example, if the senior team in an organization believes that the people closest to the work know most about it, and that we need to harness their knowledge so that problems can be solved by the people doing the work, then this thinking leads to the design of experiments to test that hypothesis and develop people at all levels. If the thinking were not aligned in that direction and the assumption made that only a few people should be coming up with solutions, then we would have a very different transformation approach. The latter would be one in which we perhaps developed a boot camp to train a select few on advanced lean techniques, creating a continuous improvement organization and identified "projects" that would give a return, but that wouldn't necessarily develop the organization thoroughly.

Therefore, we have five elements to the lean transformation framework. "What problem are we trying to solve?" This leads us to a target condition, which helps us determine the situational approach for this particular transformation. Next, we look at operational improvement, asking: "How will we improve the actual value creating work?" Of course, we want the work to improve continuously and that requires that people have the capability to do that. So, our third question is: "How will we develop people to work in new ways?"

Now we know what the problem we are trying to solve is, what the work that is required is, and what capabilities people need, we can design the leadership behaviors and management system required. The next question is "What leadership behaviors and management systems are required to lead the work in this new way?" This is a practical way to come at the issue of leadership and management, as we are closing gaps that have been identified. The final question addresses the basic assumptions and mindsets that are required. "What basic assumptions or mindsets underlie this change?"

To conclude, understanding each of the dimensions outlined in more detail is part of the future of lean research and certainly one of the next steps in the sales and service area. We argue that you have to do all five of the elements in the framework. It is a system and not prescriptive. It is about experiments to try. By asking these questions—fine-tuned to an organization's circumstances—the organization can transform faster, improving its customer fulfilment level in the core value streams. I hope that organizations seeking and asking the right questions will realize that lean can only be learned by doing and cannot be sustained via large programs from external parties. As more examples are created in this environment, it will encourage more to try. Understanding the factors that lead to organizations and individuals being successful in their efforts at implementation will play a key part in the future of lean.

Case Study: Lean Dealership in Jaeger Toyota

Jaeger Toyota is a family-owned dealer group based in Bergen, Norway. Founded in 1928, it has seven Toyota branches, three wholly owned. The firm employs 115 employees and sells almost 3,000 new vehicles per year. The company has a strong regional focus. Bergen has a population of about 450,000 and Jaeger has a market share of 16 percent of the car purchasing population.

Jaeger's lean journey started in 2006 when I accompanied them to visit Pedro Simao, in Portugal. Torgeir Halvorsen, Jaeger's Managing Director, had read some lean books as he was interested in Toyota's philosophy and management system—these included *Lean Solutions* and the Simao story. We had taken countless other dealers to see Pedro but most had not really understood the significance of what they were seeing. However, Torgeir's reaction was very different. He was already focusing on the customer—Jaeger was regularly top in customer satisfaction surveys across all Norwegian companies and in an area of full employment they were mindful of people development and retention.

Work to implement lean started shortly after the Simao visit (in 2006), initially with a pilot value stream on vehicle servicing and repair in their Asane site. Like Simao, Torgeir led the team to learn how to redesign this value stream, ably supported by Jaeger's Service Director, Rolf Paulsen. Lean thinking and the Toyota Way have been systematically disseminated throughout the organization since.

In the vehicle service and repair area, improvements have been made to the whole value stream. The improvements start with how bookings are made, parts processed, the work carried out, and the vehicle being handed back to the customer. At the start of their journey, customer fulfillment was under 50 percent, but now regularly reaches 100 percent on a day. For express service work, two technicians work on the vehicle at the same time, servicing a vehicle in an agreed sequence (with standardized work) just like technicians carrying out a pit stop in a Formula 1 race. This enables a larger proportion of customers to have a "while they wait service" which is carried out to an appointment. Not only does this smooth the flow of the work by carefully scheduling arrivals to eliminate queues, the work is passed directly to the technician, reducing handoffs. Parts and tools are pre-kitted and delivered to the technician in the service bay just as needed.

These gains create a win–win–win situation for service customers, employees, and the company. Customers' time is no longer wasted and Jaeger can handle a greater volume of business. Jaeger's technicians are significantly more productive than their competition and with more jobs being done right the first time, fewer cars are brought back for a second visit. The reduction in space required is significant too—the industry benchmark is five vehicles per ramp per day. Jaeger can carry out up to 16 vehicles per ramp per day. Such productivity improvements have meant that Jaeger has been able to stay in its existing facilities, saving millions of euros in potential redevelopment costs. The company quickly spread lean thinking to its other sites in the service operation.

Having learned simultaneously about improving the work and developing capability, Jaeger's next step was to apply lean thinking to the leadership and management system. Initially visual management was developed at the value stream level. Through this mechanism, the organization learned about the importance of making problems visible. The next logical step was to apply the same logic to the work of management. An obeya room was developed and an experiment to introduce hoshin kanri (Dennis, 2006) was conducted. Today each major function in the organization uses A3 thinking (Shook, 2008) to articulate its gaps and ensures alignment back to the overall A3 strategy for the business.

The business benefits have been substantial. The win–win–win established in the service and repair value stream is evident at the organization level. In 2006, Jaeger slightly outperformed the average for all Norwegian Toyota dealers in terms of profitability. By 2015, the gap had widened to the point where Jaeger achieves five times the profitability of the average profitability for the brand. By implementing lean, Jaeger is an outlier in monetary performance terms as well as being the class leader in quality and value for customers.

References

Brunt, D. C. and Kiff, J. S. (2007). *Creating Lean Dealers: The Lean Route to Satisfied Customers, Productive Employees and Profitable Retailers*, Ross-on-Wye, Lean Enterprise Academy.

Dennis, P. (2006). *Getting the Right Things Done: A Leader's Guide to Planning and Execution*, Cambridge, MA, Lean Enterprise Institute.

Glenday, I. (2005). *Breaking through to Flow: Banish Fire Fighting and Increase Customer Service*, Ross-on-Wye, Lean Enterprise Academy.

Shook, J. S. (2008). *Managing to Learn: Using the A3 Management Process to Solve Problems, Gain Agreement, Mentor and Lead*. Cambridge, MA, Lean Enterprise Institute.

Shook, J. (2014). *Transforming Transformation* [online]. Available at: www.lean.org/shook/DisplayObject. cfm?o=2533 (accessed February 2016).

Toyota (2001). *The Toyota Way*, Aichi, Japan, Toyota Motor Company.

Womack, J. P. (2003). Jim Womack on how lean compares with Six Sigma, re-engineering, TOC, TPM, etc. Available at: www.lean.org/womack/DisplayObject.cfm?o=710 (accessed February 2016).

Womack, J. P. and Jones, D. T. (1996). *Lean Thinking: Banish Waste and Create Wealth in Your Corporation*. New York, The Free Press.

Womack, J. P. and Jones, D. T. (2005a). Lean consumption. *Harvard Business Review*, March, 1–14.

Womack, J. P. and Jones, D. T. (2005b). *Lean Solutions: How Companies and Customers Can Create Value and Wealth Together*, New York, Simon & Schuster.

Womack, J. P., Jones, D. T. and Roos, D. (1990). *The Machine that Changed the World*, New York, Rawson Associates.

34

LEAN SOFTWARE DEVELOPMENT

Mary Poppendieck

Introduction

We were in a conference room near the Waterfront in Cape Town. "I just lost a crown from one of my teeth," my husband, Tom, declared just before I was scheduled to open the conference. Someone at our table responded, "You're lucky, Cape Town has some of the best dentists in the world." It didn't feel very lucky: Cape Town was the first stop on a 10-week trip to Africa, Europe, and Australia.

The situation was eerily familiar. A year earlier a chip had cracked off my tooth as I ate a pizza in Lima, the first stop of a 10-week trip to South America. I ate gingerly during the rest of the trip, worried that the tooth would crack further. Luckily, I made it back home with no pain and little additional damage. Once there, it took three days to get a dentist appointment. The dentist made an impression of the gap in my tooth and fashioned a temporary crown. "This will have to last for a week or two," she said. "If it falls out, just stick it back in and be more careful what you eat." Luckily the temporary crown held, and 10 days later a permanent crown arrived from the lab. Two weeks after we arrived home, my tooth was fixed.

We were scheduled to be in Cape Town for only two days. How was Tom going to get a crown replaced in two days? A small committee formed. Someone did a phone search; apparently the Waterfront was a good place to find dentists. A call was made. "You can go right now—the dental office is nearby. Do you want someone to walk you over?" As Tom headed out the door with an escort, I got ready for my presentation. Halfway through the talk, I saw Tom return and signal that all was well.

"I lost a part of my tooth, not just the crown," Tom told me after the talk. "I'm supposed to return at 3.30 this afternoon; I should have a new crown by the end of the day." The dentist had a mini-lab in his office. Instead of making a temporary crown, he used a camera to take images of the broken tooth and adjacent teeth. The results were combined into a 3D model of the crown to which the dentist made a few adjustments. He then selected a ceramic blank that matched the color of Tom's teeth and put it in a milling machine. With the push of a button, instructions to make the crown were loaded into the machine. Cutters whirled and water squirted to keep the ceramic cool. Ten minutes later the crown was ready to cement in place. Ninety minutes after he arrived that afternoon and eight hours after the incident, Tom walked out of the dental office with a new permanent crown. It cost approximately the same amount as my crown had cost a year earlier.

Lean is About Flow Efficiency

The book *This is Lean* (Modig and Åhlström, 2012) describes "lean" as a relentless focus on efficiency—but not the kind of efficiency that cuts staff and money, nor the kind of efficiency that strives to keep every resource busy all of the time. In fact, a focus on resource efficiency will almost always destroy overall efficiency, the authors contend, because fully utilized machines (and people) create huge traffic jams. These jams end up creating a lot of extra work. Instead, Modig and Åhlström demonstrate that lean is about *flow efficiency*—that is, the efficiency with which a unit of work (a flow unit) moves through the system.

Consider our dental experience. It took two weeks for me get a new crown, but in truth, only an hour-and-a-half of that time was needed to actually fix the tooth; the rest of the time was mostly spent waiting. My flow efficiency was 1.5 ÷ 336 (two weeks) = 0.45 percent. On the other hand, Tom's tooth was replaced in eight hours—42 times faster—giving him a flow efficiency of 1.5 ÷ 8 = 18.75 percent.

In my case, the dental system was focused on the efficiency of the lab's milling machine—no doubt an expensive piece of equipment. Add up all of the extra costs: a cast of the crown for the lab, a temporary crown for me, two separate hour-long sessions with the dentist, plus all of the associated logistics—scheduling, shipping, tracking, etc. In Tom's case, the dental system was focused on the speed with which it could fix his tooth—which was good for us, because a long wait for a crown was not an option. True, the milling machine in the dentist's office sits idle much of each day. (The dentist said he has to replace two crowns a day to make it economically feasible.) However, when you add up the waste of temporary crowns, the piles of casts waiting for a milling machine, and the significant cost of recovering from a mistake—an idle milling machine makes a lot of sense.

What does flow efficiency really mean? Assume you have a camera and efficiency means keeping the camera busy—always taking a picture of some value-adding action. Where do you aim your camera? In the case of resource efficiency, the camera is aimed at the resource—the milling machine—and keeping it busy is of the utmost importance. In the case of flow efficiency, the camera is on the flow unit—Tom—and work on replacing his crown is what counts. The fundamental mental shift that lean requires is this: flow efficiency trumps resource efficiency almost all of the time.

What is Lean Software Development?

To understand *lean software development*, we first need to understand lean product development. During the 1980s Japanese cars were capturing market share at a rate that alarmed US automakers. In Boston, both MIT and Harvard Business School responded by launching extensive studies on the automotive industry. In 1990 the MIT research effort resulted in the now classic book *The Machine that Changed the World: The Story of Lean Production* (Womack et al., 1990), which popularized the term "lean." A year later, Harvard Business School published *Product Development Performance* (Clark and Fujimoto, 1991), and the popular book *Developing Products in Half the Time* (Smith and Reinertsen, 1991) was released. These two 1991 books are foundational references on what came to be called "lean product development," although the term "lean" would not be associated with product development for another decade.

Clark and Fujimoto documented the fact that US and European volume automotive producers took three times as many engineering hours and 50 percent more time to develop a car compared with Japanese automakers, yet the Japanese cars had substantially higher quality and cost less to manufacture. Clearly the Japanese product development process produced better cars faster and at lower cost than typical Western development practices of the time. Clark and Fujimoto noted that the distinguishing features of Japanese product development paralleled features found in Japanese automotive production. For example, Japanese product development focused on flow efficiency, reducing information inventory, and learning based on early and frequent feedback from downstream processes. By contrast, product development in Western countries focused on resource efficiency, completing each phase of development before starting the next, and following the original plan with as little variation as possible.

In 1991, the University of Michigan began its Japan Technology Management Program. Over the next several years, faculty and associate members included Jeffrey Liker, Allen Ward, Durward Sobek, John Shook, and Mike Rother. This group has published numerous books and articles on lean thinking, lean manufacturing, and lean product development, including *The Toyota Product Development System* (Morgan and Liker, 2006) and *Lean Product and Process Development* (Ward, 2007). The second book summarizes the essence of lean product development this way:

1   Understand that knowledge creation is the essential work of product development.
2   Charter a team of responsible experts led by an entrepreneurial system designer.
3   Manage product development using the principles of cadence, flow, and pull.

It is important to recognize that even though lean product development is based on the same principles as lean production, the practices surrounding development are not the same as those considered useful in production. In fact, transferring lean practices from manufacturing to development has led to some disastrous results. For example, lean production emphasizes reducing variation—exactly the wrong thing to do in product development. The Western practice of following a plan and measuring variance from a plan is often justified by the slogan "Do it right the first time." Unfortunately, this approach does not allow for learning; it confines designs to those conceived when the least amount of knowledge is available. A fundamental practice in lean product development is to create variation (not avoid it) in order to explore the impact of multiple approaches. This is called set-based engineering (see Chapter 6 in this book, "Lean Product and Process Development" by Rossi, Morgan and Shook).

The critical thing to keep in mind is that knowledge creation is the essential work of product development. While lean production practices support learning about and improving the manufacturing process, their goal is to minimize variation in the product. This is not appropriate for product development, where variation is an essential element of the learning cycles that are the foundation of good product engineering. Therefore, instead of copying lean manufacturing practices, lean product development practices must evolve from a deep understanding of fundamental lean principles adapted to a development environment.

Lean Software Development is a Subset of Lean Product Development

In 1975, computers were large, expensive, and rare. Software for these large machines was developed in the IT departments of large companies and dealt largely with the logistics of running the company—payroll, order processing, inventory management, etc. However, as mainframes morphed into minicomputers, personal computers, and microprocessors, it became practical to enhance products and services with software. Then the internet began to invade the world, and it eventually became the delivery mechanism for a large fraction of the software being developed today. As software moved from supporting business process to enabling smart products and becoming the essence services, software engineers moved from IT departments to line organizations where they joined product teams.

Today, most software development is not a stand-alone process, but rather a part of developing products or services. Thus lean software development might be considered a subset of lean product development; certainly the principles that underpin lean product development are the same principles that form the basis of lean software development.

Agile and Lean Software Development: 2000–2010

It is hard to believe these days, but in the mid-1990s developing software was a slow and painful process found in the IT departments of large corporations. As the role of software expanded and software engineers moved into line organizations, reaction against the old methods grew. In 1999, Kent Beck proposed a radically new approach to software development in the book *Extreme Programming Explained* (Beck, 2000). In 2001 the *Agile Manifesto* (Beck et al., 2001) gave this new approach a name—"agile."

In 2003, the book *Lean Software Development* (Poppendieck and Poppendieck, 2003) merged lean manufacturing principles with agile practices and the latest product development thinking, particularly from the book *Managing the Design Factory* (Reinertsen, 1997). Lean software development was presented as a set of principles that form a theoretical framework for developing and evolving agile practices:

1   eliminate waste,
2   amplify learning,
3   decide as late as possible,
4   deliver as fast as possible,
5   empower the team,
6   build quality in, and
7   see the whole.

Although the principles of lean software development are consistent with lean manufacturing and (especially) lean product development, the specific practices that emerged were tailored to a software environment and aimed at the flaws in the prevailing software development methodologies. One of the biggest flaws at the time was the practice of moving software sequentially through the typical stages of design, development, test, and deployment—with handovers of large inventories of information accumulating at each stage. This practice left testing and integration at the end of the development chain, so defects went undetected for weeks or months before they were discovered. Typical sequential processes reserved a third of a release cycle for testing, integration, and defect removal. The idea that it was possible to "build quality in" was not considered a practical concept for software.

To counter sequential processes and the long integration and defect removal phase, agile software development practices focused on fast feedback cycles in these areas:

1   *Test-driven development*: Start by writing tests (think of them as executable specifications) and then write the code to pass the tests. Put the tests into a test harness for ongoing code verification.
2   *Continuous integration*: Integrate small increments of code changes into the code base frequently—multiple times a day—and run the test harness to verify that the changes have not introduced errors.
3   *Iterations*: Develop working software in iterations of two to four weeks; review the software at the end of each iteration and make appropriate adjustments.

4   *Cross-functional teams*: Development teams should include customer proxies and testers as well as developers to minimize handovers.

During its first decade, agile development moved from a radical idea to a mainstream practice. This was aided by the widespread adoption of Scrum, an agile methodology which institutionalized the third and fourth practices listed above, but unfortunately omitted the first two practices.

The Difference between Lean and Agile Software Development

When it replaced sequential development practices typical at the time, agile software development improved the software development process in most cases—in IT departments as well as product development organizations. However, the expected organizational benefits of agile often failed to materialize because agile focused on optimizing software development, which frequently was not the system constraint. Lean software development differed from agile in that it worked to optimize flow efficiency across the entire value stream "from concept to cash." (Note the subtitle of the book *Implementing Lean Software Development: From Concept to Cash* by Poppendieck and Poppendieck, 2006.) The end-to-end view was consistent with the work of Taiichi Ohno, who said:

> All we are doing is looking at the timeline, from the moment the customer gives us an order to the point when we collect the cash. And we are reducing that time line by removing the non-value-added wastes.
>
> *(Ohno, 1988. p ix)*

Lean software development came to focus on these areas:

1   *Build the right thing*: Understand and deliver real value to real customers.
2   *Build it fast*: Dramatically reduce the lead time from customer need to delivered solution.
3   *Build the thing right*: Guarantee quality and speed with automated testing, integration, and deployment.
4   *Learn through feedback*: Evolve the product design based on early and frequent end-to-end feedback.

Let's take a look at each principle in more detail:

1   *Understand and deliver real value to real customers*: A software development team working with a single customer proxy has one view of the customer interest, and often that view is not informed by technical experience or feedback from downstream processes (such as operations). A product team focused on solving real customer problems will continually integrate the knowledge of diverse team members, both upstream and downstream, to make sure the customer perspective is truly understood and effectively addressed. Clark and Fujimoto (1991) call this "integrated problem solving" and consider it an essential element of lean product development.
2   *Dramatically reduce the lead time from customer need to delivered solution*: A focus on flow efficiency is the secret ingredient of lean software development. How long does it take for a team to deploy into production a single small change that solves a customer problem? Typically, it can take weeks or months—even when the actual work involved consumes only an hour.

Why? Because subtle dependencies among various areas of the code make it probable that a small change will break other areas of the code. Therefore, it is necessary to deploy large batches of code as a package after extensive (usually manual) testing. In many ways the decade of 2000–2010 was dedicated to finding ways to break dependencies, automate the provisioning and testing processes, and thus allow rapid independent deployment of small batches of code.

3   *Guarantee quality and speed with automated testing, integration, and deployment*: It was exciting to watch the expansion of test-driven development and continuous integration during the decade of 2000–2010. First these two critical practices were applied at the team level—developers wrote unit tests (which were actually technical specifications) and integrated them immediately into their branch of the code. Test-driven development expanded to writing executable product specifications in an incremental manner, which moved testers to the front of the process. This proved more difficult than automated unit testing, and precipitated a shift toward testing modules and their interactions rather than end-to-end testing. Once the product behavior could be tested automatically, code could be integrated into the overall system much more frequently during the development process—preferably daily—so software engineers could get rapid feedback on their work.

Next, the operations people got involved and automated the provisioning of environments for development, testing, and deployment. Finally, teams (which now included operations) could automate the entire specification, development, test, and deployment processes—creating an automated deployment pipeline. There was initial fear that more rapid deployment would cause more frequent failure, but exactly the opposite happened. Automated testing and frequent deployment of small changes meant that risk was limited. When errors did occur, detection and recovery was much faster and easier, and the team became a lot better at it. Far from increasing risk, it is now known that deploying code frequently in small batches is the best way to reduce risk and increase the stability of large complex code bases.

4   *Evolve the product design based on early and frequent end-to-end feedback*: To cap these remarkable advance, once product teams could deploy multiple times per day, they began to close the loop with customers. Through canary releases, A/B testing, and other techniques, product teams learned from real customers which product ideas worked and how to fine-tune their offerings for better business results.

When these four principles guided software development in product organizations, significant business-wide benefits were achieved. However, IT departments found it difficult to adopt the principles because they required changes that lay beyond span of control of most IT organizations.

Lean Software Development: 2010–2015

In 2010, two significant books about lean software development were published. David Anderson's book *Kanban* (Anderson, 2010) presented a powerful visual method for managing and limiting work-in-process (WIP). Just at the time when two-week iterations began to feel slow, *kanban* gave teams a way to increase flow efficiency while providing situational awareness across the value stream. Jez Humble and Dave Farley's book *Continuous Delivery* (Humble and Farley, 2010) walked readers through the steps necessary to achieve automated testing, integration, and deployment, making daily deployment practical for many organizations. A year later, Erik Ries' book *The Lean Startup* (Ries, 2011) showed how to use the rapid feedback loop created by continuous delivery to run experiments with real customers and confirm the validity of product ideas before incurring the expense of detailed implementation.

Over the next few years, the ideas in these books became mainstream and the limitations of agile software development (software-only perspective and iteration-based delivery) were gradually expanded to include a wider part of the value stream and a more rapid flow. A grassroots movement called DevOps worked to make automated provision-code-build-test-deployment pipelines practical. Cloud computing arrived, providing easy and automated provisioning of environments. Cloud elements (virtual machines, containers), services (storage, analysis, etc.), and architectures (microservices) made it possible for small services and applications to be rapidly and independently deployed. Improved testing techniques (simulations, contract assertions) have made error-free deployments the norm.

The State of Lean Software Development in 2015

Today's successful internet companies have learned how to optimize software development over the entire value stream. They create full stack teams that are expected to understand the consumer problem, deal effectively with tough engineering issues, try multiple solutions until the data shows which one works best, and maintain responsibility for improving the solution over time. Large companies with legacy systems have begun to take notice, but they struggle with moving from where they are to the world of thriving internet companies.

Lean principles are a big help for organizations that want to move from old development techniques to modern software approaches. For example, Calçado (2015) shows how classic lean tools—value stream mapping and problem solving with five whys—were used to increase flow efficiency at Soundcloud, leading over time to a microservices architecture. In fact, focusing on flow efficiency is an excellent way for an organization to discover the most effective path to a modern technology stack and development approach.

For traditional software development, flow efficiency is typically lower than 10 percent; agile practices usually bring it up to 30 or 40 percent. Yet in thriving internet companies, flow efficiency approaches 70 percent and is often quite a bit higher. Low flow efficiencies are caused by friction—in the form of batching, queueing, handovers, and delayed discovery of defects, as well as misunderstanding of consumer problems and changes in those problems during long resolution times. Improving flow efficiency involves identifying and removing the biggest sources of friction from the development process.

Modern software development practices—the ones used by successful internet companies—address the friction in software development in a very particular way. The companies start by looking for the root causes of friction, which usually turn out to be 1) misunderstanding of the customer problem, 2) dependencies in the code base, and 3) information and time lost during handovers and multitasking. Therefore, they focus on three areas:

1   understanding the consumer journey,
2   architecture and automation to expose and reduce dependencies, and
3   team structures and responsibilities.

Today, lean development in software usually focuses on these three areas as the primary way to increase efficiency, assure quality, and improve responsiveness in software-intensive systems.

1   *Understand the customer journey*: Software-intensive products create a two-way path between companies and their consumers. A wealth of data exists about how products are used, how

consumers react to a product's capabilities, opportunities to improve the product, and so on. Gathering this data and analyzing it has become an essential capability for companies far beyond the internet world: car manufacturers, mining equipment companies, retail stores, and many others gather and analyze "Big Data" to gain insights into consumer behavior. The ability of companies to understand their consumers through data has changed the way products are developed (Porter and Heppelmann, 2015). No longer do product managers (or representatives from "the business") develop a roadmap and give a prioritized list of desired features to an engineering team. Instead, data scientists work with product teams to identify themes to be explored. Then the product teams identify consumer problems surrounding the theme and experiment with a range of solutions. Using rapid deployment and feedback capabilities, the product team continually enhances the product, measuring its success by business improvements not feature completion.

2   *Architecture and automation*: Many internet companies, including Amazon, Netflix, eBay, realestate.com.au, Forward, Twitter, PayPal, Gilt, Bluemix, Soundcloud, The Guardian, and even the UK Government Digital Service have evolved from monolithic architectures to microservices. They found that certain areas of their offerings need constant updating to deal with a large influx of customers or rapid changes in the marketplace. To meet this need, relatively small services are assigned to small teams which then split their services off from the main code base in such a way that each service can be deployed independently. A service team is responsible for changing and deploying the service as often as necessary (usually very frequently), while insuring that the changes do not break any upstream or downstream services. This assurance is provided by sophisticated automated testing techniques as well as automated incremental deployment.

Other internet companies, including Google and Facebook, have maintained existing architectures but developed sophisticated deployment pipelines that automatically send each small code change through a series of automated tests with automatic error handling. The deployment pipeline culminates in safe deployments which occur at very frequent intervals; the more frequent the deployment, the easier it is to isolate problems and determine their cause. In addition, these automation tools often contain dependency maps so that feedback on failures can be sent directly to the responsible engineers and offending code can be automatically reverted (taken out of the pipeline in a safe manner).

These architectural structures and automation tools are a key element in a development approach that uses Big Data combined with extremely rapid feedback to improve the consumer journey and solve consumer problems. They are most commonly found in internet companies, but are being used in many others, including organizations that develop embedded software. (See the case study below.)

3   *Team structures and responsibilities*: When consumer empathy, data analytics, and very rapid feedback are combined, there is one more point of friction that can easily reduce flow efficiency. If an organization has not delegated responsibility for product decisions to the team involved in the rapid feedback loop, the benefits of this approach are lost. In order for such feedback loops to work, teams with a full stack of capabilities must be given responsibility to make decisions and implement immediate changes based on the data they collect. Typically, such teams include people with product, design, data, technology, quality, and operations backgrounds. They are responsible for an improving set of business metrics rather than delivering a set of features. An example of this would be the UK Government Digital Service (GDS), where teams are responsible for delivering improvements in four key areas: cost per transaction, user satisfaction, transaction completion rate, and digital take-up.

It is interesting to note that UK laws make it difficult to base contracts on such metrics, so GDS staffs internal teams with designers and software engineers and makes them responsible for the metrics. Following this logic to its conclusion, the typical approach of IT departments—contracting with their business colleagues to deliver a pre-specified set of features—is incompatible with full stack teams responsible for business metrics. In fact, it is rare to find separate IT departments in companies founded after the mid-1990s (which includes virtually all internet companies). Instead, these newer companies place their software engineers in line organizations, reducing the friction of handovers between departments.

In older organizations, IT departments often find it difficult to adopt modern software development approaches. This is because they have inherited monolithic code bases intertwined with deep dependencies that introduce devious errors and thwart independent deployment of small changes. One major source of friction is the corporate database, once considered essential as the single source of truth about the business, but now under attack as a massive dependency generator. Another source of friction is outsourced applications, where even small changes are difficult and knowledge of how to make them no longer resides in the company. Perhaps the biggest source of friction in IT departments is the distance between their technical people and the company's customers. Since most IT departments view their colleagues in line businesses as their customers, the technical people in IT lack a direct line of sight to the real customers of the company. Therefore, insightful trade-offs and innovative solutions struggle to emerge.

The Future of Lean Software Development

The worldwide software engineering community has developed a culture of sharing innovative ideas, in stark contrast to the more common practice of keeping intellectual property and internally developed tools proprietary. The rapid growth of large, reliable, secure software systems can be directly linked to the fact that software engineers routinely contribute to and build upon the work of their worldwide colleagues through open source projects and repositories like GitHub. This reflects the long-standing practices of the academic world but is strikingly unique in the commercial world. Due to this intense industry-wide knowledge sharing, methods and tools for building highly reliable complex software systems have advanced extraordinarily quickly and are widely available.

As long as the software community continues to leverage its knowledge-sharing culture it will continue to grow rapidly, because sophisticated solutions to seemingly intractable problems eventually emerge when many minds are focused on the problem. The companies that will benefit the most from these advances are the ones that not only track new techniques as they are being developed, but also contribute their own ideas to the knowledge pool.

As micro-structured architectures and automated deployment pipelines become common, more companies will adopt these practices, some earlier and some later, depending on their competitive situation. The most successful software companies will continue to focus like a laser on delighting customers, improving the flow of value, and reducing risks. They will develop (and release as open source) an increasingly sophisticated set of tools that make software development easier, faster, and more robust. Thus, a decade from now there will be significant improvements in the way software is developed and deployed. The lean principles of understanding value, increasing flow efficiency, eliminating errors, and learning through feedback will continue to drive the evolution, but the term "lean" will disappear as it becomes "the way things are done."

Case Study: Lean Software Development in Hewlett Packard LaserJet Firmware

The HP LaserJet firmware department had been the bottleneck of the LaserJet product line for a couple of decades, but by 2008 the situation had turned desperate. Software was increasingly important for differentiating the printer line, but the firmware department simply could not keep up with the demand for more features. Department leaders tried to spend their way out of the problem, but more than doubling the number of engineers did little to help. So they decided to engineer a solution to the problem by reengineering the development process.

The starting point was to quantify exactly where all the engineers' time was going. Fully half of the time went to updating existing LaserJet printers or porting code between different branches that supported different versions of the product. A quarter of the time went to manual builds and manual testing, yet despite this investment developers had to wait for days or weeks after they made a change to find out if it worked. Another 20 percent of the time went to planning how to use the 5 percent of time that was left to do any new work. The reengineered process would have to radically reduce the effort needed to maintain existing firmware, while seriously streamlining the build and test process. The planning process could also use some rethinking.

It is not unusual to see a technical group use the fact that they inherited a messy legacy code base as an excuse to avoid change. Not in this case. As impossible as it seemed, a new architecture was proposed and implemented that allowed all printers—past, present, and even future—to operate off the same code branch, determining printer-specific capabilities dynamically instead of having them embedded in the firmware. Of course, this required a massive change, but the department tackled one monthly goal after another and gradually implemented the new architecture. However, changing the architecture would not solve the problem if the build and test process remained slow and cumbersome. The engineers methodically implemented techniques to streamline that process. In the end, a full regression test—which used to take six weeks—was routinely run overnight. Yes, this involved a large amount of hardware, simulation, and emulation, and yes, it was expensive. However, it paid for itself many times over.

During the recession of 2008, the firmware department was required to return to its previous staffing levels. Despite a 50 percent headcount reduction, there was a 70 percent reduction in cost per printer program once the new architecture and automated provisioning system were in place in 2011. At that point there was a single code branch and 20 percent of engineering time was spent maintaining the branch and supporting existing products. Thirty percent of engineering time was spent on the continuous delivery infrastructure, including build and test automation. Wasted planning time was reclaimed by delaying speculative decisions and making choices based on short feedback loops. Moreover, there was something to plan for, because over 40 percent of the engineering time was available for innovation. This multi-year transition was neither easy nor cheap, but it absolutely was worth the effort. (For more details, see Gruver et al., 2013.)

A more recent case study of how the bookmaker and software company Paddy Power moved to continuous delivery can be found in Chen (2015). In this case study the benefits of continuous delivery are listed: improved customer satisfaction, accelerated time to market, building the right product, improved product quality, reliable releases, and improved productivity and efficiency. There is really no downside to continuous delivery. Of course, it is a challenging engineering problem, which can require significant architectural modifications to existing code bases as well as sophisticated pipeline automation.

However, technically, continuous delivery is no more difficult than other problems software engineers struggle with every day. The real stumbling block is the change in organizational structure and mindset required to achieve serious improvements in flow efficiency.

References

Anderson, D. (2010). *Kanban*, Sequim, WA, Blue Hole Press.

Beck, K. (2000). *Extreme Programming Explained*, Reading, MA, Addison-Wesley.

Beck, K., Beedle, M., van Bennekum, A. *et al.* (2001). *Manifesto for Agile Software Development*. Available at: http://agilemanifesto.org/ (accessed July 2016).

Calçado, P. (2015). How we ended up with microservices. Available at: http://philcalcado.com/2015/09/08/how_we_ended_up_with_microservices.html (accessed July 2016).

Chen, L. (2015). Continuous delivery: Huge benefits but challenges too. *IEEE Software*, *32*(2), 50–54.

Clark, K. B. and Fujimoto, T. (1991). *Product Development Performance*, Boston, MA, Harvard Business School Press.

Gruver, G., Young, M. and Fulghum, P. (2013). *A Practical Approach to Large-Scale Agile Development*, Harlow, Pearson Education.

Humble, J. and Farley, D. (2010). *Continuous Delivery*, Reading, MA, Addison-Wesley Professional.

Modig, N. and Åhlström, P. (2012). *This is Lean: Resolving the Efficiency Paradox*, Stockholm, Rheologica Publishing.

Morgan, J. M. and Liker, J. K. (2006). *The Toyota Product Development System*, New York, Productivity Press.

Ohno, T. (1988). *Toyota Production System: Beyond Large-Scale Production*, New York, Productivity Press. Published in Japanese in 1978.

Poppendieck, M. and Poppendieck, T. (2003). *Lean Software Development*, Reading, MA, Addison-Wesley.

Poppendieck, M. and Poppendieck, T. (2006). *Implementing Lean Software Development*, Reading, MA, Addison-Wesley.

Porter, M. E. and Heppelmann, J. E. (2015). How smart, connected products are transforming companies, *Harvard Business Review*, *93*(10), 97–112.

Reinertsen, D. G. (1997). *Managing the Design Factory*, New York, The Free Press.

Ries, E. (2011). *The Lean Startup*, New York, Crown Business.

Smith, P. G. and Reinertsen, D. G. (1991). *Developing Products in Half the Time*, New York, Van Nostrand Reinhold/Wiley.

Ward, A. (2007). *Lean Product and Process Development*, Cambridge, MA, Lean Enterprise Institute.

Womack, J. P., Jones, D. T. and Roos, D. (1990). *The Machine that Changed the World: The Story of Lean Production*, New York, Rawson & Associates.

35

LEAN PRINTING

Ken Macro

Introduction

The printing industry has experienced great disruption over the past 500 years. Since around 1440, when Gutenberg invented the highly durable and moveable type, composed of lead, tin, and antimony, the world of communication has progressed exponentially. Gutenberg—as we think in the printing industry—was one of the first adopters to apply lean principles unknowingly. He devised a way to mass produce letters, symbols, and numbers by developing a matrix in to which he poured type metal to create fonts. These metal types could then be stored and sorted into boxes for each retrieval and replacement. Although moveable type had been invented hundreds of years earlier in China (made of clay and later weaker, less durable metals), he was the first to experiment with metals that could be easily mixed, poured into a form, cooled, and hardened quickly. This invention could be seen to have sparked the Reformation, educating communities and enhancing literacy across the globe. He was the father of printing and the first entrepreneur to launch a manufacturing industry.

In the late 1860s, Ottmar Mergenthaler, a watch maker from Germany, took note of the fact that the process of picking individual type from a drawer to form sentences and, consequently, pages for books, newspapers, ephemera, and the like, was painstakingly slow. He thought that the process would work better if there was a device that could gather matrices (forms) into one lot, which then, in turn, could generate one full line of type into one sentence that would produce a lead slug. This invention, called the Linotype, revolutionized the book and newspaper publishing industry because it significantly increased productivity and enhanced quality due to the reduction of variation. Mergenthaler's Linotype machine set the standard for productivity and utilization.

Although the Linotype machine, a marvel unto itself, was a major contributor to enhanced productivity, the process itself only produced one sheet/copy at a time. Alois Senefelder discovered that petroleum-based inks and water tend to separate. Therefore, if an image is inscribed on the surface of a stone, ink will adhere to it, and, where there is no image, water will remove the remainder of the ink from the stone. This process, known as stone lithography (or planographic process), would later evolve into the use of metal (special coated aluminum) plates that could be wrapped around a cylinder. Using the same basic principles as stone lithography, offset lithography sparked an even more efficient process for set-up (the first true attempt at set-up reduction in the printing industry). Plates with images representing four process colors (cyan, magenta, yellow, and black) on four separate units could be registered as such so that a photo-realistic rendering of an image could be registered and printed on continuously fed sheets of paper at one time. Offset lithography requires the use of three cylinders. First, a plate cylinder to hold the imaged metal plate. Second, a blanket cylinder to receive the printed image (ink) in order to make it "right side" (not reversed). And, third, an impression cylinder to apply pressure to the paper as it hits the blanket cylinder in order to pick up the printed image and transfer it to the paper. Sheet-fed offset lithography has truly become the staple in technology for commercial printers in the world and this remains true to this day.

In the 1960s, the first Xerox 914 was launched to the printing community: the first machine to utilize electro-photographic technology (also known as xerography). Chester Carlson had perfected a way in which to electrostatically charge a photoreceptive belt to attract pigmented plasticized capsules of toner particles to form the image captured through a photograph. The toner particles were then offset on to a piece of paper and fused permanently on to the surface of the substrate through pressure, heat, and an oil-based affixer.

Through the advent of xerography, originals could be made into many copies at the push of a button. Additionally, the digital printing market, as it has become known, has also evolved inkjet technology where molecular size droplets of ink can be extracted through large print heads with precise accuracy providing an opportunity to mass-produce customized one-to-one collateral known as variable data printing or imaging.

Throughout all of the innovative printing technologies made available to the commercial printing and packaging markets, the *massive push to do more, better, cheaper, and faster has never been more prevalent*; not to mention the devastating (or disruptive) effect that the Web has had on the reduction of and reliance on printed materials. The newspaper business alone has had significant decreases in readership, which in turn has decreased advertising revenue, and thus reduced print volumes. With the paradigmatic shift to view material online, printing volumes as a whole have dropped, leaving a rather large and looming surplus of equipment and an industry that is overcapacitated.

Much like many manufacturing industries, the recession of 2008 took its toll on the commercial printing industry, especially in the United States. Unfortunately, however, the concepts and tools of lean have been slow to be adapted by this industry, mostly because of its inability to move quickly in developing strategic initiatives, and its inability to direct financial sources to such initiatives. The good news is that lean is prevalent today and printers are cognizant of the shift that is required for them to remain nimble and reactive to market influxes. Moreover, they are open and dedicated to identifying waste in their production milieu and executing processes that assist in enhancing efficiencies. They are further dedicated to reducing this waste in order to improve quality and increase profitability from the center of their shop floors.

As the graphic communication industry continues to develop taxonomies of printing and imaging technologies (today it consists of planographic, porous, flexographic, relief, intaglio/gravure, and digital), more and more opportunities for variance become ever more prevalent. As Steven Spear (2009) observes in his book *Chasing the Rabbit*,

> The common problem these organizations [lagging companies] face is that they produce complex products or provide complex services; requiring many varied forms of skill and expertise. Their operations, the "systems of work" involve many people of many disciplines using equipment of various types, are correspondingly complex, requiring that the efforts and contributions of many specialists be integrated and coordinated in a harmonious fashion.
>
> *(p. xx)*

At any given time in any graphic communication enterprise, there is a cacophony of sounds emanating from the hundreds of varying printers and production equipment representing multiple technologies, all in the name of output and hard deliverables, under intense deadlines with unparalleled quality. This is precisely what the leaders of graphic communication organizations must understand with regards to *lean printing*, that the sounds must weave a fabric of harmonies in an orchestrated and flawless matter. Employing the concepts and tools of lean, coupled with the evolution of a culture that is fully committed to continuous improvement that identifies waste, optimizes processes, and empowers employees, will only ensure confidence that productivity, profitability, and its people will emerge triumphantly.

What is Lean Printing?

Lean printing is more than a set of processes, standards, or tools. It is more than an ideal. It is, however, a philosophical foundation or, in the eyes of the author, a cultural imperative. Lean printing is a great call to action that requires organizations within the graphic communication industry to reflect, analyze, research, strategize, plan, experiment, and execute concepts relating to lean manufacturing (Cooper et al., 2007). Table 35.1 highlights how lean tools are used to assist with a specific identifiable problem within the confines of a graphic communication-based manufacturing facility:

Most commercial printers do not have a long-run continuous product that they produce daily, weekly, or yearly that requires minimal to no set-up or make-ready. There are some facilities, such as Bible printers, that print only one product all year round. But most printers, by and large, print multiple products with varying degrees of complication, and specifications that have

Table 35.1 Typical problems in a printing facility and lean tools and methods to fix them

Usual printing facility problems	Lean tools and methods
Paper and ink mislabeled and misplaced.	5S, work standards, *kanban*, A3.
Issues with press set-up and cycle time.	*Kaizen* events, cycle time analysis, set-up reduction, value stream mapping.
Pre-press, press, and post-press equipment downtime and malfunction.	Total productive maintenance, A3 problem solving, 5S.
Variance with operator production and output.	Work standards.
Images not aligned properly because of printing plate registration.	*Poka yoke*, work standards, visual workplace management.
Mislabeling of chemicals and improper disposal of chemicals.	Environmental health and safety initiatives, work standards, visual workplace management, 5S.
Underutilization of equipment.	OEE (overall equipment effectiveness), *heijunka*, WIP (work-in-process) planning, workflow analysis.
Product production and delivery time fluctuates.	Value stream mapping, *takt* time analysis.
Printed stock on skids marked incorrectly and delivered to wrong production process on the floor.	WIP analysis, visual workplace management, work standards, cellular flow analysis.
Lack of experience on equipment operation.	Knowledge management initiatives, training, work standards.
Forklift and transportation accidents.	*Kaizen* events, visual workplace management, work standards, 5S, A3.

a standard set-up for one piece of equipment are traditionally rare. Within the printing production stream there is a multitude of equipment required for the completion of the product. For example, a customer orders 25,000 brochures on a certain text weight of paper. The pre-press department impositions the image on the printing plate in order to maximize coverage and eliminate waste (paper, ink, labor). The plate is specifically formulated and sized for one kind of printing press. Each company may own 5 to 50 printing presses of varying sizes. The paper or substrate chosen for the job has to be gauged and the press adjusted to accommodate the throughput and printability of the paper. It also, at times, must be cut to the desired size prior to printing on a large flatbed cutter. Once the job is printed it is sent to post-press where it is cut to finished size prior to finishing (embossing, die-cutting, gluing, mailing) and/or binding (stitching, adhesive binding, poly-bagging, wrapping, bundling, crating).

Each one of these activities (or production processes) also requires specific set-up instructions for handling the throughput of the job. Therefore, in the printing and packaging manufacturing world, variance is a multifaceted concept and often an obstacle in preparing for a successful lean experience. With regards to the 25,000 brochure order above, the standard lead time for the production of this job would take (in a lean and efficient facility) one or two days and it would require the set-up and operation of a plate imaging machine, a four-color (4C) printing press with possible coater, a cutter, a folder, a stitcher, and an inkjet addressing system. With such a vast array of equipment requirements and processes embedded, there are increased probabilities of errors and malfunctions along the production stream. Therefore, a lean approach to eliminating variance through the use of 5S, total productive maintenance (TPM), A3, work standards, visual workplace management, set-up reduction, cycle time, and takt analysis all generate great relevance on the manufacturing plant floor. However, it requires a concerted effort that is well planned and understood by every employee in the company.

Many organizations within the graphic communication industry have placed great commitment and diligence into developing lean initiatives. As a result, there have been great milestones and rewards. As many who have consulted within this industry have experienced, lean implementation planning generally launches into three distinct phases of execution. The first phase is education about lean and the creation of the "low hanging fruit" plan which looks at implementing 5S, developing a comprehensive *waste identification* initiative, and training the workforce on WIP standards. The second phase is the analysis of a job workflow using swim-lane diagrams to identify duplication of effort and possible constraints. The third phase is the development of a TPM plan, calculation of takt time, and the creation of work standards for varying equipment on the production floor. An interesting note with regards to the use of *swim-lane* diagrams: the author has discovered that because of the intensified processes associated with print production, the exercise of constructing a swim-lane diagram that outlines the meticulous stages in job completion for one product (such as a brochure, for example) provides invaluable insight to any evolving or newly developed lean team. The ability to see duplication and compounded non-value-added workflow is thus providing additional fuel for moving the lean implementation process forward.

As we have experienced these phases, Netland and Ferdows (2014) have discovered that there are four stages of performance improvement that act as a classification of manufacturing industries as they experience progress through lean implementation: 1) beginning plants, 2) in-transition plants, 3) advanced plants, and 4) cutting-edge plants (pp. 85–88). In the correlation of the two, it would be a correct assessment that most commercial printing and packaging manufacturing plants (in North America) would fall under the auspices of the beginning or in-transition stages. Again, because of the complicated nature of customized products and the multitude of equipment required to complete them, streamlining processes take time and money (the number one barrier to lean implementation, according to Jadhav et al., 2014). There are, however, a few larger corporate printing and packaging companies that have developed into the advanced stage—that is, with enhanced production efficiencies through automation, optimal OEE, and reduced lead time rates—but not always with a culture that is open and supportive to the likes of Toyota.

Fortunately, there exist educational institutions across the globe that instruct in graphic communication and have—over the past 10 years—integrated lean concepts within the classroom either through applied practices or in the development of formal production management or quality management courses. US and Canadian institutions include the California Polytechnic State University Graphic Communication program, Clemson University Graphic Communications program, Ferris State University Graphic Communications program, Rochester Institute of Technology Imaging Sciences program, and Ryerson University Graphic Communications program (Toronto, Canada), to name a few. Additionally, there are examples throughout Europe and Asia: Helsinki Metropolia University of Applied Sciences, Aalto University, Hochschule Der Media, Obuda University, Moscow University of Printing Arts, Kiev Polytechnic Institute, Artevelde Hogeschool, Beijing Institute of Graphic Communication. Furthermore, many of the supporting industry organizations such as Printing Industries of America (PIA), Epicomm (formerly NAPL), Specialty Graphics Industries Association (SGIA), and others have crafted special conferences dedicated to continuous improvement, created and offered special one-day seminars to local organizations, and developed webinars and online tutorials on various concepts and tools for their constituencies to access. The good news is that the awareness of lean printing has become more prevalent as organizations explore ways in which to eliminate wastes, enhance quality, and improve process efficiencies.

Challenges and Opportunities

In their report entitled "Exploring barriers in lean implementation," Jadhav et al. (2014) identify 24 barriers that inhibit or derail lean implementation initiatives. The top barriers "are the lack of resources to invest, the lack of top or senior management involvement and workers' attitude or resistance to successful implementation of the lean system" (p. 133). Given these common barriers, CEOs, managers, and supervisors alike must tackle these higher-level issues prior to launching any initiative that involves such a magnitude of change and individual participation. That said, there are some obstacles/barriers that are unique to the printing and packaging industry.

Manufacturing Verses Service

There remain many challenges and as many opportunities for integrating lean printing into the graphic communication industry. Obviously, the higher-ranging challenges predominately lie in the area of cultural acceptance. As with any industry, teaching management about lean concepts is counterproductive if the workforce is not also taught about lean and how it will affect each and every individual on the production floor. Additionally, many graphic communication organizations must come to terms with the fact that printing production is actually a manufacturing process. Dr. Andrew Paparozzi of the Epicomm (formerly National Association of Printing Lithographers, NAPL) writes,

> No result of our research is more significant than the growing number of companies
> that view print as a form of distributing communication . . . that needs to be viewed

as one source among many options, rather than a standalone service defined by how it is manufactured. The companies see themselves in the communications business rather than the ink-on-paper business.

(2015, p. 31)

For the past 20-plus years, the graphic communication industry has considered itself a service industry, one that services clientele in facilitating marketing initiatives. As printing companies (also known as "marketing solutions providers") attempt to generate new revenue and expand into new markets, their reliance on output technology is still imperative. To generate output without efficiencies, however, is counterproductive and unsustainable. Until the printing industry and the graphic communication industry collective agree that the output generated from their service renderings is—in fact—through a manufacturing process, many firms will still fail to see the value in initiating lean incentives.

According to Paparozzi (2015), discussions within the industry have propelled questions involving the dissemination of the revenue generated currently from lithography printing. One question posed by an industry representative was "What kind of a company wins this business?" In an online forum, there were several answers submitted: "1) The fastest because the turn times continue to shrink," and "2) The most efficient because any printer caught with old technology in the pressroom is doomed" (p. 31). This means that reliance on older technology or technology that is considered "inefficient" would be catastrophic to a printing organization of the future. However, if lean concepts such as TPM were to be analyzed, implemented, and executed, this technology would never become obsolete or ineffective. Many companies within the graphic communication industry see new technology as the answer. Had they rather just analyzed their existing processes and effectively maintained their existing technology, they would be quite competitive.

Similarly, in a recent survey conducted by Epicomm (Paparozzi 2015, p. 16), the top five concerns of CEOs and executives of printing companies in the United States (in descending order) were:

1   the ability to increase sales,
2   maintaining profitability,
3   rising cost of healthcare benefits,
4   uncertainty about where the industry, economy, and nation are going, and
5   economy and general business conditions.

The top "must-do" for executive leadership to emerge from the survey is to "be as lean as possible in order to do more with less, streamline workflow, and reduce steps" (Paparozzi, 2015). This at least shows that CEOs of graphic communication firms are beginning to see the need to ingest lean.

Utilization Rates

Another challenge is for graphic communication firms to research, calculate, analyze, and act upon utilization rate determination. In the United States, the capacity utilization for non-durable manufacturing classification of printing and support for 2015 was reported to be 63.1 percent. With such low utilization rates and overcapacity with regard to equipment and technology, this industry needs to look more inwardly and reflect upon initiating processes that enhance utilization and reduce over-capacity. As printing companies rely heavily on the news and communication sector, much disruption has been experienced in the significant decrease in printed newspaper distribution and magazine printing. As a result, press equipment is sitting idle, thus contributing to greatly affected utilization rates and OEE. As a result, companies are selling equipment or placing it in surplus as they busily scramble to identify new technologies and ancillary products that can supplement the loss of income. Others are investing time into developing new and innovative products that can be produced on the same equipment but yield new and interesting target markets.

Second, with the manufacturers of equipment that have slowly evolved automation into the newer technological products that they bring to market, efficiencies experienced from stream-lined, in-line automation will also rear their heads into the conversation. Unfortunately, lots of excess printing equipment sitting in warehouses today cannot be retrofitted with automation updates because of the expense. This requires innovative companies to relinquish capital for new equipment acquisition but not without the high scrutiny of return on investment (ROI). Therefore, great effort will be needed in comprehensive strategic planning to evolve lean effi-ciencies through equipment and technology acquisition. Regardless, this will be a primary challenge for printing companies for the next three to five years.

Profitability

Currently, according to several estimates, the printing industry (graphic communication industry) generates $640 billion in revenue that, in turn, drives $3.8 trillion worth of related services (Keen Systems, 2012). This includes magazine and periodical publishing, book publishing, finance and insurance, professional-scientific-technical services, the paper and ink industry, packaging, and equipment manufacturers. Furthermore, as logic dictates, *profit leaders* (printing companies that are financially successful) have both higher profits and fewer employees compared with *profit challengers* (firms that struggle financially) according to Dr. Ronnie Davis (2015) of the Printing Industries of America. Profit leaders utilize fewer employees per $1m in sales than do profit challengers, which equates to roughly $108,350 per employee versus $92,690 per employee working in a profit challenged company (p. 6).

It is not as great a time for newspapers and newspaper publishers, however. Sales for US newspaper publishers were at $30bn in 2013 compared with $49bn in 2005 (Statista Dossier, 2015, p. 8). The source of revenue for US newspapers is split as follows: print advertising $17.3bn; digital advertising $3.42bn; direct advertising $1.4bn; niche/non-daily advertising $1.4bn; circulation $10.87bn; and other revenue $3.15bn (Statista Dossier, 2015, p. 9). Revenue for magazine and periodical publishing in 2014 was at $38bn, down from $41bn in 2009 (Statista Dossier, 2015, p. 12).

In addition, of course, the packaging market continues to grow. As more and more products are being launched and packaged to grab the attention of the everyday consumer, the more elaborate the package, the more opportunity to increase sales. According to Marketsan Markets Strategic Analysis Services (2015), the global market for packaging printing is projected to grow to $587bn by 2020. This air of optimism is creating a great rush for printing firms to transition underutilized technology and convert it into packaging technology to enter this rather unique—yet highly competitive—market. Additionally, printers and graphic communication firms are—albeit slowly—making capital investments into newer technology that enters the packaging production space. This market would be considered an opportunity for many. However, it will require great strategy and understanding of a developed market that includes pharmaceuticals, cosmetics, and food, which will require an expedited learning curve to make the competitive edge.

The Future of Lean Printing

The graphic communication industry (for the sake of this chapter referring to the sector that represents printing manufacturing) is large, diverse, mature, lacking confidence, and unsure of the future. Inevitably, something will always need to be printed. The need will never go away. It may change drastically and may require less technology to produce it, but there will always be a need for a book, a publication, a journal, a billboard, a building wrap, a bus sign, a printed map, and printed packaging. As the web continues to house more electronic documents and generate billions and billions of pages of content, then, yes, the reliance on print will dissipate. This was said of the letterpress prints, and as of late more and more consumers are seeking out letterpress printed books and ephemera at a premium to display as craftwork and art. The same was said about vinyl records, yet there is an upsurge of interest in finding and obtaining used and new vinyl records to be played on old needle turntables.

Of course it is not healthy to reminisce of times long ago, but the lessons of the past should not be lost on the paradigmatic changes afforded to an industry in flux. For printing manufacturing—a $580-billion-dollar industry—there is profit to be had. The revenue stream may not be seeking exponential gains, but through the analysis, understanding, and application of lean principles, healthy profits are to be discovered, thus allowing for capital reinvestments into newer innovative technology responsible for creating newer markets within undiscovered industries. The future of lean printing is an imperative of the industry and is most effective when immersed slowly and simply. Based on the author's experience as a consultant in the industry, the best results have been received when a company trains on one or two simple concepts (i.e. 5S and product swim-lane diagram) and initiates a plan to execute events in which to analyze and review for further improvement.

When positive results are witnessed, there is inevitably more buy-in from management, staff, and employees alike. This has been seen in numerous small and mid-sized printing companies throughout western Canada and western United States first-handedly by the author. Since the individual impact that a lean initiative has is on everyone on the printing manufacturing floor, simplification and the building of trust have greater results than a massive push down from executives and management from the top floor. The results yield a more solidified, understanding, and collective culture of employees who are willing to engage in lean experimentation and learn more about the benefits of making their jobs safer, more productive, and contributory toward the general health and welfare of the organization.

Ingenious inventions from Gutenberg, Mergenthaler, and Senefelder were primarily developed to make a process more productive and to yield better efficiencies using technology. In the graphic communication industry, developing a lean culture and starting an implementation plan using the many concepts and tools encouraged will only supplement the scaffolding for building a lean philosophy. Once established as a philosophy, organizations will exert less energy on "asking why" and more energy on "doing how." According to Martin Joyce of Lockheed Martin, "Toyota's competitive advantage comes from educated, involved workers who are the envy of the industry because they can implement change while they do their daily jobs" (cited in Jadhav et al., 2014, p. 136). Therefore, as a philosophy, lean thinking will generate significant rewards. Print manufacturing firms dedicated to and reliant on printing technology, executing lean initiatives, will secure at least another 100 years of profit generation and quality output for future clientele.

Case Study: Lean Printing in Wayside Press, Vernon, British Columbia, Canada

Wayside Press is an established commercial offset lithography printing company of 90 years that resides in the city of Vernon in the Okanagan region of the Southern Interior of British Columbia, Canada. It has provided printing services for customers throughout western Canada. Considered a small mid-sized printing facility (fewer than 50 employees), its equipment ranges from large offset lithographic printing presses to digital presses. Over the past several years, it has also developed expertise in the area of integrated marketing communication and cross-media design. This transition required purchase, installation, and training on various ink-jet wide-format equipment and further expertise in customized mailing and targeted multichannel digital marketing execution and analysis (direct mailing, personalized email, landing pages, mobile marketing, and appropriate marketing analytical services).

As a result of attending a lean printing workshop in Edmonton, Alberta, Canada in September of 2009, Neil Perry, President and CEO of Wayside Press, decided that the company should embark on its own lean journey. As a result, he attended numerous lean training functions, viewed online tutorials, purchased several books, and contracted with Josh Ramsbottom, a consultant through the Landmark Group Center for Value Improvement at NorQuest College, Edmonton. Over a six-month period, Mr. Ramsbottom visited the facility once a month to conduct a three-day training program and to have each lean team member (nine in total) report on their individual progress on tasks they were assigned. The final deliverable of the program—the result of six months of training—was to develop, write, and sign an official *contracted lean implementation plan* (a.k.a. CLIP) for the entire company. The CLIP is a comprehensive plan authorized and written by the lean team that requires a signature and a finite timeline for accomplishing goals and charting progress.

The six-month (three-day) program consisted of three phases of lean training and application. *Phase I*: Introduction to lean fundamentals and tools such as *muda*, non-value activities (NVAs), 5S, audit zones (geographically assigned 5S checklists for supervisors on floor), voice of the customer (VOC), *gemba* walking, plan, do, check, act (PDCA), and development of a lean culture. *Phase II*: Understanding how to see problems, using A3, why-why analysis, swim-lane analysis, and understanding non-value-added processes. *Phase III*: Creating a culture of *kata* (routine): understanding a kata culture, creating work standards, evaluating lead time effectiveness, calculating cycle time, developing takt time standards, analyzing and understanding OEE and utilization rates.

Team leaders were assigned projects to manage or experiments to facilitate which they would report on each month. As a result of the team's engagement, Wayside Press was able to report the following: 1) a 20 percent reduction of the NVAs as a result of the swim-lane analysis and the elimination of duplicative processes within its production stream, 2) a 15 percent improvement in process flow (through cycle time analysis), 3) a decreased overall lead time throughput by 10 percent through process evaluation and savings of over 41,345 minutes of lost production time in one year—a total of 689 hours, 4) a trained workforce of eight employees (in addition to the nine managers on the lean team) in application of lean concepts, and 5) an improved general environmental health and safety of employees due to the newly implemented 5S audit zone program.

In addition to the savings that have been calculated from its progress thus far, Wayside Press has also accomplished several technical achievements of which it is proud: 1) created a visual management campaign that included a kanban system for replenishing boxes for paper, ink, plates, and other press supplies, 2) created audit zones and assigned personnel accordingly, 3) calculated utilization rates on equipment and analyzed effectiveness, 4) calculated floor usage costs and value, 5) engaged in A3 problem-solving activities, 6) developed applicable SMART (specific, measurable, achievable, result-oriented, and timely) statements for future planning, 6) generated fishbone diagrams for various projects, 7) created an online customer portal for business card ordering, and 8) created, authorized, and signed a CLIP.

According to Joshua Bartholomew, Controller at Wayside Press Ltd.:

> The impact of this project has been very significant for Wayside Press and the benefits have been recognized by both employees and management. We are all committed and excited to continue our lean journey in optimizing our order and production processes to eliminate waste and create efficiencies.

Through practical planning and pragmatic exploration, Wayside was able to create a company culture that accepted lean concepts but became more intrigued as it began to see results as rewards were generated. Although this was an arduous endeavor, Wayside Press has planted seeds of lean that seem to be rooted into its culture. Only time will tell of its progression; however, only this educated and committed group of people can harvest from what has been nurtured and grown.

References

Cooper, K., Keif, M. and Macro, K. (2007). *Lean Printing: Pathway to Success*, Sewickley, PA, PIA Press.

Davis, R. (2015). Profiling people cost and profitability. *Flash Report October 2015*, Pittsburgh, PA, Printing Industries of America.

Keen Systems (2012). Print is BIG: United States and worldwide industry statistics. Available at: www.printisbig.com (accessed July 2016).

Jadhav, J., Mantha, S. and Rane, S. (2014). Exploring barriers in lean implementation. *International Journal on Lean Six Sigma*, 5(2), 122–148.

Marketsandmarkets (2015). Packaging printing market: Global forecast to 2020. Available at: www.marketsandmarkets.com/Market-Reports/packaging-printing-market-153207109.html (accessed July 2016).

Netland, T. and Ferdows, K. (2014). What to expect from a corporate lean program. *MIT Sloan Management Review*, Summer, 83–89.

Paparozzi, A. (2015, January 21). State of the industry. *Executive Leadership Summit Presentation*. Epicomm State of the Industry Research.

Spear, S. (2009). *Chasing the Rabbit: How Market Leaders Outdistance the Competition and How Great Companies can Catch Up and Win*, New York, McGraw-Hill.

Statista Dossier (2015). Print media in the United States. Study ID 12527. Statista, Inc. New York. Available at: www.statista.com/chart/3563/news-sources/ (accessed July 2016).

36

LEAN RETAIL

Paul Myerson

Introduction

It has only been in the past 10 years or so that lean concepts have significantly migrated from manufacturing to other areas of business such as the office and supply chain functions. Since lean and the idea of value are focused on the customer, it is only logical that this philosophy is now migrating to the end (or more accurately, beginning) of the supply chain—the retail (i.e. business-to-consumer) environment.

There is a concept called the "last mile" in the supply chain, which refers to the final portion of product movement right up to the customer's hands. For our purposes, this encompasses movement from suppliers (i.e. manufacturers, wholesalers, and distributors) to retail distribution centers, from which a product then moves either to the store or directly to the customer. The last mile, as it is the direct interface with the consumer, is where the "rubber meets the road," where true value or waste becomes visible to the customer (and to the retailer). Taken a step further, these days some refer to the "last 10 [or more accurately, 50] yards" of the retail supply chain as being the most critical step in the process. The last 10 yards refers to product flow from a store's receiving dock to the customer's hands and the area where we can look for ways to identify and eliminate waste (White, 2015).

In this chapter, I explore ways that retailers can, and in many cases do, implement lean concepts throughout their businesses including strategic planning, merchandising and distribution, and store operations.

What is Lean Retail?

As a general definition, lean is a form of team-based continuous improvement focusing on the identification and elimination of non-value-added activities, also known as "waste," from the viewpoint of the customer. The customer may be the end consumer or the next step downstream in your supply chain.

Lean is a journey, not a short-term fix. As such, it requires that a lean culture exists that includes everyone from the executive team to hourly store and warehouse employees. To be successful, there needs to be the proper guidance, training, and support available to all employees. Management should also consider the answer to the common question of "what's in it for me?"

which can be answered in a variety of ways, ranging from a "pat on the back" to monetary rewards and career advancement.

Additionally, it is important to customize the lean tools and methodologies to your industry and company. Those that try just to "slam in" the famed Toyota Production System may lower their chances for success. This is especially critical for retailers as they have a large number of employees who are required to support the lean thinking process. There are many tools and methodologies that go under the lean "umbrella." They range from the basic ones (e.g. layout, visual workplace, etc.) to more complex ones (e.g. just-in-time inventory where inventory quantities are based upon downstream demand and less upon a forecast).

We will cover some of the major concepts and tools now, especially the ones that most closely relate to the retail environment.

The Eight Wastes Related to Retail

The supply chain, which is actually more like a "web," consists of all parties involved in fulfilling a customer request, which includes manufacturer and suppliers, transportation, warehouses, retailers, and the customers themselves (Cooper et al., 1997). While the goal of each participant is to ultimately add value to the customer, there are plenty of non-value-added activities that exist along the way. In fact, non-value-added activities could be as high as 90 percent of any process, or in lean terms "value stream" (a sequence of activities that are required to deliver a specific or family of goods or services).

It is no surprise that much of this waste can start at retail and work its way up the supply chain and become magnified through what is known as the "bullwhip effect" (see Figure 36.1) (Forrester, 1961). The bullwhip effect refers to larger and larger swings in inventory in response to changes in customer demand, as one looks at organizations further back in the supply chain for a product. So the greater the volatility of demand in retail, the greater the inefficiencies further up in the supply chain.

While inventory is considered one of the eight wastes (see Table 36.1), in general it tends to be used as a tool to cover variability in the supply chain such as late deliveries, quality issues, inaccurate forecasts, and inventory counts, etc. This results in higher than necessary inventory holding costs (i.e. interest, taxes, storage, etc.), and while in "theory" this should result in higher service levels (to a point of diminishing returns), it doesn't always accomplish that, as many

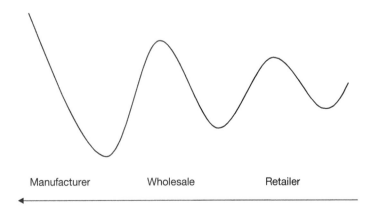

Figure 36.1 The bullwhip effect: Increasing variation in demand upstream in the supply chain

businesses still end up with too much of the wrong and not enough of the right inventory. This explains why it makes sense to start looking at the identification and elimination of waste in retail from the perspective of all eight wastes.

In general, waste is anything that does not add value to the customer (which can be viewed as the consumer or even the next step in your process). Items being stored, inspected, or delayed, products waiting in queues, and defective products do not add value; they are 100 percent waste. Many years ago, Toyota's Chief Engineer, Taiichi Ohno, as part of the Toyota Production System identified "seven wastes" of unproductive manufacturing practices, which are commonly used today in lean thinking. They have been adapted to many industries and processes over the past 20 years including both goods and manufacturing and well beyond the shop floor to include the office and supply chain and logistics functions. Table 36.1 summarizes the wastes and where they may be seen in retail.

The Inventory Dilemma

Some of the wastes are more apparent in retail than others. While inventory is necessary, especially in retail where without it we would have no business, there is a tendency to have too much of it. This is not only because of the fact that, as they say, "you can't sell from an empty wagon," but also as a means of covering variability in your supply chain. Variability can be found in a variety of forms such as over-buying from inaccurate forecasts, poor quality, inaccurate inventory counts, late deliveries, and bottlenecks where the capacity of an entire system is limited by a single or small number of components or resources. Of course, the more inventories we have, the greater our carrying costs, which include investment costs, taxes, storage, insurance, theft, and deterioration among other things and can range from 15 to 40 percent of an item's cost on an annual basis. Whether it is in the distribution center or the store, the longer inventory sits, the more it costs and the more "bad things" can happen to it, resulting in write-offs and markdowns.

Retail Methods Related to Lean

Since the late 1980s, while manufacturers have embraced the concepts of lean, producing a greater variety of items in smaller quantities, larger forward-thinking retailers such as Walmart (mass merchandiser) and Shoprite (grocery) have begun to work more closely with manufacturers to collaborate on improved forecasts and inventory planning in order to reduce the bullwhip effect mentioned earlier. The methods used have included:

- *Quick response* (QR): A just-in-time (JIT) inventory partnership strategy initiated by the US Textile Industry in 1984 between suppliers and retailers of general merchandise involving supply techniques that allow retailers to change demand in response to fashion trends and seasonal sales variation.
- *Efficient consumer response* (ECR): A strategy similar to QR started by the grocery industry in the late 1980s to increase the level of services to consumers through close cooperation among retailers, wholesalers, and manufacturers. It aimed to improve the efficiency of a supply chain as a whole beyond the wall of retailers, wholesalers, and manufacturers, to gain larger profits than each of them pursuing their own disparate business goals. Retailers place orders more frequently in smaller lots to shorten lead times and reduce inventory costs. In many cases, like QR, the supplier takes the responsibility of monitoring and replenishing the retailer's distribution center inventories with the approval of the retailer.

Table 36.1 The eight wastes related to retail

Eight wastes	Description	Waste in retail
Inventory	The largest and most apparent waste is inventory. A means of covering variability in your supply chain. The more inventory we have, the greater our carrying costs. Carrying costs include investment costs, taxes, storage, insurance, theft, and deterioration among other things and can range from 15 to 40 percent of an item's cost on an annual basis.	Whether it is in the distribution center or the store, the longer inventory sits, the more it costs and the more "bad things" can happen to it, resulting in write-offs and markdowns.
Transportation	Transportation waste includes transporting, temporarily locating, filing, stocking, stacking, or moving materials, people, tools, or information. It can be within a facility as well as between facilities.	Excess transportation can be driven by a suboptimal distribution network or inadequately laid-out distribution center, store, or office.
Motion	Motion waste refers to unnecessary motions or movements of person or machine which are not as minimized or as simplified as they could be.	Most retailers give some thought to motion waste in their stores by arranging them by departments, which are meant to maximize their revenue. This is sometimes at the inconvenience of the customer.
Waiting	We have all experienced excessive waiting in our business and personal lives. In lean terms, this refers to the time spent waiting on items needed to complete a task and can include products, information, supplies, and people.	The waste of waiting can be observed with both employees (in the store, office, and warehouse) and customers in the retail environment and can be the result of poor layout or flow, inadequate systems or training, among other things. No matter what, you end up paying employees to do a purely non-value-added activity and in the case of customers either frustrate them or (potentially) lose a sale
Overproduction	The waste of overproduction is making (or in the case of retail, buying) too much or too early. This is usually because of working with large batches, long lead times, poor supplier relations, and many other reasons. It can ultimately lead to high levels of inventory which, as mentioned earlier, can cover many other problems within your organization.	Retailers, like manufacturers, need to put more thought and training into improved collaborative forecasting and procurement processes that consider the trade-offs between holding costs and order costs (the larger the order, the greater the carrying costs, but the lower the order costs). They should better utilize the vast amount of data that is available today in *point-of-sale* (POS) and enterprise resource planning (ERP) systems both internally and externally.

Table 36.1. (continued)

Eight wastes	Description	Waste in retail
Over-processing	The waste of over-processing refers to excess effort and time spent processing either material or information that does not add value.	In retail, over-processing can occur in packaging and repackaging items, often resulting in damage and markdowns.
Defects	Defect waste can cause the rework, repair, return, or scrapping of material or information. It can be the result of not only quality defects, but data entry or human errors such as incorrect pricing or shipping the wrong item to a customer.	This can result not only in higher costs because of extra processing (e.g. returns and price adjustments), but also customer dissatisfaction.
Underutilized employees	Perhaps the greatest waste of all is behavioral waste in employees, whether due to lack of a lean culture of team-based continuous improvement or inadequate training and rewards.	As employees, especially in retail, are the direct interface to our customers, they can be our greatest resource (and a source for a competitive edge) not only in terms of identifying and solving problems, but also in terms of customer satisfaction.

- *Everyday low pricing* (EDLP): In the early 1990s, Procter & Gamble, partnering with Walmart, went to EDLP, eliminating their previous "high–low" promotional strategy in use by most retailers at the time. Over the long term, it enabled both Walmart and P&G to reduce the negative bullwhip effects caused by variability in demand driven by promotions, thereby reducing costs and improving service levels.
- *Collaborative planning, forecasting, and replenishment* (CPFR): Originated jointly by Walmart and Warner Lambert in the 1990s. CPFR is where both trading partners develop a joint business plan, including a promotion calendar, and conclude with a joint replenishment plan. The retailer and manufacturer also agree on a joint sales and order forecast (Myerson, 2014).

Problem Solving in Retail

Since excess inventory can be driven from a variety of sources, it is critical to perform root cause analysis to determine the major causes and to put a permanent solution in place before reducing inventory levels. One simple method to get to the root cause of a problem is known as the "five whys," which states that asking the question "why" five times will help you to identify the root cause. An example of the use of the "five whys" in retail is the case of a stock-keeping unit (SKU) markdown. This is illustrated in Table 36.2.

The example in Table 36.2 shows how collaboration between all parties in the supply chain could have avoided the excess waste created by a less than successful promotion. There are also other simple tools available which can be used to solve problems. The tools originally stem from "total quality management," and include, among others (Juran Institute, 1990):

- *Pareto principle*: Suggests that most effects come from relatively few causes.
- *Scatter plots*: Used for the characteristic whose behavior we would like to predict and define the area of relationship between two variables.

- *Control charts*: Used to enable the control of the distribution of variation instead of attempting to control each individual variation. Action can be taken based on trend rather than on individual variation.
- *Flow charts*: Pictures, symbols, or text coupled with lines, arrows on lines to show the direction of flow. They enable modeling of processes, problems/opportunities, decision points, etc.
- *Cause and effect or fishbone diagram*: To relate potential causes and effects.
- *Histogram or bar graph*: Graphic summary of variation in a set of data.
- *Check lists*: Data collection form that has been designed to interpret results from the form itself.
- *Check sheets*: Contain items that are important to a specific issue or situation. They are used under operational conditions to ensure that all important steps or actions have been taken.

Challenges and Opportunities in Lean Retail

When implementing a lean strategy in retail it is helpful to attack waste in three levels of the business simultaneously:

- retail strategy,
- merchandise management, and
- distribution and store operations management.

Strategic Perspective

From a strategic viewpoint in retail, inventory is purchased from a variety of suppliers, primarily manufacturers, wholesalers, and distributors. The types and quantities relate to the retailer's overall competitive strategy (e.g. luxury brands, low-cost items, etc.), which must be supported by sales and marketing, location, human resources, information systems, supply chain and logistics, and customer relationship management. If these functions are not structured and aligned strategically with the overall competitive strategy, poor service and high costs may result. In terms

Table 36.2 Five whys example in retail

Why 5: Why did the supplier produce such a large quantity of raw material?	→ Supplier hedged on purchases of a key ingredient in its product and now offers incentives to manufacturers to reduce its inventories.
Why 4: Why did the manufacturer overproduce?	→ Manufacturer ordered too much of a key raw material due to special pricing offered by the supplier. As a result, to reduce raw material inventories, there was an excess of finished goods that were offered at a discount to the distributor to move the product.
Why 3: Why did the distributor offer a large quantity discount to the retailer?	→ Distributor offered a large quantity discount to retail due to their large order of finished goods from the manufacturer.
Why 2: Why was there a promotion?	→ The retailer planned local promotion after they were given the incentives from the manufacturer and distributor.
Why 1: Why was the item marked down?	→ The item was marked down after a brief "bump" in demand due to promotion. The product was not selling well.

of the supply chain, for example, one needs to consider if a more responsive or more low-cost structure is the best option (see Fisher, 1997).

In the case of Walmart, it has primarily chosen the lower cost structure and as its supply chain is totally aligned, it is able to execute this strategy very well. A recent example of a misalignment between strategy and execution is the case of the large US retailer Target's Canadian operations (Malcolm and Horovitz, 2015). In 2015, after two years, Target announced that it was leaving the Canadian market entirely. The reasons given were that it "suffered from poor supply chain management and a misguided pricing strategy." Target didn't have an adequate distribution network to supply stores, resulting in shelves being inconsistently stocked. It also did not price merchandise as low as the company's US stores, further frustrating the consumers, many of whom had visited US Target stores in the past and were expecting similar assortments and pricing. Ultimately, its sales and distribution strategy was not fully designed (and aligned) and executed to meet its profitability goals.

Merchandising Perspective

Merchandise management is the analysis, planning, acquisition, handling, and control of the merchandise investment of a retail operation. From a lean perspective, the merchandising process should focus on the simplification and standardization of work, moving the supply chain process from a demand "push" to a customer "pull" form of replenishment and removing bottlenecks that limit overall capacity and throughput in the supply chain.

A great example of successfully implementing lean in merchandising is Zara, the world's third leading retailer with 1,160 stores in 34 countries from the United States to Japan (Newsweek, 2001):

> The success of Inditex [Zara's parent company] is based on controlling all the steps of manufacturing clothes: from design to fabric to manufacturing, distribution and sales in order to cut costs and make huge gains in speed and flexibility. And in the fashion industry, where trends change daily, flexibility is the key to a retailer's survival.

Due to its decision not to outsource most of its production, items take less than two weeks to go from design in Spain to stores worldwide, versus 24 weeks for the competition. This also allows Zara to "ship fewer pieces, in a greater variety of styles, more often and they can more easily cancel lines that don't sell as well, avoiding inventory backlogs" (Newsweek, 2001).

Store and Distribution Center Perspective

Opportunities at the store and distribution center level abound. When implementing lean at the store level, it is often easiest to think in terms of layout, operations, and customer service.

An example of a retailer that integrates lean thinking into all three aspects of its operations is Mercadona (Hanna, 2010), a Spanish supermarket chain which has truly focused on the "last 10 yards" of its supply chain, from the store's loading dock to the customer's hands. Mercadona offers low prices with personalized customer service. Its employees are paid above-average wages and receive up to 20 times more training than in the average American retailer.

According to Hanna (2010), Mercadona:

> cross-train employees so their productivity is not tied to store traffic. Cleaners can work the cash registers during busy periods, and cashiers can shelve products during

downtime. Departmental specialists can assist customers during busy periods and order merchandise and arrange their sections during slack hours.

This not only helps it to serve its customers better, but allows for more predictable schedules for employees, at least partially resulting in a very low turnover rate (3.8 percent) and high profitability. It has 43 percent fewer items per square foot than American grocery retailers, allowing for employees to "prescribe" products to customers with a two-way flow of information. Employees also look for small, daily improvements such as suggesting that suppliers modify product dimensions, making it possible for store employees to stack the product more easily and as a result for Mercadona to lower the price. Ultimately, a "continuous-improvement mentality is pervasive, from the raw materials supplier to the store worker. Every decision is made thinking about the entire supply chain—the components work together and reinforce one another" (Hanna, 2010).

The Future of Lean in Retail

The trend toward an "omni-channels" or multichannel approach to sales, where retailers deliver anything, anytime, anywhere, providing the customer with a seamless shopping experience whether they are shopping online from a desktop or mobile device (i.e. *e-commerce*), by telephone, or in a "bricks and mortar" store, has put increased competitive pressure on retailers in an already tough economy. Many forward-looking retailers such as Walmart and Staples have successfully blended this approach into an efficient, lean supply chain resulting in lower costs and higher revenues. Creative examples of a blended approach by mass merchandise retailers include the "ship to store" model to meet volatile demand by leveraging their full inventory, and electronics retailers using kiosks at hotels and airports, an approach that is most convenient for the customer. Others have either not moved quickly into an integrated approach or have not done it well, resulting in even more non-value-added activities and associated higher costs and lower revenues. It is at a retailer's own peril if they don't focus on adding value to the customer and eliminating waste through a lean philosophy, starting at the "last 10 yards," moving right up their supply chain.

Case Study: Lean Retail in Starbucks

This case study on Starbucks draws on the *Wall Street Journal* article "Latest Starbucks buzzword: 'lean' Japanese techniques" by Jargon (2009), the book *Onward: How Starbucks Fought for its Life Without Losing its Soul* by Schultz (2011), and discussions of Starbucks by Harrington (2011).

At its more than 11,000 US Starbucks stores, "there will be no more bending over to scoop coffee from below the counter, no more idle moments waiting for expired coffee to drain and no more dillydallying at the pastry case" (Jargon, 2009). Scott Heydon, the company's "vice president of lean thinking" and a 10-person "lean team" have been going from region to region reducing waste to free up time for baristas to interact with customers and improve the Starbucks experience.

Starbucks began testing lean methods in Oregon in 2008 on store operations, primarily focusing on layout, flow, and the identification and elimination of bottlenecks. In one process used for making blended drinks:

> they moved all but the most commonly ordered syrup flavors and now store pitchers closer to where the drinks are made. After learning that topping the drinks with whipped cream and chocolate or caramel drizzle at the drink station was slowing down production, they moved those items closer to where drinks are handed to customers (quote in Jargon, 2009).

The changes reduced the entire 45 second process by 8 seconds. They also cut 2 seconds off the average drive-through time.

> At another store, the barista made about 40 trips back and forth before the store opened —carrying baked goods from one end of the shop, where they were delivered, to the pastry case at the other end. Time clocked: one hour and 15 minutes. Mr. Heydon and the store's manager came up with changes including rolling a pastry rack next to the case. Efforts at other stores have shaved an average of an hour-and-a-half off the task per store per week (Jargon, 2009).

Bins of beans, which are ground in smaller batches every eight minutes, versus once per day, are kept on top of the counter so the baristas don't have to bend over; Starbucks used the "visual workplace concept" where bins are color-coded, so they can locate an individual type of coffee without having to stop to read the label. Starbucks also uses colored tape to differentiate between soy, nonfat, and low-fat milk.

This is also not just a case of a "top down" approach to implementing lean, which usually is not very successful for the longer term, as employees are encouraged to come up with their own improvements. At Starbucks, lean thinking goes beyond their stores up the supply chain. In 2008, only 3 out of 10 orders were delivered perfectly to Starbucks' stores from their warehouses. Today, 9 out of 10 orders to 16,500 stores are delivered on time, with every item included and no errors. Starbucks Supply Chain Organization's (SCO) safety performance has improved by 90 percent. In the past two years, SCO cumulative savings were over $400 million for Starbucks. In 2009, Starbucks staff named lean their most valued program of the year (Harrington, 2011).

References

Cooper, M. C., Lambert, D. M. and Pagh, J. D. (1997). Supply chain management: More than a new name for logistics. *International Journal of Logistics Management*, 8(1), 1–14.

Fisher, M. L. (1997). What is the right supply chain for your product? *Harvard Business Review*, 75, 105–117.

Forrester, J. W. (1961). *Industrial Dynamics*, Cambridge, MA, MIT Press.

Hanna, J. (2010). How Mercadona fixes retail's "last 10 yards" problem. *Harvard Business School Working Knowledge*. Available at: http://hbswk.hbs.edu/item/how-mercadona-fixes-retails-last-10-yards-problem (accessed May 2015).

Harrington, M. (2011, October 13). Strategy: The Starbucks Way: Rediscovering your mission. New Directions Consulting. Available at www.newdirectionsconsulting.com (accessed May 2015).

Jargon, J. (2009, August 4). Latest Starbucks buzzword: "lean" Japanese techniques. *Wall Street Journal*. Available at: www.wsj.com/articles/SB124933474023402611 (accessed July 2016).

The Juran Institute (1990). The tools of quality. *Quality Progress*, September, 75–78.

Malcolm, H. and Horovitz, B. (2015, January 15). Target to shutter all stores in Canada, *USA Today*.

Myerson, P. (2014). *Lean Retail and Wholesale*, New York, McGraw-Hill.

Newsweek (2001 September 9). Zara Clothing retail model based on lean inventories and market flexibility could change the future of manufacturing. Available at: www.prnewswire.com/news-releases/zara-clothing-retail-model-based-on-lean-inventories-and-market-flexibility-could-change-the-future-of-manufacturing-71974747.html (accessed July 29, 2016).

Schultz, H. (2011). *Onward: How Starbucks Fought for its Life without Losing its Soul*, Emmaus, PA, Rodale.

White, B. (2015, May 3). Last mile: The new frontier in the retail supply chain, *Industry Week*. Available at: www.industryweek.com/last-mile (accessed July 2016).

37

LEAN EDUCATION

Vincent Wiegel and Lejla Brouwer-Hadzialic

Introduction

"I taught my dog Chinese."
"Let's hear it talk."
"He can't."
"I thought you taught it Chinese?!"
"Yes, I did, but he just didn't learn."

This age-old joke nicely illustrates that education has two core processes: teaching and learning. The fact that value is created through processes that intensively involve both the "customer" (student) and the "supplier" (teacher) is highly significant. There are few domains in which customer involvement is so strong and the value creation process is to a substantial extent taking place in an environment (inside a student's mind, his or her home, the playground, etc.) that is outside the view and direct control of the supplier.

Learning and teaching are very old processes that humankind has been doing for millennia. Theories on learning and teaching are almost as old and as varied. Much has been learned about learning and teaching over all these years. When considering *lean education*, it is important to keep in mind that pedagogy has a long and rich history to which lean education needs to relate. Therefore, we believe that to understand what lean education is and its impact on education, we must begin with pedagogy. Focusing on both teaching and learning, we go along with the definition of Watkins and Mortimore (1999) in which they refer to pedagogy as more than only the teacher's role and activity. In their definition, pedagogy is "any conscious activity by one person designed to enhance learning in another" (p. 3). Ultimately, it is the learning that matters.

Currently, most of the lean education practices focus on the support processes known as "student administration." There are few lean education practices that actually engage teachers in the primary processes of teaching and learning. These mostly involve teachers who teach lean and then consider applying lean thinking to their own teaching. These teachers face challenges as they try to apply lean beyond their own course and circle of influence. They are the peers who tell their colleagues how to improve their teaching. In addition, they face the institutional inertia of schools with strong cultures, vested interests, and many governmental regulations. These are factors that, in themselves, are far from unique but make for a challenging environment when combined. Moreover, it seems that lean educators are perhaps not always the best change agents. Teaching lean and applying lean are two different things, though we would argue that good lean practitioners have to be good teachers (as well as good students!).

In this respect, we expect and hope that this chapter will appeal to all readers irrespective of the application domain they are working in. Whether we are lean academics, lean practitioners, or both, we are engaging in some form of teaching. As such, we encourage the reader to practice some *hansei* (critical self-reflection) on his or her own lean teaching practice. How "lean" is it? What lean practices are applied explicitly?

In Section 2, "What is lean education?," we consider the following four factors that shape the domain of lean education:

1   co-creation of value when the process of teaching and learning happens simultaneously; there is a need to deal with inherent variation in students;
2   lean concepts, such as customer and waste, with domain-specific denotation;
3   the relationship with domain technology (by which we mean pedagogy); and
4   the need for an integrated approach in which organizational strategy and primary and secondary processes are addressed as a whole.

These factors stem from the nature of education and have a profound impact on how lean can be applied in education.

Section 3 examines the challenges and opportunities in lean education. The challenges lean education faces can be categorized into three groups. The first group consists of the integration with pedagogy. Since education is as much about learning as it is about teaching, the study of how this learning takes place and how best to organize teaching needs to be taken into account. The view on pedagogy will affect the way processes are organized. The second group consists of the need for an integrated approach across the educational institution. The domain of education generally lacks a practice of policy deployment, which is an impediment to the implementation of lean. The third group consists of adapting lean techniques to take structural differences in the domain into account. Education is characterized by strong input variation (students have differing mental, behavioral, and cognitive abilities and attitudes) and inherent co-creation—education is as much about learning as it is about teaching. Thus, there is a need to apply varying teaching and learning strategies depending on the specific situation of the students involved. The implication is that some of the traditional lean techniques might not be well suited or may be in need of adaptation.

The close alignment of pedagogy and lean thinking offers an opportunity for stronger education. Pedagogy has a clear process focus (Wiliam, 2011; Hattie, 2012). It focuses on the goals to be achieved and the associated success criteria. Frequent checks on progress and adjustments are an integral part of the educational process. This approach has obvious similarities to the concepts of *kaizen* and improvement *kata*, and to lean thinking as process thinking. Pedagogical approaches are typically weak on the *how* of their recommendations. With its holistic, coherent, and practical outlook, lean can help in implementing pedagogy.

The alliance of pedagogy and lean opens a new perspective on education, described in Section 4, "The future of lean education," in which students "pull" the needed knowledge based on their state of development, personal abilities, and preferences. Teachers create a learning environment in which they both teach and provide the context-relevant content. Defining a target condition with its success criteria and the monitoring of progress are both key in the environment and its learning process. This learning-centered teaching process is supported through administrative processes. Lean methods are used to align strategy and support processes toward this learning environment. Short cyclic continuous improvement practices are an integral part of the educational organization. Scarce resources are freed up through the elimination of waste.

Let us state three of our "prejudices" at the start as well. First, we do not believe in learning in which students are just provided with access to all kinds of information through their tablets and look up whatever they need to know. A student needs knowledge before he can ask a meaningful question. The teacher is not just a conduit for information. She is teaching from a position of deep subject matter expertise. However, she is not "just" teaching, but also helping students reflect on their learning and creating their own learning strategies. Second, while we think that information technology (IT) has to play an important role in education as it does in almost any other sector of the economy, we do not believe IT is the main driving force that is going to propel education forward and solve its problems. The hailing of massive open online courses (MOOCs) as the solution to budget cuts (because of large-scale teaching) and quality (a few of the best teachers are producing the MOOCs) is off the mark. IT will, however, be an important enabler for a more diverse set of learning strategies. Third, lean education practices, improvement efforts, and conferences are currently focused too much on the improvement of support processes irrespective of learning and teaching. Lean education needs to always and explicitly include students and teachers and address the primary processes of education if it wants to be more than lean services applied to the domain of education.

What is Lean Education?

Lean education differs from other traditional application domains, such as manufacturing, in three dimensions (Wiegel and Brouwer-Hadzialic, 2015), in that it 1) encompasses strong co-creation, 2) faces inherent input variation, and 3) is characterized by the application of multiple, varying technologies:

1   Students are to a large extent both the consumer and the producer and thus their partici-
    pation in the process is key. Their participation is formed and facilitated through pedagogy
    adopted in the primary processes of teaching and learning. The support processes, such as
    administration and scheduling, contribute to the student's journey. These processes are an
    integral part of the total educational offering.
2   Students entering the educational system vary widely in terms of their skills, ambitions,
    knowledge, etc. These differences constitute what one could call "input variation." Such
    differences affect preferences of how information is presented and processed, group and
    individual work, timing of work, size of assignments, etc. These preferences are not merely
    individual whims but reflect physiological/mental processes. All of these affect the learning
    and teaching processes. Dealing with these variations is key in successful teaching. In short,
    some (but certainly not all) variation is inherent in the processes of education.
3   The presence of variation then requires the deployment of various technologies. In education
    technology consists of a set of pedagogies and teaching methods. A particular combination
    of these constitutes a learning–teaching strategy. Depending on the progress of students
    and the success of teaching and learning, a teacher will vary the learning–teaching strategies.
    A substantial part of a teacher's work consists of finding out what does and does not work
    for a student. Along these lines, Hattie (2012) notes as follows:

> A typical lesson never goes as planned. Expert teachers are skilled at monitoring
> the current status of student understanding and the progress of learning towards the

success criteria, and they seek and provide feedback geared to the current understanding of the students . . . . Through selective information gathering and responsiveness to students, they can anticipate when the interest is waning, know who is not understanding, and develop and test hypotheses about the effect of their teaching on all of the students.

(p. 30)

All these aspects together are reflected in a learning environment in which a student is challenged, provided with information, distracted, etc. Students and teachers work together in varying physical and digital settings to share information, comment on work, reflect, provide feedback, ask questions, and do project assignments. Lean education is geared toward the creation and improvement of this learning environment. According to Wiliam (2011),

The teacher's job is not to transmit knowledge, nor to facilitate the learning. It is to engineer effective learning environments for the students. The key features of effective learning environments are that they create student engagement and allow teachers, learners, and their peers to ensure that the learning is proceeding in the intended direction.

(p. 50)

From a lean perspective, the student is the main customer, or consumer if you will. As in any domain, there are various stakeholders. Leave out the students, however, and all other stakeholders will disappear. Even so, the student cannot always be said to be a customer in the economic sense. Students in primary and secondary schools are mostly underage and are thus not permitted to make important decisions on their own. Legally speaking, their parents are perhaps the "customer." However, in all teaching and learning processes the student is clearly the one for whom the value is produced and toward whom everything is geared. In part-time and vocational education, companies are clearly important stakeholders and might even pick up the bill. However, as in the case of parents, they are not the customer. For-profit schools might have yet another, different, relationship with their stakeholders. In all cases, however, we maintain that the underlying insights in learning and teaching remain the same.

Determining what type of students a school caters to requires strategic choices in conjunction with legal requirements. Different types of students will need different forms of support and different types of pedagogy will have different needs in terms of group size, IT facilities, and classroom organization. These are not merely economic considerations; they determine what kind of school to what kind of students an organization is. They affect all processes throughout the organization, regardless of the choices made.

Taking all above observations into consideration, we define lean education as follows: lean education is an organization-wide strategy that aims at generating value for students and supports the chosen pedagogical philosophy through:

1   alignment of the whole organization and its processes to create an effective learning environment, and
2   short cyclic continuous improvement of the learning environment and elimination of waste.

Next we consider what constitutes value and waste in education. Waste is to be found in teaching, learning, and support. Value is the provision of any materials that contain information and instructions that allow the student to acquire skills, knowledge, and attitudes, and an environment in which these can be exercised, practiced, and developed to a level desired by and suitable for the student. Paraphrasing Womack and Jones (2005), we maintain that lean education is about:

> Helping the student deciding what he wants and needs to learn,
> and subsequently teaching the student according to
> what he wants and needs to learn,
> how he wants to learn,
> when he wants to learn,
> not wasting his time,
> teaching in a stimulating environment where
> all necessary materials are available,
> easily accessible and functioning, and
> geared towards the intended goal.

Of course, we are not advocating that students should just "do whatever they wish." As in any domain, from healthcare to building, there are obvious limitations, legal, moral, and otherwise, that to some extent restrict the customer.

With this view on lean education in mind we can take a fresh look at educational practices and elucidate some key lean concepts within the context of education. Consider, for example, the waste of overproduction of information in the form of PowerPoint slides (Emiliani, 2004). We witness in our daily practice that (we) teachers love to talk about the subject we teach. Therefore, in most of the lectures (fixed time) we are the ones pushing the information and knowledge toward the students by using many slides and explanations. Even though we strive to accomplish the pedagogical goals and increase the learning output, the analysis of our own teaching practices showed that about 80 percent of what we were doing when teaching was a classroom style (fixed format) where the teacher was presenting about one slide per minute with little space for student–teacher interaction.

Note in the context of education the unevenness created through the yearly cycles of teaching, with the subsequent divisions and semesters, trimesters, etc. marked by holidays. While these divisions are to some extent legally prescribed, they are also the result of long-standing traditions that date back to pre-industrial ages. These divisions are not necessarily productive and conducive to learning. They lead to peaks in teaching and learning work and consequently overburden students and teachers. Waste is the result. For example, part-time students who work and study need to align their study with their work. For companies, the end of the year is generally a busy time. The students are very busy submitting year-end reports, closing books, etc. Teachers also tend to want to close their semester "books" and schedule exams and assignments around December and January. This causes a huge peak in both work and study. This is further aggravated by students not doing their learning throughout the year but instead cramming just before the exam. The resulting waste is that students do not really integrate much of what has been taught.

Lean education is characterized by its forms of waste. Various authors have provided insightful examples and categorizations of waste (see Emiliani, 2004; Balzer, 2010; Antony et al., 2012). The overview of these and other authors includes between 9 and 40 categories of waste. These categories are subcategories of the widespread list of eight categories.

For the domain of lean education, the notion of co-creation is important. This means that in defining waste we need to adopt the perspective of both producer (teachers and administrators) and the co-producing customer or consumer (students). In Table 37.1 we give an overview of a few examples of waste per category and role.

Table 37.1 Waste in education

Type of waste	Student	Teacher	Administrator
Transport	From one classroom or location to another.	From one classroom or location to another.	Moving files and brochures across locations.
Inventory	Material to be studied. Assignments to be completed.	Student work to be graded. Teaching materials to be prepared. Lessons to be evaluated.	Applications to be processed.
Motion	Looking for and assembling information about schedule, classroom, required reading.	Looking for students. Searching for emails.	Switching from one system to another. Looking for files.
Waiting	Waiting for feedback on essays.	Waiting for input from other colleagues on teaching materials, literature.	Waiting for information from other departments.
Overproduction	Learning/processing too many materials.	Teaching/producing too many materials.	Requesting and processing more information than needed. Producing reports that are not read.
Over-processing	Including more references than required for an assignment.	Creating convoluted file structures. Repetitive instructions.	Producing repetitive letters. Producing reports containing too much detail.
Defects	Classroom disturbances. Reading wrong materials. Re-learning lessons forgotten due to long holidays.	Incomplete or wrong teaching materials. Assigning the wrong group work.	Dealing with incomplete information.
Talent	Teaching materials geared toward average students. Looking for instructions.	Administrative work. Finding short cuts around non-functional systems.	Repeat data entry.

Taiichi Ohno called overproduction the most important form of waste in the context of mass production. In high-variety low-volume production, waiting is the main waste. For education, talent is the most important waste, including the talents of students that are not addressed or remain underdeveloped and the talents of teachers that are wasted on administration and thus are not used to develop students' talents. All other wastes are waste because they distract from the development and deployment of talent.

The application of lean thinking to education seems to fit nicely. Until recently, however, lean education initiatives were few and far between (Hines and Lethbridge, 2008). Currently, we witness rising interest at all educational levels from primary schools to higher education. There are case studies about primary and secondary education in the US and the UK as well as some on primary schools in the Netherlands and Norway (Eden, 2014; Netland, 2015), which show how lean tools are used to increase the learning output for the pupils and to improve the working environment for the teachers. Emiliani (2004) focuses on the improvement of teaching in the context of higher education. Previous studies (Hines and Lethbridge, 2008; Balzer, 2010; Antony et al., 2012; Radnor et al., 2014) have shown that lean education usually focuses on the improvement of support and administration services. One of the pioneers in this field is the University of St Andrews in Scotland, which has adopted an approach now known as "The St Andrews Model" (Robinson and Yorkstone, 2014). The number of lean education conferences and the number of conference attendees are growing, as is the number of educational institutes that engage in lean. The Lean Higher Education hub (2015) provides a nice illustration through an interactive world map detailing higher education institutions where lean continuous improvement teams are active. The number of case studies is growing. However, we are still in the very early days of lean education. A critical mass is emerging that makes it likely we will witness the development and spread of lean thinking akin to that of, for example, lean healthcare and lean construction.

Challenges and Opportunities

There are three specific challenges facing the application of lean in education. The first challenge, integration with pedagogy, is highly specific to the domain of education. We often refer to pedagogy (singular) as if there is only one theory of pedagogy when, in fact, there are many different theories. While we focus on some common features, we still ask the reader to bear in mind that this is not a chapter on pedagogy even though it plays an important role in the view on lean education.

Pedagogy is often strongly and expressly process oriented in nature. Writing about formative assessments, Wiliam (2011) observes that "assessment is the central process in instruction." In his view, teaching is about establishing where the students currently are, defining the learning goals with success criteria, and then creating a learning environment that is conducive to learning. In Wiliam's (2011, p. 45) view, "All teaching really boils down to three key processes . . .: finding out where the learners are in their learning, finding out where they are going, and finding out how to get there."

In a similar vein, Hattie (2012, p. 53) refers to the need to "share the learning intentions with the students, so that they understand them and what success looks like." The role of assessments is to decide how to take the next step. Assessments should be designed by thinking backwards from the decisions that need to be made. In lean terminology, we see target conditions, a kata, and process thinking with the end in mind. Rother (2010) describes the process of setting a target condition as starting from a deep understanding of the current condition: "once you take a step the learning process begins" (Rother, 2010, p. 124).

Writing about learning to learn, Hattie (2012, p. 104) indicates the importance of different strategies students can apply in learning: "the heart of learning to learn: it is about *intention* to use, *consistency* in appropriately using the strategies, and knowing when chosen strategies are *effective*" (emphasis in the original).

There is a lot of hansei called for on the part of the student and the teacher alike, in the type of pedagogy envisioned by Wiliam and Hattie. There is much common ground with lean thinking. Most lean practitioners and researchers seem to be missing this point when applying lean to education. Balzer (2010) and Antony et al. (2012) make this point nicely when remarking on a strong tendency to use lean speak rather than education speak. We suggest two reasons for this missing out on the common ground. One, lean practitioners often just do not take the time to consider the existing education setting. Two, lots of teachers do not teach according to the pedagogy they were once taught.

Any lasting successful attempt at introducing lean in education needs to address the primary processes. In order to do so, it needs to relate to pedagogy. In addition to the process mindset, pedagogy consists of theories on knowledge, methods to acquire knowledge, and ways to test students' knowledge. These methods are very specific to the domain of education and have little overlap with lean methods. Lean practitioners would do well, however, to take note of insights from pedagogy.

The challenge to relate to pedagogy is also a huge opportunity. Pedagogy and lean are natural allies and are very closely related on a conceptual level. This should give the lean practitioner an advantage when applying lean to the primary processes. Adopting the language of teaching and learning, following the process orientation a lean practitioner should have little problem relating to educators.

The lean contribution can be manifold. Foremost in our view are the following two contributions: seeing the whole and execution. First, teachers are often deep into the daily micro-aspects of teaching, including making sure the projector works, grading the exams, providing feedback, preparing the sheets for the next lesson, etc. It is easy to lose sight of the whole process and its end—the learning intentions. Visualizing the whole process, standardizing it, and tracking progress through visual management help the teacher to integrate activities and focus on what matters most: assessing progress and selecting learning strategies. For example, when handing out an assignment, we sometimes ask the student what grade she would like to achieve. We then discuss the various success criteria associated with the progressive grades. In subsequent discussions, progress toward the desired grade is tracked. Second, even though pedagogy explains the need to vary learning strategies, track progress, etc., it is hard to do so. Pedagogy is not always very articulate when it comes to the "how" question. With its execution-oriented tradition and techniques, lean can contribute through visual management techniques, work instructions, etc. These need to be detailed at such a level that individual students also know how to operate and use them to "pull" instructions, assignments, and information when needed and provide feedback on their progress.

A prime example of poor execution practices is the process of evaluation and improvement of teaching. Every teacher has been taught that course evaluation and improvement activities are key. Structural evaluation of courses and classes is not a common practice. The evaluation that is being done is too abstract and the cycles in which it is carried out are too long to be effective. Many courses are evaluated only at the end after the exams and tests have been done. They seldom address individual teaching sessions or materials. The evaluation is too late for the students and teachers to remember either what was done, or what did and did not work with any precision or relevance. Daily starts, rapid improvement sessions, and improvement kata are just a few lean techniques that can help conduct the needed short cyclic continuous improvement activities in education. We use, for example, smartphone apps to solicit focused student feedback on a small number of items. We act on the items and report back to the students. In parallel, we hold more in-depth interviews with a selection of students to deepen our understanding. For both approaches we experimented with the frequency of the feedback and the breadth and depth of the topics covered.

Adopting the lean techniques and showcasing them for education is a primary task for lean education practitioners that will help gain trust and support. Examples from primary schools in the Netherlands and Norway show visual improvement boards being used to solve problems, track progress, and much more (Eden, 2014; Netland, 2015).

The second challenge, the need for an integrated approach encompassing primary and secondary processes as well as strategy, is not inherent to education per se, but rather is highly typical of the situation in education. The process of teaching has always had the predominant position in education. However, it has only been loosely coupled with the secondary processes that are at best a diversion from the so-called "real job." The approach to secondary processes has been minimalist and focused on just making sure things work, i.e. the lights are on, the classes are clean, the schedule works, etc. The services provided are not considered an integral, important, and constructive part of the total value delivered.

As the scales of schools have grown, the management of the secondary processes has become increasingly removed from the primary processes. The scale and the associated costs afforded the administrators and managers of the secondary processes more influence. IT systems, upscaling schools with large numbers of students, and standardized enrollment and planning processes became more noticeable in the process of teaching, but in a negative, constraining sense. This caused a more antagonistic relationship between the colleagues involved in the support and the teaching processes.

Lean has various contributions to make in this respect. Seeing the whole both at the value stream level and at the organizational level is the overarching goal. To achieve this, applying lean techniques to map the value stream and linking primary processes and support processes contributes to integrating teaching and administration. Policy deployment (hoshin kanri) helps to integrate all efforts at the organization level. X-matrices and target trees are mostly foreign to lean education. We have found that these help administrators and educators to bring coherence to the myriad developments they are facing. Antony et al. (2012) summed up 12 of these challenges, including "lack of visionary leadership," "weak links between continuous improvement projects and strategic objectives," and "lack of communication at various levels across the higher educational institutions." Several of these challenges are also reflected in Balzer's (2010) work.

The third challenge concerns structural differences in the domain that will require reconsideration of core lean concepts and techniques. Various authors have pointed out some structural differences among the application domains (Bateman et al., 2014; Radnor et al., 2014; Wiegel and Brouwer-Hadzialic, 2015). Bateman et al. (2014) refer to the ambiguity of the pull principle when applying lean in the service sector. These differences need to be addressed as well. We have denoted three dimensions that characterize and differentiate education from the traditional domains of lean application: strong co-creation, inherent input variation, and application of multiple, varying technologies.

Co-creation is hard to capture in a traditional value stream map. Co-creation means that the consumer is also the supplier—or the input if you will—to the process. Important parts of the process are actually taking place outside the physical and digital premises of the supplier. The interaction between suppliers and customers becomes complex, frequent, and multifaceted. The customer becomes the supplier when providing feedback to fellow students or when doing exercises. The interaction is frequent, i.e. many times a day, many days a week, many weeks a year. Some interactions are synchronous, e.g. classroom teaching or one-on-one feedback, while other interactions are asynchronous, e.g. giving assignments or sending instructions through blackboard or email. Added to the co-creation is the fact that the artifacts produced vary across a wide range, including clay models, essays, project reports, and video clips. Therefore, the number and kind of "products and services" that are flowing through one value stream vary considerably. In this case, using service blueprinting as a technique to capture the value stream is probably more effective.

This also means that one needs to reconsider the concept of "takt": it should take account of student effort rather than a number of artifacts to be produced or consumed. It also needs to be formulated at the level of the individual student rather than at the classroom level. As there is inherent variation among students, both the form and pace will vary.

From this variation follows the need for the application of many different best ways to do a particular activity rather than one best standard way to do a particular activity. By activity we mean teaching a specific topic. The drive toward the reduction of variation can be counterproductive in education. Not all variation is bad and some variation just cannot be eliminated.

Interestingly, we find that the increase in variation also increases the need for standardization in order to keep the variation manageable. This idea is akin to mass customization.

The Future of Lean Education

Lean education in the coming years will function as an enabler and driver for the creation and maintenance of an effective learning environment—an environment in which the talents of students are further developed and the teachers' talents are deployed (and, of course, further developed). Lean education will bring to education the notion of a student journey that needs support through aligned processes, in terms of both primary teaching and learning processes and secondary support processes. Lean education will help visualize the student journey and identify the wastes. Through the introduction of short cyclic continuous improvement activities, students and teachers become joint student investigators of effective learning strategies. Lean education helps in the articulation of a future state and the subsequent deployment of pedagogy and process improvement at the level of both the educational institute and the individual student. An effective learning environment plays an important role in lean education. An effective learning environment is one in which the following are evident:

1   students and teachers determine the learning goals and success criteria and visualize them;
2   learning–teaching strategies are developed and deployed that fit the students' needs;
3   the progress toward the goals and the effectiveness of the strategies are tracked and adjusted when needed;
4   the student actually achieves the set goals.

Lean education, then, plays an important role in the visualization of the student journey, including the goals and progress. Through techniques such as the improvement kata and five whys, lean education helps teachers and students investigate what works and what does not. Standardization of strategies makes it easier to deploy and track their effectiveness. Lean education helps to introduce shorter continuous improvement cycles. The notion of waste in education focuses the improvement efforts.

As teaching and learning is not just about pedagogy, lean education also contributes to the improvement and alignment of all support processes. Constructing and maintaining a physical and digital infrastructure that is highly flexible and adaptable is key to the deployment of varying learning and teaching strategies. Buildings and digital environments are both far from flexible. Their design is far removed from the primary processes of learning and teaching. By focusing the physical infrastructure on different uses through, for example, single-minute exchange of die (SMED) techniques, lean can help administrators create an environment better suited to the needs of students and teachers. Helping teachers create digital content that can be accessed by students when and where they want will increase the flexibility and adaptability of the learning environment. Ultimately, support processes in lean education are organized not according to their own economic or bureaucratic logic, but instead according to their overall contribution to the learning environment and the extent to which they help eliminate the waste of talent.

As there will be practical and economic limits to flexibility and adaptability, administrators will need to make strategic decisions regarding what kind of school they want to be and which kind of students they want to serve. Defining and deploying such a strategy is not currently common practice in education. Lean expertise can thus be usefully applied in this area. School administrators' main tasks will be to align processes toward the single goal of an effective learning environment and ensure the execution of systematic, short cyclic continuous improvement activities. The lean teaching and learning that unfolds can be described as follows:

> As students mature intellectually and have experience in the classroom and in the world, they can become members of a democratic classroom. In a democracy, teachers and students co-create the syllabus. In order to be self-determining beings, students must make the key choices how the class should be run: class structure, grading, books, etc. But when students come into a course in which they have little or no knowledge, this proves to be a herculean task. This is why the course should begin with tentative guidelines suggested by the instructor. As the course progresses and students get what is going on, then the real syllabus will be co-created. . . . Teachers lead through the authority of reason, not by the reason of authority.
>
> *(Mills and Miller, 2002, p. 104)*

Case Study: Lean Education in the Bachelor of Nursing Study at HAN University

After a few years of nationwide research and redevelopment, the new body of knowledge and skills for the Bachelor of Nursing 2020 was established in the Netherlands in January 2015. The educational institutions throughout the country who offer an undergraduate curriculum in Bachelor of Nursing (BoN) were already making plans to revamp their curricula. At the HAN University of Applied Sciences (HAN), the program director of Nursing Studies had an extra challenge to manage. The curriculum has to accommodate the needs of part-time students (studying and working), including learning at the workplace and devising flexible learning routes that lead to a diploma. Furthermore, the curriculum is intended to promote and improve lifelong learning practice in the Netherlands. The Executive Board at HAN embraced and promoted lean as the philosophy that can help to achieve these goals.

The project team for Curriculum Development BoN was installed and the decision was made that the first part-time students for the new program would enroll by February 2016, meaning that the enrollment procedure would start in October 2015. This was challenging, however, since the BoN had not been running since 2013 due to low enrollment numbers. The project team's key goal was to develop a high-quality, sustainable, financially sound curriculum that adds value for the student, workplace, and society. Other HAN programs struggled with the same issues. Lean offered them a structured and integrated approach for making the changes. The project team got a lean advisor on the board to support three project leaders who looked after content, support services and administration, and project management. Together they started to build a *lean model cell* and redevelop the whole curriculum, primary and support processes.

Personas: The first step we took was getting to know the student and his or her journey from selecting a course to enrolling and later from learning to examination. Together with the curriculum developers and teachers, we interviewed about 40 potential students and described personas we used later to develop the content and define the pedagogical vision.

Vision and strategy: Together with the program management team, we went through the institute's vision and used the X-matrix to connect ambition, pedagogical vision, improvement initiatives, and goals. Decisions were made about which personas the study would focus on in the first year and what goals the program would achieve in two to three years. Moreover, the management team stated what type of nurse the study would educate.

Curriculum development: The personas together with the (pedagogical) vision and strategy statements provided the direction for the development of the curriculum. The planning and monitoring was established using the performance board meetings. The three project leaders were coached based on the improvement and coaching kata.

Support services and student administration: As creating an effective learning environment also means aligning support services and administration, special attention was given to this part. For example, enrollment needs to take into account specific workplace circumstances that will affect assignments and teaching later on. A project leader was assigned to make sure that the student journey was supported by the organizational journey and aligned with the vision and strategy as stated and deployed by the management team.

At the time we are writing this chapter, over 120 students have already enrolled solely through word of mouth, way over the number needed to start. The discussion between the management team, project team, curriculum developers, and teachers is based on the shared vision and transparency. The process has not been without hiccups, but at this moment the program is meeting the development requirements. More teaching programs at HAN University are now willing to adopt the lean approach.

References

Antony, J. Krishan, N. Cullen, D. and Kumar, M. (2012). Lean Six Sigma for higher education institutions (HEIs): Challenges, barriers, success factors, tools/techniques. *International Journal of Productivity and Performance Management*, *61*(8), 940–948.

Balzer, W. K. (2010). *Lean Higher Education: Increasing the Value and Performance of University Processes*, New York, Productivity Press.

Bateman, N., Hines, P. and Davidson, P. (2014). Wider applications for lean: An examination of the fundamental principles within public sector organizations. *International Journal of Productivity and Performance Management*, *63*(5), 550–568.

Eden, van J. (2014). Lean op een basisschool, kan dat?, *Procesverbeteren.nl*. Available at:www.procesverbeteren.nl/LEAN/Lean_basisschool.php (accessed October 28, 2015).

Emiliani, M. L. (2004). Improving business school courses by applying lean principles and practices. *Quality Assurance in Education*, *12*(4), 175–187.

Hattie, J. (2012). *Visible Learning for Teachers*, London, Routledge.

Hines, P. and Lethbridge, S. (2008). New development: Creating a lean university. *Public Money & Management*, *28*(1), 53–56.

Lean Higher Education hub (2015). Available at: www.leanhehub.ac.uk (accessed October 27, 2015).

Mills, J. and Miller, G. D. (2002). *A Pedagogy of Becoming: Abolishing Educational Welfare: Redrawing the Lines of Interdependency through Dialogue*, Editions Rodopi B.V.

Netland, T. (2015). Lean in the primary school? *Better Operations*. Available at: http://better-operations.com/2015/10/08/lean-primary-school/ (accessed October 28, 2015).

Radnor, Z., Osborne, S. P., Kinder, T. and Mutton, J. (2014). Operationalizing co-production in public services delivery: the contribution of service blueprinting. *Public Management Review*, *16*(3), 402–423.

Robinson, M. and Yorkstone, S. (2014). Becoming a lean university: The case of the University of St Andrews. In: Bergan, S., Egron-Polak, E., Kohler, K., Purser, L. and Vukasović, M. (eds), *Leadership and Governance in Higher Education: Handbook for Decision-Makers and Administrators*, Berlin, Raabe, pp. 42–72.

Rother, M. (2010). *Toyota Kata*, New York, McGraw-Hill.

Watkins, C. and Mortimore, P. (1999). Pedagogy: What do we know? In: Mortimore P. (ed.), *Understanding Pedagogy and its Impact on Learning*, London, Paul Chapman/Sage, pp. 1–19.

Wiegel, V. and Brouwer-Hadzialic, L. (2015). Lessons from higher education: Adapting Lean Six Sigma to account for structural differences in application domains. *International Journal of Six Sigma and Competitive Advantage*, *9*(1), 72–85.

Wiliam, D. (2011). *Embedded Formative Assessment*, Bloomington, IN, Solutions Tree Press.

Womack, J. P. and Jones, D. T. (2005). *Lean Solutions: How Companies and Customers Can Create Value and Wealth Together*, New York, Simon & Schuster.

38

LEAN SCHOOLS

Jan Riezebos

Introduction

Lean challenges the way we have looked at our processes and suggests taking a view from another perspective, i.e. through the lens of customer value. If we would like to apply lean to improve educational systems, a first step is to rethink customer value. Schools should identify what aspects of customer value have to be considered for a process that provides educational services, and to specify the customer requirements and constraints for the delivery of these services. Next, process descriptions of current and desired state have to be constructed, various types of waste have to be identified and eliminated, and flow has to be realized through the use of pull. Finally, an improvement cycle has to be implemented that aims at continuous improvement using a plan-do-check-act approach (Womack and Jones, 1996).

The term lean has been introduced to distinguish the approach taken by Japanese car manufacturers from the traditional mass-production approach of Western car manufacturers. Key terms of the lean approach are:

- respect-for-human (Sugimori et al., 1977; Riezebos et al., 2009),
- customer value instead of shareholder value (Emiliani, 2004),
- long-term instead of short-term strategy (Hines et al., 2004),
- flow efficiency instead of resource efficiency (Modig and Åhlström, 2014), and
- pull instead of push (Hopp and Spearman, 2004).

Lean has been applied in all kinds of processes and environments, including product development, supply chains, engineering, construction, food production, industrial services, public services, and healthcare. Applications in the field of education have been lagging behind and are still limited (Radnor and Bucci, 2011; Balzer and Rara, 2014). However, the potential for using lean improvement tools for educational processes is undoubted (Flumerfelt, 2008; Balzer, 2010; Schierenbeck, 2012; Emiliani, 2013). Therefore, it seems there is a large gap between the potential and realization of lean implementations.

In this chapter we explore the application of lean in education, particularly schools (primary and secondary education). We discuss whether the gap between the potential and the actual realization of lean might be due to the areas of education that have been involved so far in lean improvement projects. We classify projects of lean within primary and secondary education that are referred to in the literature and show what areas of education have been involved. This brings forward several challenges and opportunities for the application of lean in schools. Next, we focus on specific challenges of using lean in schools. This chapter is accompanied by an illustrative case study of a lean school.

What Constitutes a Lean School?

Education is essential to society. It challenges us to be curious, creative, to learn from the past and train ourselves in new areas, and prepare for the unknown future. In our modern society, schools are formal institutes to provide the service of education. They not only offer formal curricula and processes that help the students to acquire knowledge, competences, and an attitude that is required in order to continue their careers, but also provide an environment that facilitates learning in social interaction between students and staff. However, we should be aware that public or private schools are not the only providers of education. Some people acquire the same knowledge or skills without attending school. The processes that they have developed to acquire this knowledge or skills are equally important to study. However, in this chapter we will focus on the formal processes used in schools to provide education as a service.

Customer Value

The first question we have to address is what the intended customer value is of the educational service offered at the school. Related questions are whether students should be considered as customers or as a products of the educational process. This question has received a lot of attention in literature, but from a service operations perspective (Van Looy et al., 2003; Katzan, 2008) it is more important to understand that a customer might have various roles in a service process. It is important to distinguish between phases of the process:

1   service specification and selection;
2   service provision and transformation;
3   evaluation (quality control); and
4   benefiting.

Both the customer and the service provider will have a role in specifying the service to be offered to the customer. In some cases, the customer (i.e. student) just selects from a standardized portfolio of service offerings, while the service provider has designed the standardized service offerings according to external criteria from stakeholders such as government, higher education, labor market, etc. In other cases, the student is offered much more freedom in specifying what to learn, when to learn, how to learn, and where to learn. Program and intended learning outcomes may be designed as "tailor-made."

In operations management literature (e.g. Askin and Goldberg, 2002), the different options are denoted as *make to order* (MTO) and *engineer to order* (ETO). MTO organizations offer standardized services and start these services in general according to a predetermined schedule as soon as a batch of customers has entered the system. ETO organizations first construct (i.e. engineer) a specific process based on the demands of the customer. In order to avoid too much variation, these organizations frequently try to modify one of the available standard designs or apply a previously made design. ETO results in more variation of customer orders in the service provision process, which makes it more difficult to organize it efficiently. Operations management literature denotes this field as high mix, low volume, while the MTO field could be considered as high volume (per standardized process), low mix. Applications of lean in the field of high volume, low mix have been extensively described in the literature, primarily due to the origins of lean in the automotive industry. However, the variation in cars that are being produced in the same process is much higher than the variation that we nowadays intend to serve in schools. Hence, lean developed toward the high-mix, low-volume area over recent decades. A customer of a car specifies a perhaps unique configuration of modules. The car is being produced according to this specification in the same production line as other cars. Lean therefore offers methods and tools to facilitate mixed-model production lines and other types of high-mix, low-volume production.

The role of the customer (student) in the phase of service provision and transformation is both an active and a passive one. Active participation in the service provision and transformation is essential in learning. The idea that students learn just by being provided with inputs (i.e. knowledge, tests, etc.) in a specified sequence (like an assembly process of a product) denies fundamental characteristics of learning processes, which are based on exploration, building upon previous experiences and knowledge, while an open and safe environment, interaction, and motivation are essential preconditions.

Passive participation of students in the service provision and transformation is also present in educational processes within schools. For example, in most schools a student will receive a schedule that specifies when and where the modules or tests that she should take are offered. Otherwise, she will receive information about what material to study in order to prepare for an exam. Hence, the student is in general not involved in selecting the learning method (what and how to learn), nor the module and assessment schedule (when and where to learn). This prevents the students from being in control of the speed of learning, the social environment where learning takes place, the type of assignment that motivates or challenges his or her learning process, and so on.

The third phase of a service process is denoted as evaluation or quality control. In lean systems, evaluation of progress during service provision is considered to be of more value than just end-of-process quality control. The main reason is related to the possibility of providing feedback to previous stages in the process and feed forward to subsequent stages of the process. Note that this feedback is not directed toward the student, but the student will hopefully benefit from the feed forward that is provided to the not-yet-completed stages of the process. Next to this, it might be necessary to involve a customer actively in order to decide on adapting the specification of the intended outcomes or process for that specific customer. Based on intermediate measurements of progress in the intended transformation the customer may decide to change the desired service specification. In order to take such a decision, it might also be necessary to involve other stakeholders (e.g. parents, student counselors, teachers, etc.). However, it is an important active role of the customer to be involved in the adaption of specifications based upon the intermediate evaluation of service provision.

The final phase of a service process is when the customer benefits from the service. Note that this stage may already start when the customer enters the first stage of the process. The benefits from learning are gathered when one recognizes and specifies the desired intended learning outcomes and realizes that the gap with current knowledge and competences can be bridged by participating in the service provision. However, benefiting will in general continue after finishing school. The knowledge and skills acquired will hopefully be useful for further individual development. Further, the learning experience will also help to broaden the social network and increased access to resources or jobs that are valued by the customer. Some of these benefits will only become realized after some time, which makes it more difficult to measure. However, they should be included in specifying the customer value that customers (students) experience as a consequence of selecting the service of a specific school.

Educational Services

The second question we have to address is how lean schools will provide customer value in a more effective and efficient way. The focus in education is on delivering services that enable the student to learn a set of subjects at a specified level, master a set of skills, and acquire desired competences. As a result of this, customer value is enhanced by offering these services at the right time, in the right amount, in the right location, and at the right quality level. This is where we should start asking the question about what educational services should be distinguished in a school system.

In fact, there are numerous services offered and organized in a school. They may or may not add directly to the customer value as experienced by the students. Thus it might be wise to use a categorization of services. Literature on service management (e.g. Grönroos, 1994; Storey and Easingwood, 1998) makes the distinction between core services, facilitating services, supporting services, and augmented service offerings. Core services consist of the bundle of intangible services that are offered to meet the direct requirements of the customer, i.e. the main reason for the customer to ask for the service. In an educational context, the core services relate to learning, teaching, training, and assessment. Facilitating services are necessary to provide the main core service that is of value to the customer, i.e. without the facilitating services the core services simply can not be delivered. Think of program specification, course syllabi, classrooms, IT systems that support the primary processes, and so on. Supporting services are offered on the side to attract customers or to be distinctive on the market. The augmented service offering consists of admission, accessibility, interaction, and customer participation in provision of the service product.

We have performed a literature review in books and papers on lean in education. We limited our attention to books and papers that have the words "lean" and "education" in the title, abstract, or keyword list, and included studies of all types of educational institutes. Most studies that we found focused on colleges and none on primary education at all. Therefore, the results may not directly be transferable to all types of educational institutes, but give us an indication of what type of improvement projects have been undertaken and published by authorities in the field, and how these projects can be classified in terms of service characteristics. All cases or references to lean implementations in the education area have been classified in Table 38.1 using the classifications mentioned above.

From Table 38.1, we conclude that 75 percent of the lean improvement projects that have been described or mentioned in literature concern service activities in schools that are characterized as either facilitating, supporting, or related to the augmented service offering. It is remarkable that only 25 percent of the case studies have been published on the use of lean improvement tools for the core value-adding activities in education, as it is here the real value-adding activities can be found. This conclusion is in line with previous findings on the focus of improvement activities in the related field of total quality management (Koch and Fisher, 1998).

Case studies that apply lean in the core educational process discuss projects to improve course design or program design through emphasizing responsiveness, process design, and communication with the customer. These case studies demonstrate that it is possible to apply lean to core educational activities and processes. The lean improvement tools that have been used to improve these core educational processes have mainly focused on identifying customer value, processing redesign to reduce waste, and improving responsiveness by more frequent communication with the customer. Examples of the tools used are quality function deployment, visual controls, value stream maps, root cause analysis, standard work charts, and load smoothing. Less attention is given

Table 38.1 Analysis of lean in education projects referred to in literature

Source	Number of cases referring to educational service of type			
	Core	*Facilitating*	*Supporting*	*Augmented offering*
Balzer (2010): University of Central Oklahoma	0	7	2	3
Balzer (2010): University of Iowa	0	6	1	0
Balzer (2010): University of New Orleans	0	1	0	0
Balzer (2010): Bowling Green State University	0	0	2	2
Balzer (2010): University of Scranton	0	0	0	1
Emiliani (2004)	3	1	1	1
Emiliani (2005)	10[1]	0	0	0
Jankowski (2013)	0	1	0	0
Knight et al. (2000)	5	1	0	0
Radnor and Bucci (2011)	2	7	0	1
Stratton et al. (2007)	1	1	0	0
Thirkell and Ashman (2014)	0	2[2]	2[2]	2[2]
Waterbury (2011, 2013)[3]	2	3	3	27
Ziskovsky and Ziskovsky (2007)	3	1	0	0
Total (percentage)	**25%**	**30%**	**10%**	**35%**

Notes

[1] This is the number of cases that the author reports, but they have not been described in detail in this paper.

[2] The authors do not actually describe these cases, just refer to two or more cases in each of the non-core fields.

[3] The list of projects of Waterbury is made available for this chapter by the author and available upon request.

to the analysis of actual data that may help to improve processes for either the currently enrolled students or the next group.

Case studies that have applied lean to the facilitating services of a school describe, for example, facilities for disabled students, improved scheduling, placement services for work-based learning, and student enrollment for electives.

Case studies on supporting services are not found very frequently. The cases that we found in the literature listed in Table 38.1 focus mainly on housing facilities and sport accommodation for both students and staff.

The last category of augmented service offering is very well connected to the core and facilitating services, but is not considered to be delivering primary value to the students, i.e. it is experienced as it allows interaction with service providers, provides access to the core and supporting services, and communicates to the customers and their environment what service quality is being provided and acquired by the customers. Cases on lean in education that have been described largely address services in this category. Examples are admission and interaction with prospective students, communication with students and parents, enterprises, and govern-ment. Other services in this category focus on maintenance of resources (i.e. hiring and managing new staff) and administrative processes for accreditation.

Challenges and Opportunities for Lean Schools

This section addresses questions that should be addressed when using lean in schools, i.e. process descriptions, realizing flow, and establishing a culture of continuous improvement. These questions are considered to provide both challenges and opportunities for using lean more effectively in schools.

Process Descriptions

This question is how to describe processes and identify value-adding activities within the process. Lean suggests using value stream mapping as a tool to describe both the current state and the future state of a process (Rother and Shook, 2003). Value stream mapping uses a scheme that describes the process over time from the viewpoint of the flow unit (in schools this may be the student who flows through the process) by using symbols that describe:

- activities (both active and passive),
- movements,
- waiting,
- decisions,
- systems, and
- information flows.

For all these process elements, data is gathered to describe the essential characteristics of the activity. This data may concern the resource usage, cycle time, batch size, scrap rate, etc. The information flow describes the connection between the process and the control system that monitors the process flow. This includes the information sent to customers on the progress of the process, as well as the communication between several actors in the process in the form of feedback and feed forward.

Alongside the process elements, the average (observed) time spent in these activities or stages is also listed as the net time required to perform the value-adding part of this activity.

There is no doubt a need for a process description tool that enables communication among various stakeholders and actors in the process and helps to identify areas for improvement. However, based on the actual experiences we have with using this tool, we noticed that there are various issues that make the tool less applicable in the context of educational processes, especially if these processes concern the core services provided.

First of all, the process boundaries need to be defined. This is a decision of the team that describes the process flow. It should take into account the whole process of value creation for which the process has been designed and installed. However, many value stream maps just focus on a small part of the whole process without giving proper attention to the actual value being created. The effect might be that the redesign of the process focuses too much on inefficiencies within the narrowly defined process while losing sight of the elements of the process that result in ineffectiveness of the process.

Second, process descriptions in value stream maps tend to be very detailed and complete. The many details might cause a loss of sight on the main flow of the process. Discussions on process improvements might get stuck on changing some details or may even be prevented by first focusing on a correct presentation of all details. This is the problem of (the absence of a proper level of) abstraction. Abstraction is a modeling decision that needs to be taken prior to designing a value stream map and should relate to the primary objective of the process map visualization. It lists what flows need to be considered beforehand and what flows associated with the process can be neglected. An example is the decision to ignore the flows associated with energy or waste in the value stream map of a process. This is not to say that these secondary flows are not important to analyze, but it prevents losing sight of the primary process of value creation.

Third, descriptions of elements in the process vary in the level of aggregation. Aggregation is a modeling decision as well and concerns a statement beforehand on what time unit to use and how to round up or down toward this time unit. For example, it is no use specifying the time spent on one process element in a whole number of days, while another element is expressed in seconds. Aggregation decisions mean that all process elements are treated in the same way. A more detailed analysis of the same process in a later stage of the lean transformation may use another level of aggregation. As long as the level of aggregation is used all over the same map and is in line with the main objective of the analysis and redesign, this is no problem at all.

Fourth, value stream maps should add information flows to the regular process maps. These information flows describe and visualize the amount and type of information that is shared between participants (actors) in the process. These flows may be stored in systems like logbooks, data warehouses, spreadsheets, and so forth. It is important to identify this type of storage and retrieval system, as well as when and for what purpose (decision) the information is used. It is hence important to focus the description on recovering these aspects instead of trying to be as complete as possible. Ineffective information flows (too late, too detailed, outdated data, too many handling steps between data gathering and usage) might point toward improvement areas. Inefficient data-related activities might also be analyzed. However, most important is a focus on the requirements put in by the process itself, i.e. to use an approach that specifies data requirements for controlling the process based on providing the required customer value, i.e. on the decisions to be taken during the process by resources and participants.

Fifth, the timeline in a value stream map shows two sides of the coin with respect to the time spent on the process: the total time spent on each activity, as well as the value-adding time of that activity. This timeline results from the analysis of the various parts of the process, i.e. all data gathered on the process elements. However, some warnings on the construction and use of this timeline are in place. Lean provides tools to make a trade-off between quality, time, and cost. Quality concerns the value delivered to the customer, cost concerns the inputs and efforts made by the service provider (which may include efforts of the customer who actively participates in the delivery of the service). Time expresses how much time a customer needs to either wait or actively participate between the start and end of the process in order to acquire the required service. Lean improvements focus first of all on resolving a possible gap between the quality offered and the required quality. Next, a possible gap between the time needed and the required time is addressed. Finally, a possible gap between the actual cost and the minimal costs given the required quality and time is also addressed. If lean is used to address these performance criteria in another sequence, bad things will happen. These bad things concern not only customer satisfaction, but also employee involvement in process improvement. Now, the value stream mapping technique aims to describe first of all how quality is being delivered. However, if the improvement activities first focus on the time dimension or even on the cost dimension, then value stream maps are used for the wrong purpose.

This brings us to the last item to discuss regarding the use of value stream mapping as a lean tool in schools: waste elimination. In my opinion, this is one of the least understood concepts in lean improvement projects. Based on my previous comment on the necessary sequence of improvement activities, one should first focus on quality, then on time, and finally on cost. In most situations that I have encountered, quality improvement projects should not start with identifying waste, although waste may be present in the process. Instead of waste elimination, one should first try to enhance quality, i.e. provide customer value that is in line with the customer expectations or requirements. If there is overperformance, this may be considered a waste from the perspective of the service provider. But why first focus on eliminating this waste while there are so many areas where the actual service provided is below what is required?

However, waste elimination is important when time and/or costs need to be investigated. For all activities of students that they complete as part of the process, it is now known whether they contribute to the required customer value or not. Note that some activities, such as short breaks or holidays, may be value-adding as they help the student to process the learning acquired in preceding learning activities or periods. If these breaks are too long, they become waiting times and diminish the learning gains acquired through the preceding activities. This example makes clear that constructing and analyzing value stream maps in an educational context is not that easy to accomplish. Nevertheless, similar challenges are found in industrial processes, such as, for example, a bakery. Delays between processes are required to cool down, but if these delays are too long, the quality of the end product is lower than required. You won't find this type of example in many textbooks, but the complexity of processes is often more challenging than the examples you encounter in these textbooks. Value stream mapping may still be used both for educational as well as industrial processes, but the resulting diagrams may look more complex than the ones found in textbooks. We conclude that value stream mapping is a valuable lean tool that may be useful when improving processes, but only if used appropriately.

Realizing Flow

When redesigning and optimizing a process, lean focuses on realizing flow (Modig and Åhlström, 2014). It might be difficult to apply the concept of flow to schools (Waterbury, 2008), but think of learning as a process that needs time in order to achieve the desired outcomes. Part of this time might be value adding, another part may be considered as waste. For example, if you are taking driving lessons at a driving school, a minimum amount of time between lessons may be required in order to prevent fatigue, but if these times become to extensive or irregular, effectiveness is reduced. The same holds true for the waiting time between applying for an examination time slot and the actual examination. Realizing flow means that a process is being redesigned such that the flow units (students, products, etc.) do not have to wait unnecessarily long, so they can learn at the pace that is optimal for them and hence learn most effectively. Distractions, i.e. activities that require attention and disturb the learning, should be avoided. The same holds true for unnecessary set-up changes, movements, repetitions, scrap, etc.

In practice, organizations have to find a balance between realizing flow efficiency and realizing resource efficiency, as depicted in Figure 38.1. Traditionally, most organizations tend to focus on resource efficiency, as the resources (e.g. teachers, doctors, call center operators) are more permanently present in an organization compared with the individual customers in a process (students, patients, callers). Their longer presence and the power they have gained within the organization come with the costs the organization makes to employ them. Both effects cause a tendency to focus on resource efficiency, even where this may lead to a lower service to the customer in terms of timeliness, effectiveness, or quality.

Some organizations have to provide a flow efficient process without bothering about resource efficiency at all. Think of ambulance services, fire workers, hotels, prison labor, etc. Characteristic of such processes is that labor is available and waiting to start the process as soon as a new demand arrives. In the meantime, they may find other activities to perform, but these activities will be postponed as soon as a request to start the process is being made.

Lean aims to realize flow by moving both systems toward another extreme where they will encounter less waste and hence more efficiency. However, lean has to deal with the effect of variation in processes that circumvent the realization of both types of efficiency. Variation in processes may be encountered through the time needed to perform activities, which may fluctuate over time or differ per student or resource. Processing time variation includes set-up time

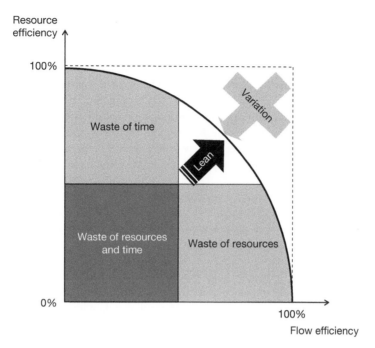

Figure 38.1   Flow and resource efficiency

Source: Modig and Åhlström (2014).

and non-availability of resources or flow units over time. It may also occur due to routing variation between flow units in the process. This routing variation may be caused by different specifications for the flow units (mixed-model production), or by quality problems (scrap and re-entrance at a previous processing step). Variation in processes may also be caused by an ineffective control of the processes, for example by batching requests and handling them together. The waiting time that the elements in the batch faced before they were processed differs due to this control policy. Large batches cause additional problems when errors are made that are only detected after completing the whole batch. Finally, variation may be caused by fluctuations in demand or supply. This type of variation affects processes through the availability of resources. It may take some time for a resource to become available for a next flow unit after completing a previous one. This cycle time of a resource is a type of set-up time that normally would be done offline (i.e. without the next flow unit being present). However, in case of peak demand, this time affects process variation and performance. The same holds true for temporary non-availability of supplies over time.

Lean attempts to increase flow and (if necessary) resource efficiency through reducing the effect of variation by buffering against or eliminating the causes of variation. Keep in mind: first flow efficiency (time), as cost (resource efficiency) comes last in a lean approach.

Culture of Continuous Improvement

Essential in a lean system is a culture for continuous improvement. This culture should be enhanced and valued by both students, staff, and management. Lean schools should be characterized by an open culture where every participant is invited to help improve the school. Typical lean tools, such as *kaizen* events, day starts, 5S policy, *poka-yoke*, *andon*, *kata*, and quality enhancement help to establish such a culture. However, these terms are not very well known in lean schools, although some have been implemented using different names.

Kaizen events are perhaps the best-known lean tool for continuous improvement (Imai, 1986). These events involve a team of participants who focus during a relatively short period of time on a typical process that needs improvement. The event is well-prepared: workshops to support the improvement process on, for example, A3 charting (Shook, 2008) and data analysis are offered alongside the event, while the multidisciplinary team addresses the issues and suggests improvements. In schools, similar systems focusing on improving core educational activities, such as assessment and teaching, are peer review teams, internal program audits, etc. However, schools may learn from the typical lean approach of very short and focused improvement events through kaizen.

Day starts among staff members are typical for most schools. In a lean context, these day starts may need a different set-up. Lean suggests a very structured set-up of these day starts in order to focus on improving a small set of process steps. The team takes responsibility for the process improvement and supports each other. Hence, it is not about socializing and sharing nor solving problems that have popped up.

Schools use a 5S policy to organize their processes and activities in a very efficient way, i.e. through a well-organized educational environment (Netland, 2015). This may impact the classrooms, virtual learning environment, offices, etc. Materials that do not contribute to the learning process or that are not being used by teachers or students should be removed from the learning environment. Menu buttons or news items in the virtual learning environment that are not adding value should be removed or moved to another location. Websites that offer materials that are outdated should be removed. 5S projects should be done in a systematic way, as the effect of a one-time exercise is not adding to a culture change at all.

Poka-yoke (Shingo, 1989) aims to prevent systematic errors. These errors might become clear through an analysis of the process. In schools, these errors may be found in all types of services. Errors when filling in forms might easily be identified, but student outcomes that are considered to be systematic underperformance might also be easily prevented by specific poka-yoke solutions. Poka-yoke tools are often developed with the team that identified the issue. They are typically easy and quick to implement, i.e. not very sophisticated or demanding in investment.

In an industrial assembly process, the andon (Shingo, 1989) provides authority to line employees to signal quality issues they encounter and if necessary even stop the whole line. Signaling may show the other employees that an urgent problem has been identified and asks for a solution. The andon signal is not provided in order to blame someone, but to share responsibility in identifying and solving problems and in the end prevent customer dissatisfaction. It is this culture of shared responsibility in identifying problems and developing solutions that is often lacking in school organizations. Andon is just a tool that cannot easily be copied to a school system. However, the underlying principle of shared responsibility for identifying and solving problems instead of blaming a specific participant in the process (whether it is the student, parents, management, support staff, or a single teacher) should be the basis of a culture for continuous improvement in lean schools.

Kata is the pillar of real management support to drive improvements in lean systems. Kata is a specific type of coaching using Socratic questions. Rother (2009) describes five steps of this coaching approach toward continuous improvement:

1   identify the ultimate target or challenge for this process;
2   identify the actual condition;
3   specify what obstacles are to be solved first in order to move toward the target;

4   define the first intermediate target to move to in the direction of the target; and,

5   identify the plan-do-check-act cycle for the first step.

The kata process requires a supportive environment that helps the problem owner to identify the answers on these five challenges. This is not to say that the environment (e.g. the management) knows the answers, but that they are able to support the problem owners to find the answers. In lean schools, coaching is often interpreted as a staff-to-student educational instrument or a management-to-staff tool to develop teachers. In kata, coaching is used to improve the system by prioritizing and addressing problems encountered in the process that prohibit an effective process. Hence, coaching may be provided by any participant in the process in order to support problem owners to work on improving the process. Thus, students may be trained to support teachers in improving the core educational service provided to them, management may be trained to help support staff in identifying solutions, etc.

Quality enhancement is the last aspect of a culture of continuous improvement in lean systems. Quality enhancement is much more effective in increasing the quality of processes than quality assurance. This is also recognized in educational processes (Betters-Reed et al., 2008). However, terminology in educational quality systems is sometimes quite confusing. For example, an interesting and valuable tool for quality enhancement in the context of core educational services is known as "assurance of learning." The essence of assurance of learning is to use data from student outcome assessment to improve the core educational process. The approach is propagated by the Association to Advance Collegiate Schools of Business International (AACSB) in their standard for educational quality (Riezebos, 2015). For example, student outcomes (such as presentations, essays, homework assignments, written exams) will be assessed (resulting in a grade for the student), but may also be used for an assurance of learning evaluation where a team of peers reviews the student outcomes on some specific identifiers for one of the selected learning gains. If the peer reviewers are dissatisfied with the average level achieved or think the variation is too large, this will have no consequences for the grades of the students for the whole module (which take into account a set of learning outcomes). However, it ought to lead to adaptations in the set-up of this module or preceding modules in the program in order to improve on this specific learning objective.

The Future of Lean Schools

We have shown that literature on the application of lean in schools has mainly referred to applications related to service activities that are characterized as either facilitating, supporting, or concerning the augmented service offering. It is remarkable that only a limited number of case studies have been published on the use of lean improvement tools for the real value-adding activities in education: instruction, assignments, and feedback.

Future research in the field of lean schools should use a broader scope of application areas where lean has been applied in the past. If researchers are not able to identify application areas in the core educational process, the relevance of lean in schools will diminish and so will the interest of educational professionals and administrators, notwithstanding the high potential of process improvements in this area.

Future research within the lean schools field might also reconsider the terminology used for other lean improvement tools, such as batching, pulling, quick changeovers (SMED), etc. It is better to broaden the scope of lean improvement activities using terminology and tools that are accepted in both primary and secondary education. Moreover, future research might enrich educational improvement approaches such as assurance of learning. It is all about a data-driven approach to improve the core educational process; hence there is a promising future for practice-based research on lean schools.

Case Study: Lean in Bærland Primary School

This case study is an extract from Netland (2015). It is used with permission of the author.

Bærland Primary School in Rogaland, Norway, has 35 employees who teach about 300 children from first to seventh grade. Since 2012, the teachers and staff at the school have learned about what lean can potentially offer a public school. They have agreed on two main objectives for their lean implementation: 1) increase the learning output by providing pupils more time for learning and teachers more time for teaching; 2) improve the working environment for the teachers by creating a more attractive working environment at the school and removing "time thieves" in administration. So far, Bærland Primary School has focused primarily on three lean practices:

1   5S workplace organization;
2   continuous improvement; and
3   standardization.

Lean School Practice 1: 5S Workplace Organization

5S (sort, set-in-order, shine, standardize, and sustain) is about maintaining an organized workspace. As a school is a public place with many users, 5S is a challenge for all users of the shared resources. Bærland uses tape markings and visual instructions ("one point lessons") to keep the school in an orderly state. The school has also implemented a solution for not accumulating material and waste over time: when a thing is not used for a while it will be marked with a date and moved to "The final resting place?," a physical place where unutilized objects are kept for a few days before being removed if not claimed.

Lean School Practice 2: Continuous Improvement

Every day, all Bærland employees gather for a five-minute morning meeting. These meetings focus on operational tasks and enable quick problem solving. The employees also hold weekly improvement meetings in front of visual team boards showing key performance indicators. Improvement suggestions and complaints are raised using post-it notes. In addtion, the school experimented with value stream mapping (for the development of local curricula) and A3 thinking for efficient communication.

Children also take part in improvement activities. At the school "class councils" have been replaced by "class improvement meetings" (from the fourth grade onwards). These meetings take place in front of visual improvement boards. The school has already implemented more than 1,200 improvement suggestions. The aim is simple: getting a little better, every day.

Lean School Practice 3: Standardization

Through standardization, Bærland Primary School tries to agree on some common practices for teaching (for example, how to start and end a class effectively), with the ultimate objective of increasing the quality of education. Teachers are encouraged to share best practice with one another with the purpose of improving the overall learning experience for the pupils. The point is to make the "desired standards of teaching" clear so one can apply them and improve the quality of teaching by experimenting with deviation from them. Admittedly, standardization is not an easy sell in a school environment, which is why Bærland allows time to discuss and learn rather than forcing it.

References

Askin, R. G. and Goldberg, J. B. (2002). *Design and Analysis of Lean Production Systems*, New York, John Wiley and Sons.

Balzer, W. K. (2010). *Lean Higher Education: Increasing the Value and Performance of University Processes*, New York, Productivity Press.

Balzer, W. K. and Rara, T. (2014). Why is the broad implementation of lean higher education failing? In: *2nd International Conference on Lean Six Sigma for Higher Education*, Arnhem.

Betters-Reed, B. L., Nitkin, M. R. and Sampson, S. D. (2008). An assurance of learning success model: Toward closing the feedback loop. *Organization Management Journal*, 5(4), 224–240.

Emiliani, M. L. (2004). Improving business school courses by applying lean principles and practices. *Quality Assurance in Education*, 12(4), 175–187.

Emiliani, M. L. (2005). Using kaizen to improve graduate business school degree programs. *Quality Assurance in Education*, 13(1), 37–52.

Emiliani, M. L. (2013). *The Lean Professor: Become a Better Teacher Using Lean Principles and Practices*, 2nd edition, Wethersfield, CT, The CLBM, LLC.

Flumerfelt, S. (2008). Is lean appropriate for schools? [Electronic version]. In: Flumerfelt, S. (ed). *White Papers*, Rochester, MI, The Pawley Lean Institute, pp. 1–6.

Grönroos, C. (1994). From scientific management to service management: A management perspective for the age of service competition. *International Journal of Service Industry Management*, 5, 5–20.

Hines, P., Holweg, M. and Rich, N. (2004). Learning to evolve: A review of contemporary lean thinking. *International Journal of Operations and Production Management*, 21(10), 994–1011.

Hopp, W. J. and Spearman, M. L. (2004). To pull or not to pull: What is the question? *Manufacturing and Service Operations Management*, 6(2), 133–148.

Imai, M. (1986). *Kaizen: The Key To Japan's Competitive Success*, New York, McGraw-Hill Education.

Jankowski, J. (2013). Successful implementation of Six Sigma to schedule student staffing for circulation service desks. *Journal of Access Services*, 10(4), 197–216.

Katzan, H. J. (2008). *Service Science, Concepts, Technology, Management: A Guide to Service Science for Academicians and Practitioners*, Bloomington, IN, iUniverse.

Knight, P., Aitken, E. N. and Rogerson, R. J. (2000). *Forever Better: Continuous Quality Improvement in Higher Education*, New Forums Press.

Koch, J. V. and Fisher, J. L. (1998). Higher education and total quality management. *Total Quality Management*, 9, 659–668.

Modig, N. and Åhlström, P. (2014). *This is Lean: Resolving the Efficiency Paradox*, Stockholm, Rheologica Publishing.

Netland, T. H. (2015). A Norwegian primary school is experimenting with the use of lean management principles to improve both learning and teaching. *Planet Lean, The Global Network Journal*, pp. 1–7.

Radnor, Z. and Bucci, G. (2011). *Analysis of Lean Implementation in UK Business Schools and Universities*, A Report by AtoZ Business Consultancy, pp. 1–74.

Riezebos, J. (2015). Assurance of learning as a lean improvement tool for higher education. In: Antony, J. and Albliwi, S. (eds), *Third International Conference on Lean Six Sigma for Higher Education*, Edinburgh, Heriot-Watt University, School of Management and Languages, pp. 76–85.

Riezebos, J., Klingenberg, W. and Hicks, C. (2009). Lean production and information technology: Connection or contradiction? *Computers in Industry*, 60(4), 237–247.

Rother, M. (2009). *Toyota Kata: Managing People for Improvement, Adaptiveness and Superior Results*, New York, McGraw-Hill Education.

Rother, M. and Shook, J. (2003). *Learning to See: Value Stream Mapping to Add Value and Eliminate Muda*, Cambridge, MA, Lean Enterprise Institute.

Schierenbeck, C. (2012). *Fixing Higher Education*, Wiesbaden, Springer.

Shingo, S. (1989). *A Study of the Toyota Production System: From an Industrial Engineering Viewpoint*, Boca Raton, FL, CRC Press.

Shook, J. (2008). *Managing to Learn: Using the A3 Management Process to Solve Problems, Gain Agreement, Mentor and Lead*, Cambridge, MA, Lean Enterprise Institute.

Storey, C. and Easingwood, C. J. (1998). The augmented service offering: A conceptualization and study of its impact on new service success. *Journal of Product Innovation Management*, 15, 335–351.

Stratton, T. D. Rudy, D. W., Sauer, M. J., Perman, J. A. and Jennings, C. D. (2007). Lessons from industry: One school's transformation toward "lean" curricular governance. *Academic Medicine*, 82(4), 331–340.

Sugimori, Y., Kusunoki, K., Cho, F. and Uchikawa, S. (1977). Toyota Production System and Kanban system: Materialization of just-in-time and respect-for-human system. *International Journal of Production Research*, 15(6), 553–564.

Thirkell, E. and Ashman, I. (2014). Lean towards learning: Connecting lean thinking and human resource management in UK higher education. *International Journal of Human Resource Management*, 25(21), 2957–2977.

Van Looy, B., Gemmel, P. and Van Dierdock, R. (2003). *Services Management, an Integrated Approach*, 2nd edition, Harlow, Pearson Education.

Waterbury, T. A. (2008). *Lean in Higher Education: A Delphi Study to Develop Performance Metrics and an Educational Lean Improvement Model for Academic Environments*, Capella University.

Waterbury, T. A. (2011). *Educational Lean for Higher Education: Theory and Practice*, Lulu.com.

Waterbury, T. A. (2013). Project list till Oct. 2013 (private communication).

Womack, J. and Jones, D. T. (1996). *Lean Thinking: Banish Waste and Create Wealth in Your Corporation*, New York, Productivity Press.

Ziskovsky, B. and Ziskovsky, J. (2007). *Doing More with Less: Going Lean in Education—A White Paper on Process Improvement in Education*, Lean Education Enterprises. Available at: www.leaneducation.com/whitepaper-DoingMoreWithLess.pdf (accessed July 2016).

39

LEAN UNIVERSITIES

Steve Yorkstone

Introduction

This chapter examines lean implementation in higher education (HE) institutions. There is evidence of lean initiatives beginning in HE in the US in the early 2000s; there is also some evidence of business process improvement activity before this time (Hines and Lethbridge, 2008; Waterbury and Holm, 2011). Today, many universities and other HE institutions are pursuing lean thinking.

The HE sector faces challenges around maintaining funding while continuing to deliver excellent services. Critics of HE assert that university operations are typically loaded with wasteful, unnecessary, and unproductive activity. On the one hand there is an apparent need for the sector to become ever-increasingly effective and efficient. On the other hand, the inherent complexity of the mission of universities would seem to present particular challenges to optimizing efficiency and effectiveness in the sector.

The Characteristics of Higher Education

Universities deliver teaching and research (see Figure 39.1). They have been around for a long time; some institutions are hundreds of years old, and yet they are still big business. Much is written about the transformative power of HE both for individuals and for businesses and economies. This is not surprising when we consider individual universities, like Waterloo in Canada, that have a significant economic impact on their regions. Waterloo plays a crucial role in anchoring the Waterloo Region Innovation Ecosystem, which generated C$18 billion in technology sector revenue and a C$84 billion deal flow in 2009 alone.

The marketplace for HE is growing and is linked to an increasing demand for highly qualified individuals, the increasing global population, and a growing appetite for research outcomes from both public and private sectors. Finance models for HE vary from institutions funded directly by student fees (often in the form of student loans) to institutions where the state directly bears the full cost of education. However, student funding is only part of the picture as institutions also draw significant income from research contracts and agreements (with private companies, charities, governments, and/or non-governmental organizations (NGOs)).

Universities are typically independent bodies, and as such the sector contains a range of operating models. These models reflect the history and purpose of each institution and are often displayed with varying levels of central control over federalized structures (Whitchurch, 2006). There are a number of factors that impact a university's operating model, including the institution's balance between research and teaching as well as the nature of the teaching and research undertaken. Given that universities are here to innovate, the border between teaching and research itself is often blurred, with some of the most attractive teaching provided by world-class researchers and some of the best students contributing to world-class research.

Modes of Teaching

Teaching is delivered at different levels, beginning with undergraduate degrees and then moving to postgraduate (or graduate) and research (or doctoral) degrees. The nature of the delivery of degrees varies, according to established methods known as pedagogies. Degrees can be delivered entirely residentially or non-residentially, and are typically delivered as a combination of both. They can be part time, full time, delivered on site, or delivered remotely via technology. They can include practical assignments, applied work, work placements, or establishing a business as part of the course. Some courses now teach over the traditional vacation period to shorten the length of time it takes to gain a qualification.

An undergraduate degree is often required for an individual to access a certain level of employment following graduation and thus serves as evidence of a level of experience and understanding of the subject at hand.

Pure research degrees operate differently. Those undertaking a research (or doctoral) degree are already experts and they work underneath an eminent expert supervisor for a number of years with the aim of adding a novel element to their field. Postgraduate students are also often involved in the business of the university; for example, they contribute by teaching undergraduate students or participate in the commercial aspects of research.

Modes of Research

The volume of research undertaken in each university varies, but for many institutions research is a necessity implied by undergraduate teaching; i.e. in order for academics to be qualified to teach at undergraduate level they may be required to be actively researching in their field. Institutions adopt different approaches to research, with some institutions developing highly applicable, close-to-market outputs, and others opting for more academic publications. Universities also undertake research that impacts culture and society at large, for example, in fine art.

The organization of research itself is largely dependent on the field in which the research is conducted. Research can be undertaken by individuals or teams and often requires significant non-academic and specialist resources.

Organizational Structures

The evolution of universities includes the development of significant administrations to support teaching and research. Universities require logistics like all businesses. However, specialist teaching and research may also require specialized facilities, laboratories, etc., all of which lead to a need for attendant supporting services and management.

Universities often provide a range of services in-house, for example provision for student accommodation. The services they offer are frequently also provided for the communities where they are located. Many universities choose to leverage their estate or brand for commercial benefit, for example, as providers of sporting facilities, conference facilities, and particularly in the US, college athletics.

Internationalization

International education is commonplace, with many students choosing to travel to study; for example, in 2013–2014 around 4.5 million students studied overseas.

Not only is studying at a foreign university a worthwhile experience in itself, students also study overseas for financial reasons, with the international economy often making traveling an affordable route to a quality degree. For instance, all publicly funded German universities have abandoned tuition fees, even for non-German students. As a significant number of German programs are offered in international languages, such as English, these institutions are particularly attractive for students from countries with high tuition fees.

In other countries, such as the UK, primarily public universities have for some time been using income from international tuition fees to support their operations, while still offering good value to students who choose to study abroad in these universities.

HE institutions are increasingly reaching out to overseas students by delivering degrees in their home countries, either through working in partnership with local educational institutions and importing lecturers and course materials (the flying faculty model) or through the establishment of satellite campuses.

The Move to the Internet

There has been significant press recently discussing the impact of the rise of courses delivered online, known as "massive open online courses" (MOOCs). Delivered to large numbers of students, these have had a far-reaching impact in that most institutions now offer some level of their delivery online.

That said, MOOCs themselves have failed, at least in the short term, to be an industry changer for HE. While it was predicted that MOOCs would open affordable education to those who would not have otherwise studied, uptake has been largely from those who already have a degree and are seeking additional qualifications. Furthermore, completion rates for most online courses are extremely low.

For now, at least, wherever it is delivered, most HE continues to be about bringing people physically together in order to create shared learning or research outcomes.

The Principle of Academic Freedom

In the context of a wide variety of institutions and operating models, one thread that unites the sector is "academic freedom," a principle that allows for freedom of inquiry without staff risking their employment or benefits. This means that, in practice, academic staff members are able to teach and research without fear, even when such activities run counter to existing orthodoxies (indeed some would argue it is the responsibility of the academic to challenge prevailing orthodoxies). Academic freedom is enshrined in law in a number of countries; however, in practice there are limits to this since academics are expected to act ethically, legally, and with limited resources.

Another thread that runs through the sector is the necessity for research to be non-standard, i.e. in order for it to be successful (indeed, marketable), it has to have never been done before. In essence, HE is a creative industry.

What is Lean Higher Education?

Universities often operate as collections of separate functions (federal in structure) rather than as highly corporate enterprises. This federal structure often leads to an emergent strategy for lean implementations, with individuals taking an opportunistic approach. That being said, it would be wrong to generalize as there are also highly successful top-down structured implementations (typically in more modern, more centralized universities). We are at a relatively early stage of understanding lean in the sector and a high level of tailoring for lean to meet the unique contexts of individual institutions currently exists.

In common with lean applications in industry, in many lean applications in HE we are seeing the non-zero-sum (i.e. win–win) aspects of lean activity being applied: resources are released from back office or administrative activity and applied to increase value for students and research outcomes.

Locating Lean within HE Organizational Structures

There is no shared acknowledgment regarding the "best" one functional area of a university that should be responsible for the implementation of lean practices, or indeed that any one area should take responsibility for implementing lean.

In practice, staff leading lean in institutions are often aligned to senior management (e.g. the principal's, vice chancellor's, or president's office), or the human resources or information technology departments. Furthermore, leadership can be provided by either academic or non-academic staff. While there is some debate about where best to site leadership for lean, where central staff responsible for lean exist they tend to be managed in administrative or support functions rather than academic functions.

It is true that lean is being applied directly to the primary institutional value streams in universities, for example those relating to teaching (Emiliani, 2015b). However, there does appear to be more effort currently focused on the improvement of supporting or back office processes (Balzer, 2010; Robinson and Yorkstone, 2014; Emiliani, 2015a).

The non-academic leadership of central lean teams, combined with this typical focus on non-academic processes, has led to the accusation that the sector is often applying "lean office" within HE (i.e. focusing on enhancing the administrative and back office processes of a university), rather than ensuring true lean HE (i.e. enhancing the teaching and/or research activity).

Different Approaches to Lean in HE

While lean in HE is as varied as universities themselves, there are several approaches emerging which are explored further below. In most implementations we see different elements of these approaches to a greater or lesser extent. Three common approaches to lean in HE are as follows:

1   *Event-driven lean in HE.* There has been a strong movement in lean HE toward event-driven lean, as seen in the University of St. Andrews for example (see case study), with improvements being driven as part of a series of "kaizen events" or "rapid improvement events." Typical in the sector, these events are supported by a central team of trained facilitators who lead activities on a project basis. Such event-driven implementation also typically aims to embed lean culture and behaviors through knowledge transfer and coaching.

This approach has the benefit of deeply introducing the staff involved in these interventions to lean tools, techniques, and behaviors. It does, however, run the risk of missing those areas not included as part of a program of activities, and thus care must be taken to ensure the broader cultural aspects of true lean are maintained.

2   *Advocate-led lean in HE.* Alternative early models focused on a small team of lean facilitators training and supporting staff at key levels in lean techniques (developing a network of advocates) and supporting them through improvement projects. This is an approach seen notably at Cardiff University.

Focusing on a relatively large group of individuals enables a broad spread across the institution at relative speed and can work to maximize behavioral and cultural impact. However, there is a risk that the initial enthusiasm will be short-lived. There is also a risk that without support for these advocates to see their organization as a whole system, any improvements could be at the expense of other internal functional areas. There is also a risk of tokenism, with these staff seen as the "lean person" rather than the wider body of staff taking responsibility for improvement themselves.

3   *Tool-led lean in HE.* In other applications, we see institutions taking elements of the lean toolkit and applying them, examples of which include the use of daily communication cells and visual management to support improvement. This is not an approach that one would imagine would work in the creative space of a university, but there is strong evidence, e.g. in the University of Strathclyde in Scotland, that this approach is having a real impact. However, it is important to note that such an approach works best when applying these tools is part of a wider initiative aiming at cultural change.

Lean and Related Approaches in HE

Other approaches related to lean that have been utilized in the HE sector include Six Sigma, systems thinking, business process mapping, and total quality management (Waterbury and Holm, 2011; Antony et al., 2012). Indeed, many more universities apply continuous improvement (and may be more lean in nature) than those that explicitly apply lean by name. As part of their assessment for programs such as "Investors in People" or "Customer Service Excellence," a large number of universities, particularly in the UK, are required to demonstrate continuous improvement activity, albeit not specific lean activity.

Examples of Tools Seen in Higher Education

Returning to lean implementations, there are a number of tools often used. The use of sticky note process mapping in a commonplace as-is and to-be model is frequently seen in HE. While some authors have attempted to redefine the classic types of waste to more aptly fit a university environment (Balzer, 2010), typical lean implementations in universities address the classic "seven plus one" wastes: transportation, inventory, motion, waiting, overproduction, overprocessing, defects, and skills.

"Affinity mapping" (Kawakita, 1982; George et al., 2004) is often seen as an approach to problem solving in university lean workshops and is often paired with a De Bono-inspired "six thinking hats" approach (De Bono, 2000) to ensure systematic analysis.

Visual management is often seen in HE through the use of whiteboards to manage information, even though this is often not acknowledged explicitly as a lean tool.

There are examples of many other lean tools being successfully deployed (albeit less commonly) in HE. For example, there is evidence of the successful application of 5S in Aberdeen University in Scotland, which includes clearing office clutter, reducing the amount of storage space needed, and making access to materials significantly easier (Paterson, 2015).

While in universities there is often not the kind of high-volume transactional data that lends itself to statistical modeling, such modeling has been seen in HE, for example, in understanding the variations in the return times of library items and in invoice processing.

It is a challenge for the sector to move beyond what we see in early lean in HE implementations, i.e. the elimination of waste from the value stream, and to move to a more advanced level of lean maturity, as demonstrated by: improving flow, truly embracing "customer" value, developing pull, and seeking perfection.

Lean as a Phenomenon of Organizational Culture

There has been recent criticism of lean in HE in online forums, i.e. that in obsessing with models or approaches, practitioners of lean in HE have missed out on lean's true nature as an enterprise-wide approach and a way of working rather than a particular tool, model, or structure.

One aspect that successful applications of lean in HE share is the common understanding of lean as an applied philosophy of work that is essentially about how people within an organization relate to each other, their common behaviors, and the culture of work.

Challenges and Opportunities

Like any industry distant from lean's manufacturing birthplace, there is some reluctance to embrace lean, typified by that familiar phrase "But we aren't like Toyota!"

Ensuring buy-in from university management is thus key. This drives a need for theoretical rigor to evidence lean as a viable improvement approach for HE and the importance of using the evidence base for lean that has been developed in industry. These challenges are shared by many organizations in the early stages of their lean experiences (Netland and Ferdows, 2014).

Organizational Cultures: HE as a Non-standard and Creative Industry

Deeply embedded within the culture of academia is the need to develop new ways of working; in the field of academic research there is a drive to produce the novel, the never-before-seen. This fundamental behavioral drive runs counter to the idea that work can be standardized and is a challenge to gaining a real understanding of lean (as standard work is a large part of many lean applications in industry).

A concept that can address this challenge is the manufacturing analogy of "runners," "repeaters," and "strangers." This model suggests that there are some things we do that are high volume and can be standardized (runners); other pieces of work that are regular and that can be standardized to some extent (repeaters); and those items of work that are infrequent and need to be treated as unique instances (strangers). The error that this concept can help us avoid is confusing one category for another and the subsequent increase in waste this causes.

So, to apply this in HE: yes, it is true that research must be unique and unprecedented (a stranger), but the purchase of the equipment required to stock the lab to produce that outcome can be done in a perfectly standardized way (a runner).

Organizational Cultures: Academic Freedom and Debate

As we know, academic freedom is a key feature of universities, and again this can be a challenge to introducing new and standard ways of working. On the one hand it is a misapplication of the notion of academic freedom to suggest that standard processes never apply to academic staff.

On the other hand, it is hardly surprising when our academic freethinkers apply their skills of critical thinking to challenge what in other sectors would be highly standardized processes.

In fact, it is the willingness to experiment with new ways of working and the reluctance to standardize across the sector that many see as fundamental to the current comparative success of the sector. Without this diversity the HE sector would not be as vibrant as it currently is; pairing this diversity with an action-orientated approach enables universities to really lead innovation.

Indeed, HE is not alone in employing highly specialist, expert levels of staff with a penchant for questioning the norm. Involving these challenging stakeholders appropriately can be a gift, provided the debate is constructive.

The "Customer Problem"

When more than two lean practitioners in HE are brought together, there is almost always an inevitable discussion revolving around the following question: "Who or what is the customer of higher education?" In order to properly define value, we need to understand who the organization is for and what its purpose is.

The simplest definition of the customers of a university is that they are those people who study within it. While using university-provided catering or accommodation, students are clearly transacting with the university as customers. However, when consuming teaching content or undergoing assessment, students do not always view themselves as a customer. Given some funding models where students do not pay for their own education, their relationship as a customer is unclear.

Many go further and suggest that the employers of graduates are the main customers of universities and that those organizations that fund research or the people that benefit from the research outcomes should be considered as customers also. At this level the "customer" of HE might then be seen as the cultures within which universities operate, which is arguably a definition almost too broad to be useful (see Figure 39.1).

Additionally, and quite rightly, many academics rail against the "commodification" of education with the assumption that universities do not provide a simple, repeatable transaction that anyone with enough income, if needed, can buy. It is often expressed that what universities

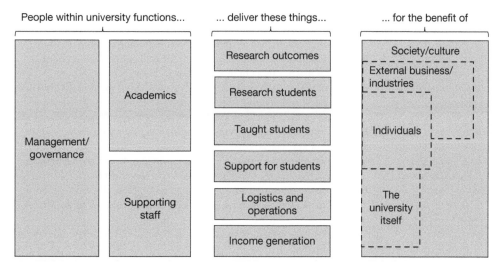

Figure 39.1 Mapping the relationship between university functions, outputs, and destinations

do is a complex act of co-creation, requiring a personal investment from all parties in a way that not all individuals are capable of undertaking. Furthermore, it has been suggested that applying capitalist models to HE undermines its ability to add value.

That said, there are elements of the market in play, as universities are in competition to attract the best and brightest students, to win research funding, and to attract and retain the most prestigious academics.

For the lean practitioner, this "customer problem" runs the risk of becoming intractable. A pragmatic and functional approach has been observed to be the best solution. Rather than endless debates around who the customer of HE is, this energy is better spent practically getting on with the business of making the experience of HE better for students, for research funders, and/or for the beneficiaries of (and those engaged in carrying out) whatever the process in question may be. The "customer problem" runs the risk of being an example of where HE's predilection for discussion acts as a significant barrier to action.

Evidencing Lean in Higher Education: The "Benefits Problem"

The business of evidencing the benefits of lean in HE is a challenge. For organizations that have complicated and diverse aims, enhancing one aspect of performance may be detrimental to another. Again, we see a propensity for discussion over action inhibiting value-adding activity.

The tensions between teaching and research (and administration) are familiar to those who work in the sector (Whitchurch, 2006; Winter, 2009), and are an instance where different organizational goals lead to tensions within an organization. There are also concerns that the very different business models and aims of HE institutions, even if consistency is achieved within one university, make shared metrics across institutions misleading.

Perhaps this is one reason that an early report on lean in HE concluded that there was a large gap in the evidence of costs and savings made using lean (Radnor and Bucci, 2011). Indeed, since

Table 39.1 Stages in "A Guide to Evidencing the Benefits of Business Process Improvement in Higher Education"

Project phase	Summary of evidencing benefits activities
Institutional preparation	Preparatory work required to agree on priorities for undertaking BPI activities and ensure consistency of approach when measuring benefits.
Project initiation	Introduction of key activities to gather high-level baseline data to inform decision making ahead of project selection and scoping activity.
Project scoping and start-up	Detailed project scoping activities to gather and capture the necessary baseline data against which future improvements can be measured. This informs whether projects should proceed.
Diagnostic	Key activities once a project is underway to maximize data collation and the buy-in of key stakeholders.
Design, trial, and implementation	Essential activities that enhance the measurement of post-improvement data and ongoing buy-in for evidencing the success of the project.
End of project	Focused on the sign-off of benefits captured so far, those that have not been realized, and the ongoing responsibilities for the realization of further benefits.
Sustainment	Ongoing benefits realization and the identification of further opportunities for improvement.

Source: Reproduced with permission from Lawrence and Cairns (2015).

that report, there remains, perhaps surprisingly, little transparent reporting around the benefits of lean in HE (Lawrence and Cairns, 2015).

Lawrence and Cairns' recent research into the barriers universities face in sharing the benefits of their lean or process improvement initiatives is enlightening. Their survey of the sector suggests that in some cases people are not measuring the benefits of their interventions, and that even when measurement is being undertaken institutions are often reluctant to share this information externally. Such reluctance stems either from fear of criticism at the amount of waste that existed in the processes before improvement or from concern that the project has not delivered the desired measurable results.

Nonetheless, Lawrence and Cairns' work led to the development of a framework for consistently measuring impact within universities, entitled: "A Guide to Evidencing the Benefits of Business Process Improvement [BPI] in Higher Education," which has been welcomed by the sector.

This framework provides a series of tools and activities based around seven project phases that complement existing project management approaches, as shown in Table 39.1.

Evidencing Lean in Higher Education: Existing Information

There is some evidence for the success of lean in HE. High-profile lean adopters have published evidence of their successes. Examples include the University of St. Andrews, which reported that over the first four years of its implementation it released the time equivalent of 24.63 full-time staff members to increase value-adding activity (Robinson and Yorkstone, 2014).

Interestingly, however, St. Andrews has more recently moved away from publishing data around savings made. It has commented that focusing purely on data detracts from its real goal of skills transfer and ensuring cultural change. Additionally, it cites the difficulties in arriving at robust and therefore fully defensible data. It has been argued that producing more data than is required to bring about improvement, while perhaps reputation enhancing, is in fact a form of over-processing.

Groups representing universities, particularly in the UK, are referencing business improvement and lean initiatives as part of their successes, which is starting to tell a story of how lean is having an impact on the sector. For example, Universities Scotland's 2015 report *Working Smarter 2015* lists six case studies of lean and process improvement across the 19 universities in Scotland. These case studies identify benefits totaling £168,000 in direct cost savings, £2.5 million of increased revenue for one named project, and a number of qualitative savings, including reduction in wait times and improved service levels (Diamond, 2015).

The growth of the number of lean implementations in HE and the interest that staff in HE have in lean (which, granted, is not a direct indicator of the benefits of lean) suggest that there is momentum behind lean and process improvement as a movement. For example, the Lean HE Hub moderates an online forum for staff interested in lean. This forum started in 2009 and has grown from around 500 members by the end of 2014 to well over 1,100 members by the close of 2015.

The Future of Lean Higher Education

In a sector where the central business is that of creatively deconstructing and reconstructing ideas, it is no surprise that crossing the knowing–doing gap (for example, relating to the customer and benefits problems) presents the sector's biggest challenge.

Despite the challenges, however, current indicators suggest that lean is in a period of growth in HE globally, with an increasing number of universities embarking on lean journeys. In early implementations we saw lean leveraging a largely bottom-up, emergent strategy to growth, yet we are now increasingly observing university leaders actively championing lean and continuous improvement initiatives.

The Evolution of Lean in Higher Education

This recent growth of lean should be tempered with a word of caution, as in some institutions, including early adopters, we are seeing lean teams restructured and their roles minimized. In a small number of instances, universities that previously employed staff to introduce lean working have chosen to go in other directions. Despite the relatively recent growth of lean in universities, it is inevitable that we are going to see more implementations change or cease altogether.

There are two ways of viewing these changes. One interpretation could be that, as some lean teams are moved into other areas of the universities, we are seeing the true lean message being diluted. As a result, the strength of the lean improvements is weakened. An alternative view could be that we are seeing lean becoming more mainstreamed into the way that universities conduct their work; and thus continuous improvement becomes business as usual.

For lean to continue to have a positive impact in the sector, the key is to take the second of these routes. In other words, it will be crucial to see a change in how the institution applies lean not as a failure but instead as a necessary evolution and an opportunity to apply learning from these experiences. Notwithstanding, at the early stages of these developments further investigation will be required as these changes play out.

Whatever approaches are taken, there are enormous opportunities to improve the way that universities undertake their work, and lean is proving to be an important part of how this happens. Importantly, lean is becoming a significant part of building a culture of HE where continuous improvement and respect for people are part of how universities work.

Universities have been described as modern-day miracles, producing amazing outcomes for individual students and enabling research critical to the development of businesses, industries, and society. This is the challenge for lean in HE: to ensure that in a rapidly changing world, our universities can continue to produce transformative outcomes in a way that benefits everyone.

Case Study: Lean at the University of St. Andrews

The University of St. Andrews founded its lean team in 2006. This was one of the earliest and most successful lean interventions in HE. Ten years later, the university continues to practice lean and is also in the business of supporting other universities (and other bodies, primarily in the public sector) in their lean implementations, both at home in the UK and globally.

This case study is based on a series of interviews conducted with staff at front-line, management, and senior levels in the university, who have been involved in St. Andrews' lean initiative in different ways. The aim is to reflect on what St. Andrews has done that has led to lean being a successful part of the university's strategy and uncover lessons that other organizations can apply.

The University of St. Andrews

The University of St. Andrews is a relatively small and highly international community (just under 8,000 students, 47 percent of whom are from outside the UK), which has recently (over the past 10 years or so) improved its standing in the league tables to become a university that now places consistently within the top five universities in the UK.

It has a traditional academic portfolio, with subjects grouped into faculties of arts, science, medicine, and divinity. Its approach to internationalization is likewise traditional, with students traveling from around the world to attend the university, which is set in a small and picturesque mediaeval seaside town.

Lean in St. Andrews: Historically

In 2006, the university had reached a time where its academic staff met global standards of excellence, following a consistent policy of investment. However, there was feedback from these academic staff that the administrative processes of the university were suboptimal.

The senior management team of the university was also at that time recognizing that while the university was able to manage its finances adequately, in the medium to longer term the university needed to seek ways to ensure that it used resources more effectively.

This led university leadership to conclude that there was a need to become more effective and efficient, to look at the way the university organized its work. The leadership team wished to undertake process improvements, rather than merely implementing new technology.

Against this background, the then Quaestor and Factor (the chief operating officer who was at that time responsible for the finance and estates functions of the university) recognized that lean was an approach that would meet these needs. He was drawn to the approach by the non-zero-sum aspect of releasing waste to increase value, and the importance that lean placed on building relationships between people.

The university commissioned an external consultancy for a significant number of months to train a small number of seconded staff in "lean office" techniques, creating a central team that was line managed as part of the university's information services (IS) division. However, this team was still very much established as an internal consultancy service independent of existing organizational structures.

After the initial three-year secondments, the team members were made a permanent feature of the university, having developed their own *lean project cycle* (see below) and demonstrated significant successes in a number of areas.

Lean in St. Andrews: Functionally

Practically speaking, the senior sponsor of the St. Andrews lean team has remained consistent since its inception. However, as of January 2016, while retaining the title "Quaestor and Factor," this role has grown to include serving as the acting chief executive officer of the university, responsible for the university's operational structures, alongside the university's acting principal, responsible for its academic delivery.

Line management of the team has remained within IS, which was initially intended as a way to ensure that technological implementations first dealt with root cause problem solving and improved business processes before applying a digital solution. While managed within IS, the lean team positioned itself very much as an internal consultancy service independent from any service or department within the university.

Lean in St. Andrews: The Process

Figure 39.2 illustrates how one staff member described (in a "rich pictures" exercise) the work of the lean team at St. Andrews, which involves taking the complicated and making it simple in order to delight the customer.

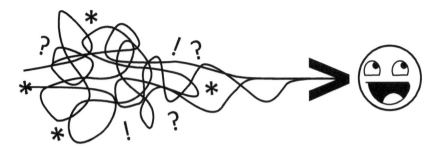

Figure 39.2 Image describing lean in the University of St. Andrews (both over time and in terms of the act of process improvement itself)

The university has been a key influencer behind an events-driven approach to lean, having designed a process that revolves around a series of interventions that progress through the following steps (Robinson and Yorkstone, 2014):

1   *Request*: An area of work is identified by a member of the principal's office, senior management, front-line staff members, or through an inquiry the lean team might make.
2   *Scoping*: It is ensured that there are clear goals, the right people are involved, and any required resources are arranged.
3   *Training*: Where required (e.g. when staff are new to lean or it is a specialist area), additional training is undertaken.
4   *Planning*: With the appropriate people, the project goal is reviewed and agreed upon. The approach, timetable, and any data requirements are also agreed upon.
5   *Redesign*: The group meets for a focused period of time with the authority to create a new process and identify and complete the actions required. This will lead to a new documented process and an action plan for any further work.
6   *Implementation*: Further actions are taken by the team members.
7   *Review*: The group meets regularly as required (often at 15, 30, and 90 days) to identify and remove any barriers to implementation
8   *Feedback*: The project is signed off as completed and feedback is gathered on the lean process as a whole.

These steps are described further in Figure 39.3.

Notwithstanding the success of this "St. Andrews Model," it is fair to say that St. Andrews' approach has always aimed to leverage these events as a starting point to drive wider cultural and behavioral change.

Lessons from St. Andrews

From the start of the lean team, it was acknowledged that lean was a "philosophy of work" rather than a series of tools or interventions, which is reflected in how staff describe the changes lean has made at St. Andrews.

When asking staff at the boardroom level in St. Andrews to reflect on the impact lean has had, they describe it as a cornerstone of the university's current success, success which has in part resulted from the breaking down of barriers between organizational functions enabled by lean. They are passionate

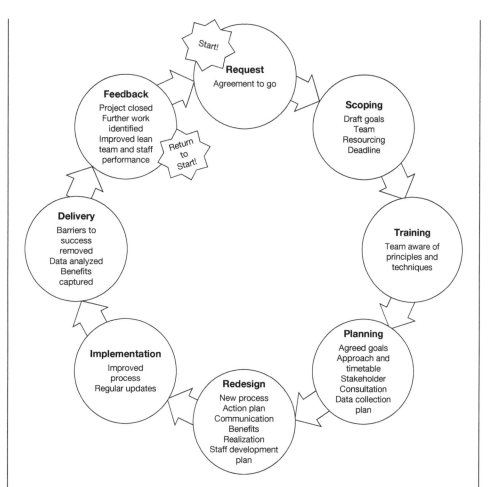

Figure 39.3 Image outlining the University of St. Andrews' process improvement project cycle

about how lean has fundamentally changed how individuals and teams communicate and problem solve together.

Despite lean's successes at St. Andrews, even after 10 years there is some evidence that not all areas of the university understand lean as an organizational cultural phenomenon—that is, as a "philosophy." Instead, they understand lean as a specific tool designed to deal with a certain type of problem. This is to be expected in an intervention-driven approach. Perhaps unsurprisingly, this perception is primarily carried by staff members who have not been involved in such interventions.

When asking a sample of St. Andrews' staff about the impact of lean on individuals, they report that when people working as part of a lean project "get it" these people then make time to support their colleagues. The staff interviewed indicated that in the longer term, also, individuals who have taken part in a lean intervention subsequently appear to adopt the principles of lean in terms of how they run their teams and how they relate to their internal colleagues. This then leads to the emergent growth of lean behaviors across networks of staff and business processes, semi-opportunistically.

That said, members of the St. Andrews lean team itself reflect that their lean journey has not been easy and that their role requires a high level of personal resilience, with a relatively high turnover of staffing during the early years of the lean team.

Summary

The lean team in the University of St. Andrews clearly demonstrates that using a lean approach works in HE, albeit that the approach is tailored to fit the sector.

While many aspects of the lean approach in St. Andrews appear to be very different from lean in other sectors, when we examine this case in more detail we can see similarities with other successful second-order lean implementations, e.g. the initial adoption of specific lean techniques in order to enable a principles-led approach and focusing on respect for people and continuous improvement.

At the time of writing, the lean team at St. Andrews was broadening its responsibility to include purview of all change projects in the university as a whole. This is an approach emerging in the sector as a whole: one of hybrid lean and project management teams. It is an approach not without its risks as it arguably supports the misperception that improvement is different from business as usual.

If St. Andrews can avoid this risk and keep working organizationally at a cultural and behavioral level, then we may yet see one of the world's oldest universities become one of the most lean.

References

Antony, J., Krishan, N., Cullen, D. and Kumar, M. (2012). Lean Six Sigma for higher education institutions (HEIs). *International Journal of Productivity and Performance Management, 61*(8), 940–948.

Balzer, W. K. (2010). *Lean Higher Education: Increasing the Value and Performance of University Processes*, New York, Productivity Press.

De Bono, E. (2000). *Six Thinking Hats Revised Edition*, 2nd edition, London, Penguin.

Diamond, I. (2015). *Working Smarter 2015*, UK, Universities Scotland.

Emiliani, B. (2015a). *Lean Teaching: A Guide to Becoming a Better Teacher*, Wethersfield, CT, The CLBM, LLC.

Emiliani, B. (2015b). *Lean University: A Guide to Renewal and Prosperity*. Wethersfield, CT, The CLBM, LLC.

George, M. L., Rolands, D., Price, M. and Maxey, J. (2004). *The Lean Six Sigma Pocket Toolbook*, New York, McGraw-Hill.

Hines, P. and Lethbridge, S. (2008). New development: Creating a lean university. *Public Money and Management*, February, 53–56.

Kawakita, J. (1982). *The Original KJ Method*, Tokyo, Kawakita Research Institute.

Lawrence, H. and Cairns, N. J. (2015). *Best Practice Guide: Evidencing the Benefits of Business Process Improvement in Higher Education*, UK, University of Strathclyde.

Netland, T. and Ferdows, K. (2014). What to expect from a corporate lean program. *MIT Sloan Management Review, 55*(3), 83–89.

Paterson, B. (2015). College of Physical Sciences NCS TRO Office 5S Improvement 10/09/2015. Unpublished A3 Report, Aberdeen, Aberdeen University.

Radnor, Z. and Bucci, G. (2011). *Analysis of Lean Implementation in UK Business Schools and Universities*. Available at: www.york.ac.uk/admin/po/processreview/ABS Final Report final.pdf (accessed May 27, 2013).

Robinson, M. and Yorkstone, S. (2014). Becoming a lean university: The case of the University of St. Andrews. *Leadership and Governance in Higher Education, 1*, 42–71.

Waterbury, T. and Holm, M. (2011). *Educational Lean for Higher Education: Theory and Practice*. Available at: lulu.com (accessed October 27, 2015).

Whitchurch, C. (2006). Who do they think they are? The changing identities of professional administrators and managers in UK higher education. *Journal of Higher Education Policy and Management, 28*(October), 1–10.

Winter, R. (2009). Academic manager or managed academic? Academic identity schisms in higher education. *Journal of Higher Education Policy and Management, 31*(2), 121–131.

PART III

A Lean World

40

A LEAN WORLD

Torbjørn H. Netland and Daryl J. Powell

Introduction

This Companion provides a deep investigation into one of the most celebrated, used, and criticized business concepts of our time, namely lean management. Today, lean seems to be on everyone's lips—not only across all functional areas of the traditional manufacturing enterprise (Part I of this book) but also in many different industries (Part II). Whereas other business concepts have proven to be short-lived and faddish, lean has maintained a strong position for almost three decades; what is more, it is gaining momentum. Lean is spreading far beyond its original environment on the shop floors of Toyota Motor Manufacturing. As Figure 40.1 illustrates, the spread of lean thinking across the enterprise and into new industries is continuing at a rapid pace. This chapter, which constitutes Part III of the Companion, discusses what the emergence of "a lean world" means for our understanding of lean in the broader sense.

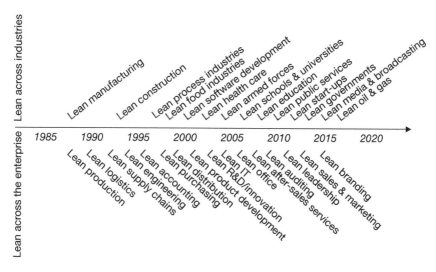

Figure 40.1 The spread of lean thinking across the enterprise and select industries

In the spirit of learning, before you read the rest of this chapter, ask yourself the following: Can an organization do lean without knowing its customers? Without aiming to reduce variation? Without paying attention to just-in-time (JIT)? Without pulling production to the demand of customers? Without paying attention to standards? If your answer was "no" to one or more of these questions, you are likely to learn something new in this chapter, just as we did in working with the 69 contributing authors in this Companion on lean management.

The various chapters describe and discuss what "lean" looks like in different settings. To our surprise, it is clear that what is lean in one setting may be completely anti-lean in another. Take "reduction of variation" as an example: many authors claim that variation is the number one enemy of lean (e.g. Bicheno, 2004; Modig and Åhlström, 2012), but as Schuh et al. (Chapter 5), Rossi et al. (Chapter 6), and Poppendieck (Chapter 34) explain, creating *more* variation is a goal in successful *lean innovation*, *lean product development*, and *lean software development*. Another example is Toyota's archetypical JIT principle. There is no doubt that this principle is appropriate for application to assemble-to-order manufacturing companies, but its legitimacy is less clear in *lean remanufacturing* (Chapter 16), *lean engineer-to-order industries* (Chapter 25), *lean armed forces* (Chapter 29), *lean policing* (Chapter 30), or *lean education* (Chapter 37), to mention a few. There are several inconsistencies like these in the common understanding of lean, and these have the potential to disrupt and ruin any lean transformation. It is therefore important to clarify what the essence of lean is as it applies in different settings; this is our goal in the present chapter.

Back to the Roots of Lean Production

As a concept, lean has evolved since it was introduced by Krafcik (1988) and made popular through the publication of *The Machine that Changed the World* by Womack et al. (1990). The MIT International Motor Vehicle Program showed that Toyota in the late 1980s used less of everything compared with its mass-production competitors but still produced more products with a higher variety, higher quality, and lower cost. Toyota's production system represented nothing less than a paradigm shift in manufacturing (Holweg, 2007). (For detailed discussions of the history and evolution of lean, see Jones and Womack, Chapter 1, Liker, Chapter 2, and Found and Bicheno, Chapter 3.) Considering Toyota's staggering performance, it came as no surprise that companies all over the world tried to replicate the Toyota Production System under the label "lean production."

The first descriptions of Toyota's production system focused on logistical and technical aspects (e.g. Sugimori et al., 1977; Shingo, 1986; Ohno, 1988). Total quality management (TQM), total productivity maintenance (TPM), and JIT logistics were essential to Toyota's performance and became an integral part of our descriptions of lean production (Cua et al., 2001). In addition, Toyota valued the principle of "respect for people," using human resource management (HRM) practices, such as teamwork, cross-training, and a coaching leadership style (Spear and Bowen, 1999; Liker and Hoseus, 2008). Based on an empirical study by Shah and Ward (2003), these four "interrelated bundles of practices"—TQM, TPM, JIT, and HRM—have come to represent one of the most used academic conceptualizations of lean production.

Developing and implementing TQM, TPM, JIT, and lean HRM practices is one way to build the foundation of lean capability in a production company. Because these four bundles of practices are complementary, they should be developed in parallel, not in sequence or isolation (Shah and Ward, 2003; Furlan et al., 2011). However, to become a lean manufacturer, it is not enough to introduce new lean practices in the workplace. Rather, the foremost characteristic of a lean production company is that it continuously challenges and improves on these practices.

That requires the meta-capability of *continuous improvement* (CI; "*kaizen*" in Toyota lingo). In our understanding, adding CI to TQM, TPM, JIT, and lean HRM practices provides a reasonable and useful conceptualization of lean production (illustrated in Figure 40.2).

Figure 40.2 is consistent with a large body of research on lean production, and the elements are similar to those of many corporate lean programs of large manufacturing companies (see Netland, Chapter 22). However, the question is whether the five elements in Figure 40.2 also provide a reasonable understanding of lean thinking when it disseminates beyond the production floor—to administration, sales and marketing, the production development department, and so on—and beyond the bounds of the manufacturing enterprise to the healthcare sector, public services, the education system, and so on. An analysis of the chapters in this book only finds CI to be considered and applied in all settings. The four other elements of lean production are more or less relevant depending on the specific situation and environment. Good examples are the biases toward JIT in *lean distribution* (see Holweg and Reichhart, Chapter 20) and toward TPM in *lean public water supply* (see Scholten et al., Chapter 32). Both of these examples make intuitive sense. Therefore, whereas the model in Figure 40.2 provides a useful conceptualization of "original" lean in production and manufacturing environments, new models are needed to understand lean in the modern extended enterprise and new industries.

Revisiting the Five Lean Principles

The five lean principles developed by Womack and Jones (1996) are perhaps the most referenced "explanation" of lean thinking and promise to be generic principles. Several of the chapters in this book (and many other articles) use the five lean principles to structure the discussion on what lean could be in a specific application area. Womack and Jones (1996) presented the five lean principles as a distillation of lean thinking. Although often used as "the definition of lean," a reassessment of the five lean principles shows that it is difficult to apply them directly in many settings

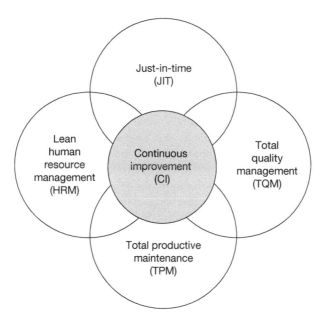

Figure 40.2   The five elements of lean production

and application areas. Below, we take a deeper look at each of the five principles in turn, which are as follows:

1   define value for the customer;
2   identify the value stream;
3   create flow by eliminating waste;
4   establish pull; and
5   seek perfection.

Principle 1: Define Value for the Customer

The first lean principle is as follows: "Specify value from the standpoint of the end customer" (Womack and Jones, 1996; Marchwinski and Shook, 2006). This has worked seamlessly in a wide selection of industries and helped many businesses change their mindset from an inward-looking resource efficiency perspective to a customer-driven flow efficiency perspective. Applying this principle first requires identifying the customers and then specifying what they value. A typical definition of a "customer" is "someone who buys a good or service from a business," for example a consumer who buys commodities in a store, a car at a dealership, a meal in a restaurant, or a haircut at a hairdresser. Business-to-business examples include an aircraft manufacturer that purchases jet engine parts from a supplier or a governmental institution that buys accounting services from a consultancy house. In all of these examples, it is not hard to identify the customer or specify what the customer values.

While this fits easily into some contexts, the first lean principle is more difficult to apply in other settings. In healthcare, for example, it is easy to look at the patient as the customer (this is even helpful and may radically improve the quality of a particular healthcare service), but the picture is not as clear cut as in the examples above (see Jones, Chapter 23). Often, the patient is not paying for all of the healthcare services she receives. Rather, the society may be the "paying customer" through governmental tax systems. Patients' next of kin are also "customers" in a sense. Furthermore, one of the biggest challenges for lean healthcare is that patients are unique individuals with partly overlapping, partly competing needs—all requesting services from the same, limited resources.

The identification of value for customers is even more difficult in the primary and higher education systems (see Wiegel and Brouwer-Hadzialic, Chapter 37; Riezebos, Chapter 38; and Yorkstone, Chapter 39). Let us take the example of a primary school. Who are the "customers" of a school? Are they the learners, the parents, the government, the taxpayers, or other groups? Some would quickly point to the schoolchildren as the customers in this setting. However, "learning" is not a commodity that can be transferred from a supplier to a customer. Rather, it is co-created in the learning process between the learner and the teacher. Hence, using business lingo, the learner is both a supplier and a customer (the same is true for many other transformational and experience-based services). In lean education, it is therefore practically impossible to deliver the highest value for each of the "customers." As Wiegel and Brouwer-Hadzialic (Chapter 37) explain, "Different types of students will need different forms of support and different types of pedagogy will have different needs in terms of group size, IT facilities, and classroom organization." For these reasons, the discussion on "value for the customer" is often a barrier to lean in the education sector.

The concept of customers and value is also difficult in many other lean application areas. Who can be identified as the customers of public services (Radnor, Chapter 28), the military

(Bateman and Hines, Chapter 29), law enforcement (Barton et al., Chapter 30), or the justice system (Martins et al., Chapter 31)? What about art, drug rehabilitation, an undertaker, or prison services? Reporting from an attempt to implement lean in Her Majesty's Revenue and Customs (HMRC), Radnor (Chapter 28) ironically asks, "Who's the customer [of HMRC]?" The answer is "everyone" (in the United Kingdom). Although it is difficult to think in terms of customers in all settings, the chapters in this book show that lean still has a lot to offer in multiple application areas.

Principle 2: Identify the Value Stream

The second lean principle is to "identify all the steps in the value stream for each product family" (Womack and Jones, 1996; Marchwinski and Shook, 2006). The limitation of this principle is noticeable in industries that make and deliver one-off, custom-made products and services (see, e.g., *lean engineer-to-order (ETO)* as discussed by Powell and van der Stoel, Chapter 25, and occasionally *lean construction*, as considered by Ballard, Chapter 24). In dynamic environments, value streams do not remain as stable as they would in a high-volume, low-variety production environment. This is particularly true of project-oriented situations, wherein project value streams are characterized as a temporary endeavor. Certainly, some projects have a repetitive nature and can easily benefit from a detailed mapping and understanding of the value stream. However, if each project has a unique value stream, a simple high-level process map may be the best thing available.

The idea of detailed process mapping, such as in "value stream mapping" (Rother and Shook, 2009), is also challenging in the education sector. Value streams are easier to identify in back-office operations, such as student admission, semester payments, and examination procedures, than in the front-office learning processes of the classroom. Perhaps this explains why lean has mostly been applied to back-office operations in this sector (Wiegel and Brouwer-Hadzialic, Chapter 37; Riezebos, Chapter 38; and Yorkstone, Chapter 39). Moreover, in other sectors with extreme variation (often human-centered sectors), such as sales, emergency departments, police work, armed forces, and sports, value stream mapping is often most useful in the back-office support processes rather than the core value-creating processes.

Principle 3: Create Flow by Eliminating Waste

The third lean principle is as follows: "Make the value-creating steps occur in tight sequence so the product will flow smoothly toward the customer" (Womack and Jones, 1996; Marchwinski and Shook, 2006). From a productivity perspective, flow is always smart (Schmenner, 2001)—and it is an integral part of both mass production and lean production. Creating flow is easier in automotive assembly operations (Found and Bicheno, Chapter 3), *lean mining* (Ghodrati et al., Chapter 26), and *lean public water supply* (Scholten et al., Chapter 32) than in *lean branding* (Busche, Chapter 13), *lean remanufacturing* (Pawlik et al., Chapter 16), and *lean dealerships* (Brunt, Chapter 33), to give some examples. The flow principle is also extremely difficult to achieve in knowledge-based work, such as product and software development (Rossi et al., Chapter 6; Poppendieck, Chapter 34).

In Toyota lingo, the third lean principle is about "*muri*," "*mura*," and "*muda*." Toyota regards the reduction of waste ("muda"; that is, everything that does not add value to the customer) as important but asserts that an organization can only reap the real benefits of waste reduction *after* resources are shielded from overburden ("muri") and unevenness ("mura"). Unfortunately, this wisdom has not reached all organizations that seek to implement lean; although the objective of the third principle is to create flow, it is often interpreted simply as "reduction of waste" due to an overemphasis on muda at the expense of muri and mura. Waste reduction seems to have immediate appeal in all settings that are new to lean because we can all see "wastes" or inefficiencies in our workplace. Even if the customer is hard to identify, there is always waste that can be pointed out. Therefore, one of the first things that usually happens when lean is introduced into a new area is that authors and consultants propose new classification of wastes for the specific area. This is usually based on Taiichi Ohno's categorization of seven sources of waste, namely transportation, inventory, motion, waiting, overproduction, overprocessing, and defects. Examples are included in this book in the chapters "Lean Innovation," "Lean Sales and Marketing," "Lean After-sales Services," "Lean Retail," "Lean Justice," and "Lean Universities." Perhaps this signifies the infancy of lean in these application areas.

Principle 4: Establish Pull

The fourth lean principle of Womack and Jones (1996) is as follows: "As flow is introduced, let customers pull value from the next upstream activity" (Marchwinski and Shook, 2006). However, as we shift our focus from the factory floor at Toyota to other settings, the way in which this principle is operationalized requires a reconsideration of pull as a concept. A traditional pull system, such as the *kanban* system, authorizes value-adding activities to take place based on the consumption of *materials*. However, some settings are better off if free *capacity* in the production system is what pulls in a new order. This can be demonstrated through applying the drum-buffer-rope principle of bottleneck control theory, as in the theory of constraints (Goldratt and Cox, 1984). A good example of this can be found in the chapter on *lean maintenance, repair, and overhaul* (Srinivasan, Chapter 27), which integrates the theory of constraints with lean.

In Chapter 29, Bateman and Hines suggest the term "demand readiness" instead of pull in the context of public services, for example when a patient "pulls" services from a healthcare provider. Again, this definition of pull considers the state of the process, while the capacity of the process is not consumed without a clear signal or requirement from a customer. The process is itself "demand-ready," and no work is carried out unless there is a clear customer signal (avoiding overproduction). Thus, we can conclude that it is a combination of the state of the system and the flow-controlling mechanism (authorizing consumption of capacity) that creates the distinction between push and pull in the wider context.

Principle 5: Seek Perfection

Finally, the fifth lean principle is as follows: "Continuously improve the processes" (Womack and Jones, 1996; Marchwinski and Shook, 2006). Our analysis of the chapters in this Companion shows that this principle is the most versatile of the five lean principles. Creating a culture of continuous improvement is essential for the success of a lean transformation in any industry. According to Jones (Chapter 23), "What distinguishes lean from other process improvement methodologies is its focus on developing the capabilities of the front-line teams . . . to manage and continuously improve their work." The ability of all employees to reflect on current ways of working and to improve these continuously is the only means by which the significant results one would expect from a successful lean implementation can be achieved. The next question is how to make employees able to engage in continuous improvement. The authors of the chapters in this Companion agree that this requires a culture of *learning*. We dedicate the next section—"the essence of lean"—to learning and how to achieve it.

The Essence of Lean

We suggest that the essence of lean—as it applies to all functional areas of the enterprise and different industries and sectors—is continuous improvement, with learning at its core. Hence, present-day lean thinking is ultimately about creating the learning organization (e.g. Senge, 1990; Garvin, 1993). A precondition for this is developing a long-term perspective. In addition, fostering organization-wide learning requires a special form of leadership. We call these the three essential Ls of lean—learning, a long-term perspective, and leadership.

Learning

Just as rapid learning cycles are the essence of lean innovation (Schuh et al., Chapter 5), lean software development (Poppendieck, Chapter 34), and lean start-up (Ries, 2011), the success of the Toyota Production System (TPS) was very much built on a scientific method of learning (Liker, Chapter 2). It is not without reason that the TPS has been called "the thinking production system." Through many small scientific experiments, Toyota updates its standard operating procedures to represent the state of the art and quickly trains all employees in the new and better standards. To accomplish this, Toyota uses Deming's plan, do, study, act (PDSA) cycle, as this approach encourages continuous reflection and improvement among all employees. The trick is to go beyond "know-how" to create a deep understanding of "know-why." Furthermore, because learning occurs when the outcome of an experiment is the predicted result, successful lean organizations exhibit a no-blame culture, as "failure" and problems are a necessary and valuable part of any learning process. Improvement without a focus on learning is *not* lean thinking.

Long-term Perspective

A successful lean transformation requires a long-term perspective. Unfortunately, creating lasting improvement is often *not* the starting point of many lean initiatives. Rather, cost cutting is considered as the main driving force for the implementation of lean in most industries that are new to the concept. A few examples are healthcare (Jones, Chapter 23), the mining industry (Ghodrati et al., Chapter 26), public services (Radnor, Chapter 28), the armed forces (Bateman and Hines, Chapter 29), police departments (Barton et al., Chapter 30), and the printing industry (Macro, Chapter 35). Budget cuts are also a driving force in many other sectors that have recently encountered lean, including airlines, banking, broadcasting, governments, insurance, law firms, oil and gas, telecoms, and so on. The problem is not that practical "lean" tools and techniques do not deliver quick cost-cutting results. They can do that. Rather, the issue is that these results will not last. Although value stream mapping workshops and "waste walks" can cause rapid changes, the benefits soon wear off if continuous learning is not part of the transformation. Application of methods without a long-term perspective on learning is *not* lean thinking.

Leadership

Creating a learning organization is easier said than done. Thirty years of trial and error related to implementing lean in many sectors has taught us that it necessitates a special form of leadership, namely "lean leadership" (see Liker, Chapter 2; Ballé, Chapter 4; Brunt, Chapter 33). Ballé argues that lean leadership is a set of *practices* and not a theory or principles; it cannot be done in an office, outsourced to consultants, or summarized in a boardroom presentation. Perhaps the three most essential lean leadership practices are as follows: 1) go observe directly at *gemba*, 2) always challenge the current state of affairs by asking questions, and 3) develop a coaching leadership style (Spear, 2004; Rother, 2010; Liker and Convis, 2011). Often, this requires a complete shift in how management is performed, which again explains many failed attempts at lean transformations. This is also the fundamental message behind the "lean transformation framework" (Shook, 2014), presented in detail in this book by Brunt (Chapter 33). Regardless of where a lean transformation begins, the lean transformation framework promises to set a premise for *any* successful enterprise transformation.

Jones (Chapter 23) points out that as soon as you tell someone what to do, you take away that person's responsibility to learn. Admittedly, developing lean leadership capabilities can be more difficult in some organizational cultures than in others. In this Companion, we can read that the strong hierarchical cultures of the police force (Barton et al., Chapter 30) and the military (Bateman and Hines, Chapter 29) are hurdles for lean transformations in these sectors. The healthcare and education sectors have similar challenges due to their strong profession-centered cultures, where doctors, teachers, and professors would like to preserve power (Jones, Chapter 23; Riezebos, Chapter 38; Yorkstone, Chapter 39). Technically, however, these characteristics should not stop these industries from developing lean organizations. Discussing lean healthcare, Jones reminds us that "lean uses the same scientific method to diagnose and treat organizational problems as doctors use to diagnose and treat medical problems." Examples like the Consorci Sanitari Del Garraf in Spain (case study in Chapter 23) and Bærland primary school in Norway (case study in Chapter 38) show that it is also possible to develop lean cultures outside the traditional manufacturing environment. A lean journey without dedicated and engaged leaders, however, is destined to fail.

Conclusions

We started this chapter by asking a few questions relating to the characteristics of a lean organization, as follows: Can an organization do lean without knowing its customers? Without aiming to reduce variation? Without paying attention to JIT? Without pulling production to the demand of customers? Without paying attention to standards? If you are thinking of *lean production* (i.e. the TPS), the correct answer to all of these questions should be "no." However, it should be clear by now that the answer to any of the above questions could be "yes" in a different sense. It is not easy to define "customers" in primary education, yet we have *lean schools*. Reduction in variation can hamper innovation, yet we have *lean innovation*. JIT and pull production are not easy to apply in law enforcement, yet we have *lean policing*. Different students' learning processes are non-linear and non-standard, yet we have *lean education*. Hence, what is lean in one setting may not be lean in another. It is clear that a one-size-fits-all approach to lean is a strategy for failure. Thus, managers must tailor lean to the characteristics of the specific industry and organization.

The common characteristic of lean that we found across all application areas in this book was continuous improvement. Lean—cut to the core—is about creating a culture for continuously improving the operations of a business or organization. Everybody in the organization should be engaged in improvement activities using problem-solving methods. We suggest that any lean transformation—regardless of the sector and application area—is dependent on the three essential Ls of lean: learning, a long-term perspective, and leadership.

References

Bicheno, J. (2004). *The New Lean Toolbox: Towards Fast, Flexible Flow*, Buckingham, Production and Inventory Control, Systems and Industrial Engineering Books.

Cua, K. O., Mckone, K. E. and Schroeder, R. G. (2001). Relationships between implementation of TQM, JIT, and TPM and manufacturing performance. *Journal of Operations Management, 19*(6), 675–694.

Furlan, A., Vinelli, A. and Dal Pont, G. (2011). Complementarity and lean manufacturing bundles: An empirical analysis. *International Journal of Operations & Production Management, 31*(8), 835–850.

Garvin, D. A. (1993). Building a learning organization. *Harvard Business Review, 71*(4, July–August), 78.

Goldratt, E. M. and Cox, J. (1984). *The Goal: Excellence in Manufacturing*, Croton-on-Hudson, NY, North River Press.

Holweg, M. (2007). The genealogy of lean production. *Journal of Operations Management, 25*(2), 420–437.

Krafcik, J. F. (1988). Triumph of the lean production system. *Sloan Management Review, 30*(1), 41–51.

Liker, J. K. and Hoseus, M. (2008). *Toyota Culture: The Heart and Soul of the Toyota Way*, New York, McGraw-Hill.

Liker, J. K. and Convis, G. L. (2011). *The Toyota Way to Lean Leadership: Achieving and Sustaining Excellence Through Leadership Development*, New York, McGraw-Hill.

Marchwinski, C. and Shook, J. (2006). *Lean Lexicon: A Graphical Glossary for Lean Thinkers*, Cambridge, MA, Lean Enterprise Institute.

Modig, N. and Åhlström, P. (2012). *This is Lean: Resolving the Efficiency Paradox*, Stockholm, Rheologic.

Ohno, T. (1988). *Toyota Production System: Beyond Large-Scale Production*, New York, Productivity Press.

Ries, E. (2011). *The Lean Startup: How Today's Entrepreneurs Use Continuous Innovation to Create Radically Successful Businesses*, Lake Arbor, MA, Crown Books.

Rother, M. (2010). *Toyota Kata: Managing People for Continuous Improvement and Superior Results*, New York, McGraw-Hill Professional.

Rother, M. and Shook, J. (2009). *Learning to See: Value Stream Mapping to Create Value and Eliminate Muda*, Brookline, MA, Lean Enterprise Institute.

Schmenner, R. W. (2001). Looking ahead by looking back: Swift, even flow in the history of manufacturing. *Production and Operations Management, 10*(1), 87–96.

Senge, P. M. (1990). *The Fifth Discipline: The Art and Practice of the Learning Organization*, New York, Doubleday.

Shah, R. and Ward, P. T. (2003). Lean manufacturing: Context, practice bundles, and performance. *Journal of Operations Management, 21*(2), 129–149.

Shingo, S. (1986). *Zero Quality Control: Source Inspection and the Poka-Yoke System*, Cambridge, MA, Productivity Press.

Shook, J. (2014). *Transforming Transformation*. Cambridge, MA, Lean Enterprise Institute.

Spear, S. (2004). Learning to lead at Toyota. *Harvard Business Review, 82*(5), 78–86.

Spear, S. and Bowen, H. K. (1999). Decoding the DNA of Toyota Production System. *Harvard Business Review, 77*(5), 95–106.

Sugimori, Y., Kusunoki, K., Cho, F. and Uchikawa, S. (1977). Toyota Production System and kanban system: Materialization of just-in-time and respect-for-human system. *International Journal of Production Research, 15*(6), 553–564.

Womack, J. P. and Jones, D. T. (1996). *Lean Thinking: Banish Waste and Create Wealth in your Corporation*, New York, The Free Press.

Womack, J. P., Jones, D. T. and Roos, D. (1990). *The Machine that Changed the World*, New York, Rawson Associates.

INDEX

Diagrams, drawings and pictures are given in italics.